D1570086

Luis F. Ladaria

The Living and True God

THE MYSTERY OF THE TRINITY

CONVIVIUMPRESS

SERIES TRADITIO

2009

The Living and True God.
The Mystery of the Trinity

Original Title: El Dios vivo y verdadero.
El misterio de la Trinidad
© SECRETARIADO TRINITARIO 1998.

Translation: The Living and True God.
The Mystery of the Trinity
© Convivium Press 2009.
All rights reserved
Todos los derechos reservados.
For the English Edition.

http://www.conviviumpress.com
sales@conviviumpress.com
ventas@conviviumpress.com
convivium@conviviumpress.com

7661 NW 68th St, Suite 108,
Miami, Florida 33166. USA.
Phone: +1 (786) 8669718
Teléfono: +1 (786) 8798452

Edited by Rafael Luciani
Translated by Evelyn Harrison
Revised by Doris Strieter and Thomas Strieter
Designed by Eduardo Chumaceiro d'E
Series: Traditio

ISBN: 978-1-934996-06-5

Printed in Colombia
Impreso en Colombia
D'VINNI, S.A.

The Living and True God

THE MYSTERY OF THE TRINITY

Contents

11

«Unitas in Trinitate». The One God in the Trinity. Properties and modalities of action *page* 417

Prologue

The theology of the Trinity has lately been the object of renewed interest. A quick look at the most common bibliography is enough to convince us of this. Some specialized bibliographies show even more clearly the abundance —impossible to cover in full— of studies that address this topic from different points of view[1]. They are not absent either in the main Western languages, as the reader can easily see in general bibliography, treatises and manuals that roughly correspond to the characteristics of this volume. An obvious question emerges as to the reason for yet another work that will contribute, at least to a certain extent, to making this tangled jungle of publications even more impenetrable. The question is even more difficult to answer in the case of the author, because of his clear belief that the contribution that he offers will certainly not deserve to be qualified as decisive, and even more so, it is probable that it will not significantly influence the final course of theology.

However, when a professor teaches at an international center and has a very high number of students, the lectures that he offers begin to travel easily, with no possibility at all of control, throughout the whole world by means of the notes taken by students, which by the way, have a doubtful reliability. The unpleasant consequences that can be derived from this fact are quite evident. Offering a clear point of reference, first and foremost to students, has been my main purpose for writing this book. I will feel quite satisfied if I am able to attain this goal. Nevertheless, if the effort is also useful for others, my joy will be considerably greater.

Two main concerns have guided me when writing this book. In the first place, I hope to offer considerable positive information, primarily from the main data of the New Testament and the tradition and teachings of the Church, on the mystery of the one and triune God who has been revealed in Christ. However, I must also refer to the main systematic contributions on this topic that have guided theological reflections throughout history or that exert a considerable influence

---

1   The volume devoted to the Trinitarian bibliography by the journal *Estudios Trinitarios* 25 (1991) covering the years 1976 to 1990, is especially significant. This is the case of the different contributions of X. Pikaza (New Testament), E. Romero Pose (Patristic), M. M. Garijo-Guembe (orthodox theology and pneumatology), S. del Cura Elena (Catholic and Protestant systematic thought), E. Schadel (the Trinity as a philosophical problem) totaling approximately 4463 titles. Even though there are inevitable repetitions, this is still an impressive figure. Some authors emphasize that due to reasons which are quite easy to understand, these lists are not comprehensive. It is quite instructive to compare this bibliography with the one published by this same journal in its issue 11 (1977), even though the chronological and numbering criteria applied to the titles are less clear in the latter case. Cfr. as well, Cozzi A., «L'originalità del teismo trinitario. Bibliografia trinitaria» in *ScCatt* 123 (1995) 765-840.

on current times. In the second place, I must mention the concern of coordinating all this abundant material, so as to prepare a coherent synthesis that evidences the intrinsic relationship between the different issues that I have addressed. The mystery of God cannot be understood by our human reason. Nevertheless, this does not keep the teachings that the Church offers us on this issue from being highly and deeply harmonious. Every theological reflection should attempt to emphasize this internal coherence —the *nexus mysteriorum* that was mentioned in the First Vatican Council (DS 3916), even though, in many cases, it is not possible to eliminate this paradox. This will simply be a continuous reminder that the effort of believing in order to give a reason for hope (cfr. 1Pet 3:15) can never be mistaken for the pretension of submitting everything to the rule of our reason.

From the oldest writing of the New Testament I have taken the title of this work (cfr. 1Thess 1:9). This is the God whom, according to Paul, we Christians adore. Life and truth (truthfulness) are divine properties that were already emphasized in the Old Testament and that acquire their full meaning in the revelation of Jesus.

There is no need to insist on the importance that the biblical data, especially that of the New Testament, should have in the case of every theological exposition, and specifically when dealing with the topic that we are addressing and studying in this treatise[2]. The New Testament gives testimony of Jesus who reveals the Father to us, and after his resurrection and exaltation he sends over his disciples the Spirit that has rested upon him. I have devoted considerable space to the doctrinal evolution of the first centuries, which is of the utmost importance for our treatise. By framing this work within the great Western tradition, even though very good ecumenical reasons also compel us to look to the East, I could never ignore the Trinitarian theology of Saint Augustine and Saint Thomas Aquinas who must also receive significant attention. This is basically due to the concern to which I have referred before, of offering sufficient historical information, without which it is impossible to understand the theology of the West, including its most recent theological thinking. Nevertheless, this is also the case, and even more importantly so, due to the intrinsic value of many of its institutions. Let us not assume that the determining influence that these institutions have exerted in the past and in the present has been out of mere chance. Even though we must not attach the same significance to all their statements, we cannot

---

2 In general terms, I have resorted to the translation of the Jerusalem Bible.

disregard their most crucial and decisive contributions. At any rate, these will not be the only voices to which we will be listening. We cannot assume that the ante-Nicene tradition has simply been overcome by a dogmatic development that has required ideas which were not known in the first three centuries. Years of study have enabled me to become familiar with the thought of Hilary of Poitiers, who was so highly praised by Augustine[3], and who is still frequently forgotten despite the value that very important experts have attached to him[4]. The fact that I have cited the Cappadocian Fathers, especially Basil of Caesarea, requires less justification. Going into the Middle Ages, we cannot forget the influence that Richard of St. Victor has had of late. Thus, we will also pay attention to this author, even though much of what has been written on the social model of the Trinity requires an in-depth critical revision.

As will be explained in greater detail in the first chapter, this work is aimed at assembling the classical contents of the treatises *de Deo uno* and *de Deo trino*, although with a clear preference for the second one. We will focus our attention on the contents of the faith of the Church and less on the «context» in which this faith is now professed and witnessed[5]. This is by no means out of contempt for these current issues, the importance of which cannot be overlooked, but in view of the fact that I am aware of my personal limitations and because of the nature I would like this work to have. Only based on the knowledge of the central core of the Christian faith in the one and triune God can we study with success the other problems that are intimately related to God.

So that this volume could be kept within reasonable limits for a work of this nature, I have tried to be quite sober in my presentation, and I have attempted not to multiply bibliographic references that can easily be accessible from the ones that I offer. Rather, I have been more generous with my quotations of classical and modern authors because I believe that nothing could be a substitute for direct access to the texts, and this is basically what I have tried to achieve.

Prologue

17

3 Cfr. for example *Contra Iulianum* I 3,9 (PL 44,645); *Trin* VI 10,11 (CCL 50,241). Saint Thomas Aquinas also very frequently cited Hilary in his treatise on the Trinity in the *Summa*.

4 ORBE A., «El estudio de los santos Padres en la formación sacerdotal» in LATOURELLE R. (ed.), *Vaticano II: balance y perspectivas. Veinticinco años despues (1962-1987)*, Salamanca 1989, 1037-1046. See on page 1043: «without denying the value of Saint Ambrose, Saint Hilary will always be dogmatically more instructive, although more difficult to grasp. The one who is able to be an expert in the teachings of the Bishop of Poitiers is able to make considerable progress in the field of patristics. This is even more the case than if he or she were to simultaneously extend the field of study to cover all the Western Fathers (except for Saint Augustine)».

5 Cfr. AMATO A. (ed.), *Trinità in contesto*, Roma 2003; also cfr. CODA P.-TAPKEN A. (eds.), *La Trinità e il pensare. Figure, percorsi, prospettive*, Roma 1997.

This work has been possible due to the encouragement and the assistance of many colleagues, friends, and students. I would especially like to mention two of them who took the trouble of reading the manuscript even before I had the final version and who encouraged me to publish it: Msgr. Eugenio Romero Pose, Auxiliary Bishop of Madrid and Father Angel Anton, professor of the Faculty of Theology of the Pontifical Gregorian University. I extend to both of them, as well as to many others whom I cannot mention, my deepest gratitude.

Abbreviations

AAS	Acta Apostolicae Sedis.
AG	Second Vatican Council, Decree *Ad Gentes.*
Ang	Angelicum (Roma).
Aug	Augustinianum (Roma).
BAC	Biblioteca de Autores Cristianos (Madrid).
Cath	Catholica (Münster).
CCL	Corpus Christianorum. Series Latina (Turnhout).
CEC	Catechism of the Catholic Church.
CSEL	Corpus Scriptorum Ecclesiasticorum Latinorum (Wien).
DS	Denzinger-Schönmetzer, *Enchiridion symbolorum, definitionum et declarationum de rebus fidei et morum,* 34 ed., Barcinonae 1967.
DV	Second Vatican Council, Dogmatic Constitution *Dei Verbum.*
EphThLov	Ephemerides Theologicae Lovanienses (Bruges).
EstEcl	Estudios Eclesiásticos (Madrid).
EstTrin	Estudios Trinitarios (Salamanca).
FP	Fuentes Patrísticas (Madrid).
GCS	Die griechischen christlichen Schrifsteller der ersten drei Jahrhunderte (Leipzig).
Greg	Gregorianum (Roma).
GS	Second Vatican Council, Pastoral Constitution *Gaudium et Spes.*
LG	Second Vatican Council, Dogmatic Constitution *Lumen Gentium.*
LThK	*Lexikon für Theologie und Kirche,* 2 ed., Freiburg 1957-1965.
MunThZ	Münchener Theologische Zeitschrift (St. Ottilien).
MySal	*Mysterium Salutis. Fundamentos de la dogmática como historia de la salvación,* Madrid 1969ff.
NA	Second Vatican Council, Declaration *Nostra Aetate.*
NRTh	Nouvelle Revue Théologique (Louvain).
PG	Patrologia Graeca (Paris).
PL	Patrologia Latina (Paris).
RET	Revista Española de Teología (Madrid).
RevTh	Revue Thomiste (Paris).
RM	John Paul II, Encyclical *Redemptoris Missio.*
RSPhTh	Revue des Sciences Philosophiques et Théologiques (Paris).
RSR	Recherches de Science Religieuse (Paris).
RThLou	Revue Théologique de Louvain (Louvain).
ScCat	Sources Chrétiennes (Paris).

TheolSt	Theological Studies (Baltimore).
TheoPhil	Theologie und Philosophie (Freiburg).
TWAT	*Theologisches Wörterbuch zum Alten Testament*, Stuttgart 1973ss.
WA	Martin Luther, *Werke. Kritische Gesamtausgabe*, Weimar 1883-1949.
WiWe	Wissenschaft und Weisheit (Düsseldorf).
ZthK	Zeitschrift für Theologie und Kirche (Tübingen).

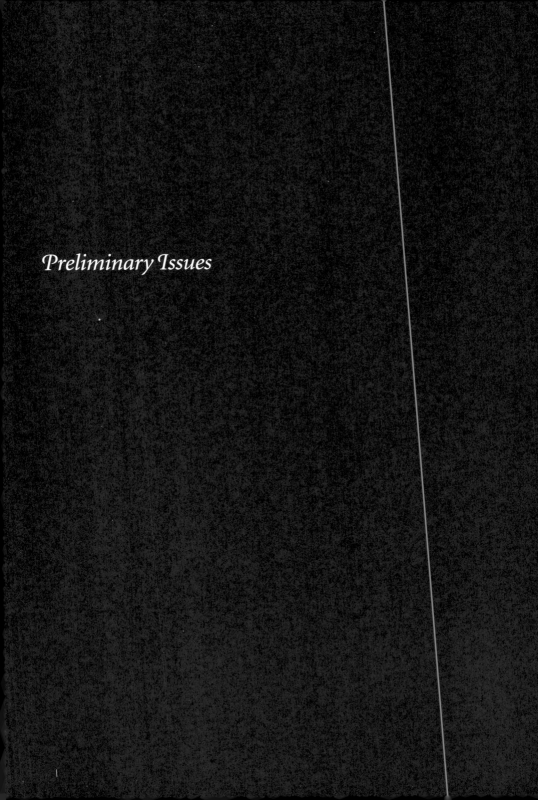

Preliminary Issues

Introduction to the treatise

1

God is revealed as the primary subject of theology

It does not seem difficult to justify that the treatise on God is the one that deserves fully and in the most *strictu sensu* the qualification of «*theological*». It is quite clear that only based on a set of all the theological treatises can we really have a comprehensive idea of the Christian mystery of God and of the salvation that the Father wants to bestow upon us in Jesus Christ his Son and in the Holy Spirit. There is no doubt, however, that in view of the fact that the truths he has willed to reveal to us for the sake of our salvation are directly related to God himself (cfr. DV 2.6), he has a priority over all the other issues that will be the subject of study in theology. All of these truths will receive their ultimate light from God himself. Hence, in the study of the treatises of God we find ourselves in the very center of theology.

At the beginning of his *Summa Theologiae*[1], Saint Thomas deliberates on the need for a doctrine of God founded on revelation, one that is, hence, differentiated from the philosophical disciplines. The fundamental reason that he offers to justify the existence of this doctrine is that God is the purpose of human existence. In effect, human beings are directed toward God, to a purpose that goes beyond the capacity of reason to understand. It is precisely toward this purpose that people should aim their actions, so that they can truly be saved. Thus, it has to be an end or a purpose that they know in advance, that is *praecognitus* by human beings. To this end, there is a need for a doctrine founded on revelation, so that humanity may know all those things that go beyond reason and that refer to this ultimate goal. Revelation was necessary also for a second reason: even those truths about God that people can know through the light of reason are difficult and require considerable research. They are not within the grasp of all. One does not reach this knowledge without the combination of many mistakes. Because of this, it was necessary for us to receive some understanding of them through divine revelation. The First Vatican Council, in its constitution *Dei Filius*, echoed these reasons that Saint Thomas had already set forth (cfr. DS 3004-3005). In due time, we will address this issue in greater detail.

---

1 *STh* I 1,1: «Utrum sit necessarium, praeter philosophicas disciplinas, aliam doctrinam haberi».
   Cfr. this article for what follows.

The convenience of revelation is founded solely on the purpose to which humanity is destined by God. Hence, it is not a matter of acquiring a new knowledge simply out of curiosity. As stated in the Second Vatican Council (DV 6), it is a knowledge that has God himself as its subject, along with the eternal decrees of his will with respect to the salvation of the world. Therefore, the need for knowledge about God founded in revelation is based on the fact that he is the only purpose of humanity, the end to which human beings are drawn even without knowing him, and the only one who can calm the restlessness of their hearts[2].

According to the terminology of Saint Thomas, the knowledge that is derived from revelation and that people accept as an act of faith is *sacra doctrina*, and although it is different from the other human disciplines, it nevertheless deserves the name of «science»[3]. This special science has God as its subject; it is *theologia—sermo de Deo*[4]. The subject of this science is directly related to the finality of this same science. In other words, it is directed toward helping humans attain their goal, which is none other than God. Hence, theology has to do with God himself, because even though it addresses so many other issues, it studies them all *sub ratione Dei*. At any rate, God is the subject of theology because it deals directly with God himself, or, because it deals with other things insofar as they are related with and drawn toward God[5]. Therefore, what we are intending to do is, in *strictu sensu, sermo de Deo*. If we approach all the theological issues with both trembling and fear, it would be even more the case when addressing this specific one. The speculative effort cannot be separated from the attitude of listening and contemplating. This meditation or contemplation should not be regarded as something different from theology. Rather, it is precisely what should

---

2 AUGUSTINE, *Conf.* I 1,1 (CCL 27,1): «Fecisti nos ad te et inquietum est cor nostrum donec requiescat in te».

3 *STh* I 1,2: «Et hoc modo sacra doctrina est scientia: quia procedit ex principiis notis lumine superiore scientiae, quae scilicet est scientia Dei et beatorum». Once again, the reference made to God is of the utmost importance for determining the «scientific» nature of theology. Obviously, we understand that we are not addressing the complex problem of the scientific nature of theology. Cfr. CODA P., *Teo-Logia. La parola di Dio nelle parole dell'uomo. Epistemologia e metodologia teologica*, Roma 1997, 171-190.

4 *STh* I 1,7. Theology has God as its object, although God is also in a way its «subject». Theology departs from revelation of what God himself tells us and has as a principle, as Saint Thomas reminded us, the same knowledge of God.

5 *STh* I 1,7: «Omnia autem pertractantur in sacra doctrina sub ratione Dei vel quia sunt ipse Deus; vel quia habent ordinen ad Deum, ut ad principium et finem. Unde sequitur quod Deus vere sit subiectum huius scientiae. Quod etian manifestum fit ex principiis huius scientiae, quae sunt articuli fidei, quae est de Deo»; ibid. *ad* 2: «Omnia alia quae determinantur in sacra doctrina, comprehenduntur sub Deo».

guide the theological effort so that it is not driven away from its authentic objective of helping us attain our ultimate goal, which is none other than God.

Following the guidelines that we have stated thus far, in this treatise we will address the God revealed in Christ. The rich set of current problems and issues about God, as well as the opening of humanity to God, will only be discussed marginally in order to avoid repetition of statements that have already been addressed in the treatises on natural theology or other works that specifically analyze this broad and complex set of problems[6].

We must state as a guide and as the basis for our work some key texts included in the prologue of the gospel according to John:

> The Word became flesh, he lived among us, and we saw his glory, the glory that he has from the Father as only Son of the Father, full of grace and truth... From his fullness we have, all of us, received —one gift replacing another, for the Law was given through Moses, grace and truth have come through Jesus Christ. No one has ever seen God; It is the only Son, who is close to the Father's heart, who has made him known (John 1:14, 16-18).

In his coming into this world, enabling us to know the glory that corresponds to him as the only Son of the Father, Jesus Christ has revealed to us God whom no one has been able to see and who dwells in unapproachable light that is inaccessible to any human being (cfr. Exod 33:20; 1Tim 6:16). He enables us to know God by having us share his life, offering us his fullness, communicating to us his grace and his truth. The revelation of God in Christ is not a simple communication of «truths», but rather, it entails the giving of his own life. It is an authentic «self-communication» of God. Because of this fact, the attitude of faith is of the utmost importance in order to have access to this divine revelation. In Jesus we cannot only see the Father, but we also find at the same time the only way that leads to him (cfr. John 14:6-9).

This is what shapes the theological nature of our treatise which begins with the revelation evidenced in Christ and accepted through faith by the faith of the Church[7]. In effect, any knowledge that human beings can have of God is based,

---

6   Among the very extensive bibliography on this issue, we can refer to DE S. LUCAS J., *La búsqueda de Dios en el hombre*, Madrid 1994; ALFARO J., *De la cuestión del hombre a la cuestión de Dios*, Salamanca 1988.

7   Significant titles of some treatises that emphasize these aspects are: KASPER W., *Der Gott Jesu Christi*, Mainz 1982; and recently, SCHEFFCZYK L., *Der Gott der Offenbarung. Gotteslehre*, Aachen 1996.

in one way or another, on the fact that he has revealed himself and enabled us to know him. In due time, we will address the theological problem of the access of human reason to God. In the meantime, it will suffice to point out that whenever people search for God, the initiative lies in God himself, and it is guided by his providence and by his hand, even when we may not know it[8]. The knowledge of God that human beings can acquire as derived from creation comes from the ongoing testimony that God gives us of himself (Second Vatican Council, DS 3). In addition to this testimony of creation, the constitution *Dei Verbum* 3 refers to a divine manifestation that our first Fathers enjoyed; indeed, it is a manifestation on a higher level than that of creation itself, as it relates to salvation on a higher order to which they were destined *(supernae salutis)*. The revelation of the Old Testament to the chosen people is undoubtedly another step further in the self-revelation of God through which he has been acknowledged as the «only, living and true God, a provident Father and a fair judge» (DV 3). In this way, God was paving the way for the gospel; but only through Christ will this revelation reach its fullness, because the Word that enlightens all people alike has been sent by the Father «so that he could dwell among them and reveal the secrets of God» (DV 4)[9].

God is the subject of theology insofar as he is the purpose of humanity, because the revelation that was fulfilled in Jesus has no other object than God and the truth of our salvation. Hence, we must look to Jesus in order to know God the Father. By revealing God to us as Father he enables us to know him as the Son. We can have access to this mystery in the Spirit of God, «and nobody is able to say "Jesus is Lord", except by the Holy Spirit» (1Cor 12:3).

The revelation of God as the Father of Jesus, which implies the revelation of Jesus as the Son of God and God as the Father, and the Holy Spirit as gift of the Father and of Jesus who introduces the Son into the intimacy of the life of the Father, is the revelation of the one and triune God. The doctrine of divine unity in Trinity and Trinity in unity that the Church has developed is the direct consequence of the God whom Jesus has enabled us to know. We are not facing an appendix or a secondary matter of theology or faith, but rather, its deeper core, because here we are faced with the mystery of God that is revealed as the only purpose to which people are drawn and the one where they can reach their fullness.

---

8 Augustine, *Soliloquiorum Lib.* I 1,3 (PL 32,870): «Deus, quem nemo quaerit nisi admonitus».

9 DV 4: «With all his presence and manifestation, with his words and works, signs and miracles; and, mostly, with his death and glorious resurrection from the dead, and finally, by sending the Spirit of truth, he completes the revelations and confirms with the divine testimony that God lives with us».

2

The originality of the Christian idea of God

For the reasons that we have just stated, in the confession of the one and triune God we have the focal point of the Christian faith. Christianity stands beside the major monotheist religions. It follows the tradition of the Old Testament, and it is considered to be the legitimate heir of the religion of Israel in which the unity and unicity of God make up the fundamental truth (cfr. Exod 20:1ff; Deut 6:4, etc.; Mark 12:29; John 17:3). Islam came into existence after Christianity, and it has strongly maintained the monotheism of the tradition of the Old Testament, rejecting the Christian Trinity as a deviation.

Precisely, however, because Christian monotheism, which we must affirm with all our strength, is that of the triune God, it cannot be identified as easily with the monotheism of Judaism or that of Islam. The ultimate unity of God, the greatest that we can think of, is in itself plural[10]. Hence, even though this statement is partly true, we cannot affirm without any nuances that the one God can be known by reason, while the divine Trinity must be the object of revelation. In fact, through reason we can reach the knowledge of the one God, as has also been the case of other religions mentioned before and perhaps others in the world that have also been able to reach this idea without the definitive revelation in Christ. However, the God that is known in Jesus Christ is the one and triune God. Unicity is not only prior to the Christian revelation, but rather, along with it, it receives a new sense which is far more profound. There is no divine unity without Trinity and vice versa. The divine unity that Christianity affirms is the *unitas in Trinitate*, but we cannot understand the Trinity without bearing in mind the divine unity, *Trinitas in unitate*[11]. The God revealed in Christ is at the same time the one God and the triune God.

---

10 Christian theology is always aware of this problem. We will, however, address this in Chapter 10 on the unity of God. Cfr. MANARANCHE A., *Il monoteismo cristiano*, Brescia 1988. This problem should not be neglected in the Christian dialogue with Jews and Muslims.

11 Lateran Council, year 649 (DS 501): «Si quis… non confitetur… trinitatem in unitate et unitatem in trinitate». SCHEFFCZYK L., *Der Gott der Offenbarung. Gotteslehre*, 343ff, 344: «…Christian faith in the Trinity was always understood as the highest form of faith in one God». Cfr. GREGORY OF NAZIANZUS, *Or.* 25,17 (SCh 284,198).

From the very beginning we must be extremely clear and aware of the great originality of the idea of the Christian vision of God. We will develop this idea throughout our exposition. This does not mean that outside the scope of the Christian faith we cannot know anything about God. Faith itself tells us otherwise. The revelation of the Old Testament is an integral part of the Christian message, even though only in the light of Jesus can it receive its ultimate and definite sense. There are seeds of the Word and rays of the truth, as well as presence of the Spirit, in so many cultural traditions and religions[12]. God can be known by the works of creation (cfr. Wis 13:1-9; Rom 1:19-23), which can lead to the certainty of his existence with the light of reason (cfr. DS 3004). The Christian faith, which cannot be the result or consequence of rational deduction, must be justified before reason itself. However, the depth of the mystery of God is only known through Christian revelation, whereby Jesus tells us everything that he has heard from his Father (cfr. John 15:15). The acknowledgement of the possibility of a true knowledge of God outside the scope of faith should not lead us to minimize the originality of the Christian message and its vision of God. Only against the background of the Trinitarian mystery is it possible to understand the incarnation and the fact that God is made a human being and shares our condition in everything except for sin (cfr. Heb 4:25), including his death, even the death on the cross (Phil 2:6-11). Likewise, only because God is one and triune, can we think that he enables all of us to share in the fullness of his life.

Having reached this point, we must go one step further. The revelation of God in Jesus, the Christian revelation of the one and triune God, is a confrontation with an even greater mystery. In fact, it would be easier to understand a God who would present himself as simply unipersonal. He would be less mysterious than our one and triune God, revealed as such in the incarnation of the Son. Therefore, we must not think that the revelation of God, made a reality in Christ, will «explain» to us the being of God or will make his mystery a mystery that we can take in. «The God who sends his Son into the world, the God who manifests his love by delivering him to death, appears before us even more mysterious and inscrutable»[13]. In this way, the Christian revelation appears as the most immediate confrontation with the mystery of

---

12 Cfr. Second Vatican Council, NA 2; AG 9.11; OT 16. Also JOHN PAUL II, *Redemptoris Missio*, 28-29; 55-56; and International Theological Commission, *Christianity and the Religions*, Città del Vaticano 1997, 40-45.

13 JOHN PAUL II, in his audience dated 25-9-95; cfr. *Insegnamenti di Giovanni Paolo II* 8,2 (1985) 764.

God[14]. In all this mystery, we must see the definitive nature of the manifestation of God in Christ. The closest proximity to God means the greatest possibility of seeing his inscrutable greatness. A mystery is not simply what is irreconcilable or incompatible with our experience; neither is it what we do not know and what we might even get to know some day, but the mystery is God himself. God is the holy mystery that comprises it all. The greater the revelation of God, the greater his mystery will be. Knowing that we do not know is even more imposing because it confronts us with the immense greatness of God, and this is not despite his proximity, but precisely as a result of it. This could even be applied to the beatific vision itself:

> What is known about God is known under the premise that it is not understandable. What is known about God is really known in the ultimate of human knowledge only when its mysterious nature is acknowledged at the highest level. The supreme knowledge is the knowledge of the supreme mystery as such[15].

This is the reason why the revelation of the mystery of God in Christ does not solve the issue of God, but rather confronts us in a more radical way with the mystery of what God himself is. However, we are confronted with him, although he gives himself to us and although he is within our reach, because he accepts us and takes us. It is the radical immanence of the holy mystery, and not its remoteness, that makes us grasp his full splendor. Therefore, in Jesus we have the revelation of the mystery of God when we contemplate the glory that corresponds to him as the only Son of the Father (cfr. John 1:14). In the mystery of Christ that the Father reveals to us, we are faced with the expression of the unfathomable mystery of God who paradoxically can reveal himself to us in the proximity of his Son made man, and the greater his transcendence, the closer he can be to us.

---

14 Von Balthasar H.U., *Teodramática 3. Las personas del drama: el hombre en Cristo*, Madrid 1993, 486: «A purely transcendent God (in case such a God might exist) would be an abstract and purely negative mystery. However, a God who could also be immanent in his transcendence is a concrete and positive mystery: insofar as he comes close to us, we begin to acknowledge how high he is above us, and insofar as he reveals himself to us, we really begin to understand how incomprehensible he is».

15 Rahner K., «Sobre el concepto de misterio en la teología católica» in *Escritos de Teología* iv, Madrid 1964, 53-101, esp. 83. In the Christian tradition, this aspect has been greatly emphasized, as for instance, by Gregory of Nazianzus, *De vita Mos.* ii 162 (SCh 1bis, 210): «This is precisely what the true knowledge of what we are searching for consists: seeing by not seeing»; ii 233 (266): «This is the real vision of God: the one who sees him will never be satiated in his desire to see»; idem 235;239 (268;270).

The mystery of the love of God is the main element of divine revelation. All this is an invitation to praise and glory, to adoration, and not a negative affirmation, because the God whom we cannot grasp and who is beyond and above us, turns to us. The concealment of God is the concealment in his revelation, the concealment of his glory in the passion and death of Jesus Christ, which is the ultimate manifestation of the love of God for the world. The revelation of the mystery, that is, the revelation of our salvation, cannot be more than God himself[16]. The revelation of the mystery of God, that is, Christ himself, gives us the fullness of wisdom and knowledge: «… until they are rich in the assurance of their complete understanding and have knowledge of the mystery of God in which all the jewels of wisdom and knowledge are hidden» (Col 2:2-3).

This is precisely what appears in Jesus: the love of God, greater than we can even contemplate, manifested to humanity. God so loved the world that he sent his only Son (John 3:16) to die for us. It is the revelation of the abyss of love; it is the incomprehensibility of the incomprehensible immanence, which responds from the depths to the expectations of the human heart. It is a hope that humans can never attain by themselves. This realization is precisely the revelation of the one and triune God. This is the God who in his incomparably greater proximity manifests his incomparable incomprehensibility and vice versa. The revelation of God is the mystery of our salvation; it is participation in God's own life.

Here we are faced with the mystery of *Deus semper maior,* related to the mystery of the love of God. In the New Testament, in the writings of John in particular, we find several «definitions» of God[17]. Among them, mention can be made of 1John 4:8,16: «God is love»[18]. The whole of Trinitarian theology can be understood as a commentary on this phrase, and in fact, we will simply try to decipher its meaning and sense throughout our exposition. As related to the God who is manifested in Christ, the first epistle of John implies the love that God is in himself.

---

16 Cfr. KASPER W., *Der Gott Jesu Christi*, 165-167.

17 The inadequacy of the term is clearly evident. God is by definition the «infinite », the one who knows no limit. Hence, according to John 4:24, God is spirit. The notion of spirit precisely indicates what is uncontrollable, what humans cannot encompass. According to 1 John 1:5, God is light, an idea that clearly points, as well, to the fullness without any limits.

18 Cfr. SCHNACKENBURG R., *Cartas de San Juan*, Barcelona 1980, 256-264 (El amor como esencia de Dios). SÖDING TH., « "Gott ist Liebe", 1 Joh. 4:8-16 als Spitzensatz Biblischer Theologie» in SÖDING TH., (Hg.), *Der lebendige Gott. Studien zur Theologie des Neuen Testaments* (Festschrift W. Thüsing), Münster 1996, 306-357.

Herein lies the distinct newness of the concept of the biblical God and, above all, the Christian God. The Aristotelian God is the unmoved mover, the end of all things, the one who attracts them. He is love, although not the lover[19]. Being omniperfect, he cannot love because loving tends towards possessing. The God revealed in Christ offers us the dimension of love as a bestowal of himself[20]. It is precisely the radical nature of his giving himself to us that evidences the never-ending condition of the God who loves us. The mystery of God that appears before us in his revelation is, above all, the mystery of his infinite love. This is the love that the Trinitarian doctrine of the Church tries to analyze in greater depth. Hence, it is not at all surprising that recent documents of the Church present to us the mystery of the one and triune God as the central mystery of Christianity:

> The mystery of the Holy Trinity is the core mystery of faith and of Christian life. It is the mystery of God himself. Hence, it is the source of all the other mysteries of faith. It is the light that enlightens us. It is the most fundamental teaching in the «hierarchy of the truths» of faith. «The history of salvation is the same history of the path and the modality with which the true and one God —the Father, the Son, and the Holy Spirit— is revealed to humanity, alienated by sin, reconciling them and uniting them to a "Yes"»[21].

This verification takes us directly to the next point that we must address.

---

19 Cfr. Aristotle, *Metaphysics* XII 7-9,1072-1074. Cfr. the edition edited by Reale G. (ed.), 562-584.
20 Cfr. Jüngel E., *Gott als geheimnis der Welt*, Salamanca 1984, 464 (esp. edition 433): «... the collation "God is love" is a statement that preserves the divinity of God».
21 CEC 234, translation based on the typical edition, *Catechismus Catholicae Ecclesiae*, Città del Vaticano 1997, 71. The idea is summarized in ibid. 261, with the significant conclusion of the strict necessity for the revelation of this mystery so that we can know it: «The mystery of the Holy Trinity is the core mystery of the faith and of the Christian life. Only God can reveal it to us, revealing himself to us as the Father, the Son and the Holy Spirit» (ibid. 78). Other Christian confessions also confess the centrality of the mystery of the one and triune God. Hence, the World Council of Churches defines itself as follows: «The World Council of Churches is a fellowship of churches that confesses the Lord Jesus as God and Savior according to the Scriptures, and these churches try to respond together to their common vocation for the glory of the only God, the Father, the Son and the Holy Spirit». Cfr. Vercruysse J., *Introduzione alla teologia ecumenica*, Casale Monferrato 1992, 51.

3

The core nature of the faith in the One and Triune God

If faith tells us that God is the only purpose of humanity and also points to the fact that the originality of the Christian conception about him lies in the ultimate characteristic of being the God of love, or the one and triune God, it should not surprise us that this confession is the very core of the Christian faith. According to the mandate of Jesus in Matthew 28:19, baptism is administered in the name of the Father and of the Son and of the Holy Spirit. This fact itself points to the significance of faith in the triune God because in his name one enters the community of believers. Almost all the old professions of faith, the symbols, have a Trinitarian structure[22]. We will refer specifically to the Symbols of the Apostles and the Symbols of Nicaea-Constantinople. The confession of faith in Father, Son, and Holy Spirit precedes the professions of other truths when these are introduced[23]. Other formulas have a bipartite, Trinitarian-Christological structure[24]. In these cases, the Trinitarian part takes the first place. The Trinity is in the very center of the Christian liturgy, in the Eucharistic celebration, and in that of the other sacraments. The Eucharistic prayer is always addressed to the Father[25], and it ends with a doxology in which the three persons are mentioned: «Through Christ, with Christ and in Christ». The prayers are usually addressed to the Father, through Jesus Christ in the unity of the Holy Spirit. In order to avoid any subordinationist interpretations, the formula of praise and glory to the Father, through the Son in the Holy Spirit, gave way to the one that we use more frequently nowadays: «Glory be to the Father, and to the Son and to the Holy Spirit», which underlines the equal dignity of the three persons[26]. The Trinity has also been placed in the very heart of the life of the Church in the Sec-

---

22 Likewise, the «rule of faith» presented by the ancient writers: cfr. for instance, IRENAEUS OF LYONS, *Adv. Haer.* I 10,1 (SCh 264,154-156); *Adv. Prax.* 2,2 (Scarpat,144-146), and others.

23 Cfr. the examples mentioned in DS 1-64. Some of these symbols are under a question that reflects the same scheme (cfr. DS 36; 61-64).

24 Cfr. DS 71-75. Especially significant among these symbols, is the so-called «Quicumque», DS 75, which dates back probably to around the first half of the fifth century.

25 According to the ancient formula of the Council of Hippo of 393: «cum altari adsistitur semper ad Patrem dirigatur oratio». Cfr. NEUNHAUSER B., «"*Cum altari adsistitur semper ad Patrem dirigatur oratio*". Der Kanon 21 de Konzils von Hippo 393. Seine Bedeutung und Nachwirkung» in *Aug* 25 (1985) 105-119.

26 Cfr. BASIL OF CAESAREA, *De Spiritu Sancto* I 3 (SCh 17bis,256). Both formulas are correct according to the Bishop of Caesarea.

ond Vatican Council. This is the Church summoned to unity: «Hence, the whole Church manifests itself "as a throng assembled around the unity of the Father, and of the Son and of the Holy Spirit"»[27] (LG 4).

Undoubtedly what is in the very heart of faith and in the life of the Church should also be in the very heart of Christian awareness. Only with the background of the Trinitarian doctrine can we understand the salvation of Christ. Without it, Christology is a mere functionality which, as it turns out, ends by destroying the function itself. Indeed, if we are to limit our concern to the meaning for us of Jesus or God, without wondering what they are on their own, this would be equivalent to losing sight of the meaning of Christian salvation itself. If we do not address what the divine mystery of the Father who sends his Son and the Holy Spirit is in itself, as well as the unity of the three who are the only God, why should we attribute to Christ a distinct and unsurpassable nature? In which intrinsic relationship with the mystery of Christ do we find the gift of the Spirit? Why has the salvation of the whole world been fulfilled in Christ? What is, in short, this salvation that has been characterized on so many occasions as participation in the divine life? All these questions are highly significant, and they cannot be answered without relying on an adequate vision of the mystery of the one and triune God. We arrive at the mystery of God by means of the history of salvation, although the demand for shedding light on this mystery also comes from the *historia salutis* itself, which would lack any foundation without this consideration of what God himself is.

4

The Trinity falls into «Oblivion»

The Christian doctrine of God will always be searching for a balance between divine unity and divine Trinity. Neither a simply monadic God nor tritheism is compatible with the revelation of the New Testament. Maintaining the balance between these two poles has not been an easy task, and it is still not so. It is a fact that in the Western world, both preaching and the catechesis about the one and triune God have not always been successful. The divine Trinity has been simply

---

27 CIPRYANE OF CARTAGHE, *De orat. dom.* 23 (PL 4,553); AUGUSTINE, *Sermo* 71, 20,33 (PL 38,463f); JOHN OF DAMASCUS, *Adv. iconocl.* 12 (PG 96,1358). Cfr. SILANES N., *La Iglesia de la Trinidad. La SS. Trinidad en el Vaticano II,* Salamanca 1981.

regarded as a mystery that cannot be understood, rather than as the foundation and the beginning of our salvation. In this same theology, the doctrine of the Trinity has suffered a certain degree of «isolation» in some periods of time. Once we have stated that God is one and triune, this statement has been practically put aside, or at least, it has not been as effective with respect to the development of a considerable number of the remaining issues that are related to it[28]. It has not always been easy to grasp the sense of these teachings. There is no doubt that at certain points in time, there has been evidence in wide strata of believers of a certain decrease in the sense of the originality of Christian monotheism and of the Christian vision of Christ.

Different factors have contributed to this result. The Enlightenment had searched for universal reason and had been quite critical with historical religion, and more specifically with Christianity. How can the salvation of all of us depend on a concrete event that many do not even know or cannot have the remotest possibility of knowing? Is not there some sort of an injustice on the part of God who enables a considerable number of human beings to be ignorant of Christ[29]? All these questions necessarily lead to the underestimation of Christianity and of every positive religion. The uniqueness of the Christ event will thus undoubtedly be something secondary, because what really matters is the religion of reason. This is a starting point for many of the major ideas about God.

In this respect, I. Kant is worth special mention. This author set forth his ideas mainly in his work *Die Religion innerhalb der Grenzen der reinen Vernunft* (Religion Within the Limits of Pure Reason). According to him, the true Church should be universal. It cannot be based on a historical revelation that would necessarily be very specific. Hence, only pure religious faith, based on reason, can be acknowledged as the true one[30]. What religion declares as a mystery can be limited to reason itself, and especially to its moral dimension. When there are biblical texts that do not only go beyond reason but can also be considered to be

---

28 Cfr. RAHNER K., «Advertencia sobre el tratado dogmático *De Trinitate*» in *Escritos de Teología* IV, Madrid 1964, 105-136, esp. 107-110, 117. The situation described by the German theologian fortunately no longer corresponds to that of current times. Also, in 1981, the International Theological Commission in its document *Theology-Christology-Anthropology* pointed to the fact that the Trinity was not duly taken into account by the authors of the neo-scholastic school in order to «understand the Incarnation and the deification of men»; cfr. Comisión Teológica Internacional, *Documentos 1980-1985*, Toledo, s.f. p. 12. See the Latin text «Theologia-Christologia-Anthropologia» in *Greg* 64 (1983) 5-24.

29 These and similar questions were addressed by J.J. Rousseau. Cfr. SULLIVAN F.A., *Salvation outside the Church? Tracing the History of the Catholic Response*, New York 1992, 104-108.

30 Cfr. *Die Religion*..., in KANT I., *Gesammelte Werke* IV, Berlin 1913, 115.

at odds with practical reason, they have to be interpreted in favor of the latter. This is what happens with the Trinity: «From the doctrine of the Trinity... we simply cannot derive anything for practical life, even when we believe that we are understanding it immediately, and far less when we are convinced that it goes beyond our capacity to understand». It makes no difference if in God there are three or ten persons, «we cannot derive from this differentiation any different rule that determines his behavior»[31]. Hence, what is imperative is a solely rational interpretation of the Trinity. Indeed, these teachings do not only go beyond, but they even go against practical reason. As a result of this, what the Christian doctrine of the one and triune God refers to as three persons, are simply these three attributes of God who is holy, benevolent, and just. As the creator of heaven and earth, he is the holy legislator. As the one who rules over and supports mankind, he is benevolent. He is the just judge who enforces his holy laws[32]. Hence, the Trinity is redirected towards the practical demand of «vocation», «satisfaction» and «choice» by God. It is «vocation» because humanity is called to a divine status, not as a result of the dependence derived from the creation, but by virtue of a law of freedom. It is «satisfaction» because human beings are morally corrupt, and thus they need God to compensate for what is missing in their human capabilities. It is the demand for «choice», by means of which God grants us celestial grace, not due to the merits of humanity, but as a result of his unconditioned decree[33].

The only Supreme Being, unipersonal although with the plurality of attributes, is the Father adored insofar as he loves the world; the Son insofar as he becomes a model for humankind; and the Holy Spirit insofar as he looks for agreement and consensus among humanity and shows a love founded on wisdom[34]. Talking to a God of three persons would be polytheism. Hence, it is no longer a matter of three persons, but a triple person as to «*summum ens, summa intelligentia, summum bonum*»[35]. With these assumptions, it is quite clear that Jesus Christ cannot be, in our reason, God in the *strictu sensu*, but a «divine man», the sublime ideal of innate virtue. In fact, «in the manifestation of the God-man, what is submitted to our senses or what can be known through experience is not

31 *Der Streit der Fakultäten* in *Gesammelte Werke* VII, 38-39.
32 Cfr. *Die Religion ...*, 139f.
33 Cfr. *Die Religion ...*, 142ff.
34 Cfr. *Die Religion ...*, 145ff.
35 Cfr. MILANO A., *La Trinità dei teologi e dei filosofi*, in PAVAN A. - MILANO A. (eds), *Persona e personalismi*, Napoli 1987, 120.

precisely the object of sanctifying faith, but rather the model that exists in our reason»[36]. Therefore, it seems that the same historical figure of Jesus is ultimately considered irrelevant.

Developing the Kantian philosophy of religion goes beyond the scope of this treatise, although it is worth referring to this significant example in order to see how Trinitarian theology is the first thing that disappears when we are looking for a God and a religion that are valid for all and that are also subject to the laws of reason as the supreme rule. Undoubtedly, the Church fought against this rationalism, although the necessities of the struggle sometimes led to the ground of the opponent. The apologetic concern forces us to remain in a field of common ideas. In this way, the peculiarity of the Christian God is pushed into the background to a secondary point in time once it has been evidenced that the revelation of God is possible. The contents of this revelation, and specifically the characteristics of the God who reveals himself in the incarnation, do not appear in the foreground of this confrontation.[37] A certain conception of the relationship between nature and grace may have helped shape this vision of things. Nature, and along with it the idea of God that can be attained through reason, would have a reason in itself. This supernatural revelation adds new contents to a horizon that would have sufficient sense per se. Hence, the Trinity would be added to an idea of the one God that could be considered per se as the natural purpose of men. What has brought the genuinely Christian idea of the love of God to the foreground of the interest in the Trinity has been the crisis of this rational idea of God— the appearance of atheism.

Nevertheless, the issue of the relative oblivion of the Trinitarian dogma also has more ancient intra-theological roots. Ante-Nicene theology was greatly

36 KANT I., *Die Religion*, 139. The same also in *Der Streit der Fakultäten* in *Gesammelte Werke* VII, 39: «The situation is exactly the same (as in the Trinity, cfr. footnote 31) for the doctrine of the incarnation of one person of the divinity. Indeed, if this God-man is not presented as the idea of mankind that from eternity meets with God in his complete moral perfection, pleasing to him…, but as the divinity that dwells corporally in the real man and that acts in him as a second nature. Hence, this mystery has no practical relevance for us, because we cannot expect of ourselves to act the same as God, and thus he cannot be an example for us».

37 Cfr. LATOURELLE R., *Teología de la Revelación*, Salamanca 1969, 242ff. According to this author, the treatises about revelation that date back to the turn of this century «soon address the problem of the possibility of revelation without noticing that it is not a matter of just any revelation, but a specific revelation that comes to us by means of history and the incarnation…». GONZÁLEZ DE CARDEDAL O. *La entraña del cristianismo*, Salamanca 1997, 71: «Theologians who wanted to refute this image of God were finally attracted to it when they accepted the assumptions of the debate».

Trinitarian in its formulations, and mostly so when considering the development of the saving economy. However, it was not always fully clear, at least in the case of subsequent times, regarding the implications of the Trinitarian dogma, specifically as it related to the equal dignity of the persons. As a result, this great theology acquired some positions that could be accused of a certain ambiguity from the point of view of the events that followed. Specifically, this refers to the tendency of considering the Son and the Holy Spirit «subordinated» in a certain sense to the Father, although their divine condition is clearly affirmed. The Arian crisis forced an in-depth reformulation of this issue. The fact that the divinity of the Son (and of the Holy Spirit) was denied meant going back to a monotheism where there was only place for one divine person, that of the Father. The orthodox affirmation of the divinity of the Son and of the Holy Spirit led to the strong emphasis on the unity of the divine essence, which was manifested in the unity of the *ad extra* actions. When the problem of subordination is eradicated from the realm of theology, what emerges is the problem of the relevance of the Trinitarian dogma and its relationship with the history of salvation[38]. The legitimate and necessary affirmation of the unity could have led to forgetting, to a certain extent, the relevance that the different persons also have in the *ad extra* actions of the only God with respect to us[39]. Insisting on the unity of the essence of the only God and on the likeness of the three persons can never make us forget the differences between them, because that is what makes the history of salvation possible, and it is thus reflected in this history. The only God whom Christians profess has to appear from the very beginning as a triune God who reveals himself in his relationships with us. The fact that there is only one God and only one beginning for all creatures does not mean that this is an undifferentiated beginning. If we say, following the Catechism of the Catholic Church (cfr. footnote 21), that the Trinity sheds light on all the mysteries of faith, this should have its consequences in each one of the theological topics.

---

38 Cfr. on this scope of problems, ANGELINI G., «Il tema trinitario nella teologia scolastica» in *ScCat* 116 (1990) 31-67.
39 An example of this relative oblivion. THOMAS AQUINAS in *STh* III 23,2 even affirms that the invocation of the «Our Father» is addressed to the three divine persons and that it is convenient for the full Trinity to adopt humans as the children of God. Cfr. AUGUSTINE, *Trin.* V 11,12 (CCL 50,219).

5

About the structure of the treatise

⌁

It is no longer common to see in recent treatises the classical distinction between a section that addresses the *De Deo uno* and another one that addresses the *De Deo trino*[40], which distinction is ultimately derived from the systematic approach of Saint Thomas who analyzes first what corresponds to the essence of God and subsequently, the distinction between the persons[41].

This division has been very successful throughout the centuries. It was further accentuated in the times of the Renaissance and during the Baroque period, and it has easily given the impression that it is responsible for an extremely drastic distinction between those truths that reason can grasp and those that can only be known by way of divine revelation. In Thomas, we study the divine essence along with its attributes and the knowability of God, and so forth. Hence, the first part of this treatise, and to a certain extent even the second one, as the first one has already set the pace and the «tone» of the presentation, are centered around the «himself» of God, and they are barely related to the saving mystery. The *de Deo uno* turned into a basically philosophical treatise[42]. After having attempted to recover its theological contents, it strongly insists on the revelation of God in the Old Testament. Nevertheless, it is quite obvious that the division between revelation of the one God in the Old Testament and of the triune God in the New Testament would be too simple, and hence, inexact. This is the case because the revelation of the Trinity is an actual deepening of the divine unity itself, and it is by no means a simple juxtaposition. Therefore, the division in both treatises between the one God and the triune God seems to be far more difficult, if not impossible. Additionally, some of the classical sections of the *de Deo uno*, specifically the divine attributes or properties, are better understood if we bear in mind the triune God, the communion of persons, and not only a divine

---

40 This distinction is very clearly maintained as well in the title of Rovira Belloso J.M., *Tratado de Dios uno y trino*, Salamanca 1993. A distinction is maintained in some manuals that address the set of dogmas. Hence, Müller G.L., *Katholische Dogmatik. Für Studium und Praxis der Theologie*, Freiburg-Basel-Wien 1996, although it does not respond to the common division between the one God and the triune God. Cfr. footnote 46.

41 Cfr. *STh* I 2, *prol.* Thomas is consistent with this distinction throughout his treatise. Still, Lombardo P., *Liber Sententiarum* I, combines those issues that in time will be the treatises of *De Deo uno* and *De Deo trino*.

42 Cfr. Stagliano A., *Il mistero del Dio vivente*, Bologna 1996, 320f.

abstract essence[43]. It is also far easier to reflect on the very nature of this divine essence once we know that it is possessed by the Father, Son, and Holy Spirit. On the other hand, the growing concern of beginning with the *historia salutis,* and hence with the revelation of God in Jesus, is what makes this division even more difficult. Therefore, following the prevailing line thought in past times, we will attempt to integrate the two areas of problems. We will attach a very marked and clear preference to those that belong to the *de Deo trino* in the traditional distinction. Nevertheless, we will attempt to show, as has been traditionally the case, that the Trinity and the divine unity are two equally original aspects of the essence of God that can never be seen as one separated from the other. We will focus our attention from the very beginning on the one and trine God, the «triune» God[44].

Our systematic starting point will be the revelation of God in Christ. As we have already stated, there is no other way to grasp the profound mystery of the true God. In the life of Jesus, in the revelation of the «economic Trinity», we see opening before us the mystery of the immanent Trinity. After a systematic reflection on the economic and immanent Trinity, we will focus our attention on the manifestation of the Trinity in the life of Jesus and in the first Christian community. The evolution of the Trinitarian doctrines until the second council of Constantinople and the medieval councils will be the next step. However, we will leave the studies of Saint Augustine and of the most important medieval theologians for the section that addresses the systematic reflection. We will begin with the classical concepts of processions and relationships that will pave the way and lead us to the study of the «person», which is the key notion of Trinitarian theology. We will study the classic ideas and the modern problems around this concept. From this, we can move to the significance of the affirmation of the three persons in the one God. God the Father, Son, and Holy Spirit in their personal properties will be analyzed subsequently. Only after this will we address briefly the unity of the divine essence and the properties of God, along with the natural knowledge of God and the language of analogy. In fact, I believe that once

---

43 In this respect, the statements of AUER J., *Gott, der Eine und Dreieine,* Regensburg 1978; SCHEFFCZYK L., *Der Gott der Offenbarung. Gotteslehre,* Aachen 1996, are quite interesting.

44 The normal term for referring to the Trinity in the German language is *Dreieinigkeit.* Hence, it combines Trinity and unity in the same word. In the Latin languages, we need to resort to neologisms in order to express this idea. KASPER W., *Der Gott Jesu Christi,* Mainz 1982, 381: «Der eine Gott ist… der dreieine». GRESHAKE G., *Der dreieine Gott. Eine trinitarische Theologie,* Freiburg-Basel-Wien 1997.

we have studied the Trinity of persons, it is easier to address the issue of the divine essence and the properties of God. This is an essence that is possessed by the three persons and an essence of the properties of God who is in himself love and communion[45].

6

The treatise about God in theological systematic thought

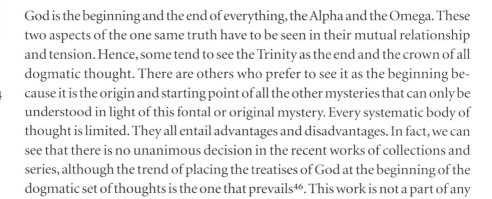

God is the beginning and the end of everything, the Alpha and the Omega. These two aspects of the one same truth have to be seen in their mutual relationship and tension. Hence, some tend to see the Trinity as the end and the crown of all dogmatic thought. There are others who prefer to see it as the beginning because it is the origin and starting point of all the other mysteries that can only be understood in light of this fontal or original mystery. Every systematic body of thought is limited. They all entail advantages and disadvantages. In fact, we can see that there is no unanimous decision in the recent works of collections and series, although the trend of placing the treatises of God at the beginning of the dogmatic set of thoughts is the one that prevails[46]. This work is not a part of any

45 I do not agree with the opinion that tends to identify the one God with the Father. There are clear conclusions that can be derived from the article written by Rahner K., *Theos im Neuen Testament* («*Theos* en el Nuevo Testamento» in *Escritos de Teología* I, Madrid 1963, 93-167), on the fact that in the New Testament God refers to the Father and that God is the God of the Old Testament. Hence, we do not follow the idea that whatever must be said about God is simply said about the Father. The Father is simply the Father in his relationship with the Son and the Holy Spirit, and the three of them make up the only God. Cfr. the paragraphs devoted to the Father and the divine unity in chapters 10 and 11.

46 Hence, in Schneider Th. (Hrsg.) *Handbuch der Dogmatik*, 2 volumes, Düsseldorf 1992, the Trinity appears at the end, even though it has preceded the treatises about God (cfr. the Italian translation *Nuovo corso di dogmatica*, Brescia 1995). The collection that will begin to be published, *Katholische Dogmatik*, of Scheffczyk L. - Ziegenaus A. places the treatises of God (cfr. number 7), the first one published in the second volume of the series, after the introduction. A similar decision was adopted in his time by Auer J. - Ratzinger J., *Kleine katholische Dogmatik*. The treatise of God also appears at the beginning of the dogmatic information in *Mysterium Salutis*. Pannenberg W. has also placed it at the beginning of the dogmatics in his *Systematische Theologie*. Müller G.L., *Katholische Dogmatik. Für Studium und Praxis der Theologie*, Freiburg-Basel-Wien 1996, includes a chapter on the revelation of God the creator as the God of Israel and the Father of Jesus Christ, after anthropology and creation. They are followed by Christology and Pneumatology, and after these treatises, the Trinity is like a conclusion of a theological-Christological block, before Mariology, eschatology, ecclesiology, and the sacraments. Likewise, Beinert W. (Hrsg.), *Glaubenszugänge. Lehrbuch der kath. Dogmatik*, Paderborn-München-Wien-Zürich 1995, places the treatise of God at the beginning, combining the subjects of the two traditional treatises (Breuning W., *Gotteslehre* Volume I, 201-362). In our times, the *Sapientia*

series, and hence this problem is not as important. However, I believe that there are good reasons to include these treatises at the beginning of theological studies and closely related to Christology.[47] I believe that the reasons set forth by W. Kasper in the final pages of his theological treatise *Der Gott Jesu Christi* (*The God of Jesus Christ*)[48] are quite correct and accurate. The treatise about God, and concretely about the triune God, must be included at the beginning of dogmatic presentation because it addresses a topic that will come up again under multiple variations. The issue becomes thematic among the many topics of dogmatic thought. In a way, it is the grammar of the other topics of the dogmatic presentation, the basic affirmation of theology (*Grundsatz*) that can never become an adjunct (*Zusatz*). We must run the risk that everything is not well understood from the beginning. In all other respects, many of the topics that are the object of study will not be exhausted once and for all in this treatise. We will have to return to them on other occasions[49].

We will attempt to ensure that the treatise of God revealed in Christ is not a speculation devoid of significance for life. At every point in time, we must see the theological relevance of the various affirmations within the context of the faith of the Church and of Christian life. As we have already suggested, we will constantly have to open ourselves to the adoration of the holy mystery which we cannot fully grasp. However, at the same time we will not refrain from addressing the inherent difficulties of the subject we are studying. Faith attempts to understand, not through a superfluous speculation, but because there is a need to believe more profoundly and to give a better reason for our hope. It is faith that leads to understanding (*crede ut intelligas*), but the latter, if correct, can only enrich faith itself (*intellige ut credas*). By exercising this intelligence, in this as well as in other theological fields, we face times of difficulty and dryness.

Fidei collection places it at the beginning of the dogmatic treatises. The *Corso di Teologia Sistematica* places it after the introductory volume and that of basic theology. LAURET B. - REFOULÉ R. (eds), *Initiation à la pratique de la Théologie*, 5 volumes, Paris 1982, place it at the end of the dogmatic presentation (volume 3, 225-276). Regarding some aspects of the history of this issue, see SCHEFFCZYK L., *Der Gott der Offenbarung. Gotteslehre*, 206-210.

47 Cfr. COLOMBO G., «"Teocentrismo" e "cristocentrismo"» in *Teologia* 6 (1981), 293-306, esp. 295. We cannot talk about the Christian God ignoring Jesus Christ, nor can we talk about Jesus Christ before talking about God.

48 Cfr. number 44; especially interesting are pages 379 and 380 of this work.

49 PANNENBERG W., *Teología Sistemática* I, Madrid 1992, 362: «The doctrine of creation, Christology, and the doctrine of reconciliation, ecclesiology and eschatology are all part of the complete development of the doctrine of the Trinity… On the contrary, the Trinitarian doctrine of God is an anticipated summary of all Christian dogmatic thought».

We cannot refrain from this either. Only with appropriate efforts will we discover the wealth of the great insights of those who have preceded us, in order to feel more enlightened by the mystery of love which surrounds us, and we will be able to know better the God in whom «we live, and move, and exist» (Acts 17:28).

The relationship between the «economic» Trinity and the «immanent» Trinity

From the economic Trinity to the immanent Trinity

The brief introduction to the treatise has enabled us to see that simply by the revelation that took place in Christ we have access to the knowledge of the one and triune God. Hence, our starting point can only be the saving economy, and more specifically, whatever the New Testament tells about Jesus Christ, who by revealing the Father to us also reveals himself as the Son. Subsequently, after his resurrection, he sends, on behalf of the Father, the Holy Spirit who has descended on him in baptism and given him the strength to fulfill his mission. Therefore, the «economy» is the only way in which we can acquire the knowledge of the «theology»[1]. A brief reflection on the relationship between the two will help us analyze, in greater depth and relying on further information, the history of the Trinitarian revelation.

The relationship between the economy and the theology has recently been amply discussed in theological studies. This basically stemmed from the formulation set forth by K. Rahner of the so-called «fundamental» axiom of Trinitarian theology. «The economic Trinity is the immanent Trinity and vice versa»[2]. Or, stated in other words, the one and triune God is revealed in the «economy», just as he is in his immanent life, that is, by means of the revelation of Christ we have a real access to «theology». The formulation of this principle and the discussions it has sparked have led to a renewed awareness of the theology of this ancient truth: only from the revelation that was evidenced in Christ can it make sense to talk about the triune God. We say that the truth is old. The Trinity is a truth based on faith, not inferable from any knowledge of God that we can acquire as a result of the things that have been created. This is explicitly the opinion

---

1 This last one is frequently referred to in Latin as *dispositio, dispensatio.* Cfr. the work *Catechism of the Catholic Church* (CEC), number 236, which refers to this old distinction of the Fathers. At any rate, it is worth noting, as we will see in due time, that these words are not always given the same significance.

2 «El Dios trino como principio y fundamento trascendente de la historia de la salvación» in *MySal* II/1, Madrid 1969, 359-449; here 370. Cfr. also for what follows, ibid. 370-371. Even before this, RAHNER K. had set forth similar ideas in «Advertencias sobre el tratado dogmático *De Trinitate*» in *Escritos de Teología* IV, Madrid 1964, 105-136. I do not simply set forth here the doctrine of Rahner, but rather, taking as a starting point his reflections and the discussions to which they have given rise, I will try to clarify the issue of the knowledge of the divine Trinity starting from the revelation of this Trinity in the history of salvation.

of Thomas Aquinas, among many others[3]. It is evident that we cannot consider things otherwise. Efforts initiated by Augustine and continued in medieval theology aimed at finding in created realities the imprints and traces —*vestigia*—[4] of the Trinity, sometimes giving the impression of being rational deductions, but which are frequently simply attempts at explanations that presuppose the universe of faith, and which certainly we cannot understand based on our current categories[5]. Even so, they can show from the light of faith in Jesus that the one and triune God from whom everything comes is not far from us or from our world. Even though the principle of the non-inferability of the Trinity from creation prevails, we can find in our human experience certain elements that open us, at least initially, to the profound sense of what we are when enlightened by faith. The «seeds of the Word», the fragments of the truth that the Logos has spilled over the world[6], are undoubtedly related as well to the Trinity, even though they are not revealed explicitly.

«No one has ever seen God. It is the only Son, God, who is close to the Father's heart, who made him known» (John 1:18; cfr. 1Tim 6: 16). The revelation of the mystery of God in all its depth only occurs in Jesus Christ. Only by means of faith in him do we have access to this mystery. Only if we believe in him as the Son of God can we see in him the Father (cfr. John 14:9). This revelation gives us access to the mystery of God because he himself is the mystery of our salvation. The Second Vatican Council points out a clear connection between the revelation of God and the revelation of the saving truth (cfr. Second Vatican Council, *Dei Verbum* 2.6). Only God is the salvation of humanity. As a result of this, the knowledge of the triune God, as a truth based on faith, is only accessible to us through the revelation that was carried out by Jesus, because God himself is revealed in him. This implies that the God who is revealed to us appears before us just as he is. Otherwise, there would not be a true revelation. The Christian revelation is the revelation of God and of his saving plan and intention. In fact, according to the *Dei Verbum* constitution, this revelation takes place with words

---

3 Cfr. S*Th* I q. 32, a.1. Cfr. CEC 237.
4 Cfr. SCHEFFCZYK L., *Der Gott der Offenbarung*, 384ff.
5 Cfr. SIMMONS W., *Trinität und Vernunft*, Frankfurt Main 1972; BONANNI S., «Abelardo e il problema della conoscenza della Trinità. Riflesssioni a partire della lettura della Theologia Scholarium» in *Philologica* 4 (1995) 97-111.
6 Cfr. JUSTIN, *Apol.* I 5,4; (Wartelle, 104;160); II 7,7; 8,1-3; (206;208); CLEMENT OF ALEXANDRIA, *Protr.* I 6,4; X 98,4 (SCh 2bis,60;166); *Ped.* I 96,1-2 (FP 5,260); cfr. in footnote 12 of the previous chapter references to documents of the Second Vatican Council and of John Paul II.

and works, most especially those of Jesus: «... with the fact itself of his presence and with the manifestation that he fulfills in himself with words, with works, with signs and with miracles, and especially with his death and his resurrection from the dead, and finally, when he sends the Holy Spirit, he fulfills and completes the revelation...» (dv 4; cfr. ibid. 2). The revelation of God, as a saving revelation in itself, is evidenced in the execution per se of our salvation by the action of Christ. The two aspects cannot be separated[7]. We know the mysterious and luminous reality of the triune God as a result of the saving revelation that Christ makes of himself. Hence, the way in which the Trinity appears before us in the economy of salvation has to reflect how it is in itself[8]. This is the reflection that seems to prevail. Otherwise, the salvation of humanity would not be God himself. We would have to look for it elsewhere, or otherwise the God who is revealed and who saves us would not be the one that he is in himself, which obviously is not in agreement with the Christian faith.

It does not seem that this line of reasoning can be opposed to the principle of the unitary action of three divine persons with respect to the world and with respect to humanity, *ad extra*, in such a way that this manner of acting as a unit cannot reflect the Trinity in itself. Undoubtedly, it is necessary to maintain the principle of the unitary action of God. It would make no sense that the divine persons acted «separately» one from the other. However, at the same time, we must avoid giving excessive explanations about this principle that do not bear in mind that the only beginning —that is God— always has the distinction in himself. In every instance of God acting outside himself, *ad extra*, the three divine persons act in unity. God is the only and one beginning of creation and of the history of salvation; we cannot talk about three beginnings. However, this cannot lead us to assume that this sole beginning is in itself indistinct. On the contrary, we know very well that it is not so and that it does not act outwards as

---

7 Cfr. ALFARO J., «Encarnación y revelación» in *Revelación cristiana, fe y teología,* Salamanca 1985, 65-88.

8 RAHNER K., «El Dios trino como principio y fundamento...», 371: «The phrase is indeed exact: the doctrine of the Trinity and the doctrine of the economy (doctrine about the Trinity and doctrine about salvation) cannot be distinguished adequately». As can be noticed, the identity does not rule out certain distinction, although it is not truly adequate. The distinction between the economic Trinity and the immanent Trinity is seen already in BARTH K., *Kirchliche Dogmatik,* I/1, München 1935, 352; and 503: «We have followed the rule, and we consider that it is of the utmost importance. Likewise, the statements about the reality of the modalities of being divine "basically by themselves" cannot be different as to the contents that have to be made precisely regarding the reality in the revelation».

such. It is also worth noting that the principle of the unitary action of God outwards was always moderated by the use of the doctrine of «appropriations». According to traditional theology, in the action of the one God, the different persons are also included in the language of the Scriptures of the Church under those modalities of acting that more directly correspond to what in the internal life of God is «typical» of that person[9]. Naturally, this assumes certain knowledge of what is inherent to each person within the Trinitarian life. Furthermore, in view of the fact that the Trinity is the object of faith and cannot be assumed in a purely rational way, but can only be known in the light of revelation, only by means of the saving way of acting of each person can we know what corresponds more directly to that person in the internal life of God. Hence, the principle of the unity of actions *ad extra* cannot exclude any intervention of the persons as such. Based on what we have just mentioned, it seems that it explicitly assumes the opposite[10].

Additionally, there is an event whereby we know that there is an outward action through which the person acts in a differentiated manner: the incarnation[11]. Only the Son has hypostatically assumed the human nature. It is not a matter of stating that the other two persons have not taken part in this event. We know quite well that this is not the case. The Father is the one who has sent the Son into the world, and this is also an inherent way of acting by the person of the Father (cfr. John 3:17, 34; Rom 8:3; Gal 4:4). On the other hand, the Holy Spirit who comes upon Mary enables the incarnation (cfr. Luke 1:35; Mark 1:20; DS 150). In the incarnation and throughout the life of Jesus on earth, as well as in his resurrection and exaltation to the right hand of the Father and in the gift of the Spirit that follows, we see a differentiated way of acting by the divine persons in saving history. It is precisely this differentiation which enables us to know them. We

---

9 Cfr. THOMAS AQUINAS, *STh* I q. 39, a.7, who defines appropriation as «the manifestation of individuals by means of their essential attributes». The essential attributes are those that correspond to the unique divine essence. It is clear that whatever we say here about appropriations does not pretend, by any means, to challenge its use and legitimacy. It is only a matter of making everyone realize that only in the light of what is typical of the persons, can we «appropriate» in them what corresponds to the three of them. In our chapter on the idea of the person, we will talk again about the «appropriations».

10 Cfr. the summary of the pneumatology of Athanasius and the Cappadocians in VON BALTHASAR H.U., *Theologik III. Der Geist der Wahrheit*, Einsiedeln 1987, 114-116. It is worth noting that the CEC 258 sets forth that each person carries out the common operation according to his personal property. To this end, the author bases his ideas on the II Council of Constantinople (DS 421, a text that we will analyze in due time).

11 Cfr. RAHNER K., «El Dios trino como principio y fundamento…», 372ff.

cannot think that the coming of Jesus Christ into the world is an exception in the way of God's acting with respect to us. Rather, we have to state quite the opposite. In Jesus Christ we have the culmination of this acting, as well as the paradigm and the foundation of everything that God does for us. Everything has its consistence in the beloved Son in whom we have redemption and pardon for our sins. Everything has been done through him and leads to him (cfr. Col 1:13-20).

We can ask ourselves, does the incarnation, precisely of the Son, sent by the Father, reflect something of the internal Trinitarian life, of what the persons are? How does this fact, which is a basic element in the saving economy, show something of the internal life of the Trinity? Because of the reasons to which we have already referred, it is clear that this revelation has taken place in Christ. Is it of no significance that it has been like this, or, in other words, could it have been done any other way? Or perhaps does this fact tell us something of what God is in himself?

Throughout the centuries, the common doctrine has been that any of the divine persons could have incarnated, even though the doctrine has always insisted on the «convenience» of the incarnation of the Son. For instance, this is what the two great Scholastic masters, Bonaventure and Thomas Aquinas believed[12]. However, this opinion is far from being accepted peaceably or from being considered clearly and definitely proven[13].

---

12   Cfr. BONAVENTURE, *In III Sent.* 1,1,4, although the convenience of the incarnation of the Son is also highlighted in ibid. 1,2,3; THOMAS AQUINAS, *STh* III q.3, a.5; the convenience of the incarnation of the Son in ibid. q.3 a.8. Saint Thomas states that regardless, in the case of the incarnation of the Father we cannot be talking about a «mission».

13   An historical note could be illustrative in this respect. Frequently (for instance, RAHNER K., «El Dios trino como principio y fundamento…», cfr. 374; also in *Grundkurs des Glaubens*, Freiburg-Basel-Wien 1976, 213) it is said that Saint Augustine would have been the first in stating this possibility. However, it does not seem that this is the case. Without having directly posed this question, he shows a sensitivity to the correspondence between the economic and the immanent Trinity, *Trin.* IV 20,28 (CCL 50,199): «Pater … non dicitur missus, non enim habet a quo sit aut ex quo procedat». Nevertheless, it is interesting, ibid. IV 21, 32 (205): «Quia etiam si voluisset deus pater per subiectam creaturam vissibiliter apparere, absurdissime tamen aut a filio quem *genuit*, aut a spiritu sancto *qui* de illo *procedit* missus diceretur»; the widest context addresses the theophany, and in the immediate plane, it is shown that the Son and the Holy Spirit, although sent by the Father, are not less than he because of this. The hypothesis of the incarnation is not considered directly. ANSELM, for reasons that can seem to us somewhat outlandish today, shows the inconvenience of the incarnation of the Father or of the Holy Spirit: *Ep de Inc. Verbi* 10 (SCHMITT, ed.), v. 2, 25-28; also *Cur Deus Homo?* II 9 (SCh 91,376f.). LOMBARD P. *Sent.* III 1, 1-2, addresses in the first place the convenience of the incarnation of the Son to affirm, after this, the possibility of the incarnation of the Father and of the Holy Spirit. Most probably, he is the first one to state this possibility. Let us note that the great scholars have changed the order in which he addresses the problem.

We could assume that if the Son has incarnated, it is because he is in himself the revealer of the Father, by being his perfect image (cfr. 2Cor 4:4; Col 1:15; also John 1:18; 14:9)[14]. We do not need to address the issue of whether the Father or the Holy Spirit could have incarnated, because the revelation does not offer us enough support for those speculations[15]. Nevertheless, some of the reasons that have been proposed in order to set forth the theoretical possibility of the incarnation of any of the three persons can give way to some reflection. In fact, one of the main reasons that led Thomas Aquinas to state the possibility of the incarnation of any of the three divine persons was the fact that the *ratio personalitatis* is common to the three persons, even though the personal properties of each one of them are evidently different[16]. However, addressing now some issues that we will analyze in greater detail and with more time later on, we can truly doubt that the term «person» or *hypostasis* means exactly the same when we apply it to the Father, to the Son, and to the Holy Spirit. The «numbers» in God are always a source of problems. Everything in him is unrepeatable[17]. Undoubtedly, the terminology of the three persons, consecrated by tradition, is not only legitimate, but also necessary. In one way or another, we will have to refer to the «three» that are mentioned in the formula of baptism and in our confessions of faith[18]. Nevertheless, we have to be aware of the difficulty entailed by the use of the plural number when applied to God. If this is the case, it would be legitimate to think that the communication of God to the world can be made under the

---

14 The condition of the image is included in the reasons that point to the convenience of the incarnation of the Son, both in the case of Thomas and in the case of Buenaventura (cfr. the works that have been quoted in footnote 12). The old Fathers of the Church have insisted considerably on this idea of the image, without posing the idea that we are addressing now: *Adv. Haer.* IV 6,6 (SCh 100, 450): «visibile Patris Filius»; cfr. also 6,7 (450ff.); CLEMENT OF ALEXANDRIA, the Son is the *prosopon* of the Father, *Paed.* I 57,2 (FP 5,192); *Strom.* V 24,1 (SCh 278,80); VII 58,3 (GCS 17,42); *Exc. Theod.* 10,5; 12,1; 23,5 (SCh 23,80;82;108). TERTULLIAN refers to the Son as the «facies» of the Father, *Adv. Prax.* 14, 8-10 (Scarpat, 180-182), even though it is a very difficult text. We will analyze again some of these texts when addressing specifically the person of the Son (Chapter 10).

15 This topic is not usually an issue for reflection among current authors. This theoretical possibility of the incarnation is defended by SALVATI M.A., *Teologia trinitaria della croce*, Leumann, Torino 1987, 98-104. In the discussion of the opposite opinion of K. Rahner, in *MySal* II/1, 375-378; also see *Grundkurs des Glaubens*, Freiburg-Basel-Wien 1976, 213-214.

16 Cfr. footnote 12.

17 Cfr. VON BALTHASAR H.U., *Theologik III. Der Geist der Wahrheit*, Einsiedeln 1987, 110-113, with abundant patristic quotations on this issue: cfr. mainly BASIL OF CAESAREA, *De Spiritu sancto*, 18, 44-45 (SCh 17bis, 402-408); also see MOLTMANN J., *Trinität und Reich Gottes*, München 1980, 204, speaks of the Trinitarian principle of unrepeatability, *Einmaligkeit*. Without discussing here the correct use of the principle, we must agree that it points to a real problem. We will address this issue again in our chapter devoted to the idea of the person (Chapter 9).

18 Cfr. AUGUSTINE, *Trin.* V 9,10; VII 4,7 (CCL 50,217; 256-257).

modality of an hypostatic union because this modality is suitable to the modality of being, *hypostasis,* of the second person, while the communication of the Holy Spirit does not take place in this sense because it would not correspond to the personal characteristics of the Holy Spirit[19].

In the opinion of Rahner, all this has important effects on anthropology. It is the second Adam, Jesus Christ, who is the one who gives significance to the first Adam(cfr. Rom 5:14; 1Cor 20-22, 45-49). The incarnation shows us the ultimate truth of human beings. There is a fundamental and internal relationship between the Logos and human nature. On the one hand, we find the Son as Logos —Word— who by his very essence is the «utterable», the word of the Father where he can manifest himself and discover himself freely in what is not divine. On the other hand, when this communication of the Logos with what is not divine takes place, it is simply because the Logos takes on human nature. Hence, this is not a mask that the Son of God has taken from outside, or behind which he hides. Rather, by virtue of its own origin, it is in itself the symbol of the Logos himself. In this way, «with an ultimate ontological authenticity we can and must state as follows: man is possible because the alienation of the Logos is possible»[20].

From the concrete modality as God, giving himself to us in the entire life, death, and resurrection of his Son and in the outpouring of the gift of his Spirit, he has revealed himself to us, and we can think that in that way of acting we are shown a part of his intimate being. God has revealed himself in the saving dispensation. Therefore, it is quite legitimate to think that this way of acting corresponds to his way of being in the fullness of his intra-Trinitarian life.

We must also bear in mind the concrete salvation that the Son of God has brought to us with his incarnation[21]. This salvation consists in the fact that we, in the Holy Spirit, become children of God. Once again, we are faced with the opinion of a widespread school of thought in ancient times. The unity of the *ad extra* action of the persons gives rise to the idea that we are the children of all the Trinity. On another path, we go back to the issue of the relative oblivion or irrelevance of the Trinitarian doctrine in the field of theology, a fact to which we

19 Cfr. RAHNER K., «El Dios trino como principio y fundamento… », 374. Even though between question marks, Rahner uses stronger expressions than the ones that I have used: «the peculiarity of this communication, insofar as it is determined by the peculiarity of the second person»; «depends on the nature itself of the third person».
20 RAHNER K., «El Dios trino como principio y fundamento… », 378; also cfr. from the same author, *Grundkurs des Glaubens,* Freiburg-Basel-Wien 1976, 211-225.
21 Cfr. RAHNER K., «El Dios trino como principio y fundamento… », 376. Also KASPER W., *Der Gott Jesu Christi,* Mainz 1982, 335.

have already referred. We know that one of the statements of Saint Thomas is the true foundation of this doctrine[22]. Despite this fact, it is difficult to find bases for this opinion in the New Testament, which is constantly assuming the opposite (cfr. Gal 4:4-6; Rom 8:14-16; Matt 5:45; 6:1,9,14 etc.; Luke 11:1-2). There is an intrinsic relationship in the Holy Spirit between the divine sonship of Jesus and ours[23]. «Grace» is not basically a gift of God, but the gift of God himself, the gift of the Holy Spirit, a *gift* by *antonomasia*, and even more so, the «gift person»[24]. Hence, we can think of a personal indwelling of the Holy Spirit in those who are just. Here we can see the distinction of the persons in the way in which God acts with respect to us, and based on this, we can discover the characteristics that are inherent to the Father, to the Son, and to the Holy Spirit in the internal life of the Trinity. God is communicated to us precisely as he is in himself. The one and triune God is our salvation and our savior[25].

Finally, the first part of the thesis of the identification between the economic and the immanent Trinity —that is, «the economic Trinity is the immanent Trinity»— tells us that God is the one who gives himself to us and who does not simply offer us gifts, even though we can believe they are indeed very important. If he should not give himself to us as he is, he would not be giving himself. If he did not manifest himself as he is, he would not be revealing himself to us. All this is not founded on the clear statement of a text from the Scriptures, but rather on the «spirit» of the latter. The love of God is manifested in the fact that he has given us his Son for the salvation of the world (John 3:16f; cfr. 1John 4; Gal 4:4; Rom 8:3,etc.). The Father sent the Spirit of the Son into our hearts (Gal 4:6), or the risen Jesus Christ gives us the Spirit on behalf of his Father (John 15:26), or the Father, in the name of Jesus Christ (John 14:26; 14:16). We must think that with this way of acting and communicating himself, God enables us to know him as he is. Thinking that he might have done things otherwise would simply be speculation, and the revelation offers no basis for this thinking. Hence, there is a correspondence between the economic and the immanent Trinity. They are the same. They are not distinguished to any degree. In this respect, there is no doubt that the postulate set forth by Rahner —at least, the first part— is both legitimate

---

22 Cfr. footnote 39 in the previous chapter. Also on the filial adoption, cfr. *STh* III 32,1; 45,4; *STh* I 33,3.
23 Cfr. LADARIA L.F., *Teología del pecado original y de la gracia*, Madrid 1993, 231-266.
24 Cfr. JOHN PAUL II, *Dominum et Vivificantem*, 10.
25 Although it is true that this title is generally attributed to Jesus Christ, the New Testament also attributes it to God the Father: cfr. for instance, 1Tim 1:1; 2:3; 4:10; Titus 1:3; 2:10; Jude 25.

and necessary. It has been fruitful for Catholic theology because it has contributed to the rediscovery of the soteriological implications of the dogma of the Trinity, its key nature in theology, and its relevance and significance for the Christian life. The International Theological Commission gives credence to the acceptance, at least in principle, in Catholic theology of the «fundamental axiom», when it states as follows:

> For this reason, the fundamental axiom of current theology is expressed quite well with the following words: the Trinity that is manifested in the economy of salvation is the same immanent Trinity, and the same immanent Trinity is the one that is freely and graciously communicated in the economy of salvation. Consequently, in both theology and catechism, we have to avoid any *separation* between Christology and the Trinitarian doctrine…[26].

Only against the background of the Trinity can Christology be understood, if we do not want to reduce it to a mere functionality that results in the complete loss of its significance. God shows himself to us in Jesus as he is. In this sense, Christology and the Trinitarian doctrine are inseparable.

2

From the Trinity to the Economy. The «identity» between the immanent Trinity and the economic Trinity

Although the first part of the axiom of Rahner has been accepted without difficulties in Catholic theology, difficulties have soon emerged as a result of the interpretation of the «vice versa», which is not free from the possibility of misunderstandings. Indeed, even though it is quite clear that the revelation of the Trinity in the saving economy is founded on the immanent Trinity, the latter might exist without its economic manifestation. Therefore, we have to determine what this axiom does not mean. In the first place, we have to stress that the economic communication of the immanent Trinity is free and

---

26 Commissio Theologica Internationalis, «Theologia-Christologia-Anthropologia» in *Greg* 64 (1983) 5-34; translation into Spanish in Comisión Teológica Internacional, *Documentos* 1981-1985.

gratuitous[27]. In other words, the identity does not mean that the immanent Trinity only exists in the economic Trinity, that God is triune insofar as he communicates himself to humanity, or that the Trinity of persons is the result of his free decision for the purpose of this *self-communication*. It is not difficult to see that this cannot be the case. The immanent Trinity communicates freely and gratuitously in the economy of salvation. The incarnation of the Word is the supreme gratuitous act of God. Likewise, creation, pointed in fact toward incarnation, is also gratuitous. God is not perfected with it[28] or with the saving economy. God does not need either humanity or the world. Only with the differentiation between the Trinity in itself and its communication can this divine freedom be preserved. Hence, a certain distinction (though not a separation) is inevitable[29]. The immanent Trinity is not fulfilled or dissolved in the economy. It has fullness in itself, regardless of the creation and the saving work. If this were not the case, our own salvation would be compromised. God would not be able to save us because he would have to achieve his own fullness, and ultimately, «save himself». Only if the transcendence of God is guaranteed, even affirming his profound immanence to this world, can the saving economy be really what it is. The immanent Trinity is the transcendent foundation of the economy of salvation.

As an example of the limited attention given to this principle, the philosophy of G. Hegel is usually quoted in this context. At least according to some interpretations, this philosophy would lead to certain confusion between the Trinity itself and its saving manifestation. In an attempt to overcome the displacement of faith to a higher sphere of reason, Hegel wants to include God and the Trinity under the analysis of philosophy[30]. For him, God is «spirit», absolute activity, a

27 This is clearly stated by RAHNER K., «El Dios trino como principio y fundamento… », 380. This communication is «free and not appropriate». The International Theological Commission (cfr. text referred to in the previous footnote) uses the same terms. Cfr. also for the discussion of the axiom, KASPER W., *Der Gott Jesu Christi*, 333ff. See also SCHEFFCZYK L., *Der Gott der Offenbarung*, Aachen 1996, 294-312, on the identity and distinction between the economic Trinity and the immanent Trinity.

28 Cfr. First Vatican Council, Constitution *Dei Filius* (DS 3002).

29 A distinction that K. Rahner himself recognizes when he states that the economic and the immanent Trinity are not adequately differentiated; cfr. footnote 7.

30 Cfr. HEGEL G.W.F., *Vorlesungen über die Philosophie der Religion III* (ed. LASSON G.), Leipzig 1929, 53ff. It is clear that we cannot start here a long presentation. See SPLETT J., *Die Trinitätslehre G.W.F. Hegels*, Freiburg-München 1965; BRITO E., *La christologie de Hegel*, Paris 1983; GRECO C., «La mediazione trinitaria dell'unità di Dio nella filosofia della religione di G.W.F. Hegel» in MUCCI G. (ed.), *Ecclesiologia e cultura moderna. Saggi teologici*, Roma 1979, 299-351. Brief summaries will be found in MILANO A., «La Trinità dei teologi e dei filosofi: l'intelligenza della persona in Dio» in PAVAN A.-MILANO A. (eds.), *Persona e personalismi*, Napoli 1987, 1-286, 149ff; ÁLAVAREZ

pure act and full subjectivity. The understanding of this God-spirit means that, in view of his essence, he makes himself an object of himself in order to subsequently overcome this differentiation through love[31]. In this way, the Trinity is no longer a mystery for speculative thought. Concretely, this means that at the beginning we find what is abstract and what is general. The Father is a subject in himself, who encompasses everything outside the world and outside its finite nature and beyond time in the thought of eternity. God determines himself in the other one, the Son, the object in himself, the specificity, the consciousness grasped in the relationship with the other one, and hence, divine history, descending and appearing as a phenomenon. Finally, in the third one, the Holy Spirit, what is general turns into a concrete idea. In the history of the world, the reality of God does not remain abstract. Rather, he develops himself, and this is evident in the finite nature that returns him to the infinite[32]. Thus, the Trinity means that God, an infinite subjectivity, comprises in himself the contradiction and also the solution, the differentiation and the annulment of the latter[33]. In this way, God is one and triune, eternal life in the emptying and returning to himself. Because of this, the triune God means that God is love. In love, the person abandons his special features in order to expand and acquire concrete personality. In the case of Hegel, this development seems to emerge from the lack rather than from the overabundance of the divine being. God is not without the world, the Son is not without the incarnation[34], and the Holy Spirit is not such without the Christian

---

GÓMEZ M., «Hegelianismo» in PIKAZA X. - SILANES N. (eds.), *Diccionario Teológico. El Dios cristiano*, 597-611; and, also in KASPER W., *Die Gott Jesu Christi*, 323f; VON BALTHASAR H.U., *Gloria* 5, Madrid 1988, 524-549; GRESHAKE G., *Der dreieine Gott*, 136-141. It is evident that we are not attempting by any means to make a broad presentation of such a complex problem.

31 Cfr. HEGEL G.W.F., *Vorlesungen über die Philosophie der Religion* I 41f; cfr. SPLETT J., *Die Trinitätslehre G.W.F. Hegels*, 120. Hegel defines love in this way in *Vorlesungen* III 75: «Love is the differentiation (*Unterscheiden*) of two. In spite of this, ultimately, they are not different one with respect to the other». In the death of Christ, we see the greatest sign of the love of God to humanity. In this death, God reconciles the world and is reconciled with himself. The resurrection of Christ as a denial of denial is a moment of the divine life itself. Cfr. GRECO C., «La mediazione trinitaria dell'unità di Dio nella filosofia della religione di G. W. F. Hegel», 441.

32 Cfr. GRECO C., «La mediazione trinitaria dell'unità di Dio nella filosofia della religione di G.W.F. Hegel», 340.

33 Cfr. SPLETT J., *Die Trinitätslehre G.W.F. Hegels*, 54; 108-109.

34 SPLETT J., *Die Trinitätslehre G.W.F. Hegels*, 144: «However, if this God should not remain in a thought without reality, he must go out beyond itself to the Son and to the world. This is not simply the Son, but it is his negative moment. And, as stated by Hegel, with this the Son not only turned into the truth of the world (cfr. *Vorlesungen über die Philosophie der Religion* I, 186), but also the world turns into the truth of the Son. Indeed, only in him is his essence released: being a denial and *vis à vis* (*Gegenüber*) and only from this real opposition does the absolute essence as a concrete Spirit emerge».

community[35]. There is no *ad intra* life without *ad extra* activity. The processions and temporary missions are not always clearly distinguished[36]. The Trinity is a unity that is only fulfilled in the process of reciprocal giving. God is not God without the world. It is precisely according to his essence that he is the creator of the world[37]. Hence, the differentiation between the Trinity in itself and the economic Trinity seems only abstract. In order to be more specific, we should say that the two are the same thing. Even though this process in itself does not mean anything new, beyond ensuring oneself that the real truth will appear only at the end[38]. In this way, Hegel has called attention to the importance of eschatology, the final consummation of history.

The First Vatican Council (DS 3024) formulated canon 4 of the constitution *Dei Filius* against pantheism in its different modalities. No doubt, «Hegelianism» was in the minds of the Council: «Si quis dixerit … Deum esse ens universale seu indefinitum, quod sese determinando constituat rerum universitatem in genera, species et individua distinctam, a.s.», although from other points of view we will see throughout our treatise the manner in which this issue of the immanence of God to the world and the necessity of the world for his full realization, as well as the eschatological perspective of the «plenitude» of God, will appear in other more recent theologians[39].

Positive and negative aspects are combined in this vision. The insistence on the personal nature of God and on the God of love, and the relationship between the immanent Trinity and the saving economy, are among the aspects that we will see many theologians develop. The contribution of Hegel to the restatement of these problems cannot be denied. At the same time, the ambiguities that this concept presents appear; on the one hand, the lack of a clear differentiation between the immanent Trinity and the economic Trinity that makes us think that in his economy God is finally full in plenitude; on the other hand, the attempt at

---

35 Cfr. SPLETT J., *Die Trinitätslehre G.W.F. Hegels*, 65f: «The Spirit is in the third element … he is his community».

36 SPLETT J., *Die Trinitätslehre G.W.F. Hegels*, 145, «In view of the fact that for Hegel the immanent Trinity is only realized as economic Trinity, the distinction between both of them disappears: there is no interlocutor to whom the revelation of God can be addressed. The economy turns into the immanent "way out of oneself" of the divine development itself».

37 HEGEL G.W.F., *Vorlesungen über die Philosophie der Religion* I 148: «Without the world God is not God»; cfr. also ibid. III 74.

38 Cfr. *Vorlesungen*, III 65,72-74; cfr. KASPER W., *Die Gott Jesu Christi*, 324.

39 Cfr. PANNENBERG W., «La teología de la Trinidad en Hegel y su recepción en los teólogos alemanes» in *Est Trin* 30 (1996) 35-51.

reaching the Trinity based on a philosophical analysis that poses the problem of the relationship of this knowledge with the only way of access to the divine mystery, the revelation that God makes of himself. The mystery of the triune God that transcends this world can be known only by means of the economic Trinity, in other words, by means of the revelation of Jesus Christ. The saving mystery that is God himself is only accessible to us by virtue of free divine communication.

Consequently, the «identity» between the immanent Trinity and the economic Trinity cannot be explained in terms of the fulfillment or realization of God in the economy or in terms that lead to a confusion between the doctrine of the Trinity and Christology[40]. However, we also have to bear in mind a second aspect of this issue. Just as the immanent Trinity is not identical with the development of the economy of salvation, nor is it «dissolved» in it, neither is it «exhausted» in the saving dispensation in which it freely and graciously communicates. This means that in its saving self-communication God enables us to see more closely his unfathomable mystery, and he does not eliminate it. God actually gives himself to us, although his being is infinitely greater than what we can receive. Y. Congar has pointed out this problem most relevantly when he wonders whether we can state that God commits and reveals *all* his mystery in the self-communication he makes of himself[41]. We cannot penetrate all the mysteries of the intradivine life, of the unity and of the distinction of the persons, of the generation of the Word, and of the procession of the Spirit, and so forth. Only in the eschatological consummation will God enable us to know him fully in his total self-giving. We will see him face to face, as he is (cfr. 1Cor 13:12; 1John 3:2)[42]. On the other hand, the self communication that is fulfilled in history entails an element of *kenosis* and cross. It entails an emptying that forces us to assume a distinction

---

40 Cfr. for instance, SCHOONENBERG P., «Spirit christology and Logos christology» in *Bijdragen* 38 (1977) 350-375; *Der Geist, das Wort und der Sohn. Eine Geist-Christologie*, Regensburg 1992, 183ff and 195ff, and others; according to Schoonenberg, in the incarnation there would be a full «personalization» of the Word as the Son and of the Spirit as the Spirit of the Son.

41 Cfr. CONGAR Y., *El Espíritu Santo*, Barcelona 1983, 457; cfr. also 454-462. The clarifications are accurate, even though Congar does not seem to always take into account the statements of Rahner on the unwarranted nature and the freedom of the divine self-communication.

42 Evidently, there is a qualitative difference between our knowledge of God in the beatific vision in the other world and our current knowledge. This is clearly shown in the biblical texts that have been quoted; cfr. also DS 1000, among others. (We could give a much longer list of the biblical or teaching passages). In spite of this fact, it is still possible to state that even then, we will not be able to fully embrace God. Cfr. THOMAS AQUINAS, *Expositio super symbolum apostolorum, 12*, in *Opus. Theol. 2*, that quotes in turn Saint Augustine: «Totum gaudium non intrabit in gaudentibus, sed toti gaudentes intrabunt in gaudium». GRESHAKE G. *Der dreieine Gott*, 519: «The clear manifestation of God per se presupposes the end of history».

between the economic Trinity and the immanent Trinity[43]. The *forma servi* actually has been taken on by Jesus, although the *forma Dei* also belongs to him, and we cannot know fully its contents in our present condition.

Therefore, the identification between the economic Trinity and the immanent Trinity has to be understood in the sense that on the one hand, God gives himself to us and is revealed to us just as he is in himself, although he does it freely. In other words his being is not realized or perfected in this self-communication. On the other hand, God maintains his mystery in this revelation, and his greatest closeness will be the most direct manifestation of his highest greatness. These two explanations that are directed toward a correct interpretation of the axiom in fact have much in common.

> The economic Trinity actually appears as the interpretation of the immanent Trinity, which nevertheless, by being the foundational principle of the first one, cannot simply be identified with it. Indeed, in that case, the immanent eternal Trinity runs the risk of simply being the economic Trinity. In a clearer explanation, we can say that God would run the risk of being absorbed in the process of the world and of not being able to attain himself except through that process[44].

Undoubtedly, God takes care of the world. The dogma of the Trinity in its deepest inner self entails, as any dogma, a soteriological quality. On the one hand, God takes care of the world as God. «He does not turn into "love" in order to have the world as his "you"… but because he is already "love" in himself, and he is so beyond the world»[45].

We have already referred to the document of the International Theological Commission: *Theology. Christology. Anthropology.* We quoted this as it relates to the first part of the basic axiom that the Commission seems to claim as its

43 Cfr. CONGAR Y., *El Espíritu Santo*, 460; from the same author, *La parola e il soffio*, Roma 1985, 131.
44 VON BALTHASAR H.U., *Teodramática III. El hombre en Cristo*, Madrid 1993, 466.
45 VON BALTHASAR H.U., *Teodramática III*, 467. Cfr. also *Teodramática 4. La acción*, Madrid 1996, 205-204. Cfr. also among the recent catholic authors, WERBICK J., «Dottrina trinitaria» in SCHNEIDER TH. (ed.) *Nuovo corso di dogmatica*, Brescia 1995, vol. II, 573-683, 624-636; STAGLIANÒ A., *Il mistero del Dio vivente. Per una teologia dell'Assoluto trinitario*, Bologna 1996, 482-493; HILBERATH B.J., *Pneumatologia*, Brescia 1996, 196-200; GONZÁLEZ M., *La relación entre Trinidad económica y Trinidad inmanente. El «axioma fundamental» de K. Rahner y su recepción. Líneas para continuar la reflexión*, Roma 1996. Cfr. LAFONT G., *Peut-on connaître Dieu en Jésus-Christ?*, Paris 1969, 171-228. Throughout our presentation we will also see how some Protestant theologians have posed this issue.

own. We can now report what it states regarding the second part which is, at the same time, a good balance within the discussion of Catholic theology around this topic:

> … in both theology and catechism, it is necessary to avoid every *separation* between Christology and the Trinitarian doctrine… Likewise, we must avoid any immediate *confusion* between the event of Jesus and the Trinity. The Trinity has not merely turned into the history of salvation through the incarnation, the cross, and the resurrection of Jesus Christ, as though God needed a historical process in order to be triune. Hence, we must keep a very clear distinction between the immanent Trinity, in which freedom and necessity are identical in the eternal essence of God, and the Trinitarian economy of salvation, in which God fully exercises his own freedom without any need of nature.
>
> The distinction between the economic Trinity and the immanent Trinity fully coincides with the real identification of both of them. The economy of salvation states that the eternal Son in his own life takes up the "kenotic" event of birth, of human life and of death on the cross. This event, in which God is revealed and communicated fully and permanently affects, in a certain way, the being himself of God the Father because he is the God who carries out these mysteries and who lives them as his own, and also with the Son and the Holy Spirit. Indeed, God the Father is not only revealed to us and communicates freely and graciously in the mystery of Jesus Christ by means of the Son and in the Holy Spirit, but as the Father, together with the Son and the Holy Spirit, leads the Trinitarian life in a most profound manner, and at least in our opinion, in an almost new manner (*quasi novo*), insofar as the relationship of the Father to the incarnated Son in the consummation of the gift of the Spirit is the same relationship that makes up the Trinity. The condition of the possibility of certain events is present in the internal life of God because of the unintelligible freedom of God that we find in the history of salvation of our Lord Jesus Christ.
>
> Hence, the great events in the life of Jesus express for us openly and efficiently in a new way the colloquium of the eternal generation where the Father tells the Son: «You are my Son, today I have fathered you» (Psalm 2:7; cfr. Acts 13:33; Heb 1:5, 5:5; Luke 3:22)[46].

---

[46] Commissio Theologica Internationalis, «Theologia-Christologia-Anthropologia» in *Greg* 64 (1983) 10-12. I have resorted to the translation from the edition *Documentos* 1981-1985, 12-13, although modifying it to a certain extent.

We have already referred to the illegitimacy of the *separation* between Trinitarian doctrine and Christology. However, in view of the fact that we have to save the precedence of the immanent Trinity, because this is the one that is communicated in the history of salvation, we also have to avoid any *confusion* between the event of Jesus Christ and the Trinity, as though only on account of this event the Trinity would be posited as such. The terms of the Christological definition of the Council of Chalcedon (without confusion, without separation; cfr. DS 302) helped separate, and at the same time maintained united, the plane of the divine life and that of the saving economy. If, in the first one, freedom and necessity (which certainly cannot be conceived as ours) are identified with the divine nature in a way that it is unknown to us, in the second one, the category of necessity fully disappears. We are faced with the completely free design of God that is undoubtedly founded in what he is in himself, although it excludes any internal or external necessity. Hence, freedom does not mean that the saving economy will not have its deep roots in the divine being.

The necessary, though not adequate, distinction between the economic Trinity and the immanent Trinity «coincides» with the identity of both of them. There are not two «trinities». On the one hand, the immanent Trinity contains the foundation, the condition of the possibility of the saving economy. However, on the other hand, and here lies, in my opinion, one of the most valuable aspects of this document, it is stated that the kenotic event of the incarnation and death is taken up by the eternal Son in his life. Insofar as the Son takes up in his life these events, they affect the being of God the Father, who cannot live on his own, with the Son and the Holy Spirit living in themselves in the events of the temporal life of the incarnated Son. This means that the life of the Trinity, which is not posited by virtue of these events, is lived based on them in an «almost new» way[47]. In other words, even though, as related to the saving economy, the category of necessity has no place, the former, once it has been freely decided by God, «affects» the divine life of the immanent Trinity. God has not willed to be without us. This does not mean that the Trinity is perfected by the economy or that the economy gives the Trinity something that the Trinity had been lacking.

[47] HILARY OF POITIERS, *Trin.* IX 38 (CCL 62,412) already talked about the «Dispensationis novitas», the «newness» brought about by the saving economy in the relationships between the Father and the Son. Cfr. as well, the reflections of GRESHAKE G., *Der dreieine Gott*, 323f, according to whom the immanent Trinity has turned into the economic Trinity forever. He also warns against the danger of dissolving the being of God in history (ibid.). We also have to preserve, at the same time, the divine transcendence and the fact that God is «affected» by the incarnation.

The newness lies in the fact that the Son has entered as man into the relationships that make up the Trinity. Jesus who was born has also died and has risen from the dead. God lives the saving mysteries as his own, not as something that is alien to him. The economy does not constitute the triune God; neither does it not perfect him, although this does not mean that it is meaningless to him. The immanent Trinity, in the sovereign freedom of its love, is the foundation of the history of salvation. Nevertheless, in turn, the latter has certain «repercussions». It has an effect on the divine being. The saving mysteries are mysteries that are characteristic of God. He himself, and only he, is the one who acts in them, and only these mysteries can reveal him to us by making us share his life.

Part one

A look at History

The revelation of God in Christ and the preparation in the Old Testament

The revelation of God in the life of Jesus. A theological-biblical study

Our previous chapter, which dealt with the relationship between the economic Trinity and the immanent Trinity, has pointed out the path we will follow when developing our treatise. In the formulation of the axiom of the «identity» between both of them (although with the reservations and nuances that we have suggested), we always start with the economic Trinity. This is what the document of the International Theological Commission, to which we have referred, does in a concrete way: «The Trinity that is manifested in the economy of salvation is the immanent Trinity». All this is simply the direct consequence of what we have been saying from the beginning of this exposition: the Trinity is a truth to which we only have access from revelation as the starting point. The methodological consequences that follow are clear, and they are founded on the New Testament: there is no other path that leads to the Father if it is not through Jesus (cfr. John 14:5-6). We must begin with the revelation of the economic Trinity because only by means of it can we have the possibility of examining in greater depth the mystery of the being of God, although always with a clear awareness that it is completely impossible to embrace and understand fully this mystery. Only by beginning with God who is turned toward others (the economy of God) can we reach God in himself (the theology). Nevertheless, we should never forget that from eternity God has been God for us in his intimate life and that he has never desired to exist only for himself but has always desired to make us share in his fullness. This path is the one that Catholic theology commonly follows today.

Hence, we will begin by taking into account the historical revelation of God, which reaches its culmination in the «missions» of the Son and of the Holy Spirit. To this end, we must deal primarily with the data offered by the New Testament. However, we do not intend to address in isolation what is told in the New Testament about God or about the Trinity. Rather, we are also —and primarily— intending to study the way in which the mystery of God has been revealed in the life of Jesus Christ (the revelation in the facts and in the deeds to which we have already referred) from his coming into the world, to his resurrection and exaltation to heaven and the effusion or outpouring of the Holy Spirit. Therefore, we will attempt to set forth, at least partially, a theology of the mysteries of the life of Jesus Christ from the point of view of the revelation of the mystery of God[1]. To this end, we will further extend our biblical study by including some data re-

---

1   We try not to repeat contents that are more pertinent for Christology manuals. At any rate, the points of contact are evident, and it is impossible to determine with precision the boundaries between one and the other.

garding the tradition and contemporary theological reflections. The latter will also contribute interesting elements and intuitions that will help us better grasp the revelation of God in Jesus Christ. Hence, our purpose is not merely historical, but rather, systematic.

A highly significant text from the letter to the Galatians can be an excellent guide in our exposition. It is the one that shows the «Trinitarian» structure of salvation related to the fact that God the Father sent his Son Jesus Christ and the Holy Spirit:

> But when the completion of the time came, God sent his Son, born of a woman, born a subject of the Law, to ransom the subjects of the Law, so that we could receive adoption as sons. As you are sons, God has sent into our hands the Spirit of his Son crying out, «Abba, Father!» (Gal 4:4-6).

In light of the fact that the Father has sent Jesus his Son into the world and has also sent into our hearts the Spirit of his Son, God has made us his children and has created us to share his life. In this way, he has opened to us the mystery of the one and triune God. We have already had occasion to realize that our knowledge of God is related to the gift of himself which God offers us. God has been revealed to us when he came to us, when he sent us his Son and his Holy Spirit. The New Testament refers to this double «mission». Both the Son and the Spirit have been sent by God, and the text of Galatians that we have just quoted connects these two parallel «missions». In different stages of our exposition we will keep in mind the difficulty implied when we apply the plural to God. However, in this case, we must also be aware of the problem. Nevertheless, here, more so than in other instances, it is the language of the New Testament that authorizes us to make use of the plural. It even induces us to use it. Exactly the same term is used to refer to the action of sending the Son and the Holy Spirit into this world (ἐξαπέστειλεν). It is clear, on the other hand, that the characteristics of each mission are quite different. Reference is already made to this in the passage from Galatians to which we are alluding, where it mentions that the Holy Spirit has been sent «into our hearts». If the mission of Jesus coincides with his incarnation, with his entrance into human history in order to share the life of humanity, and for this reason, it is a specific event in time and space, the mission of the Spirit has a certain quality of continuity. The Spirit is sent into the heart of each believer. This mission also has an invisible nature if we do not consider the effects of the outpouring of the Spirit on the day of Pentecost (Acts 2:1ff; cfr. also Acts 4:31; 10:44-46), and it cannot be limited to either time or space. Even in those cases of the outpouring of the Spirit in the book of Acts which do not exhaust the multiplicity of effects of the mission of the Spirit, the characteristics of these effects are quite different from those of Jesus. The two «missions» must be seen in their mutual relationship. This will be evidenced in the arguments that follow. We will begin with the mission of the Son, mentioned in the first place in the Galatians text.

1

God sent his Son

God has sent Jesus Christ, his Son, into the world. This concept is repeated frequently in the New Testament with different formulations and nuances (in addition to Gal 4:4, and without attempting to be exhaustive, cfr. Mark 9:37; Matt 10:40; Luke 4:43; 9:48; Rom 8:3; John 3:17; 5:23; 6:57; 8:42; 17:18; and passim in John; 1John 4:9f; 4:14). God (the Father) takes the initiative in this mission. The love of God for humankind is the only reason why he sends his Son to the world: «This is the revelation of God's love for us, that God sent his only Son into the world that we might have life through him» (1John 4:9; cfr. John 3:16). These texts of God's missions, which on many occasions are close to those that state the preexistence of Christ, imply and assume knowledge of the entire life of Jesus Christ. From the life of Jesus, from his deeds and his words through his death and resurrection, we have attained the understanding that he is the Son who has been sent to the world by the Father, and not the other way around. In turn, in Jesus Christ the Son, we know the Father. The two terms are strictly correlative. It is in the historical appearance of Jesus Christ the Son that the revelation of God as Father takes place.

1.1. GOD, THE FATHER OF JESUS CHRIST

New Testament revelation assumes Old Testament revelation. In the Old Testament, God has been revealed as the God of the covenant which he established with the people of Israel, his chosen people —a covenant of love, founded on divine predisposition. This God is also the creator of all things and hence, God of all peoples. This God, which the New Testament already clearly assumes as being known, at least to a certain extent, is the one who is revealed to us as the «Father» in Jesus Christ his Son. The God of the Old Testament is, consequently and preeminently, the one to whom we Christians refer as the Father. The God who sent Jesus is identified with the God of Israel (cfr. Mark 12:26; 12:29par; Deut 6:4f; Matt 4:10; 1Cor 8:6; 1Tim 2:5; John 5:44; 17:3). The New Testament refers to this God of Israel in the immense majority of cases when it talks about «God»[2]. He is the God whose proximity is announced by Jesus when he proclaims the imminence of the coming of the Kingdom, related to his own person (cfr. Mark 1:15; Matt 4:17; 12:28; Luke 11:20; 17:21, among many other places). We will see something similar in the usage of the ancient Church which still follows the liturgy to a considerable extent. Founded on the usage of Jesus and his explicit teachings, we Christians call this God «Father». Before taking time to study the idea of the divine Fatherhood in the New Testament, a quick look at the Old Testament will enable us to determine the originality of this way of addressing God which is inherent in Jesus Christ, and consequently, accounts for the originality of the Christian usage of that designation[3].

First and foremost, we must realize that the Old Testament does not resort in any great degree to the idea of fatherhood in order to refer to God, perhaps because this might appear linked to representations that are incompatible with the faith of Israel[4]. In addition to this general reservation, we must also bear in mind that there are very limited occasions when the idea of the Fatherhood of God is related to creation, or when it is considered to be founded on the latter (cfr. Mal 1:6; 2:10, more clearly; Isa 45:10f; cfr. also, although not as closely, Ps 29:1; 89:7). The idea of divine Fatherhood linked to creation can be corrupted when it is applied to the idols: «who say to a piece of wood, "You are my father" and to a stone, "You gave birth to me"» (Jer 2:27).

---

2   Cfr. the classic article of RAHNER K., «Theos en el Nuevo Testamento» in *Escritos de Teología* I, Madrid 1963, 93-168; also SCHLOSSER J., *Le Dieu de Jésus. Etude exégétique*, Paris 1987, 30-34.

3   Cfr. for what follows MARCHEL W., *Abba, Père! La prière du Christ et des chrétiens*, Rome 1971², 23-36; 50-62; by the same author, *Dieu Père dans le Nouveau Testament*, Paris 1966; JEREMÍAS J., *Abba y el mensaje central del Nuevo Testamento*, Salamanca 1981, 19-35; BYRNE B., *Sons of God — Seeds of Abraham*, Rome 1979; SCHLOSSER J., *Le Dieu de Jésus. Etude exégétique*, 105-122; GARCÍA LÓPEZ F., «Dios Padre en el Antiguo Testamento a la luz de las interpretaciones recientes de la religión en Israel» in AA. VV., *Dios es Padre*, Salamanca 1991, 43-57; GRELOT P., *Dieu. Le Père de Jésus-Christ*, Paris 1994.

4   Cfr. MARTÍN VELASCO J., «Dios como Padre en la historia de las religiones» in AA. VV. *Dios es Padre* (cfr. previous footnote), 17-47 with subsequent bibliography. The name is useful for designating the relationship of God with the world and humanity, as to its origin. In other occasions, it tries to explain God in himself, *ad intra* (cfr. pages 29-31).

The people of Israel have not often considered the Fatherhood of God within a universalistic perspective, but rather, relate it with the predisposition that God has shown and still manifests, with the departure —the exodus— from Egypt, the covenant, the promised land, and so forth. Hence, Israel is the son and the first-born son of God (cfr. Exod 4:22f; Deut 14:1f; 32:5; Ps 103:13, «As tenderly as a father treats his children, so Yahweh tenderly treats those who fear him»; also Isa 1:2f; 30:19: Jer 3:4,19,22; Hos 11:1); God is, hence, the «Father» of the people whom he has chosen (cfr. Deut 32:5f with the metaphor of the creation as the work of the potter, which, based on the context, seems to refer to the formation of the chosen people far more than to creation in general; Jer 31:9; Isa 63:16; 64:7, once again with the use of the image of the potter). In some of these latter passages, in addition to the statement that God is «Father», there are expressions that are very close to the invocation as such: «you, Yahweh, are our Father» (Isa 63:16; 64:7; Jer 3:4). In the Old Testament, different aspects of divine Fatherhood are emphasized, ranging from control over all things to teachings and the care for the chosen people. Furthermore, what is most specifically stressed is his love, so that we can state that Yahweh is a «father with the womb of a mother»[5]. Hence, the maternal features clearly appear in Isa 49:15: «Can a woman forget her baby at her breast, feel no pity for the child she has borne? Even if these were to forget, I will never forget you». And specifically, Isa 66:13: «As the mother comforts her child, so I shall comfort you». God indirectly appears as mother in the words used by Moses to address God in Num 11:12-13: «Was it I that conceived all these people, was I their father for you to say to me, "Carry them in your arms like a foster father carrying an unweaned child to the country I swore to give their fathers"»? The approach of the figures of both father and mother are found in Ps 27:10; Jer 31:15-20 (cfr. possible feminine features in Deut 32:18; Job 38:8; 66:8). According to Ps 68:6, God is father of the fatherless, defender of widows. The personal trust and the loving care that God has for human beings acquires here a more significant role. In this passage, as well as in others that we have just quoted,

77

---

5 Cfr. García López F., «Dios Padre en el Antiguo Testamento a la luz de las interpretaciones recientes de la religión en Israel», 52ff; Armendáriz L., «El Padre materno» in *EstEcl* 58 (1983) 249-275; Del Cura S., «Dios Padre / Madre. Significado e implicaciones de las imágenes masculinas y femeninas en Dios» in *EstTrin* 26 (1992) 117-154; Briend J., *Dieu dans l'Ecriture*, Paris 1992, 71-90; Amato A., «Paternità —maternità di Dio. Problemi e prospettive» in Amato A. (ed.), *Trinità in contesto*, Roma 1993, 273-296; in these studies we will find a subsequent bibliography. Cfr. John Paul II, *Dives in misericordia*, 4, note 52; cfr. AAS 72 (1980) 1189f, with reference to the vocabulary and the texts of the Old Testament. John Paul I had already stated the idea in his famous statement on September 10th, 1978; cfr. *Insegnamenti di Giovanni Paolo I*, Città del Vaticano 1979, 61f.

this emotion predominates over the people of Israel who belong to him. We have already referred to some texts which, relating to divine Fatherhood, also talk about the people of Israel as «son». It is clear that the two ideas are reciprocal. Nevertheless, it is also worth pointing out that these passages are less in number than those that refer to God as Father.

In addition to the texts in which divine Fatherhood refers to the people of Israel in general, we find others in which it is a concrete individual, with special significance among the chosen people, who appears as the «son» of God (cfr. 2 Sam 7:14; 1Chr 22:10, regarding the descendent of David; Ps 2:7, referring to the anointed one; David is also the son of God according to Ps 89:27). Also, in these cases, the feature of love is the prevailing one when talking about the Fatherhood of God and the divine Sonship of the persons to whom he has entrusted a special mission.

In wisdom literature, the Fatherhood of God is also in relationship with concrete persons —the just— although frequently these are only comparisons (cfr. Prov 3:12; Ps 2:16; 11:10)[6]. On the contrary, a direct invocation of God as Father appears under this context, combined with the title of Lord, in Ecclesiasticus (What is the abbreviation?) 23:1,4; and in Wis 14:3, without any additions or supplements. This explicit invocation of God as Father is especially rare in the writings of the Old Testament, and it only appears in relatively later stages. At any rate, it is clear that the Old Testament avoids excessively literal or material conceptions of divine Fatherhood. The transcendence of God and the unsuitability of our concepts when referring to him are always borne in mind[7]. In the Judaism of Palestine in the second half of the first century after Christ, we find this invocation both as related to individuals and with respect to the community, although it is normally together with other names and titles that dilute its meaning to a certain extent. It does not seem that concrete individuals frequently invoke God as Father during the times prior to Jesus Christ. Only with Jesus Christ will the Fatherhood of God appear in its full power.

In fact, the revelation of this Fatherhood is one of the basic issues, if not the core, of the message of the Gospel. This revelation seems to be essentially limited to the person of Jesus, who not only talks about God as his Father, but also

---

6 Sometimes maternal features are also discovered, or at least, the female features in the figure of Wisdom, for instance Ecclesiasticus 14:22ff and especially, 15:2ff. The identification of Wisdom with the Spirit could also point in the same direction.
7 PHILO OF ALEXANDRIA, *De opif. mundi* 171 (Oeuvres 1,256); *De prov.* II 15 (Oeuvres 35, 226-230), uses the comparison of God who is worried about human beings like a father.

invokes him as such, and in this way, he clearly expresses the awareness of his closeness to God and the familiarity and immediacy of his relationship with him[8]. It is a rightful extrapolation to go from there to the awareness of his Sonship, of the specificity of his relationship with the Father. Based on this information, we move closer to the central core of the mystery of the person and work of Jesus Christ. A depth that has never been even suspected before is revealed to us in him regarding the Fatherhood of God and the Sonship that results from it. This sheds a new light on the mystery of the divine being. Jesus has awareness of an original and unique relationship with God on which he ultimately bases his desire that his message is both heard and accepted. In a sense, which is indeed unique, God is his Father. When he addresses God, Jesus Christ uses the term «Abbá» —Father— which seems to be a term used by those who lived during his times within the framework of their family life, which, however, does not imply that it is simply the language used by children. The synoptic gospels only report this original term in Aramaic once in the mouth of Jesus Christ (Mark 14:36, the prayer of Jesus in the Garden; cfr. also Rom 8:15; Gal 4:6, where the term appears on the lips of the believers). But the mere fact that the original word has been preserved, even disregarding its use in the precise circumstance[9], points to the fact that it was used by Jesus Christ and that the first Christians have attached considerable significance to the concrete term used by him to address God and have invoked it in their plea for illumination regarding the mystery of his person.

On all the occasions when, according to the synoptic gospels[10], Jesus has God as his intermediary, he calls him «Father» (Mark 15:34; Matt 27:46, which is not exactly an exception, because it is a quotation from Ps 22:2). Here, we can also leave it as parenthetical if this information from the synoptic gospels corresponds exactly to the usage of Jesus[11]. Among these invocations that are presented to us in the synoptic gospels, special mention must be made of the «hymn of joy» in which the Father is praised (cfr. Matt 11:25-27; Luke 10:21-22), one of the very few occasions when Jesus refers to himself as the «Son» in the synoptic gospels (cfr.

---

8 Cfr. JEREMIAS J., *Abba y el mensaje central del Nuevo Testamento*, 37-73; SCHLOSSER J., *Le Dieu de Jésus*, 208f, and the other works that have been quoted in footnote 3.

9 Cfr. SCHLOSSER J., *Le Dieu de Jésus*, 130-139; 203-209.

10 Cfr. the in-depth analysis of SCHNEIDER G., «El Padre de Jesús. Visión bíblica» in *Dios es Padre* (cfr. footnote 3), 59-100.

11 Cfr. *ibid.* 205 that qualifies the known thesis of JEREMÍAS J., *Abba y el mensaje central del Nuevo Testamento*, 66.

also Mark 13:32). Along with the intimacy with God that the passage reflects, it also emphasizes the revealing function of Jesus, founded on reciprocal knowledge (cfr. also, John 10:15). In turn, the initiative, the approval and consent of the Father to whom Jesus Christ surrenders, is also expressed. In fact, it is impossible to isolate the invocation of God as Father from the attitude of Jesus Christ as Son who surrenders to the Father with trust at every point in time, and mostly, during his death (cfr. Luke 23:46).

The revealing function of Jesus Christ, his obedience to the will of the Father, and his continuous reference to the Father will be more insistently emphasized, if possible, in the fourth gospel[12]. «Father» in the lips of Jesus Christ in the gospel of John is the normal way of referring to God, while «Son» in the same gospel is the normal way in which Jesus refers to himself. The Father is the one who has sent Jesus Christ into the world (cfr. John 5:36-37; 6:44; 6:57; 8:18; 12:49; 14:24). Jesus «comes» from him or has «come forth» from him (John 8:42; 13:3; 15:17-28). The Father has marked him with his imprint (6:27). With this mission of his Son, God the Father has evidenced his love for humanity (John 3:16f; 1John 4:7-21), and this fact opens before us an unsuspected perspective to know the being and the essence of God.

The Father is also the one whom Jesus knows (and vice versa, John 10:15) and reveals (John 14:8; cfr. 1:18; 12:45; 17:6,26), the one whom Jesus obeys (John 4:34; 5:19f; 5:38-40; 12:49, among others). Even more so, the Father is the one for whom Jesus lives and whose life he shares with humanity (John 5:26; 6:57). He is the one to whom Jesus returns once he has fulfilled the actions that he had to carry out in this world (cfr. John 13:1; 14:28; 17:4-5; 20:17). The Father has given Jesus the power which he possesses (John 5:19ff), and most specifically, the power to bring the dead back to life, to judge, and to do whatever he himself does. The Father testifies on behalf of Jesus (John 5:37), he loves him, and Jesus Christ the Son returns this love (John 3:35; 5:20; 14:31; 15:9). Likewise, he will also love those who keep and observe the commandments of Jesus (John 14:21.). The Father is the one who glorifies the Son, as the Son glorifies the Father (John 17:1ff). The Father and Jesus Christ are one, and this is the unity all the believers are told to share (John 10:30; 17:21ff). Jesus Christ intercedes before the Father on behalf of

---

12 In the «corpus iohanneum» and primarily in the fourth gospel, we can find more than half of the references to God as the Father that we find throughout the entire New Testament (141 out of 261). Cfr. a global vision of this issue in CAPDEVILA i MUNTANER V.M., «El Padre en el cuarto evangelio» in *Dios es Padre*, (cfr. footnote 3) 101-139.

all of us once he has risen from the dead to heaven (John 14:13.16; 16:24ff; 1John 2:1; cfr. also Rom 8:34; Heb 4:14ff; 7:25; 9:24). These brief indications are enough to give evidence to how the Father is the constant point of reference for Jesus Christ. No aspect of his life or of his actions is explained without the Father. Jesus Christ constantly focuses on and lives in reference to God the Father who is the one who has full primacy over the entire life of Jesus. The communion between both of them is complete.

It is said that the initiative of creation comes from God the Father (we find the two names specifically combined in 1Cor 8:6). All comes from him and through the only Lord Jesus Christ (cfr. Rom 11:36). This initiative of God the Father in creation places us, on the one hand, in continuity with the Old Testament, although it also shows us, on the other hand, the innovation: the God who is the Creator is the Father of Jesus, and he does everything through the Son (cfr. Col 1:15ff; Heb 1:2-3; John 1:3,10). The initiative of the mission of Jesus to the world, as well as his second coming, also emerge from God the Father (1Tim 5:14; Acts 3:20). The Fatherhood of God is especially related to the resurrection. Paul sees God as the Father of the resurrected Lord (cfr. 2 Cor 1:3; 11:31; Eph 1:17; Phil 2:11; Rom 6:4). Since then, the Christian God is simply the Father of Jesus Christ (Eph 1:2-3; 1Pet 1:3: «Blessed be God the Father of our Lord Jesus Christ»). The title of «Father» of Jesus Christ is, hence, definitively incorporated within the confession of the Christian God. Our profession of faith begins by proclaiming only one God, the Father Almighty. At the end of the age, Jesus will hand over the kingdom to God the Father, and when all things have been surrendered, this very same Jesus Christ, to whom everything has been submitted, will be subjected, so that God will be all in all (cfr. 1Cor 15:24-28).

In the entire life of Jesus Christ, and specifically in his death and resurrection, we see the revelation of God as Father. For this reason, we cannot stop addressing this issue here because we have barely begun to discuss it. In our study of the mysteries of the life of Jesus we must inevitably return to different aspects of the revelation of the Father. As we have seen, he is the one who has sent Jesus Christ, but he is also the total and constant point of reference for the whole life of Jesus. However, from the very beginning, we will also find ourselves confronting the activity of the Holy Spirit. The revelation of the three divine persons takes place simultaneously. It is also worth noting, before going any further, that the revelation of God as the Father who sends Jesus Christ is equivalent to the revelation of God as love. In view of this context, and as a result of this revelation, God, primarily the Father, is defined as «love» in John 4:8 and16:

> My dear friends, let us love each other since love is from God and everyone who loves is a child of God and knows God. Whoever fails to love does not know God, because God is love. This is the revelation of God's love for us, that God sent his only Son into the world that we might have life through him. Love consists in this: it is not we who have loved God, but God loved us and sent his Son to expiate our sins…. We have recognized for ourselves, and put our faith in, the love God has for us. God is love, and whoever remains in love remains in God and God in him (1John 4:7-10,16).

From the saving economy, we go to the being itself of God: «That God is *love* in his most profound self is something that the author discovers in the *divine action,* and undoubtedly, in the most extraordinary fact that he sent his Son to the world of death in order to give life to men»[13]. Hence, love also turns into the distinctive feature of the children of God, and mainly, of the Son par excellence who is Jesus Christ. There is an intimate relationship between love and divine Sonship. Even though the thinking of John seems to move here towards the participation of humanity in the love of God, there is no doubt that there is a clear Christological mediation of this love. It is precisely this Christological mediation that shows the special relationship of this revelation of love with Jesus Christ and how in the conveying of the latter through us we can see this evidence of love, this «divine definition»: «God loves to such an extent that he gives what is most dear to him so as to save men. In this giving and giving himself, in this compassion and this desire to save, lies real love, and it is precisely this love that makes up his essence»[14]. In the love that is evidenced precisely in the self-giving of Jesus we can anticipate a new way of being the love of God *ad intra.* The New Testament, and more concretely, these passages from the first letter of John, open up the mystery of the intra-divine life from the revelation that has taken place in Jesus.

---

13 SCHNACKENBURG R., *Cartas de San Juan*, Barcelona 1980, 257: Especially page 259: «The God of the new covenant is by its very essence the merciful love that gives everything and that communicates himself».

14 Cfr. SCHNACKENBURG R., *Cartas de San Juan*, 269.

The Fatherhood of God and the Sonship of Jesus Christ are in strict reciprocal relation. In light of the fact that Jesus Christ has lived «in Sonship», he has revealed God as the Father, and he has revealed himself as Son of God. As a result of the Father-Son correlation, it is clear that we cannot draw an exact line that separates what we have said about the Father in the previous pages and what we will say here about Jesus Christ, the Son. Some examples will suffice, because it is not our intent to repeat what is usually studied in treatises on Christology[15].

It does not seem that Jesus frequently called himself «Son», unlike what has been the case of the very frequent, if not habitual or constant, use of the term «Father» when referring to God. We have already mentioned the so-called «hymn of joy in praise of the Father», one of the culminating moments in the synoptic gospels that show us the relation of intimacy and closeness of Jesus with God the Father. In this text, Jesus calls himself the «Son»: «No one knows the Son except the Father, and no one knows the Father except the Son...» (Matt 11:27; Luke 10:22). We also find this designation in the words of Jesus Christ in the so-called ignorance in the *lógion* of Mark 13:32par: «But as for that day or hour, nobody knows it, neither the angels in heaven, nor the Son; no one but the Father». Likewise, we do not find in a single instance the reference of Jesus calling himself the «Son of God», unlike what is the case of other persons (he does not even do it directly in Matt 26:64). Nevertheless, the limited use of this title by Jesus himself can be accounted for by the fact that he does not preach about himself but about God. The Kingdom that Jesus feels he has been called to announce belongs to the Father. His revelation as the Son is indirect from this point of view. As we have already mentioned, in the gospel of John we see a considerable increase in the frequency of passages in which Jesus refers to himself as the Son.

According to the synoptic gospels, Jesus Christ is proclaimed Son of God by the voice of the Father during the baptism and the transfiguration (cfr. Mark 1:11par). Let us note that the title «Son of God» is already present in Peter's confession of faith (Matt 16:16, although not in the parallel writings of Mark 8:29 and Luke 9:20), in a messianic sense. With the words «If you are Son of God...» (without the article), the devil starts his insinuations in order to tempt Jesus

---

15 Cfr. KASPER W., *Jesús el Cristo*, Salamanca 1978, 134-137; AMATO A., *Gesù il Signore. Saggio di cristologia*, Bologna 1988, 121f; O'COLLINS G., *Gesù oggi. Linee fondamentali di cristologia*, Cinisello Balsamo 1993, 87f; by the same author, *Christology. A Biblical, Historical and Systematic Study of Jesus Christ*, Oxford 1995, 113-135.

Christ (cfr. Matt 4:3,6; Luke 4:3,9); the vision of the divine Sonship in the eyes of the tempter and that of Jesus Christ differ considerably. Jesus Christ is also proclaimed after his death as the Son of God by the centurion who was guarding him (cfr. Mark 15:39; Matt 27:40).

The title of «Son» (of God) points, more than any other one, to the ultimate identity of Jesus, as it emphasizes his unique relationship with God the Father. It is used by Paul (1Thess 1:10; Rom 1:3,4,9; 8:3,29,32; 1Cor 1:9,15,28; Gal 1:15f; 4:6; 2Cor 1:19, «the gospel of his Son»; Eph 4:13; Col 1:13), although far less frequently than that of «Lord», which is more adequate in expressing the condition of Jesus Christ glorified in his relationship with the community. Paul could have resorted to an idea which he had already found in the Christian community. The key aspect in this respect is that this title is used whenever mention is made of the relationship of Jesus Christ with God. This also implies a reference to his function as mediator of salvation[16]. Hence, there is an intimate connection between the relation of Jesus Christ with God and his condition as savior of the world. Theology and the economy of salvation are already united from the very beginning in the perspective of the New Testament. The doctrine of the divine Sonship of Jesus Christ has been established from early days, and it would not be correct to limit it to those aspects that are merely functional. The latter cannot be isolated from the relationship of Jesus Christ with God that the title emphasizes.

We have already mentioned that in the gospel of John, «Son» is the normal designation used by Jesus Christ to refer to himself, in correlation with extensive use of the term «Father» employed by Jesus Christ when referring to God. As in the rest of the New Testament, this filial relationship of Jesus Christ with the Father is the only one of its kind in the writings of John. Jesus Christ is the «Son» by *antonomasia*, ὁ Υἱός, vis à vis others who are τέκνα. In some passages of John he is also the «only Son» (John 1:14,18; 3:16,18; 1John 4:9). Thus, this uniqueness is even further emphasized. According to the first ending of the gospel of John, the purpose of his writings is to show that Jesus is the Christ, the Son of God.

This special relationship of Jesus Christ with God, by virtue of which he is his «Son», already existed at the beginning of his public life (cfr. Mark 1:1, «the beginning of the gospel about Jesus Christ the Son of God»), and even at the beginning of his existence on this earth (cfr. Luke 1:35). Nevertheless, the Christology of the earliest times also evidenced the full realization of this divine Sonship at

---

16 Cfr. HENGEL M., *El Hijo de Dios*, Salamanca 1978, 25-30.

the time of the resurrection, with its definitive enthronement of Jesus Christ as Lord (cfr. Rom 1:3f; Phil 2:11; Acts 2:14ff; 13:32-34). The passage of Rom 1:3f, probably a reproduction of a confession of the pre-Pauline faith, is characteristic of this awareness: Jesus is presented as the Son of God in verse 3. This Jesus Christ, who is at every point in time the Son of God, is the only subject of a history that takes place in two times or in two contrasting phases. On the one hand, he is born from David according to the flesh in his earthly existence, but on the other, he has also been made Son of God in power, by virtue of the Spirit of holiness through the resurrection from the dead. We will analyze this passage again in due time. In the mean time, let us remember two issues. In the first place, Jesus Christ, from eternity the Son of God, lives in a certain way as a man in history through his Sonship. In the resurrection he, who is from the very beginning the Son of God, is made the Son of God in power. In the second place, the «Spirit of holiness» intervenes in this story[17]. This story of the divine Sonship of Jesus as a man is related to the activity of the Spirit in Jesus the Christ. At the beginning of this chapter, we referred to the fact that in the different mysteries of the life of Jesus, we see the revelation of the Trinitarian mystery. We will briefly analyze some of these mysteries, but before doing so, once we have seen the relationship between Jesus and the Father, we will briefly focus on our participation as Christians in this relationship, because the Father of Jesus is also our Father, and we are his children.

1.3. GOD, FATHER OF ALL

The Fatherhood of God is revealed to us in the mission of Jesus, the Son, sent into the world. As set forth in Gal 4:4-6, the text that will be the guide in our exposition, this Fatherhood has the purpose of ensuring that humans receive this sonship. Hence, the sending of the Son and the divine sonship of human beings are in close relationship. This is also stressed in the texts of First John which we already have seen (cfr. 1John 4:9,14). God, who is the Father of Jesus, also wants to be the Father of humanity. Jesus himself initiates us into his relationship of sonship with the Father. According to Mathew and Luke, he teaches his disciples to address God using the invocation «Our Father» (Matt 6:9; 11:2) in this prayer which has remained as the example and paradigm of every Christian prayer. In

---

17 This is the only time when Paul uses this term; in general terms, he refers to the «holy spirit». According to SCHLIER H., *Der Römerbrief*, Freiburg-Basel-Wein 1977, 26f, the expression could be equivalent to «spirit of glory». In due time we will see how these two ideas are related in the New Testament and in the tradition.

other places we can also see that Jesus, addressing his disciples, refers to God as «your Father» (cfr. Mark 11:25; Matt 6:32; Luke 12:30; Matt 5:48; Luke 6:32; Luke 12:32; Matt 23:9)[18].

Just as the divine Sonship of Jesus Christ is reflected throughout his existence, the acknowledgment of the Fatherhood of God must also have its effects on the concrete life of the disciples. In effect, the disciples must love and do good to all people alike, without any distinction whatsoever, imitating the merciful Father who causes rain to fall on the just and the unjust and the sun to rise on the bad and the good (cfr. Matt 5:45-48; Luke 6:27-36). Although it is true that in these texts, mention is made *strictu sensu* of God the Father only with respect to the disciples, it is also worth stating that according to them, God behaves with an attitude of love (and hence, in a certain sense, of Fatherhood) with respect to all people. There is an undeniable relationship between the Fatherhood of God with respect to Jesus and the Sonship of Jesus, on the one hand, and to that of the disciples, on the other. Only because Jesus is the Son of God and calls him Father can he teach the disciples to invoke him in these terms and to lead their lives as his children. He is the one who introduces them to this father-son relationship. However, it is worth noting that the divine Sonship of Jesus and that of the disciples are never equivalent. There is no mention in the New Testament of an «our Father» in which Jesus includes himself under the same conditions with other people. The relationship of Jesus Christ with the Father is unique and unrepeatable. This is evidenced in his words and in his behavior, and most specifically, when he prays in solitude (cfr. Luke 5:16; 6:12, etc.). Nevertheless, precisely because of its unrepeatability, the Sonship of Jesus Christ is the basis for the sonship of his disciples.

According to Paul, the Holy Spirit is the bond that relates the divine Sonship of Jesus Christ with ours. It is the Spirit himself who cries out in us «Abbá» (Gal 4:6) or who makes us say it (Rom 8:15). An important aspect of the predestination of all people in Jesus Christ, even from before the creation of the world, is also divine Sonship (cfr. Eph 1:5), which certainly cannot be lived without the gift of the Spirit (cfr. ibid. 13). Jesus Christ is explicitly mentioned in other passages in which Paul speaks of God also as our Father, which points to the association of our sonship to his Sonship (cfr. 2Cor 1:2f; Gal 1:3f; 1Thess 1:1-3; 3:11-13; 2Thess 1:1; 2:16).

---

18   These are the texts that JEREMÍAS J., *Abba y el mensaje central del Nuevo Testamento*, 46-52 states as probable authentic words of Jesus. At any rate, for us it is relatively indifferent to know to what extent we are, or are not, facing the «*ipsissima verba Iesu*».

In the writings of John, most specifically his first letter, we can also read that the believers have been born from God or have been begotten by him. Hence, God is also the Father of those who believe in Jesus Christ with the new title of son, because they have been begotten by his action to the life of faith (cfr. John 1:12f; 1John 2:29; 3:9; 4:7; 5:14, 5:18; cfr. also the birth from above by the Spirit in John 3:3ff). The divine sonship that is already real will be, in its fullness, an eschatological gift (cfr. 1John 3:2). The life and the love that Jesus has from the Father are destined to be transmitted to his disciples. Hence, God is the Father insofar as he is the beginning, in a very real way, of the eternal life of humankind mediated by Jesus Christ (cfr. John 6:57; 15:9 passim). The relationship and the distinction between the Sonship of Jesus Christ and our sonship is also expressed in John (cfr. John 20:17).

This is not the ideal place to develop in depth the topic of the Fatherhood of God with respect to humanity and the divine Sonship[19], which instead finds its place in treatises on grace. In this first approach to the biblical revelation of God as Father, we are simply interested in emphasizing how from the Fatherhood with respect to Jesus, other perspectives open. In the first place, we can see this clearly with respect to the believer, although in the second place, the Fatherhood of God already acquires universal dimensions in the New Testament. Strictly speaking, the name «Father» is only adequate for referring to God: «You must call no one on earth your "Father"…» (Matt 23:9). In a more direct relationship with the Fatherhood as related to Jesus, Paul says: «kneeling before the Father, from whom every Fatherhood in heaven or on earth is named…» (Eph 3:14). The Father of Jesus Christ is the only God of all humanity, both Jews and Gentiles (cfr. Rom 3:29-30). He is the creator from whom all things exist (cfr. 1Cor 8:6). If initially, the names of Father and Son are used in an analogical sense derived from worldly reality, in a second way, once the mystery that Jesus Christ reveals to us is known, it is clear that divine Fatherhood is the main analogous element of the whole idea of Fatherhood. Everything has its beginning in the Father of Jesus Christ. In essence, the name Father only corresponds to him in a mysterious and always differentiated manner related to Jesus and to all other people. God is the «Father of all» (Eph 4:6). We have mentioned that in the Old Testament there are very few texts which relate the Fatherhood of God to creation. In the New Testament, we find very few passages that have a universal

---

19 Cfr. LADARIA L.F., *Teología del pecado original y de la gracia*. Madrid 1993, 231-266.

perspective, in which the motif of creation is barely suggested. Nevertheless, it is worth emphasizing that they are not in a direct continuity with the texts of the Old Testament to which we have referred. The code has changed. The paradigmatic Fatherhood of God is founded on his relationship with Jesus and in his divine Sonship. On the contrary, in the ancient Church, we will instead find some direct references to God as Father in relation to creation. However, it is worth noting that these texts are already under the influence of the writings, or at least, the spirit of the New Testament, and because of this, the designation of God as Father as it relates to his creating action cannot be seen a priori as separated from the message of the New Testament, although it is not directly responding to the usage of this Testament.

1.4. JESUS CONCEIVED BY GRACE THROUGH THE HOLY SPIRIT

According to the gospels of Matthew and Luke, the incarnation of Jesus Christ takes place through the Holy Spirit (cfr. Matt 1:20; Luke 1:35). Hence, the Holy Spirit acts at the point in time when Jesus Christ comes into this world sent by the Father. It is worth stating, by the way, that according to the gospels, at that precise moment, the Holy Spirit comes directly upon Mary and not on Jesus (cfr. Luke 1:35). Nevertheless, the «holiness», which is an effect of this divine action, is attributed to Jesus Christ from the very first instance: «and so the child will be holy, and will be called Son of God» (ibid). Even though this is not stated in a clear way, everything points to the fact that from the moment of the incarnation, the Holy Spirit is present in the life of Jesus, the Son who is incarnated according to the plan of the Father[20]. His origin in this most distinctive action of God shows the transcendent, divine nature of the personhood of Jesus Christ. The creative activity of the Holy Spirit (cfr. Gen 1:2; Wis 1:17) reaches here its highest manifestation. Upon descending upon Mary, the Holy Spirit enables the incarnation of the Son. In this sense, his action «precedes» that of the Son. On the other hand, everything appears to point to the fact that the Spirit is present in the humanity of Jesus Christ, created by the fact itself of the assumption of the Son into the hypostatic union[21]. From that point of view, this presence of the

20 Cfr. SHÜRMANN H., *Das Evangelium nach Lukas I*, Freiburg-Basel-Wien 1982, 54; the divine Sonship of Jesus that is referred to at that point in time is even prior to his messianic mission. Cfr. as well, BOVON F., *Das Evangelium nach Lukas I*, Zürich-Neukirchen-Vluyn 1989, 76; BORDONI M., *La cristologia nell'orizonte dello Spirito*, Brescia 1995, 205ff.

21 According to the elegant formula «ipsa assumptione creata», inspired in AUGUSTINE, *Contra sermonem Arian*, 8 (PL 42,688): «nec sic adsumptus est ut prius creatus post assumeretur, sed ut ipsa assumptione crearetur»; followed almost textually by LEO THE GREAT, *Ep.* 35,3 (PL 54,807).

Spirit has to be considered logically (though not chronologically) «subsequent» to the hypostatic union of the Son[22]. Nevertheless, it is worth noting at the same time that the public activity of Jesus Christ moved by the Holy Spirit and the subsequent gift of the same Spirit are not related, neither in the New Testament nor in the primitive tradition of the Church, to this instance of the virginal conception of Jesus by the action of the Spirit, but rather with the coming of the Spirit upon Jesus in the Jordan[23]. It is this mystery in the life of Christ to which we must now turn our attention.

1.5. THE BAPTISM AND ANOINTING OF JESUS[24]

1.5.1. *THE NEW TESTAMENT AND THE FATHERS*

We mentioned at the beginning of this chapter that we wanted our starting point to be the manifestation of the Trinitarian mystery in the life of Christ. Undoubtedly for the New Testament, Jesus Christ is the Son of God, the only begotten, and hence in a strict sense, he does not share with anyone this condition as Son. Nevertheless, Jesus Christ is also «anointed» with the Spirit; he is the «Messiah», the «Christ». Besides being the Son, Jesus Christ is the Anointed, the bearer of the Spirit. In the text of the letter to the Galatians, which is a guide for this chapter, and in which we have seen the parallelism between the mission of the Son and that of the Spirit, we must notice that the Spirit is also called «Spirit of his Son». The mission of the Holy Spirit is related to the fact that Jesus Christ has been the bearer of the Spirit.

The synoptic gospels speak about the baptism of Jesus in the Jordan by John the Baptist (cfr. Mark 1:9-11par). With some noteworthy differences which will not be addressed here, there are two important ways in which we see a concurrence between the three gospels: the descent of the Holy Spirit upon Jesus (Luke 3:21 adds the significant information of the coming of the Spirit while Jesus was

---

22 This double aspect of the action of the Spirit is not always taken into account by theologians; cfr. KASPER W., *Jesús el Cristo*, 310; followed by BORDONI M., *La cristologia nell'orizonte dello Spirito*, 227; cfr. LADARIA L.F., «Cristología del Logos y cristología del Espíritu» in *Greg* 61 (1980) 353-360.

23 Cfr. CONGAR Y., *El Espíritu Santo*, Barcelona 1983, 42; CANTALAMESSA R., «"*Incarnatus est de Spiritu Sancto ex Maria Virgine*". Cristologia e pneumatologia nel simbolo constantinopolitano e nella patristica» in *Credo in Spiritum Sanctum. Atti del Congresso Teologico Internazionale di Pneumatologia*, Roma 1983, 101-125.

24 I based the subsequent foundations of what follows on my articles: «*Humanidad de Cristo y don del Espíritu*» in *EstEcl* 51 (1976) 321-345; «*La unción de Jesús y el don del Espíritu*» in *Greg* 71 (1990) 547-571, as well as in the article quoted in footnote 22.

praying) and the voice from heaven that proclaims that he is the Son of God. Undoubtedly there is a relationship between these two points. The first information is also included in the fourth gospel (cfr. John 1:32-34). Also, for John this descent and the *permanence* of the Spirit in Jesus show that he is the Son of God (cfr. John 1:34). Jesus is presented as sent by God, his «Son», sent to the people of Israel, and he is endowed with all the power of the Spirit that is necessary for him to fulfill his mission, a power that responds to the unique relationship which unites him with God[25]. As of that moment, Jesus begins his public life; he preaches the Kingdom of God and confirms with his signs and wonders that this kingdom has now emerged among humankind. According to the New Testament, this occasion of baptism is of utmost importance. Jesus has been anointed with the Holy Spirit for his mission, which he is to carry out in order to fulfill what the prophets have said[26].

Clearly making reference to the specific moment of the baptism of Jesus Christ, the New Testament has referred to the «anointing» of Christ with the Spirit. The gospel of Luke recounts in the words of Jesus Christ himself the passage of Isa 61:1-2: «The Spirit of the Lord is upon me, because he has anointed me…» (Luke 4:18-19), and in Acts 10:37-38 we read: «You know what has happened all over Judea, beginning in Galilee after the baptism that John preached, how God anointed Jesus of Nazareth with the Holy Spirit and power. He went about doing good and healing all those oppressed by the devil, for God was with him». There seems to be no doubt that the anointing refers to the baptism in the Jordan[27]. Hence, the New Testament seems to know these two moments that are chronologically differentiated: the incarnation of Jesus Christ by the act of the Spirit and by virtue of which he is already «holy» from the very first moment, and the anointing, located in point of time at the Jordan, after which Jesus is

25 Cfr. LENTZEN-DEIS F., *Die Taufe Jesu nach den Synoptiken,* Frankfurt am Main 1970; McDONELL K., «Jesus' Baptism in the Jordan» in *TheolSt* 56 (1995) 209-236; YILDIZ E., «El bautismo de Jesús como teofanía trinitaria» in *Diálogo Ecuménico* 31 (1996) 81-106.

26 Cfr. DE LA POTTERIE I., «L'onction du Christ» in *NRTh* 80 (1958) 225-252; CANTALAMESSA R., *Lo Spirito Santo nella vita di Gesù. Il mistero dell'unzione,* Milano 1988, 15f: « I Vangeli senza l'episodio iniziale del battesimo di Gesù sarebbero come gli Atti degli Apostoli senza il racconto iniziale della Pentecoste: mancherebbe ad essi la chiave di lettura per comprendere tutto il resto»; CHEVALLIER M.A., *Aliento de Dios. El Espíritu Santo en el Nuevo Testamento I,* Salamanca 1982, 151, also relates to the baptism the communication of the Spirit to the Messiah: «This is maintained in the case when the divine spirit intervenes as creator of life [in the incarnation], in another case, as a power communicated to the heroes of God, in general, and to the Messiah, in particular».

27 Cfr. also Acts 4:26-27 (cfr. Ps 2:1-2), which also seems to relate the anointing to baptism; on the other hand, in Heb 1:9 the quotation of Ps 45:8 seems to refer to the resurrection of Jesus Christ. At no point in time is the «anointing» related to the conception by the act of the Holy Spirit.

solemnly proclaimed the Son of God (although let us also remember Luke 1:35) and begins his mission of preaching and evidences through his actions that he is moved by the Spirit of God.

In the theology of the earliest fathers of the Church, the anointing of Jesus Christ has always held a distinctive place. This anointing means in the first place that Jesus receives upon himself the Spirit which he is to give to the Church. Ignatius of Antioch, although he refers directly to the anointing at Bethany (cfr. Mark 14:3par), states that the Lord poured ointment on his head to inspire incorruption in the Church[28]. Furthermore, already with the explicit mention of the baptism in the Jordan, Irenaeus states that, as the Word of God was man, from the root of Jesse and a descendant of Abraham, the Spirit of God rested upon him and anointed him to proclaim the gospel to the poor[29]. And after this in the same context: «The Spirit of the Lord was upon him, the Spirit of the one who has been announced by the prophets, who was going to anoint him so that we could be saved upon receiving the abundance of his anointing» [30]. Some points of these passages must be emphasized. In the first place, we must emphasize the identity of Jesus Christ who is anointed and who is the Word of God and not simply a man. On the other hand, he is anointed in his humanity[31], not as God, however, because it is clear that as God he did not need the anointing[32]. As a man, neither did Jesus need baptism for the forgiveness of his sins. However, this does not mean that baptism and anointing have no meaning for Jesus Christ. As we have just seen, Irenaeus states that Jesus must receive anointing in order to fulfill his mission of proclaiming the gospel to the poor. At the same time he points out, as was already the case of Ignatius of Antioch, that this anointing was directed toward the Church, toward human beings. In the humanity of Jesus Christ, the Spirit «had to get used» to being among humanity[33]. Even Irenaeus will see in the name of Christ, in the Spirit's relationship with Christ's baptism

---

28 *Ephesians* 17:1 (FP 1:129f). Even though this passage refers to the anointing at Bethany, mention is made of the baptism of Jesus immediately after in 18:2 (ibid.); cfr. ORBE A., *La unción del Verbo*, Roma 1966, 5-13.

29 Cfr. *Adv. Haer.* III 9,6 (SCh 211,206-208). Irenaeus quotes in this context Isa 61:1f and Luke 4:18.

30 Cfr. *Adv. Haer.* III 9,3 (SCh 211,110f). Cfr. ORBE A., *La unción del Verbo*, Roma 1966, 5-13.

31 ATHANASIUS, *Serap.* I 6 (PG 26,541): «When the Lord was baptized as man, on account of the flesh that he bore… it is said that the Holy Spirit came upon him. And when he gave it to his disciples he said…» (John 20:22); cfr. *Serap.* I 4 (537).

32 We cannot offer many details about the topic of «no-need» which is so frequent in the Fathers. Cfr. ORBE A., *La unción del Verbo*, 46-52.

33 *Adv. Haer.* III 17,1 (SCh 211,330); 18,7 (364-370); IV 14,2 (SCh 100,542-544), the man had to get used to the Spirit.

in the Jordan, a clear manifestation of the Trinity: «In the name of Jesus Christ we also imply the one who anoints, the one who is anointed and the ointment used for anointing. The Father anointed him, the Son was anointed in the Spirit which is the anointing… and this means the Father who anoints, the anointed Son, and the Holy Spirit which is the ointment»[34].

The «identity» of the Spirit in whom Jesus is anointed is still an open issue during the first Christian centuries. We cannot assume that we are always explicitly dealing with a «third person», because in the early Christian days, the idea of the Spirit is still vague. It is clear, at any rate, that this Spirit is a divine force which comes from the Father and which qualifies Jesus Christ, the incarnated Word, so that he can fulfill his mission[35].

Nevertheless, we must acknowledge that this rich theology of the anointing of Jesus Christ will disappear relatively soon from the consciousness of the Church. What will prevail is a current that will tend to identify it or to simply reduce it to the incarnation. In this way, the fact that the Spirit rests or reposes on Jesus will tend to be mistaken for the hypostatic union and will not be considered as a theological aspect which is relevant in itself. Several views have fostered an underestimation of the presence of the Holy Spirit in Jesus Christ. In the first place, mention can be made of the danger of adoptionism in its early modalities (Jesus is a mere man, and he is adopted as Son of God by the gift of the Holy Spirit; or, as set forth in some gnostic currents, a man upon whom the divine force descends in the Jordan, a force that would even have abandoned him at the time of his death). Later will come the dangers of Arianism (Jesus has a need for the Spirit, and hence, he is not God). Finally, we could point to the extreme modalities of the Christology of Antioch (the necessity of the Spirit in the man Jesus for his union with the divine persons). Perhaps this current of thought is already insinuated from the time when the Trinitarian dimension of the anointing is no longer emphasized (the Father anoints Jesus with the Spirit), and rather, what is

---

34 *Adv. Haer.* III 18,3 (SCh 211,350-352). It is worth noting that this text has been almost fully reproduced by BASIL OF CAESAREA, *De Sp. sanc.* 12,28 (SCh 17 bis, 344), and by AMBROSE OF MILAN, *De Sp. sanc.* I 3,44 (CSEL 79,33). The moment of this descent of the Spirit in his baptism is not a problem for any of them. It is also quite clear for these authors that Jesus receives the Spirit as man; cfr. texts in LADARIA L.F., *La unción de Jesús y el don del Espíritu*, (cfr. footnote 24), 565.

35 Cfr. LADARIA L.F., *La cristología de Hilario de Poitiers*, Roma 1989, 105-115; ORBE A., *Introducción a la teología de los siglos II y III*, Roma 1987, 662-665; by the same author, *Estudios sobre la cristología cristiana primitiva*, Madrid-Roma 1994, 500-507.

stated is that the Son as God is the one who gives the Spirit to the humanity which he has assumed and which belongs to him as God[36].

We can easily move from this assumption to the pure and simple confusion of the incarnation and the anointing. What is frequently quoted in this context is a significant passage of Gregory of Nazianzus:

> He is «Christ» (the Anointed) because of his divinity. This is the anointing of his humanity which sanctifies it, not by acting, as in other «anointings», but with the full presence of the one who gives the anointing, and by virtue of this presence, the one who anoints is called man, and the anointed is called God[37].

In addition to being interesting examples of «language communication», these texts show quite clearly the fact that the anointing of Christ is «reduced» to a hypostatic union. It is no longer the Spirit who anoints the Word made man, but the divinity anoints the humanity. Even though we do not intend to assign such a clear identification, Saint Augustine also thought that it was impossible that Jesus would have been anointed with the Holy Spirit in the Jordan. The baptism in the Jordan has the value of an announcement of everything that has already been a reality from the first moment in the life of Christ, and at the same time it prefigures what the reality of the Church will be[38]. The opinion of Saint Thomas does not seem to disagree significantly. The action of the Word and that of the Holy Spirit appear to be quite different at a certain point in time, but it does not seem that Saint Thomas had explicitly reflected on the relationship be

---

36 Cfr. ATHANASIUS, *Contra Arianos* I 46-47 (PG 26,108-111), even though it is still clear that the gift of the Holy Spirit affects the humanity of Jesus for the sanctification of all people.

37 *Or.* 30,21 (SCh 250,272); also 30,2 (ibid. 228): «the divinity is the anointing of the humanity»; cfr. also *Or.* 10, 4 (SCh 405,304). Although somewhat more clear and with different nuances, GREGORY OF NYSSA, *In illud Tunc ipse filius* (PG 44,1320): «The Logos —joining the flesh—— raised it to the properties of the Logos by receiving the Holy Spirit which the Logos possessed before the incarnation». The influence of Gregory of Nazianzus is clearly evidenced in JOHN OF DAMASCUS, *De fide orthod.* III 17 (1070); IV 14 (1161); 18 (1185), although with more nuances and clarifications in IV 6 (1112); 9 (1120).

38 *Trin* XV 26,46 (CCL 50A,526f): «Nec sane tunc unctus est Christus spiritu sancto quando super eum baptizatum velut columba descendit; tunc enim corpus suum, id est ecclesiam suam praefigurare dignatus est… Sed ista mystica et invisibili unctione tunc intellegendus est unctus quando *verbum* dei *caro factum est* (John 1:14), id est quando humana natura sine ullis praecedentibus bonorum operum meritis deo verbo est in utero virginis copulata ita ut cum filio fieret una persona… Absurdissimum est enim ut credamus eum cum iam triginta esset annorum… accepisse spiritum sanctum». Together with the pre-figuration of what happens in the Church, the pre-figuration of what happens in our baptism; cfr. GREGORY OF NAZIANZUS, *Or.* 39 1; 14-17; 20 (SCh 358,151; 178-188; 194); AMBROSIUS, *De Spir. sanc.* I 3,44 (CSEL 79,33)

tween the grace of the union and the fullness of the grace of the Spirit[39]. The idea of the anointing of Jesus with the Spirit had practically disappeared in the West. When it was remembered, it was simply to incorporate it virtually into the incarnation. The anointing is simply the fullness of the divinity of the Logos which joins the humanity and really lives in it[40]. The Church had not been able to take into account this aspect of the revelation of the Trinity in the life of Jesus Christ.

1.5.2. *THE RECENT APPROACHES*

The presence of the Spirit in Jesus has been emphasized in various ways in contemporary theology. However, this is not the time to address all the lines of thought that have been set forth in this respect[41]. We will simply refer to some important Catholic authors who have attempted to harmonize this information with the Christology of the incarnation that has been reflected in the New Testament and in the tradition of the Church.

In my opinion, credit can be attributed to H. Mühlen, who reformulated the issue in the systematic field after some biblical and patristic studies had already placed it in the historical plane. The incarnation and the anointing of Jesus Christ must be distinguished, and at the same time, they need to be articulated and coordinated[42]. In this distinction, Mühlen begins with an ecclesiological concern —that of failing to consider the Church as a continuation of the incarnation of

39 Cfr. *STh* III, q.6, a.6, the habitual grace of Christ is an effect of the grace of the union; III q.34, a.1, the sanctification of the humanity of Christ is present from the very first instant, and also without mention made of the Holy Spirit. However, in III q.39, a.2, it is stated that Christ did not need the baptism of the Spirit, because from the very first instant he was full of the «grace of the Holy Spirit». Cfr. also, II-II q.14, a.1. On the ecclesial dimension of the anointing in Saint Thomas, cfr. BORDONI M., *La cristologia nell'orizonte dello Spirito*, 243.

40 In this respect, see SCHEEBEN M.J., *Die Mysterien des Christentums*, Freiburg 1951, 276. What this author affirms is indeed interesting, ibid.: «When the Fathers say that Christ has been anointed with the Holy Spirit this only means that the Holy Spirit has come down upon the humanity of Christ with the Logos from which he comes, and that, as an outflow or perfume of the anointing —*that is the Logos himself*— he anoints and disseminates his aroma in his humanity» (I included the italics). However, a greater degree of differentiation can be found in LEO XIII, in his encyclical letter *Divinum illud munus*, of the year 1897 (cfr. DS 3237). Cfr. also, PIUS XII, *Mystici Corporis*; cfr. AAS 35 (1943) 206f; 219, from the first instant of his incarnation, the Son has adorned the human nature which is essentially bound to him with the fullness of the Holy Spirit.

41 There have been several attempts at replacing the traditional theology of the incarnation with a «Christology of the Spirit». Probably the most meaningful example in this respect has been LAMPE G.W.H., «The Holy Spirit and the Person of Christ» in SYKES S.W. - DAYTON S.P. (eds.), *Christ, Faith and History*, Cambridge 1972; by the same author, *God as Spirit*, Oxford, 1976.

42 Cfr. for what follows, MÜHLEN H., *Una Mystica Persona*, München-Paderborn-Wien 1968⁴, especially, 173-200; also pages 244.250.252; by the same author, *Der Heilige Geist als Person*, Münster, 186, 206f.

the Logos— which indeed is an issue rife with problems. It is quite clear that the once-only occurrence of the incarnation of the Logos can be subject to questioning with this conception. According to Mühlen, the Church should be seen rather as a continuation of the anointing of Jesus Christ with the Holy Spirit. In this way, a difference arises between the incarnation and the Church, and it is derived from the two missions of the Son and the Holy Spirit. According to the Holy Scriptures, there is a differentiation in time between these two missions. That of the Son takes place at the precise time of the incarnation, while that of the Holy Spirit takes place when he is sent to descend upon Jesus in the Jordan. Nevertheless Mühlen believes, inspired by thoughts in Saint Thomas, that this succession in time could be considered as a mere logical succession. Despite the biblical affirmations, he believes that there are dogmatic reasons which enable us to locate at the same point in time of the incarnation, the anointing of the humanity of Christ, which corresponds with the mission of the Holy Spirit. Consequently, there would be a chronological coincidence between the two events, although logically the anointing assumes the incarnation, and hence the latter precedes the former. Therefore, from the very first moment of his incarnation, Jesus had the fullness of the Holy Spirit and the fullness of grace. This does not mean that we cannot speak of a «history» of grace (and of the presence of the Holy Spirit) in Jesus Christ, but it would only be a growth in the manifestation of this grace[43]. On the other hand, the Spirit who descends upon Jesus at the time of the incarnation is the Holy Spirit who has the Son as his origin. Jesus as a man receives his own Spirit[44]. Even though a relevant significance is granted to the death and resurrection of Jesus, specifically as it relates to the gift of the Spirit to all humanity by the glorified Lord, the time of the baptism is not granted more value than its being the public delegation of what existed from the time of the incarnation itself[45].

It is absolutely necessary to maintain the key idea of the distinction between the incarnation and the anointing, which addresses a relevant aspect of the tradition. Jesus is the incarnate Son of God, and he is also at the same time the «Christ», the Anointed, the bearer and the giver of the Spirit. The action of the

---

43 Cfr. MÜHLEN H., *Una Mystica Persona*, 147f.
44 MÜHLEN H., *Una Mystica Persona*, 244, based on CYRIL OF ALEXANDRIA, *Com. in Joel* II 35 (PG 31,380); Cyril seems to place the descent of the Holy Spirit on Jesus in his baptism at the Jordan, according to this passage.
45 Cfr. MÜHLEN H., *Una Mystica Persona*, 249-257; *Der Heilige Geist*, 206.

Spirit in Jesus during the time of his earthly life is also emphasized, which is another element that we must set aside for future chapters. On the one hand, what is posed is the problem of whether the coincidence in time between the incarnation of Jesus and the anointing —or in other words, the exclusively revealing nature of the baptism of Christ— does justice to the data of the New Testament, not only as it relates to the «chronology», but also to the most profound intention of the authors. We must also ask ourselves if the Trinitarian dimension of the anointing of Jesus is duly emphasized. As we could see in the earliest tradition, the Father is the one who anoints Jesus in his humanity, and not the Son.

In a more elaborated manner, H. U. von Balthasar has also addressed this issue[46]. The action of the Holy Spirit upon Jesus Christ is clearly evident in the New Testament. If at first we saw the Spirit as the one in whom Jesus has been anointed as the Messiah, there was a need very early to antedate the beginning of the action of the Spirit on him to the time of his conception so that the Lord is not considered simply as a prophet[47]. In this way, there is a certain «precedence» of the Holy Spirit with respect to Christ, which is primarily emphasized in the incarnation, because it is the Holy Spirit who makes this possible, although his work is also evident in other moments in the life of Jesus. If after the resurrection Christ sends the Holy Spirit, in some way Christ has been «sent» previously by the Spirit[48]. In the economy of salvation there is a «Trinitarian inversion» that does not alter the «order» of the intra-divine life, although it shows how, because of the needs of the saving dispensation, the mutual relationships of the second and third persons change to a certain extent[49]. In this way, it is the Spirit who is the one who acts in the incarnation of the Son, and he «precedes» him in the economy. The Holy Spirit is at the same time the Spirit of the Father and of the Son. As Spirit of the Father, he is sent to the Virgin, and at the same time the Spirit of the Son moves him to enable Sonship to take place. The Spirit who comes upon Jesus and who impels him shows the «immanent» moment of the Spirit who

---

46 Cfr. Von Balthasar H.U., *Theologik III. Der Geist der Warheit*, Einselden 1987, especially 28-53 and 151-188.

47 Cfr. Von Balthasar H.U., *Theologik III*, 156; cfr. also, 41ff.

48 It is clear that the term is used in a rather inadequate way. According to the New Testament, only the Father sends his Son to the world. Nevertheless, it is worth pointing out the odd formulation made by the XI Council of Toledo (DS 538): «Missus tamen Filius non solum a Patre, sed a Spiritu Sancto missus esse credendus est... A se ipso quoque missus accipitur...»

49 Cfr. Von Balthasar H.U., *Theologik III*, 41.166-168.187. Also cfr. Bulgakov S., *Il Paraclito*, Bologna 1987, 437. The order of the activity of the *hypostases* in the world is inverse to that of their intra-trinitarian order, their *taxis*.

comes from the Father[50]. Von Balthasar also shares the belief that the incarnation and the anointing coincide in time and that the «anointing» of the humanity of Christ coincides with the divine nature on the one hand, and with the Holy Spirit on the other[51]. In the well-known expression of Irenaeus, the «two hands of the Father» —the Son and the Spirit— act in a differentiated way, although always one with the other. On the other hand, von Balthasar seems to attach to the baptism of Jesus a value that is more than a revelation of the presence of the Spirit which would have taken place from the beginning. From the moment of his baptism, the Spirit «sweeps» over Jesus (*ihn… über-schwebt*) in order to turn him during his whole life into the one who receives the disclosures of the Father[52].

More obviously in favor of the chronological and logical succession of the New Testament, Y. Congar, who on several occasions has addressed this matter, also refers to this issue[53]. He underlines the historicity of the work of God, the succession of events in time, the «newness» which we must respect. The self-communication of God in Jesus is evidenced in different historical stages, which are qualitative moments of this communication. More specifically, in the gospel we see successive moments of the descent of the Spirit upon Jesus:

> As to Jesus, we will have to be very careful to avoid any adoptionism. We affirm that he is ontologically the Son of God by the hypostatic union, from the moment when he was conceived, and that he is the temple of the Spirit from that very same moment, sanctified by the Spirit in his humanity. Nevertheless, guided by the intention of respecting the subsequent moments or stages of the history of salvation and of granting all its due reality to the texts of the New Testament, first we intend to show in the baptism, and afterwards in the resurrection and exaltation, two moments of new *actions* of the *virtus* (of the efficiency) of the Spirit in Jesus when he is made (and not only declared) by God the Messiah-Savior, and subsequently, the Lord[54].

---

50 VON BALTHASAR H.U., *Teodramática 3. Las personas del drama. El hombre en Cristo*, Madrid 1993, 477. In this work, he also refers to the Trinitarian inversion, 173ff.
51 Cfr. VON BALTHASAR H.U., *Theologik III*, 168ff.
52 VON BALTHASAR H.U., *Theologik III*, 187; cfr. also, 220.
53 Cfr. CONGAR Y., *El Espíritu Santo*, Barcelona 1983, 42-46; 598-607 (the last pages reproduce a previous article, «Pour une christologie pneunatologique» in RSPhTh 63 (1979) 435-472; also, *La Parole e il Soffio*, Roma 1985, 108-125.
54 CONGAR Y., *El Espíritu Santo*, 606. Also, CANTALAMESSA R., «Incarnatus est de Spiritu Sancto» (cfr. footnote 23): by the same author, *Lo Spiritu Santo nella vita di Gesù* (cfr. footnote 26), 13-16.

M. Bordoni gives a similar opinion: it is not enough to consider the symbolic value of the baptism of Jesus. Theology must shed light as well on the reality of the anointing of the baptism of Jesus as an event in the Spirit which has really taken place in him, both in the Christological and in the ecclesiological sense, because the gift of the Spirit that Jesus received is also destined for the Church[55].

Consequently, we can see that Catholic theology of the last decades has recovered the distinction (while at the same time the profound relationship) that the New Testament shows us between the incarnation of the Son and his anointing in his humanity by the Holy Spirit. There are two aspects which still do not appear to have gained general agreement, although I believe that we have the elements to find a solution: the chronologic moment of the anointing (in the incarnation or in the Jordan) and its active subject (the Father or the Son himself).

As related to the moment of the «anointing» of the assumption of Jesus as the Messiah, we have examined the clear differences among the authors whom we have briefly explored. Should we attach preference to the moment of the incarnation or to that of the baptism of Christ[56]? It does not seem that, when faced with the quite clear statements of the New Testament and of the earliest tradition of the Church, we can pose any serious objections. The «anointing» of Jesus takes place in the Jordan, as we have already seen. This is the reference point for the messianic action of Jesus and the subsequent giving of himself to humankind[57]. It must be clearly stated that the sanctification of the humanity of Jesus by the act of the Spirit in the first instance is not under discussion because of this fact. Ever since the incarnation, Jesus is personally the Messiah, the Christ (cfr. Luke 2:11; also Matt 1:1; 1:16; 1:17; 1:18). But only after the outpouring of the Spirit and his manifestation to men and women in the Jordan will he begin to exercise his messianic function. His baptism has a meaning for Jesus, the incar-

---

55 Cfr. BORDONI M., *La cristologia nell'orizonte dello Spirito*, Brescia 1995, 238ff.

56 The *Catechism of the Catholic Church* (CEC) addresses on different occasions the baptism and the anointing of Jesus. Cfr. numbers 438, 453, 535, 536, 565, 695, 727, 741 and 1224. On the one hand, special mention is made of the fact that, from the first instant, Jesus is the «Christ» and that from the incarnation, he has the fullness of the Spirit. However, on the other hand, it sets forth that Christ is anointed and consecrated in his baptism at the Jordan and that he receives the Spirit who will remain upon him.

57 A patristic tradition insists on the fact that at the time of the coming of Christ every activity of the Spirit must cease because he must be received, from that moment, solely from the Spirit as his only source. At the Jordan, the Spirit descends upon him, destined to make the subsequent fulfillment, the gift after the resurrection: cfr. JUSTIN, *Dial. Tryph.* 87-88 (BAC 116,458-462); also, TERTULLIAN, *Adv. Iud.* 8,12 (CCL 2,1362); *Adv. Marc.* V 8 (CCL 1,598); cfr. ORBE A., *La unción del Verbo*, 39-60.

nated Son. It is only a manifestation for others of something he already possessed[58]. Without falling at all into adoptionism, we can see moments of «something new» in the historical path of Jesus the Son towards the Father, which will end in the resurrection.

The Holy Spirit descends and rests upon Jesus who is in his person the Son. The Spirit acts in Jesus. At every point in time, he is the driving force and the guide in his historical path as Son towards the Father. It is worth calling attention to the idea of von Balthasar regarding the Holy Spirit as the «mediator», to a certain extent, of the will of the Father with respect to Jesus. In the Spirit, Jesus obeys, although in freedom, the plans and the intentions of the Father[59]. The statements made in the gospel to the action of the Spirit in Jesus are quite significant. It is the Spirit who encourages Jesus to go to the desert to be tempted after the baptism at the Jordan (cfr. Mark 1:12par, with significant differences in the synoptic gospels; according to Luke 4:1, Jesus goes to the desert «filled with the Holy Spirit»); in the same Spirit, Jesus starts his ministry (Luke 4:14: «Jesus with the power of the Spirit returned to Galilee»); and we have already noticed the role of the Spirit in the quotation from Isa 61:1f, as stated in the words of Jesus in Luke 4:18. Furthermore, by virtue of the Spirit of God, Jesus drives out demons, and with this, he shows that the kingdom of God has arrived (cfr. Matt 12:28; cfr. Luke 11:20 which speaks, as it is well known, of the finger of God). This same idea is evidenced in Mark 3:22; 3:28-30: Jesus does not drive out the demons by the prince of demons, but by the Holy Spirit. The fact of not acknowledging this presence is blasphemy against the Holy Spirit. In Matt 2:18-21, Jesus refers to Isa 42:1-4 (first song of the Servant) which speaks, among other things, of the presence of the Spirit in the servant of the Lord. Jesus rejoices in the Holy Spirit (Luke 10:21). Finally, by the «eternal Spirit» he offers himself to the Father in his passion and in his death (cfr. Heb 9:14). Hence, the action of the Spirit in Jesus is

---

[58] The International Theological Commission also refers to the anointing during the baptism in the Jordan: Commissio Theologica Internationalis, «Questiones selectae de Christologia» in *Greg* 61 (1980) 609-632, especially 630. The Spanish text of the International Theological Commission used by Ladaria: *Documentos 1970-1979*, Madrid 1983, 225-247, 245: «After this, when he was baptized in the Jordan (cfr. Luke 3:22) he was anointed by the Spirit in order to fulfill his messianic mission (Acts 10:38; Luke 4:18)»; also JOHN PAUL II, *Dominum et Vivificantem*, 19, seems to locate the messianic anointing of Jesus in the Jordan; cfr. as well ibid. 40.

[59] Effectively, the Spirit is completely opposite to constriction. BORDONI M., *La cristologia nell'orizonte dello Spirito*, 239, following R. Cantalamessa, most adequately points to the fact that it is not enough to ratify the human freedom of Jesus, but we also have to bear in mind his effective exercise in the dynamic nature and tension that leads to the fulfillment of the original project of the Father.

not disinterested in Jesus' fulfilling his life of Sonship in compliance with the mission that the Father has entrusted him. Basil of Caesarea has summarized in this way the different affirmations made in the New Testament:

> The plan of salvation for men… who can doubt that it is fulfilled with the grace of the Holy Spirit? … And after this, those things that are related to the coming of the Lord in the flesh [were fulfilled] by the Holy Spirit. In the first place, he shared the same flesh of the Lord, turning it into anointing, and in an inseparable way, as has been written: «The man on whom you see the Spirit come down and rest is my beloved Son» (John 1:33; Luke 3:22). And: «Jesus of Nazareth who was anointed by God with the Holy Spirit» (Acts 10:38). And after this, all the activities of Christ depended on the presence of the Holy Spirit[60].

Thus, Jesus, anointed at the Jordan, can begin his public life and his mission[61]. Hence, it seems more consistent (although without forgetting a presence of the Spirit in Jesus and his personal condition as Messiah from his coming into the world) to place in the moment of his baptism the messianic anointing that empowers him for the exercise of his ministry among humanity.

The second controversial point of which we have spoken is the one that refers to the active subject of this anointing. Is it the Father or the Son himself who anoints his humanity? Having seen the testimonies of the New Testament and those of the earliest Christian tradition, it does not seem sufficient to think that the Logos anoints his humanity with the Spirit that he possesses and that belongs to him. It is above all, the Father who carries out this anointing. It does not seem typical of the overall sense expressed in the New Testament to say that the Son anoints his own humanity at the Jordan. We must also note that the descent of the Spirit upon Jesus, his messianic anointing, has to be seen in relation to the voice from heaven which proclaims Jesus as his Son: «You are my Son the beloved; my favor rests on you» (Mark 1:11; Luke 3:22; cfr. Matt 3:17), or even: «Today I

---

60 BASIL OF CAESAREA, *De Spir. Sancto* 16,39 (SC$_h$ 17,386), cfr. also ibid. 19,49 (418-420); AMBROSE OF MILAN, *De Spir. Sancto* III 1,2.5-6 (CSEL 79,150-151); JOHN PAUL II, *Dominum et Vivificantem*, 40: «In the sacrifice of the Son of man, the Holy Spirit is present and acts in the same way as he acted in his conception, when he entered this world, in his hidden world and in his public ministry».

61 BOVON F., *Das Evangelium nach Lukas I*, 180, on the baptism of Jesus: «That the Holy Spirit has acted in the miraculous birth of Jesus does not mean for Luke that the Messiah has already reached his perfection. For his mission (more than for himself) he now receives the assent and the assistance of the divine force»; cfr. ibid. 220, on Luke 4:18.

have fathered you» (Ps 2:7; variant of Luke 3:22). The identity of Jesus as Son is manifested at this moment, and the descent of the Spirit cannot be separated from the fulfillment of the work of Jesus as the Son of God which he must carry out by order of the Father. Hence, the moment of his baptism is of the utmost importance for the revelation of the Sonship of Jesus in full personal identification with the mission that has been entrusted to him by the Father[62].

Related to this problem, we also must view the «identity» of the Spirit which descends upon Jesus. We have referred to the difficulties of patristic theology in this precise identification. It is quite evident that today we cannot have doubts regarding this identity. The Holy Spirit descends upon Jesus. He is the Spirit of the Father and of the Son. Nevertheless, not everything has been said with this phrase. There is a «history» of the revelation of the mystery of God, of the Trinitarian mystery, and consequently of the mystery of the Holy Spirit. At the time of the baptism, the Spirit is not fully manifested as the Spirit of the Son. This full manifestation will take place at the time of the resurrection. In due time, we will again address this issue. The New Testament never refers to the Spirit of the Son or of Jesus when speaking about the Spirit which descends upon him at the Jordan and the Spirit through whom Jesus is anointed. However, in the human life of Jesus, something is revealed by the fact that the Holy Spirit is also the Spirit of the Son: Jesus possesses the Spirit as something that belongs to him, and not just as something that is received from the outside[63]. In view of the fact that it is the Spirit of the Father who is the one who comes upon him, Jesus is encouraged to carry out his mission. In light of the fact that he is the Spirit of the Son, the latter, with internal freedom, is obedient to the Spirit of the Father who guides him. The Holy Spirit is not a mere external principle for Jesus, but rather, someone who dwells in him and remains in him as his natural place. In this availability of the Son in free obedience to the Father, we see the historical manifestation of the eternal Sonship of Jesus. In the full manifestation of this Sonship in the resurrection, we will also see the full evidence of the identity of the Spirit as the Spirit of the Father and of the Son, because at this point in time, this is what the resurrected Jesus is able to give.

---

62 Von Balthasar H.U., *Teodramática* 3, 194.205; the identification of Jesus with his mission and the definition of who he is to God as it is related by the voice in the baptism; also cfr. ibid. 187.209.
63 Cfr. González de Cardedal O., *La entraña del cristianismo*, Salamanca 1997, 714-719.

It is true that to a certain degree, at the time of the baptism of Jesus, all of us already received the Spirit when Jesus received him upon his head[64]. However, at the present time, the gift granted to all of us has still not been made effective. The Spirit has not yet revealed all of his potentiality and has not manifested himself fully in his effects as will happen on Pentecost, after the resurrection and exaltation of the Lord to the right hand of the Father. However, the baptism of the Lord is a moment of manifestation of Jesus the Son in his anointing in the Spirit by the initiative of the Father. For this reason, it is a very important time in the history of the manifestation of the triune God.

We must also bear in mind the moment of the transfiguration of the Lord which reminds us in so many aspects of his baptism. The new proclamation of Jesus as Son of God, in very similar terms to those of the baptism (cfr. Mark 9:7; Matt 17:5; 9:35), undoubtedly plays a key role. Hence, we see the final goal of the glory (cfr. Luke 9:32) that the way of Jesus must take, which necessarily leads through death.

1.6. THE TRINITY AND THE CROSS OF JESUS

If in the Paschal mystery of the death and resurrection of Jesus his life reaches its culminating moment, it should come as no surprise that precisely in this moment the manifestation of the triune God also takes place. We have already suggested how the delivery of Jesus to his death, which purifies us from sin, is fulfilled by virtue of the eternal Spirit (Heb 9:14), probably to be identified as the Holy Spirit who is referred to in the epistle in this context (9:8). The Spirit has been compared to the fire of the sacrifice by virtue of which Jesus fulfills his total offering to the Father[65]. Undoubtedly in the Paschal mystery we have the key moment of the revelation of the mystery of the God of love, of the Fatherhood and the divine Sonship through the Holy Spirit. The love that Jesus has for us sinners was manifested in his death, as was equally the love of the Father (cfr. Rom 5:6-10; 8:32-35). The Paschal mystery always has to be seen in the unity of death

64 Cfr. besides the texts already quoted, ATHANASIUS, *Contra Ar.* I 46-48 (PG 26,108-113); also HILARY OF POITIERS, *In Mat.* 2:5-6 (SCh 254,108-110); cfr. LADARIA L.F., *La unción de Jesús y el don del Espíritu*, 563ff.
65 Cfr. VANHOYE A., «L'Esprit eternal et le feu du sacrifice en He 9,14» in *Bib* 64 (1983) 263-274; states to this purpose JOHN PAUL II, *Dominum et Vivificantem*, 40: «The Son of God, Jesus Christ as man… enabled the Holy Spirit, who had already intimately impregnated his humanity, *to transform it into a perfect sacrifice* by means of the act of his death, as a victim of love in the cross… The Holy Spirit acted in a special way in this absolute self-giving of the Son of men to transform the suffering into a redeeming love».

and resurrection. Only in an attempt to make things easier, will we first address the revelation of the mystery of love in the cross[66], and from this, we will go on to the resurrection.

1.6.1. THE REVELATION OF THE TRINITY IN THE CROSS IN CONTEMPORARY THEOLOGY

In the field of Catholic theology, the ideas of von Balthasar on this issue have raised great interest and have been analyzed and further expanded in different writings, but particularly in his theology of the Paschal mystery published in *Mysterium Salutis*[67].

Von Balthasar states that according to the New Testament, Jesus accepts death for us in full obedience and agreement to «be delivered». Nevertheless, it is said of the Father that he delivers Jesus his Son, and with this he shows us that he loves us (cfr. Rom 8:32; John 3:16). Christ also loves us (Rom 8:35; Gal 2:20; Eph 5:1), and when he delivers himself over to death, he evidences at the same time his love and the love of the Father for us. Because of this, «the theology of this delivery does not permit any other framework than the Trinitarian one». The fact that God «delivers» up his Son has to be understood in a powerful sense and not as a simple «sending» or «gift»; «rather, the Father fully delivered Christ to his fate of dying»[68]. The obedience of Jesus to the point of death is the response to this initiative of the Father. Already in the beginning of the passion the «*reduction in oboedientiam*» is the essential feature of the prayer in the garden, the only purpose of which is saying «yes» to the will of the Father and waiving his own will. The whole sense of the prayer rests on giving priority to the will of the Father, rather than his own will[69].

---

66 Ample information on this topic will be found in SALVATI G.M., *Teologia trinitaria della croce*, Torino 1987; CIOLA N., *Teologia trinitaria. Storia-Metodo-Prospettive*, Bologna 1996, 165-197. Cfr. the considerations on the importance of the Paschal mystery for the theology of the Trinity in LAFONT G., *Peut-on connaître Dieu en Jésus-Christ?* Paris 1969, 234f.

67 VON BALTHASAR H.U., «El misterio pascual» in *MySal* III/2, 143-335. The following notes refer to this work if it is not otherwise stated. It is quite clear that here we cannot make a broad presentation of his thought. We mostly center on the Trinitarian aspects. Cfr. MARCHESI G., *La cristologia trinitaria di Hans Urs von Balthasar*, Brescia 1997, 524-534.

68 VON BALTHASAR H.U., «El misterio pascual» in *MySal* III/2, 212. Von Balthasar quotes in this context ALTHAUS P., *Das Kreuz Christi*, in his *Theologische Aufsätze* I, Göttingen 1929, 1-50. Cfr. also VON BALTHASAR H.U., *Teodramática 4. La acción*, Madrid 1995, 294ff.

69 Cfr. VON BALTHASAR H.U., «El misterio pascual» in *MySal* III/2, 207f.

However, the glory of God appears in the suffering of Jesus, in the total *kenosis*: «the light of God's glory brings glory on the face of Jesus Christ» (2Cor 4:6)[70]. This does not mean for von Balthasar that the realism of the passion is eliminated. On the contrary: «There is no need to soften everything that is related to the cross of Christ, as though the crucified, without suffering any disturbance or commotion in his union with God, would have simply taken this time to recite the psalms and would have died in the peace of God»[71]. The cry of abandonment and forsakenness that is conveyed by the evangelists (Matt 27:46; Mark 15:34) is not simply the recitation of Ps 22. Rather, it shows in all its power the real experience of abandonment. This sense of abandonment cannot be less than the one that has been experienced by many in both the Old and the New Testaments. For instance, Irenaeus, as opposed to the Gnostics, set forth the principle according to which Christ could not demand from his disciples those sufferings that he himself had not experienced (cfr. *Adv. Haer.* III 18, 5-6)[72]. The unity of the cross and the glory, which is characteristic of the theology of John, enables us to see in the image of the crucified the last elucidation of the God whom no one has ever seen (cfr. John 1:18). Although in the light of the glorification that has already begun at this moment in the crucified Jesus, we have as a result the ultimate revelation of God.

We still must determine the scope of this forsakenness of Jesus by the Father that will paradoxically reveal to us the mysteries of divine love. The abandonment of Jesus by God cannot be duplicated, just as the Son cannot be duplicated[73]. Specifically, this means that Jesus in his forsakenness and total passivity, which is the consequence of the experience of «Holy Saturday» (not only with respect to the pain of the cross that would reach its end with death), has even lived the personal experience of one who is condemned. This personal experience «should be none other than the one demanded by an authentic solidarity in the *Sheol*, without any saving light, because every light of salvation comes exclusively from the one who was supportive until the very end; and if he can convey that light it is

[70] VON BALTHASAR H.U., «El misterio pascual» in *MySal* III/2, 218.
[71] VON BALTHASAR H.U., «El misterio pascual» in *MySal* III/2, 220. Cfr. also *Teodramática 3. Las personas del drama. El hombre en Cristo*, Madrid 1993, 485f.
[72] Cfr. VON BALTHASAR H.U., «El misterio pascual» in *MySal* III/2, 222f.
[73] VON BALTHASAR H.U., «El misterio pascual» in *MySal* III/2, 192.

because he vicariously relinquished it»[74]. As the author states, it meant «experiencing sin as such», which accounts for his utter impotence and passiveness:

> Now Christ belongs to the *refaim*, the «powerless». Now he cannot begin an active struggle against the «forces of hell», nor can he «be triumphant» subjectively because both things imply life and strength. Nevertheless, his extreme «weakness» can and should coincide with the purpose of his vision of the second death, which coincides, in turn, with pure sin per se, unrelated to any concrete person and not incarnated in a living existence, but detached from any individualization and contemplated in its plain and simple reality, *as* sin[75].

Hence, we are faced with the worst manifestation of abandonment and *kenosis* of the Son. In the distinction, and even the «opposition», between the will of the Father and of the Son (cfr. Mark 14:36par), as well as in the abandonment on the cross, there is clear evidence of the «economic» opposition between the divine persons, although this same opposition is the ultimate manifestation of all the unitary action of God[76], the internal logic of which is evidenced in the inseparable unity between his death on the cross and his resurrection. The full revelation of the Paschal mystery takes place in the resurrection, although it was prepared in the opposition of wills in the garden, as well as in the abandonment of

---

74 Von Balthasar H.U., «El misterio pascual» in *MySal* III/2, 256. Cfr. all the context 252ff, especially 253: «If the Redeemer, on account of his solidarity with the dead, spares them the experience of being dead (as to the pain of the damage) by enabling a celestial light of faith, hope and love to always shine in the "abyss", it is because he took for himself the burden of all this experience». However, in *Theologik II. Wahrheit Gottes*, Einsiedeln 1985, 315, n.1, the author seems to abandon the notion of «solidarity with the dead».

75 Von Balthasar H.U., «El misterio pascual» in *MySal* III/2, 256. Cfr. also in Kehl M. - Loser W. (herausgegeben von), *In der Fülle des Glaubens. Hans Urs von Balthasar Lesebuch*, Freiburg-Basel-Wein 1981, 158: «Nevertheless, on Holy Saturday we remember the descent of the dead Jesus to hell. In other words (and simplifying this considerably), we see his solidarity in the "no time" with those who are lost and away from God. For them, this choice, by means of which they have chosen their "self" rather than the disinterested and altruistic love of God, is definitive. This definitive nature of death is the one to which the dead Son descends, by no means active at this point, but rather deprived from the cross of every power and initiative of his own, as the one that is fully disposed of, lessened and weakened to pure matter, totally indifferent in the obedience of the corpse, incapable of any active solidarity and any "preaching" to the dead. He is dead because of love together with them, and precisely in this way, he breaks the absolute solitude that is assumed for the sinner: the sinner, who wants to be "condemned" far from God, finds God again in his solitude, although this is the God of the absolute powerlessness of love…». Cfr. also *Theologik II* (cfr. previous footnote), 314-329.

76 Cfr. Von Balthasar H.U., *Teodramática 4*, 220-224, the abandonment is also a moment of the «conjunction» of the persons. This conjunction always underlies the separation.

the cross[77]. The intra-divine Father-Son relation is evidenced in the history of the passion. From this economic «separation» we can understand to a certain degree the total giving up of the Son by the Father, which is, in a way, a first intra-divine «separation» that is always exceeded by the union in the Spirit of love. Naturally, these considerations have to be completed in the light of the resurrection. Hence, we will address this in our next exposition.

In parallel with what we have seen in our study of the anointing of Jesus, we also must retain here as a value that we cannot surrender, the consideration of the history of the passion as an event between the Father and the Son in the Holy Spirit, and hence, in its unavoidable Trinitarian dimension. It does not suffice to see this as an issue of the relation between humanity and divinity in Christ, even though this dimension cannot be absent; however, it must be framed within the mystery of the father-son relationship. Jesus, the Son, is the one who feels abandoned by the Father and not only in «his humanity». We must also retain the reality of the abandonment and the darkness that Christ experiences in his passion. The power of the affirmations about Jesus made sin for us should not be minimized. All the love of the Father that delivers the Son in his love for the world, and all the love of the Son who gives himself up in this obedience, even when faced with anguish and darkness, in solidarity with sinners who are absent from God, is evidenced here. The step from this point to the affirmations that we have quoted regarding Holy Saturday and to the abandonment by God, even to the extremity of experiencing the separation of the condemned, is simply one step that I would not dare take on my own. Holy Saturday has been lived as a time of hope. Furthermore, it has instead been regarded in the tradition as the moment of salvation that Jesus offers to those who experience separation from God in Hades[78].

The theology of the cross has been a main issue in the case of M. Luther. It comprises the revelation of God. In his thesis in the Heidelberg Disputation, he points out that the true theologian is not the one who looks upon the invisible things of God through creation, but rather, the one who comprehends the visible and mani-

---

77 Cfr. Von Balthasar H.U., «El misterio pascual» in *MySal* III/2, 279.287.

78 Cfr. Grillmeier A., «Der Gottessohn im Totenreich Soteriologische und christologische Motivierung der Descensuslehre in der älteren Christlichen Überlieferung» in *Mit Ihm und in Ihm. Christologische Forschungen und Perspektiven*, Freiburg-Basel-Wein 1978, 76-174; Orbe A., «El "*Descensus ad inferos*" y San Ireneo» in *Greg* 68 (1987) 485-522. The same Von Balthasar *Theologik* II, 316, refers to that triumphant Christ who descends to hell according to the images of the Eastern Church, and he is aware that he takes a step away from that tradition.

fest things of God seen through the passion and the cross[79]. It is not strange that Protestant authors have followed this path. The relation between the cross and the Trinitarian mystery has been studied especially by J. Moltmann and E. Jüngel.

Moltmann has done so primarily in his very well known work, *The Crucified God (Der gekreuzigte Gott)*[80]. His main concerns are on the one hand, to leave behind the extremely limited scheme of the theology of the two natures of Christ that only revolves around the relation between the humanity and the divinity, leaving aside the Trinitarian dimension of Christology; on the other hand, he is also intent on emphasizing the inadequacy of theism when attempting to explain the triune God and the Paschal mystery. In regard to the aspect that we are now discussing, the formulas of the New Testament constitute the starting point in the reflection of the author, most specifically those of Paul and John, on the «delivery» of Jesus by God for the salvation of those «who are without God», and the definition of the God of love who appears as it relates to that delivery in 1John 4:8 and 4:16. The love that is referred to here is realized in the cross. «God is love» means that he exists in love, and he exists in love in the event of the cross. In the cross, the Father and the Son are profoundly separated in the abandonment of Jesus, and at the same time, they are also most profoundly united in the delivery. The Spirit comes out of this event between the Father and the Son that justifies those «who are without God», fills the abandoned with love, and brings back the dead to life. What happens in the cross happens first and foremost «between God and God». It brings about a most profound separation in God himself, because God abandons God (the Father abandons the Son), thus contradicting himself. However, in God there is evidence of a profound unity that is obvious in the Spirit who is united with the Father and with the Son. It is the Spirit who must be understood as the Spirit of the delivery of the Father and the Son, and at the same time, it is the Spirit who brings about love for abandoned humanity and who gives life to the dead[81].

---

79   *Thesis* 19-29 (WA 1,354): «Non ille vere theologus dicitur, qui invisibilia Dei per ea, quae facta sunt, intellecta conspicit, sed qui visibilia et posteriora Dei per passiones et crucem intelligit»; other significant expressions: «Crux sola est nostra theologia» (WA 5,176): «Crux Christi unica est eruditio verborum Dei, theologia sincerissima» (ibid. 216); cfr. BLAUMEISER H., *Martin Luthers Kreuzestheologie. Eine Untersuchung anhand der Operationes in Psalmos (1519-1521)*, Paderborn 1995, especially 98ff.

80   MOLTMANN J., *Der gekreuzigte Gott. Das Kreuz Christi als Grund und Kritik christlicher Theologie*, München 1972. Also *Trinität und Reich Gottes. Zur Gotteslehre*, München 1980. We cannot continue here the debate that has emerged as a result of these works.

81   Cfr. MOLTMANN J., *Der gekreuzigte Gott*, 229-232.

These phrases enable us to begin to realize that the Spirit «becomes» in the event of the cross. Undoubtedly, we cannot fail to acknowledge other statements set forth by Moltmann regarding the «constitution» of the Trinity, in which he refers to traditional concepts. Nevertheless, the relationships between the economic Trinity and the immanent Trinity are not always set forth with the clarity for which we would hope[82]. Moltmann continues his reflections on the mystery of the cross in this way:

> We have interpreted here the event of the cross as an event between persons, where these persons set up their reciprocal relationships. In this way, we have not only seen one person of the Trinity suffer, as though the Trinity were already «at the disposal» (*vorhanden*) of itself, in the divine nature… This starting point is new with respect to tradition. It overcomes the dichotomy between the economic Trinity and the immanent Trinity, as well as between the nature of God and his internal «tri-unity». In this way, the Trinitarian thought is necessary for fully perceiving the cross of Christ… Thus, the Trinitarian doctrine is simply the summary of the history of the passion of Christ and of its significance for the eschatological freedom of faith and the life of oppressed nature (*verdrängt*)[83].

Hence, the «*historia salutis*» is not a matter of indifference within the life of the Trinity, and most specifically, in the cross of Jesus. Moltmann also insists on the abandonment of Christ on the cross, which entails the abandonment of God, absolute death, so that what is not divine is destroyed. This abandonment is such that it turns into a total opposition: «*Nemo contra Deum nisi Deus ipse*»[84]. In the opinion of Moltmann, the salvation of the world is fulfilled in this Father-Son «opposition» which means abandonment of the Son. The Spirit of life comes out of this «story» between the Father and the Son[85].

Therefore, we must not assume a concept of God. It must rather be based on the concept that is shown here. We must understand what God is from the cross of Jesus. Those who speak of him from the Christian point of view must tell the story of Jesus as a story between the Son and the Father. Thus, God is not a di-

---

82 Cfr. MOLTMANN J., *Trinität und Reich Gottes*, 165f,168f,175f,178-193, with the distinction between the constitution of the Trinity and the life of the Trinity.

83 MOLTMANN J., *Der gekreuzigte Gott*, 232.

84 MOLTMANN J., *Der gekreuzigte Gott*, 233. The expression comes from Goethe: cfr. VON BALTHASAR H.U., *Teodramática* 3,486.

85 Cfr. MOLTMANN J., *Der gekreuzigte Gott*, 233.

verse nature nor a celestial person, but an «event». Nevertheless, he is not an event of community with humanity (*Mit-menschlichkeit*), but rather the event of Golgotha, the event of the love of the Son and the pain of the Father that gives way to the Spirit who appears opening the future and creating life[86]. Moltmann also wonders what the meaning is, then, of the personal God? Indeed, one cannot pray to an event. The answer is that there is no personal God as a person projected in heaven. However, there are persons in God: the Father, the Son, and the Holy Spirit. Hence, we pray «in» this event: «through the Son we pray to the Father in the Holy Spirit»[87]. The loving Father raises or provokes the perfect correspondence in the equally loving Son and creates in the Holy Spirit the correspondence of love in the humanity which is opposed to him. All of this takes place in the cross. In the cross, God fully expresses his unconditional love that is full of hope. As a result of this, the Trinity «is not a circle that closes onto itself in heaven, but rather an eschatological process, open to all people in the world, which emerges from the cross of Christ»[88]. In the cross, Jesus is rejected by the Father; he suffers the death of those who are without God so that we can all have communion with him. Moltmann speaks very powerfully about the abandonment of Jesus who, in his agony, will even reach the experience of hell. In fact, he even speaks about a Trinitarian «conflict» in the separation between the Father and the Son: «In the cross, the Father and the Son are separated to such a degree that they interrupt their relationship. Jesus dies without God…»[89]. However, in this separation, the Holy Spirit is the bond of union that links both the separation and the union of the Son and the Father. In this respect, Moltmann addresses the old tradition of the Holy Spirit as love and the bond of union of the Father and the Son, and he applies it to his conception of the cross of Christ as a radical separation of the Father and the Son, whereas the Holy Spirit continues to be the bond of union. Here we can see in the gift or giving of the Son the figure of the Trinity: the Father who delivers his only Son to an absolute death for us; the Son who delivers himself for us; and the common sacrifice of the Father and the Son which takes place in the Holy Spirit who unites and bonds the Father and the abandoned Son[90].

---

86 MOLTMANN J., *Der gekreuzigte Gott*, 233f.
87 MOLTMANN J., *Der gekreuzigte Gott*, 234.
88 MOLTMANN J., *Der gekreuzigte Gott*, 235f.
89 MOLTMANN J., *Trinität und Reich Gottes*, 93; cfr. also *Der gekreuzigte Gott*, 265; also page 230: «the Father in the abandonment of the Son also abandons himself and suffers the death of the Son; in the case of the Father, the death of the Son also corresponds to the death of his Fatherhood».
90 MOLTMANN J., *Trinität und Reich Gottes*, 98-99.

Undoubtedly, the depth of the Trinitarian life is evidenced in the cross of Christ, and we would not be wrong if we sought to see in this supreme moment of love the path to penetrate the mysteries of the divine being. In the giving of Jesus we see the gift itself of the Father. In this sense, we can also see the positive aspect of the thoughts of Moltmann. At any rate, we must ask ourselves if the God against God of Moltmann can be justified in the light of the New Testament, which even as it tells us of, and does not disguise, the anguish and the darkness experienced by Jesus, also speaks to us about his obedience to the will of the Father and his trustful giving over to him. On the other hand, some doubts have been raised about the «constitution» of the Trinity in the cross[91]. Our subsequent reflections will force us to analyze these topics again.

We have also mentioned E. Jüngel as one of the Protestant authors who wishes to contemplate the mystery of God in the cross of Christ. His line of thought has some points of contact with that of Moltmann, although it is characterized by a higher degree of complexity. In the introduction to his main work, *God as the Mystery of the World*[92], Jüngel clearly poses the problem that he wishes to address: «For the Christian accountable to the word "God", the Crucified is precisely something akin to the real definition of the word "God". Therefore, Christian theology is basically a theology of the Crucified»[93]. Faced with the ideas of an impassible, distant God —as has been mentioned as a fact in Christian theology and that may have even given way to atheism— another alternative is required. We reach the idea of God from the harshness of faith in Jesus Christ[94]. Jüngel indeed finds a problem in the view of classical metaphysics, although he sees good reasons for it. Nevertheless, he believes that by following this way one does not grasp what is crucial. Contemporary humans are allergic to the idea of a God whom they see as «absolute», necessary, and the like, in such a way that, when faced with his sovereignty, love and mercy turn into subordinate and secondary properties[95]. The place in which the being of God is fully revealed is in the death and resurrection of Jesus. In the death of Jesus God has faced death. The sovereignty of God must rest basically on love, and as a result of this it is

---

91 Cfr. Akcva J., *An den dreieinen Gott glauben*, Frankfurt am Main 1994, 224; Von Balthasar H.U., *Teodramática 4*, 398ff.

92 Jüngel E., *Gott als Geheimnis der Welt. Zur Begründung der Theologie des Gekreuzigten im Streit zwischen Theismus und Atheismus*, Tübingen 1977 (*Dios como misterio del mundo*, Salamanca 1984).

93 Jüngel E., *Gott als Geheimnis der Welt*, 15.

94 Cfr. Rodríguez Garrapucho F., *La cruz de Jesús y el ser de Dios*, Salamanca 1992, 95.

95 Jüngel E., *Gott als Geheimnis der Welt*, 52.25.

necessary to think about suffering. In the baptism of Jesus, a voice was heard. Nevertheless, at Golgotha God remained silent[96].

We must face the problem of the «death of God». However, what is the sense of this discourse? In the death of Jesus, the last word is not one of darkness. Rather, light illuminates the darkness of death. In the cross of Christ, God is revealed to us as an uncontainable movement toward the deepest levels of earthly misery. This clearly changes our ideas about the omnipotence of God. God has been most intimately affected by the death of his Son, and hence this shows that grief and death have been defeated at their roots. God himself goes to death; in the death of the man Jesus God delivers divinity to the blow of death, so that in the grief of death, he is God for humanity[97]. In the crucified we can know God. This gives way to the thesis of Jüngel of the crucified as *vestigium trinitatis*[98]. With the death of Jesus, a new relationship between humanity and God begins because the being of God is revealed in all the depth of his life only with the death of Christ[99]. God is shown to us as God with his victory over death. «Faith … announces and narrates the tension between eternal life and temporal death that determines the being himself of God in the history of Jesus Christ. He reflects and confesses history within the concept of the one and trine God»[100]. In other passages, Jüngel speaks about the identification of God with the crucified. Faith in the man Jesus, crucified for us as the Son of God, assumes identifying God with Jesus and the Trinitarian self-differentiation of God. It is an identification within the distinction, because if it were not for this differentiation, God would be trapped in his own death. However, God appears before us as the victor in this death. For this reason, God is the one who can bear in his being the annihilating force of nothingness —that denial which is really death— without being annihilated in it[101].

The Christian God is the God capable of exposing himself to nothingness; this is the way he shows himself, and he is defined as love in the cross of Jesus. «The special eschatological event of the identification of God with the man Jesus is at the same time the most intimate aspect in the mystery of the divine being.

96 Cfr. Rodríguez Garrapucho F., *La cruz de Jesús y el ser de Dios*, 99-100.
97 Cfr. Jüngel E., «Das dunkle Wort vom "Tode Gottes"» in *Evangelische Kommentare* 2 (1969) 133-138; 198-202; cfr. Rodríguez Garrapucho F., *La cruz de Jesús y el ser de Dios*, 109-110.
98 Cfr. Jüngel E., *Gott als Geheimnis der Welt*, 470ff.
99 Cfr. Jüngel E., *Gott als Geheimnis der Welt*, 471.
100 Jüngel E., *Gott als Geheimnis der Welt*, 471.
101 Cfr. Jüngel E., *Gott als Geheimnis der Welt*, 298.

In the special event of the identification of God with the crucified, God is expressed as the one who is in himself from eternity»[102]. In other words, God does not turn into love in the instant of the death of Christ, but rather, the divine love is manifested in this moment. The phrase «God is love» (the risk of self-surrender, the risk of nothingness) is the interpretation of the self-identification of God with the crucified man Jesus[103].

Jüngel speaks of the history of God, explaining that this history of love revealed in Christ is precisely God himself. God is at the same time the lover and the beloved. This is possible because of the Trinitarian distinction —Father and Son. However, this is still not love itself[104], which only is evidenced when love opens to a third party. God is the event itself of love opening to a third person, the Spirit, who is differentiated from the Father and the Son. The event of love is evidenced when God the Father, separating himself from the beloved (Son), not only loves himself, but he also includes someone totally different from him (world and humanity) by action of the Spirit. God possesses himself by giving himself. His self-possession is the event of his gift, the giving of himself. The history of God in Christ, as the history of his love, is God himself. The essence of love is the always greater capacity of separation. The cross of Jesus is in the center of the revelation of God as love, insofar as it reveals God as Trinity: the lover is the Father; the beloved is the Son who delivers himself, and by delivering himself, he reaches the other different one (the human being marked by sin and death). The Spirit is the one who enables this separation to be overcome including death in the divine life of God. «The bond of love is what binds together the Father and the Son in such a way that the human nature is introduced in this relationship of love through God the Spirit»[105]. In this way, the identification of God with the man Jesus of Nazareth is the joint action of the Father, of the Son, and of the Holy Spirit. Thus, God is love. Human love emerges because the other one is worthy of love. In God, it is the opposite way around. God is love, and he goes to the one who is astray, the one who in himself is not worthy of love[106]. God shows us what he is in his coming to humanity. Because of this fact, the Christian faith in the Trinity is not based only on the few Trinitarian texts

---

[102] JÜNGEL E., *Gott als Geheimnis der Welt*, 299.
[103] JÜNGEL E., *Gott als Geheimnis der Welt*, 446.
[104] Cfr. JÜNGEL E., *Gott als Geheimnis der Welt*, 448.
[105] JÜNGEL E., *Gott als Geheimnis der Welt*, 450.
[106] JÜNGEL E., *Gott als Geheimnis der Welt*, 250ff.

that we find in the New Testament, but in the cross of Jesus. Without the history of the life and passion of Christ, the materials of the New Testament give us a possibility for developing the Trinitarian doctrine, although the latter is not at all necessary[107].

Hence, the death of Jesus is an event between God and God, «in such a way that the abandonment of Jesus by God appears as the work that is most originally characteristic of God»[108]. God himself «occurred», («*Gott ereignete sich selbst*») in this death[109]. If, in the resurrection, God has identified himself with this dead man, this enables us to state that he also identified himself with him in the cross and in abandonment. For this reason, the *kerygma* of the resurrection announces the crucified one as a self-definition of God[110]. In this revelation as love, we see the open-handedness (*Selbstlosigkeit*) of God, who does not wish to love himself without loving the creature. The «abandonment» is an integral part of the revelation of the Trinity. When God places himself on the side of the abandoned by God, he has distinguished himself and has been capable of giving the world the reconciliation and the salvation that the world could never have given itself. God reconciles the world with himself insofar as in the death of Jesus he is an antithesis as God the Father and God the Son, without ceasing to be either of the two[111]. The Spirit is the union and the power that gives the possibility of human correspondence to the being of God, that is, faith. The essence of the relationships within God is love. The essence of God is giving (*Dahingabe*). Hence, in the cross, this is seen as an «overflowing» of the divine being when, in the death of Jesus, God delivers himself for all people. God does all of this out of love, and consequently out of his own free will. In love, the reference to himself and to the other are not challenged; both things go together. Love overflows, and in this way God is love in his Trinitarian being. The being of God as a Trinity of persons is comprised of relationships. These are the essence and the existence of God. The Father is the one who loves from himself; love is offered to the other one who is the Son, and there is no love for the Son without love for humanity and the world. In the love of the Father for the Son we find the foundations of the love for the world and for humanity as the last word of creation. The delivery of the Son, who

---

107 JÜNGEL E., *Gott als Geheimnis der Welt*, 480f.
108 JÜNGEL E., *Gott als Geheimnis der Welt*, 496.
109 JÜNGEL E., *Gott als Geheimnis der Welt*, 497.
110 JÜNGEL E., *Gott als Geheimnis der Welt*, 498; at the same time, it defines the man Jesus as Son of God.
111 JÜNGEL E., *Gott als Geheimnis der Welt*, 504.

is God himself, gives witness to the love of the Father. God has not willed to be himself without the world; but not only does God deliver the Son. The Son also freely gives himself; he delivers himself. Hence, there is correspondence in God. In Jesus, love reaches its height, the highest realization, and because of this, the manifestation of the Trinity also reaches its highest level[112].

The delivery of the Father in the Son is not an annulling antithesis, because the Spirit, preserving the distinction between the Father and the Son, is the unity of the divine being as that event which is love itself. The Spirit «*vinculum caritatis*» is also the gift to the world. The Spirit is the eternally new relationship of the Father and the Son which opens the divine love to others and includes humanity in the Father-Son relationship[113].

Within this context, Jüngel refers to the axiom of Rahner about the identification between the economic Trinity and the immanent Trinity. The relationship between this axiom and theology beginning with the crucified one is shown as evident. Nevertheless, in my opinion, it is not clear whether for him the economy manifests what the immanent life of the Trinity has been forever, or whether in this event God really «takes place» in the most precise sense of the word[114]. Undoubtedly, the saving economy is the one that attracts Jüngel's attention. In his case, the immanent Trinity is in an area of semidarkness.

Jüngel believes that he has destroyed the ideas of the absolute nature, the impassibility and the immutability of God that had led to contemporary atheism by resorting to the distinction between God and God that is founded on the cross of Jesus Christ. Atheism has fought against theism, but also against the Christian idea of God. Is it clear that by eliminating theism the Christian God would be easier for people to understand? With respect to the Paschal mystery, it is quite clear that the cross evidences the love of God, and that in this sense it is decisive for understanding the Trinity. Jüngel speaks of the abandonment of the Son by the Father, but he has not expressed this in the drastic terms of «opposition» between the two of them that we saw in the case of Moltmann.

We have devoted some space to these authors because undoubtedly they have had an influence in recent times. In order to complete our theological panorama, and before briefly deriving our conclusions regarding this issue, it is absolutely necessary to refer to a document of the International Theological

---

112 Cfr. JÜNGEL E., *Gott als Geheimnis der Welt*, 504-506.
113 Cfr. JÜNGEL E., *Gott als Geheimnis der Welt*, 512-514.
114 Cfr. JÜNGEL E., *Gott als Geheimnis der Welt*, 506-514.

Commission. Although this document has been accepted, certain institutions which are in tune with the authors that we have quoted earlier, have also shown great care and discretion and have avoided any extremes. The document entitled *Select Christology Issues* (1979) makes a marginal reference to this problem to justify the use of the idea of «substitution» in Christology and soteriology, and it states as follows:

> Human beings have been created so that they can be integrated into Christ, and hence, into the Trinitarian life, and their alienation from God, although considerable, cannot be as much as the distance between the Father and the Son in his kenotic annihilation when he emptied himself (Phil 2:7) and in the state in which he was forsaken by the Father (Matt 27:46). Here we are dealing with the economic aspect of the relationship between the divine persons, and the distinction between them reaches its highest level (in the identity of nature and of infinite love)[115].

There are two issues that deserve brief comments. In the first place, this document addresses the topic of the abandonment of Jesus by God, although there is no speculation whatsoever on the consequences of this abandonment beyond death. Within the context of the vicarious substitution, reference is made to the alienation of God from sinful humanity. Likewise, it is stated that the distance between the Father and the Son in the kenotic emptying of the latter and in his forsakenness by the Father is still greater than that of the sinner[116]. In other words, from this context it seems that we must understand the sinner in this world as not definitively separated from God. Within the soteriological context, other speculations would make no sense.

In the second place, reference is made to the economic manifestation of the immanent distinction of the persons. The abandonment of Jesus by the Father, which in the whole context seems to be considered «real» and not only apparent, clearly shows the distinction between the divine persons. This distinction always must be seen in the unity, as the text clearly states. Nevertheless, there is

---

115 Commissio Theologica Internationalis, *Questiones selectae de christologia* (cfr. footnote 58), 629. I have used the Spanish text of the International Theological Commission, *Documents* 1970-1979, 244.

116 Cfr. Von Balthasar H.U., *Teodramática* 4, 471: «Speculating about the final nature or the infinity of his pain is a futile undertaking. The only thing that is clear is that the expiatory torture must be framed within the inscrutable death of his abandonment by the Father, and from this point, it has already been shown that the Trinitarian rupture goes beyond and includes all the distances that separate God from sinner». Cfr. also ibid. 466f.

no explanation as to whether in that moment of abandonment the unity is expressed in any manner whatsoever. We have seen that the theologians to whom we have referred mention the Holy Spirit. We could also think about another type of «abandonment», in the trusting abandonment of Jesus into the hands of the Father, which is also expressed in the words of a psalm that appears in the gospel of Luke: «Father, into your hands I commit my spirit» (Luke 23:46; cfr. Ps 31:16). However, no such mention is explicitly made in the text[117].

1.6.2. CONCLUSIVE REFLECTION

What can we say about the Trinitarian revelation in the mystery of the cross? Above all, we can state that in fact, the point at which the highest degree of the love of God for us is shown is precisely when Christ is delivered on the cross, and that fact cannot be insignificant for the revelation of who God is. Throughout his life, Jesus is the one who enables us to know God. Hence, it seems coherent to believe that this supreme moment of his existence tells us something which is indeed very decisive about the love of God, and consequently, the life of the triune God. A constant affirmation in the New Testament (cfr. for example, Rom 5:8; 8:32-39) is the fact that the death of Jesus Christ is the greatest manifestation of the great love of God for us and the effective realization of this love. It is undeniable that this fact tells us something about the being of the God of love in himself.

This love is evidenced in the capacity that God has of placing himself in the situation of the sinner: «For our sake he made the sinless one a victim for sin» (2Cor 5:21). God looks for and finds the sinful human being, reaching him wherever he is[118]. We have referred to the distance between the Father and the Son

117 The same Commission analyzed the topic again two years later in the document *Theology-Christology-Anthropology*, which we already know: Comisión Teológica Internacional, *Documentos* 1980-1985, 7-26. See page 25f: «Perhaps we must say the same thing about the Trinitarian aspect of the cross of Jesus. According to the Holy Scriptures, God has freely created the world, knowing in the eternal presence —no less eternal than the generation of the Son— that the precious blood of the immaculate Lamb Jesus Christ (cfr. 1Pet 1:19; Eph 1:7) would be spilled. In this sense, the gift of the divinity of the Father to the Son has a very close correspondence with the gift of the Son to the abandonment of the cross. Nevertheless, as the resurrection is also known in the eternal plan of God, the grief of the "separation" is always overcome by the joy of the union and the compassion of the trine God in the passion of the Word is really understood as the work of the most perfect love in which we must rejoice. On the contrary, we have fully excluded from God the Hegelian concept of "negativity"». Latin text «Theologia-Christologia-Anthropolgia» in *Greg* 64 (1983) 5-24, esp. 23f.

118 VON BALTHASAR H.U., *Teodramática 2. Las personas del drama: el hombre en Dios*, Madrid 1992, 252f: «The world and humanity are created in the Son; the loss of humanity toward a finite nature without a way out seems to appear in the center, latent and hidden up until now, of the plan of God for this world: the possibility of the infinite freedom of following the path of him who has gone straight until the last twist of his damnation».

entailed by the «abandonment» of God. Jesus can experience a distance from the Father, which is greater than that of any other person who feels separated from God in this life. Only the Son, who experiences as no one else the love of the Father and is one with him, can experience to this degree the darkness that the difficulty of accepting the ways of the Father and what the Father has planned for him can entail. We must understand the realism of «Abba, Father, for you everything is possible. Take this cup away from me. But let it be as you, not I, would have it» (Mark 14:36par). The experience of Jesus in the solitude of his passion is, in this sense, unique. In this way he can reconcile the world with God, or even better, in him, the Father can reconcile the world with him (cfr. 2Cor 5:18-19). Nevertheless, although it is possible to think about the reality of a moment of darkness for Jesus in his relationship with the Father, it is also worth pointing out that even in this situation, Jesus invokes the Father as «Abba» and puts the mysterious will of his Father before his own. The sinner escapes from God in disobedience. Jesus accepts onto himself the consequences of this sin by obeying and acting according to the plan of the Father. This is indeed a key difference. Some authors state that it is quite possible that Jesus spoke the whole of Psalm 22 on the cross. Although this psalm begins by expressing the sense of abandonment and helplessness, it ends with a clear cry of trust in God[119]. If Jesus has been able to experience and express «all the grief and anguish of the Son of God when he was faced with the consequences of the mission he had received from the Father and that he had accepted, he is also expressing his full solidarity with sinful humanity out of love»[120]. Nevertheless, this solidarity cannot lead us to see him simply as another sinner[121]. The relationship of Jesus with the Father is always surrounded by mystery, and at the moment of death, this mystery can grow only greater. The information of the New Testament gives us different approximations for this mystery, which is certainly not disclosed.

We must also dwell on the fact that eschatology has emphasized an issue that also has been strongly emphasized by the authors to whom we have especially referred. It is not enough to think about the voice of abandonment as one «of humanity». In any interpretation we may give to this difficult passage, we are always dealing with the voice of the Son who addresses the Father. It is certainly

---

119 In this respect, for example Kasper W., *Jesús el Cristo*, Salamanca 1976, 146; Pesch R., *Das Markusevangelium* II, Freiburg-Basel-Wien 1984, 494-495.

120 Vives J., *Si oyerais su voz*, Santander 1988, 164.

121 Cfr. González de Cardedal O., *La entraña del cristianismo*, 578; cfr. the entire context.

the voice of the Son as man, incarnated and stripped of his rank for us. Nevertheless, at the time of the passion and the death, as in all the other moments in the life of Jesus Christ, it is precisely his relationship with the Father which is at the forefront. The whole history of Jesus, as well as that of his passion, death and resurrection, is the history of the relationship of the Son —indeed as man— with the Father who has sent him into the world and whom he obeys unto death. We are faced with the scope of the relationship between the divine persons and not only between the two natures of Christ.

The Father has delivered the Son into the world. He has delivered him to death. He has been handed over to men (cfr. Matt 17:22). There is a similarity between the formulas of the delivery and those of the sending or the mission to which we have referred, even though they are not fully equivalent. Nevertheless, we must be careful not to think that the Father has delivered the Son to death in the way that men have done so. The Father delivers his Son, handing him over to sinners; he does not act mercilessly before the suffering of Jesus. He accepts the death of his Son at the hands of men because he respects our freedom, and in this way he offers us the greatest evidence of his love. God the Father, the one who begets the Son, cannot directly wish his death. Therefore, it is necessary to clearly specify the different nuances of the «delivery» in the New Testament. God does not deliver his Son to death as his enemies do (cfr. for example, Mark 3:19par; 15:15par; Luke 24:10)[122].

However, this «delivery» to death, which indeed is part of the plan of God, does not lead Jesus to rebel, but to act fully in correspondence. Jesus also hands himself over out of love: «Who loved me and gave himself for me» (Gal 2:20), as the Apostle said (cfr. among others, Eph 5:2; 5:25). Likewise, the love of God for humanity is evidenced in his delivery. As a result of this, we are dealing with the love of the Father and the love of the Son and with the full correspondence of the Son to the decision of the Father. The love of God the Father and the love of Christ for humanity are, hence, seen as united in Rom 8:32-39. Jesus in his passion not only suffers abandonment, but he also commends his spirit into the hands of the Father (Luke 23:46) because from the very beginning of his life on earth he has descended to do his will (Heb 10:7; cfr. 2:6-8; John 4:34; Mark 14:36par). Therefore, we cannot speak in a meaningful manner of an intra-divine «conflict». If the abandonment of Jesus by the Father can express the «distance», the differ-

---

122 Cfr. DURRWELL F.X., *Le Père. Dieu en son mystère*, Paris 1988², 62ff.

entiation of the persons in God, which has reached its maximum level, the obedience of the Son, the acceptance of the plans of the Father, and radical trust in him, show the deep unity and divine communion. The two aspects must be seen in their unity. Any separation, although it can be seen and thought of as very important, cannot make us forget that the Father and the Son are purely in reference one to the other.

The authors whom we have quoted undoubtedly referred to the union between the Father and the Son that is manifested in the Spirit, as well as to the «separation» and the darkness of the passion. Even though they sometimes do not mention this expressly, to this end they resort to the old tradition of western theology that goes back at least to Augustine who sees the Holy Spirit as the bond of union between the Father and the Son. We have already mentioned the sacrifice of Jesus to the Father through the «eternal Spirit», according to Heb 9:14. In the delivery of Christ to death and to the darkness that might have surrounded this moment, we also see the expression of the communion of love between the Father and the Son in the Holy Spirit.

Everything that we have said about this revelation of the triune God in his love for humanity at the time of the passion and death of the Lord makes sense in the light of the resurrection. In it, we clearly see the «yes» of God to Jesus, which is by no means the annulment or cancellation of his earthly life, but rather, the clear evidence of the continual and perpetual value that this has in the eternity of God. The resurrected Jesus appears bearing the signs of the passion. The life of the Trinity is not lived as though the Son would not have introduced his humanity in his glory. We cannot minimize this certain «new dimension» that God has introduced into his own life in his completely free will by the assumption of the humanity taken up by his Son.

Nevertheless, before attempting a study of the resurrection, it is pertinent in conclusion to reflect briefly on the cross and death as it relates to the Trinitarian revelation. In the cross of Christ, God evidenced his love until the end to give humanity the possibility of living until the end within this delivery and surrender. The person who lives in this way reflects even more the being of God, the abyss of the divine love that Jesus has shown to him. God is the final end of the human being who is called in Christ to be in his image in a perfect likeness. The more God gives human beings the possibility in the Spirit of love to love until the end, the more the human being will reach the deepest fullness of salvation. By reflecting and living the love of God, people are placed on the path that takes them to God as their end. It is salvation as the highest fullness of humanity — certainly by a gift of God, although this gift is rendered more fully by being based on the depth of the human's being.

1.7.   THE RESURRECTION OF JESUS, THE REVELATION
       OF THE ONE AND TRIUNE GOD

To begin with, we must point out the fact that the initiative for the resurrection according to most of the texts of the New Testament is the act of God the Father (cfr. Rom 6:4; 8:11; 10:9; 2Cor 4:14; Eph 1:20, etc.). The expression used by the gospels, ήYέρθη, «he has raised from the dead», can also be understood as a way of pointing out the divine action). In some passages we also see the difference between the action of the men who killed Jesus, and God who raises him from the dead: «[Him] you took and had crucified and killed by men outside the law» (Acts 2:23-24; cfr. also Acts 3:15; 4:10; 10:39). In this way, God shows himself in his divine power. Faith in the resurrection of Jesus is not simply a supplement to faith in God, but rather it is the embodiment of faith in the Christian God. The power to give life to the dead and the power to call into being what does not exist, with a certain priority in the case of the former, go together according to Rom 4:17[123]. In both cases, God acts directly and immediately. God is the Father of Jesus, and as we have already had the occasion to evidence, he shows this Fatherhood when he raises him from the dead (cfr. Gal 1:1, among others.). The omnipotent power of God is shown in this Fatherhood. We might even say that in the light of the resurrection of his Son, he identifies with it[124]. Many passages of the New Testament offer evidence in this respect (2Cor 1:3; 11:31; Eph 1:17; Phil 2:11, among others).

In the same way, the texts of some psalms that are included in the New Testament also emphasize the initiative of God the Father in the resurrection. Among them, mention can be made of Ps 110:1, «take your seat at my right hand», one of the passages of the Old Testament that has been more frequently quoted directly or indirectly in the New Testament (cfr. Mark 12:36par; 14:62par; Acts 2:34; 5:31; 7:55; Rom 8:34; 1Cor 15:25; Eph 1:20; Heb 1:13; 10:12f; 1Pet 3:22). Jesus was exalted by the Father, and thus he shares his glory[125]. Likewise, in Acts 13:33 (cfr. Heb 1:5; 5:5),

---

123 That is also the only text of the New Testament which specifically mentions the creation out of nothing; cfr. 2 Maccabees 7:28, where mention is made of the creation from nothing in a context of the hope of the resurrection.
124 Cfr. DURWELL F.X., *Le Père*, 175.
125 Cfr. SCHIERSEE E.J., «La revelación de la Trinidad en el Nuevo Testamento» in *MySal* II/1, 138: «Within the apocalyptic mindset of Judaism, "sitting at the right hand of God" is what is the most supreme

Ps 2:7 is applied to the risen and exalted Jesus: «You are my son; today I have fathered you». Hence, the resurrection is interpreted in terms of giving birth. In fact, in this moment Jesus acquires the condition of Son of God in all his power (cfr. Rom 1:3-4). Therefore, this is the filial exaltation of the man Jesus. If the Fatherhood of God is related to the resurrection, it is also natural that the divine Sonship of Jesus is evidenced in the fact that he was raised from the dead by the Father. We have already mentioned that the Fatherhood and the Sonship are correlative. This full condition of the Son is related to the exaltation of Jesus and his enthronement as Lord (cfr. Acts 2:14ff; 3:34ff; Phil 2:11). We saw previously that the condition of the Son pertains to the relationship with the Father, and the title of Lord refers rather to his relationship with humanity. Nevertheless, the two aspects must be seen in light of their mutual implication, precisely in connection with the resurrection[126]. The Sonship of Jesus enables our sonship (cfr. Gal 4:4-6; Rom 8:29), and on the other hand, his relationship as Son of the Father is the basis of the dignity and supremacy of Jesus over everything.

In some passages of the gospel of John, it seems that the resurrection is attributed to the initiative of Jesus. Hence, in John 10:17: «The Father loves me, because I lay down my life in order to take it up again. No one takes it from me; I lay it down of my own free will, and as I have power to lay it down, so I have power to take it up again; And this command I have received from my Father» (cfr. also 2:19-21, the words about the destruction of the temple). Nevertheless, in the text that is quoted, the reference to the Father is clearly manifested. Other texts of the gospel of John emphasize the initiative of the Father in the glorification of Jesus (cfr. John 12:23; 12:28; 13:31-32; 17:1; 17:5; among others). In the case of the fourth gospel, the Paschal mystery is the acquiescence of Jesus to the Father who has entrusted everything to his hands (cfr. John 13:1,3; 14:28; 20:17). Hence, the gospel of John is not an exception that departs from the prevailing thought evidenced in the New Testament.

The Fatherhood of God and the divine Sonship of Christ which are evidenced in the resurrection (which in turn offers the key to understanding the whole life of Jesus), pave the way for understanding the immanent Trinity. They do so by affirming that Jesus existed prior to his incarnation. In other words, his divine life in the heart of the Father, does not depend on the economy of salvation, but

and definitive reference that we can make of a being who is not equal to God, from all the points of view».

126 Cfr. MAGGIOLI B., «La Trinità nel Nuovo Testamento» in *ScCat* 118 (1990) 7-30.

on the contrary, is its only foundation. The divine Sonship which Jesus lives out in this world and which is fully evidenced in the resurrection is consequently based on the same divine being, on a relationship with the Father prior to his human existence. Only in the light of «being born» to the divine life in the resurrection has the New Testament, and based on it, the tradition of the Church, referred to the existence of the Son from the beginning in the heart of the Father who has begotten him eternally (cfr. John 1:1ff; 8:58; 17:5; 17:24; Rom 8:3; Phil 2:6; Gal 4:4; Eph 1:3ff; Heb 1:2, among others). Only with this divine existence of Jesus prior to the incarnation can the saving economy find its foundation in the being himself of God, and hence it can be the communication of the life of God to the world. Jesus has always been the Son of God and has not just become his Son in his resurrection or at some prior moment in his mortal life[127].

We have seen that the New Testament speaks of the resurrection in terms of begetting. In view of the fact that the human life of Jesus «affects» the intra-trinitarian life, or in other words, that the assumption of the human nature by Jesus Christ is irrevocable, the full incorporation of Christ, in his humanity as well, into the divine life is necessary. Only if he is fully the Son of God also with respect to his human nature, can he truly be the Son. This reality led to the extremely profound statements by Hilary of Poitiers on the relationship between the eternal begetting and the resurrection:

> … so that the one who was before the Son of God and also Son of men, and being the Son of man he was begotten as perfect Son of God; in other words, so that he could take back and receive in his body the glory of eternity by means of the power of the resurrection, as begotten, he asked his Father again for this glory (cfr. John 17:5)[128].

Once the incarnation has taken place, the resurrection is a necessity for the same eternal begetting, and indeed is its expression or manifestation.

The unity of the Father and the Son is evidenced in the resurrection and the exaltation of Jesus. Likewise, the pouring out of the Holy Spirit cannot be perceived apart from the resurrection and exaltation. The Holy Spirit is the gift of the Father and the Son, which, while expressing the union of the two, also shows

---

127 For this entire scope of the problems, see: KUSCHEL K.J., *Generato prima di tutti I secoli? La controversia sull'origine di Cristo*, Brescia 1996.

128 HILARY OF POITIERS, *Tr. Ps.* 2,27 (CSEL 22,57); cfr. also *De Trinitate* IX 38 (CCI 62A,412); cfr. LADARIA L.F., «Dios en Hilario de Poitiers» in *EstTrin* 24 (1990) 443-479.

the specific significance of the *Pneuma* for the divine breadth of function together with the Father and the Son. Before attempting to address the mission of the Spirit, however, we must point out that the Holy Spirit intervenes in the resurrection of Jesus, and the initiative lies within the Father. Not many texts refer to this, although they are indeed significant[129]. The clearest text among the ones we know is Rom 1:4: «Who, in terms of the Spirit and of holiness was designated Son of God in power by resurrection from the dead». The divine Sonship of Jesus, who is the Son at every point in time (Rom 1:3), takes place in power by virtue of the Spirit. The Father raises Jesus in the Spirit. This Spirit of God, which in the Old Testament is a creating force that empowers people, is now a force of resurrection (cfr. Ezek 37:5ff, still in a figurative sense). In Rom 8:11, also, even though in fact, mention is only made directly of the action of the Spirit in terms of our resurrection, we cannot rule out that indirectly the same idea is expressed in the previous passage: «If the Spirit of him who raised Jesus from the dead has made his home in you, then he who raised Christ Jesus from the dead will give life to your own mortal bodies, through his Spirit living in you». At any rate, it is worth pointing out the designation applied here to the Holy Spirit. He is the Spirit of the one who raised Jesus from the dead. In the Paschal mystery the Father and the Spirit are definitively «portrayed in their characteristic nature».

The resurrection of Jesus and the Spirit are also interrelated in other passages (1Tim 3:16; 1Pet 3:18), whereas in Rom 1:3-4, the life of Jesus in the flesh and in the spirit are contrasted. The earthly life of Jesus is contrasted over against the divine life of the resurrection in the Spirit of God. Jesus himself in his resurrection has been made a «life-giving spirit» (1Cor 15:45)[130]. Undoubtedly, this is not a personal identification of Christ with the Holy Spirit, but rather, we are dealing with the fact that Jesus in his resurrection is with God and has been filled with the Holy Spirit with God, and he has turned into a source of life for all those who believe in him. If the first Adam has been the source of earthly life, a life that ends in death, Jesus, the second and definitive Adam, is the source of the Spirit of the definitive life that now fills his perfectly deified and glorified humanity in total communion of life with the Father. The risen Jesus takes his place at the side of the Creator and gives life. Therefore, there is a clear relationship

---

129 Cfr. CONGAR Y., *El Espíritu Santo*, Barcelona 1983, 603; CHEVALLIER M.A., *Souffle de Dieu. Le Saint-Esprit dans le Nouveau Testament* II, Paris 1990, 277-308.
130 On the Spirit who gives life, see also 2 Cor 3:6 and John 6:63.

between the deification of the humanity of Christ and the outpouring of the Spirit who descended upon him at the Jordan and which he now has in fullness.

According to Acts 2:33, Jesus, raised from death and glorified at the right hand of God, received from the Father the Spirit whom he poured out upon the apostles on the day of Pentecost. The full possession of the Spirit by Jesus, which enables his outpouring and his giving himself to humanity, is a manifestation —we might even say that it is the *first* manifestation— of the full communion of Jesus with the Father, of his Sonship, and hence, of the divine Fatherhood. The theology of recent times has recovered this leitmotif from the old traditions[131]. This brings us to a topic that we can by no means separate from the one that we have been addressing up to now: the «mission» — the sending of the Spirit following the resurrection of Jesus. At the same time, we will set forth some basic lines of thought concerning the pneumatology of the New Testament.

2

God sent the Spirit of his Son into our hearts

2.1. THE SPIRIT, GIFT OF THE FATHER AND OF THE RESURRECTED JESUS

According to the biblical text that has been a guide for us in this chapter, Gal 4:4-6, «God has sent into our hearts the Spirit of his Son». We have already pointed out the parallelism between the mission of the Son and that of the Spirit, as reflected in this passage. Nevertheless, we can and must now add something else: this sending of the Spirit has no significance without the glorification of the Son. It is precisely the «Spirit of his Son». For this reason, this mission is related to that of the Son which ends in the resurrection. Our previous reflections have already guided us in the sense that Jesus in his resurrection fully receives the Spirit. This is so to such a degree that we can say that he has «made himself spirit» (in terms that we have already explained). Hence, the mission of the Spirit depends on this reality. Indeed, resorting to various expressions, the different writings of the New Testament address the outpouring of the Spirit as being related to the glorification and exaltation of Jesus. Hence, this emphasizes that there is

---

131 VON BALTHASAR H.U., «El misterio pascual» in *MySal* III/1, 288: «Ever since the Father raises Jesus from death and both pour out their common Spirit, the Trinitarian mystery is revealed in its depth, although its clear depth is what opens us to the fact that God cannot be encompassed».

an intrinsic relationship between these two missions that are not simply juxta-posed. Jesus, the Son sent into the world, is the source of the Spirit for humanity.

Before continuing any further, it is helpful to clarify several issues. In the first chapters of the gospel of Luke, mention is made on several occasions to the action of the Spirit on the characters who intervene in the gospel of Jesus' infancy (in addition to the incarnation by action of the Holy Spirit): Luke 1:41 — Eliza-beth; 1:67, Zechariah; 2:25-27 — Simeon. No doubt we have to think that this action of the Spirit has been possible due to the coming of Jesus into the world, although it has different characteristics from those at the outpouring on Pente-cost. It is an occasional presence in specific people, a circumstantial action of the Spirit that reminds us of the way in which he had already acted on the prophets in the Old Testament (cfr. 1Pet 1:11, according to whom the prophets already had the Spirit of Christ within them)[132]. Hence, it does not seem that these cases would oppose the general statement of the relationship that the New Testament sees between the glorification of Jesus and the gift of the Spirit.

Let us analyze this briefly in the different writings. According to Luke 24:39, Jesus will send the promise of the Father once he has ascended into heaven. The announcement of the coming of the Spirit, without concretely stating who will send him, is repeated in Acts 1:5 and 1:8. Evidently, the coming of the Spirit in 2:1ff is the fulfillment of that promise. It seems that the sending of the Spirit is attributed to God the Father in Acts 2:17ff. On the other hand, Acts 2:33, which we have already quoted, refers to the fact that Jesus has received from the Father the promised Spirit whom he pours out in abundance. The quotation from the prophet Joel in Peter's speech on Pentecost (cfr. Acts 2:17ff; Joel 3:1-5) manifests the conviction that with the resurrection and ascension of the Lord the moment has come for the universal outpouring of the Spirit, without limits or frontiers, which the Old Testament could only prophesy for an undetermined future. Hence, the Spirit is seen as the eschatological gift, and in addition to fostering evangelization, the Spirit gives the joy of praising the Lord (Acts 2:4; 2:11). For John, the gift of the Spirit is a consequence of the glorification of Jesus in his hu-manity. This is stated clearly in John 7:37-39: «Jesus exclaimed: "Let anyone who is thirsty come to me! Let anyone who believes in me come and drink! As the Scripture says, 'From his heart shall flow streams of living water'". He was speak-

---

132 Cfr. Bordoni M., *La cristologia nell'orizonte dello Spirito*, 208; also Chevallier M.A., *Aliento de Dios I*, Salamanca 1982, 170f. In the following chapters, we will briefly address the action of the Spirit according to the Old Testament.

ing of the Spirit which those who believed in him were to receive; for there was no Spirit yet, because Jesus had not yet been glorified» (John 7:39). The Spirit was already present in Jesus during the time of his earthly life (cfr. John 1:32-33), but only after his glorification can he be shared. The gift of the Spirit to the Church and to the disciples is an inseparable consequence of the glorification of the Lord. Jesus spoke about the Spirit primarily when he addressed his disciples during the last supper, in other words, when his death and resurrection to which his outpouring is related were close at hand. The concrete texts which announced the coming of the Spirit are also very clear that it is good for the disciples that Jesus leaves, because otherwise the Paraclete will not come to them (cfr. John 16:17). As to the subject agent of the mission of the Spirit, these passages from the farewell discourse offer some variations. The Father will give him upon the request of Jesus (cfr. John 14:18), or in his name (14:26). The Spirit proceeds from the Father, but Jesus will send him from the Father (John 15:26). He will take from what Jesus has in common with the Father (John 16:14-15). Therefore, we cannot ignore the intervention of Jesus in the outpouring of the Holy Spirit, even though the Father is the ultimate source of this mission. As we have said, this gift of the Spirit requires the going away of Jesus to the Father, his glorification. Jesus risen from the dead is the one who gives the Spirit on Easter evening, breathing on the disciples (cfr. John 20:22)[133]. Nevertheless, the unique theology of the exaltation and the glorification seen in John, which assumes that both have already begun with the death of Jesus in the cross, lifted up over the earth (cfr. John 3:13-14; 8:28; 12:32), also enables us to think that at the time of his death, Jesus, besides dying, anticipates receiving the Spirit (John 19:30 παρέδωκευ τό Πυεῦμα)[134]. The water and the blood from the side of Christ (cfr. John 19:34) have also been interpreted as a reference to baptism and the Eucharist. Indirectly, we also cannot exclude a reference to the Spirit leaving the body of Jesus (cfr. John 7:38)[135], which had been his receptacle during all his lifetime[136].

133 According to John 1:33 Jesus baptizes in the Holy Spirit.
134 Recently in this sense, LEON-DUFOUR X., *Lecture de l'évangile selon Saint Jean* IV, Paris 1996, 159, Also SIMOENS Y., *Selon Jean 3. Une interpretation*, Bruxelles 1997, 487.
135 Cfr. DE LA POTTERIE I., *Christologie et pneumatologie dans S. Jean*, in the Commission Biblique Pontificale, *Bible et Christologie*, Paris 1984, 271-287. The possibility of this symbolic interpretation is also accepted by SCHNACKENBURG R., *El evangelio según san Juan* III, Barcelona 1980, 359. The sacramental symbolism is also accepted by SIMOENS Y., *Selon Jean 3*, 856. Likewise by SCHELLE U., «Johannes als Geisttheologe» in *Novum Testamentum* 40 (1998) 17-31; esp. 24.
136 This interpretation underlies the theology of the Fathers. For Hippolytus, the open side of Christ is like a vase of perfume that is broken, and hence, the ointment of life is spilled; cfr. ZANI A., *La cristologia di Ippolito*, Brescia 1983, 597-607.

We do not find in Paul a chronological succession similar to that of Luke and John which emphasizes the close relationship between the exaltation and glorification of Jesus and the gift of the Spirit. Nonetheless, some of the texts that have been examined have pointed out that this link exists. In his resurrection Jesus turns into a «life-giving spirit» (1Cor 15:45). Paul usually uses the term «Spirit» without anything added to it, although he also uses «Spirit of God» and «Holy Spirit». However, together with these most frequent designations, in Paul, and to a lesser extent in other writings of the New Testament, a series of terms are used which emphasize the link of the gift of the Spirit to Jesus[137]. Hence, in the text that we already know from Gal 4:6, mention is made of «Spirit of his Son». The phrases «spirit of adoption» (Rom 8:15), «Spirit of Christ» (Rom 8:9; 1Pet 1:11); «of Jesus Christ» (Phil 1:19), «of the Lord» (2Cor 3:17), and «of the life in Jesus Christ» (Rom 8:2) are also used. In Acts 16:7, mention is made of the «Spirit of Jesus». The link that exists between the glorified Jesus and the Holy Spirit is also emphasized. The Spirit is also called the «Spirit of the Lord» as well as «Lord» (cfr. 2Cor 3:16-18).

With the gift of the Holy Spirit as a consequence of the glorification of Jesus, there is an «innovation» in the action of the Spirit. Undoubtedly, as witnessed in the Old Testament, the Spirit had already acted before the coming of Jesus, but now he appears in all his potential. The New Testament shows this new situation which can be clearly evidenced in the effects of the gifts of the Spirit. The Fathers have explicitly reflected on it in order to explain the reason for the concrete effects of the outpouring of the Spirit. It is the newness of the risen Jesus that is communicated to men and women in the Spirit. This is stated by Irenaeus of Lyons: «(the Holy Spirit) realizes in them (men) the will of the Father and renews them from their oldness in the newness of Christ»[138]. The relationship between the newness of Christ and that of the Christian through the gift of the Spirit has been also emphasized by Origen:

---

137 Cfr. among the most abundant bibliography PENNA R., *Lo Spirito di Cristo. Cristologia e pneumatologia secondo un'originale formulazione paolina*, Brescia 1976. Cfr. page 271f regarding the use of different terms.

138 IRENAEUS OF LYONS, *Adv. Haer.* III 17,1 (SCh 211,330): «…voluntatem Patris operans in ipsis et renovans eos a vetustate in novitate Christi»; cfr. the follow-up 17,3 (334f); «… Spiritus Dei qui descendit in Dominum… quem ipse iterum dedit Ecclesiae, in omnem terram mittens de caelis Paraclitum»; also III 9,3 (110f); IV 33,15 (SCh 100,844): «… et semper eundem Spiritum Dei cognoscens etiamsi in novissimis temporibus nove effusus est in nos… ».

Our Savior, after the resurrection, when what is old had already passed away and all the things had become new, being himself the new man and the firstborn from the dead (cfr. Col 1:18), and once the apostles had also been renewed by faith in his resurrection, said: «Receive the Holy Spirit» (John 20:22). This is in effect what the Lord and Savior himself said in the gospel (cfr. Matt 9:17), when he denied that new wine could be placed into old wineskins, and rather, commanded new wine skins to be made. In other words, men should walk in newness of life so that they would receive the new wine —the newness of the grace of the Holy Spirit[139].

Similarly, Hilary of Poitiers also emphasized quite clearly the identity of what Jesus has in fullness and what he bestows:

With expectation the prophet announces that God must be exalted above the heavens (cfr. Ps 57:6). And, because after having been exalted to the heavens, he had to fill everything with the glory of his Holy Spirit, (the psalmist) adds: «your glory over all the earth» (Ps 57:6). Indeed, the gift of the Spirit poured out over all flesh was going to give testimony to the glory of the Lord exalted to the heavens[140].

These few testimonies suffice to show how, in the old Church, there has been a clear awareness, not only of the temporal succession, but also of the internal relationship that exists between the resurrection of Jesus and the gift of the Holy Spirit. The two «missions» are intrinsically united in their diverse characteristics.

---

139 ORIGEN, *De Principiis* I 3,7 (SCh 252,158): «Sed et salvator noster post resurrectionem cum vetera iam transissent et facta fuissent omnia nova, novus ipse homo et primogenitus ex mortuis, renovatis quoque per fidem suae resurrectionis apostolis ait: *Accipite Spiritum sanctum* (John 20:22). Hoc est nimirum quod et ipse Salvator dominus in evangelio designabat cum vinum novum in utres mitti posse veteres denegabat (cfr. Matt 9:17), sed iubebat utres fieri novos, id est homines in novitate vitae ambulare (cfr. Rom 6:4), ut vinum novum, id est Spiritus sancti gratiae susciperent novitatem». And also ibid. II 7,2 (SCh 328): «Video tamen quod praecipuus spiritus sancti adventus ad homines post ascensionem Christi in caelos magis quam ante adventum eius declaretur. Antea namque solis prophetis et paucis, si qui forte in populo meruisse, donum sancti spiritus praebebatur; post adventum vero salvatoris scriptum est adimpletum esse quod dictum fuerat in propheta Iohel…» (Acts 2:16; Joel 3:1-5).

140 HILARY OF POITIERS, *Tr. Ps.* 56,6 (CSEL 27,172): «Ex voto ergo propheta praenuntiat exaltari super caelos deum. Et quia exaltatus super caelos impleturus esset in terries omnia santi spiritus sui gloria subiecit: et super omnem terram gloria tua: cum effusus super omnem carnem spiritus donum gloriam exaltati super caelos domini protestaretur». Cfr. LADARIA L.F., *El Espíritu Santo en san Hilario de Poitiers*, Madrid 1977, 157ff. Also NOVACIAN, *Trin.* XXIX 165-166 (FP 8,248f): «Unus ergo et idem Spiritus qui in prophetis et apostolis, nisi quoniam ibi ad momentum, hic semper. Ceterum ibi non ut semper in illis inesset, hic ut in illis semper maneret; et ibi mediocriter distributus, hic totus effusus, ibi parce datus, hic large commodatus. Nec tamen ante resurrectionem Domini exhibitus, sed per resurrectionem contributus».

In the gift of the Spirit offered by the Father through the risen Jesus, we can see fully the «identity» of the Spirit both in the richness and in the variety of his effects. If in the actions of the Spirit in Jesus during his earthly life his state of being as Spirit of God (the Father) is emphasized —something that is also inherent in Jesus because he remains in his own area of purpose— now it is also clear that he is at the same time the Spirit of the Son, of Jesus. The effects that will be shown from now on also depend on this fact. The Second Vatican Council has very clearly expressed the meaning for the Church and for all humanity of the fact that the Spirit who is given to them is precisely that of the Spirit in Jesus:

> In order that we can be unceasingly renewed in him (cfr. Eph 4:23), we were granted the possibility of sharing his Spirit —one and the same in head and in members— who revitalizes, unifies and moves the whole body of the Church, and his acts could be compared by the Holy Fathers over against the action of the principle of life —the soul— in the human being (LG 7; cfr. also AG 4).

Jesus has imprinted his seal in the Spirit[141]. We will see this more concretely in the different actions of the Spirit according to the New Testament.

2.2.   THE GIFT OF THE SPIRIT AND ITS EFFECTS AFTER
       THE RESURRECTION OF JESUS

Undoubtedly, we cannot go into detail when we address the pneumatology of the New Testament. We will simply offer some essential data that can guide us in our subsequent systematic reflections[142].

---

141 BASIL OF CAESAREA, *De Spirito sancto* 18,46 (SCh 17,410): «(The Holy Spirit) as Paraclete has the nature (χαρακτηρίζει) of the goodness of the Paraclete that has sent him». Already mentioned in ATHANASIUS, *Serap.* I 23 (PG 26,565): «The seal bears the form of Christ who is the one who seals and who is shared by all those who are sealed».

142 For additional information, cfr. SCHÜTZ CH., *Introducción a la Pneumatología*, Salamanca 1991; CHEVALLIER M.A., *Aliento de Dios. El Espíritu Santo en el Nuevo Testamento* I, Salamanca 1982; *Souffle de Dieu. Le Saint-Esprit dans le Nouveau Testament* II, Paros 1990; CONGAR Y., *El Espíritu Santo*, Barcelona 1983, spanish edition 41-89; LAMBIASI F., *Lo Spirito Santo: mistero e presenza. Per una sintesi di pneumatologia*, Bologna 1987; FERRARO G., *Lo Spirito Santo e Cristo nel vangelo di Giovanni*, Brescia 1984; HORN F.W., *Das Angel des Geistes. Studien zur paulinischen Pneumatologie*, Göttingen 1992; FEE G.D., *God's Empowering Presence. The Holy Spirit in the Letters of Paul*, Peabody, Massachussets 1994; WEINANDY TH., *The Father's Spirit of Sonship*, Edimburgh 1995; O'NEIL J.C., «The Holy Spirit and the Human Spirit in Galatians» in *EphThLov* 71 (1995) 107-120.

It will be quite sufficient to begin with a brief word about terminology. We have already referred to the abundance of designations of the Holy Spirit in the writings of Paul, specifically as related to the link of the Spirit with Jesus. In other chapters of this book we will refer to the specific terminology of other authors of the New Testament. For now, I simply wish to point out that the designation «Holy Spirit», used normally to refer to the third person of the Trinity, is almost an innovation in the New Testament. It appears in the New Testament approximately seventy times, while in the Old Testament we only find it on three occasions in the Hebrew Bible and on two others in the book of Wisdom[143]. To the newness of the action of the Holy Spirit, the New Testament responds with a terminological innovation which is appealing but not absolute.

2.2.1. SYNOPTIC GOSPELS AND ACTS

130   Mention is made of the Holy Spirit in the New Testament primarily because of his effects. In this chapter we have already referred to the acts of Jesus. In the New Testament it is stated that the Spirit is the inspirer of the prophets of the Old Testament (cfr. Mark 12:36par; 1Pet 1:11, etc.). This action is already seen as referring to Jesus because he is the object of the announcement of the prophets. As related to future action, in the case of the disciples, the synoptic gospels primarily stress the Holy Spirit's assistance in times of persecution (cfr. Mark 13:11; Matt 10:19-20; Luke 12:11). This *lógion*, transmitted in several contexts, is one of the few direct references made of the Spirit by the Lord in his preaching (cfr. also Mark 3:29)[144].

In the book of Acts, the Holy Spirit plays a key role. The Holy Spirit is the gift promised by God for the end-times (cfr. Luke 24:49; Acts 1:4; 2:16ff; 2:33,39, among others). For the apostles, the Holy Spirit will be first and foremost the promise that will prepare them for their testimony to Jesus, «made by God Lord and Messiah» (Acts 2:36; cfr. 1:8; 2:32; also, Luke 24:46-49). This is the testimony offered by the apostles, perhaps by all the disciples and by Peter who gives it on their behalf on the day of Pentecost (cfr. Acts 2:1ff). Those who listen to him receive the baptism of the Holy Spirit (cfr. 2:38). The Spirit is the one who makes Peter give testimony before the Sanhedrin (4:8; cfr. 5:32). Stephen also speaks

---

143 Cfr. Ps 51:13; Isa 53:10-11; Wis 1:4; 9:17.

144 It is commonly stated that Jesus has not spoken often about the Holy Spirit in his preaching. In fact, in the gospel according to Mark, Jesus refers to the Spirit only in the three passages that are quoted in this paragraph. It has been precisely the experience of the outpouring of the Spirit on Pentecost that has given the first Christians the understanding of the key role of the Spirit in the plan of salvation and also in the life of Christ.

before his accusers before being stoned «filled with the Holy Spirit» (Acts 7:55; already according to Acts 6:5, Stephen is full of «faith and the Holy Spirit»). «The Spirit is the agent of every courageous testimony»[145]. The scene on the day of Pentecost that determines the beginning of the apostles' preaching is followed by other similar ones in which the Spirit is also shown in his visible effects: Acts 4:31, «all began to proclaim the word of God fearlessly». According to Acts 8:14-17, the apostles laid hands on the people of Samaria, and they received the Holy Spirit. Also according to Acts 19:1-5, when Paul laid his hands on the disciples of Ephesus, they began «to speak in tongues and prophesied».

By the action of the Holy Spirit the preaching of the apostles became universal. The Spirit pointed out to Peter the presence of the men sent by the centurion Cornelius (cfr. Acts 10:19). The Holy Spirit fell upon the gentiles who were listening to the words of Peter in the house of the centurion (Acts 10:44-45; cfr. 11:15; 15:8), and hence the water of baptism cannot be withheld «now that they have received the Holy Spirit just as we have» (Acts 10:47). In this way, the Holy Spirit accompanied and preceded the evangelizing action. The Holy Spirit was in the very origin of preaching to the gentiles, as well as in testimony before the Israelites. The Spirit aided the apostles in their responsibility of guiding the Church (Acts 15:28: «It has been decided by the Holy Spirit and by ourselves»). He sent them to preach at a place (Acts 13:2; 13:4), or kept them from going to another one (cfr. Acts 16:6-7). He warned Paul and appointed the shepherds of the Church (Acts 20:23, 28). Consequently, the Holy Spirit is the one who guided the Church, the apostles, and the remaining disciles in their preaching and testimony about Jesus. Without his action, the evangelizing work of the Church would not have taken place. Luke primarily saw the Spirit in this «external» action of the Church. Nevertheless, we should not forget that together with these texts, which are the majority from the quantitative point of view, the action of the Spirit is also evidenced when the marvels of God are proclaimed (Acts 2:4, 2:11, a fact that can be related to Luke 1:42; 1:67; 2:25; 10:21, in which Jesus rejoiced in the Holy Spirit)[146]. The emerging churches are built, and they grow in number «encouraged by the consolation of the Holy Spirit» (Acts 9:31). The other authors of the New Testament to whom we will now again refer also insisted on this interior action of the Holy Spirit in the believer.

---

145 CHEVALLIER M.A., *Aliento de Dios*, 201; cfr. HAYA PRATS G., *L'Esprit, force de l'Église. Sa nature et son activité d'après les Actes des Apôtres*, Paris 1975.
146 Cfr. BORDONI M., *La cristologia nell'orizzonte dello Spirito*, 75.

Undoubtedly, it is somewhat more complex to attempt to determine the action and the effects of the Spirit in Paul. Let us begin with the text that we have quoted on so many occasions in this chapter: Gal 4:6: «You are sons, God has sent into our hearts the Spirit of his Son crying "Abba Father!"»[147]. The Spirit of Jesus gives us the possibility of addressing God with the word that Jesus used. It is not possible to have a life of sonship without the action of the Spirit in us. Only if we are guided by the Spirit of God can we be and live like children of God:

> All who are guided by the Spirit of God are sons of God; for what you receive was not the spirit of slavery to bring you back into fear; you received the spirit of adoption, enabling us to cry our «Abba, Father!». The Spirit himself joins with our spirit to bear witness[148] that we are children of God. And if we are children, then we are heirs, heirs of God and joint heirs with Christ... (Rom 8:14-17).

This text, which is parallel in more than one respect to the one above, confirms and completes his teachings. The Holy Spirit —the Spirit of Jesus— creates in us the attitude of sonship, the «spirit» of adopted sons, contrary to the attitude of the slave, who lives in fear. If in the text of Galatians it is the Spirit who cries in us «Abba, Father!», here it is the believer, the one who does so directly by virtue of the «spirit», which the Spirit of God creates in us. Adoption entails inheritance, in view of the fact that the Son, and hence the heir himself, is Jesus alone (cfr. Heb 1:2). We are his co-heirs. Indirectly, we are being told that our sonship by virtue of the Holy Spirit is a participation in the life of Christ the Son. Here, the possession of the Spirit is not related directly to the inheritance that awaits us, although this connection is found in other passages of the *corpus paulinum*. Hence, the Spirit is the pledge of our inheritance (Eph 1:14; cfr. shortly before, the same idea of sonship in Eph 1:8. According to Eph 4:30, we were sealed by the Holy Spirit for the day of redemption). According to 2Cor 1:22, God gave us the spirit in our heart as a pledge (cfr. 2Cor 5:5; Rom 8:23). He is the guarantee of our future life. This idea can be related to the one we already know of the Spirit as agent of our future resurrection in the image of Christ (cfr. Rom 8:9-11).

147 In general terms, it is believed that according to this passage, the Spirit does not produce Sonship itself, but that he is rather an immediate consequence of it, and it is necessary for the relationship with God that this adoption or Sonship entails. Cfr. Penna R., *Lo Spirito di Cristo*, 219ff.
148 Or also: «The Spirit gives witness to our spirit that we are sons of God».

The Spirit is received by faith, not from the works of the law (Gal 3:1-2; 3:5; 3:14). This same Spirit is the one who enables us to confess Jesus as our Lord (1Cor 12:3: «Nobody is able to say "Jesus is Lord" except by the Holy Spirit»). The Spirit, in turn, is the one who enables us to know God, «he explores the depths of God», related to the mystery of Christ, which is not known to human wisdom (1Cor 2:10-14). The Holy Spirit also guarantees the correct understanding of the word of God, the ultimate sense of which has been revealed by Christ in whose image we are made through the Spirit (2Cor 3:14-18). The Holy Spirit is the beginning of life in Christ, which is opposed to life according to the flesh, the life according to sin which Christ has defeated by his death. Hence, Christians do not live according to the flesh but according to the Spirit (Rom 8:2-5; 8:9; 8:12-13; Gal 5:14-25). In the writings of Paul, the expressions «in the Spirit» and «in Christ» are equivalent (cfr. Rom 8:1-4; 8:9; 1Cor 6:11; Eph 2:21-22; Gal 2:17, cf. with 1Cor 6:11; 2Cor 2:17; 1Cor 12:3; Phil 3; Rom 14:17)[149]. In this way, he shows the close relationship between God and the Holy Spirit. God, by giving us the Holy Spirit, has inspired love in us, evidenced in the fact that he has delivered his Son to death for us while we were still sinners (Rom 5:5). This is the love with which God loves us, and not the love with which we love him (cfr. Rom 8:32ff). The Spirit is given to us in baptism (1 Cor 6:11; 12:13; Titus 3:5), and this is how we are identified with Christ's death and resurrection (Rom 6:3ff; Col 2:12).

The Spirit acts in people not as an external force, but from within our being because he dwells in us; he has been given to the believer. In 1Thess 4:8, the following idea appears for the first time: God has given his Holy Spirit to us. The Spirit is the ultimate gift of God, as we will be able to see shortly in greater detail. The presence of the Spirit relates to each of us in that he indwells each of us as his own body; that is, we are his own being (cfr. 1Thess 4:4-8). In 1Cor 6:19, in a similar context, we are told that our body is a temple of the Holy Spirit. This condition is related to our union with Jesus, and we are members of his body. We become one in the same «Spirit» with him (cfr. 1Thess 6:15ff). The Spirit who dwells in us is at the same time the power of Christ that brings us closer to him[150]. Being the temple of the Holy Spirit and being a member of Christ is in fact the same thing. According to 1Cor 3:16, we are the temple of God because the Spirit lives in us. The presence of the Spirit in us is equivalent to that of Christ (cfr. Rom 8:9ff).

---

149 Cfr. the parallelisms pointed out by CONGAR Y., *El Espíritu Santo*, 67.
150 Cfr. PENNA R., *Lo Spirito di Cristo*, 279.

Paul, however, does not believe that the presence of the Spirit in each of us is for our personal well-being. This presence also has an ecclesial dimension in that the Holy Spirit distributes as he wishes the gifts and *charismata*. They are diverse for each one of the members, but they all contribute to the building up of the body of Christ (cfr. 1Cor 12:4ff; Rom 12:4ff; Eph 4:11ff). The action of the same Spirit creates the unity of the Church. Christ is present in it by means of his Spirit. Both when we see the believer in his personal uniqueness and when we see the Church as a whole, the Spirit is always in reference to Christ. He makes us participate in his relationship with the Father and live in sonship according to the life that Jesus has given us. He makes us members of the body of Christ, which grows into the fullness of Christ himself (cfr. Eph 1:23; 4:13).

2.2.3. THE WRITINGS OF JOHN

134 Things do not change radically in the gospel when compared with the letters of John, even though there are different nuances. In Jesus' farewell discourse, in the passages with which we are already familiar, we find two characteristic designations when referring to the Holy Spirit: the «Paraclete» and the «Spirit of truth». As to the «Paraclete» (advocate, counselor, cfr. John 14:16; 14:26; 15:26; 16:7), he is always with the disciples and assists them in their testimony of Christ, and he himself gives testimony within each believer, convincing the world with respect to sin, unrighteousness and condemnation because the world has not believed in Jesus (cfr. 16:7ff). As to the «Spirit of truth» (cfr. John 14:17; 15:26; 16:13; 1John 5:6, «the Spirit is the one who testifies and the Spirit is truth»), he reminds the disciples of what Jesus has said. He must guide the disciples into the full truth and will announce to them what will come. He does not speak for himself, but he listens to Jesus, receives what is his, and communicates it. Hence, it is not the introduction of a new truth that will take the place of the truth of Christ, but rather, one that the Spirit keeps alive among the disciples — the word and the presence of Jesus himself. Also for John, the Spirit «gives life» (John 6:62) and is the origin of a new birth for humanity (cfr. John 3:3-8).

According to the first letter of John, the Spirit (the holy oil for the anointing, χρίσμα) takes us to the true knowledge of God and of Christ which the world cannot reach (cfr. 1John 2:20ff). The Holy Spirit is also the guarantor of the true confession of Christ, especially in that he has come into the flesh (cfr. 1John 4:2), and of the permanence of the faithful in love (1John 4:12ff). In the writings of John, the Spirit is also in relation with Christ, which means that his action cannot be considered as simply instrumental, that is, simply as that of a witness[151].

2.2.4. CONCLUSION: THE RELATIONSHIP OF THE SPIRIT WITH JESUS

According to the New Testament, the Holy Spirit is connected with Jesus because Jesus who has risen from the dead and ascended to the right hand of the Father is precisely the one who sends the Spirit, together with God the Father himself, to humanity. Furthermore, he is connected with Jesus because all his effects on both the Church and humanity also are in reference to Jesus. The Spirit builds the body of Christ, encourages preaching and testimony about Jesus, makes us live the life of children of God, and conforms us to the image of Christ. The Spirit is given to us as the Spirit of Christ and also as the Spirit of God. We cannot understand his acts if we do not bear that in mind. The Christ-Spirit relationship cannot be interpreted in the sense of a «subordination» of the Spirit to Christ, or, as we suggested previously, a merely instrumental function. We cannot do so because of the fact that the Spirit has descended on Jesus before he gave the Spirit to humankind. Rather, in the two missions of the Son and the Spirit —in their mutual implication— we see the work of salvation that has the Father as the only initiator and the only source: «God our Savior; he wants everyone to be saved and to reach full knowledge of the truth. For there is only one God, and there is only one mediator between God and humanity, himself a human being, Christ Jesus who offered himself as ransom for all» (Tim 2:4-6). The Father has carried out his saving plan with the unique mediation of Jesus Christ his only begotten Son. Nevertheless, this event of Christ takes place «in the Spirit». Jesus has carried out all his acts with the presence of the Holy Spirit, and the salvation he brings us only reaches humans by the action of the Spirit himself, the effects of whom we have just listed. The Holy Spirit *universalizes* and renders efficient, for all times and all places, the work of Christ which has been carried out at a specific time and place[152]. By universalizing it, he *updates it,* making it present, as is primarily the role of the sacraments. Likewise, by updating it,

---

151 Cfr. PORSCH F., *Pneuma und Word. Ein exegetischer Beitrag zur Pneumatologie des Johannesevangelium,* Frankfurt Main 1974, 405-407. Also in John we can determine a list of parallel situations between the acts of Jesus and those of the Holy Spirit, cfr. CONGAR Y., op. cit. 84.

152 We do not mean to say that the action of Christ is not intrinsically universal. The universality of Jesus and that of the Spirit are in mutual relationship, and one cannot be adequately distinguished from the other.

it is *internalized* in human beings, and most especially in the believers[153]. However, the action of the Spirit is not limited to the visible scope of the Church. The saving will of God has no bounds, as the mediation of Jesus does not have any bounds or limits. For this reason, the act of the Spirit cannot know any bounds either. The Second Vatican Council states this in GS 22:

> This does not apply only to Christians, but also to all those people of good will in whose heart grace acts invisibly. Christ died for all of us, and the ultimate vocation of man is, in reality only one; it is divine. Therefore, we must support the argument that the Holy Spirit offers every one of us the possibility of being associated with this Paschal mystery in a way that God knows[154].

The universal saving influence of the risen Jesus is exercised in the Holy Spirit, who is the scope and the means for salvation to be realized in Christ.

2.3. THE PERSONAL NATURE OF THE HOLY SPIRIT ACCORDING TO THE NEW TESTAMENT

The problem of the «personal» nature of the Holy Spirit according to the New Testament is discussed frequently. In fact, although the Father and Jesus his Son appear with characteristics that we can qualify, always analogically, as «personal», we cannot say the same thing with due clarity with respect to the Holy Spirit. Congar aptly points out the difficulty that emerges when trying to characterize the Spirit as a «person»: the Holy Spirit never says «I»[155]. In order to pose this situation adequately, we must bear in mind that there is no need to perceive the Holy Spirit as a «personal» being with the same characteristics as those of the Father and of the Son. As we already know, everything in the Trinity is unrepeatable.

Nonetheless, having said this, we cannot minimize certain indications that enable us to consider in all the writings of the New Testament that the Holy Spirit is to a certain extent an individual and not an impersonal force. According to the Acts of the Apostles, the Holy Spirit «prevented» Paul and Silas from going to Bithynia, or to preach the message in Asia (cfr. Acts 16:6-7). He also asked

---

153 Cfr. GONZÁLEZ DE CARDEDAL O., *Jesús de Nazaret. Aproximación a la cristología,* Madrid 1975, 558.

154 Cfr. also JOHN PAUL II, *Redemptoris Missio,* 28-29, according to which we must distinguish, without separating them, a unique action of the Spirit in the Church and a universal action.

155 Cfr. CONGAR Y., *El Espíritu Santo,* 10. Even though in one place in the New Testament he speaks directly: Acts 13:2. At least, he does not utter the word "I" in front of the Father and the Son; cfr. DURRWELL F.X., *L'Esprit Saint de Dieu,* Paris 1983, 156.

Barnabas and Paul to be set apart for him (Acts 13:2). The Holy Spirit warned Paul of the hardships that awaited him (Acts 20:23). He told Peter that he should go with those who were looking for him at the command of Cornelius because the Spirit had sent them (Acts 10:19). The Spirit made decisions in the Council of Jerusalem, together with the apostles and the elders (Acts 15:28). The Spirit himself was the one who entrusted the presbyters of Ephesus with their mission (Acts 20:28).

In the writings of Paul, mention is also made of the personal features of the Spirit. The Spirit examines the depths of God (cfr. 2Cor 2:14;) he judges things (ibid. 14), and he comes to our aid (Rom 8:26). In Eph 4:30 we are exhorted not to grieve the Holy Spirit of God. The Spirit is sent, as Jesus is sent (Gal 4:6). It is quite clear that each one of these texts taken separately is not much evidence, because there can be different types of «personifications», and Paul uses them. However, all of them together at least are pointing in the same direction.

Clearly, more personal features of the Spirit are also found in the gospel according to John. The Spirit is sent; the Spirit teaches, remembers, gives testimony, convinces the world, tells what he has heard, and so forth (cfr. John 14:16-17; 17:26; 15:26; 16:7-11; 16:13-14). According to the book of Revelation, the Spirit speaks to the churches (cfr. Rev 2:7; 2:11 etc.; cfr. also 14:13; 22:17). It is difficult to attribute all these actions to a mere impersonal force. In general terms, we can state that in the New Testament, the Holy Spirit appears, although not in the same degree as the Father or Jesus, as a «person» (using these words very carefully), as «someone», rather than as something, as someone endowed with freedom and not as a mere instrument without initiative. On the other hand, we must bear in mind that, both in the writings of Paul and in those of John, there is a remarkable parallelism between the actions that are attributed to Jesus and those that correspond to the Holy Spirit[156]. If there is a similarity and even a coincidence in the actions, there should also be such a coincidence in the characteristics of both of them.

---

[156] Cfr. the tables of CONGAR Y., *El Espíritu Santo*, 67f; 83f. Cfr. also WEHR L., «Das Heilswirken von Vater, Sohn und Geist nach den Paulusbriefen und dem Johannesevangelium. Zu den neutestamentlichen Voraussetzungen der Trinitätslehre» in *MünThZ* 47 (1996) 315-342.

The Son and the Holy Spirit in relation to the only God in the New Testament

After our analysis of the different stages of the life of Jesus in which, revealing the Father, he has shown himself as the only begotten Son in the Spirit, we must end with a reflection about the monotheism of the New Testament and the Trinitarian structure of salvation, as presented by the writings of the New Testament.

In the first place, we must emphasize that the Christology and the pneumatology of the New Testament are not an obstacle which stands in the way of the strict monotheist faith that Jesus and the apostles have inherited from the Old Testament and proclaimed without reservations. As we have already stated at the beginning of this chapter, this one and only God is revealed to us in the New Testament as the Father of Jesus. He, the only begotten and God-sent, appears on many occasions united with the only God in faith and in confession: cfr. John 17:3; 1Cor 8:6; 1Tim 2:5; Rom 10:9. Divine titles are used frequently in preaching about Jesus and in some texts; many of them are quite significant. He is even called «God». According to the prologue of the gospel of John, the Logos was God. The word θεός is used with an article, as a predicate, while God is referred to as ὁ θεός (cfr. John 1:1f). A possible reading of John 1:18 is «only begotten God» (instead of Son), and the article is also missing here. In John 20:28, we find the confession of faith of Thomas: «My Lord and my God» (ὁ κύριος μου καί ὁ θεός μου) with the article preceding the two titles. We read in 1John 5:20: «We are well aware also that the Son of God has come and has given us understanding so that we may know the One who is true. We are in the One who is true as we are in his Son Jesus Christ. He is the true God and this is eternal life». The divinity of Jesus is clearly affirmed together with that of the Father and is related to it. The Father is the true God, but this is also the case with the Son. Also with respect to him, we use this article: *the* true God. The title of «Son», which here we find united with that of God, is the one which in the New Testament and the tradition will be explained in greater depth with the identity of Jesus. The relationship of these titles shows that Jesus shares in the being of God as the Son. This is probably the passage that most explicitly affirms the divinity of Jesus in the New Testament[157]. We must also note that in the gospel according to John, the following expres-

---

[157] Cfr. SCHNACKENBURG R., *Cartas de san Juan*, Barcelona 1980, 312-314.

sion appears frequently in the words of Jesus: «I am» (cfr. John 5:35; 8:24; 8:27; 8:58; 13:19; 18:5-6), which reminds us of Exod 3:14.

Likewise, some Pauline texts seem to refer to Jesus as God. This is the case in Rom 9:5: «... to them belong the fathers, and out of them, so far as physical descent is concerned, came Christ, who is above all God, blessed for ever». It seems that Christ is called God, and this is what the rhythm of the phrase makes us believe, although we cannot rule out the fact that the end of the verse is an exclamation addressed to the Father. According to Titus 2:13, we are «waiting in hope for the blessing which will come with the appearing of the glory of our great God and Saviour Christ Jesus Christ». Similar expressions are found in 2Pet 1:1: «the saving justice of our God and Saviour Jesus Christ». It would seem far fetched to think that «God» refers in these cases to the Father and that the «saviour» is Jesus, although this cannot be ruled out totally.

Hence, Jesus is presented with full clarity to us as «God» in some texts of the New Testament, although in others we cannot eliminate a shadow of doubt. Nevertheless, these passages, not many, indeed, are not the only important ones for our purpose. We must read them as part of the complete message of the New Testament which introduces Jesus to us in his unique and unrepeatable relationship with the Father that leads to the mystery of salvation which God intended from eternity. Jesus, after the resurrection, lives in full communion with God, sitting at his right hand, and this mystery is before creation in the glory of the Father.

We can state something similar regarding the Holy Spirit. In this case, we do not have any explicit statement in the New Testament that talks about his divinity. Indeed, some of the texts that we have mentioned in the previous paragraphs are difficult to explain if we do not assume this divinity. For instance, the Spirit explores the depths of God (1Cor 2:10-12); «this Lord is the Spirit», commonly refers to the Holy Spirit (2Cor 3:17). Nevertheless, once again it is precisely the association with the Father and the Son in this saving mystery which regards the Spirit more clearly as God and not as creature. The work of salvation, which Christ has carried out once and for all (cfr. Heb 7:27; 9:12; 10:10), does not bear its fruit in human beings if the action of the Holy Spirit is absent.

Rather than a doctrine prepared around the idea of the Trinity, the New Testament clearly shows us a Trinitarian structure of salvation: an initiative that comes from the Father who sends Jesus into the world and delivers him to death (in terms that we know) and raises him from the dead; the obedience of Jesus who out of love delivers himself for us; and the gift of the Spirit through Jesus coming from the Father after the resurrection which prepares human beings for a new life and for being conformed with Jesus in his body which is the Church. Without the joint, and in turn, specific, intervention of each of these «three», neither the world nor any one in particular can attain salvation.

There is a line that could be described as «descending»: Father-Son-Holy Spirit, from God to humanity. There is another line in the New Testament which corresponds to it and which could be referred to as «ascending»: the gift of the Spirit sent into our hearts uniting us to Jesus, and by means of Jesus, we have access to the Father. Spirit-Son-Father would be the order of the way that leads human beings to God, made possible because God manifested before has come to us in his Son and his Spirit. In this way, in the Holy Spirit who unites us all by means of Christ, we have access to the Father: «Through him [Jesus], then, we both [Jews and Gentiles] in the one Spirit, have free access to the Father» (Eph 2:18). The Son and the Holy Spirit appear in the New Testament united with the only God. We will see this more explicitly when we examine some triadic texts in which mention is made of the Father, the Son and the Holy Spirit.

3.1. SOME TRIADIC TEXTS

In the New Testament there are Christological confessions of faith that frequently include mention of the Father (cfr. Phil 2:11; Rom 10:9; 1Cor 15:3-5). Other passages, even though they are not a confession of faith, show a triadic structure. The Father, the Son, and the Holy Spirit appear together in them. In the case of the New Testament, these texts are a point of arrival, far more than a point of departure. When we combine the three «persons» in a brief formula, they show the peculiar unity among them that is seen throughout the New Testament. In them, there is a synthetic manifestation of the Trinitarian structure of the divine action which we find throughout the New Testament, and it is the way that can lead us to reflections about the Trinity per se. There are numerous texts in which, one way or another, we can find signs of this structure. Many of them have already been quoted in our previous exposition. Because of this, we will now simply refer to those in which this structure appears in a more explicit way.

First, we must focus on the baptismal formula, according to Matt 28:19: «Go, therefore, make disciples of all nations; baptizing them in the name of the Father, and of the Son, and of the Holy Spirit». There is no need to insist on the significance that this fundamental text has had on the tradition and the life of the Church. It affirms at the same time the plurality of the persons and the unity of the three (the name in singular)[158]. Whether the liturgical use of the primitive Church may have influenced definitively the form of this verse is still an open issue. Unlike what we will see in the following passages, this text offers us the order that will be traditional when listing the three persons and that responds, in time, to the saving historical order —«the descending order» to which we have recently referred. Because of this same fact, the «baptized» refers to the Father, to the Son, and to the Holy Spirit. This baptismal mandate must be related to the baptism of Jesus in the Jordan[159].

2Cor 13:13: «The grace of the Lord Jesus Christ, the love of God and the fellowship of the Holy Spirit be with all of you». In our current liturgical practice, the farewell word of Paul has turned into a welcome greeting[160]. The «grace» can be identified with Jesus Christ himself. In the New Testament, the Father is the first one who loves us, and he is the source of love. The Holy Spirit is the source of communion or fellowship between God and humanity, and at the same time between people. Both elements can be present in the intention of Paul (generally objective and subjective).

1Cor 12:4-7: «There are many different gifts, but it is the same Spirit; there are many different ways of serving, but it is always the same Lord; there are different forms of activity, but in everybody it is the same God who is at work in them all». The order here is the «ascending one», to which we have alluded. The gifts or *charismata* are related specifically to the Holy Spirit; the «ministries» to the «Lord» (it is worth noting the correspondence between service and Lord); but everything comes finally from God the Father, the only beginning.

Gal 4:4-6, the text that has been our guide in this chapter, also offers us a good example of the triadic text. The initiative of the mission of the Son and the Spirit comes from the Father in its order and mutual interaction.

We could mention again the texts of the Paraclete in the gospel of John. Other Pauline texts also show with more or less clarity a Trinitarian rhythm: Rom 8:14-17; 1Cor 6:11; Eph 2:18; 4:4-6; 2Thess 2:13-14; Titus 3:4-7; also 1Pet 1:2, among

---

158 Maggioli B., «La Trinità nel Nuovo Testamento» in *ScCat* 116 (1990) 7-30, esp. 29: «Questa formula trinitaria matteana è importante, perché non solo afferma la distinzione delle Persone, ma anche la loro unità (*nel nome*, al singolare). E mostra come l'esistenza cristiana si svolga per intero, fin dall'inizio —dal battesimo, appunto— nell'ambito dell'azione della Trinità».

159 Cfr. Gnilka J., *Das Matthäusevangelium* I, Freiburg-Basel-Wien 1988, 78f.

160 Cfr. 1Cor 16:23; Gal 6:18; Phil 4:23 among others, in which Paul only talks about the «grace of Jesus Christ». The formula of 2Cor is an expansion and a more explicit reference to this other more traditional way.

others. This is by no means an all-inclusive list. All the passages state that in the awareness of the authors of the New Testament, the Father, the Son, and the Holy Spirit are all united in a very special way. The subsequent reflection of the Church will have to explain what we have here *in nuce* and how this unity of the three is not opposed to monotheism, but rather it is its most legitimate and genuine expression.

These early «Trinitarian» texts should not be seen as the only point of departure of the Trinitarian doctrine of the Church. They only make sense in light of the economy of salvation that God, revealed as Father of Jesus, carries out with his mediation and in the Spirit. It is the experience of the life of Jesus[161] and of the first moments of the life of the Church that lead us to combine these «three». On the one hand, Jesus reveals God to us as Father and gives us the Holy Spirit who has come down and rested upon him. On the other hand, only based on his relationship with the Father and the anointing of the Spirit, by virtue of which he has carried out the mission entrusted to him by the Father himself, do we know who is Jesus, the Son of God, the Lord and the Christ. Hence, faith in Jesus cannot be expressed in all its dimensions if it is not in association with Father, Son, and Holy Spirit. In this sense, we mention that these formulas are more a point of arrival than a point of departure. Nevertheless, as they are present in the New Testament, and in a way, the synthesis of its message, they are, especially the baptismal formula, a natural point of reference for subsequent reflection, although united and never separated from the history that gave them their origin and from which they extract their meaning.

4
Final reflections and conclusions

Our attempt in this chapter has not only been to carry out a biblical study, but rather a biblical-systematic study. We have not been focused only on explaining what we are told about the Trinity in the New Testament, but also on the way in which the mystery of God is revealed in the life of Christ and in the first Chris-

---

161 MONDIN B., *La Trinità mistero d'amore. Trattato di teologia trinitaria*, Bologna 1993, 91: «La sperienza trinitaria di Gesù diviene anche la sperienza trinitaria della sua Chiesa. E come la sperienza trinitaria stà al centro della vita di Gesù, similmente la sperienza trinitaria stà al centro della vita della Chiesa».

tian community. This revelation of the mystery of God is not neutral «information», but the insertion of the human being into the divine life (cfr. Eph 2:18). To this end we have resorted to biblical data, and we have also turned to the patristic tradition and systematic reflection on this data. We have attempted to offer a theology of some mysteries of the life of the Lord from the point of view of the revelation of God in them. In concluding this chapter, we will now attempt a brief summary of the results that we have reached.

• The revelation of the triune God is not evidenced only in words, but also when the Father sent his Son and his Spirit into the world. The text in Gal 4:4-6 has been a guide for us, and it is especially significant. The salvation of humanity consists in «adoption», and the missions of Christ and the Spirit are aimed at making this possible.

• These two missions are not independent, but rather, they are related intimately. They are two inseparable moments in the implementation of the saving plan of God. Their internal articulation is discovered in the life of Jesus Christ.

• The New Testament and the tradition of the Church have reached the conclusion, founded on the information about the life, death and resurrection of Jesus, that he is the Son of God who has come into this world. Nevertheless, Jesus is not only the incarnate Son of God, but also the bearer of the Spirit. This is what leads to our theology of the anointing. We have stated that during a long period of time, this anointing was mistaken for the incarnation, and hence the biblical information of Jesus possessing the Spirit with whom he has been anointed took a secondary role in theological reflection. Current theology has made a clear distinction between all these fields following the old tradition of the Fathers. The Spirit has acted on Jesus who is personally the Son. Through the action of the Spirit, Jesus has delivered himself to death and has risen from the dead. The initiative is ultimately that of the Father.

• The Paschal mystery of the death and resurrection of Jesus acquires special significance in the revelation of the mystery of God. The capacity of the Son of God to come out of himself to go and seek lost humanity where it was, in separation from the Father (the mystery of «abandonment»), should not make us forget that Jesus delivers himself out of obedience, putting his trust in the hands of his silent Father. In any case, what is shown here is the love of God the Father and the Son for all of us. With the intervention of the Holy Spirit, the Father is the main agent in the resurrection of Jesus. This resurrection is clear evidence of the unity of the Father and the Son. The outpouring of the Holy Spirit follows the resurrection and exaltation of Jesus. The Spirit is sent by the Father and by the Son. This shows that Jesus, risen from the dead, in his distinction from God the Father, participates fully in the Father's life. Jesus sends the Spirit whom, as we have seen, he also receives from the Father.

• The considerations above have enabled us to see that this presence of the Spirit in Jesus is something dynamic, as dynamic as the historical path that takes him to the Father when he is man. By virtue of this, the Spirit whom Jesus gives is his. It is his in the sense that it comes from him once he is risen from the dead, but also in the sense that the Spirit is the one who has acted upon him. He is the one who can create in people what he has made in the human nature of Christ. Jesus is the perfect man. Only through their insertion in the Trinitarian mystery can human beings reach their fullness as children of God with Jesus and like Jesus. The Son of God has been made man so that human beings could be children of God. None of this is possible without his Spirit.

• The salvation that the Father wills to grant humanity has been realized and is realized by means of Christ and through the action of the Holy Spirit. This saving work manifests the unity of the three. Because of this, in the New Testament we already begin to see the presence of triadic formulas, which synthetically show this Trinitarian dynamics of salvation. Only the saving economy opens before us the path to the reflection of what God is in himself.

What we will study in the following chapters when addressing the history of the two dogmas is simply the effort of the Church to safeguard this *kerygma* of the New Testament and to plumb its contents. The greater precision or speculative depth that we might acquire does not mean that this history will say more than we can find in the New Testament. Indeed, by preserving and correctly interpreting these messages, we can justify the great efforts made within the scope of theology, from the first times until now, to show the coherence of the faith in the one and triune God.

The preparation for the revelation of the Triune God in the Old Testament

This brief chapter could indeed serve as an appendix to the previous one. Throughout the analysis and exposition that we have just completed, we referred on certain occasions to the Old Testament. The purpose of this has been either to show the uniqueness of Jesus with respect to himself, or to convey how certain categories of the Old Testament are used in the New Testament in order to render the revelation of Jesus easier to understand. At the same time we have maintained the originality of the message of the New Testament, as well as the permanent validity of the Old Testament for Christians. The distinction between these two Testaments cannot make us forget that they are deeply and profoundly united[1]. We have already pointed out in our introduction that it would be extremely simplistic to believe that the revelation of the Old Testament reveals to us the one God and that the New Testament reveals to us the triune God. Nevertheless, this statement is indeed true to a certain extent. In their most profound unity, the Old and the New Testaments have progressively brought to us the revelation of God, addressed in the first place to his chosen people, and subsequently, through Jesus, to all the nations without any distinction whatsoever. Undoubtedly, the Old Testament does not enable us to know God in the inscrutable mystery of his triunity. Nevertheless, it is not alien to it either. It is obvious that we cannot look for clear affirmations about the Trinity in the texts of the Old Testament (for instance, in the plural that appears in Gen 1:26, «Let us make man…»), as we have done in the history of theology and as we will have the occasion to see in our theological analysis. However, the promises of the presence of God amidst his people and his nearness to humanity, especially to those who are poor and defenseless, undoubtedly prepare us for the revelation of the presence of his Son sharing with us amidst our condition.

The whole of the Old Testament, as it leads toward the coming of Jesus, prepares for the definitive revelation of the one and triune God. A complete presentation of the subject of God in the Old Testament would undoubtedly go beyond the objective that we wish to attain in this treatise. A random selection of topics would be interesting per se, but it would not make much sense in a book such as this. Among a multitude of aspects that might be taken into account, I will simply address two of them that seem to be especially relevant in order to enlighten the message of the New Testament. They are the revelation of the name

---

1 Cfr. DV 16 which refers to the famous phrase of Saint Augustine, *Quaest. in Hept.* 2, 73 (PL 34,623): «Quamquam et in Vetere Novum lateat, et in Novo Venus pateat».

of God to Moses and the existence in the different writings of the Old Testament of certain «mediators» who make the presence of God known in a unique way amidst his people and in the world, without a clear and adequate distinction made between them and God.

1

The revelation of the name of God

The importance that has already been attached from the perspective of the Old Testament to the revelation of the name of God (Yahweh) on Mount Horeb and on the other hand, the relevance that the following passage has had in the Christian tradition from the very early days, prompts us to focus on this issue at this point:

> God said to Moses: «I am he who is». And he said, «This is what you are to say to the Is-raelites, "I AM has sent me to you"». God further said to Moses, «You are to tell the Israelites, "Yahweh, the God of your ancestors, the God of Abraham, the God of Isaac, and the God of Jacob, has sent me to you. This is my name for all time, and thus I am to be invoked for all generations to come"» (Exod 3:14-15).

Among the different names of God in the Old Testament, that of «Yahweh» has primacy granted by the fact that it is a name that has been revealed by God himself[2]. With this designation, God has revealed himself for us to know him. Nevertheless, the name cannot be taken separately from the events that go along with the revelation. Yahweh does not reveal himself in his mystery as he is, but primarily as the one who will be showing and revealing himself to Israel in order to liberate Israel, as he had shown and revealed himself before to the patriarchs whom he had guided. Only in this way will he reveal something about his essence. He who is God in himself will be manifested in the «relative and efficient presence: "I will be there (for you)"»[3]. Hence, the name Yahweh points to the future

---

2 Cfr. MARANGON A., «Dios» in ROSSANO P., RAVASI G., and GIRLANDA A., *Nuevo Diccionario de Teología Bíblica*, Madrid 1990, 441-463, especially, 444ff. In the case of the Old Testament, there is also frequent mention (approximately 2,800 times, although far less than that of Yahweh, which appears 6,800 times) of the name of El or Elohim (this second form is used far more frequently). This is a name that Israel has taken from its environmental culture and has continued using in order to underline the universality of its God Yahweh.

3 VON RAD G., *Teología del Antiguo Testamento I. Teología de las tradiciones históricas de Israel*, Salamanca 1969, 235; cfr. also the entire context.

orientation of the actions of God who will be with his people. The name of God will be enriched with the different historical experiences. Nevertheless, we must bear in mind that the being and the acts of God are related and that they are not contradictory. In his concrete way of acting, God will enable us to know his being. This is the case when he guides the chosen people, when he liberates his people from Egypt, —an event that almost immediately follows this revelation of his name— and throughout the subsequent history of the people of Israel. God announces that his intentions will be manifested and evidenced in his future actions, which at this point in time, he still refuses to reveal. «What God wishes to make Moses understand is an expression of his being God that will be manifested according to his plan»[4]. Hence, the name of Yahweh is equivalent to «I am the one who exists», not in the sense of the dogmatic definition of an abstract monotheism, but in that of a practical monotheism. Yahweh is for Israel the only one who exists because he is its only savior. He is the one who will take the people from Egypt (cfr. Exod 3:19-11)[5]. Hence, this points to the frequent interpretation of the name of Yahweh as «I will be with you»[6]. What is God in himself will be known based on what he will be for his people[7].

4   CHILDS B.S., *Il libro dell'Esodo. Comentario critico — teologico*, Casale Monferrato 1995, 91; ibid. 92: «God has revealed himself to Moses with his eternal name. This is the name that, starting at this point in time, the people will remember in the *cultus* for generations to come. The name is not revealed to satisfy the curiosity of Israel, but in order to be the instrument of a continuous adoration». ZIMMERLY W., *Manual de teología del Antiguo Testamento*, Madrid 1980, 18-19: «The name Yahweh should not be interpreted from the isolated verb *hyh*, but from the figure of speech: "I am the one who am". This figure of speech must be compared against the authoritarian sentence contained in Exod 33:19: "I who show favors to whom I will, I who grant mercy to whom I will". In this figure of speech, we see how the sovereign freedom of Yahweh clearly resounds, and not even at the time of revealing his name is he within the reach of man… According to the affirmation contained in Exod 3:14, even when he refers to himself by his own name and reveals this name to men, Yahweh is still "the Free One", the one who could only be fully and completely understood in the freedom of his own self-introduction». Ibid., 19-20. «In the only passage in which the Old Testament attempts to offer an explanation of the name of Yahweh, it rejects an "explanation" of the name that will lock it in the cage of a definition. The Old Testament tries to express that one can only talk about Yahweh by carefully observing how he manifests himself (in his acts and in his precepts and commands)».

5   Cfr. DE VAUX R., *Historia antigua de Israel* 1, Madrid 1975, 343,345; cfr. in general, pages 330-347.

6   ROVIRA BELLOSO J. M., *Tratado de Dios uno y trino*, Salamanca 1993, 233, states that in Matt 28:20: «Look, I am with you always: yes, to the end of time», Christ fully complies with this plan that God has designed from the very beginning. DE VAUX R., *Historia antigua de Israel* 1, 347: «Exod 3:14 potentially contains the events and developments that the continuation of revelation will convey, and within this perspective of faith, there is justification for the profound meaning that theologians will read in it. Still, as stated in the Bible: "I am the Existing One" is echoed and commented upon in the last book of the Scriptures: "I am the Alpha and the Omega," says the Lord God, "who is, who was, and who is to come, the Almighty" (Rev 1:8). The same name of Jesus (cfr. Matt 1:20) points to this continuity: God is with his people to save them».

7   Cfr. SESBOÜÉ B., *Jésus-Christ l'unique médiateur 2. Les récits du salut*, Paris 1991, 74 ; cfr. also VON BALTHASAR H.U., *Gloria 6*, Madrid 1988, 58.

This God who reveals his name to Moses, and through him to all his people, is the only one who will liberate Israel and who will manifest his power in the events of history that are to follow. The people of Israel will celebrate this God and will make the solemn covenant, by virtue of which Israel will always be his people and a portion of his inheritance: «When the Most High gave the nations each their heritage… he assigned the boundaries of nations… but Yahweh's portion was his people, Jacob was to be the measure of his inheritance» (Deut 32:8-9). «For he is our God and we the people of his sheepfold, the flock of his hand» (Ps 95:7). This excludes the worship of other gods, as expressly stated in Exod 20:2-3, with the first «word» of the commandments: «I am Yahweh your God, who brought you out of Egypt, where you lived as slaves. You shall not have other gods to rival me». This claim of Yahweh, the Lord, of being the only God for his people is the foundation itself of the radical monotheism that already clearly points to the existence of only one God (and not merely to the fact that Israel cannot worship more than one God), as will be more clearly set forth by the prophets at the end of the exile —the exodus— and in the book of Deuteronomy. This is the case, for instance, in Deutero-Isaiah, which clearly refers to the reason for the revelation of the name of Yahweh in the Exodus:

> You yourselves are my witnesses, declares Yahweh and the servant whom I have chosen, so that you may know and believe me, and understand that it is I. No god was formed before me, nor will be after me. I, I am Yahweh, and there is no Saviour but me (Isa 43:10-11)[8].

Hence, he acknowledges and meditates in his heart that Yahweh the Lord is the only God and that there is no other in heaven and here on earth (Deut 4:35; cfr. Deut 4:6; 7:9)[9].

---

8 Cfr. also among other places, Isa 42:8; 44:6-8: «I am the first and I am the last… You are my witnesses. Is there any God except me? There is no Rock; I know of none»; 45:5-6: «I am Yahweh, and there is no other…»; 45:18-19,21; 46:8. These affirmations find their prelude in Jer 31:35; 32:17,27: «I am Yahweh, the God of all humanity». Regarding the relationship of this explicit monotheism and the development of faith in the creation, cfr. LADARIA L.F., *Antropología teológica*, Casale Monferrato, Rome 1995, 18ff.

9 The stages in the evolution of monotheism evidenced in Israel are summarized in VORGRIMLER H., *Doctrina teológica de Dios*, Barcelona 1987, 59f: A first phase is noted by the fight against the god Baal in the 9th century B. C. that was started by the prophet Elijah. Only Yahweh can be worshiped. The second phase was noted by Hosea, towards the year 740 B. C. Yahweh has to be worshiped and all other gods should be despised. A third phase is the cultural reform of Hezekiah (728-699), characterized by the struggle against the worship of images in the Northern kingdom.

We already saw in the previous chapter how in the New Testament, and specifically, in the gospel of John, the revelation of the name of God in the exodus would be a means for expressing the profound divine identity of Jesus.

2

The mediators in the Old Testament

Clearly, the transcendence of God is a constant in the teachings of the Old Testament, but it is also a core doctrine that he acts and is present amidst his people. This has already been evidenced in our previous exposition. Among the means that are used in the writings of the New Testament to maintain the tension between the transcendence of God and his mysterious nature on the one hand, and his capacity to make himself present in the world on the other hand, special mention must be made of some «quasi-divine» mediators. In their multiplicity of forms, they enable us to discern the internal wealth of the divine being, a pre-assumption of the variety of these external manifestations. It is clear that we must not think of these beings as God, although in certain moments, these mediators may appear almost as «hypostatized». We must not make hasty Trinitarian readings of the Old Testament. Nevertheless, without forcing the text in any manner whatsoever, it would be quite fair to interpret these mediations as explicit preparatory instances leading toward the revelation of the triune God in the New Testament. This appreciation is even more legitimate because in fact, the Old Testament itself and the tradition of the Church have referred to these figures, known by readers who are familiar with the writings of Israel, in order to enlighten the newness of the revelation of the Gospel. This is particularly the case in empha-

The fourth phase is the reform of Josiah (641-609) with the centralization of the *cultus* in Jerusalem. Zephaniah, Ezekiel, and Jeremiah agreed to join and commit to this monotheist movement. The fifth and last phase, after 586, with the exile, leads to monotheism: there is no other God than Yahweh in absolute terms. This is the way in which it appears in Deuteronomy and in Deutero-Isaiah. Cfr. also SATTLER S. - SCHNEIDER TH., «Dottrina su Dio» in SCHNEIDER TH. (ed.), *Nuovo corso di dogmatica*, Brescia 1995, volume I, 65-144, especially on this topic, 84-92; VAN CANGH J.M., «Les origines d'Israel et la foi monoteiste: institution et/ou charisme» in MELLONI A. - MENOZZI D. - RUGGIERI G. - TOSCHI M. (eds.), *Cristianesimo nella Storia. Saggi in onore di G. Alberigo*, Bologna 1996, 35-88; LANG B. (Hrsg.), *Der einzige Gott. Die Geburt des biblischen Monotheismus*, München 1981; HAAG E. (Hrsg.), *Gott der Einzige. Zur Entstehung des Monotheismus in Israel*, Freiburg 1985; STAGLIANÒ A., *Il mistero del Dio vivente. Per una teologia dell'Assoluto trinitario*, Bologna 1996, 129-163; CODA P., *Dio Uno e Trino. Rivelazione, esperienza e teologia del Dio dei cristiani*, Cinisello Balsamo, 13-81.

sizing the identity of Jesus Christ and of the Holy Spirit, as well as the fact that they belong within the divine scope in their distinction with respect to the Father. Bearing in mind these assumptions, we will offer some brief descriptions of these concrete «mediating» figures[10].

Mention is made in the Old Testament of the *angel of the Lord, the angel of Yahweh*. This expression points to a special quality of some of the beings that appeared designated as «angels» who are next to God and who praise him (cfr. Ps 103:20)[11]. This angel of God appears as the one who helps and leads Israel when the chosen people leave Egypt in the pilgrimage across the desert (cfr. Exod 14:19; 23:20; 23:23; 32:34; 33:2; Num 20:16). This angel can also be a judge or a figure that inflicts a punishment (cfr. 2 Sam 14:17; 24:16ff). He is sent to the prophet Elijah in his flight to Mount Horeb (cfr.1 Kgs 19:5ff) and at other times during his prophetic ministry (cfr. Kgs 1:3,15). From our point of view, some passages in which the «angel of the Lord» cannot be adequately distinguished from God himself are of special interest, because indeed, both his appearance and his language are those of God. This is evidenced, for instance, when he appeared to Hagar in Gen 16:7, 9f, 13, as well as to Jacob in Gen 31:11,13. In these cases, the angel of the Lord begins to speak, and subsequently this angel is identified with the Lord himself. In the passage of the theophany at Mount Horeb, prior to the revelation of the name of God to Moses (Exod 3:2,4ff), we see the same phenomenon. Also in this case, when the angel appears before Gideon in Judges (6:11f,14), he is, in actuality, God himself. Although the figure of the «angel» is not fully identified with God, it nevertheless cannot be clearly distinguished from God, and this, at any rate, helps emphasize the incomprehensibility of the one who is manifested through this appearance.

The figure of the *word of God*[12], which appears in several contexts, acquires an even greater significance. Above all, we must bear in mind the importance of the word of God addressed to the prophets, the one that they hear and that encourages them to preach and to convey it to the people (cfr. Isa 6:9; Ezek 10:5; Jer 1:11; Amos 1:4,7,etc.). The prophets begin their exhortations with the expression: «Thus says Yahweh…». Or also: «The word of Yahweh came to me…». This

---

10 Cfr. SCHULTE R., «La preparación de la revelación trinitaria» in *MySal* II/1, 77-116, especially in 93-102; SCHEFFCZYK L., *Der Gott der Offenbarung*, Aachen 1996, 146-153.

11 Cfr. also FREEDMAN D. N. - WILLONGHBY B. Z., «*mal'ak*» in TWAT 4, 895-904.

12 Cfr. SCHMIDT W.H., «*dabar*» in TWAT 2, 89-133; GERLENMAN G., «*dabar*» in JENNI E. - WESTERMANN C., *Dizionario teologico dell'Antico Testamento* I, Torino 1978, 375-383.

word is powerful and irresistible; it gains control over the prophet (cfr. Amos 3:8; Ezek 2:8ff; and above all, Jer 20:8ff), transforming him and turning him into a God-sent person.

In addition to being a prophetic word, the word of God is teaching; it is a revelation and a mandate of the Lord. The «commandments» of the Decalogue are «words» (cfr. Exod 20:1; 24:3,4,8; 34:27f)[13]. Moses is the first one to receive the words, and he is in charge of conveying them to the people (cfr. Exod 3:4; 4:2; 5:3, and so forth). Because of these words, the people of Israel have been made the «people of God» (Exod 24:8; 34:27). In Deuteronomy, all of these elements appear especially clearly. The divine prescriptions that Moses conveys to the people show the grandeur of God (Deut 4:5ff). This word is the promise of salvation if the people fulfill their promise faithfully (cfr. Deut 4:1ff; 5:1ff; 6:17; 34:1ff, among others).

Finally, the word is the executor of the will of God in creation[14], although it also guides the people. Hence, the word participates in the divine power. The creation by the power of the word is clearly evidenced in Ps 33:6: «By the word of Yahweh the heavens were made…»; Wis 9:1: «God of our ancestors… who by your word has made the universe». In a more indirect way, it is stated in Gen 1:3ff that everything comes to existence by the word of the Creator: «God said…» (cfr. also Isa 48:13, among others). The word of God becomes a present and living magnitude that God sends in order to liberate those who entreat for assistance (cfr. Ps 107:20) and in whom the just trust (cfr. Ps 119:81,114,147; 130:5). The word is sent to the world in order to fulfill the will of God: «For as the rain and snow come down from the sky and do not return before having watered… so it is with the word that goes from my mouth: it will not return to me unfulfilled, or before having carried out my good pleasure and having achieved what it was sent to do» (Isa 55:10f). «He sends his word to the earth, his command runs quickly» (Ps 147:15ff). When God utters his word, this produces the intended effect (cfr. Ezek 12:25ff).

Divine *wisdom*[15] is another of the figures of the Old Testament that prepares for the revelation of the triune God. This «wisdom» refers in the first place to the range of honest and just human action that is only possible if God grants it. Be-

---

13 Cfr. SCHMIDT W.H., «*dabar*» in *TWAT* 2, 110ff.

14 For more information, see LADARIA L.F., *Antropología teológica*, 82-84.

15 Cfr. GILBERT M., «*Sabiduría*» in ROSSANO P. - RAVASI G., *Nuevo diccionario de teología bíblica*, Madrid 1990, 1711-1728, especially 1723ff.

cause of this fact, it is a divine gift (Job 12:13) that humans can only attain as a gift of God for which they have to entreat (cfr. Gen 3:5ff; 1 Kgs 3:12; Prov 21:30). This wisdom, this understanding, is present in the creation of the world (cfr. Jer 10:12; Prov 3:19; Ps 104:24). A person is «wise» when he accepts and adapts to the wisdom of God, because before the Lord, human wisdom has no value (Prov 21:20). Hence, the beginning of knowledge and wisdom for a person lies in the fear of God (Prov 1:7; 9:10). Some texts in which wisdom appears as «personified» are especially significant for us. We can presumably identify in these passages the eternal plan of creation that grants the world its order. For instance, what is offered to us in this sense in Proverbs 8-9 is most interesting:

> Yahweh created me, first fruits of his fashioning, before the oldest of his works. From everlasting I was firmly set, from the beginning before the earth came into being... I was beside the master craftsman, delighting him day by day, ever at play in his presence, at play everywhere on his earth; delighting to be with the children of men (Prov 8:22-31).
>
> Wisdom has built herself a house, she has hewn her seven pillars; she has slaughtered her beasts, drawn her wine... (Prov 9:1-2).

Ecclesiasticus 24 also offers several similar characteristics. «Wisdom speaks her own praises, in the midst of her people she glories in herself, She opens her mouth in the assembly of the Most High ...» (Ecclesiasticus 24:1-2; cfr. as well the rest of the verse). Finally, we quote the passage of the book of Wisdom:

> For within her is a spirit intelligent, holy, unique, manifold... For Wisdom is quicker to move than any motion; and she is so pure, she pervades and permeates all things. She is a breath of the power of God, pure emanation of the glory of the Almighty... For she is a reflection of the eternal light... (Wis 7:22-26; cfr. the rest of the book of Wisdom)[16].

---

16 Regarding the sense of the «personification» in these texts, GILBERT M., «*Sabiduría*» in ROSSANO P. - RAVASI G., *Nuevo diccionario de teología bíblica*, Madrid 1990, 1726 states: «The main problem is that of knowing how to express divine transcendence or immanence. Wisdom expresses, mostly in Wis 7-9, this immanence or presence of God in the world and in the souls of the elect, the just, and in this latter case, we are not far from the Christian concept of grace. Nevertheless, this divine presence also grants the world its coherence (Wis 1:7), its sense, and its meaning. We can limit the concept of the order of the world to this idea, resorting in this respect to Prov 8:22-31, unless we see there the project of creation and the project of salvation of God, a project that is considered prior to its fulfillment. God is made present in history, and specifically in the history of Israel, and that presence is what we call revelation, according to the original design of God».

It is worth noting that in this last text there is an approximation of the ideas of wisdom and spirit that is not typical, in general terms, of the book of Wisdom (cfr. Wis 1:4-7). This paves the way for the next idea that we must study in the following pages.

The *spirit* is the last figure of «mediation» that we must address. This term has many meanings. As it is well known, initially it points to space and to wind, which cannot be controlled by human beings. Because of this, it can easily be related to energy and to the divine power which is superior to any human force[17].

The Spirit is connected to the creative force of God. Even though this is not the earliest characteristic of the Spirit, some texts that talk about this cosmic power are very old. Hence, for instance, it is the wind that God blows which separates the waters of the Red Sea, opening the way for the Israelites (Exod 14:21; cfr. 15:8); the cosmic power is at the service of the salvation of the people (cfr. also, Exod 10:13). Even more directly, the Spirit appears in relation to creation in Gen 1:2; the Spirit of God sweeps over the waters. According to Gen 8:1, the wind that God sends separates the waters after the deluge. In Ps 33:6 the creative power is emphasized as related to the word. According to Wis 1:7, «The Spirit of the Lord fills the world», the Spirit of the Lord being in very close relationship with Wisdom (cfr. ibid. 1:6), to which we have just referred. With respect to this cosmic function in creation, we must mention the importance of the Spirit for life in general, and for the life of humanity in particular, which always depend on the action of God (cfr. Job 27:3; 33:4; 34:14). Especially significant is Ps 104:29f: «Turn away your face and they panic, take back their breath and they die... Send out your breath, and life begins; you renew the face of the earth».

In the oldest historical books we frequently see the Spirit of God as the force that bursts within specific persons in an unexpected way in order to carry out different activities. In this way, according to the book of Judges, it is the Spirit that drives these leaders of the people (cfr. Judg 3:10; 6:34; 11:29; 13:25; 14:6, 19; 15:14). There are similar characteristics in the acts of the Spirit in the first book of Samuel (i.e. the Spirit that comes upon Saul in 1Sam 10:6,10; 11:6). The Spirit also rushes down on some groups of prophets (cfr. 1Sam 10:10). Similarly, it rushes upon David and remains on him more than on his predecessors (1Sam 16:13; cfr. 16:14; 2Sam 23:1-2).

---

17 Cfr. among the abundant bibliography, SCHÜTZ CH., *Introducción a la Pneumatología*, Salamanca 1991, 159-167; CHEVALLIER M.A., *Aliento de Dios*, Salamanca 1982, 25-39; HILBERATH B.J., *Pneumatología*, Brescia 1996, 29-50; CONGAR Y., *El Espíritu Santo*, Barcelona 1983, 29-40.

The Spirit also acts on the prophets. Prophecy itself is attributed to the Spirit, especially after the exodus (Exod 22:2; 3:24; 11:1,5,24; Hosea 9:7; in retrospect, Zech 7:12; Isa 63:11). The most characteristic bearer of the Spirit will be the Messiah, the anointed of Yahweh upon whom the Spirit will rest. This idea already appears in Isaiah (cfr. Isa 11:1ff; 28:5ff). Additionally, the servant of Yahweh will be the one who will receive this gift which is linked to the announcement of salvation to the nations (cfr. Isa 42:1ff; 61:1). The messianic era will be characterized by a general possession of the Spirit that will no longer be the legacy of just a few (cfr. Isa 2:4-6; 44:2). In the case of the prophet Joel, the universal outpouring of the Spirit is seen together with the events of the day of Yahweh, a definitive eruption of God in history, a moment in which all will prophesy (Joel 3:1ff; cfr. Acts 2:17ff).

The Spirit is the beginning of new life, of moral renewal, for the people and each individual. Primarily in the prophet Ezekiel, we find this idea on several occasions. «...I shall give them a single heart and I shall put a new spirit in them; I shall remove the heart of stone from their bodies and give them a heart of flesh...» (Ezek 11:19; cfr. 18:31; 36:26f). The return from exile and the reestablishment and reconstitution of the people is presented by the same prophet with the metaphor of resurrection by action of the Spirit that vivifies dry bones (Ezekiel 37:1-14; v. 14: «[I will] put my spirit in you, and you revive, and I resettle you on your own soil. Then you will know that I, Yahweh, have spoken and done this — declares the Lord Yahweh»). Other writings also speak of this presence of the Spirit in the depths of human beings, who are in this way internally transformed, although always depending on this divine presence: «God, create in me a clean heart; renew within me a resolute spirit, do not thrust me away from your presence, do not take away from me your spirit of holiness» (Ps 51:12-13)[18]. In a similar way, according to the book of Wisdom, the Spirit, virtually identified with Wisdom itself, dwells inside human beings. (cfr. Wis 1:4-6; 9:17).

In the Old Testament there is a process of personification as related to the Spirit, although less marked than in the case of the book of Wisdom. The Spirit of God gradually ceases to be a passing force that erupts in human beings in exceptional moments with an external and sporadic action, and becomes instead a principle that, by maintaining its transcendence, turns into something which is inside people to renew them in their behavior and to enable life faithful to God and to his covenant.

---

18 This is one of the few passages where the expression appears in the Old Testament. Cfr. footnote 143 of the previous chapter.

Without attempting to see an anticipated revelation of the divine Trinity in the Old Testament, we can offer evidence that all these figures prepare for this revelation. The verification will be justified *a posteriori*. The New Testament and the Christian tradition, as stated before, have referred to these mediating figures. The first three of them, primarily the Word and Wisdom[19], have mostly helped interpret the saving function and affirm the divinity of Jesus. The continuity, even the terminological continuity, of the Spirit of God in the two Testaments does not deserve any special comments. Nevertheless, we should not underestimate the innovation of the presence of the Spirit in Jesus, the Christ, the Messiah, announced and expected by the prophets, and the gift of his own Spirit that the Lord, once risen from the dead, gives to his Church and to all humankind.

[19] However, we will see that some Fathers, for instance Irenaeus, have combined wisdom with the Holy Spirit. The book of Wisdom, as noted before, is a precedent for this connection.

The history of Trinitarian Theology and Dogma in the ancient Church

The Apostolic and the Apologetic Fathers

A difficult journey of reflection which began in the apostolic era and continued through the end of the fourth century enabled the formulation of the key elements of the dogma of the Church concerning the one and triune God and more specifically, the divinity of the Son and the Holy Spirit in the unity of being with God the Father, thus comprising the one and only God. In a highly summarized manner, we will continue in this part of our treatise to explore the evolution of this dogma[1], concluding with a brief review of the most important magisterial documents on the topic of the Trinity that were written in subsequent times.

1

The Apostolic Fathers

The oneness of God is a basic constant of the New Testament. At the same time however, the New Testament presents to us the Son and the Holy Spirit united with the Father in the saving act and in the formula of baptism. Jesus Christ, the only begotten Son, is the only mediator between God and humanity and also is presented as united with the Father in the act of creation. The Holy Spirit is closely united with the Father and the Son when he fulfills the work of salvation. Hence, it should come as no surprise that from the very beginning, these «three» are manifested as united in the Christian writings. As is the case in the New Testament, in the old patristic writings «God» is, in general terms, the Father. He is the initiator in creation and in salvation. He is the one who sends the Son and the Holy Spirit. Indeed, when the writings that can be traced back to the earliest Christian times are judged from the point of view of subsequent dogmatic evolution, there are considerable gaps and inexactness. Despite this fact, they are testimony of a faith that is always in search of formulations that could more adequately express what goes beyond words and human concepts.

---

1   In addition to the bibliography that we will be quoting, see COURTH F., *Trinität. In der Schrift und Patristik*, Freiburg-Basel-Wien 1988; SESBOÜÉ B. - WOLINSKI J., *Le Dieu du salut*, Paris 1994; DEL COVOLO E. (ed.), *Storia della Teologia I*, Bologna 1996 ; *Dio nei Padri della Chiesa* (Dizionario di Spiritualità Biblico-Patristica 14), Roma 1996; STUDER B., *Dios Salvador en los Padres de la Iglesia*, Salamanca 1993.

In the letter to the Corinthians by St. Clement, the Bishop of Rome (†circa100), we find clear evidence of the Roman theological environment at the end of the first century. Trinitarian formulas are present during the time of Clement, already more so than is Trinitarian theology. Some quotations of the clearest texts follow: «Why have you sown discord among you… Do we not have only one God, only one Christ, and only one Spirit of grace that has been poured into us»[2]? It is indeed quite curious that the discord in the Church is precisely what gives way to this triadic formula. Nevertheless, this formula does not emphasize the unity of the three, as might be expected, but rather that each of them is «unique». The three are also mentioned in other writings: «Because God lives and the Lord Jesus Christ lives, and the Holy Spirit lives, so do the faith and the hope of the chosen ones»[3]. Clement knows the only God ($\theta\epsilon\acute{o}\varsigma$), the Father next to whom is the Lord Jesus Christ who is invoked together with the Father. The mention made of the Spirit in the third place in these passages should not be interpreted in the strict sense of Trinitarian theology. However, it shows that the tradition of combining the three names is prevalent, which means that the three of them are united in the consciousness of the believers[4].

The Father is called $\theta\epsilon\acute{o}\varsigma$, $\delta\epsilon o\pi o\tau\acute{\eta}\varsigma$, Lord of creation. The divine Fatherhood refers frequently to the creation: «Let us turn our eyes to the Father and Creator of all the cosmos… The heavens moved by his rule…»[5]. Mention is made only once of the Father in relation to Christ: «Let us turn our eyes to the blood of Christ and acknowledge that it is precious to God, his Father…»[6].

Christ exists before his incarnation. The Holy Spirit already spoke about him, and he himself already speaks in the Old Testament[7]. Nevertheless, there is no precise idea of his pre-existence. As we have already seen, the Holy Spirit has been poured out on all Christians. He has spoken in the Old Testament[8]. Like

---

2   *1 Clem.* 46,6 (FP 4,130).

3   *1 Clem.* 58,2 (144); cfr. as well 42,2-3 (124); 1,3-2,2 (70). In this last one, mention is made of the pouring out of the Spirit, as is the case in 46,6.

4   MARTÍN J.P., *El Espíritu Santo en los orígenes del cristianismo*, Zurich 1971: «Clement… shows no signs of having understood in depth these literary formulas that he himself repeats. Nevertheless, we count on these texts as evidence of the lines of a developing trait that goes beyond the intelligence or the mentality of each of these witnesses».

5   *1 Clem.* 19,2-20,12 (96-100); this is a beautiful text on the creation.

6   *1 Clem.* 7,4 (FP 4,70); very indirectly speaks about the generation of the Son (Cfr. Ps 2,7); also ibid. 36,4 (118).

7   Cfr. *1 Clem.* 16,2.15 (90;92).

8   In addition to 16,2, cfr. also 8,1; 13,1 (80;88).

wise, Paul and Clement write under the guidance of the Spirit[9]. There are, however, still no clear formulas about the divinity of the Holy Spirit.

Let us briefly refer to the so-called «second letter of Clement», from the middle of the second century. In this epistle, God appears as Father in relation to his sending of Jesus Christ into the world: «To the only invisible God, Father of truth, who sent us the Savior and leader to immortality, through whom truth and celestial life were manifested...»[10]. We must think of Jesus as God, so that we highly value our salvation[11].

1.2. IGNATIUS OF ANTIOCH

In the martyr Saint Ignatius (†circa 110) we find some points of contact with Clement of Rome. He also connects, in a way, the unity of the Church and the «Trinity»: «...strive to remain firm... in faith and love, in the Son, in the Father, and in the Spirit, in the beginning and in the end. Yield to the authority of the Bishop and to one another as Jesus Christ yielded to the Father according to the flesh, and the apostles to Christ, to the Father, and to the Spirit»[12]. Christians are «stones of the temple of the Father, all laid within the edifice of God the Father, raised to the highest by the mechanism of Christ —the cross— and aided by the Holy Spirit who is the hoist...»[13]. Hence, the three «persons» are involved in building the Church and in the salvation of the faithful. There are also statements that point to monotheistic faith. There is no need to stress that the only God who is mentioned is the Father, who is frequently called by this name[14].

Jesus Christ is directly called «God» on some occasions[15]. He is also «the knowledge (*gnosis*) of God»[16], although incipiently, some passages seem to pose the problem of the procession of the Son, as for example, «Jesus Christ came from only one Father (ἀφ' ἑνός πατρός προελθόντα)»[17]. After saying this,

---

9 Cfr. 47,3 (130); 63,2 (152).

10 *2 Clem.* 20,5 (FP 4,208). Is this celestial life related in any way to the Holy Spirit? Cfr. 14,5 (200): the Holy Spirit gives life and incorruptibility; cfr. MARTÍN J.P., *El Espíritu Santo...*, 161; mention is made of God our Father in 14,1 (196).

11 Cfr. 1,1 (174); cfr. 1,7; 2,7 (176;178). Here we see in advance an argument that will be used later in the times of the Arian crisis. Within this context, Jesus is called Father: 1,4 (174).

12 *Mag.* 13,1-2 (FP 1,136).

13 *Efes.* 9,1 (FP 1,112). Ibid. 9,2 (112f): «You are all bearers of God and bearers of the temple, bearers of Christ, bearers of what is holy».

14 Cfr. *Magn.* inscr.; 3,1; 8,2 (FP 1,128;132); *Filad.* 8,1; 9,1 (164;166); *Efes.* Inscr. (102).

15 Cfr. *Efes.* inscr. (102); 7,2, «God made flesh» (110); *Rom.* 3:3 (152).

16 *Efes.* 17,2 (120).

17 *Magn.* 8,2 (132).

Ignatius specified that God has manifested himself through Jesus Christ who is his Word that comes out of the silence[18].

The Holy Spirit is present in the incarnation and in the baptism of Jesus[19]. What Ignatius also tells us is that this Spirit, who acts on Jesus and who is communicated to the Church, «comes from God (ἀπό θεου όν)», and this is why he does not deceive us[20].

1.3. THE LETTER OF PSEUDO-BARNABAS

The epistle of Barnabas, from the end of the first century or early second century, gives evidence of the knowledge of the preexistence of Christ before the incarnation. God precisely addressed Christ when, as stated in Gen 1:26, he said: «*Let us make* man…»[21]. This exegesis was widely accepted in patristic times. Jesus is referred to on two occasions as the «Beloved»[22]. He is also the *kyrios*, the Lord, who endured his fate by delivering his flesh to destruction[23]. The Spirit which is poured out on us comes from the abundant source of the Lord[24]. This may be a reference to baptism. Prophecy is also attributed to the action of the Spirit[25].

1.4. THE DIDACHÉ

In the Didaché, which comes from the end of the first century, we find on two occasions the formula of baptism that appears in Matt 28:19[26]. The prayers contained in the celebration of the Eucharist are addressed through Jesus Christ to the Father[27]. The Didaché presents a Christology with archaic features in which

---

18 *Magn.* 8,2 (ibid.): «λόγος ἀπό σιγης προελθών». Are these remembrances of gnostic theology, at least with respect to terminology? Cfr. ORBE A., *En los albores de la exégesis iohannea* (*Ioh* 1,3), Romae 1955, 37-40.

19 *Efes.* 18,1: «The Christ, our God, from the lineage of David and of the Holy Spirit…»; cfr. 17,1 (120). We have referred to these texts in the third chapter.

20 *Filad.* 7,1-2 (164); a new coincidence, in this last issue, with Clement of Rome.

21 Cfr. *Ep. de Bernabé* 5,5; 6,12 (FP 3,168;176).

22 Cfr. 3,6; 4,8 (160;164); cfr. IGNATIUS OF ANTIOCH, *Esm.* Inscr. (FP 1,170); HERMAS, *Pastor*, Comp. IX 12,5 (FP 6,252).

23 *Ep. De Bernabé* 5,1 (168).

24 *Ep. De Bernabé* 1,3 (150).

25 Cfr. 6,14 (178); 9,7 (190), Abraham saw Jesus «in Spirit». Many Fathers have used the same expression. Cfr. LADARIA L.F., *El Espíritu en Clemente Alejandrino*, Madrid 1980, 27f. Jacob also saw «in Spirit» the figure of the future people, 13,5 (208).

26 In *Did.* 7,1-3 (FP 3,96).

27 Cfr. *Did.* 9,1-4 (98).

Jesus is shown as the «servant»[28]. Apart from the lines contained in Matt 28:19 we have found no mention of the Spirit.

1.5. THE «SHEPHERD» OF HERMAS

The existence of an adoptionist Christology in the «Shepherd», probably written during the first half of the second century, has been frequently defended. The basis for this interpretation is a difficult passage in which the Holy Spirit and the pre-existing Christ seem to be identified in a certain way:

> The pre-existent Holy Spirit, who created the whole of creation, God made to dwell in flesh, which he chose. This flesh, in which the Holy Spirit dwelt, served the Spirit well, and he walked in holiness and purity without defiling the Spirit at all. And because he lived in a good and pure manner and because he labored cooperatively with the Holy Spirit in every respect and behaved strongly and courageously, he was assumed into partnership with the Holy Spirit. God was pleased with the behavior of this flesh, while having the Holy Spirit on earth, because it did not defy him. He took the Son and the glorious angels as fellow counselors so that the flesh itself, which had irreproachably served the Spirit, had a place to dwell so that it did not appear to have lost the reward for his service. Indeed, every flesh in which the Holy Spirit has dwelt will receive its reward if it remains spotless and pure[29].

The traditional interpretations that were used to find an unsatisfactory Trinitarian and Christological reflection in this text have recently been the subject of discussion[30]. The purpose of these interpretations was not seen as addressing the Son of God, who is not mentioned in any part of the passage, but rather the Holy Spirit, the one who is united with humanity and whom humans must obey in order to be saved. Only in the final reference to the Son, along with the glorious angels, is specific mention made of the Son of God. He is seen as the mediator of salvation, although on very few occasions, if any, is mention made of the incarnation and the Son's historical work. The Son of God is transcendent and glorious, although he is never given the title of Lord, no doubt in order not to compromise rigorous monotheism. This interpretation, however, has not been

---

28 Cfr. *Did.* 9,3 (98); 10,2 (100); the «Name» also appears: 10,2-3 (100): «We thank you for your holy Name»; «You have created the universe as a result of your Name».
29 HERMAS, *Pastor*, comp. B 6,5-8 (FP 6,198f).
30 Cfr. HENNE PH., *La christologie chez Clément de Rome et le Pasteur d'Hermas*, Fribourg 1992.

fully accepted. It seems that we cannot rule out a certain Christological interpretation of the text which has been the most common interpretation. The son of the parable could be the «spirit» who pre-exists in God, although he is not the Holy Spirit as a third person. On many occasions, the divine nature, specifically that of Jesus, has been referred to as «Spirit» during the first Christian centuries[31].

In the case of the Apostolic Fathers we have found some triadic formulas, but we cannot speak of a highly complicated Trinitarian theology. Nevertheless, the theology of the relationship between the Father and the Son is somewhat more developed. The existence of Christ prior to the incarnation is ratified, and he is even called «God» with a certain frequency. The Spirit is related to prophetic inspiration and to the conception of Jesus, and in some cases he is seen as poured out upon us, probably alluding to baptism. Gradually the same repetition of the triadic formulas, in the first place that of Matt 28:19, will lead us to a deeper analysis of the contents that are expressed in them.

2

The Apologetic Fathers

With the Apologetic Fathers, the Church gradually and slowly started on the path of Trinitarian reflection per se. The main concern of these theologians was, on the one hand, to defend the faith among Christians in order to protect it from possible misunderstandings, while on the other hand, to set forth the coherence of Christianity vis a vis Jews and pagans. This forced them to initiate a speculative effort which was no longer a repetition of the traditional formulas, and neither was it merely the announcement of salvation in Jesus. Precisely, the concern for the latter leads us to ask ourselves the reason for the transcendent salvation offered to us by God. At the beginning, the reflection revolved around the Father-Son relationship. Later, the Holy Spirit will be introduced gradually. Nevertheless, the generation of the Logos, the Son of God, was to a greater extent the main concern of the Apologetic Fathers in the issue that we are now addressing.

---

31 Cfr. a summary of this condition under analysis in Ayan J.J., *Hermas. El Pastor* (FP 6), Madrid 1995, 35-41. Cfr. also Simonetti M., «Il problema dell'unità di Dio a Roma da Clemente a Dionigi» in *Studi sulla cristologia del II e III secolo*, Roma 1993, 183-215; esp. 187ff; Steward A. - Sykes, «The Christology of Hermas and the interpretation of the fifth similitude» in *Aug* 37 (1997) 273-285.

Saint Justin, philosopher and martyr who died in Rome circa 165, must be the first of these Fathers to deserve our attention, because he is no doubt the most significant of the Apologetic Fathers. Monotheism was an undisputed issue, a conviction that the philosopher shared with Trypho the Jew, his interlocutor in the *Dialogue*[32]. God always exists in the same way: immutable and the cause of everything that exists[33]. He is, at the same time, the «unbegotten (ἀγέυυητος) Father of the universe. No name has been given to him because everything that bears a name implies that there is someone older who gave him that name. The "names" of Father, God, Creator, Lord, Master, are not really names, but designations derived from his benefits and from his acts»[34].

The mention made of the Father, however, appears together with that of the Son. This is how the text that we have just quoted continues: «As to the Son, the only one who can strictly speaking be referred to as the Son, the Word who is with him before all creation and who is begotten from the beginning when God created and ordered all things by his power, is called Christ because of his anointing and because God ordered all things through him»[35]. Here we are faced with the idea of a «generation», a metaphor that is fostered with the name of the Son which is taken from the New Testament. The Son, or Word, is with God before all creation (cfr. John 1:1-3). We can think that his «generation» is related to creation, in other words, the Word came into existence when God created all things through the Word. This is the Son of God who as God began to exist. The one who was born from Mary does not begin to exist at that point in time. The Son of the Creator of the universe pre-existed as God (being God, θεός ὄυ) and was begotten as man from a virgin[36]. The fact that the Son existed before human birth is shown in his presence in the theophanies of the Old Testament, which are re-

---

32 Cfr. *Dial. Tryph.* 1,4 (BAC 116,301).

33 *Dial. Tryph.* 3,5 (306).

34 *2 Apol.* 6,1-2 (ed. Wartelle, 204). Frequently, mention is also made of the Father as he relates to creation, as we can see in CLEMENT OF ROME; cfr. for example, *Dial. Tryph.* 74,1.3 (BAC 116,435); 76,3-7 (438ff), through Christ we can know the Father.

35 *2 Apol.* 6,3 (ed. Wartelle, 204); a clear distinction with respect to the human generation that will be referred to in the following lines, ibid. 46 (204): «Jesus is the name of a man… Because … the Word was made man and was born by the will of God the Father…».

36 Cfr. *Dial. Tryph.* 48,2 (BAC 116,381); in other places mention is made of the Son or Logos as God, in general without the preceding article; *1 Apol.* 63,15 (Wartelle, 186): *Dial.* 56,1.4 (394); 61,1 (409); 63,5 (414); 126,2 (523).

ally manifestations of the Son, according to the well-known thesis of Justin, who would have so many followers during the first Christian centuries[37].

Jesus, the Word, is the Son of God in a very real sense. This is what leads to the frequent mention made of his generation, in contrast with the unbegotten Father. Jesus Christ is indeed the only Son born from God, begotten by «him who is God and Father of the universe»[38], being his Word, the first-born and power from God (πρωτότοκος καί δύναμις)[39]. How does this generation take place?

God, beginning before all creation, begot certain rational power from himself[40] which is also referred to as Glory of the Lord by the Holy Spirit, and on some occasions, Son… All of these different designations are the result of being at the service of the will of the Father and of having his being engendered by the decision of the Father. And do we not see something similar in us? In fact, when we utter a word, we coin the word, not by an excision, so as to decrease the reason that there is in us when we utter it. We also see something very similar in one fire that is lit with another one, without decreasing the one from where we took the flame… The word of wisdom will be the one that gives me its testimony, because it is God engendered from the Father of the universe…[41].

We must retain some elements of this important passage. In the first place, we must retain the intellectual and not the physical generation. God produces a rational power that we see identified with his wisdom. In the second place, this generation is intellectual, and as such, it is not a blind process, but instead it comes from the will of the Father. Perhaps we must establish a relation between this desire and the fact of a generation related to the creation of the world. Theology must continue laboring in order to reach the clear conclusion that the generation of the Son belongs to the being itself of God and that it is not the result of a contingent decision, and that despite this, it is still free. Finally, the generation does not take place as a result of a material splitting or division. It does not decrease the

---

37 Cfr. *Dial. Tryph.* 50,1ff; 56,1ff (385ff; 394ff); *1 Apol.* 63,1ff (184ff).

38 *Dial.* 63,3 (414); once again the Fatherhood in relation to creation; it seems that from this we go to the Fatherhood with respect to the Word.

39 *1 Apol.* 23,2 (128); ibid. 21,1 (126, the word πρώτου γέννημα, the first offspring of God. On the Apology, cfr. MUNIER CH., *Justin. Apologie,* Fribourg 1996.

40 γεύέυυηκε δύυαμιυ τιυα ἐξ ἑαυτοῦ λογικήυ. Cfr. ORBE A., *Hacia la primera teología de la procesión del Verbo,* Romae 1958, 565 and following; SIMONETTI M., *Studi sulla cristologia del II e III secolo,* Roma 1993, 75.81. Cfr. also *Dial. Tryph.* 62,4 (412), offspring coming from the Father, προβληθέυ γέννεημα; there may be a gnostic influence in the terminology.

41 *Dial. Tryph.* 61,1-3 (409).

being of the Father as explained by the metaphor of one fire that lights another fire. It is worth noting that without being exactly identical, there is a similarity between this metaphor and that of the «light of light» of the Council of Nicea. This begotten one, (γέυυημα), who was with the Father before all creation, is the one who elicits the words of Gen 1:26, according to the exegesis of Pseudo-Barnabas that we already have seen[42]. Hence, there is a real distinction between the two. The Son truly is different from the Father. He is not confused with him.

This distinction of the «persons» was strongly emphasized by Justin when he also ratified the unity of the Son with the Father:

> This power would be indivisible and inseparable from the Father, in the way in which [the adversaries] say —the light of the sun that illuminates the earth is inseparable and indivisible from the sun that is in the sky. And just as the sun, when it sets, takes the light along with it, hence… in the same way, whenever the Father wishes, he gives from himself some power, and when he wishes he takes it back to himself… This power… is not only different on account of the name, from the light of the sun, but it is also numerically another (αριθμώ έτερόυ)[43], and I have mentioned that this power is engendered by the Father by his own power and will, and not as a division or splitting, as though the substance of the Father would be divided… I thus gave the example of the fires…[44].

The well-known topic of the generation through power will reappear again. Nevertheless, this generation gives origin to a different substantial existence from the Father. Despite this clearly established distinction and the divine condition of the Word, the fact that this is another god, as stated by Trypho, is clearly ruled out[45]. Regardless, the speculative problem of unity and diversity is still not addressed in an objective manner.

When faced with this theology of the Logos, which has already been structured with an outstanding profoundness, mention is made of the Holy Spirit only as related to the saving economy. What is stressed is his acting as a prophetic

---

[42] *Dial. Tryph.* 62,1ff (411ff). Cfr. on this passage, compare also, ORBE A., *Procesión*, 669ff.

[43] The same expression is used in *Dial. Tryph.* 129,4 (528).

[44] *Dial. Tryph.* 128,3-4 (526f). Cfr. ORBE A., *Procesión*, 580ff.

[45] Cfr. *Dial.* 50,1; 55,1-2; 56,3 (385;392f;394). Cfr. on this matter HENNE PH., «Pour Justine, Jésus est-il un autre Dieu?» in *RSPhT* 81 (1997) 57-68.

Spirit[46]. The Spirit has also acted in the life of Jesus. The incarnation is the work of the Spirit, although in this case there is a certain amount of confusion with the Son[47]. The Holy Spirit has descended on Jesus in his baptism, without Jesus having any need for this, so that after descending on Christ, the Spirit can be poured out on all Christians[48].

Finally, we must mention some triadic formulas that we find in doxological and liturgical contexts, which show that the Trinitarian faith has been developed in the *cultus* and in the life of faith of the Church, as for example, «We worship the maker of the universe... Jesus Christ... who we have learned is the Son of the true God and whom we have in the second place, as well as the prophetic spirit whom we have in the third place»[49]. The baptismal triad also appears on certain occasions[50]. The doxology that has as its purpose «God and Father of the universe, in the name of his Son and by the Holy Spirit» also appears in a Eucharistic context[51]. Justin even pictures the Trinity in the writings of Plato, who «gives the second place to the Word that comes from God and that from God is said to be disseminated as an "X form" in the universe; and the third one to the Spirit who moved over the waters» (cfr. Gen 1:2)[52]. Nevertheless, the reflection on the unity of the three has not yet been developed.

2.2. **TATIAN**

The intuitions of Justin will be developed by the other Apologetic Fathers. If this philosopher insisted on the fact that the Father was not diminished because of the generation of the Son, the main concern of his disciple Tatian († after 172) was to show that this generation does not mean a separation in God, and that as a result of this, monotheism is maintained. Justin was aware that Jesus is not another god, although he still did not give a clear and articulated answer to this objection of Trypho the Jew. Tatian did so in a fundamental passage of *Ad Graecos*:

---

46 Cfr. *1 Apol.* 31,1; 61,13 (136;184); *Dial.* 38,2 (364); 113,4 (499), Joshua already received the strength of the Spirit from Jesus; 25,1 (341), the Holy Spirit speaks by word of Isaiah; 34:1 (356), dictates a psalm to David.

47 Cfr. *1 Apol.* 33,5-6 (142); cfr. *Dial.* 100,5 (479).

48 Cfr. *Dial.* 87-88 (458-462). Cfr. ORBE A., *La unción del Verbo*, Romae 1961, 21-82.

49 *1 Apol.* 13,1-3 (112); cfr. also 6,1-2 (104), mentioning the angels after Jesus.

50 Cfr. *1 Apol.* 61,3; cfr. ibid. 11-13 (182-184).

51 *1 Apol.* 60,3 (188f.); cfr. 67,2 (190).

52 *1 Apol.* 60,5-7 (180); cfr. the whole context. On those passages cfr. MARTÍN J.P., *El Espíritu Santo*, 243ff; in more general terms, AYÁN J. A., *Antropología de san Justino*, Santiago de Compostela-Córdoba, 1988; also MEIS A., *La fórmula de fe "Creo en el Espíritu Santo en el siglo II. Su formación y significado*, Santiago de Chile 1980, 157-179.

God was in the beginning; but we have received from the tradition that the beginning was the power of the Word (cfr. John 1:1). The master of the universe (δεσπότης) … when the creation had not yet been completed, was alone. However, since all the power of what is visible and invisible was within him, everything was founded by him from himself through the power of the Word. Furthermore, the Word (προπηεδα)[53] emerges by the will of his singularity. And the Word, which did not come out of the void, is the first work of the Father. We know that he is the beginning of the world; but this was not the result of a division (ἀπόκοπήν), but of participation (μερισμόν), because what is divided ends by being separated from the initial object or subject. Nevertheless, what is the result of participation and takes the nature of a dispensation (ὀικουομία) does not take away anything from the place from where it is taken. Because in the same way that many fires can be lit from one same torch, and not because many are lit, does the light of the first one decrease, in this same way the Word, coming from the power of the Father, did not leave the one who had engendered him without reason (*alogos*) … the Word, engendered in the beginning, after matter was made, engendered our creation…[54].

Tatian referred to the metaphor of fire, which had already been used by Justin, in order to explain the generation of the Son. The Father is not diminished with this generation because this is no physical division, but rather a participation in his being. Because of this, the Father is never left without reason. Likewise, the will of the divine single being is the basis for the origin of the generation of the Word.

Another fundamental element that we find in Tatian is the definition of God as Spirit (cfr. John 4:24)[55]. However, it is clearly stated that it is not the Spirit which permeates matter[56], but the creator of the material spirit and of the forms of matter itself. The Word, never referred to as the Son, participates in this spiritual condition. «The celestial Word —a spirit that comes from the spirit and the Word of rational power, imitating the Father who engendered the Word— made man in the image of the immortal one…»[57].

---

53 Probably, according to ORBE A., *Procesión del Verbo*, 592, Justin would reject this «emerges» because it might give the impression that it could go back. We have seen how Justin rejected this possibility. Therefore, Tatian would probably accept the comparisons of Tertullian that we will refer to later; cfr. ibid. 584ff.

54 TATIAN, *Ad Graecos* 5 (BAC 116, 578f).

55 TATIAN, *Ad Graecos* 4 (577).

56 Cfr. also TATIAN, *Ad Graecos* 12 on the different «spirits» (258ff).

57 TATIAN, *Ad Graecos* 7 (580); cfr. also the continuation of the text.

The spiritual condition of God is in the Word which in this way possesses the same «nature» of God. This spiritual condition enables the generation to be understood in terms that are not material. Nevertheless, in addition to the «God-spirit», Tatian also refers to the «Spirit of God» which can dwell in the human body and which gives human beings their perfection[58]. However, this Spirit is not related to the Father and to the Son in the divine life. Therefore, in the case of Tatian, what we see is some sort of «binitarianism». Next to the Father is the personal Logos who participates in the divinity and in the spiritual condition of the former. The Spirit, the legacy of God who dwells in us, does not appear directly associated with them.

2.3. ATHENAGORAS

In Athenagoras (second half of the second century), as was already the case in Justin, and unlike what was the case in Tatian, we find again the ternary formulas. It is worth offering a deeper analysis of a long passage in which the triadic structure is clearly visible, and which in a way, could be a clear recognition of the beginning of Trinitarian speculation:

> We confess only one God, uncreated, eternal and invisible, impassible, incomprehensible, and boundless… surrounded by light and beauty and spirit and ineffable power, by whom (υφ᾽ον) everything has been created by means of (δια) the Word that comes from him (παρ᾽αυτον), and everything has been ordered and is maintained. Because we also recognize one Son of God… We do not perceive God as Father and his Son in the way in which many poets imagine and envision… but rather we see that the Son of God is the Word of the Father in both thought and act, because through him (πρός αυτοῦ) and by means of him everything has been made, and the Father and the Son (ευός ουτος του πατρός καί τοῦ υίοῦ) are only one. And in light of the fact that the Son is in the Father and the Father is in the Son (cfr. John 10:38; 17:21-33, among others) by the unity and power of spirit[59], the Son of God is the intelligence and word of the Father… The Son is the first begotten (γέννημα) of the Father, not as a fact (γευόμευου), because from the very beginning God, who is eternal intelligence, had in himself the Word, and this is entirely rational. On the contrary, he came (προελθών) [from God] when all material

---

58 TATIAN, *Ad Graecos* 15 (593): «The perfect God is free from flesh; nevertheless man is flesh; the bond of flesh is the soul and what retains the soul is the flesh. And if this is made as a temple, God wants to dwell in it by means of the Spirit that is his legacy».
59 Without the article; here we are referring to the essence of God, as we could see in Tatian.

things were formless and the land was inert… And this agrees with our reasoning of the prophetic spirit: «Yahweh… created me, the first fruits of his fashioning, before the oldest of his works» (Prov 8:22). And in all truth, the same Holy Spirit, who acts in those who speak prophetically, as we say, is an emanation of God[60], going forth and returning as a ray of sun… Then, who will not be surprised to hear that those who confess only one God the Father, one God the Son, and one Holy Spirit are called atheists when they show their power in unity and their diversity in order (τάξις)…[61].

This text contains many issues that may generate significant comments. To begin with, and as we have already mentioned, we could refer to the triadic structure that gives direction to this whole long passage, as well as the final formula which is more concise. The unity of the Father and the Son is strongly emphasized. It seems to be based on mutual indwelling and community of spirit. It resorts to Prov 8:22 when referring to the begetting in relation to the creation. The Word has been engendered for the commencement of the works of God, but the Word is not created, because God is always rational. Hence, there is a reference to the immanent logos that exists in God before the generation. Theophilus of Antioch is even more precise with respect to this idea. The Holy Spirit is united with the Father and with the Son. Nevertheless, there is still a certain amount of ambiguity in the idea of emanation —*aporroia*— that comes out and goes back to the origin as a ray of sun. We know that Justin rejected this idea in regard to the Logos. The Holy Spirit is not specifically called God, as does happen, conversely, in the case of the Father and the Son at the end of the passage. The dogmatic development addressed the issue of the divinity of the Spirit after the issue of the divinity of the Son had been addressed. However, despite these limitations, there is a final issue that is worth stressing: the attempt at discerning the plane where we should look for divine unity and the plane where we should take into account the difference or diversity of the three. Unity is seen in the power, in the *dynamis*. On the other hand, diversity is seen in the «order», the *taxis* that is evidenced between the three. This order shows that the three are not interchangeable in all aspects, and consequently there is a difference between them[62].

---

60 Απόρροια (cfr. Sab 7,25); cfr. also the same metaphor in *Legatio pro Christianis* 24 (687).

61 ATHENAGORAS, *Legatio pro Christianis* 10 (BAC 116,659-661). Athenagoras has stated before that there is only one God, ibid. 7 (656f).

62 Some expressions are repeated in *Leg. pro Christ.* 24 (687f): «We confess God and the Son, his Word and the Holy Spirit, unified according to power, the Father to the Son and to the Spirit because the Son is intelligence, word and wisdom (σοφία) of the Father and the Spirit is emanation

Unity and diversity are expressed in similar terms somewhat later:

> …the desire to know the true God and the Word that comes from him (παρ᾽ αὑτοῦ), whatever the communion (κοινωνία) between the Father with the Son, whatever the Spirit may be, whatever the union (ἑνωσις) of such great things, whatever the diversity within the unity of the Spirit, of the Son and of the Father[63].

The problem to which we alluded as Trinitarian in *strictu sensu* is once again posed here, although still in an incipient manner. Nevertheless, Trinitarian theology through all times would wonder about the uniqueness and diversity of the Father, the Son, and the Holy Spirit. Direct reference is made to the generation of the Son by the Father, but the issue of the Spirit proceeding is not yet addressed.

Other triadic formulas attribute to the Spirit a cosmic function due perhaps to stoic influences. «Indeed, if Plato is not an atheist… neither are we for knowing and confirming God through whose Word everything has been made and through whose Spirit everything has been maintained united»[64]. Here, the reference to the action of the Spirit in prophecy could not be absent, as it was quite a common conviction during those times[65].

2.4. THEOPHILUS OF ANTIOCH

We owe in the first place the Greek term τρίας to the *Ad Autolicum* by Theophilus († circa 186). Translated into Latin, this term would be *trinitas,* and it was used to refer to the Father, the Son, and the Spirit. «The three days that precede the creation of the heavenly bodies are a symbol of the Trinity, of God, of his Word, and of his Wisdom»[66]. It is worth noting that in this case, Wisdom does not refer to the Son, as we have seen up until now, but to the Holy Spirit. The same will be evident in the writings of Irenaeus of Lyons. However, there are certain doubts in this respect in the case of Theophilus. In one passage, Wisdom appears next

---

(ἀπόρροια) as the light of fire…». Some add after «according to power», «different according to the *taxis*».

63 *Leg. pro Christ.* 12 (663f).
64 *Leg. pro Christ.* 6 (655); cfr. also, in a rather less obvious way, ibid. 5 (653f). SIMONETTI M., *Studi sulla cristologia,* 89, states that when the Spirit is introduced into the life of the Trinity, these cosmic functions, which are then attributed only to the Son, disappear. This is what really happens in the text that has been quoted. There are still some doubts in the theology of the Spirit.
65 Cfr. *Leg. pro Christ.* 7 (657).
66 *Ad Autolicum* 2,15 (805).

to the Logos and seems to be identified with the Logos[67], but in others, it takes the place of the Spirit clearly differentiated with respect to the Logos[68]. Not much is said about the Holy Spirit or the Spirit of God in other contexts, although the inspiration of the Scriptures is attributed specifically to the Spirit[69]. For Theophilus, also, the Fatherhood of God is used in reference to creation[70]. It also affirms the monarchy and the uniqueness of God that is evident in the creation itself[71].

Nevertheless, the aspect which we are most interested in emphasizing, as related to Theophilus, is his doctrine of the two phases of the Word, the immanent Logos (ἐνδιάθετος) in the Father before the generation itself, and the spoken Logos, emanated (προφορικός) when God engendered the Logos to create the world through him.

The Word is always immanent[72] in the heart of God (ἐνδιάθετουευ καρδία θεοῦ), since before creating anything, the Word was his counselor because it was his mind and thought. And when God willed to do whatever was deliberated upon, he engendered this Word as spoken (προφορικόυ), the firstborn of all creation, not emptying and becoming devoid of his Word, but engendering the Word and always conversing with the Word[73].

In this way, the eternity of the divine Logos, which existed before being spoken, is protected, and the difficulty that could be entailed by the fact that the Father was reasonless and devoid of wisdom before the generation is eliminated. In the case of the authors whom we have studied previously, we have seen some reference to this problem that is clearly formulated in this work. Theophilus has explicitly differentiated these two stages of the pre-existing Logos (accord-

---

67 *Ad Autolicum* 2,10 (796); in this context, the Logos is also called «spirit». Union of Word and Wisdom, also in 2,22 (813); in both cases, reference is made to 1Cor 1:24; 1:30, Christ the power and wisdom of God. Cfr. SIMONETTI M., *Studi sulla cristologia*, 92.

68 *Ad Autolicum* 2,18 (808), God tells the Logos and Wisdom «let us make man...» (Gen 1:26). Here, we already see the Trinitarian expansion of the interpretation that was started by Pseudo-Barnabas. Cfr. also I 7 (774), where the same distinction is evidenced in the context of the creation of the world and commenting on Ps 32:6, one of the most commonly used passages in patristic theology to affirm the intervention of the entire Trinity in creation. Hence, it seems that we can state that in Theophilus there is a Trinitarian faith which is solid enough even if not perfectly developed.

69 Cfr. *Ad Autolicum* 1,14; 2,9; 3,17 (781;795;857).

70 Cfr. *Ad Autolicum* 1,4 (786); 2,22 (814): the father of the universe is the one who engenders the Word.

71 Cfr. *Ad Autolicum* 1,6 (773-774); 1,11 (778); 2,28 (819).

72 Cfr. also *Ad Autolicum* 2,10 (796); the immanent Logos in his heart.

73 *Ad Autolicum* 2,22 (813). Theophilus seems to refer to John 1:1, to the Word in God; the uttered Word seems to be stated in John 1:3; ibid. (813f). Cfr. concerning the Trinitarian theology of Theophilus, URIBARRI BILBAO G., *Monarquía y Trinidad. El concepto teológico «monarchia» en la controversia «monarquiana»*, Madrid 1996, 105-129.

ing to the thinking of those times), and the words he used for that purpose have become technical terms for referring to them.

His doctrine of the Logos is especially significant for the doctrine of the Apologetic Fathers. No doubt it is inspired partly, although not exclusively, by the prologue of John, and it has also undoubtedly gone beyond what that biblical text states. At the same time, it has shed light on the true divine Sonship of Jesus without explaining the «generation» based on human and animal models. Hence, the generation of the Word is seen as a process that is in keeping with the divine spiritual nature. The historical transcendence of this theology of the Apologetic Fathers has indeed been considerable. All the theories of the generation of the Son as a process of the intellect, which we will have occasion to see in the pages that follow, are based on it, at least indirectly. Its limitation, which will not finally be overcome even after the Council of Nicea, will be the lack of clarity concerning the «eternity» of this generation. In any case, this explanatory model enables us to affirm the divinity of the Logos as the Son of God, united with the Father. On the other hand, we should not forget that insisting on the action of the Logos in creation has enabled us to see the universal nature of the creative mediation of Christ, so that we can see Jesus as the power of reason behind the universe and also see the presence of his seeds throughout creation. Justin has developed this issue with special care. The theology of the Spirit is not as precisely developed in these authors, but we cannot forget the attempt of Athenagoras to analyze this issue, although in a very incipient manner, united with the Father and the Son in the Trinitarian life. On the other hand, Theophilus considers the Spirit the recipient, together with Son, of the Word of God in Gen 1:26 and also includes him in the divine *triad.*

The theology of the second century and the third century

At this point, we will begin to analyze the great theology of the last years of the second century and into the third century. We will primarily, although not exclusively, address three important figures: Irenaeus of Lyons, Tertullian, and Origen. We owe to them the considerable development of Trinitarian theology during this period of time. The meaning of unity and diversity in God, which was already the subject of an early reflection in Athenagoras, will be studied in greater depth with the development of a specific terminology. Furthermore, the theology of the Holy Spirit will become even more explicit, and although with somewhat more uncertainty, we will see the Father and the Son as being more united, not only in the economy of salvation, but also in the divine life itself.

1

Irenaeus of Lyons

Saint Irenaeus, Bishop of Lyons († 202-203), although born in Smyrna, is a bond of union between the East and the West. He did not follow the thought of Greek philosophy, as was the case with the Apologetic Fathers; but rather, he was concerned with the internal threat that gnosticism could be for faith. When faced with the complicated doctrines of gnosticism, which could only be understood by select people, Irenaeus emphasized that the faith of the Church is available to all. In his writings, the Bishop of Lyons offered us abundant formulations of Trinitarian faith[1], together with others that are limited to the Father and to the Son, without mentioning the Holy Spirit[2].

Many of his texts show the Trinitarian structure of salvation with formulations that frequently have their origin in the Holy Spirit who leads human beings to the Son, who in turn gives them access to the Father: «…the Spirit who prepares man for the Son of God, the Son that takes him to the Father, the Father who gives him the incorruptibility for eternal life which is granted to all because they see God»[3].

---

1 Cfr. *Adv. Haer.* I 10,1 (SCh 264,154); IV 33,7 (SCh 100, 818); V 20,1 (SCh 153,254); *Demons.* 3;6;10 (FP 2,56;62-64;75-77); we reproduce one of these formulas, IV 6,7 (SCh 100,454): «… in omnibus et per omnia unus Deus Pater et unum Verbum [Filius] et unus Spiritus et una salus omnibus credentibus in eum». Cfr. FANTINO J., *La théologie d'Irénée. Lecture des Écritures en réponse à l'exégèse gnostique. Une approche trinitaire*, Paris 1994, especially 283-309.
2 Cfr. among other passages I 3,6 (SCh 264,62); III 1,2 (SCh 211,24); 4,2 (46f); 16,6 (312); cfr. SIMONETTI M., *Studi sulla cristologia*, 97ff.
3 *Adv. Haer.* IV 20,5 (SCh 100,638f), cfr. also ibid. 6 (644); *Demons.* 7 (FP 4,65f); V 36,2 (SCh 153,460): «et per huiusmodi gradus proficere, et per Spiritum quidem ad Filium, per Filium autem ascendere

The Son and the Spirit already participated in the creating act of the Father. According to some passages, God is aided by the Logos[4]. Still, according to others, he relies on the assistance of the Logos and Wisdom —the Son and the Spirit— who are the two hands of God, according to the well known expression of Irenaeus[5]. Therefore, there is a basic correspondence between the creating act and the act of salvation. Everything comes from only one God (as compared with the thesis of Marcion) who does everything with his Son (the Word) and his Spirit (Wisdom). As we have already anticipated, Irenaeus identifies the Spirit with Wisdom. He addresses Wisdom further in cosmological contexts and the Spirit in soteriological contexts[6]. Wisdom is firmly grounded in faith in the Father, the Son, and the Holy Spirit. However, how are the three related in the divine life itself?

Irenaeus is quite moderate when he speaks about the generation of the Logos. He avoids the analogies of human psychology. Rather, he resorts to Isa 53:8 (according to the LXX): «Who could speak of his generation»[7]? Hence, he does not follow the line of thought of the Apologists. In view of the fact that he waives every speculation on the topic, it is quite difficult to determine the when and the how of the generation of the Word in the case of Irenaeus. Is it in relation with creation? This is something which is quite difficult to answer directly. This generation is from eternity because from eternity, at least ever since time began, ever since creation began, the Son has coexisted with the Father[8].

---

ad Patrem»; IV 38,3 (954): «Patre quidem bene sentiente et iubente, Filio vero ministrante et formante, Spiritu vero nutriente et augente…».

4 Cfr. *Adv. Haer.* II 2,4 (SCh 294,38); 27,2 (266); III 8,3 (SCh 211,94).

5 Cfr. *Adv. Haer.* IV praef. 4 (390); 7,4 (462f), God has not needed the ministry of the angels to create human beings; the same in 20,1 (626); V 1,3; 6,1; cfr. ORBE A., *Teología de san Ireneo* I, Madrid-Toledo 1985, 112ff; *Demons.* 5 (60-62).

6 Cfr. SIMONETTI M., *Studi sulla cristologia*, 100.

7 «Generationem eius quis enarrabit?»; cfr. *Adv. Haer.* II 28,5 (282); also *Demons.* 70 (FP 2,187). In the original, this phrase is not related at all to the problem that we are addressing: «Which of his contemporaries was concerned?», is the translation of the Jerusalem Bible. This verse has also been used in the tradition to point out the incomprehensibility of the virginal generation of Jesus. Cfr. in this sense *Adv. Haer.* III 19,2 (374); IV 33,11 (830). This is the way in which it seems to be interpreted by JUSTIN, *Dial. Tryph.* 43,3 (BAC 116,372); 63,2 (413); 68,4 (425); 76,2 (437); 89,3 (462); also TERTULLIAN, *Adv. Marc.* III 7,6 (CCL 1,517); *Adv. Iud.* 13,22; 14,6 (CCL 2,1389;1393).

8 Cfr. *Adv. Haer.* IV 20,3 (632): Wisdom was also with him before creation (ibid.): cfr. also II 25,3 (254), God had no need to be glorified by humans because before them the Son and the Spirit were also there; also IV 14,1 (538); III 18,1 (342); cfr. ORBE A., *Procesión del Verbo*, 197-198; *Introducción a la teología de los s. II y III*, Roma 1987, 50ff; *Estudios sobre la teología cristiana primitiva*, Madrid-Roma 1994, 5ff. *Demons.* 10; 43 (PP 2,78; 148-152), are texts that have posed a certain difficulty. See the *status quaestionis* in IRENAEUS OF LYONS, *Demostración de la predicación apostólica*, ed. ROMERO POSE E. (FP 2), Madrid 1992, 75-77; 148152. Cfr. also SCh 406,96.

For Irenaeus, the Son is God[9]. He truly participates in the divinity and comes from the Father. Nevertheless, the Bishop of Lyons retains the name ὁ θεός for the Father, following in this respect the tradition with which we are already familiar. Irenaeus believes that the divinity of the Son —which is not questioned— is compatible with a certain «subordination» to the Father. However, he has not reached the point of affirming a totally «perfect» consubstantiality between both[10], because the Son is not the same as the Father in all his attributes. Irenaeus is not a supporter of *homoousios* because this idea is too materialistic and gnostic[11]. The Son is the only one who gives us the knowledge of the Father. This aspect is especially significant in the theology of Irenaeus: «The Son is the knowledge of the Father»[12]; *visibile Patris Filius;* the Son is what is visible of the Father[13]. The fact of the revelation of the Father by the Son implies the unity of both. The Son is the only one who understands the Father. Nonetheless, the knowability of the Son compared with the unknowability of the Father can imply in certain respects that the Son is inferior to the Father[14].

If we cannot rule out the possibility that the generation of the Word is related to creation, it should not surprise us that for Irenaeus, as well as for the authors whom we have analyzed up to this point, God is «Father» by virtue of creation itself. The Father of the world is also the Father of Jesus who becomes our Father out of love: «That is the Demiurge: Father out of sincere affection, Lord out of power, our Author and maker out of wisdom»[15]. In many other instances, Irenaeus talks about the fatherhood of God as related to his love for us, because he gives us in Jesus his Son the knowledge of God[16].

---

9 Cfr. *Demons.* 47 (156).
10 Cfr. ORBE A., *Procesión del Verbo,* 659; he is not an exception in this regard as related to others of his time.
11 In *Adv. Haer.* II 17,2.3.4 (158.160), etc. *Eiusdem substantiae* is used in controversy with the Valentinians; cfr. ORBE A., *Procesión del Verbo,* 660ff.
12 *Demons.* 7 (FP 2,68); cfr. also the context that we partially know.
13 *Adv. Haer.* IV 6,6 (448f): «Et per ipsum Verbum visibilem et palpabilem factum Pater ostendebatur; etiamsi non omnes similiter credebant ei, et omnes viderunt in Filio Pater: invisibile etenim Filii Pater, visibile autem Patris Filius».
14 *Adv. Haer.* IV 4,2 (420): «Et bene qui dixit ipsum immensum Patrem in Filio mensuratum: mensura enim Patris Filius, quoniam et capit enum»; IV 20,1 (624): «Igitur secundum magnitudinem non est cognoscere Deum: impossibile est enim mensurare Patrem».
15 *Adv. Haer.* V 17,1; cfr. ORBE A., *Teología de san Ireneo* II, Madrid-Toledo 1987, 121ff. All the acts of God as demiurge are loved by him as Father.
16 Cfr. *Adv. Haer.* IV 20,1.4-5 (625.635-641); *Demons.* 8 (69-70); cfr. ORBE A., *Procesión,* 129.

We have seen how the Holy Spirit is united with the Father and with the Son in the confession of faith, and his role is very important in the creation and salvation of humanity. He is always eternal, everlasting. In other words, he can give eternal life to human beings, unlike the breath of life, the soul, which only gives them worldly temporal life[17]. As to the life of the Spirit in the heart of the divinity, Irenaeus is even more moderate in terms of the Son; but we can discover something about the divine property of the Spirit if we bear in mind the characteristics of his action:

> [The Father] did not need any help in making what has been made and for arranging the issues that referred to men. Rather, he had an abundant ministry that is impossible to describe. He is served in every aspect by his Son (*progenies*) and his figure (*figuratio*) —in other words, the Son and the Spirit, the Word and the Wisdom to whom all the angels are subjected[18].

The «making» and the «arranging» refer to the activity of the Son and of the Spirit, respectively. There is a difference between them when they are at the service of the Father. The *figuratio* of the Spirit is closer to the likeness to which Gen 1:26 refers. What belongs to the Spirit is assimilation from God the Father. He perfects in the dynamic order the act of the Word that is in charge of the «making». The Son is the image, the paradigm of creation. On the other hand, the Holy Spirit does not have any «form» whatsoever. He possesses the dynamism to vivify the act of the Son as his divine essence. Wisdom grants coherence to things; it is the principle of configuration, *figura ornamentorum*[19], which grants the substances that have been created even more divine adornment, which perfects them in their arenas of activity.

For Irenaeus, the creating Wisdom to which Prov 8:22 and following verses refer is the Holy Spirit and not the Son[20]. According to this, the Spirit would not aid the Father directly but would aid the Son who is the one who directly carries out the creation. The Son carries out the economy of the Father on humanity, while the Spirit assists him in order to enable us to achieve full likeness and di-

---

17 *Adv. Haer.* v 12,2: «afflatus igitur temporalis, Spiritus autem sempiternus», cfr. Orbe A., *Teología* I, 546f.

18 *Adv. Haer.* iv 7,4 (464). Cfr. for what follows, Orbe A., *Introducción*, 123-126.

19 Cfr. *Adv. Haer.* iv 20,1 (626), the differentiation in the functions of the Father, the Son, and the Spirit in creation.

20 Cfr. *Adv. Haer.* iv 20,3 (362).

vine assimilation. If the Spirit that we first possess today has made us call out «Abbá Father» (cfr. Gal 4:6), we can easily imagine what all the grace of the Spirit that will be given to humanity coming from God will do to us. «He will make us in his image (God), and he will realize the approval of the Father, as he who models men in the image and after the likeness of God (cfr. Gen 1:26)»[21]. In this way, we always have the Spirit associated with the work of the Son, with the creating mediation. He leads us to perfection, to the perfect likeness of God, of human beings created ever since the beginning in the image of the Son. The Word grants the Spirit to all living beings, according to the will of the Father. On the one hand, we have the creating act, but mainly the gift of spiritual sonship. «While the Father himself bears the weight of creation and of his Word, the Word, sustained by the Father, gives the Spirit to all beings, in accordance with the will of the Father, to some of them by creation…, to others by adoption»[22].

This differentiation in the saving economy might lead to something akin to the «immanent Trinity». A. Orbe writes an interesting page about the procession of the Holy Spirit, as seen by Irenaeus[23]. He sees a parallelism between the creation of Eve from the side of Adam, because it was not good for Adam to be alone, and Sophia, who comes from the Logos, and who is the divine «aid» offered by nature itself for protecting the work of the Logos and for endowing the world with harmony and life:

> The dream of the Logos —the origin of Sophia— will be simply the change of direction in the dynamism of his Son. Rather than looking towards God, in communion of life with him, the Son had to look toward the future dispensation in order to originate the personal and divine Wisdom of the world. Drawing an analogy with the origin of Eve, we now understand the nature of the origin of the Holy Spirit coming from the Logos. This is not a generative way of proceeding. It is closely related to the Logos, and it proceeds from its substance directly or indirectly under the influence of God the Father[24].

---

21 Cfr. *Adv. Haer.* v 8,1; cfr. the comment of Orbe A., *Teología* 1, 376ff.
22 *Adv. Haer.* v 18,2; cfr. Orbe A., *Teología* ii, 212ff; the Word that is given by the Spirit is the Word-man, supported by the Father as a creature. Cfr. also Orbe A., *Estudios sobre la teología cristiana primitiva*, Madrid 1994, 116f.
23 Cfr. Orbe A., *Estudios sobre la teología…*, 120-122.
24 Orbe A., *Estudios sobre la teología…*, 122.

Drawing an analogy with the creation of Eve from Adam, the Logos will be the immediate substratum from which the Father takes Sophia, the Holy Spirit[25]. Hence, we would have the Spirit associated with the Father and with the Son in the very heart of the Trinity, coming in the last expression from the former, although directly from the Son, for the perfection of the creating and saving act that he must carry out. The Spirit belongs to the immanent Trinity because from the very first moment the Spirit participates in the creation, although the distinction within the economic Trinity does not seem to have yet been fully attained.

2

Tertullian

186   Tertullian († after 220) was the one who coined the Latin Trinitarian vocabulary. He addressed and completed the set of problems that the Apologists had posed. The problem of unity and diversity in God is posed by him at a highly speculative level. His main work from the point of view of Trinitarian theology is the *Adversus Praxean*[26]. Praxean is presented at the beginning of the work as a *patripassian* who states that «the Father has come down to the Virgin, he himself has been born from her, has suffered; in summary, he is Jesus Christ himself»[27]. And further ahead, «in time the Father was born and suffered, the same omnipotent God is called Jesus Christ»[28]. Vis à vis this error, Tertullian sets forth the *regula fidei:*

> Nevertheless…. we believe in only one God, although with this dispensation that we refer to as "economy", which means that the only God also has one Son, his Word, that came from him and through whom everything came to be and without whom nothing was done (cfr. John 1:3-4). [We believe] that this Son was sent by the Father to the Virgin and was born from her —man and God, Son of man and Son of God— and was called Jesus Christ; that he suffered, died and was buried; that he was raised on the third day in accordance with the scriptures (cfr. 1Cor 15:3-4); that he was raised from the dead by the Father and taken again to heaven where he is sitting at the right hand

---

25 The tradition of the feminine nature of the Spirit is the one that is the foundation for this Adam-Eve-Logos-Sophia analogy.

26 I will quote him according to the edition of SCAPAR G., Q.S.F. TERTULLIAN, *Contro Prassea*, Torino 1985.

27 *Prax.* 1,1 (142).

28 *Prax.* 2,1 (144).

of the Father; and that he will come back to pass judgment on the living and the dead. After this, keeping his promise, he sent the Holy Spirit —paraclete, sanctifier of the faith of those who believe in the Father, in the Son, and in the Holy Spirit[29].

Hence, we must ratify the divine unity, which does not mean that the Father, the Son, and the Holy Spirit are the same. The divine unity that we are addressing here is evidenced in the development of the «economy». First and foremost, the unity is an intra-trinitarian reality, although it is seen in relation with the saving economy which is derived from it, beginning with the creation. God is one,

…because he comes from one in the unity of the substance, and at the same time, the mystery of the economy is protected, which determines the unity in the Trinity in the order of the three —the Father, the Son, and the Spirit. Nonetheless, they are three not because of their status, but because of their grade; not because of the substance, but because of the form; not because of the power, but because of the manifestation. However, the three are of one substance, one state and one power[30], because only one is God and from him these grades, forms, and manifestations are distributed in the names of the Father, the Son, and the Holy Spirit[31].

As we implied in previous paragraphs, this basic and important text shows us the already explicit reflection on the planes where unity and diversity in God take place. Unity is the starting point, a unity guaranteed by the Father from whom everything comes. This unity is based on the «substance», on the substratum of what the «three» are, vis à vis the mystery of the economy, which, as we already saw in the rule of faith, points toward the unfolding of the trinity of the «persons». The unity of substance also means unity in the *status* and in the *potestas*. The three participate in the same being that is originated in the Father. They belong to the same divine order, and they share the same power. On the other hand, diversity is evidenced at the level of *gradus*, of *forma*, and of *species*. This series of distinctions falls within another order that does not affect the radi-

29 *Prax.* 2,1 (144-146); cfr. *de praescr. haer.* 13 (CCL 1,197-198).
30 Athenagoras already placed in the *dynamis* the unity of the three; cfr. the text referred to in footnote 61 of the previous chapter.
31 *Prax.* 2,4 (146); cfr. also 19,8 (198); on these concepts, cfr. the introduction of SCARPAT G., to the edition of *Adv. Prax.* 84-98; URIBARRI BILBAO G., *Monarquía y Trinidad*, 169ff; the basic references are the studies of BRAUN R., *Deus Christianorum. Recherches sur le vocabulaire doctrinal de Tertullien*, Paris 1962; MOINGT J., *La théologie trinitaire de Tertullien* (4 volumes), Paris 1965-1969.

cal unity of God that Tertullian wants to clearly ratify. On the contrary, these distinctions are the concrete way in which we must understand this unity. Hence, the unity that in itself leads to the Trinity does not mean a destruction of the former, but rather, the way in which it is set up[32]. Together with the concept of *unitas* and in contraposition to it, we have that of *trinitas*, a key term that will be most commonly mentioned in the history of theology and that is the Latin equivalent to the Greek τρίας, with which we are already familiar. Hence, the divinity of the one God must be understood in this «economy»[33]. The one «monarchy», the one government, is not destroyed because a king has ministers and officers. Even less so will it be divided, because of the simple fact that God has a Son who himself shares in the monarchy, although it still belongs to the one who holds it[34]. God suffers no dispersion whatsoever due to the fact that the Son and the Holy Spirit hold the second and the third place, sharing (*consortes*) the substance of the Father[35]. The Son who comes from the substance of the Father («non aliunde deduco sed de substantia Patris»), and who does nothing without the will of the Father, does not destroy the unity of God. The same thing happens with the Holy Spirit, the third grade that comes from the Father and the Son («non aliunde puto sed a Patre per Filium»)[36]. The monarchy is not destroyed, but it is clear that the Father and the Son (and the Spirit) are not the same[37].

These three, united although not identified in all aspects, are frequently called «persons»[38] by Tertullian, and this is another term that will be greatly transcendent in Trinitarian theology and in Christology. In any case, we must be careful at this point not to see a complete development of the subsequent contents of this idea[39]. John 10:30 leads us to a distinction between the unity of substance

---

32 *Prax.* 3,1 (146f): «…expavescunt, quod oikonomiam numerum et dispositionem trinitatis divisionem praesumunt unitatis, quando unitas, ex semetipsa derivans trinitatem, non destruatur ab illa, sed administretur».

33 Cfr. *Prax.* 3,1; 11,4; 12,1 (146;168;170).

34 Cfr. *Prax.* 3,2-3 (148); cfr. on this issue, URIBARRI BILBAO G., *Monarquía y Trinidad*, 153ff.

35 Cfr. *Prax.* 3,5 (148).

36 *Prax.* 4,1 (150).

37 Cfr. *Prax.* 4,2-4 (150), on the delivery of the kingdom and the submission of Christ to the Father according to Cor 15:24-28; the one who delivers the kingdom and the one the kingdom is delivered to are two.

38 Cfr. among other places, *Prax.* 7,9; 9,3; 11,4.7; 27,11; 31,2 (158;162;168;170;226;236).

39 On the one hand, Tertullian faces the Latin use of calling individuals «persons»; on the other hand, the physical description of the interpretation introduces the literary fiction of characters who talk. In this way, the expression «in the person of» someone is used. Nevertheless, this is not the case here: the divine beings are really distinct. The one who speaks is different from the one who is addressed in this speech. With all these elements, and based on the different words

and personal differentiation. «The Father and I are one (*unum*)». Jesus does not refer to the personal identity, but to the unity in the divinity[40]. The three, united in substance and nevertheless distinct, are *cohaerentes*[41].

In order to explain this unity of the three, while at the same time pointing out the distinction, Tertullian has used a series of comparisons that have had a great influence on the tradition, either by being approved or rejected. A passage in chapter 8 of the *Adversus Praxean* is of the utmost importance in this respect:

> The trunk is not divided from the root, nor the river from the source, nor the ray from the sun, and neither is the Word separated from God. Therefore, according to the image offered by these examples, I confess that I talk about two — God and his Word, the Father and his Son, because the root and the trunk are two things, although united; and the source and the river are two manifestations (*species*), although undivided; and the sun and its ray are two forms, although linked (*cohaerentes*). Everything that comes from one thing must be something different to that from which it comes, although not separate, because when there is a second one, there are two things, and when there is a third one, there are three. The third one is the Spirit with respect to God and to the Son, as the third one with respect to the root is the fruit that comes from the trunk, and the third one with respect to the source is the stream that comes from the river, and the third one with respect to the sun is the spark that comes from the ray. At any rate, nothing gets away from the origin that grants it its properties. Hence, the Trinity, derived from the Father by the linked and related grades, is not an obstacle that stands against the monarchy, and it protects the *status* of the economy[42].

We can realize immediately how the words that we have already seen used in other texts to refer to what is common and to what is proper of each one of them are repeated here: *species, forma*, and at the end, also *gradus* and *status*. These are

---

that correspond to the Father and to the Son, we reach the conclusion that these two are real. Hence, they are called persons (as is also the case of the Holy Spirit). We will address the final development of this concept; cfr. MILANO A., «La Trinità dei teologi e dei filosofi. L'intelligenza della persona in Dio» in PAVAN A.- MILANO A., *Persona e personalismi*, Napoli 1987, 1-284, especially 11ff.

40 *Prax.* 25,1 (218): «Qui tres unum sunt, non unus, quomodo dictum est: *Ego et Pater unum sumus*, ad substantiae unitatem, non ad numeri singularitatem»; also 8,4 (160).

41 *Prax.* 12,7 (172): «ubique teneo unam substantiam in tribus cohaerentibus»; 25,1 (218): «Connexus Patris in Filio et Filii in Paracleto tres efficit cohaerentes».

42 *Prax.* 8,5-7 (160-162): cfr. the entire context, especially the previous one. Cfr. also 22,6 (206), «radius ex sole», «rivus ex fonte», «frutex ex semine»; mention is only made of the Father and of the Son. It is the same in *Apologeticum* 21,10-13 (CCL 1,124f).

terms that show the distinction between the persons. Nevertheless, they also show the unity of the three that is expressed in the term *trinitas*. The Trinity has the Father as its only origin, and it is not an obstacle that stands against the monarchy. In turn, it also defends the «economy» that is the specific modality of the unity of God. The Father, the Son, and the Holy Spirit are different from each other, and at the same time, they are inseparable. There is no division between them, although there is a distinction, so that each of them is really «another one»[43].

The expressions of Tertullian as related to the unity and the diversity of the three seem to imply a certain grading between them, although the common divinity is maintained:

> The Father contains all the substance; the Son is a derivation and a portion of the whole, as he himself tells us: «For the Father is greater than I» (John 14:28). In the psalm, he is also praised as inferior: «Little less than the angels» (Ps 8:6). In this way, the Father is different from the Son by being greater than the Son, because one is the one who begets and the other is the begotten; one is the one who sends and the other is sent; one is the one who makes another one through whom everything is made[44].

The distinction between the two is evidenced in their diverse functions in the creation and in the salvation of humanity. This leads to the intra-trinitarian distinction of the one who begets and of the begotten. All the substance is in the Father, and in the Son there is a derivation or *portio*. It does not seem to us that we must understand this term in the material sense, but rather in the sense of participation[45]. We are concerned here with the participation in the whole that is found in the Father in fullness. Nevertheless, this does not mean that the fullness of the divinity is found in the Son in the same way as in the Father. The biblical texts to which we have referred might lead us to think about a certain «inferiority» and not only as it relates to the personal distinction between the Father and the Son. The doctrine of the procession of the Word (and *a fortiori* of the Holy Spirit), which we will address very briefly at a later time, shows the difficulty of a total participation of the Son in the divinity of the Father. However,

---

43 *Prax.* 9,1 (162): «alium esse Patrem et alium Filium et alium Spiritum».

44 *Prax.* 9,2 (162).

45 ORBE A., *Hacia la primera teología de la procesión del Verbo*, Roma 1968, 592; MOINGT J., *Théologie trinitaire* III, 940ff. The *portio* also appears in 26,3.6 (220); *derivatio* and *portio* are united once again in 14,3 (178f).

we must clearly specify that this will by no means imply that the divinity itself is compromised.

Something must be said about the problem of the generation of the Son. If Irenaeus was prudent in this respect and rejected the analogy of the human mind according to the model of the Apologists, this is not the case with Tertullian. For him, the human psyche turns into the model based on which we can understand from where the Son proceeds. All this is justified because the human mind is an image of the divine spirit. Hence, the way in which the mind operates is used to explain what happens in the being of God[46]. We can identify some phases in the procession of the Logos.

In an eternal phase, the divine intellect contemplates itself; it is the divine intellect from eternity, without beginning. As Tertullian says, at the beginning God was alone; there was nothing beside him; but following this statement he corrects himself to a certain extent. He was not alone, because he had within himself his reason, that is, his own mind[47]. The intellect is oriented toward God himself. No passage of the Scriptures refers directly to this stage.

The second phase takes place before time, in preparation for the saving economy. The Logos, out of a free and positive will of God, contemplates itself in the light of the thought of the saving economy, where he will be known by others. This is the idea of an economy of salvation that, to a certain degree, is the transition between the contemplation of God in himself and the formation of personal wisdom.

In the third phase, also before time, we see the beginning, the conception, still inside God, and we have the internal personal word, the *endiáthetos logos* that Tertullian refers to as *sophia*[48]. This is the time to which the Scriptures refer in Prov 8:22, «Yahweh created me, the first-fruits of his fashioning…». God willed to produce in his substance and externally what he had determined in himself with his wisdom, his reason and his word. Things were already set forth, even made, in respect to the mind of God[49]. There was a need for them to appear and to be recognized in their form and in their substance.

---

46 Cfr. for the following text, ORBE A., *Introducción*, 96ff.
47 *Prax.* 5,2 (152): «Ceterum ne tunc quidem solus; habebat enim secum quam habebat in semetipso, rationem suam scilicet… Qua ratio, sensus ipsius est».
48 Cfr. *Prax.* 6,1ff (154); also 7,1 (156); cfr. *Adv. Herm.* 45,1 (CCL 1,434).
49 *Prax.* 6,3 (154). «Nam, ut primum Deus voluit ea quae cum sophia et ratione et sermone disposuerat intra se, in substantias et species suas edere, ipsum primum protulit sermonem, habentem in se individuas suas, rationem et sophiam, ut per ipsum fierent universa per quem erant cogitata atque disposita, immo et facta iam quantum in Dei sensu…».

The first day God created light (Gen 1:3). This is the moment of the perfect birth of the uttered, engendered word that comes from God. In this moment «the word itself receives its form and adornment, its sound and its voice, when God says: "Let there be light" (Gen 1:3). This is the perfect birth of the word, when it comes from God»[50]. Precisely when the word comes forth from God he makes him his Father[51], and hence he turns into Son, first-born, engendered before all things and only-begotten as the only-begotten by God. Ps 44:2, «eructavit cor meum verbum bonum» and 2:7, «tu es filius meus, ego hodie genui te», also apply to this moment[52]. This word has wholeness. It is differentiated from the Father. The Father and the Son are two. Hence, it is not a useless or empty word. It could not be so because nothing empty or devoid of substance or inconsistent can emerge from God. It cannot be deprived of the consistency through which the creating mediation will give consistency to all things[53].

The Word, born as the only begotten Son of the Father, is «spirit». In other words, he shares the common substratum of the divinity and the nature of the Father. In this way «the spirit is the substance of the Word, and the Word is the action or working of the spirit»[54], a common divine substratum. Hence, this is the way in which the Son's own personality is distinguished along with the spiritual substance that he has in common with the Father.

In Tertullian, we also see the problem of knowledge of the Son, as we evidenced before in the case of Irenaeus. This Son is knowable with a knowability that is prior to the incarnation. Hence, the theophanies of the Old Testament, as was the case for Justin and Irenaeus, show the Son. This visibility, vis à vis the invisibility of the Father, seems to be based on a certain «inferiority» of the Son. We

---

50 *Prax.* 7,1. The text continues like this: «conditus ab eo primum et cogitatum in nomine sophiae —*Dominus condidit me initium viarum* (Prov 8:22)—, dehinc generatus ad effectum —*cum pararet caelum, aderam illi* (Prov 8:27)—, exinde eum Patrem sibi faciens, de quo procedendo Filius factus est…».

51 *Prax.* 10,2-3 (164): «Atquin pater filium fecit et patrem filius… Habeat necesse est pater filium ut pater sit, et filius patrem ut filius sit»; Let us retain these ideas that will be basic further ahead for developing the doctrine of relationship, which is such a cornerstone of Trinitarian theology. *Prax.* 11,1 (166): «…illum sibi Filium fecisse sermonem suum». He has caused his Son by his word, engendering him. Cfr. ORBE A., *Estudios,* 3ff.

52 Cfr. *Prax.* 7,1-2 (156).

53 Cfr. *Prax.* 7,5-8 (156-158).

54 *Prax.* 26,4 (220): «Nam et spiritus substantia est sermonis et sermo operatio spiritus, et duo unum sunt». The Son is spirit coming out from the God with the personal form of Sophia; cfr. ORBE A., *Estudios,* 27ff.

cannot contemplate the sun, but we can see its ray[55]. In this way, the Son is the one who makes us know the Father, the Son being the one in whom the face of the Father is visible[56].

Something must be said about the Holy Spirit. On many occasions, mention is made of the Spirit as the «third»[57]. As we already saw in the *regula fidei* of *Adversus Praxean* 2, the Spirit is sent by the Son risen from the dead. All these aspects are emphasized in the following passage:

> He (Jesus) poured the gift (*munus*) received from the Father, the Holy Spirit, the third name of the divinity and the third name of the majesty, preacher of a sole monarchy and interpreter of the economy…, master of all truth, who is the Father, the Son, and the Holy Spirit according to the Christian mystery[58].

Tertullian continues to speak of the origin of the Spirit and about his divine condition. The Holy Spirit comes from the Father through the Son, «non aliunde puto quam a Patre per Filium»[59], as the Son comes from the substance of the Father. As we have already seen, the Word, the *sermo,* subsists in the common divine substratum. The Spirit, in a sense, would turn out to be the divine nature of the substratum. The fact of being *sermo* cannot be communicated, although the substratum by its own nature is communicable; hence, the communication of the Spirit that comes from the Father through the Son[60]. The *a Patre,* of the Father, would point toward two things: a) the remote and universal principle of the Holy Spirit, and b) the main agent in the causality itself of the Son. God the Father acts as a remote principle and also as a main agent in the procession of the Spirit *ex Filio.* The «spirit» can finally only be derived from the Father, and this is the Spirit that the Son is capable of emanating from himself, as the water that goes from the river to the stream or to the water course that is derived from

---

55 *Prax.* 14,3 (178f): «…invisibilem Patrem intelligamus pro plenitudine maiestatis, visibilem vero Filium agnoscamus pro modulo derivationis, sicut nec solem nos contemplari licet… radium autem eius toleramus oculis pro temperatura portionis»; cfr. the whole chapter 14 (178-182), on the revealing Son.

56 Cfr. *Prax.* 14,9-10 (182), a highly complicated text.

57 We have already seen in *Prax.* 8,5-7; cfr. also, 13,5.7 (176) and the passages that we will quote later.

58 *Prax.* 30,5 (236); 9,3 (162): «ut tertium gradum ostenderet in Paracleto…»; also 25,1, the Paracleto will receive Jesus as he receives the Father. Likewise, in 11,10 (170); 31,1-2 (236f), the Holy Spirit united with the Father and with the Son in the only divinity.

59 *Prax.* 4,1 (150).

60 Cfr. ORBE A., *Estudios…*, 106ff. Also for the following text.

it, and ultimately, from the source; or like the sun that is, in short, the source of the light that the ray can communicate to the spark, as well as other analogies and images described by Tertullian, of which we are also well aware[61].

As was the case with Irenaeus, so also in the writings of Tertullian, the differentiation between the Son and the Spirit can be reflected in the difference that exists between the image and the divine likenesses in human beings. Likeness is to the image what the personal Spirit is to the *sermo*. The Holy Spirit paves the way for the mediation of the Son and does not have any «form». He makes the human being, in his dynamism and life, similar to God. The Father carries out the first creation, formless; the Son, founded in his wisdom, carries out the second creation; and the Spirit inspires or vivifies the beings that are configured through the Word. Hence, by act of the Spirit the perfect likeness of the incarnated Word is attained, and this is the first model of the human being according to Tertullian. The creation of the human being is in this way an act of the Trinity. Tertullian, as had been the case before with Theophilus of Antioch, expanded the Holy Spirit, the third person, the «let us make» of Gen 1:26, which only referred to the Son, according to Pseudo-Barnabas[62].

We have seen that the Holy Spirit is gift, *munus*. We must retain that idea which will be widely addressed by the subsequent tradition. It is the gift that makes Jesus. It is interesting that the Father-Son-Spirit relationship emphasizes a parallelism: the Son is called *vicarius* of the Father because he makes him visible[63]. The same term applies to the Holy Spirit with respect to Christ. It is what makes him present and carries out his work among humanity[64].

---

61 ORBE A., *Estudios…*, 106: «The Word, in possession of its own Spirit, derived from the paternal *Pneuma*, is capable of emanating —from the Spirit himself— another one, a third one and granted "ipso facto" subsistence. And as assumed according to the analogy of the *fons / flumen / rivus*, they all have water as the common substratum. Hence, in his Trinitarian application, the *Pneuma* is assumed as a common substratum… As the *Pneuma* of the Son comes from the *Pneuma* of the Father, that of the personal Spirit comes from the Spirit of the Son. Hence, as the *Pneuma* of the Son does not come "in equal terms" from the *Pneuma* of the Father, but as a *portio totius*, by participation in him, in this same way, the *Pneuma* of the personal Spirit does not come "in equal terms" from the *Pneuma* of the Son, but as a participation in this *Pneuma* (very much like the *portio portionis totius*)».

62 *Prax.* 12,3 (170f): «Immo quia iam adhaerebat illi Filius secunda persona, sermo ipsius et tertia… ideo plurale pronunciavit: "faciamus"… Cum quibus enim faciebat hominem et quibus faciebat similem, Filio quidem qui erat induiturum hominem, Spiritu vero qui eran sanctificaturum hominem, quasi cum ministris et arbitris ex unitate trinitatis loquebatur»; cfr. 12,1-2 (170). Cfr. ORBE A., *Introducción*, 122f.

63 *Prax.* 24,6: «vicarium se Patris ostenderet, per quem Pater et videretur in factis et audiretur in verbis…».

64 Cfr. *De virg. Vel.* 1,4 (CCL 2,1209); *De praes. Haer.* 13,5 (CCL 1,198).

Tertullian offers us quite a complicated Trinitarian theology. Although he wants to maintain the divine unity in *Praxean* that he so much insists upon, he also emphasizes that this is not affected by the intra-trinitarian economy by means of which the Father communicates his divine nature —his «spirit»— to the Son, and by means of him, to the Holy Spirit. These three are one because of their substance, their «state», and their power.

3

Hippolytus of Rome

Our mission now is not to address the complicated issues of the authorship of the works attributed to Hippolytus, but simply to make some comments about the theology of *Contra Noetum* that will help us complete our panorama of the theology at the beginning of the third century.[65]

The Son, for Hippolytus, is «logos, spirit, and strength»[66]. The designations come from the tradition. The Father, who is spirit, engenders from his bosom a spiritual fruit, the Logos, which hence has a divine origin and a substantial unity with God. The divine Logos does not compromise the divine unicity, as Noeto, who has a patripassian inclination just like Praxean, believes. God is originally alone. There is nothing coeval with him. He creates because he wills to do so, and likewise he engenders the Logos according to his will[67], although out of his substance. From the beginning, the Logos lives in the heart of the Father. There is a unity of God and in God, an undivided distinction between the Father and the Son. God, even though being alone, was multiple, because he was not devoid of the Logos nor of wisdom; he was not devoid of strength, nor of will. Everything was in him, and he was everything[68].

The creating act is the first step in the distinction between God and the Logos. When he willed it, as he willed it, in the time that had been approved, God manifested his Logos, by means of whom he made all things[69]. Hence, there is a rela-

Chapter 6

195

65 Regarding the date when this work was written, cfr. Uribarri Bilbao G., *Monarquía y Trinidad*, 236-280. I quote the *Contra Noetum*, Butterworth R. (ed.), London 1977.

66 Cfr. *C. Noetum* 4,11 (55); cfr. 1 Cor 1:24; also Justin, *1 Apol.*14,5; 33,4.6 (Wartelle, 114;142); cfr. Orbe A., *Introducción*, 100ff.

67 Cfr. *C. Noetum* 10,3 (69); 16,4 (83); cfr. Zani A., *Cristologia di Ippolito*, Brescia 1984, 62.76.

68 Cfr. *C. Noetum* 10,2 (69).

69 Cfr. *C. Noetum* 10,3-4 (69); cfr. Zani A., *Cristologia di Ippolito*, 76f.

tionship between the Logos, which is the result of the will of the Father, and the created universe, which is the result of the same divine will. «Out of his own will, God utters the personal Logos, and by means of the Logos he then builds the world»[70]. Hence, God engenders the Logos in the order of the creation of the world. The divine will that engenders the Logos does not separate the Logos from the Father. The unicity of God is compatible with the economy. Hippolytus, as was also the case before with Tertullian, resorts to John 10:30, «the Father and I are one», to underline the unity and the diversity of Jesus and the Father[71].

As the Lord of creation, God gives forth his own intellect so that with this manifestation the world can be saved. Therefore, there is a relationship between the giving forth of the Logos for creation and the sending of the Logos to the world for salvation. The Logos turns into a persistent force, so that in turn it can be revealed salvifically in the incarnation. Hence, there is a relationship between the eternal procession and the human generation of Mary. The bosom of the Father is for the generation *secundum Spiritum*, precisely what the bosom of Mary is for the generation *secundum carnem*. The two of them take place when the Father wills it. According to what has been set forth, the first birth is directed toward the second one. The generation of God turns the Logos into «spirit», in distinction although not in separation from the Father. «Spirit» points to his nature; Logos is a personal name. The generation of Mary turns Jesus into man, flesh, because the Logos was *asarkós* before the incarnation. After the incarnation, he appears as the perfect Son of God, from the Spirit and from Mary[72]. Hence, «Son» is the name of the incarnate one. For Hippolytus, the δύναμις of God descends into the flesh, not the Father himself: «I came from the Father and have come» (John 16:28). Therefore, the personal distinction between the Father and the Son is maintained[73].

Nevertheless, there is a unity of δύναμις[74] that guarantees the unity of God. By virtue of the same power and force, the Father decides and the Son fulfills the will of the Father. There is a similarity with the union and a distinction of the same «spirit». The *dynamis* is at the same time the Father-Logos and the nature itself of God. The generation of the Son is differentiated from human and animal

---

70 ORBE A., *Estudios…*, 10.
71 Cfr. *C. Noetum* 7,1 (61); ZANI A., *Cristologia di Ippolito*, 96.
72 *C. Noetum* 4,10-11 (54-55).
73 Cfr. *C. Noetum* 16,2 (81); ORBE A., *Introducción*, 103ff; ZANI A., *Cristologia di Ippolito*, 140ff.
74 *C. Noetum* 7,1 (61), there are two πρόσωπα but only one δύναμις; also 11,1 (71), there is only one force that comes from the Father.

generation precisely because of the individual «distinction», according to the same divine spirit. In this way, God and the Logos are not two gods, but they are distinguished as light from the light, water from the fountain, and ray from the sun. One is the δύναμις that is derived from the whole, the *dynamis*-Logos that comes from the Father[75]. We have seen that Hippolytus speaks of two πρόσωπα as related to the Father and the Son[76], but never about three, so that the term «person» does not apply to the Holy Spirit. On the other hand, he refers to the «triads»[77] at the same time as he also uses some triadic formulas. «Through him (the Logos) we know the Father, we believe [in him] in the Son, we adore him in the Holy Spirit»[78]. In *Contra Noetum*, the theology of the Holy Spirit is clearly less developed than in Tertullian.

After the study of these Western authors, we must direct our attention to Alexandria in order to study the great Origen who set the standard for the noted theological school of that city, also as it related to Trinitarian theology.

4
Origen

The theology of Origen (†circa 254) is especially rich and complex regarding not only the issue we are addressing, but many other issues as well. Without attempting to be exhaustive, we will simply analyze some aspects that can shed a light on the evolution of Trinitarian theology. We will begin with a text that is a commentary on the gospel according to John, leading us to the broad field of problems that were addressed by this theologian from Alexandria:

See how the problem that troubles many can be solved because, by trying to be pious, out of fear of acknowledging two gods, they succumb to erroneous and impious opinions, either because they deny that the individuality of the Son is different from that of the Father —even though they profess as God the one they call the Son, at least by

75 *C. Noetum*, 11,1 (71); ZANI A., *Cristologia di Ippolito*, 141ff. Let us note the use of the similar comparisons to those of Tertullian, although in the latter they are more amply developed.
76 Cfr. *C. Noetum* 7,1 (61); 14,2-3 (75), in which he refers to the grace of the Spirit as the «third economy».
77 Cfr. *C. Noetum* 14,8 (77).
78 *C. Noetum* 12,5 (73); cfr. also 9,2 (67); 14,6 (75f): «we cannot think in the only God if we do not believe in the Father, the Son and the Holy Spirit»; different formulas are repeated throughout chapter 14 (75f).

name— or because when denying the divinity of the Son, they admit that his individuality (ἰδιώτητα) and his personal substance (οὐσία κατὰ περιγραφήν) are, in their inherent characteristics (ἰδιώτητα), different from those of the Father.

It is necessary to tell them that *the God* is God himself (αὐτοθεός), and that for this reason, he is also the Savior, as stated in the prayer to his Father: «And life eternal is this, to know you, the only true God» (John 17:3), although it would be more appropriate not to speak of *the God,* but *God,* because all is deified by participation in his divinity, with the exception of God himself (αὐτοθεός). Therefore, in an absolute manner, the first-born of all creation (cfr. Col 1:15), as he is next to God and is the first one to be impregnated with his divinity, is the one that most deserves honor among all those who also are gods…, because he grants them the possibility of turning into gods, taking from God the principle to deify, and in his goodness, making them share his liberality with the others.

Hence, God is the true God. The other gods that have been made according to him are like reproductions of a prototype. On the other hand, the archetypal image of these multiple images is the work that is next to God and remains always God, because God would not be God if he were not next to God, if he would not persevere in the uninterrupted contemplation of the depths of the Father[79].

As can be seen, many topics emerge from this rich passage. Above all is the relevant position of the Father, the only one who is «God in himself»[80]. The Son in other places is called the kingdom, justice, wisdom, reason in itself, but never *autotheos.* He is the «second God» (δεύτερος θεός)[81]. Being *the* God, with the preceding article, only pertains to the Father (cfr. John 1:1).

The text that we have quoted clearly shows the transcendence of the Father over everything that has been created. Only God the Father is transcendent over all. He is the ἀρχή, the beginning, as everything is derived from him[82]. He is also

79 ORIGEN, *In Iohannes* II 2,16-18 (SCh 120,216f); cfr. ibid. 149 (304f). Cfr. the comment of PELLAND G., *A propos d'une page d'Origène. In Joh.* 2,16-18, in DUPLEIX A. (dir.), *Recherches et Tradition. Mélanges patristiques offerts a Henri Crouzel,* Paris 1992, 189-198. In addition to the studies that we will be quoting, see WIDDICOMBE P., *The Fatherhood of God from Origen to Athanasius.* Oxford 1994.

80 As also the principle of all goodness that is shared by the Son and the Spirit, *Princ.* I 2,13 (SCh 252,140-142).

81 The second God appears in *C. Celsum* V 39 (SCh 147,118); *In Joh.* VI 39,202 (SCh 157,280). *C. Celsum* ibid. (120), the Son is reason in himself, wisdom and justice; the *autobasileia* appears in *In Mt.* XIV 7 (GCS, *Oratio* Wer X, 289). Cfr. ORBE A., *Hacia la primera teología de la procesión del Verbo,* Romae 1958, 420; also FÉDOU M., *la Sagesse et le Monde. Le Christ d'Origène,* Paris 1995.

82 Cfr. *Princ.* I 2,13 (SCh 140f); Cfr. SIMONETTI M., «Sulla teologia trinitaria di Origene» in *Studi sulla cristologia del II e III secolo,* Roma 1993, 109-143.

greater than the Son and the Holy Spirit. They are transcendent with respect to other beings, but they are surpassed by the Father. We can even mention a passage —indeed exceptional— that seems to compare the distance that separates the Son and the Holy Spirit from the Father, thus separating all creatures from them[83]. This further accentuates the singular position of the Father. At any rate, divinity, in its Trinitarian articulation, is clearly distinguished from the creatures. Only God has in himself substantially goodness and sanctity. The Son and the Holy Spirit are united with the Father from this point of view[84].

The Father, the beginning of everything, has internally engendered the Son. In the case of Origen, we find the first clear affirmation of this co-eternal generation with the being of the Father[85]. The Logos is from the very first moment the Son and has a subsistence of his own, even though it is incorporeal. There is no reason whatsoever for God not to have willed, or not to have been able, to always be the Father and to engender the Son[86]. No doubt, the divine immutability helps this conception. God is the Lord from eternity. He is effectively *pantokrator*, not only the one who can do everything in the abstract, παντοδυναμός. According to this, God has engendered the Son from eternity, he has willed to be and he has been the Father, because from eternity he has been the Lord of all creation, although he did not begin as creator. Hence, we could deduce that creation is eternal. Origen believes that an intentional co-eternity seems to suffice. From eternity the creation is made in wisdom. It is preformed and prefigured in it. This wisdom is identified with the Son, with the Logos[87].

Unlike the creation, however, personal wisdom exists as such and is not simply prefigured. God is always light (cfr. 1John 2:5), and the only-begotten is always the brilliant glare of that light[88]. This is what clearly determines the eternal procession of the Son, although there might subsist a certain relationship between the generation and the creation. In the case of Origen, it is clear that God

---

83 *In Joh.* XIII 25,151 (SCh 222,112-114): «We state that the Savior and the Holy Spirit are not comparable to all the beings that have been made, but that they go beyond them with an infinite transcendence; but they, in turn, are surpassed by the Father just as, or even more so, than the Son and the Holy Spirit go beyond the other beings». Cfr. SIMONETTI M., *Studi sulla cristologia*, 118.

84 Cfr. *Princ.* I 5,5 (SCh 252,192); in creatures, sanctity is accidental. Cfr. RIUS CAMPS J., «Orígenes y su reflexión sobre la Trinidad» in *La Trinidad en la tradición prenicena*, Salamanca 1973, 189-213, 199ff.

85 Cfr. *Princ.* I 2,3f (112-16); I 2,9; (130); IV 4,1 (SCh 268,400-402). Cfr. ORBE A., *Procesión*, 165ff.

86 *Princ.* I 2,2-3 (112-116); cfr. ORBE A., *Procesión*, 169.

87 *Princ.* I 4,4f (170-172): «In sapientia omnia facta sunt, cum sapientia semper fuerit, secundum praefigurationem et praeformationem erant in sapientia ea quae protinus substantialiter facta sunt». Cfr. also ibid. I 2,2f (112-116).

88 *Princ.* I 2,7 (124).

is not God before being Father; he is eternally the Father of the Son. Hence the Logos, engendered from eternity, is also the Son from eternity. The idea of the brilliant glare of the light has been developed by Origen in order to explain the Father-Son relationship in the saving economy:

> The glare of this light is the only-begotten Son, who comes from this light inseparably as the glare of light and illuminates all the creatures… In this sense, because he is the way and leads to the Father… in the same way as he is truth, life or resurrection (cfr. John 14:6; 11:26), we must also understand consequently the work of the radiance, because by the glare you recognize and you feel what light itself is. And this glare, when offered to mortal and weak eyes in the most serene and gentle way shows them and enables them to become accustomed to gradually and to bear the clarity of light, because it removes from them what obstructs or hinders their vision…; it makes them capable of receiving the glory of the light, also turned into a sort of mediator that will help men reach the light[89].

Thus, the Son manifests God to humanity. He is the splendor that makes God known. This can lead us to the intra-trinitarian relationships of the Father and the Son. Wis 7:25, and the following passage offers the theologian from Alexandria the occasion to develop a rich doctrine on the relationship of the Father and the Son[90]. The power of the Father is manifested in the breath that has no beginning. The emanation of the Almighty means that over whatever he exerts his omnipotence, it subsists. Hence, there is no omnipotence prior to the emanation that comes from it. The Son, emanated from God, shares the glory of the Omnipotent from eternity. God is light in eternity, and Wisdom is the glare of this light without any beginning or end. Other terms are less important with respect to the key issue of the light that is developed here. In the case of this type of affirmation, «breath of the power of God; emanation of the glory of the omnipotent; splendor of the eternal light; reflection of the power of God; image of his goodness», the expressions that refer to the Father show his transcendence:

---

89 *Princ.* I 2,7 (124). Cfr. ORBE A., *Estudios sobre la teología cristiana primitiva*, Madrid 1994, 41ff.
90 Let us remember the text: «Wisdom is a breath of the power of God, a pure effluvium of the glory of the Almighty…. It is a reflection of the eternal life, a spotless mirror of the activity of God, an image of his goodness». The comment of ORIGEN on this passage is found in *Princ.* I 2,912 (128-140). As we can easily assume, the second series of affirmations refers to the Father according to Origen, while the first one refers to the Son or subsistent personal Wisdom; cfr. ORBE A., *Estudios*, 44-52.

power, glory, eternal light, goodness. Those related to the Son indicate mediation and possibility of knowledge by human beings: breath, emanation, splendor, reflection, image… They are graces oriented to humanity, and not to God. The relationship of the Father to Wisdom is gratuitous; the fact that the Son proceeds from God is not «necessary», except only in the fact that the Father opts for the creation and the deification of humanity. All this is to their benefit. He does not pass on to the Son all the light or all the power of the Father, and so forth, which does not keep this Wisdom from having its origin in God himself. He is certainly God and not creature. God emits Wisdom with the same freedom with which he creates the world in which Wisdom exercises the mediating function.

In the text used at the beginning of this presentation on Origen we found the affirmation, strange at first sight, that the Logos is God because it is always with the Father contemplating him[91]. We must explain somewhat further the problem of the generation of the Logos, an eternal generation that as we saw, although it is free, is linked to the creating and deifying will of God.

The Logos is God by virtue of generation. There is an essential difference between the participation of the Logos in the divinity and the participation that is granted to creatures. Besides being divine, the Logos is a *hypostasis* on its own, as also suggested in the text on the commentary of John that has been our guide. The individuality of the Son, his *idiotes*, is different from that of the Father. It is the glare of the light, although it possesses a personal subsistence. On the one hand, the Son is natural, not adopted. But on the other hand, we have pointed out the freedom of his generation. Insofar as God the Son comes from the mind of the Father, as a person he comes from God's will. He is Son because of the will of God, and «Son» is the title of his personal subsistence[92], which leads to the formula *tamquam a mente voluntas*, the Son proceeds from the Father as the will from his mind[93]. This procession is a free activity in view of the correlation of the Logos to creation. The Father is absolute simplicity; however, this is not the case with the Son, in view of the plurality of his relationships with creation. His personality is in accordance with his economy. Hence, it follows that his generation is free in itself and in the concrete way of being of the Logos, as a function of the economy freely chosen by the Father. In the opinion of Origen,

---

91 *In Joh.* II 2,12 (SCh 120,215): «The Word is God because the Word is with God» (John 1:1).
92 Cfr. ORBE A., *Procesión*, 499.
93 Cfr. *Frag.* in GCS IV, 662; ORBE A., *Procesión*, 388ff; RIUS CAMPS J., «Orígenes y su reflexión sobre la Trinidad», 205f.

as well as in that of the Apologetic Fathers, the Son is the Son of the love of the Father (cfr. Col 1:13). He subsists because of the will of God, although he comes from God's mind, which will be the basic distinction with respect to the Arians: the divinity of the Son is by no means compromised by this «will» of the Father in his generation[94], as he comes «from God» in a completely different way than other beings come from him, because they exist as a result of creation out of nothing.

For us, the Son is the truth that reveals the Father to us[95]. As such, the «food» that he needs is the fulfilling of the will of the Father. Only he can make us understand the will of the Father; and also from this point of view, the Son is the Father's image[96]. Hence, all the being of the Son is oriented toward humanity, toward manifesting the thought and the will of the Father. Likewise, the fulfillment of the fatherly will is part of the condition of the «image» of the Son. For this reason, this divine will is the choice food of the Son himself by virtue of which he is what he is[97].

These ideas undoubtedly pose a problem for us. The Logos is God through the fulfillment of the fatherly mandate, by continuously being turned toward him and contemplating him, as stated in the text of *In Iohannis* at the beginning of our presentation. Is the Logos a «person» rather than strictly «God»[98]? When faced with the fatherly simplicity, the multiple relations of the Son with the world, the multiplicity of his *epinoiai* show the complexity of the Son in his person, all of which are directed toward the saving dispensation.

In principle, there is no reason why the Logos should have to be divine. Nevertheless, the Logos is God. Even though Origen apparently has not expressly posed this problem, the text that we have already mentioned, *In Joh.* II 18, provides us an answer in principle. In the Logos, there is a first phase of personal formation or development and another one of divine formation. In the first phase,

---

94 Cfr. *Princ.* IV 4,1 (SCh 268,402); I 2,6.9 (SCh 252,122.130).
95 Cfr. ORBE A., *Procesión*, 420.
96 Cfr. *In Joh.* XIII 36,228ff (SCh 222,154ff); ORBE A., *Procesión*, 420.
97 Cfr. CROUZEL H., *Théologie de l'image de Dieu chez Origène*, Paris 1956, 91; ORBE A., *Procesión*, 427;429: « Origen assumes that the total communication of the paternal will to the Son explains his personal subsistence by effect of the will of the Father, as his divinity by virtue of the paternal thought... that was passed on to him».
98 Cfr. ORBE A., *Estudios*, 36ff.

God projects in the person of the Son the perfections and graces that constitute himself. In the second phase, the Son turns his eyes to God in order to receive the communication of life with him, the deification[99]. «The saving mediation to which he is summoned claims its communion of essence and life with the Father. Hence, by looking outward as a creative mediator, he does not necessarily have to be God; by looking inward as a saving mediator, he has to be God»[100].

Therefore, the Logos is directed toward the creation and toward the saving economy. Strictly for creative mediation, he would not need to be God, but he does need to be so for the saving mediation. Only if he is God in himself can God deify. His divinity is constantly «fed», so to speak, with the contemplation of the fatherly abyss, of the only beginning, ἀρχή, of everything. He would lose it if, in an impossible situation, he would cease to feed constantly from this source. The Son lives out of this from eternity, because God has willed always to be the Father and creator.

What type of unity and diversity exist between the Father and the Son? Tertullian speaks about the union of the «spirit», the common divine substratum. Origen reflects less on the divinity itself. It is not clear whether the definition of the «spirit» of God has any relevance in his writings[101]. Certainly, between the Father and the Son there is no identity of subject. They are two, as we have seen in this respect. The unique qualities of the Father and of the Son are different. Is there a distinction according to the essence? It seems that also in this respect, the two «persons» differ, not because there is no consubstantiality between them, but because we must distinguish the unshared substance from the shared one. The Son has a shared essence with the Father, which brings with it life, immortality, and so forth. These properties are of the essence of the Father, but in the Father there is a perfect simplicity, while in the Son there is multiplicity. The distinction according to essence is based on participation and not on the fact

99 ORBE A., *Estudios*, 37-38: «The first one takes place when God projects in the person of the Son all the perfections and graces (*epinoias*) that comprise him; all of them directed outwards with the dynamism that is summoned to act in the dispensation that has been created. The person created like this, consistent, outside the bosom of God, is not separated from him. Otherwise, he would not be God. When feeling personally created —as looking outwards— and by knowing he is called to mediate divinely between God and men, he turns himself to God looking for the communion of life with him. He looks to God, and his eyes receive without any divisions what is divine. He is deified for the benefit of those for whom he was created a person. He keeps the gaze of God because only from his eyes he receives what is divine and which he will afterwards communicate to the future universe».

100 ORBE A., *Estudios*, 39; cfr. RIUS CAMPS J., «Orígenes y su reflexión sobre la Trinidad», 205f.

101 Cfr. ORBE A., *Procesión*, 441; with more nuances, SIMONETTI M., *La teologia trinitaria…*, 111ff.

that they are of a diverse nature naturally[102]. Contrary to what is set forth by the Patripassians, in some passages Origen strongly insists on the diversity of the persons.[103] In summary, we could say that according to Origen, the unity between the Father and the Son is dynamic in nature. It is founded on the unity of will and of action more than on categories of essence[104]. It is the saving concern, more than the concern for the life of the Trinity in itself, which characterizes Origen's approach

We will complete our brief overview of the Trinitarian theology of Origen by speaking of the Holy Spirit. Only the Son comes directly from God and is engendered by him. On the one hand, the Holy Spirit is not engendered, but he is not un-begotten either, as the Father alone is without beginning[105]. He comes from the Father through the Son (cfr. John 1:3), but from eternity. Because of this, he has the substantial potential for good. He is the first of the beings made through the Word, although different from creatures in *strictu sensu* because he has not gone from nothingness to being. His existence is eternal, as is that of the Son:

> As to us, convinced as we are, that there are three *hypostases* —the Father, the Son, and the Holy Spirit— and believing that none of them, except for the Father, is un-begotten, we believe that the Holy Spirit has a preeminent position over all that has been made through the Logos, and in the order, he is the first of the beings derived from the Father through Christ[106].

In this way, we have a «descending» line: Father-Son-Spirit that is emphasized on different occasions. The Holy Spirit, made through the Son, also receives the teaching through him[107]. The Father has a greater scope of power than the Son and the Son a greater one than the Spirit[108]. Together with this lineal, vertical conception in a growing «subordination», there are other texts in which the Son

---

102 Cfr. *In Joh.* II 23,149 (SCh 120,304-306); Cfr. ORBE A., *Procesión*, 440ff.

103 Cfr. *In Joh.* X 37,246 (SCh 157,530).

104 Cfr. SIMONETTI M., *La teologia trinitaria*, 122f; quotations of *In Joh.* XIII 36,228 (SCh 222,154); *C. Celsum* VIII 12 (SCh 150,200), in which mention is also made of unity by concord, harmony, identity of will; etc. Cfr. also RIUS CAMPS J., *El dinamismo trinitario en la divinización de los seres racionales según Orígenes*, Roma 1970, that underlines the functional concern of the Trinitarian doctrine of the writer from Alexandria. At any rate, in some places, mention is made of the unity of the substance: *Princ.* I 2,6 (SCh 252,122); IV 4,1 (SCh 268,402).

105 Cfr. *In Joh.* II 10,73ff (SCh 120,252ff); *Princ.* praef. 4 (SCh 252,82), shows doubts about the «generation».

106 *In Joh.* II 10,75 (SCh 120,254-256).

107 Cfr. *In Joh.* II 18,127 (290).

108 Cfr. *Princ.* I 3,5 (SCh 252,154f).

and the Spirit appear as coordinated among themselves in relation with the Father[109]. Hence, we would have these two diverse Trinitarian schemes[110], although the first one should prevail. In fact, the subordinated function that is attributed to the Holy Spirit in the Trinitarian theology of Origen depends on the fact that according to him the Logos exhausts the whole of the mediating function between God and the world. From this point of view, there does not seem to remain any place for the Spirit. Nevertheless, in the tradition, the Spirit is united with the Son. Therefore, he must be placed at the side of Christ in the mediating act. He could not be a simple subordinate of Christ, nor could he be a repetition of him. Following the tradition, the Spirit is attributed with the sanctification of humanity[111] and the inspiration of the Scripture. On the other hand, the saving functions that are assigned to the Spirit are not exclusive, because they are also carried out by the Son.

The being of the Spirit and his function in the salvation of humanity appears primarily in a passage of *In Joh.* to which critics attach a special relevance. It is precisely the continuation of what we have just quoted, presenting us the Holy Spirit as the first of the beings made by the Father through the Son:

> I believed that, so to speak, the Holy Spirit offers the matter of the gifts of grace (χαρισμάτων) granted by God to those who are called saints by God and by the Spirit's participation in God. This issue of the *charismata* that we have already addressed would come from the activity of God the Father (ἐυερισμάτων ἀπό τοῦ θεοῦ), would be ministered by Christ (διακονουμένης ὑπό τοῦ χριστοῦ) and would have its own consistence in the Holy Spirit (νφεστώσης δέ κατά τό ἅγιον πυεῦμα)[112].

If the Word acquires coherence by the will of the Father (*tamquam a mente voluntas*), we can assume[113] that the Spirit acquired it by means of the Word, as the first of the effects that are specifically related to the Word's creating act

---

109 Cfr. *Hom. In Is.* 4,1 (GCS, *Or. Ver.* VIII, 257-259).
110 Cfr. SIMONETTI M., *La teología trinitaria*, 130ff, also for the text that follows.
111 *Princ.* I 3,6ff (154ff).
112 *In Joh.* II 10,77 (SCh 120,256); cfr. SIMONETTI M., *La teologia trinitaria*, 132f; ORBE A., *La unción del Verbo*, Romae 1961, 533ff. A parallel passage in *Princ..* I 2,7 (160): «Est alia quoque Spiritus sancti gratia, quae dignis praeatatur, ministrata quidem per Filium, inoperata autem a Patre, secundum meritum forum qui capaces eius efficiuntur».
113 Cfr. ORBE A. *Unción*, 533ff, for the text that follows.

(although different from creatures). According to this, the Son gave coherence to the divine matter that he had first received from the Father as paternal energy destined one day for human beings and which he was in charge of consolidating, taking it out from himself in order to make with it the subsistent material, graces and gifts meant for the cosmos and especially for the Church. Rather than creating it *ex nihilo*, as he specifically made the creatures, God consolidated by means of the Son that divine energy that had been poured on him to be destined for the universe. When did this happen? Origen does not give us this information. It must have been before his pouring forth into the cosmos prior to the times of the *ornatus mundi*. It is an axiom, based on the universal affirmation of John 1:3 that the Spirit was made through Christ. Hence, the *hypostasis* of the Holy Spirit is subordinated to the will of Christ, but always according to the plan of the Father. This is the way in which the incarnation of the Word grants subsistence in the human nature of the Son of God who already subsists in his divine nature before the creation of the world. Hence, the outpouring of the Spirit (in the Jordan, in the upper room, and on Pentecost) enables the human nature to subsist in the *hypostasis* (although not by personal union, as in the case of the Word) that the Holy Spirit had from before and that is now given to humans[114].

In this way, Origen presents to us the articulation of the three persons — Father, Son, and Spirit— united in the confession of faith and in the work of salvation. The modality of the unity of the three is not emphasized on many occasions. We have already quoted an important passage in which the Father, the Son, and the Holy Spirit are mentioned together as three *hypostases*[115], three different subsistences in the heart of the divinity. In the case of Origen and in that of Greek theology in general, this term has the meaning that it has in Tertullian, and derived from him, in Latin theology, which is the typical word for «person». The term τρίας or *trinitas* is undoubtedly not frequent in Orígen, but this does not mean that Trinitarian theology does not exist. Hence, passages with Trinitar-

---

114 RIUS CAMPS J., *Orígenes...*, 207: «Unlike the Son, the Spirit has not come from a generation. God has not conceived him in his bosom by means of the seed of his desire. Hence, we cannot adequately call him "Son of God". On the other hand, the Holy Spirit could be considered as the main "making" of the Father, carried out through the Logos, Son of God. The indefinite and shapeless Spirit of the divinity has been molded by contact with the individuality of the Son, thus acquiring a form and a constitution of his own».

115 *In Joh.* II 10,75 (SCh 120,254): «... persuaded as we are that there are three *hypostases*, the Father, the Son, and the Holy Spirit...»; cfr. also *In Mt* XVII 4 (GCS, *Or.* Wer. x 624); also *Com. Ep. Rom.* VIII 5 (PG 14,1169), the three are not a simple name.

ian rhythm are not absent in his writings[116]. Even with imperfections and imbalances, the contribution of Origen to the development of Trinitarian theology cannot be disregarded. Although it seems to relate to the procession of the Word to creation, the affirmation that this procession is eternal, and hence that God does not make himself Father, is undoubtedly of the utmost importance. The unity of the three is less emphasized than the divine character they have, perhaps because the writer from Alexandria is quite moderate in his characterization of the divinity as such. The distinction between the *hypostases* will be a characteristic of the subsequent theology of this author. Taken to an extreme, an extreme that would undoubtedly be inadmissible for Origen, it will give rise to the heresy of Arius.

5

'Novatian[117]

We will not address the agitated personal life of Novatian, Roman priest and «antipope» († 257). He wrote his *de Trinitate* in the capital of the Empire, when the Church was still in a normal situation, between the years 240 and 250. We will simply limit our analysis to some aspects of his Trinitarian theology.

God is Creator, Lord and Father of all creation. «We recognize and know that God is Creator of all things, Lord by his power, Father on account of creation».[118] Still, for Novatian, following the line of thought that is familiar to all of us, the fatherhood of God is related to the creation, but the generation of the Son is also taken into account. The Father, source of everything, without ceasing to be the only God, has a Son who also is God. «He who proceeds from the one by whose will all things have been made, is undoubtedly God coming from God; and as Son, he is the second person after the Father, without taking from the Father the

---

116 Cfr. Simonetti M., *La teologia trinitaria*, 135-138, that refers, among others, to *Hom Jer.* 8,1; *In Joh.* 32,16,187-189; *In Mt.* 12,20; 12,42, etc. Likewise, these are texts that have been preserved in Latin, where we cannot exclude a Trinitarian base in the original, although admitting possible modifications in the translation.

117 Cfr. Simonetti M., *L'unità di Dio a Roma: da Clemente a Dionigi*, in *Studi sulla cristologia…*, 183-215, especially 203-208.

118 *Trin.* 3,17 (FP 8,80); 1,1 (58): «The rule of the truth requests before all that we believe in God, Father, and omnipotent Lord, in other words, most perfect creator of all things»; concerning the only God, cfr. also 2,11-12 (72-74); 3,18 (82); 30,176 (260); 31,182 (264), etc.

fact that he is the only God»[119]. Therefore, the divinity of the Son does not mean that there are two gods. Novatian perhaps takes from Tertullian the designation of «person» that he applies to the Father and to the Son[120]. Everything that the Son is he receives from the Father. «Everything that is not his own, comes from himself because he is begotten, but from the Father, because he is engendered. And this is the case either as Word, or power, or wisdom, or light, or Son»[121]. Insofar as he receives from the Father, the Son is «less» than the Father. «Because he receives sanctification from the Father, he is less than the Father. Therefore, if he is less than the Father, he is not the Father, but the Son»[122]. The difference and the subordination come from this generation[123]. Novatian is not clear yet about the «moment» of the emanation of the Word. The Word exists from eternity. As begotten, he is always in the Father; otherwise, the Father would not always be Father[124]. Nonetheless, at the same time it seems that he follows the tradition of the free decision of the will of the Father in the generation. «Hence, when the Father willed it, he proceeded from the Father and the one who was in the Father, because he was of the Father, was later with the Father…»[125]. Perhaps we are faced here with an outstanding approximation of the formulation of the idea of the eternity of the generation of the Son, even though this step has not taken place clearly.

Novatian confesses the divinity of the Son in subordination and dependence from the Father who has begotten him. The two are united, so this radically rules out the possibility of two gods. The union does not imply personal identity, as Sabellius, who followed the Patripassian tradition, would like. They are only one thing, *unum* (cfr. John 10:30), in likeness, in combination, in love of the Father who loves the Son, in harmony, and in charity[126]. This union is not explained in

119 *Trin.* 31,187 (272); 31,189 (275): «…owing his origin to God, he could not bring about discord in the divinity as to the number of two gods, the one who when he was born had his origin in whom is the only God».
120 Cfr. *Trin.* 26,145 (224); 27,151 (236).
121 *Trin.* 31,189 (274).
122 *Trin.* 27,152 (236).
123 Cfr. SIMONETTI M., *L'unità di Dio a Roma: da Clemente a Dionigi*, in *Studi sulla cristologia del II e III secolo*, Roma 1993, 183-215, 205, the subordination seems a criterion for making a difference between the persons. Cfr. also the context, 203-208.
124 Cfr. *Trin.* 31,184 (268-270); also 31,185 (270), the Son is *simul minor*.
125 *Trin.* 31,186 (270-272). It seems that mention is made here of the double stage of the Word, immanent and *prolaticio* that we know. Also 31,183 (264): «Ex quo [Patre] quando ipse voluit, sermo Filius natus est».
126 *Trin.* 27,149-150 (230-234). Cfr. also 28,155ff (238ff), against the Sabellian interpretation of John 14:9.

terms of substance but of love and harmony, although clear mention has been made of the generation which seems to imply something more. The formulations of Novatian in this respect are not always satisfactory, but we have seen very similar formulations in Origen. His adversaries are the Sabellians, and he must insist on the diversity between the persons when opposing their views. It has been discussed whether, according to Novatian, at the end of time, when Jesus delivers the Kingdom to the Father, the personal subsistence of the Son will continue, or rather, whether he will be «reabsorbed» into the Father. It seems that we must tend to favor the eternal persistence of the person of the Son[127].

The problems of the relationship of the Son with the Father were those primarily addressed by Novatian throughout his analysis and work. Nevertheless, he devoted Chapter 29 of his work *de Trinitate* to the Holy Spirit. He does not refer to the Holy Spirit as a person nor does he say he is God. However, because of the effects that are attributed to the Spirit, his divine character is quite clear. What is most important is what he says about the Spirit's full manifestation and contribution as it relates to the resurrection of Jesus. It is given prominence that the Holy Spirit is the same in the Old and in the New Testament. Nevertheless, the Holy Spirit's partial contribution in earlier times is followed after Christ by the full outpouring, which is only made possible because the Spirit dwells in Jesus *plenus et totus*[128]. The contribution made by Christ corresponds now to the promise made to the prophets[129]. The Holy Spirit is an object of faith[130] and is united with the Father and with the Son in the triadic formula seen at the end of Novatian's work, and which is also a summary of this treatise[131]. However, nothing is specifically explained about the Trinity, nor does the term which had already been used by Tertullian appear there.

209

---

127 The specific text is *Trin.* 31,192 (278-280): «totam divinitatis auctoritatem rursus ex subiectione sui illi remittit, unus Deus ostenditur verus et aeternus Pater, a quo solo haec vis divinitatis emissa, etiam in Filium tradita et directa, rursum per subiectionem Filii ad Patrem revolvitur. Deus quidem ostenditur Filius, cui divinitas tradita et porrecta conspicitur, et tamen nihilominus unus Deus Pater probatur, dum gradatim reciproco meatu illa maiestas atque divinitas ad Patrem, qui dederat eam, rursum ab illo ipso Filio revertitur et retorquetur…»; Cfr. SIMONETTI M., op. cit., 207; PELLAND G., «Un passage difficile de Novatien sur 1 Cor 15:27-28» in *Greg* 66 (1985) 25-52; ORBE A., *Estudios…*, 102f; URIBARRI BILBAO G., *Monarquía y Trinidad*, 423ff.

128 *Trin.* 29,168 (252): «… posteaquam Dominus baptizatus est, super eum venit et mansit, habitans in solo Christo plenus et totus, nec in aliqua mensura aut portione mutilatus, sed cum tota sua redundantia cumulate contributus, ut ex illo delibationem quandam gratiarum ceteri consequi possunt…».

129 Cfr. *Trin.* 29,163-172 (246-256); Cfr. ORBE A., *Estudios…*, 527-636.

130 Cfr. *Trin.* 30,163 (246).

131 *Trin.* 30,173 (256): «Haec quidem de Patre et de Filio et de Spiritu Sancto breviter sint nobis dicta…».

6

Dionysius of Alexandria and Dionysius of Rome

Up to this point, we have studied the most qualified representatives of the theology of the East and the theology of the West. Rome and Alexandria will be directly confronted in the discussion between Dionysius of Alexandria and Dionysius of Rome. A brief summary of this confrontation will help us understand some assumptions of the Arian crisis. In effect, if the unity of the triune God was strongly emphasized by Western authors, Alexandrian theology, as we have seen in Origen, was directed more toward a greater distinction of the *hypostases*, placing less emphasis on the divine unity. This difference of emphases is stressed in the discussion to which we will now refer and which took place around the years 257 to 260. In his desire to oppose the Sabellians, it seems that Bishop Dionysius of Alexandria scandalized the faithful —the followers of his church— with proposals that were extremely subordinationist. As a result of this, they went to the Bishop of Rome, who was also named Dionysius, and presented him with a series of accusations. These accusations have been transmitted to us by Athanasius[132]. They can be summarized as follows:

Dionysius separates the Son from the Father.

He denies the eternity of the Son. God was not always Father, nor did the Son always exist. God was without the Logos; the Son did not exist before being engendered, and hence he is not eternal.

He names the Father without the Son and the Son without the Father.

He does not accept that the Son is consubstantial with the Father (ὁμοούσιον τῶ πατρί)[133].

He says that the Son is a creature of the Father, ποίημα, who has been made, and hence has come to be. In order to establish the relationships of the Father with the Son he uses ambiguous comparisons, such as the farmer with respect to the grapevine or the sailor with respect to the ship. The Son, as creature, did not exist before he was made.

---

132 ATHANASIUS, *De sent. Dyon.* (Opitz, Ath. Werke II/1, 46-67); cfr. the summary of those accusations in GRILLMEIER A., *Jesus der Christus* I, Freiburg-Basel-Wien 1979, 285.

133 This is indeed a curious accusation which by no means anticipates the vocabulary of Nicaea. The term *homoousios* did not enjoy prestige and had even been rejected in the sentence of Paul of Samosata. It had a modalist tint that denied the personality of the Son.

The theology of Dionysius of Alexandria reminds us of Origen and is based on three individual subsistent entities (*hypostases*) in the Trinity, more than in the unity between them. As related to the issue of the eternity of the generation of the Son, he seems to revert to a stage that is prior to the theology of Origen.

In his response to the accusations against his colleague (cfr. DS 112-115)[134], the Roman Dionysius did not include innovations and novelties, but instead he sought a middle ground between those who defend Sabellianism and those who divide the Trinity.

First and foremost, Dionysius of Rome sees that there is a need to defend the «monarchy» against those who stand for three powers (*virtutes*, δύναμεις), for three separate *hypostases* (μεμερισμένας) and who even reach the point of affirming three divinities. The monarchy seems to be interpreted here in the sense of divine unity or monotheism. In this unity, the three would be included, one way or another, always under the primacy of the Father, as will be clarified hereafter. In the first place, the movement that is antagonized by Dionysius of Alexandria destroys the «holy monad», when it affirms that to a certain extent there are three gods. Nevertheless, on the other hand, Sabellius blasphemes when he says that the Son is the same as the Father and vice versa.

Dionysius of Rome believes that the divine Logos must of necessity be united with the Father of the universe and that the Holy Spirit remains and dwells in God[135]. What we are addressing here is the unity of the Son and of the Holy Spirit with God the Father. Furthermore, it is necessary that the divine Trinity is recapitulated and united into one (εἰς ἕνα — it is worth noting that the masculine gender is used) in its highest point, in other words, in the God of all things, the *pantocrator*. The God of all things is without doubt the Father, because in a previous paragraph mention was made of the Word united with the God of all, and exactly the same terms are used. According to Dionysius, Marcion divides and cuts the monarchy into three beginnings, and this is the reason why his doctrine is not that of the disciples of Christ, but of the devil[136]. Although the Holy Scripture talks about the Trinity, it never affirms that there are three gods (DS 112).

---

134 The text has been conveyed to us also by ATHANASIUS, *De decretis Nicaenae synodi* c. 26 (Opitz, Ath. Werke II/1.22-23). To facilitate things, I will quote DS. Cfr. about the current *status quaestionis*, URIBARRI BILBAO G., *Monarquía y Trinidad*, 458-489.

135 The same terms are not used for referring to the Father, to the Son, and to the Holy Spirit, perhaps in order not to excessively push the argument; cfr. SIMONETTI M., *L'unita di Dio...*, 211.

136 Regarding the exactness in attributing these doctrines to Marcion, cfr. PIETRAS H., «La difesa della monarchia divina da parte del papa Dionigi († 268)» in *Archivum Historiae Pontificiae* 28 (1990) 335-342, esp. 339.

Pope Dionysius also denies that the Son is a creature. His generation is not a creation. If he were a creature, there would have been a time when he did not exist. On the contrary, he affirms that Jesus exists from eternity in the Father (cfr. John 14:10-11). As the Son is the word, strength and wisdom of God (John 1:14; 1Cor 1:24), we cannot understand that the Father has been deprived of this before the creation of the Son (DS 113). As related to what is stated in Prov 8:22, «Yahweh created me», it is mentioned that the term «create» has many meanings, and that in the Scripture the mysterious generation of the Lord (DS 114) has never been construed in terms of a specific creation.

Dionysius of Rome argues that we cannot divide into three divinities the «admirable and divine unity (μόναδ)». On the contrary, it is absolutely necessary to maintain the divine Trinity and the holy *kerygma* of the monarchy. We must believe in the Father, in the Son, and in the Holy Spirit. The Word is united with the God of all things. (This is the third time that this expression appears). In order to ratify this statement, mention is made of John 10:30, without any reference being made to the difference between the *unum* and the *unus* that we saw in Tertullian, Hippolytus, and Novatian, and also to the «I am in the Father and the Father is in me» that we read in John 14:10 (DS 115).

The text does not delve into great detail about the major theological delineations. First and foremost, Dionysius of Rome wants to reject the division or separation of the triad that leads to the affirmation of three gods. He defends the «monarchy», understood in the traditional sense of the Father, who alone is at the beginning. He does not use any term that points out the difference between the three. More concretely, we can say that he does not recognize the language of the three *hypostases*, although he also defends at the same time the monarchy and the «triad» that has the Father as its highest point. The existence *ab aeterno* of the Son is at least suggested «in the Father». If no special theological innovation is found in this response, it is worth pointing out the balance between the Sabellian and the tritheist extremes. In view of the context of the controversy, the dangers that are derived from the latter are those that are primarily taken into account.

Dionysius of Alexandria defended himself from the accusations of his detractors[137]. He denied the fact that he separated the Father from the Son. He added the Holy Spirit, telling where and through whom he comes. He reaffirmed

---

[137] Cfr. ATHANASIUS, *De sent. Dyon.*; GRILLMEIER A., *Jesus der Christus I*, 287ff ; PIETRAS H., «L'unità di Dio in Dionisio di Alessandria» in *Greg* 72 (1991) 459-490.

at the same time the unity and the Trinity. The Son is the splendor (Heb 1:3); he is the wisdom of God (1Cor 1:24). The relationship between the Father and the Son shows that they are always one with the other. Hence, the generation from eternity; there was no time when God was not Father. As in the case of Origen, the Son is Logos, Wisdom, Power. It is not that God was first without the Son and then later he came to be, but that the Son owes his existence to the Father[138].

Of special interest is the issue of the splendor of the Father and the Son as «light of light»[139]. We are already partially familiar with the history of this expression. Dionysius of Alexandria stressed the splendor, as Origen did. Considering the Son as light, as reflection, is proof that the Father is not separated from the Son. Mention is also made of breath and outpouring (cfr. Wis 7:25). These ideas came from Origen, but Dionysius did not want to get involved and committed to the idea of the will of the Father as causing the generation of the Son. In view of the fact that the texts have been transmitted to us within an anti-Arian context, the issue of the reliability of this transmission is still an open question.

Another of the accusations against the Bishop of Alexandria referred to the Son as the «work» of God, ποίημα. Dionysius defended himself by stating that he had called God the Father of the Son and not the one who made him. Athanasius defended Dionysius, saying that he had referred to the humanity of Jesus[140]. Nevertheless, this does not seem to be exact, because Dionysius talked about the Father-Son relationship, although not directly in terms of the incarnation. However, Dionysius made a distinction between the different terms and spoke of the «work», although not about the creature of the Father. He also said that the Son comes from the Father. Dionysius responded in the same way to the accusation that he did not use the term *homoousios*. It is not found in the Scripture. Nonetheless, he also mentioned that his conclusions were close to the meaning of this term because he had said that sons differ from fathers only in the fact that they are sons. Likewise, the plant has the same nature as the seed or the river has the same nature as the fountain[141]. The monad and the Trinity are affirmed at the same time[142].

138 Cfr. ATHANASIUS, *De sent. Dyon.* 15,1 (57).
139 Cfr. ATHANASIUS, *De sent. Dyon.* 15,2-5 (57).
140 ATHANASIUS, *De sent. Dyon.* 21,2.3 (62); GRILLMEIER A., *Jesus der Christus I*, 288f ; PIETRAS H., «L'unità di Dio in Dionisio di Alessandria», 478ff.
141 Cfr. ATHANASIUS, *De sent. Dyon.* 18,2-3 (59-60).
142 ATHANASIUS, *De sent. Dyon.* 17,2 (58); cfr. also the fragments transmitted by BASIL OF CAESAERA, *De Sp. sanc.* 29,72 (SCh 17bis, 504).

We have certainly found different emphases in the two main characters in this controversy, although it does not seem that the positions are unyielding. The two were concerned about maintaining the divine unity and the divine Trinity at the same time. With the radical Arian view of the distinction between the Father and the Son, the former will be affirmed to the detriment of the latter. It is possible that Arius could find points of support in Dionysius of Alexandria, in isolated phrases of his context. Nevertheless, it would be very difficult to say the same thing about his ideas as a whole. However, in this interesting episode, the problem that was later to be debated in Nicaea was already the subject of discussion more than half a century before.

The Arian Crisis and the Council of Nicaea. The Anti-Arian Struggle of the Fourth Century

The Arian crisis will give way to the first serious definition of the Church, not only regarding the Trinitarian controversy, but also in general terms. It is still significant that for the first time in history the Church compromised its authority specifically to safeguard the full divinity of Jesus Christ. We might say that the first issue that was the subject of this doctrinal declaration was precisely the central issue of faith: the ultimate identity of Jesus the Savior, and along with this, the meaning of Christian monotheism. Indirectly, the problem of the divinity of the Holy Spirit is also set forth and will be solemnly affirmed, although in a less explicit way, at the first Council of Constantinople.

We will begin by addressing some aspects of Arian thought, and prior to discussing the Council of Nicaea we will briefly analyze the theological panorama of the first half of the fourth century. At that time there were many who, although with more moderation, tended toward the line of thought defended by Arius; others, on the contrary, favored a strong conception of the unity of God in which the eternal subsistence of the *hypostasis* could be compromised.

1

The Doctrine of Arius

Arius was a priest from Alexandria who was born around the year 260. His preaching created difficulties because he argued that Christ was a creature, although indeed not a creature like all the rest; he was a privileged one, but a creature nonetheless. In other words, he clearly denied Christ his divine condition. His main concern was affirming the unicity of God, and in his opinion, this unicity would be compromised if the divinity of the Son were accepted. On the other hand, he believed that the concept of the generation was too material because it would imply a loss, or some sort of a decrease, in the Father. He also wanted to oppose Sabellianism by affirming the real personal subsistence of the Son. The letter that Arius addressed to the Bishop Alexander of Alexandria is a good summary of his doctrine:

> We know only one God, the only uncreated (unbegotten), the only eternal, the only without beginning, the only true, the only immortal, the only entirely good, the only powerful…. This God engendered an only-begotten Son before all the centuries, by means of whom he created the centuries and all things; born not in appearance, but

in all truth; abiding by his will, immutable and unalterable; a perfect creature of God, although not just one more among his creatures; perfect making and creation, although not as other creations.... As we said, he was created by the will of the Father before time and before the centuries, and he received both his life and his being from the Father, and the Father glorified him by making him share his being... the Son was derived from the Father outside of time, created and made before the centuries. Nothing existed before he was born, but he was born before time, before all things, and he received his being only from the Father. Nonetheless, he is not eternal, nor coeternal, nor uncreated together with the Father...[1].

As we can see, for Arius it was a matter of emphasizing the unique and unrepeatable position of the Father. The Father has a nature of his own and a different *hypostasis* from that of the Son. Therefore, no one can be consubstantial with him. Only the Father is without beginning, and in this, he is radically differentiated from the Son who, as all creatures, has his beginning in the will of the Father.

The Son is called «begotten». As such, he cannot be co-eternal because he had a beginning. There cannot be two uncreated beings. Hence, the Son must have a beginning, and this is what leads to his nature as a creature. Arius spoke of the generation of the Son by the Father, but in real terms, as clearly stated in the context, this is really a creation[2]. On the one hand, he referred to generation before time, because there is no time without creation. Nevertheless, on the other hand, what he insisted on was the absence of co-eternity. He used expressions such as «before he existed», and the like. Therefore, even though the Son has been created by the Father before all time, he has indeed begun to exist. Consequently, the Father has begun to be Father. This is the basic issue. The Son has a «temporal» beginning because only the Father is without beginning. Arius did not understand how the Son could have his beginning in the Father if he was co-eternal with the Father.

---

1 Text conveyed by HILARY OF POITIERS, *Trin.* IV 12-13; VI 5-6 (CCL 62,112-114; 199-202); ATHANASIUS, *Syn.* 15,1 (Opitz II/1, 242-243).

2 Regarding «creating» and «generating», cfr. SIMONETTI M., *La crisi ariana nel IV secolo*, Rome 1975, 53; the identity of the meaning of the two verbs is assumed, leading it towards «create». Also see GRILLMEIER A., *Jesus der Christus im Glauben der Kirche* I, Freiburg-Basel-Wien 1979, 369, regarding the confusion between ἀγένητος, the one that has not come to be, and ἀγέννητος, not generated. From this point of view, everyone who has been «generated» has come to be, has ultimately been created; cfr. also HANSON R.P.C., *The Search for the Christian Doctrine of God*, Edinburgh 1988, 203ff, regarding the initial confusion of the two terms.

Arius rejected any form of generation that could seem material or «animal». The Son is not part of the Father, nor does he emanate from the Father. Likewise, there is no common substratum between the two of them. At a certain point in his writings, he deliberately did not wish to use the preposition *ex* that pointed, according to him, toward a «material nature»[3]. Consequently, the Son does not proceed from the *ousia* (essence) of the Father. This free and voluntary «generation» of the Son is, hence, a «creation». If, as related to the voluntary nature of the generation of the Son, Arius opted for the line of continuity with the previous tradition, this was not the case in relation to the decisive issue of the non-authentic generation that was simply a creation for him. The Son comes from nothing; he has been created *ex nihilo*, even though it is repeated that his creation is not like that of other creatures. This Son who, based on the premises of Arius, is given this name quite inadequately, is the one who will carry out the creation. His «generation» depends on the creation itself.

Nevertheless, the Son is called «God», although this is a lesser god. The term is only used in the figurative or metaphorical sense and not in the real sense. The arguments set forth in John 10:30 and 14:9 and the verses that follow, which have been used in the earlier tradition to underline the unity of the Father and the Son, were interpreted by the followers of Arius in the sense of «belonging», of union of will, although not of participation of the Son in the divinity of the Father[4].

There are biblical passages that were brought up in the Arian controversy which at first glance seem to point to the fact that the new doctrines supported by the representatives of Arias were correct[5]. Special mention must be made of the passages that speak about the oneness or unicity of God: 1Tim 2:4-5; John 17:3; Mark 10:18. No one is good; only God is good. Those passages that point to the fact that the power of Jesus comes from the Father (John 3:35; 5:22) are also significant. The Son is the first-born of all creation according to Col 1:15 and Prov 8:22. «Yahweh begot me, the first fruits of his fashioning» was one of the texts in which the Arians found the strongest support and the one that would acquire greater significance in the subsequent controversy which was evidenced throughout the fourth century. These passages that apparently speak about the Son as a

---

3 Cfr. SIMONETTI M., *La crisi ariana nel IV secolo*, 48ff, and also the following paragraphs. Cfr. also the letter to Alexander that has been already quoted, ARIUS, *Ep.* 1,2 (Opitz, *Urkunden*, 2). Regarding the voluntary nature of the generation of the Son by the Father, cfr. ibid. 4 (3).
4 Cfr. SIMONETTI M., *La crisi ariana nel IV secolo*, 50.
5 Cfr. SIMONETTI M., *La crisi ariana nel IV secolo*, 52f.

creature are related to those that speak of human beings in general as children of God (for instance, Isa 1:2; Ps 81:7). In this way, attempts are made at establishing a certain parity between Christ and us. Undoubtedly, the texts that showed the suffering and the anguish of Jesus were also important for the Arians, among them, Matt 26:38: «my soul is sorrowful to the point of death». On the other hand, it is quite odd that John 14:28, «the Father is greater than I», which would seem to be the quintessential subordinationist text, was not used by Arius and his followers to begin with. A certain «inferiority» of the Son as engendered by the Father was accepted by all, and hence, the fact that the Father was «greater» than the Son fit perfectly well, as we have had the occasion to see, in the orthodox schemes. Furthermore, this verse showed that we can draw a comparison between the Father and the Son (which would be impossible between different orders of magnitude), and hence in a way, this favored the consubstantiality of both. Later, when the Church has a clearer awareness that the divinity of the Son (and of the Spirit) rules out any type of inferiority, the discussion around this text will be crucial in this controversy.

In real terms, the Arian doctrine implied interpreting Christianity in light of the Hellenic schemes of thought that prevailed at that time, specifically during Middle Platonism. This meant ignoring or considerably reducing the originality of Christianity. Recently there have been countless investigations into this issue[6]. Some passages written by Arius are interesting: «The Son of God has his age, his magnitude, the when and the coming from whom». «The Father is alien to the essence of the Son (ξένος κατ᾽ οὐσίαν) because he is without beginning. Let us remember that the μονάς existed before the existence of the δύας…»[7]. These phrases, taken from the *Thaleia* of Arius, point toward a considerable relationship with well-known philosophical models and can explain to a certain extent the ideological background of both Arius and his followers: absolute primacy of the one, the μονάς, identified with God the Father from whom everything comes. The idea, or Logos, comes second; it is the *Nous*, the Demiurge[8]. Finally, comes the matter that the Demiurge produces.

---

6 Cfr. the summary of HANSON R.P.C., *The Search for the Christian Doctrine of God*, 84-94; for the most recent discussion, cfr. STEAD CH., «Was Arius a Neoplatonist?» in *Studia Patrística* XXXII, Leuwen 1997, 39-52.

7 ARIUS, *Thaleia*, in ATHANASIUS, *Syn.* 15 (242-243); cfr. GRILLMEIER A., *Jesus der Christ I*, 362-363.

8 Cfr. the text of NUMENIUS mentioned by GRILLMEIER A., *Jesus der Christ I*, 364: «the second (God) who is double in himself forms in himself the idea and the world because he is the Demiurge» (cfr. EUSEBIUS OF CAESAREA, *Praeparatio Evangelica* XI 22,544; PG 21,905).

Although not necessarily in identical terms, this line of thought found an echo in Arius. By unilaterally stressing the divinity of the Father and the subsequent denial of the divinity of the Son, who is the mediating Logos of creation (and *a fortiori,* that of the Holy Spirit), Arius denied any direct relationship between God and the world. The creation has been carried out by the Son who is not God. The Son and the Holy Spirit themselves, as creatures, cannot cause any direct access of human beings to God. Neither does God come to humanity, nor can human beings, consequently, reach God. The God-world relationship is the one that is at stake when we speak of the Father-Son relationship. Hence, the Son is the cosmic mediator. Arius did not speak of the revelation that God brings us, nor about his saving mediation; however, these concepts are clearly consistent with his premises. The problems faced by Arius were primarily derived from his desire to combine the Christian *kerygma* of Father, Son, and Holy Spirit with cosmological schemes of thought in which the mediation is lowered to the level of creature. This is what led to the rupture from many elements in the Christian tradition, to which in fact Arius was not fully alien. The relationship between creation and the procession of the Logos is not new, as we all know. Nevertheless, distinctions between the immanent and the spoken Logos, and speculations regarding the participation of the Son in the Father's own life ensured his belonging to the divine scope, although he was engendered by the will of the Father. In fact, many of the difficulties faced by the first centuries of Christian reflections seem to be «solved» here in an extremely simple and radical way. The extreme position of Arius runs the risk of enclosing the faith within previous philosophical schemes. Because of this fact, the reaction of the great Church in Nicaea has been perceived as a true «de-hellenization» of Christianity[9].

We cannot end these brief notes without addressing the problem of the human soul of Jesus, which was not really addressed in the early Arian controversy.[10] Quite possibly, it was precisely the concern for guaranteeing the real suffering of Jesus, the reality of his body being like ours, which really made Arians deny

---

9 Cfr. RICKEN F., «Nikea als Krisis der altchristlichen Platonismus» in *TheoPhil* 44 (1969) 321-351. Today it is practically impossible to maintain the thesis of the dogmatic development of the early Church as a phenomenon of progressive accommodation to the Hellenic schemes of the times.

10 According to GRILLMEIER A., *Jesus der Christ I*, 374ff, during the early times of the Arian controversy, this problem was evident only in some circles (Eustatius of Sebaste). Not until the year 360, however, will the problem emerge. AUGUSTINE will also realize that they have not taken into account this aspect in their struggle against the Arians. «In eo autem quod Christum solam carnem sine anima suscepisse arbitrantur, minus noti sunt» *C. haer.* 49 (PL 42,39).

the divinity of Jesus, even though they strongly favored the idea of divine impassivity. Hanson[11] stated that the Arians were faced in general terms with all the harshness of the scandal of the cross without looking for a way out in the «peculiarity» of the humanity of Christ to which the Nicenes sometimes resorted. Naturally, they had no need to do so because the subject of these pains and anguishes for them is not the Son of God himself. This insistence on the reality of the sufferings of Christ, both physical and moral, can be the foundation for denying his divinity. If we ignore the human soul of Christ, all of this anguish must fall directly on the Logos. From this perspective, the union of God with the flesh of Christ is indeed very difficult to accept. There is no place whatsoever for the suffering of the Logos «in his humanity as man»[12]. The Trinitarian problem of the divinity of the Son is then closely related to the Christological issue of the integrity of the human nature taken up by the Logos. The Holy Spirit was only marginally part of the discussion at this time. Undoubtedly, if the divinity of the Son is denied *a fortiori*, we must deny the divinity of the Spirit. The problem will come up in a reflexive way only later, around the year 360. In summary we can say that in the case of Arius and his followers, there is no immanent Trinity that is the foundation for the economy of salvation. In this respect, they basically coincided with the Sabellians who, on the other hand, were their great adversaries.

2

A first response to Arius: Alexander of Alexandria

Alexander, Bishop of Alexandria, took a stand with respect to what his presbyter Arius had said. We know of only two letters in which he set forth his reactions to the doctrine of Arius[13]. Here, we will simply summarize briefly the basic points of this response.

Alexander insisted on the eternity of the generation of the Son. There is no interval in which God exists without having engendered or begotten the Son. The Logos is «in the beginning», and consequently the relationship that unites him

---

11 Hanson R.P.C., *The Search for the Christian Doctrine of God*, 122.

12 Cfr. Hanson R.P.C., *The Search for the Christian Doctrine of God*, 117-122, and mostly, Grillmeier A., *Jesus der Christ I*, 374-385.

13 Cfr. Simonetti M., *La crisi ariana nel IV secolo*, 55-60; Hanson R.P.C., *The Search for the Christian Doctrine of God*, 140-145.

to the Father exists forever. The Father is always Father and the Son is always Son[14]. The generation is real, although ineffable. In addition to Isa 53:18[15], a passage that we have already seen quoted in this respect, Alexander referred to Psalms 109:3 and 44:2[16]. This insistence on the eternal generation evidences the influence of the thinking of Origen. Alexander continued to admit the voluntary nature of the generation[17], and he kept to a minimum all the expressions that could have a subordinationist tint. He referred to the Son as image of the Father and used the well-known metaphors of light and gleam, while at the same time emphasizing the similarity and not the differentiation. In every aspect, the Son is in the image of the Father. The only difference lies in the fact that the Father begets and the Son is begotten. In this respect, the use of John 14:28, «the Father is greater than I» is interesting. Precisely to emphasize the likeness: the Father is certainly greater, but the mere fact that the comparison can be made points to the fact that they have the same nature[18]. Therefore, the Son is God. Alexander also briefly mentioned the confession of the Holy Spirit together with the Father and the Son. The Spirit has already renewed the elect of the Old Testament as well as those of the New Testament[19]. He did not add anything else about the third person.

For the Bishop of Alexandria there was no technical idea of asserting the unity of the Father and the Son. The Father and the Son are still two *hypostases*, as evidenced in the writings of Origen and Arius, without analyzing this theory in greater depth. Nevertheless, the divinity of the Son was affirmed without any question, but not his nature as creature.

After this initial response to the issues posed by Arius, the Church will react in a more solemn and decisive way at the Council of Nicaea. However, before addressing and analyzing this Council, we will briefly dwell on two interesting writers of the early fourth century, Eusebius of Caesarea and Marcellus of Ancyra, who in their contrasting positions will aid us in understanding the theological environment that prevailed at that time and the different obstacles that the Council had to overcome.

---

14 *Ep.* 2,26ff (Opitz, *Urkunden*, 23-24).
15 Quoted by ALEXANDER in *Ep.* 2,21 (23).
16 *Ep.* 11,11 (9).
17 Cfr. the fragment addressed in Opitz, *Urkunden*, 22; SIMONETTI M., *La crisi ariana nel IV secolo*, 59.
18 Cfr. *Ep.* 2,48.52 (27-28); the Father is greater because he begets the Son exactly in his image.
19 Cfr. *Ep.* 2,53 (28).

cℐℴ

(The Son) is the head of the Church, and his head is the Father. He is the only God, Father of the only-begotten Son, and the only one who is also the head of Christ himself. In view of the fact that only one is the beginning and the head, how could there be two gods instead of being only one, the one that does not have anyone above him or anyone who is his source? He who possesses, as his own without beginning and without being begotten, the divinity of the power of the monarchy has made his Son participate in his divinity and his life[20].

This text shows the theological inclination of this great historian of the Church († 339). We can see the clear difference with respect to Arius when Eusebius affirmed the divinity of the Son, although his main concern was that of maintaining the unique position of the Father, the only one who retains the «monarchy». Following the ideas of Origen, we can see that he made a distinction between the three *hypostases* in a descending order, although certainly clearly affirming the divinity of the Word begotten by the Father in an inexpressible and indescribable way[21].

In this way, according to Eusebius, the Father is the πρόρος θεός[22], the first God, the only really good God[23], the only true God[24], because only he is unbegotten. He is, speaking in negative terms, unutterable, incomprehensible, and indescribable. He is absolutely and complete transcendent[25].

---

20 Cfr. EUSEBIUS OF CAESAREA, *Eccl. Theol.* I 11 (GCS Eus W. IV, 69-70); the continuation of the text on the incarnation and the exaltation of Jesus (70) is interesting and worth analyzing: «when he submitted him to all things, when he sent him…, he gave him orders and rules, he taught him; when he delivered him everything, he glorified and exalted him, he declared him king of the universe and gave him the power to judge… And the only begotten Son, obeying (this only God) stripped himself of his own self, humbled himself, turning himself obedient… to this God to whom he begs, obeys, offers his gratitude… confesses that this God is greater than he and teaches to believe in him as the only God…»; cfr. very similar ideas in II 7 (104). Cfr. SIMONETTI M., *La crisi ariana nel IV secolo*, 61-66; GRILLMEIER A., *Jesus der Christ I*, 301-326, and the paragraphs that follow.

21 Cfr. among others *Dem. Ev.* IV 6; V 1 (GCS Eus. Werke VI, 158-160; 210-213); *Eccl. Theol.* I 1-2.10 (62-63; 68).

22 *Dem. Ev.* V 4,11 (225); cfr. IV 2,2 (152).

23 *De. Ev.* V 1,24 (214).

24 *Dem. Ev.* V 4,9 (225).

25 A list of the designations of the Father and the Son can be seen in GRILLMEIER A., *Jesus der Christ I*, 305.

Together with the transcendent Father, the Son is God by participation; he is the second God, δεύτερος θεός[26]. He is the creator and penetrates everything, revealing the Father already in the theophanies of the Old Testament, and he saves the world[27]. He has been begotten by the will of the Father for the purpose of creation[28], but his generation is not the result of the division of the fatherly essence[29]. It is clear at any rate that he is not created. The divinity of the Son is not alien from, nor unconnected with that of the Father. Eusebius also referred to Origen's terminology of the ray of light, the outflow, the emanation[30], although it seems that for him the generation is not eternal[31]. On the other hand, he insisted strongly on the Son as image of the Father, the only perfect image in the likeness of the Father in everything[32]. In his case, there is a clear difference between the divine filiation of the Son and our sonship. Neither did he did accept the Arian interpretation of Prov 8:22 that we should not read «has begotten me», but «has possessed me»[33]. For Eusebius, the Son is lesser than the Father according to John 14:28, and he interpreted this passage in similar terms to those we have already seen[34].

Eusebius did not speak to a great extent about the Holy Spirit within the framework of the divinity and as it relates to Trinitarian theology. On one occasion he mentioned that the Spirit has been created by the Father through the Son. He seemed to deny the Spirit the condition of God[35].

Hence, the theology of Eusebius proceeded within the framework of a certain ambiguity, a certain «theological penumbra», according to the felicitous expression of A. Grillmeier[36]. If, on the one hand, he affirmed quite clearly the divinity of the Son —and in this respect he disagreed with Arius— on the other

26 *Dem. Ev.* v 30,3 (249); cfr. SIMONETTI M., *La crisi ariana nel iv secolo*, 62; GRILLMEIER A., *Jesus der Christ I*, 305.
27 Cfr. *Dem. Ev.* iv 2-6 (151-160); v 6.13 (229-230; 236-237); *Eccl. Theol.* II 21 (130-131), III 3 (146).
28 Cfr. *Dem. Ev.* iv 3,7 (153); cfr. GRILLMEIER A., *Jesus der Christ I*, 310.
29 Cfr. *Eccl. Theol.* II 14 (115), as opposed to Marcellus of Ancyra; *Dem. Ev.* v 1,11 (212).
30 Cfr. *Eccl. Theol.* I 8.9.12 (66.67.72).
31 Cfr. GRILLMEIER A., *Jesus der Christ I*, 310; R. FARINA, *L'Impero e l'Imperatore cristiano in Eusebio di Cesarea. La prima teologia politica del Cristianesimo*, Zürich 1966, 39.
32 Cfr. *Dem. Ev.* iv 2.3.6 (152-154;160); v 4.10-15 (225-226); *Eccl. Theol.* II 7 (104), among others.
33 Cfr. *Eccl. Theol.* III 1-2 (138-149); also *Dem. Ev.* v 1,6 (211).
34 Cfr. *Eccl. Theol.* I 11; II 7 (70;105).
35 *Eccl. Theol.* III 6 (164): «Only the Son, honored with the paternal divinity…has made all things… even the Paraclete Spirit himself (cfr. John 1:3; Col 1:16)… The Paraclete Spirit is not God nor is his Son… he is one of those who were created by means of the Son»; cfr. LADARIA L.F., *El Espíritu Santo en san Hilario de Poitiers*, Madrid 1977, 322.
36 LADARIA L.F., *El Espíritu Santo en san Hilario de Poitiers*, 300.

hand, this divinity was for him a second order divinity. It seemed that the Holy Spirit was excluded from the divine condition, even in the somewhat diminished way that corresponds to the Son. Thus Eusebius did not attain a clear formulation of the Trinitarian faith and still remained with Binitarianism. Nevertheless, if he overstated his case because of his excessive separation of the three *hypostases*, in his great adversary Marcellus of Ancyra we can evidence the opposite trend.

4

Marcellus of Ancyra

If Eusebius of Caesarea, with all the due distinctions that we have already emphasized, could be considered somewhat close to Arius, Marcellus of Ancyra (†circa 374) strongly emphasized the unity of the three divine persons. He did not deny the Trinity, but he did tend to distort it and obscure it somewhat for the purpose of opposing Arianism[37]. The problem is not whether the Son is God or not, but to what extent he has a personal subsistence of his own. Marcellus attempted to save the unicity of God[38]. Even before the world existed, the Logos was already in the Father as his δύναμις. The Logos is the power of God[39]. He is one with the Father in οὐσία and *hypostasis*[40]. The classical passages of John (10:30 and 14:9 among others) were interpreted by Marcellus in the sense of personal unity. It is the opposite extreme to that of the union of wills that we saw in Arian thought[41]. In the «let us make» of Gen 1:26, the Father has addressed his «mind» —in reality, himself[42]. The Logos is the mediator in creation, but instead, as a power of the Father and not as a different *hypostasis*. The texts of the unicity of God, for instance Deuteronomy 6:4, to which the Arians resorted in order to exclude the Son from the divinity, were used by Marcellus to integrate him into the unity of the Father. The Son is one (not only one thing) with the Father, and hence there is only one God. In the sense of the unity of the Father and his Logos as well, we must understand the revelation of the name of God in Exod 3:14[43].

---

37 We know of the thought of Marcellus primarily from the book of Eusebius, *Contra Marcellum* (GCS, Eus. Werke IV, 1-58). In this same volume we can see fragments of Marcellus (185-215).
38 Cfr. fragment 75-78 (200-202).
39 Fragment 73 (198).
40 Cfr. Eusebius, *C. Marc.* I 1,5 (4).
41 Fragment 74 (199-200).
42 Fragment 58 (195); *C. Marc.* II 2, 41-42 (42-43).
43 Cfr. Simonetti M., *La crisi ariana nel IV secolo*, 67. Fragment 61-63 (196-197); 77-78 (201-202).

The generation of the Logos and similar terms contained in Prov 8:22 and the verse that follows, refer to the human generation of Jesus. Only at this point in time does the Son clearly turn into «person». Jesus has called himself the «son of man», and thus the affirmations that we find about him in the Scriptures refer to his humanness and not to his divinity. At the time of the incarnation, the divine monad has been expanded into a dyad, and subsequently into a triad with the outpouring of the Spirit[44]. Following the line of thought mentioned before, the affirmations about the Son in Col 1:14 and the following passages, his condition as image, and the like, refer to his human nature[45]. Hence, we go back to the Asian and African traditions of Irenaeus and Tertullian, which are indeed closer to the intention of the letter to the Colossians, although evidently the conception of these authors is quite different from that of Marcellus. In his line of interpretation of Trinitarian theology, we must include the theology of the endtime. His interpretation of 1Cor 15:24-28 is well-known, and it has given rise to considerable discussion[46]. The delivery of the kingdom to the Father implies the end of the kingdom of Jesus, which began when he came into this world. The soteriological function, in view of which the Father has sent his Son into the world, has come to an end. The Logos has not ceased to exist, but he finds himself in the same situation in which he was before the creation of the world. He returns as «energy» to the God from whom he left[47]. Marcellus set forth his doubts about the final fate of the humanity of the Logos. Having finished his saving mission, there is no reason for this humanity to be united with the Logos[48]. Nevertheless, this point is not totally clear. Those who opposed the doctrine of Marcellus regarding the end of the kingdom of the Son were a determining factor for inserting in the symbol of Constantinople the phrase «and his kingdom will have no end». We will address this again in due time.

---

44 Fragment 66-70; 76-77 (197-198; 201). There can be no Trinity if it does not have its origin in the monad (fragment 60). The Logos and the Spirit are different in the unity. Among the last references in the bibliography about Marcellus, cfr. SEIBT K., *Die Theologie des Markell von Ancyra*, Berlin-New York 1994; cfr. the critical note of SIMONETTI M., «Sulla teologia di Marcello di Ancira» in *Rivista di Scienza e Letteratura Religiosa* 31 (1995) 257-269; Seibt, among other things tends to consider the divine sonship of the Logos occurring before the incarnation, vis à vis the thesis that has been primarily maintained.

45 Cfr. fragment 91-95 (204-205).

46 Cfr. PELLAND G., «Le théologie et l'exégèse de Marcel d'Ancyre sur 1 Co 15:24-28. Un schème hellénistique en théologie trinitaire» in *Greg* 71 (1990) 679-695.

47 Cfr. GRILLMEIER A., *Jesus der Christ I*, 436f.

48 Fragment 119-121 (211); cfr. SIMONETTI M., *La crisi ariana nel IV secolo*, 71.

Without having attempted a rigorous chronological presentation, we have described the lines of thought that revolve around Nicaea and that enable us to duly interpret within its context the symbol of this important Council. We have seen how the thought of Origen regarding the three *hypostases* has had a great influence, although this thinking has received an exaggerated interpretation which led to the separation between the participants, as evidenced in the extreme position of Arius and in the more moderate stance of Eusebius. On the other hand, mention must be made of the strong emphasis on the divine unity evidenced in Marcellus that generated problems regarding the modality of the eternal existence of the Trinity itself. Hence, some have considered him as the heir of Sabellianism. Ranging between the two lines of thought of Arius and Marcellus, the theology of the great Church was faced with the need to find its own way, and this need reached its most qualified expression in the Council of Nicaea.

5

The Symbol of Nicaea (325)

Undoubtedly, with the symbol of Nicaea we reach one of the basic issues and landmarks —if not the decisive one— in the development of Trinitarian dogma. It goes beyond the scope of this treatise to describe the historical issues as to why this assembled council was called and held[49]. Regarding the origin of the Nicene formula, Eusebius affirmed that its base was the symbol of his Church, and he himself submitted it to the assembly. It is assumed that some additions were made, specifically ὁμοούσιος. It does not seem, however, that this information from Eusebius can be fully worthy of acceptance. A preparatory proceeding for the Council of Nicaea was the Synod of Antioch held at the beginning of the year 325, which had already addressed the Arian problem. Indeed, the anathemas attached to the symbol of Antioch seem to anticipate those of Nicaea[50]. Nevertheless, whatever the influences, what we are interested in analyzing is the text of the Council of Nicaea:

---

49 Details can be seen in SIMONETTI M., *La crisi ariana nel IV secolo*, 78ff; HANSON R.P.C., *The Search for the Christian Doctrine of God*, 152ff.

50 Cfr. SIMONETTI M., 83; HANSON R.P.C., 164; KELLY J.N.D., *Primitivos credos cristianos*, Salamanca 1980, 250ff.

We believe in one God, the Father Almighty, Maker of all things visible and invisible.

And in one Lord Jesus Christ, the Son of God, begotten of the Father the only begotten; that is, of the essence (οὐσία) of the Father, God of God Light of Light, very God of very God, begotten, not made, being of one substance (ὁμοούσιου) with the Father; by whom all things were made both in heaven and on earth; who for us men and for our salvation, came down and was incarnate and was made man; he suffered and the third day he rose again, ascended into heaven; from thence he shall come to judge the quick and the dead.

And in the Holy Ghost.

But those who say: «There was a time when he was not» and: «He was not before he was made»; and «he was made out of nothing», or «he is of another substance or essence» (ὑποστάσεως ἡ οὐσίας), or «the Son of God is created», or «changeable» or «alterable», they are condemned by the holy catholic and apostolic Church (DS 125-126).

We must briefly comment on some of the most outstanding aspects of the text[51]. The first article refers only to God, the Father Almighty. What is beyond any doubt is that the designation of «God» refers primarily to the Father in the early days of the Church. We have already had the occasion to verify this. God the Father has been the Father of Jesus in the New Testament. However, in the second and third centuries, a relationship was established between the fatherhood and the creation of all, and in fact, the Father is here the almighty, the maker of all things. The formulation is frequent in the symbols of the first centuries. The idea of the «one» God and Father and the making or creation of all things are united in 1Cor 8:6. The Greek «*pantocrátor*» is not translated exactly as «omnipotent» or «almighty». He is not only the one who can do everything, but the one who maintains it and reigns in his transcendent power. No mention is made of an abstract property, but rather of the real exercise of this power. Nevertheless, we would not be interpreting the first article of the creed correctly if we were to think that it is only related to what is cosmic. The Trinitarian structure of the symbol reveals to us that the divine Fatherhood is affirmed mostly in the relationship with the Son. As we have already pointed out, only the revelation of God as Father of Jesus, witnessed in the New Testament, has enabled us to speak of God the *Father* as the maker of all things.

51 Cfr. on the text and its transmission DOSSETTI G.L., *Il simbolo di Nicea e di Costantinopoli*, Rome 1967. In addition to the works to which we have been referring, cfr. SESBOÜÉ B., *Le Dieu du salut*, in *Histoire des Dogmes* I, Paris 1994, 103-120, on the structure of the symbols, and especially as related to the peculiarities of the symbol of Nicaea in 343ff.

The second article is devoted to the Son, using the incarnation as a starting point: «one Lord Jesus Christ» (cfr. 1Cor 8:6). All the statements that follow refer to Jesus Christ. He is the «Lord». There are many places where the titles of Christ and Lord are combined (cfr. Phil 2:11; Rom 5:1; 7:25, among others). It is stated to begin with that this Lord Jesus Christ is the Son of God. The expression is based on the New Testament. The article continues with the eternal origin of Jesus, «begotten of the Father». These terms belong to the ancient tradition. The generation of the Son is unique and unrepeatable; it is that of the «only-begotten» (cfr. 1John 1:14 1:18; 3:16; 4:9). This clarification was quite frequent in the ancient symbols. Stating that the Son has been begotten is equivalent to saying that he is «of the essence of the Father». Here it is a matter of stressing the real sense of the generation, which should not be understood as something material, as though the Son were a part of the Father[52]. The Arians rejected the generation because they thought that it meant the splitting or the division of a part of the Father, but it is possible that they could have agreed with this interpretation of «only-begotten».

The following expressions are more generic: «God of God, light of light». We have already addressed some of the history of these comparisons, which introduce in God the distinction without any lessening or decrease of the unity. Nevertheless, the expression «true God of true God» is clearly contrary to what the Arians believed, as they only agreed to refer to the Son as God in a generic way, construing, as well, the name Son in a generic way. The symbol emphasizes that the Son is God in *strictu sensu*, by virtue of the making or generation[53]. «Begotten not made» is a new clarification. The generation that gives being to the Son is different from creation by means of which beings that we know come into existence. Going somewhat further, we could say that Arius could also have accepted this idea because he made the distinction between the generation or creation of the Son from the Father alone and the creation or making of the other things through the action of the Son and by the will of the Father. However, the expressions of the Council go beyond these. It is a matter of making a clear distinction between the two modalities of coming into existence, without accepting any other difference between the two. This is the main purpose of the terms Father and Son in the New Testament. The making or generation of the

---

52 Cfr. EUSEBIUS OF CAESAREA, *Ep.*, 3, 9-10, to the community of Caesarea (cfr. Opitz, *Urkunden*, 45); SIMONETTI M., *La crisi ariana nel IV secolo*, 89.
53 Cfr. GRILLMEIER A., *Jesus der Christ I*, 407f.

Son is not a creation from nothing. This is stated in the analogy with human generation or making, although only taking the comparison so far, in that in God we find the main analogy with every fatherhood and every sonship.

«Of one substance with the Father». The phrase of one substance —consubstantial— is the most characteristic term of Nicaea, and it will give way to countless controversies. It is probably also the most directly anti-Arian formula[54], while at the same time it is one that could bring about considerable difficulties because of its ambiguity. The discussion clarified that the term does not apply to God as it does with corporal or earthly beings. Thus, the integrity of the essence of the power of the Father is guaranteed[55]. Arius could not accept it, even with these exceptions and clarifications. The difficulty that still prevailed was that *homoousios* is a term not found in Scriptures. On the other hand, the ambiguity of *homoousios* comes from the ambiguity of *ousía*, which could point to the individual essence or to the common essence of all beings having the same specie. Consequently, if we understand the *ousía* in the first sense (that is, stressing the unity of the Father and the Son), *homoousios* could be Sabellian, and in fact this was the stance taken by the Arians and Semi-Arians when they opposed the term. Nevertheless, the fact that it could be interpreted with various meanings could itself have made it acceptable to all. Most specifically, some could interpret it in a very strong sense of the unity of the Father and of the Son. However, there was also the possibility of interpreting it in a generic sense, in that the *ousía* of the Son is like that of the Father, and as a result of this, it could simply be possible to see in the term the affirmation of the divinity of the Son[56]. At any rate, it is clear

---

54 Arius expressly denies *homoousios* in the *Thaleía*; cfr. ATHANASIUS, *Syn.* 15,3 (Opitz, Ath. Werke II/1, 242): «he is not equal (to the Father) nor of his own substance».

55 Cfr. EUSEBIUS, *Ep.* 3,12-13 (45-46); cfr. SIMONETTI M., 89; HANSON R.P.C., 164ff.

56 Cfr. in SIMONETTI M., 89ff, a summary of the history that we are addressing: Origen used the term according to a fragment that has only been preserved in the translation of Rufinus, who has attempted to «normalize or standardize» the affirmations of Origen according to the sense of Nicaea. The controversy of the two Dionysiuses added another aspect to this situation. Dionysius of Alexandria was accused of not accepting it. However, Dionysius of Rome did not take up the accusation. At any rate, the former defended himself by saying that he had not accepted it out of fear of running the risk of Sabellianism. He was aware of the polemics and accepted it after *pro bono pacis*, in a sense of a generic essence, as a human father and a human son. We know that Paul of Samosata used it to deny the Son his personal subsistence. It was not used by Alexander of Alexandria. It was also alien to the terminology of Origen who insisted on the personal subsistence of the Son, and it was also alien in his followers who, as he had done, defended the three *hypostases*. It is very difficult to believe that the proposal could have come from this line of thought. Possibly it came from the West, where there was less concern for defining the personal subsistence of the Son. The possibility of interpreting it in the generic sense (Dionysius) could have led the followers of Origen to accept it.

that a third choice is excluded between the transcendent God and the world. The Son is God as is the Father, and by him God himself is in direct contact with the creature.

Therefore, it is necessary to acknowledge that the sense of *homoousios* is not fully clear from the beginning. What is denied is even more important than what is affirmed. The Son is God like the Father; he is not a second God. He has the same divinity received from the Father. The universal creating mediation of the Son closes this part of the creed (cfr. 1Cor 8:6; John 1:3; Col 1:16, which specifically mention all things in heaven and earth). The generation is not seen in direct relation with this creating act. Post-Nicaene theology further clarified this idea. For the time being, it is quite clear that the mediator of creation is God as Father.

After the eternal generation, and following the common line of thought of the symbols, the human generation or making of Jesus is addressed. It does not seem that repetition «was incarnate and was made man» should be considered as a precise affirmation of the soul of Christ. This issue, which later caused even more agitation in the controversies with Apolinarius of Laodicea, had not yet been explicitly posed in those times. Nevertheless, the human nature of Jesus was emphasized together with his divinity, which had already been addressed immediately before. Although we must confess the divine birth of Jesus, we must also confess the human one that takes place «for us men and for our salvation». All the creeds reproduce the core of the *kerygma* of the New Testament, the death and the resurrection of Jesus (cfr. 1Cor 15:3-4) and his ascension to heaven. Likewise, the confession of the exalted Jesus sitting at the right hand side of the Father is frequent in the New Testament, although this last issue is not explicit in Nicaea (cfr. Acts 2:33; Rom 8:34; 1Pet 3:22; Heb 1:3, among others). In this part of the symbol, there is no special originality either, as also no mention is made of the second coming to judge the living and the dead (cfr. Acts 10:42).

A very brief reference is made of the Holy Spirit, without any comments. The Spirit is united in the Christian confession of faith to the Father and Son, but absolutely nothing else is added. We will see how this aspect is addressed in Constantinople.

Anathemas completed this formulation of faith. The most radical expressions of the Arians were condemned, such as «there was a time when he was not» and «he did not exist before he was engendered», which opposed the eternity of the Son, and mainly, «he was made out of nothing», which was the clearest denial of his divinity. According to Eusebius of Caesarea[57], these formulations about the eternity of the Son left open the possibility of the distinction between a generation in power and a generation in act, which was the line of thought of Marcellus of Ancyra and other bishops who did not want to talk about the generation before the incarnation. On the other hand, those who followed the line of thought of Eusebius had difficulties in a generation *ab eterno* —as was already taught by Origen— which for them could be equivalent to the denial of the generation. Likewise, those who said that the Son is mutable or alterable were condemned. Arius himself defended the immutability of the Son. The key issue is the last one: the Son has not been made of that which did not exist (out of nothing, which is the method of creation). He is not derived from any other essence or *hypostasis* which is not that of the Father. This is the repetition of what has already been said in the symbol. Nevertheless, what is interesting in the anathema is that mention is made of the *ousía* or *hypostasis* as being equivalent. This leads then to the problem of whether we must understand *ousía* in the sense of individual essence, and as a result, possibly giving the impression that we are dealing with the same *hypostasis*. In other words, this would mean that the Son does not have a personal individuality. Therefore, because of this, some considered that the *homoousios* was Sabellian[58]. At any rate, this lack of clarity and these difficulties show us that we are evidencing the beginning of the road that will take us from the year 325 almost to the end of the fourth century. It is to be expected that only time would help determine with precision the new terms used for pointing to a specific line and direction of thought, although still without a precise and well delimited content.

Hence we can see the points that were never specified clearly in Nicaea, as well as those issues that were still open-ended. In order to have a more complete picture of the theological situation, we can also suppose that at that time a clear doctrine of the ecumenical council or of its magisterial authority, and so forth, had still not been determined. Precisely, beginning with Nicaea, this doctrine would

---

57 This had been clarified by Constantine, according to Eusebius *Ep.* 3,16 (Opitz, *Urkunden*, 46); Simonetti M., *La crisi ariana nel IV secolo*, 93.

58 Cfr. Simonetti M., *La crisi ariana nel IV secolo*, 94, who pointed out a possible distinction between the uses of *ousía* and *homoousios*. The first one is always understood in the sense of the individual essence: the Son is begotten of the essence of the Father who is, thus, distinguished from the Son. On the contrary, the *homoousios* involves the Son in the paternal *ousía*. The derivation of the Son from the paternal *ousía* does not necessarily imply that his is different, but that he participates in the *ousía* of the Father. In fact no mention is made of an *ousía* of the Son.

begin to be developed. It is clear that we cannot judge, based only on our current criteria, the discussions and even the opposition that arose as a result of the council of Nicaea.

6
The vicissitudes after the Council of Nicaea

In this treatise we cannot attempt a detailed analysis of the complex history of the fourth century, during which both the strictly doctrinal aspects as well as those of imperial policy were of decisive importance. There was an endless series of synods, and in each of them a different group or party prevailed, each of which had addressed the Trinitarian problem and had consequently prepared its own symbol of faith[59]. Our interest will revolve around the great theological figures who have analyzed in depth the contents of the faith proclaimed in Nicaea. We will only attempt a brief historical overview to aid us in understanding the doctrinal evolution during the time between the Council of Nicaea (325) and the first Council of Constantinople (381)[60].

6.1. EVENTS THAT TOOK PLACE UNTIL THE DEATH OF CONSTANTINE IN 337

Arius had died one year before Constantine. Athanasius had been elected to the Episcopal see of Alexandria in the year 328, when Alexander died. The election was unanimous, although some Semi-Arian sources stated that there were some intrigues and scheming in the election. After the year 328, many Arians as well as Arianizers who were followers of the ideas of Eusebius of Caesarea regained the grace of the Emperor and for the most part made their ideas felt in the East. Even Arius was rehabilitated. Marcellus of Ancyra, who favored ideas that were completely contrary to those set forth by Arianism, was deposed for the first time from his see. Athanasius, who followed the Nicene trend, endured the same fate.

---

59 A long list of these vicissitudes can be seen primarily in the cited works: SIMONETTI M., 99-434; also in HANSON R.P.C., 181-386; KELLY J.N.D., 315-351.
60 I was inspired primarily by the summary of SESBOÜÉ B., *Le Dieu du Salut*, 250ff, completed by SIMONETTI M., *La crisi ariana*, especially 99-267.

When Constantine died, his sons Constantius and Constans began their reigns in the East and in the West. Constantius was Semi-Arian, while Constans was Nicene. Marcellus of Ancyra, in a statement addressed to Pope Julius (341, Council of Rome), clarified that the kingdom of the Son will have no end and that the Son will reign forever with the Father. The Logos was already called the pre-existent Son, but Marcellus avoided talking about the generation of the Son who was at that time still considered a *dynamis*, as was the case in the previous period. In Rome, in the year 341, the Church was very indulgent with Marcellus, and his anti-Arianism was enough to rule out any suspicion.

During that same year, 341, a council was held in Antioch against Pope Julius. Vague and not radically Arian terms were used on that occasion. What prevailed were both the anti-Sabellian and the anti-Marcellian concerns. It was affirmed that the Son has been begotten before all time, and the extreme Arian articles were condemned and denounced, although there were important changes with respect to Nicaea. For example, it was stated that the Son is not a creature like other creatures and that he has not been begotten as they have been. Arian formulas were reproduced, while at the same time different elements of the symbol of Nicaea were discussed. Mention was made of the three *hypostases* united in harmony. As we can clearly see, many problems arose as a result of the ambiguity of the expressions and formulations.

What was incorrectly referred to as the fourth formula of Antioch was submitted in the year 342 to the Emperor Constans in Treveris. It is briefer than the previous one, and no mention is made of the three *hypostases* or of *homoousios*. Likewise, this formula does not refer to «true God from true God». The same anathemas are maintained as in Nicaea. Another important position is found in the symbols of Sardica of the year 343. Easterners and Westerners prepared their symbols separately. The Easterners wanted to maintain that the Father has begotten the Son out of his own power or will, as opposed to what Marcellus set forth, because the expansion of the monad into a triad was «natural». On the other hand, theologians of the West underlined the divine unity and referred to a *hypostasis* of Father, Son, and Holy Spirit. To this end, they based their arguments on texts such as John 10:30 and 14:9, which we have seen were interpreted with more nuances by the great authors. The formulas of Antioch in the year 344 and those of Sirmio of the years 349-350 and 551 were excessively Semi-Arian. Upon the death of Constans in the year 350, the whole empire was entrusted to

Constantius. Because of this, the Semi-Arian party also acquired more strength in the West. Synods were held in Arles and Milan (353 and 355) in order to address orthodoxy which was a source of controversy, although the synods were manipulated by the emperor. Hilary of Poitiers expressed resistance in Gaul, but his final fate was exile, as was also the case for Pope Liborius and the elderly Ossius of Cordoba. This was followed by the subsequent depositions of Athanasius. Around the years 557 to 560, the Arian victory seemed to be complete and resounding[61]. The symbol of Sirmio of the year 557 would account for the greatest victory of the Semi-Arian line of thought. No mention was made of *homoousios*, and instead they strongly insisted that the Father is greater than the Son because of his dignity, his glory, and his majesty. The Father has no beginning. The symbol of Sirmio said that nothing is known about the generation of the Son, using Isa 53:8 almost in the sense of denial and not of a reverent silence. The term substance was not used because it is not included in the Scriptures.

6.3.   TOWARD A CHANGE IN THE SITUATION

Beginning around the years 358 and 360, these same excesses led to schism. However, at the synod of Sirmio, held in 358, no formula of faith was produced, although the «Homoiousian» thesis prevailed. In other words, the Son is «like the Father in regard to the *ousía*». Even though the terms did not correspond exactly with those of Nicaea, they were indeed not far from them. In the synod of Ancyra in 358, as a result of the efforts of Basil of Ancyra, the formula «ὁμοιούσιος κατ' οὐσίαν» had been proposed. In the fourth council of Sirmio of the year 559, an agreement was reached regarding the generic formulas, although it did not please anyone.

In the year 359 the councils of Westerners and Easterners were held separately in Rimini and Seleucia[62]. While the Westerners moved along lines that are quite close to Nicaea and accepted the term *substantia*, the Easterners proscribed the use of the Greek equivalent «οὐσία» because it is not found in the Scriptures. In the East, the Semi-Arians were the ones who won, and as a consequence of a complex combination of turns of events, they were encouraged by

---

61 It is worth remembering the famous phrase of JEROME, *Dial. Contra Luciferianos* 19 (PL 23,172): «The whole world wept and was utterly frightened of being Arian». HILARY OF POITIERS, *Trin.* VI 1 (CCL 62,196): «In almost all the provinces of the Roman Empire many churches had already been infected by the disease of this venomous and spiteful preaching, and they were alike pervaded by it because of the prolonged repetition of these teachings…».

62 Cfr. SIMONETTI M., *La crisi ariana nel IV secolo*, 313-349.

the Westerners to approve a series of ambiguous formulas which, under an orthodox appearance, did not actually reject completely the basic Arian thesis of the creation of the Son. In fact, while anyone who asserted that the Son existed without question before all times (and not only before the centuries) was anathematized, those who mentioned that God the Son is like other creatures were also condemned. We already are acquainted with the Arian matrix of this affirmation.

Supporting these events were the doctrinal stances of their main advocates. The most radical Arians continued with their extreme theses, called *anomeas*, because they wanted to avoid all mention of any similarity or likeness between the Father and the Son. Aetius and Eunomius were the most representative names of this second generation Arianism. Their theses were indeed radical. According to them, in view of the fact that what characterizes the divine nature is the lack of generation, the begotten Son cannot be God. The Son has been created, although not as other things are, because he is greater than all of them. Prov 8:22, «the Lord created me...» was a basic point of support for this group; so also was John 14:28, «the Father is greater than I», which was now interpreted in the sense of a difference in substance. At the beginning of the Arian controversy, this passage still helped affirm the divinity of the Son as to his being begotten by the Father who is «greater» than he. Now, in view of the fact that according to the orthodox position the divinity of the Son is equal to that of the Father in everything, the text in John 14:28 is used by the Arians to deny his divinity.

Less known, although equally important, was the group of the «homeos» who were content to just state the generic likeness between the Father and the Son (ὁμοίωσις), although without making any comments about the issues regarding the substance (cfr. the formulas to which we have referred in the synod of Sirmio of the year 357).

«Homoiousians» stated, as we have already shown, that the Son is «like the Father according to his essence». They did not dare affirm the *homos*—the equality or the identity of essence— although they did mention essence together with likeness, in order to save in this way the subsistence of the Son. Basil of Ancyra and George of Laodicea were among the representatives of this line of thought. For them, *homoousios* would confuse the Father and the Son because the «Son» is a word suggesting consubstantiality. He is truly begotten, unlike humans who are children of God by adoption. There is one divinity, only one *basileia*, only one beginning. What is spoken about in Prov 8:22, instead of simply implying a creation out of nothing, helps to clarify the understanding of generation. It eliminates the connotation and implication of «passing on» something, as is the case with bodily generation. Human generation produces a fellow creature. Therefore it is not enough simply to speak about unity of will between the Father and the Son. In comparison, when speaking of fellow creatures, one's fellow human being is not identical with the one with whom he is similar. In like manner, the prerogatives of the divinity of the Son are similar, but not identical with, those of the Father. The Holy Spirit also subsists from the Father through the Son. These are the key ideas of the «Homoiousians». Beginning with the early decade of the sixties, there was a greater union between these groups and the Nicenes[63], and the followers of the thesis set forth in the council increased in number. A remarkable change took place within a few years[64]. The «Homoiousians» had contributed considerably to the final victory of the thesis of Nicaea. For this reason the term «Semi-Arians» that has been used to refer to them through the centuries does not seem to be adequate. The classification is not so simple. This has been clearly shown in this brief review of the events of the conflicted fourth century. At this point in our study we can address the great theological figures of that time, who in the East and in the West have contributed decisively to the victory of the Nicene faith: Athanasius of Alexandria and Hilary of Poitiers.

7

Athanasius of Alexandria

Let us begin with Athanasius († 373) to whom we have already referred in the previous section. His life was marked by five exiles as a consequence of the ecclesiastical and political vicissitudes to which we have briefly referred. We will focus now on some of the aspects of his theological contribution.

As did his predecessor Alexander, Athanasius resorted to the metaphors used from the beginning by Origen in Alexandria, which are so well known to all of us: the Son is image, splendor (ἀπαυγάσμα), imprint (χαρακτήρ) (Heb 1:2),

---

63 This union was greatly encouraged by Hilary of Poitiers who tried to attract these more moderate groups in order to form a common front against the more radical Arians. Cfr. *De syn.* 85-89 (PL 19,536-542).
64 Later on we will briefly address the main events of the years 360-380, prior to the date when the council of Constantinople was held.

truth, wisdom. He also used the metaphors of the ray of the sun and of light[65]. In view of the fact that God can never be without what belongs to him, the Son has to be eternal as the Father and hence has to exist forever[66].

For Athanasius —and here we undoubtedly find a key contribution to the Christian doctrine of God— the Trinity does not depend on the creation of the world. It exists in its fullness of life independently from the creation. It is not necessary for God to produce first an intermediary or Demiurge in order to create the world. It is clear that Athanasius developed the traditional thesis of the Son as mediator in creation, which we have already witnessed in the New Testament. Nevertheless, this mediator is God from all eternity, just as the Father is, and not begotten to that end. He has not existed in order to be the cause of creation, but we have been created by him. Even without the creation, the Son would always exist at the side of the Father[67]. There is no necessity to resort to any type of «inferiority» of the Son to explain the creative mediation. There is a direct God-world relationship, unlike that which the Arians believed. The Son is the *ousía* of the Father[68]. In the Father and in the Son, there is only one divine nature, one and the same, a unity of essence[69].

This union of the Son with the Father, which is not dependent on creation, is what led Athanasius to believe that there is not a substantial logos and wisdom inherent in the divine essence, nor a logos and wisdom that would come from the existence of the personal Logos. On the contrary, the true God is the power and the wisdom and the Word of the Father. It is wisdom per se, power, light per se, truth per se… The only Son is the most perfect image of the Father[70].

---

65 Cfr. among others *C. Arian.* I 20-21;24;27 (PG 26,53-56;61;68) III 3-4 (328-329). In addition to the works to which we have been referring, see also KANNENGIESSER Ch., *Le Verbe de Dieu selon Athanase d'Alexandrie*, Paris 1990; WIDDICOMBE P., *The Fatherhood of God from Origen to Athanasius*, Oxford 1994; SESBOÜÉ B. - MEUNIER B., *Dieu peut-il avoir un Fils. Le débat trinitaire du IV siècle*, Paris 1993, 19-130.

66 Cfr. *C. Ar.* I 19-20 (52-53).

67 Cfr. *C. Ar.* II 29-31 (208-213). Cfr. SIMONETTI M., *La crisi ariana nel IV secolo*, 268f.

68 Cfr. *C. Ar.* I 15 (44); the Son is ἐκ τῆς οὐσίας of the Father; ibid. I 16 (45), ἐκ τῆς οὐσίας αὐτοῦ γέννημα; cfr. I 20;26 (53;65); III 6 (332f), in the Son lies the fullness of the divinity of the Father, and the like; cfr. HANSON R.P.C., 438; SIMONETTI M., 270f.

69 *C. Ar.* III 3-4 (328-329): they are one in the uniqueness and in the characteristic attributes of their nature, as well as in the identity of divinity itself τῇ ταὐτότετι τῆς θεότητος. This would be most typical of Athanasius when pointing out the unity; cfr. SIMONETTI M., 275f. He does yet not use technical terms to refer to the difference in the persons.

70 Cfr. *Contra Gentes*, 46 (PG 25,93).

The generation of the Son by the Father does not mean any splitting, dividing, or passing on of something. God is certainly incorporeal. Nevertheless, despite this, generation is the adequate word to point out the way in which the Son proceeds from the Father and not the word creation. The co-eternity of the Father and the Son is based on the fact that the essence of the Father was always complete, without any need for someone to add what already belongs to his essence. The Son is the offspring of the Father; he alone is his Son. Human beings procreate after their birth, and this is due to the fact that their nature is incomplete. Nothing of this sort occurs in the case of God. His generation is eternal because his nature is complete[71]. This co-eternity of the Son corresponds to his perfect divinity in nature and truth (φύσει καί άλήθεια), and not by grace (κατά χάριν), as also happens in the deification of human beings[72].

Proverbs 8:22 was also a subject for discussion and analysis in the case of Athanasius. The «creation» of wisdom «for his fashioning» points to his physical birth and not the substance of Son. This physical birth makes sense only because God can rescue us once God's progeny have been made imperfect because of sin. In this way, the «creation» of the human nature of the Son takes place to complete his work[73]. The incarnation is necessary for human beings to be deified and to have access to the Father: «the man united to a creature; in other words, if the Son would not have been true God, he would have not been able to be deified, and the man could not have been in the presence of the Father if the one who had taken his body was not the true Word of the Father by his very own nature»[74]. As we can see, the soteriological argument played a leading role in the Trinitarian discourse of Athanasius. The true salvation of humanity cannot be fulfilled if the savior is not the true Son of the Father.

The divinity of the Son is clearly affirmed as he is begotten and not created, co-eternal with the Father. The one who generates and the one who is generated have always existed; the Son belongs to the Father according to his essence, κατ' ούσίαν, and is not a part of the Father. The human generation is temporal; the divine one is eternal. In the discussion with the Arians, the problem of the voluntary nature of this generation was posed. It is quite clear that for the Arians,

---

71 *C. Ar.* I 14 (41); also I 26.28 (65-68.69); *De decr. Nic. Syn.* 11-12 (Opitz, Ath. W II/1, 9).

72 Cfr. *C. Ar.* I 39 (92-93); II 59 (272-273); we are not *physei*, but *thesei* children; cfr. SIMONETTI M., 271. The true filiation is the guarantee of our salvation as this one can only take place if it is an act of God himself; cfr. *Or. De Incar. Verbi*, 13.54 (PG 25,120;192).

73 Cfr. *C. Ar.* II 66-67 (285-291).

74 *C. Ar.* II 70 (296).

the generation (properly stated, the creation) takes place because the Father wills it. The eternity of the generation and the fact that it is naturally unrelated to the creation or the plan of creating cast doubts on the problem of the will with which the Father begets his Son. Is then the generation something forced upon God? According to Athanasius, the difference between orthodox theology and the theology of the Arians is not the will with which the Father begets, but rather the nature that gives origin to the generation. In fact, the Arians saw the free generation and the generation in time as being the same, and the Son did not exist before his generation. Nevertheless, in the case of orthodox theology, we cannot speak of the moment prior to the generation or of a prior decision for the reason that this prior moment does not exist because of the coeternity of the Father and the Son. However, this does not mean that the Father would not have willed the generation of the Son, as though freedom and necessity could be in opposition to God. Rather, we must think very much to the contrary:

> If the Son exists by nature and not by will, is it perhaps that he has not been willed by the Father and that he exists against his will? Absolutely, not. The Son is loved by the Father…. Because as his goodness has not begun out of his will, although at the same time he cannot be good without will or without a plan… likewise, the existence of the Son, even though it has not begun out of will, is not involuntary nor lacking in consent. Indeed, in the same way that the Father loves his own *hypostasis*, so also he loves that of the Son, who is of his own essence…[75].

Hence, there is not something involuntary in God, as necessity and will are not related in him as they are in us. It is worth noting that the will with which the Father loves the Son is the same that leads him to love himself. Consequently, the generation is eternal and necessary, which does not mean at all that it is involuntary. On the other hand, without the divinity of the Son, there cannot be real salvation of the creatures. How is the divinity of the Father and of the Son related according to Athanasius? How is the unity and the difference between the two articulated? What use is made of the key term of Nicaea: *homoousios*? All of these speculative problems of Trinitarian theology had not yet been fully clarified in the thought of Athanasius.

---

75 *C. Ar.* III 66 (461); cfr. the previous chapters, 61ff (452ff); in the Word, the Father wills all things.

The *homoousios* seems to mean «equal nature» for Athanasius[76]. The Bishop of Alexandria still did not resort to this term in his early writings, although he explained and defended its use in *De decretis Nicenae Synodi*[77]. In *De Synodis*, he preferred the term to «*homoiousios*». While pointing to the equal substance, the term also denotes the origin of the *ousía* of the Son, engendered from the *ousía* of the Father[78]. The origin and the union should not be understood as separation in a material way, but with the metaphor of the ray and the sun: «We are not talking about two gods, but about one God that exists as a form of the divinity, as a relationship between the light and the ray»[79]. For Athanasius, *homoousios* meant that the Son is God, that he comes from the Father, and hence, that the two have the same essence. There is a fatherly substance from which the Son emerges as a perfect image. Thus, the unity of the two is explained in terms of the unity of light and its reflection[80].

Therefore, the only substance of the Trinity that Athanasius defended is the substance of the Father. He was less concerned about the issue of the unity of substance of the Father and the Son. Hence, we will not find the technical language of the difference between the *hypostases* in the unity of the substance. These were not the categories that Athanasius addressed. He was far more interested in affirming the divinity of the Son (and of the Holy Spirit) than «Trinitarian monotheism»[81]. In other words, the issue as to how the three are only one God will instead be the main concern of the Cappadocians. Nevertheless, it is clear that this does not mean that the unity of the Trinity is fully removed from his perspective:

There is only one modality of the divinity (εἶδος τῆς θεότητος) that is also in the Logos. Only one God is God the Father... who is also present in the Son... and who is

---

76 Cfr. SIMONETTI M., *La crisi ariana nel IV secolo*, 274.

77 1.3 and mostly 20 (Opitz, Ath. Werke II/1,1.3.17); the term means that the Son is not only in the likeness of the Father but also shares in the same things that come from the Father's likeness.

78 Cfr. *Syn.* 41.48 (Opitz, Ath. Werke II/1,226-227;272-273); the Son and the Father are one in *ousía*. He also uses the term in *Serap.* II 5.6 (PG 26,616-617) in reference to the Father and the Son. The consubstantiality is derived from the fact of the generation. He does not seem to address in greater depth the modality of the divine unity. In *Serap.* I 27 (PG 26,593), it is also said that the Holy Spirit is consubstantial with the Father and the Son.

79 *Syn.* 52,1 (275); HANSON R.P.C., *The Search for the Doctrine of God*, 441.

80 Cfr. HANSON R.P.C., *The Search for the Doctrine of God*, 441ff; also PIETRAS H., «L'unità di Dio in Atanasio di Alessandria. Una descrizione dinamica della Trinità» in *Rassegna di Teologia* 32 (1991) 558-581, especially pages 565,567,572.

81 This has been addressed in PANNENBERG W., *Teología Sistemática I*, Madrid 1992, 296-298.

also in the *Pneuma*, because all things operate by means of the Logos in him (the Spirit). Hence, we confess that God is only one in the Trinity[82].

In addition to a few citations such as the one to which we have just referred, the Athanasian teachings on the Holy Spirit are found in his letters to Serapion. In these letters, in which the doctrine based on the Holy Spirit is developed, instruction on the Trinity is also completed. In fact, the Spirit, who is of God and not a creature,[83] belongs to the one, eternal, and immutable Trinity…[84]. The Trinity is the only God[85]. The operational unity of the Trinity where the persons are differentiated shows that the three are inseparable. This unity of action is evidenced in sanctification and in creation[86]. The most interesting thing that we are told about the Holy Spirit is that he belongs to the Son. In this way, two parallel relations are established, namely: Father-Son and Son-Holy Spirit[87]. The Holy Spirit belongs to the Son in the same way as the Son belongs to God. On some occasions, it is said that he is (ἴδιον) of the Son or the Logos, but also of God (or the Father)[88]. He is consubstantial (ὁμοούσιον) with the Father and with the Word[89], although it is never said directly that he is God[90]. The Spirit is from God, given by the Father through the Son:

82 *C. Ar.* III 15 (353); about the *eidos* of the Father in the Son, also III 16 (356-357); cfr. also III 3-5 (328-332), although no mention is made of the Holy Spirit. Once again, he speaks of the eternal Trinity, although without mentioning the Spirit in I 17.19 (48-49).

83 Cfr. *Serap.* 1,3ff, (PG 26, 536ff), and especially I 21-27 (580-593); the Spirit ponders the depths of God (1Cor 2:11); he sanctifies and is not sanctified; he vivifies and does not receive life; he is unction; he divinizes, and so forth; the arguments are repeated in *Serap.* III (ibid. 525-637).

84 Cfr. among others, *Serap.* I 28-30 (596-600); III 6 (633); IV 7.12 (648; 652-653), and the like.

85 *Serap.* I 14 (565): «… one is the grace that, originated in the Father by means of the Son, is fulfilled in the Holy Spirit. There is only one divinity, only one God who is beyond everyone for all and in all (cfr. Ephesians 4:6)»; I 16 (569): «One is the divinity and the faith of the holy Trinity»; cfr. IV 7 (648), and so forth.

86 This shows the divinity of the Spirit; cfr. the previous footnote and also, *Serap.* I 12.20.23.28.30-31 (561.577.584.596.601); III 5 (632), the divinity of the Spirit is repeated frequently in the prepositions: *of* the Father, *through* the Son, *in* the Holy Spirit. Concerning the sanctifying Spirit, cfr. DIDYMUS THE BLIND, *De Sp. Sanc.* 5,19; 53,231 (SCh 386, 160; 352).

87 Cfr. *Serap.* I 20 (576-580) regarding the unity with the Son as the Son with the Father; I 21 (580), about the τάξις and φύσις of the Spirit with respect to the Son, as of the latter with respect to the Father; III 1 (525), the «property» of the Son with respect to the Father is like that of the Holy Spirit with respect to the Son; the Holy Spirit is the image of the Son, I 20; I 24; IV 3 (577.588.641).

88 I 25.32 (589.605); the Spirit is inherent in the Logos and in the divinity of the Father; IV 4 (641), is inherent in the substance of the Word and can only be inherent in God; it is not alien to the substance and divinity of the Son.

89 Cfr. *Serap.* I 27 (593).

90 Although in *Serap.* I 31 (601), it is said that the Spirit is acknowledged as God (θεολογούμενον) together with the Logos; in I 28 (596) the same term is used with reference to the three of the Trinity.

The Spirit is given and sent on behalf of the Son, and he is also one and not many....If the Son, the living Word is one, so there must be a living perfect energy that is sanctifying and enlightening which is his gift. It is said that this energy comes from (ἐκ) the Father (cfr. John 15:26) because it shines, it is sent, and it is given on behalf (παρά) of the Logos who is from the Father, as we have confessed[91].

As we have already mentioned regarding the relation between the Father and the Son, neither is there a speculative solution in regard to the union of the Spirit with the Father and the Son, his «proceeding», and the like. Nevertheless, without any doubt we already find in these letters a remarkable development of pneumatology founded in the clear affirmation that the Spirit is God, consubstantial with the Father and the Son, and that as such, he belongs to the one and indivisible Trinity. His saving act, together with the Father and the Son, is the definitive proof of his divinity.

8

Hilary of Poitiers

The starting point for Hilary († 367) in his Trinitarian reflection is the formula of baptism as mentioned in Matt 28:19, which affirms the divine unity that has its source in the Father and also in the Trinity (a term that he used infrequently):

He sent them to baptize in the name of the Father and of the Son and of the Holy Spirit, in other words, in the confession of the author, of the only begotten and of the gift. Only one is the author of all things because «there is only one God, the Father, from whom all things come and for whom we exist, and one Lord, Jesus Christ, through whom all things come and for whom we exist» (1Cor 8:6). And only one Spirit, gift in all... Nothing will be missing in such a great perfection where, in the Father, the Son and the Holy Spirit, we find the infinite nature in the eternal, the revelation in the image, the enjoyment of the gift[92].

---

91 *Serap.* I 20 (580); cfr. I 22 (581).
92 *Trin.* II 1 (CCL 62,38).

The «three» are briefly characterized in this key passage. The Father is first and foremost the *auctor*, from whom everything comes. This term is repeated very frequently. To him corresponds the infinite and eternal being. In him, ultimately, lies the power. The Son is characterized as the image, as the perfect revelation of the Father. This designation is quite frequent in Hilary, along with other similar ones (form, figure of the Father)[93]. The Holy Spirit is already characterized from the beginning as a gift. We will address this issue again at the end of these pages.

The Son, word of the Father, is the consistent word and not a *flatus vocis*. Rather, this word is real and has in itself a real subsistence. «This Word is a reality, not a sound; a substance and not simply an expression; God and not emptiness»[94]. Precisely because Hilary wanted to maintain the true consistency of the Son, he did not believe that the traditional metaphors of Tertullian about the river and the ray of sun were enough[95]. On the contrary, light coming from light was his preferred comparison to give assurance about the real subsistence of the Son, while at the same time he is from the Father from whom he has been born[96].

As opposed to the Arians, who spoke of the «Father» and the «Son» without giving those names from the Scriptures their true value, Hilary insisted that they reflect reality. The Father is the Father and the Son is the Son in a real way, although in a different way with respect to everything related to human fatherhood. Between the two of them, there is a unity of nature based on the fact that the Father has begotten the Son. For Hilary, the difference between the two is expressed in different biblical passages, specifically 1Cor 8:6 that speaks, according to Hilary, about the *Deus ex quo* and about the *Deus per quem*. This distinction will help Hilary see already in action the Father and the Son with differentiated functions in the creation of the world and of humans according to Gen 1:1 and the verses that follow[97]. Nevertheless, in the creation itself, we also see the unity of substance, because the Father and the Son together make humans in «our» image, after «our» likeness (cfr. Gen 1:26). In other words, the two

---

93 Cfr. *Trin.* II 8 (45); III 23 (95); VII 37 (304-305), etc. In the creating mediation and in the saving mediation beginning with the theophanies of the Old Testament, the Son, frequently called the Word, reveals the Father.

94 *Trin.* II 15 (53); cfr. VII 11 (270-271).

95 Cfr. *Trin.* IX 37; cfr. HILARY OF POITIERS, *La Trinidad*, (LADARIA L.F. ed.), Madrid 1986, 463f, on the use of these metaphors by other authors.

96 Cfr. *Trin.* VI 12 (209-210); VII 29 (296-297).

97 Cfr. *Trin.* IV 16-22 (117-125); V 4-10 (154-160).

of them do it at the same time[98]. Therefore, the generation is the foundation of the unity of the Son and the Father, although Hilary, as had also been the case before with Irenaeus, resorted to Isa 53:8 (*generationem eius quis enarrabit?*) in order to avoid any speculations about the way in which this generation is carried out[99].

However, without resorting to too many details, Hilary showed us that he had a coherent idea about fatherhood and generation. The Son is not a creature. He has received the nature given to him from the Father because generation in God means that he begets and gives everything he has:

> According to the laws of nature, the one who has only one portion cannot be the whole. The one who proceeds from the perfect is perfect because the one who has everything has been given everything. And we do not have to think, either, that he has not given all because he still has it all, nor that he does not have it because he has given it away[100].

Hence, the generation does not mean a rupture or a decrease in the case of the Father. The reason for this lies in the simplicity of the divine nature that can be communicated in the ineffable generation which is carried out fully. The Father can give everything that he possesses without being deprived because of that which he gives. All this is due to the understanding of the divine life (cfr. John 5:26) which excludes every limitation to its fullness:

> … as the Father has life in himself, he has also given the Son the possibility of life in himself. With this he [Jesus] has intended to clearly indicate the unity of the nature (*unitas naturae*) that he has by virtue of the mystery of his birth. When referring to that which the Father has, he has intended to say that he has the Father himself in him; because God does not exist, as men do, as a compound of elements, in such a way that there is a difference between what he [Jesus] possesses and he [the Father] himself who possesses it. Rather, everything that he is, is life, in other words, perfect, complete, infinite nature; not formed by unequal elements, but living in all his being. And this na-

---

98 Cfr. *Trin.* IV 18-19 (121-122); V 8-9 (158-159).
99 Cfr. *Trin.* II 10-11 (47-49); III 17 (88-89); cfr. also VI 16 (214-215); IX 26 (399-400); in XII 8 (584-585) he determines how we should not understand in an anthropomorphic and excessively crass way the the term «womb» of Ps 110:3.
100 *Trin.* II 8 (46). As we can see, Hilary reacts here against the idea of the *portio* of Tertullian.

ture is given as it is possessed, and even though this means the birth of the one to whom it was given, it does not imply a diversity in the substance, because the nature is given as it is possessed (*cum talis data est qualis et habetur*)[101].

Being simplex in the highest sense, God can give himself fully. Even more so, he can only give himself to the Son in this way. Thus, according to Hilary, the idea itself of the divine generation eliminates from its very roots any subordination. A partial communication of the divine nature is contradictory. God, who is totally simplex, is also wholly and entirely Father. He is Father in everything that he is. The reflections of Hilary concerning divine Fatherhood are one of his greatest contributions to the Christian doctrine of God:

> At every point in time, God only knows how to be love, only how to be Father. And he who loves has no envy and he who is the Father is fully so.... The Father is everything because he exists; he possesses himself fully in the one for whom he is not only partly Father[102].
>
> In an incomprehensible and indescribable way, before any time and any age, he begot the only begotten from the unbegotten substance that is in him, and he gave his Son, born from him by means of his love and his power, everything that God is[103].

On two occasions, we see the idea of love united to that of self-communication in the sense that the Father makes the Son from his divine being. God is entirely Father; he is not only partly so. Everything in him is giving, love, thus ruling out any envy of communicating to the other one everything he is and he has. It would not make sense that if he could give himself fully, he did not do so. Therefore, the Father is the infinite capacity of communication, the infinite capacity of love. For this reason the Son must be equal to the Father in his divine nature, fully God in everything except in fatherhood. The divine nature that the Father originally possesses is also possessed by the Son, although it is received. Nevertheless, this is without any degeneration because nothing alien is included in this generation. The divine nature is maintained without variation[104]. From

---

101 *Trin.* VIII 43 (356). On the definition of God as life and total self-possession and also full giving, cfr. also *Trin.* VII 27 (294); *Syn.*19 (PL 10,495), among other places; cfr. LADARIA L.F., «Dios Padre en Hilario de Poitiers» in *EstTrin* 24 (1990) 443-479, especially 454f.
102 *Trin.* IX 61 (440). Also II 6 (43): *Pater tantum est.* The exclusion of the envy of God in the generation of the Son is seen also in VI 21 (220); cfr. GREGORY OF NAZIANZUS, *Or.* 25,16 (SCh 284,194-196).
103 *Trin.* III 3 (74).
104 Cfr. *Trin.* IX 36 (410); VIII 41 (354).

this starting point, we understand the interpretation that Hilary made of John 14:28, «the Father is greater than I». The Father is greater only because he gives and because he is the beginning. But the Son is not lesser because he receives it all[105]. And this total gift of the Father is not only that of eternal generation; it is also that of the perfect glorification of the humanity of Jesus in the resurrection, by virtue of which the eternal Son of God becomes fully Son also in the human nature that he has assumed[106].

Because the divinity which the Son receives is only from the divinity of the Father, he is not a second God next to him. The Father and the Son are only one thing (cfr. John 10:30), because one comes from the other[107]. But we still do not find the technical explanation for *homoousios*. Stating that the Son is consubstantial with the Father is equivalent for Hilary of saying that he is «God of God», to affirm that the Son has been born and is not a division of the unbegotten God. He is first begotten, in every sense equal to the Father, and his essence is not different or dissimilar[108]. In other places, mention is made of the equal nature[109]. The unity of the Father and of the Son is not only that of harmony or will, but of nature, of honor, and of power[110]. We have already mentioned the work of mediation that Hilary took up with the «Homoiousians». In his theological interpretation of *homoiousios*, he tended to identify similarity of nature with equal nature[111], the only divine nature of the Father and of the Son.

Hilary did not go beyond this in his explanation of the levels of development in which we would have to look for unity and diversity in God. The interpretation of John 10:30, following the line of thought of Tertullian with which

---

105 *Trin.* IX 54 (433): «Therefore, if on account of his authority as giver the Father is greater, is it then that by the gift conferred the Son is lesser? Certainly the one who gives is greater, but the one who is granted, being one thing with him, is not lesser»; IX 56 (435-436): «The Father is greater as he is the Father; but the Son is not lesser as the Son». We will see this same interpretation in other authors. Another explanation of the difficult text at that time was that the Son was lesser than the Father because he was incarnated. This is an interpretation which has less theological interest. Cfr. SIMONETTI M., «Giovanni 14,28 nella controversia ariana» in *Kyriakon* (Festschrift J. Quasten) I, Munster 1970, 151-161.

106 *Trin.* IX 54 (433): «Hence, the Father is greater than the Son. And, certainly, he is greater because he gives him all that he is in himself and grants him being in the image of himself… and having been born from his glory, Christ according to the spirit (according to his divinity), grants Jesus Christ again being in his glory as God according to the flesh after having died», cfr. also IX 56 (436).

107 Cfr. *Trin.* V 11 (162).

108 Cfr. *Syn.* 88 (PL 105,540).

109 *Trin.* VII 15 (276), *aequalitas naturae,* that only birth guarantees.

110 Cfr. *Trin.* VIII 19 (330); cfr. also the following chapters.

111 Cfr. *Syn.* 89 (541); «The real likeness or similarity is in the truth of the nature. The truth of the nature in one and the other is not opposed to the *homoousion*».

we are familiar, assists us in distinguishing the common nature of the persons[112]. However, this vocabulary is still not used in a coherent way, or with technical precision[113].

The concept of the Fatherhood of God which we have set forth entails the understanding that the generation of the Son is eternal. Otherwise, God would not always be Father, or only Father. The Son has received his birth from the eternity of the Father[114]. In view of the fact that the generation is eternal, God is not alone, nor has he ever been alone or solitary. Contrary to what Sabellius had set forth, Hilary strongly insisted on this characteristic[115]. Likewise, Hilary was highly interested in the literal and correct interpretation of Prov 8:22 and the verses that follow: «The Lord created me, the first born of his fashioning…», contrary to the Arians who based their arguments on this passage in order to refer to the Son as a creature. For Hilary, it was not only about the creation of the human nature of Jesus, but about the human manifestations of any other type adopted by the Son from the beginning in the different theophanies in the Old Testament. The road to salvation begins with them, and only with the human birth of Jesus can salvation be fulfilled. With a clear differentiation in the unique and definitive event of the incarnation, the theophanies already indicate a certain acceptance by the Son of a reality that has been created. Therefore, according to Hilary, in the Old Testament, Wisdom, created for the works of God, already exists. In other words, Wisdom exists to make himself manifest to God by means of creation. These «works» will culminate in the incarnation[116].

Even though the theology of Hilary regarding the Holy Spirit is extremely rich in its historical saving aspect, it is not clear as it relates to the Trinitarian aspect. Regardless, it has been clearly established that the Spirit is united with the Father and with the Son in the confession and that he is God and not creature[117]. As we have seen in the text which we quoted when we began these lines, the Spirit is characterized mainly as «gift». He is the gift of life itself from Christ risen from the dead, which is communicated to human beings. Hilary barely addressed the dogmatic difficulties regarding the Spirit that Athanasius had the opportunity to analyze in his letters to Serapion; but it is clear, nevertheless, that the Spirit

---

112 Cfr. *Trin.* VII 22-31 (286-298).
113 Cfr. SMULDERS P., *La doctrine trinitaire de saint Hilaire de Poitiers*, Romae 1944.
114 Cfr. *Trin.* IV 6 (105).
115 Cfr. *Trin.* IV 17 (119-120); VII 39 (307); VIII 36 (349).
116 Cfr. *Trin.* XII 35-50 (605-621).
117 Cfr. *Trin.* XII 55 (625).

has not been created, although the Spirit is not begotten. He is the Spirit of God and of Christ. Without explaining the meaning of the formula, he repeated on several occasions that the Spirit comes from the Father, through the Son[118].

With Athanasius and Hilary, the faith expressed at Nicaea was not only defended, but was also taken to deeper levels, and light has been shed on it. Their contribution in maintaining the true doctrine in East and West has been priceless. Other events contributed to a decisive loss of influence of the Arians during the years 361-381. We will refer to them briefly in the following section.

9

The main events from the year 361 to the year 381

250   Emperor Constantius died in the year 361. Emperor Julian, the Apostate, precisely because he had abandoned Christianity, followed a policy of greater freedom in ecclesiastical issues. Beginning in that year, the Arian controversy entered a new phase that had already been taking shape in the times immediately preceding. In that same year 361, the Council of Paris addressed the legitimacy of the use of *homoousios*, thus eliminating the Sabellian sense. In 362, Athanasius was again in his see in Alexandria. A council held that same year has entered history because of the synod letter known as *Tomus ad Antiochenos*. Saint Athanasius decidedly intervened in the drafting of this letter. This letter clarified the simple fact that referring to «three *hypostases*» is not necessarily Arian or thritheistic, while at the same time, it points out that «one substance» or *ousía* is not necessarily Sabellian. Even though no positive contribution was offered, by clarifying this terminology, many difficulties and misunderstandings were eliminated. The three *hypostases* do not mean three gods. What they mean is that in the Trinity there are not only three names, but «three» really existing and subsisting persons. Parallel to this, those who supported only one *hypostasis* in the divinity did not want to be Sabellians and eliminate the Son and the Holy Spirit. Rather, they clarified that as these two proceeded from the Father, they were only one *ousía* and nature with him[119]. Either group could be seen as orthodox. At that time,

---

118 Cfr. *Trin.* XII 54-57 (624-627); cfr. LADARIA L.F., *El Espíritu Santo en san Hilario de Poitiers*, Madrid 1977, especially 293-308. Some texts written by Hilary about the Spirit pose some difficulties because they seem to deny the unity of substance of the Spirit with the Father and the Son; hence *Syn.* 32 (PL 10,505A); cfr. LADARIA L.F., 312-319.

119 Cfr. *Tomus ad Antiochenos*, 5-6 (PG 26,800-802).

this was paving the way for the subsequent formulas that would precisely combine and harmonize these two statements that seemed incompatible.

In the year 363, several Bishops of Antioch addressed a letter to the Emperor[120]. They explained *homoousios* by saying that the Son has been begotten from the *ousía* of the Father and is in his likeness in substance ὅμοιος κατ᾽οὐσίαν. The term *ousía* has been introduced in order to avoid the idea of the creation of the Son. The *homoousios* is accepted, although the explanation given for it is in the «Homoiousian» sense. Regardless, it is quite important that the Nicene term was accepted by some who until very recently had openly been Semi-Arians.

Beginning in the year 369, Emperor Valente favored the Arians once again. Nevertheless, this policy really forced «Homoiousians» from the East to accept *homoousios* as an indispensable condition of having some support in the West. By the year 370, Basil of Caesarea was also part of this battle. Despite the support of Valente, this rebirth of Arianism did not last long, and the way was opened for the triumph of the Nicene faith due to the work of the Cappadocians.

Before addressing the Cappadocians in our analysis, we must point out some texts written by Pope Damasus around 374, which can give us an idea of the situation of Trinitarian theology at that time. In these texts the Trinity, which has only one majesty, one divinity, and one οὐσία, is confessed. Nevertheless, at the same time, according to Damasus, three persons, who always remain and are never decreased or reintegrated in the unity, are also affirmed. The Word is not only uttered but born from God. He is true God of true God, begotten, true light of true light. He is not lesser than the Father. He is the splendor and image, the one who shows the Father (cfr. John 14:9). The Holy Spirit is *unius usiae, unius virtutis* with God the Father and with our Lord Jesus Christ. He cannot be separated from the Father and from the Son, perfect in everything, in power, honor, majesty, and divinity, and we adore him together with the Father and the Son (cfr. DS 144-147)[121]. In this way, mention is made of the three «persons» and of their unity.

The issue of the Holy Spirit began to be posed explicitly around the year 360. As we have seen, Athanasius had already devoted his attention to this issue[122].

---

120 Cfr. SIMONETTI M., *La crisi ariana nel IV secolo*, 374.

121 Regarding the precedence of these writings of Damasus, cfr. the introduction to the text of DS 144-147. It is possible that some of these statements about the Holy Spirit are a response to a letter from Basil.

122 SIMONETTI M., *La crisi ariana nel IV secolo.*, 362ff; HANSON R.P.C., *The Search for the Doctrine of God*, 738-748.

The affirmation of the divinity of the Spirit and the discussion around the Trinitarian formula are very closely related. The issue of the Spirit is set forth as a result of the doctrines of Macedonius, who was expelled from Constantinople in 360. He affirmed that the Holy Spirit is the servant of God, like the angels, and not *homoousios* with the Father. Among the Macedonians, the first to make a name for themselves were the «Pneumatomachians» (enemies of the Holy Spirit)[123], although both groups ended by being in agreement on their understanding of the Holy Spirit. The contribution of the Cappadocians was of the utmost importance both as related to the issue of the divinity of the Spirit and with respect to the Trinitarian formula of one essence and three hypostases. We will begin our next chapter with them.

---

[123] Cfr. ATHANASIUS, *Serap.* I 32 (605), who uses the verb *pneumatomaxein*; and BASIL OF CAESAREA who talks about the «Pneumatomachians», *De Sp. Sancto* 11,27; 21,52 (SCh 17bis, 340;432).

The Cappadocian Fathers. The formulation of the Trinitarian Dogma in the First and Second Councils of Constantinople

C

Athanasius in the East and Hilary in the West have been the great defenders of the dogma of Nicaea. They were the ones who showed the incongruence of the Arian position, both from the point of view of the true meaning of the Fatherhood of God, and from the standpoint of the salvation that God offers to humanity —the participation in the divine Sonship of Christ. Nevertheless, as we have shown, neither of them analyzed in depth the significance of *homoousios*. Likewise, neither one of them offered a speculative explanation regarding the problem of the unity and the personal distinction in God. This endeavor was addressed by the Cappadocians, who also played a very important role in the development of pneumatology, and even more concretely, in the reflection on the unity of the Holy Spirit with the Father and the Son in the only divinity. This is an issue to which Hilary barely referred, although it was taken up by Athanasius in his letters to Serapion. We will address these two problems in this chapter when we undertake a brief analysis of the Trinitarian thought of Basil of Caesarea, Gregory of Nazianzus, and Gregory of Nyssa.

Before beginning this analysis, and precisely in order to duly understand the thinking process of these Fathers, we must briefly address the development of the Arian doctrines by turning to someone who may have been the most prominent representative of this school of thought in the second half of the fourth century —Eunomius († after 392). It is worth stating that both Basil and his brother Gregory of Nyssa —both of them authors of treatises titled *Contra Eunomium*— were forced to confront Eunomius and stand strongly against his ideas. For this reason, the *Apology* of Eunomius, written shortly after the year 360, is a necessary reference for understanding the religious thinking of his illustrious adversaries. The key thought in Eunomius was that of defining God as the «ungenerated», that is, the unbegotten. This state of being «ungenerated» pertains to the substance of God. It is not difficult to discover the intention of this statement. The whole tradition has affirmed that the Son has been begotten by the Father. By insisting on this absence of generation as the characteristic and specific nature of God, Eunomius denied the divinity of the Son. Let us now analyze the foundations of the argument set forth by Eunomius:

> We have confessed only one God, both in keeping with and according to the natural understanding and following the teachings of the Fathers. He has not been produced either by himself or by any other one. Indeed, any of these two hypotheses is impossible because, according to the truth, that which creates must preexist that which is cre-

ated, and the one who is produced must be second with respect to the one who is producing him. Then, it is not possible that one thing can be previous or subsequent to itself. In the same way, it cannot be previous to God.... If it has been shown that no one exists before him and that no thing exists prior to him, but rather that he is the one before all, it is because being ungenerated befits his nature. In other words and expressed in better terms, he himself is the ungenerated substance[1].

God cannot be the one who comes from another one. At the time when theology had already clearly affirmed the eternal generation of the Son, Eunomius insisted on affirming, once again, that anyone who comes from another one is subsequent in time and follows the one he comes from. Therefore, the Son cannot be God.

As a result of this, God is ungenerated. Nevertheless, we cannot use this term according to human concepts. Calling God ungenerated is not a deprivation or a loss; it is not taking away from him something that he had had before. He is in himself the «unbegotten substance»[2]. Being ungenerated, he cannot beget and cannot make anyone share his nature, which is precisely that of being ungenerated. In the divine substance there is no room for any differentiation or separation.

On the other hand, nobody can say that the Son is not lesser than the Father if it is the case that the Son himself has mentioned this (cfr. John 14:28). This is now one of the points of support for the Arian argumentation that has something to which Nicene orthodoxy must respond. The Son is lesser than the Father because he is not ungenerated. Therefore, there can be no communion of substance between the two of them. It is impossible to be at the same time unbegotten and begotten. Once you have been begotten, you exist above all by decision of the Father. It is not possible that the Son has been begotten when he existed. Otherwise, he would have existed as ungenerated before being begotten. Nevertheless, in this hypothesis, what need did he have of generation? It is therefore impossible that the Son existed before being begotten. If the substance of the Father does not admit to any generation, the Son must be a creature —undoubtedly greater than the rest— and the most apt minister to fulfill the will of the Father[3].

---

1 EUNOMIUS, *Apol.* 7 (SCh 305,244f); cfr. ibid. 8.9 (245f,250). On this issue, see SESBOÜÉ B.-MEUNIER B., *Dieu, peut-il avoir un Fils? Le débat trinitaire du IV siècle*, Paris 1993, 147ff.
2 Cfr. *Apol.* 8 (246f).
3 Cfr. *Apol.* 14-15 (260-264).

According to Eunomius, it is absolutely irrational to deny that the Son is a creature, although he is not the same as others who have been created through him. However, Eunomius also referred to the Son as «God», as had already been the case with the first Arians. Nevertheless, in this respect, we are clear about the meaning that this term had for them. According to Paul, the Son is the image of the Father, although this is not an image of substance but of activity. The entire and full power of the Father is discovered in his creating mediation[4]. Eunomius did not say a great deal about the Holy Spirit, other than that he is the third in order, in dignity, and in nature (ἀξιώματι καί τάξει καί τήν φύσιν). He cannot be the first one in regard to his nature, because only the Father is the first. Furthermore, he cannot be the only-begotten either, because this title pertains to the Son[5]. These points of reference are quite sufficient, and now we can proceed to study the thinking of Saint Basil of Caesarea.

1

Basil of Caesarea

Basil (c. 330-377 / 379) was the first of the Cappadocians and the one who established the guidelines and criteria that were to be followed by this school of thought. In his treatise, *Contra Eunomius,* he responded to Eunomius' radical Arianism. The Bishop of Caesarea based his considerations on the mysteries of the deity, and hence he believed it was impossible to define the divine substance, something that Eunomius had assumed to do. God cannot be defined; he is only known through the Son and the Holy Spirit[6]. We know from the Scriptures that Jesus referred to himself in many ways and by many names: light, shepherd, vineyard, and path. He does so to point out his different activities and the variety of the benefits he brings to us. We can say something similar about God the Father; we call him ungenerated or unbegotten and also incorruptible[7]. As we can see,

---

4 Cfr. *Apol.* 22-24 (278-284).

5 Cfr. *Apol.* 25 (284f); he has been made by the will of the Father and by the energy of the Son.

6 Cfr. *C. Eun.* I 14 (SCh 299, 220). Cfr. for the following SESBOÜÉ B.-MEUNIER B., op.cit., 163f; on the Trinitarian theology of Basil, DRECOLL V.H., *Die Entwicklung der Trinitätslehre des Basilius von Cäsarea,* Göttingen 1996; SESBOÜÉ B., *Saint Basile et la Trinité,* Paris 1998.

7 *C. Eun.* I 7 (SCh 299,188-192); cfr. also *De Sp. Sanc.* 8,17 (SCh 17bis,302-304); we can see in these texts an influence of the doctrine of the *epínoiai* of Origen, although with certain differences with respect to the theologian from Alexandria; cfr. ORBE A., *La Epinoia. Algunos preliminares históricos de la distinción kat'epínoian (en torno a la filosofía de Leoncio Bizantino),* Rome 1955; SIEBEN H.S., «Vom Heil in den vielen "Namen Christi"» in *TeoPhil*73 (1998) 1-28.

the words «ungenerated» or «unbegotten» do not say it all. All of these names offer us only an obscure and limited knowledge of what God is, of his way of being, and of his divinity (ὅπως), rather than of his τό τι, his real being. Terms such as «ungenerated» or «unbegotten» are only our attempts to learn more about «how» God is and not «what» he is. Terms cannot describe what God is in himself. There are no exceptions to this rule[8].

Basil also stated that the names that we find in the Scriptures are not «ungenerated», «unbegotten», and «begotten», but rather, «Father» and «Son». If we further pursue the thinking of Eunomius, the vocabulary of the Gospel disappears. If God is not capable of conveying his nature to the Son whom he begets, the Father and the Son are not really what these words imply, and as a result of this, the words themselves in the Gospel lose their value. If the Father and the Son do not have the same nature, we cannot understand how Jesus could say, for instance, that whoever sees me sees the one who sends me, and whoever has seen me has seen the Father (cfr. John 12:45; 14:9)[9]. In the opinion of Basil, the likeness of the Son to the Father does not lie in the activity, as Eunomius believed, but in his divine nature itself. If God the Father has no form or figure due to his simplicity, the Son does not have them either. If the substance does not have any form or figure, the likeness does not lie in the form or in the figure and can only be in the substance itself. The identity of the substance is manifested in the equality of power (cfr. John 5:19; 1Cor 1:24)[10]. Faced with the objection that can come from the words of the Lord «the Father is greater than I» (John 14:28), Basil followed the classical interpretation that was quite common among the representatives of Nicene orthodoxy: the Father is greater as Father, because he is the «cause» and «beginning» of the Son who has been begotten from him. Nevertheless, the fact that the Son carries out the activities of God points to the identicality of their nature[11].

However, after this refutation, founded on the sense of the biblical texts, Basil initiated another type of speculative argumentation that would have major consequences on subsequent Trinitarian theology. Eunomius based his denial of the divinity of the Son on the fact that he is «begotten», that he is an «offspring»

8 C. Eun. I 15 (224f); «unbegotten» cannot be the name of the substance because it is negative; ibid. 11 (210).
9 Cfr. C. Eun. I 17-18 (232-238).
10 Cfr. C. Eun. I 23 (254).
11 Cfr. C. Eun. I 24-25 (256-262): if they were not equal in substance, the activity of the Son, as that of the Father, would be out of proportion to his nature.

of the Father. In view of the fact that he is begotten, he could not have the same nature as the unbegotten Father. Well then, Basil responded, a distinction has to be made between two types of names —those that are absolute and those that are relative names. Some point to what a thing is in itself (human, horse, ox), while others point to what one thing is in relation to another one (son, slave, friend). It is evident that γέννεμα, offspring, belongs to the second category. It does not tell us what the Son is in himself, but it points to his relation with the Father. That is why it cannot mean the essence of the Son, just as «unbegotten» cannot mean the essence of the Father. Similarly, the names Father and Son are applied to God and to humans, when indeed God and humans are different with respect to each other. This is possible because these names are relative, and in view of this, they do not describe what those to which they refer really are in themselves. Such terms simply point out the relationship that unites them. Because of this fact, they can be applied to beings that are quite different, and nobody would think that when we apply the same terms to God and to humans we are affirming that God and humans have the same substance. In the same way, the word γέννεμα, offspring, is also a relative term. It is always the offspring «of» someone. If we believe that «offspring» tells about the substance of something, then it would be that all offspring are consubstantial[12]. The consequence that can be derived from this is quite clear: the names «father» and «son» and other relative terms do not point to the substance, but to the relationship. Therefore, they can be applied to beings that are very different. There is no doubt that Basil was indeed brilliant in this refutation. He not only destroyed the reasoning of Eunomius, but he also laid the foundation for future Trinitarian theology which would combine the unity of the divine essence with the plurality of the persons, precisely derived from the distinction between the absolute and the relative names.

Therefore, father and son are two relative names, and they apply mutually to each other. There is no father without a son, and there is no son without a father. For this reason, if God the Father is eternal, so his Son must also be eternal. We saw that Eunomius was unable to think of the Father as the beginning of the Son without giving this «beginning» a temporal nature. Basil set forth a distinction between the relation of precedence and chronological succession. This was something that the Nicene tradition had done before him. Hence, the Son can be at the same time eternal and begotten. In order to affirm the eternity of the

---

12 Cfr. *C. Eun.* II 9-10 (SCh 305, 36-40); cfr. SIMONETTI M., *La crisi ariana nel IV secolo*, 464.

Son, Basil used an argument based on John 1:2, «the Word *was* with God». This imperfect tense points toward a time that has no beginning. If we start with this «was» we cannot go to a previous moment where the Son did not exist[13]. «The Son exists from all eternity, united, as begotten, to the Father who is unborn»[14].

It would make no sense to consider the unbegotten and the begotten who has received his being from him as having a diverse nature. There can be no difference in nature between ungenerated and generated light[15]. On the other hand, the activity of the Son corresponds with the nature of God; the Only Begotten is the image of the substance of the Father[16]. Therefore we cannot question the divinity of the Son. Likewise, the Holy Spirit cannot be considered a creature either[17], and together with the Father and the Son he is in the divine triad. Once we have clearly established this, we must proceed a step further. How can these three, being different, have the same divinity?

The three persons have only one nature, and they are only one God. The three are uncreated. The Father is not derived from any cause. The Son shines as the only begotten of the ungenerated light. In turn, the Son cannot be understood if he is not understood through the illumination of the Spirit[18]. There are not three ultimate beginnings; the only beginning is the Father, who gives everything without receiving in return and without losing anything and who creates through the Son and perfects the creation in the Spirit[19]. The Father and the Son (and we can add the Holy Spirit) are different according to the properties of their persons (τήν ἰδιότητα των προσωπών). They are one and one (εις καί εις). Nevertheless, according to the community of their nature (κατά δέ τό κοινον τής φύσεως), they are only one[20]. Hence, there is a unity in their substance (οὐσία), although they possess different properties which do not break the common substance:

---

13 *C. Eun.* II 12.14-15 (44f,50-60); Hilary already used the same argument: *Trin.* II 13 (CCL 62,50-51). Cfr. LADARIA L.F., *Il prologo di Giovanni nei primi libri del De Trinitate di Ilario di Poitiers*, in PADOVESE L. (ed.) *Atti del III convegno di Efeso*, Roma 1994, 157-174, 166.

14 *C. Eun.* II 17 (66).

15 Cfr. *C. Eun.* II 27 (112-116).

16 Cfr. ibid. II 31 (128-132).

17 Cfr. *C. Eun.* III (SCh 305,144-174). We will speak again on the topic of the Spirit, developed primarily in the *de Spiritu Sancto*.

18 Cfr. *de Sp. Sanc.* 26,64 (SCh 17bis, 476); *Ep.* 38,4, COURTONNE (ed.) 1,84.

19 Cfr. *de Sp. Sanc.* 16,38 (376-378), see the whole context. In other places, mention is made of the Father as the root, the source, etc.; cfr. HANSON R.P.C., *The Search for the Doctrine of God*, 693.

20 *De Sp. Sanc.* 18,45 (406).

If you want to accept what is true, that is, that the begotten and the unbegotten are distinctive properties to be perceived in their substance which leads us by the hand to the clear understanding of the Father and the Son without any confusion, then you will not fall victim to the danger of impiety and you will maintain coherence in your reasoning. Indeed, the properties, as characteristics and forms taken into account in the substance, constitute a distinction between what is common, in view of the characteristics that make them specific, although they do not sever what is common in the essence. For instance, the divinity is common, although paternity and filiation are properties (ἰδιώματα), and we can see and understand the truth based on the combination of the two elements —the common and the distinctive. In this way, when we hear about ungenerated light, we think about the Father, and if we hear about a begotten light, we understand the idea of the Son. As light and light there is no opposition between them, but as begotten and unbegotten, they are seen as contrasting. Such is the effect and the nature of the property —that of showing the otherness in the identicality of their essence (οὐσία)[21].

The doctrine of relationships, which here is not addressed directly and specifically, and that of properties, which we have addressed superficially[22], are combined in this passage. In the unity of the divine essence, characterized as light according to tradition (a doctrine that is echoed in Nicaea), the Father and the Son are distinguished by the relative properties. «The property has as its content a relationship, and this relationship points to the divine subject as such»[23].

We have seen here a difference between *ousía* (frequently the term *physis* is used as an equivalent) and properties. The term ποστασις has not yet appeared as opposed to οὐσία. Basil would slowly arrive at the formulation which would be imposed in time on the Trinitarian formula. The acceptance of the three *hypostases* depends on having a clear and impartial understanding of *homoousios*. This word shows the property of the *hypostases* in their perfect sameness in nature, because one thing is always consubstantial with something, and hence the word itself implies the distinction[24]. The Father, the Son, and the Holy Spirit exist,

---

21 *C. Eun.* II 28 (118-120); cfr. also, among others, *Ep.* 38,3 (182f); 210,3-4 (II 192f).
22 Cfr. also *C. Eun.* II 4 (118-120) regarding the common substance of human nature and the distinction of the personal properties of Peter and Paul.
23 SESBOÜÉ B., *Le Dieu du salut*, Paris 1994, 289.
24 Cfr. *Ep.* 52,3 (I 136); cfr. SESBOÜÉ B., *Le Dieu du salut*, 298.

in the instance of each one of them, in his own *hypostasis*[25]. Speaking about one *hypostasis* could cause people to think of Sabellianism. Each of the persons or *hypostases*, in the unity of the divine essence, has his unyielding peculiarity — the fatherhood, the sonship, and the sanctification:

> The same difference that exists between essence and *hypostasis* is the one that exists between what is common and what is individual. This is the case, for instance, in the difference between humanity in general and a specific human being. For this reason, we recognize only one essence in the divinity...; on the contrary, the *hypostasis* is specific. We recognize this in order to have a distinct and clear idea about the Father, the Son, and the Holy Spirit. In fact, if we do not take into account the natures or characters defined for each of them —the paternity, the filiation, and the sanctification— and if we do not confess our faith in God according to the common understanding of God's being, it would be impossible for us to profess our faith as we should. Therefore, we must combine what is specific and what is common, and in this way, we must confess our faith. What is common is divinity; what is specific is paternity. After this, we must combine these understandings and say: I believe in God the Father. We must do exactly the same thing in the confession of the Son and the same with respect to the Holy Spirit[26].

This text has already enabled us to analyze the issue of the divinity of the Holy Spirit, united with the Father and the Son in the traditional formulas. Basil devoted his famous work, *de Spiritu Sancto,* written in 375, to this issue. Following the line of thought that we already have seen in the case of Athanasius, he opposed the *pneumatomachi* when they affirmed that the Holy Spirit is a creature and when they stated that the Holy Spirit cannot be a subject of adoration together with the Father and the Son in view of the fact that they are worshiped and glorified «in» the Spirit[27]. Nevertheless, Basil showed that the New Testament

25 Cfr. *Ep.* 125,1 (II 32). Even in the case of Basil, this would be the opinion of the Fathers of Nicaea. References to the formula of one *ousía* and three *hypostases* are found in VOICTORINO M., *Adv. Ar.* II 4 (SCh 68,408;450), who conveys it in Greek terminology. Cfr. SIMONETTI M., *La crisi ariana nel IV secolo,* 513, who points to Porfirius as a possible source, through the *de Trin.* attributed to Didymus.
26 *Ep.* 236,6 (III 53f); cfr. 214,3-4 (II 204f); cfr. SESBOÜÉ B., *Le Dieu du salut,* 300; SIMONETTI M., *La crisi ariana nel IV secolo,* 515f; cfr. also *de Sp. Sant.* 17,41 (394); 18,44-45 (402-408); the Father, the Son, and the Holy Spirit are only one God, and they cannot be «added up» in order to give way to tritheism. «In the κοινωνία of the divinity lies the unity».
27 Cfr. *de Sp. Sanc.* 1-2 (250-262). Cfr. on this treatise, DÖRRIES H., *De Spiritu sancto. Der Beitrag des Basilius zum Abschluss des trinitarischen Dogmas,* Göttingen 1956; CAVALCANTI E., *L'esperienza di Dio nei Padri greci. Il trattato «Sullo Spirito Santo» di Basilio di Cesarea,* Roma 1984; LUISLAMPE P.,

applies to the Father, to the Son, and to the Holy Spirit the different prepositions «of», «through», and «in», in such a way that their use cannot lead us to deduce a difference in nature among the three[28]. No preposition is exclusive of one person. On the other hand, the Spirit appears united with the Father and with the Son in the baptismal faith. Hence, he cannot be separated from them[29]. The union with the Father and the Son in the external action of these three persons also indicates that he is not a creature[30]. Specifically, the Spirit acts in creation; the Father creates it all through the Son and perfects it in the Holy Spirit[31]. There is also unity in the saving action. The Spirit is the one who distributes the gifts, the Son is the one who sent him, and the Father is the source and the cause of all good[32]. The Spirit is primarily involved in divinizing. In Basil we may well find the most beautiful text in all patristic literature on the divinization that the Holy Spirit works on the believer:

> He, enlightening those who have been purified from all stains, makes them spiritual by means of communion with him. And, as limpid and transparent bodies, when hit by a ray, themselves turn into brilliant sources that reflect another ray, in this way, the souls that have the Spirit in them are enlightened by the Spirit. They turn fully spiritual and convey to others their grace. This is the origin of their knowledge of future things, their understanding of the mysteries… their likeness with God; the fulfillment of their wills: turning into God[33].

The greatness of the Spirit is also shown when he acts in Jesus himself[34]. Because of all these reasons, Basil insisted on the inseparability of the Holy Spirit from the Father and the Son. He referred to the term *koinonía* in order to address

---

Spiritus vivificans. Grundzüge einer Theologie des Hl. Geistes nach Basilius von Caesarea, Münster 1981; POUCHET J.R., «Le traité de S. Basile sur le Saint Esprit. Milieu originel» in RSR 84 (1996) 325-350 ; POUCHET J.R., «Le traité de Basile sur le Saint Esprit. Structure et portée» in RSR 85 (1997) 11-40 ; Basilius von Cesarea. Über den Hl. Geist, übersetzt und eingeleitet von H.J. Sieben (Fontes Christiani 12), Freiburg-Basel-Wien, 1993.

28 Cfr. among others *de Sp. Sanc.* 4-5; 7-8 (268-284; 298-320).
29 Cfr. *de Sp. Sanc.* 10,24.26 (332.336); 12,28 (344f); 27,67 (488).
30 *De Sp. Sanc.* 22,53 (440f), κοινωνόν ἐστι των ἐνέργειων; the Spirit is also difficult to know, as is the case of the Father and the Son (cfr. John 14:17, the world cannot receive him because the world does not know him).
31 *De Sp. Sanc.* 16,38 (376-384); Basil is primarily based on Ps 32:6.
32 Cfr. *de Sp.Sanc.* 16,37 (376); 19,49 (418-422).
33 *de Sp.Sanc.* 9,23 (328); other texts on the effects of the Spirit that show indirectly his divine character in 9,22 (322-326); 15,36 (370-372).
34 *de Sp. Sanc.* 19,49 (418-420); 12,28 (344) and especially 16,39 (386).

this union. In a significant passage he talked about the κοινωνία ἐκ φύσεως by means of which the Spirit is named together with God[35]. He also alluded to the *koinonía* of the glory[36]. Through the only Son, he is united with the only Father; he is of the Son according to the nature[37].

Furthermore, he is «divine according to his nature»[38]. For this reason, the Holy Spirit must be glorified with the Father and with the Son[39]. There is no difference in grade between the Father, the Son, and the Spirit, because reference is never made in the Scripture to a first, a second, or a third one, nor does it address them as one, two, and three, thus avoiding polytheism[40]. Nevertheless, at no point did Basil refer directly to the Spirit as God, or as *homoousios* with the Father and the Son[41], although on some occasions he spoke about the consubstantial Trinity[42]. The Holy Spirit comes from God as a breath of his mouth, although we cannot understand this divine breath in an anthropomorphic manner. He is not begotten nor is he a creature. Although it is clear that he belongs to God, his existence is indescribable[43].

---

[35] *De Sp. Sanc.* 13,30 (352); cfr. also 16,38 (376), once again about the κοινωνία.

[36] *De Sp. Sanc.* 24,55 (450); κοινωνόν in the activities, 22,53 (440) already quoted, 27,68 (488).

[37] *De Sp. Sanc.* 18,45 (408). Basil related the Holy Spirit to the Son, although vaguely, also in reference to origin. All the power of the Son is put in motion for the *hypostasis* of the Holy Spirit, just as that of the Father is put in motion for the generation of Son; *C. Eun.* II 32 (134); cfr. also II 34 (142). Cfr. SIMONETTI M., *La crisi ariana nel IV secolo*, 479f. The sanctifying capacity and the sovereign dignity go from the Father through the Son to the Spirit: *de Sp.Sanc.* 18,47 (412); as the comforter, he bears the nature of the goodness of the comforter from whom he comes, 18,46 (410).

[38] *De Sp. Sanc.* 23,54 (444): θειον τη φύσει. This is probably the affirmation that comes closer to the direct confession of the divinity of the Spirit. Cfr. also *Ep.* 159 (II 86f).

[39] Cfr. *de Sp. Sanc.* 18,46 (410); 25 (456-464), etc.

[40] Cfr. *de Sp. Sanc.* 18,44.47 (402.414), cfr. *C. Eun.* III 1-2 (146-152).

[41] Cfr. letter number 71 written by BASIL (I 166f), as related to letter number 58 written by GREGORY OF NAZIANZUS (GCS 53,52-54); on the reasons for this reservation, cfr. SIEBEN H.J., *Basilius von Cesarea, Über den Hl. Geist.*, (cfr. no.27) 42ff; the traditional explanation was the tactical one: Basil did not want to exasperate his adversaries. Sieben rather thought that Basil still did not believe that the divinity of the Spirit was part of the linking *kerygma*. It sufficed for him to affirm that the Spirit is not a creature.

[42] *De Fide,* 4 (PG 31,688); and also concerning the Son consubstantial with the Father and to the Holy Spirit, see *Ep.* 90,2 (I 196); more references in HANSON R.P.C., *The Search for the Doctrine of God,* 818f.

[43] *De Sp. Sanc.* 18,46 (408), the *trópos tés hypárcheos* of the Holy Spirit is ineffable.

Gregory of Nazianzus († 389 / 390) also posed the problem of the divine unity and of the distinct nature of the *hypostasis* because of their properties. We will first see how he characterized the persons, and then we will analyze some of his key texts that focused on the unity of the divinity. For Gregory, the Father is without beginning, unbegotten. The Son is begotten without beginning, and the Holy Spirit is the one who proceeds without being begotten[44]. In a similar formulation, the Father is the unbegotten, the Son is begotten, and the Holy Spirit is the one who comes from the Father (ἐκ τοῦ πατρός ἐκπορευόμενον)[45]. The most remarkable change with respect to what we see in Basil relates to the property of the Holy Spirit that the Bishop of Caesarea saw in sanctification, in other words, the Spirit is more in relationship with us than in relation to the first two persons. On the contrary, Gregory based his arguments on John 15:26 when referring to the «procession» of the Holy Spirit from the Father in order to point to the origin of the third person. He was the first one to use this biblical understanding, which after that moment would turn into a technical term in Trinitarian theology. The characteristic property of the Spirit lies in this procession from the Father. Hence, this property refers to the relationships *ad intra* and not to his acting in us. Gregory added that the Spirit proceeds from the Father but not as begotten; being begotten is what is typical of the Son[46].

The three persons are eternal; they have never begun to exist, but this does not mean that the three are *anarchoi*, without beginning[47]. The only one who has no beginning is the Father, while the Son has been begotten, and the Holy Spirit proceeds from the Father. The Father never began to be Father because he has always had the Son. For the same reason, the Son never began to be a Son.

---

44 Cfr. *Or.* 30,19 (SCh 250,266).
45 *Or.* 29,2 (180); cfr. 39,12 (SCh 358,174); 25,16 (SCh 284,196).
46 *Or.* 31,8 (290): «… as he proceeds from the Father, he is not a creature, while insofar as he has not been begotten, he is not Son… You ask me, what is procession? Tell me what is the condition of unbegotten or ungenerated that is typical of the Father and I will explain to you… what the generation of the Son and the procession of the Spirit are…» The fact that one uses specific formulas does not mean that one fully understands what one is intending to describe with them.
47 Cfr. *Or.* 29,3 (182); 25,15 (SCh 284,194).

Being begotten and existing from the beginning are not contradictory[48]. Between the one who begets and the one who is begotten there is an identicality with respect to their nature. There is no difference in οὐσία. The understanding of generation itself forces us to think along this line. On the other hand, if the Father is the only unbegotten, the honor of being the Son is not lesser because he is the Son of that Father[49].

As was the case with Basil, Gregory resorted to the category of relationship in order to set the foundations for the unity of the nature of the Father and of the Son. These two terms —«Father and Son»— do not define the essence, nor the action (ἐνέργεια), but precisely the relationship between both. The names «Father» and «Son» point to the ὸ οφυία, the equal nature of the two[50].

The Son is the first begotten, not because in fact he is unique, but because he is the only generation, since nothing is repeated in God. The Son is the «brief definition of the nature of the Father»[51]. In turn, there are different designations for the Son: Wisdom, power, truth, seal of the Father, image, light, and life, among others. All of them are founded on consubstantiality with the Father[52]. On the other hand, the Spirit is also God and is *homoousios* (with the Father and with the Son)[53]. Gregory did not hesitate to apply this term to him.

Gregory's speech number 31 on the Holy Spirit (theological speech number 5) offers some of the richest synthetic texts on his Trinitarian theology, as he affirms the equality of the persons as opposed to any subordinationism:

> What is the Spirit lacking… so that he can be Son?… On the other hand, the Son lacks nothing either to be Father, because the condition of Son does not entail any lack, and he is not the Father because of that reason… These words do not point to a lack or to a decrease in terms of essence (κατὰ τήν οὐσίαν). «Not having been begotten», «having

---

48 *Or.* 29,5-6 (184-188). Also 31,4 (280-282), on the eternity of the Spirit. The generation of the Son is not a function of creation. We would be offending God if we were to think that he had to beget the Son in order to carry out his creation: *Or.* 23,6 (SCh 270,294); cfr. also 23,7 (294-296).

49 *Or.* 29,3.5.6.10-12 (SCh 250.182.184.196-200). Also 30,20 (266-268).

50 *Or.* 29,16 (210).

51 *Or.* 30,20 (268).

52 Cfr. *Or.* 30,20 (268).

53 *Or.* 31,10 (292; also *Or.* 12,6 (SCh 405, 360). Gregory seemed to take up the criticism directed at Basil (cfr. no. 41) for not having reached or not having dared to set forth a clearer formulation; cfr. MORESCHINI C., *Dios Padre en la especulación de Gregorio Nacianceno*, in *Dios es Padre*, Salamanca 1991, 179-202, 192. Cfr. also DIDYMUS THE BLIND, *De Sp. Sanc.* 17,81; 29,130f; 32,145; 53,231 (SCh 386,218;266;280;352), the Spirit is God and consubstantial with the Father and with the Son (we have to bear in mind that we do not have the original text of this work of Didymus).

been begotten», and «proceeding» refer in the first place to the Father, in the second place to the Son, and in the third place to the one who is precisely called the Holy Spirit. Thus the distinction between the three *hypostases* in one nature is preserved without confusion (ἀσύγχυτον), in only one nature (ἐν τῇ μίᾳ φύσει), and in the only dignity of the divinity. The Son is not the Father because the Father is only one, but because he is the same thing with the Father. Likewise, the Spirit is not the Son because he comes from God, because only one is the only begotten, but he is the same thing as the Son. The three are only one being as to divinity, and the only being is three as to their properties (Εν τα τρία θεότητί καί τό ἐν τρία ταῖς ἰδιότησιν)[54].

As we can see, Gregory strongly insisted on the unity of the divine essence possessed by the three. The three are the only and unique divinity[55]. Nevertheless, the distinction of the *hypostases*, characterized by their properties, is also clear. The unity and the trinity in God must be affirmed at the same time. One or the other aspect appears before our eyes according to our point of view:

> When we turn our attention to the divinity (τήν τηεότετα) as well as to the first cause and to the «monarchy», this unity appears before us. When we look at those in whom we find the divine nature, those who come from outside time and with equal honor from the first cause, then it is three that we adore[56].

«Three diverse properties, only one divinity, undivided in glory, honor, essence and dominion (*basileia*)»[57]. This can be the summary of the Trinitarian theology of Gregory of Nazianzus. Gregory strongly insisted on divine unity, even more

---

54 *Or.* 31,9 (290-292).
55 Therefore in *Or.* 39,11 (SCh 358,170-172): «Three on account of the individualities or *hypostases*... but one as relates to the substance: this is the divinity. In view of the fact that the three persons are divided without division —if I am allowed to express my thoughts in these terms— they are united in the division. In fact, the divinity is one in three and the three are one in whom the divinity resides; or to be more precise, they are the divinity». Cfr. on this emphasis, HANSON R.P.C., *The Search for the Doctrine of God*, 699f; SIMONETTI M., *La crisi ariana nel IV secolo*, 321. Nevertheless, it is also said that the Father is the only beginning. and that by virtue of this only beginning, there is only one God, cfr. *Or.* 20,7 (SCh 270,72); also *Or.* 25,15-16 (SCh 284,194-196); 29,2 (SCh 250,180); 42,15 (SCh 384,82), the unity of the three is made by the Father not for them to be mingled, but united.
56 *Or.* 31,14 (302-304); also 29,2 (178): «We worship the monarchy, not a monarchy delimited by only one person... but a monarchy made up of the same dignity of nature, agreement of thought, identity of movement, and return to the unity of those who come in it...». But in *Or.* 25,15 (SCh 284,194), the «monarchy» seems to refer to the three.
57 Cfr. *Or.* 31,28.

so than Basil. The unity of the essence as possessed by the three appears to be stronger than the unity that comes from the Father. Nonetheless, this other perspective is not absent. There is also concern for avoiding the confusion of the *hypostases*. In this way, Gregory did not seem to fully accept the traditional metaphors of sun and fountain because he believed that the subsistence of the Son and that of the Spirit are not sufficiently guaranteed[58].

Gregory depicted in a masterly text many of the activities and actions of the Holy Spirit according to the Holy Scriptures, as an evidence of his divine nature:

> On the other hand, I feel worried and alarmed when I consider the abundance of titles and of all the names that have been deeply insulted by all those who attack the Holy Spirit! He has been called Spirit of God (1Cor 2:11), Spirit of Christ (Rom 8:9), mind of the Lord (1Cor 2:16), Spirit of the Lord (Wis 1:7; 2Cor 3:17), the Lord himself (2Cor 3:17), Spirit of adoption (Rom 8:15), of truth (John 14:17; 15:26), of freedom (2Cor 3:17), Spirit of Wisdom, of understanding, of counsel, of strength, of knowledge, of mercy, of fear of the Lord (Isa 11:2); because he has created all these things, he fills all things with his substance, he contains all the things, *he fills the world* (Wis 1:7) with his substance but he is not containable by the world as to his power; he is good (Ps 142:10), righteous (Ps 50:12), guide (Ps 50:14); he sanctifies (1Cor 6:11) by his nature and not by the decision of the other and he is not sanctified; he measures and he is not measured (John 3:34); we participate in him (Rom 8:15) but he does not participate; he fills (Wis 1:7), and he is not filled; he is all-embracing (ibid.), he is not contained; he is the down payment of our inheritance (Eph 1:13-14), he is glorified (1Cor 6:19-20); he is mentioned along with [the Father and the Son] (Matt 28:29); he gives rise to a threat (Mark 3:29); he is the finger of God (Luke 11:20); he is the fire (Acts 2:3), as God (Deut 4:24), to show what I believe is consubstantial with him.
>
> He is the Spirit who creates (Ps 103:30), who recreates by means of baptism (John 3:5; cfr. 1Cor 12:13) and by means of the resurrection (Ezek 37:5-6, 9-10.4). He is the Spirit who knows all things (1Cor 2:10), who teaches (John 14:26), who blows where he wills and how he wills (John 3:8), who guides (Ps 142:10), who speaks (Acts 13:2), who sends (Acts 13:4), who sets apart (Acts 13:2), who shows wrath (Job 4:9), who is tested (Acts 5:9), who reveals (John 16:13), who enlightens (John 14:26), who gives life (John 6:63; 1Cor 3:6), or rather, who is light and life itself, who makes us temples (1Cor 3:16; 6:19), who divinizes us (ibid.), who makes us perfect (John 16:13), who precedes baptism (Acts

58 Cfr. *Or.* 31,31-32 (338-340).

10:47) and is searched for after baptism, who acts as God acts (1Cor 12:4-6; 12:11), who is divided into tongues of fire (Acts 2:3), who distributes gifts (1Cor 12:11), who gives apostles, prophets, evangelists and teachers (Eph 4:11). He is intelligent, manifold, clear, agile, keen, irresistible, unstained (Wis 7:22), which means that he is the supreme Wisdom, the one who acts in multiple ways (cfr. 1Cor 12:11), the one who pervades and penetrates all things (Wis 7:24), the free and immutable being (Wis 7:23); he who is all-powerful, he who is all-seeing, pervading all spirits, although they be intelligent, pure, and very subtle (ibid.). I refer to the holy souls, the angelic powers, as well as the prophets (Wis 7:27) and the apostles at the same time but not in the same places (Wis 8:1), because they are dispersed here and there, which shows that nothing circumscribes the Spirit[59].

Few synthetic passages can be found in which the wealth of the action of the Spirit according to the Scripture is better expressed. In this varied way of acting in the economy of salvation, we see the consubstantiality of the Spirit with the Father and with the Son. At the same time, Gregory, as was the case before with Basil, resorted to the presence of the Spirit in Jesus to show his grandeur and his dignity, and finally, his divinity[60].

3

Gregory of Nyssa

The youngest brother of Basil, Gregory of Nyssa (†circa 395), was also involved in this issue of Eunomius regarding the difference in nature between the begotten and the unbegotten[61]. Gregory's answer will be that the divine generation is always an eternal act. There is nothing in God before or after. Like his brother Basil, Gregory argued based on John 1:12 that in the beginning the Logos *existed* and *was* next to God. The imperfect tense points to continuity and indicates that the Logos has no beginning, just as God has no beginning[62].

59 *Or.* 31,29 (332-336). I have resorted to the translation made by J. R. Díaz Sánchez-Cid, in GREGORY OF NAZIANZUS, *Los cinco discursos teológicos*, Madrid 1995, 259-262, although with slight modifications.
60 Cfr. *Or.* 31,29 (332): Christ is begotten, he precedes him; Christ is baptized, he gives testimony; Christ is tempted, he leads him back (to Galilee?); Christ performs miracles; he is with him.
61 Cfr. SIMONETTI M., op.cit., 464f. *C. Eun.* III 1 67-72 (Jaeger II,27-29), Eunomius makes the mistake of identifying essence with generation. On Gregory, we can refer to: GREGORY OF NYSSA, *Teologia trinitaria*, MORESCHINI C. (ed.), Milano 1994; POTTIER B., *Dieu et le Christ selon Grégoire de Nysse*, Namur 1994.
62 *Contra Eunomio*, III 2, 18f (Jaeger II, 58).

Gregory also addressed the characteristics that are typical of each of the persons in the only and unique divine nature. The basic distinction appears between the uncreated and the created beings, with the former being the divine persons. At this point, there is no difference between these persons. Being uncreated is held in common by the divine persons, and it is only the divine nature that possesses this characteristic. The characteristics that are typical of the persons are, in the case of the Father, that of not being begotten, and in the case of the only begotten Son, that of being begotten. The Holy Spirit has communion of nature with the Father and the Son, τῆς φύσεως τήν κοινωνίαν, although the distinctive sign that characterizes the Spirit is not being begotten or unbegotten. The Spirit is distinguished from the Son because he does not have the subsistence of the Father as the only begotten, but rather he has manifested himself through the Son[63].

Gregory of Nyssa explained one essence and three *hypostases* by resorting to the comparison, indeed ambiguous to a certain extent, with the unity of the human essence which he affirmed with great insistence. Peter, James, and, John are one in essence, having only one nature, even though each possesses the properties of the person *(hypostasis)* which pertain to each of them. In a similar way, we can understand the three persons in God: the *ousía* is one, in the typical characteristics of the *hypostases*[64]. In our normal language, we say «three men» to refer to Peter, James and John, but in them «only one is the man»[65]. Gregory believed that it was a true abuse to name in the plural those who are not divided by nature, but rather by traditions[66]. Is traditions the correct word here? Even more so, the three divine persons have the one same *ousía* or essence[67]. Therefore, we must confess that God is one according to God's essence, although in the recognizable characteristics of the *hypostases* they are three, and in view of this, we profess faith in Father, Son and Holy Spirit, distinguishing them, although without confusing them. The particularity of the *hypostasis* enables us to see the distinction of the persons, *prosopa*, and the only name that we believe in (God) shows the unity of the essence[68].

---

63 Cfr. *C. Eun.* I 278-280 (Jaeger, I 107-109); cfr. SIMONETTI M., *La crisi ariana nel IV secolo*, 517f.

64 GREGORY OF NAZIANZUS had already resorted to this argument, although not as strongly, *Or.* 31,15.16 (SCh 250,304-306); cfr. also BASIL, *Ep.* 38,4 (181f).

65 *Quod non sunt tres dei* (Jaeger III,1, 54); cfr. ibid. (40).

66 Ibid. (39).

67 *Ad Graecos* (Jaeger III 1,22).

68 Cfr. *Ref. Conf. Eun.* 6.12.13 (Jaeger II, 314-315; 317-318); cfr. HANSON R.P.C. *The Search for the Doctrine of God*, 725f. The one God appears to be the Trinity according to *Quod non sunt…* (42). On the understandings of *ousía* and *hypostasis*, cfr. POTTIER B., *Dieu et le Christ*, 95f.

However, this divine essence is unknowable. We know God not because of his nature but because of his activity. The name «God» (θεός), according to the etymology accepted by Gregory, comes from θεάομαι, to see. Consequently, God is «the one who sees», the one who has the capacity to see in the world. This ability is attributed by the Scriptures to Father, Son, and Holy Spirit[69]. Gregory was indeed aware of the objections that could be raised against his argument. According to Gregory the unity of the three refers to the common activity that they carry out. But if this activity is exercised or practiced by three who have the capacity to see, then we should be talking about three gods. Gregory of Nyssa responded that in the common action of three persons there cannot be one unity as there is in the one that exists in the divine action in the world. This is begun by the Father, carried out by the Son, and perfected by the Spirit in total unity of both will and action. The three will the same thing and carry out the same thing. There is only one will of the Father that is fulfilled by the Son and the Spirit. No action is carried out separately. There is no interval or interruption in the action of the three, just as there is no interruption in their life[70]. The divine unity also has this dynamic and concrete aspect.

There is one order, one *taxis* of the persons, but this order does not affect the equality in the divinity. The Son is united with the Father, and he does not lose his dignity due to the fact that the Son comes from him. The order of enumeration does not entail any diversity of nature. The same thing must be said of the Holy Spirit[71]. His divine nature is known by its effects, which are the same as those of the Father and the Son. He has the same properties that they have, and for this reason he cannot be a creature[72]. It has been stated on many occasions that the Spirit is divine or that he has a divine nature[73]. Like Basil, Gregory also saw a relationship with the Son in the origin of the Spirit. Nevertheless, we must bear in mind that we cannot always assume a clear distinction between what was

---

[69] Cfr. *Quod non sunt…*, (42-48).
[70] *Quod non sunt…*, (46-53). Cfr. also BASIL, *Ep.* 38,4 (I 86).
[71] *C. Eun.* I 197-204; 690-691 (I 310-312;464); cfr. HANSON R.P.C., *The Search for the Doctrine of God* 729ff; POTTIER B., *Dieu et le Christ*, 313-378.
[72] Cfr. *Ad Eus. de Trin.* (Jaeger III 1,7-11); Christ has been anointed with the Holy Spirit; ibid. (14-16); *De Fide* (65-67); *Adv. Mac. De Sp. Sanc.* (100); ibid. (112) for the same understanding of the anointing; cfr. HANSON R.P.C., *The Search for the Doctrine of God*, 784f.
[73] *Adv. Mac. De Sp. sanc.* (90.92.94.101); the Spirit is united in everything with the Father and with the Son (100). He has κοινωνία of nature and honor with the Father and the Son (90). The Spirit is united with the Father and with the Son in the creative and saving action; these are formulations that are quite similar to those of Basil (cfr. 100.106.109).

later to be called «procession» and «mission». Hence, the Spirit comes or proceeds from the Father, and he is received from the Son[74]. The Holy Spirit has his purpose in the Father through and with the Son[75]. The divine life is transmitted to the Son through generation and to the Holy Spirit, through the Son, by procession. This is a summary of the thought of Gregory of Nyssa in this respect.

The Cappadocians insisted on the full divinity of the Son and the Spirit, without admitting any subordinationism. From the moment when the generation of the Word was not seen as a function of the creation, a decisive step forward was taken to consider the equal dignity of the three in the unity of the divine essence. The authors who came immediately after the Council of Nicaea had already paved that way. On some occasions, this might give the impression that after this point in time, the Trinitarian speculation grew apart somewhat from the saving economy which is the only proper way to understand the Trinity. Nevertheless, in short, the reality of the salvation of humankind can only be guaranteed with the proper profession of faith in the one and triune God. The contribution of the Cappadocians to Trinitarian theology certainly has been most relevant. In addition to addressing the speculative problem of unity and trinity in God, they openly affirmed the divinity of the Holy Spirit. In doing so, they paved the way for the first Council of Constantinople (year 381), the second of the ecumenical councils, which we will now begin to analyze based on these previous assumptions.

4

The first Council of Constantinople

To a certain extent, the theological developments of the fourth century, beginning with the Council of Nicaea, had their high point in the first Council of Constantinople. In this council, the *fides nicena* was completed, primarily regarding the article devoted to the Holy Spirit and the recognition of his divinity, even though it is not directly affirmed, as well as his unity with the Father and

---

74 *Adv. Mac.* (97); he is of the Father and of Christ, ibid. (89-90). Cfr. Pottier B., *Dieu et le Christ*, 357f.

75 Cfr. *C. Eun.* I 378-379 (1 138;180); *Ref. Conf. Eun.* 190-192 (II 392-393), against the Eunomian modality of understanding the procession through the Son; Basil, *Ep.* 38,4 (85.86). The Spirit as the third lamp that is lit from the first one by means of the second one, *Adv. Mac.* (93); *Quod non sunt . . .* (56); the «mediation» of the Only Begotten: Simonetti M., *La crisi ariana nel IV secolo*, 499f.

the Son manifested in the honor and adoration he receives. Although there is information about it, we have not had access to the *tomus* that explains the contents of the symbol. Nevertheless, there are still countless elements that help us clarify the sense of the most important affirmations of this council (cfr. DS 150).

As was the case with the symbol of Nicaea, so with the symbol of Constantinople, there is a question as to whether a previous symbol had been accepted (and to what extent), or whether the one that we know was actually produced in the sessions of the council[76]. This issue is not of the utmost importance for us. We will basically be analyzing the most significant modifications with respect to the Nicene symbol which is already known.

In the article devoted to the Father, it is added that he is the Maker «of heaven and earth», although that does not seem to be an especially significant innovation. The universality of the control and rule of the Father over everything is underscored.

More relevance can be attached to the changes in the second section of the symbol in which it is added that the generation of the Son is before all time, before all worlds. The idea of eternal generation was addressed in the anathemas of Nicaea which now disappear; and what is most important, the words «that is, of the essence (*ousía*) of the Father» are eliminated so as to further clarify the words «begotten of the Father». With the distinction between *ousía* and *hypostasis* which was still unknown in Nicaea (cfr. the anathemas) and which had been introduced during the debates that took place in the fourth century, these words could have caused confusion. After the affirmation of the universal creative mediation, the phrase «both in heaven and on earth» is eliminated to be consistent with what was added to the first article to which we have just referred.

The references to the historical life of Jesus are enriched. Above all, it is said that the incarnation takes place «[by] the Holy Ghost of the Virgin Mary». References are added to the crucifixion and to the burial of Jesus. The resurrection is «according to the Scriptures». Jesus who ascended into heaven «is seated on the right hand of the Father». The second coming will be «with glory». Likewise, «whose kingdom shall have no end» is added to rule out the possible ambigui-

---

76 Cfr. HANSON R.P.C., *The Search for the Doctrine of God*, 815-817; ABRAMOWSKI L., «Was hat das Nicaeno-Constantinopolitanum mit dem Konzil von Konstantinopel zu tun?» in *TheoPhil* 67 (1992) 481-513; SESBOÜÉ B., *Le Dieu du salut*, 273-277. Also regarding the symbol, RITTER A.M., *Das Konzil von Konstantinopel und sein Symbol*, Göttingen 1985; DOSETTI G.L., *Il simbolo di Nicea e di Costantinopoli*, Roma 1967.

ties of the interpretation of Marcellus of Ancyra on the delivery of the kingdom to the Father, the end of the kingdom of the Son, and the final fate of the human nature of Jesus.

The most transcendent innovations refer to the Holy Spirit. Unlike Nicaea, in this case what is said is τό πνεῦμα τό ἅγιον. The article is repeated; the Holy Spirit is holy. What is not said is «only one Holy Spirit», as happens with the Father and the Son. The differentiation can already be found in Nicaea. Basil talked about the «unicity» of the Holy Spirit, together with that of the Father and the Son[77].

The concrete affirmations about the Holy Spirit have a clear biblical inspiration. The Spirit is Lord (2Cor 3:17)[78]. In the New Testament, the title is applied primarily to God the Father and to Jesus Christ. Hence, its use by the council points toward placing the Holy Spirit on the same level of dignity with the first two persons. On the other hand, «giver of life» is a qualification that is applied in the New Testament primarily to the Spirit (cfr. 2Cor 3:6; John 6:63; in 1Cor 15:45, it refers to Jesus born from the dead who is made «a life-giving spirit»). We already saw how Athanasius argued against the nature of the Spirit as creature, based on the fact that he gives life and does not receive it. Without any doubt, mention is made not only of the creative function of the Spirit, but also of his sanctifying action and communication of divine life. The Spirit «proceeds from the Father». Reference to his «essence», which was mentioned in relation to the generation of the Son, has been eliminated, as we have already shown. The affirmation of the council drew inspiration from John 15:26, although this is not a literal quotation because the council replaces the preposition παρά with the preposition ἐκ. In 1Cor 2:12, we can read that the Spirit is ἐκ του θεου. With this change of prepositions, the text does not distance itself from the direct biblical inspiration. It is clear that there is a parallel between the generation of the Son «from the Father» and the «proceeding» of the Spirit also «from the Father». By affirming his proceeding from the Father, the intention is to show, above all, that the Holy Spirit is divine and not a creature[79]. It would be anachronistic to see in the text of the symbol a reference to the problems of the *filioque* that would be brought up later. This is an issue that was alien to the mentality of those times.

---

77 *De Sp. Sanc.* 18,45 (sСh 17bis,408). On the pneumatology of the symbol, cfr. De Halleux A., *La profession de l'Esprit Saint dans le Symbole de Constantinople*, in *Patrologie et œcuménisme*, Loeuven 1990, 322-337.

78 Cfr. Basil, *de Sp. Sanc.* 21,52 (434).

79 Hence, already in Athanasius, *Serap.* I 15 (pg 26,565), the procession from the Father contrasts the Holy Spirit with creatures, specifically the angels.

«Who with the Father and the Son together is worshiped and glorified». The influence of Basil is evident because, as we have seen, he protested against the subordinationist use that was made of the prepositions[80]. The *isotimia* is actually equivalent to consubstantiality. Finally, it is said that the Holy Spirit «spoke through the prophets». This is an understanding which we already find in the New Testament and in the oldest tradition, as we have had occasion to show. It is an action that is typical of the time of the Old Testament. The «newness» of the Spirit as a gift of Jesus, which is implied in the *vivificantem,* is not emphasized. Let us remember that mention has been made before of the action of the Spirit in the incarnation, although other actions typical of the time of the New Testament are not specified[81]. At any rate, it is clear that it is the same Spirit who has acted before and after Christ. The Spirit is not called God nor is the Spirit *homoousios* with the Father *directly.* In this respect, the coincidence with Basil is also evident.

We will not dwell on the aggregate statements on the Church, baptism, and the resurrection of the dead, because they are not directly our focus at this point. We can explain them through the presence of these issues in the creeds in which Constantinople may have found its inspiration.

Even though the various affirmations of the Council of Constantinople regarding the Holy Spirit differ in style from those applied to the Son, they reflect the firm conviction of the divinity of the third person, equal to that of the Father and of the Son. The contribution of the council to the development of the Trinitarian dogma is, consequently, decisive. It is comparable to that of the Council of Nicaea which proclaimed the full divinity of the Son and his consubstantiality with the Father.

The symbol of Constantinople was not very well known in the years that immediately followed the council. The common opinion at that time seems to have been that Constantinople merely confirmed the faith of Nicaea. Hence, the Nicene symbol was the only point of reference in the theological controversies at the end of the fourth century and the beginning of the fifth century. It was at the Council of Chalcedon (year 451) where this symbol was acknowledged and presented as belonging to the Council of Constantinople, attributing to it the same significance that had been first granted to the creed of Nicaea.

---

80 Cfr. *de Sp. Sanc.* 5;10;25;27;29 (272-284;332-338;456-464;478-490;500-518), etc.
81 Other creeds refer to the Spirit descending at the Jordan and to other actions mentioned in the New Testament: he spoke through the apostles, he dwells in the saints; cfr. DS 44;46.

In general terms, what Trinitarian theology is derived from the Council of Constantinople and the precedent of Cappadocian theology? The symbol of Constantinople included the Nicene *homoousios*. What meaning does the symbol give to *homoousios* in the new theological context, which is certainly more refined in its terminology? M. Simonetti[82], following the observations of M. Ritter[83], stated that in Nicaea, the identification between *ousía* and *hypostasis* has led us to interpret *homoousios* as indicative of the numerical identity of the divine essence. Despite the rather inadequate example of humankind and concrete humans, the Cappadocians regarded the divine essence in a specific and real way. Basil's formula appeared as an attempt to combine the stress on the unicity of God of Western thought, which would be the origin of *homoousios*, with the distinction of the *hypostases*, which had been defended by the «Homoiousians». Basil conceived of the divine essence as concrete and real, precisely as did the authors of the symbol of Nicaea. Nonetheless, he also insisted on the distinction of the three *hypostases* in which the unique concrete divine essence is articulated. Hence, *homoousios* should be understood in the light of this evolution, in the sense of numerical unity which would point to the divine essence itself and not merely to the generic unity. In this sole divine essence we see the integration of the articulation of the three persons, refining Nicene theology, which will further accentuate unity[84].

5

From the First to the Second Council of Constantinople[85]

Trinitarian dogma was defined in its essential features by the first Council of Constantinople, which offered a clear, although indirect, definition of the divinity of the Spirit who is Lord, and who proceeds from the Father and is wor-

82 Simonetti M., *La crisi ariana*, 541.
83 Ritter M., *Das Konzil von Konstantinopel* (cfr. no. 76), 270f.
84 Hanson R.P.C., *The Search for the Doctrine of God*, 735f, seems to opt for a more generic form of the Trinity. The analogies of the Cappadocians would go from what is specific to what is general, although this metaphor should not be taken in an extremely strict sense. At the same time, following Prestige G.L. (*God in Patristic Thought*, London 1936, 233), he underlines that the unity of the three is not only founded on the person of the Father, but rather, that even without taking directly into account the origin, the three are in a real sense one in themselves.
85 Unlike what we have done up until now, we will not now attempt to address the subsequent development of the Trinitarian «"theology"», but rather only the most important doctrinal statements. We will leave the study of this theological evolution —specifically the ideas of Saint Augustine who has been so determinative for Trinitarian theology in the West— for the systematic chapters that will follow.

shiped and glorified together with the Father and the Son. Nevertheless, later in time, there were other solemn declarations that are worthy of our attention. Before analyzing them, we must briefly study two important documents which followed immediately after the Council of Constantinople: the letter from the bishops of the East to Pope Damasus and the *tomus* of the latter, as a result of the Roman Council of the year 382.

In the letter from the bishops of the East to Pope Damasus and to the bishops of the West assembled in Rome in 382, in which they excused themselves for not having been able to attend the council summoned by the Damasus, we read as follows:

> [The profession of the faith of our baptism] teaches us to believe in only one divinity, power and essence of the Father, the Son and the Holy Spirit, in their equal and eternal honor and sovereign power, in three perfect *hypostases* or in three perfect persons. Hence, we do not give way to the pests of Sabellius who mistook the *hypostases* and eliminated the properties, and we attach no more significance to the blasphemy of the Eunomians, the Arians, and the *Pneumatomachi*, who divided the essence, the nature, and the divinity and introduced a subsequent or created nature —or, even a different essence— in the uncreated, consubstantial (*homoousios*), and coeternal Trinity[86].

In this text we also see the result of the work of Basil of Caesarea and his followers. The unity of the *ousía* is affirmed in the distinction of *hypostases* or persons[87] who really subsist. We will see how some of these formulations will also be used by the second Council of Constantinople.

The *Tomus Damassi* is made up of a summary of the Trinitarian faith and a series of anathemas that condemned the different errors that had appeared. We point to some of the most important affirmations for us: Father, Son, and Spirit are only one divinity, power, majesty, authority…. They are at the same time three true, equal, always living «persons» who contain it all, who do it all… and who save it all (DS 172ff).

---

86 Cfr. the text in ALBERIGO G. (ed.), *Les Conciles oecuméniques* II, Paris 1994, 81; cfr. SIMONETTI M., *La crisi ariana nel IV secolo*, 550 ; SESBOÜÉ B., *Le Dieu du salut*, 301, states that this is the first time that what would later be the dogmatic formula of Trinity appears in an official text.

87 The equivalence of these concepts is already found in the Cappadocians. Specifically, Gregory of Nyssa very frequently uses the *prósopon*.

The Council of Chalcedon (year 451), in the manner of the formula of union between Cyril of Alexandria and the bishops of the school of Antioch of the year 433 (DS 272), made a distinction between the two generations of the one Christ, the only begotten Son: the eternal generation from the Father before time according to the divinity, and the temporal generation from Mary according to the human nature (DS 302).

The formula of the unity of the essence in the Trinity with the *hypostases* will be definitively approved by the second Council of Constantinople (year 553). We will not address the complicated vicissitudes of its history[88]. The council primarily addressed Christological topics, although the first canon is Trinitarian:

> If anyone does not confess only one nature or substance (φύσιν ἤτοι οὐσίαν) of the Father, the Son, and the Holy Spirit, only one might and power, one consubstantial Trinity (τρίαδα ὁμόσιον), only one divinity worshiped in three *hypostases* or persons (πρόσωπα), this is anathema. Indeed, there is only one God and Father from whom all things come, only one Son through whom all things exist, and only one Holy Spirit in whom all things are (DS 421).

The text is made up of two parts. The first part is a summary of Trinitarian theology which has laboriously attempted to adequately combine the levels of the unity of essence and the distinction of persons in God. The second part, indeed having a more direct biblical inspiration, refers to the unity and distinction in the activity of God *ad extra*. The unity in God is found in the divine essence; the *ousía* or *physis* is the unique specific substance of the divinity; and the unity of power corresponds with this unity of essence. We saw in Nicaea and Constantinople the understanding of the Son as consubstantial with the Father. Here they speak of the consubstantial Trinity, as was already the case with the Eastern bishops in the year 382. The equality of the three persons is in the foreground, and the emphasis is on the same divinity and the same nature of the three and not simply on the «equal» nature, as in the classical example of the three men. The only and unique divinity is worshiped *in* three *hypostases* or persons. They are three truly subsistent entities, not three who appear as such. Therefore, in God, and without detriment to the unity of the essence, we have the distinction

---

88 Cfr. SESBOÜÉ B., *Le Dieu du salut*, 417-428; GRILLMEIER A., *Jesus der Christus im Glauben der Kirche* II/2, Freiburg-Basel-Wien 1989, 459-484.

of three persons. The one divinity is not the sum of the three persons, although the unity of the divinity lies solely in that of the consubstantial Trinity.

The unity in the Trinity also appears in the second part of the text inspired by 1Cor 8:6, with the gathering together of the Holy Spirit *in* whom all things are. The formulas of Athanasius, and also those of Basil, are reproduced almost literally. These are the formulas that addressed the unity of action of the three, although at the same time they contain the personal distinctions in this unique and joint action. It is worth noting that on these three occasions, the «only one» is repeated. Each one of the persons is unrepeatable and is God entirely[89].

6

The medieval Councils

Even though we will have occasion to quote them in our systematic study, we must mention at this point some of the most important ecumenical councils of the Middles Ages that address Trinitarian issues.

The first of them is the Fourth Lateran Council of the year 1215 which confesses the following:

> …that there is only one true, eternal, boundless, immutable, incomprehensible, omnipotent and ineffable God, the Father, the Son and the Holy Spirit; three persons although one completely simple essence, substance or nature. The Father does not come from anyone, the Son only from the Father, and the Holy Spirit from the two at the same time. Without beginning, he exists always and without an end. The Father begets, the Son is begotten, and the Holy Spirit proceeds. They are consubstantial and equal among themselves, together omnipotent and eternal… (DS 800).

Even when the divine unity that will characterize the medieval councils was stressed, it was affirmed that the only God is the Father, the Son, and the Holy Spirit. Other affirmations about creation followed which were in contrast with

---

89 Many of the concepts are repeated in the Lateran Synod of the year 649: «Si quis secundum sanctos Patres non confitetur proprie et veraciter Patrem et Filium et Spiritum Sanctum, trinitatem in unitate et unitatem in trinitate, hoc est, unum Deum in tribus subsistentiis consustantialibus et aequalis gloriae, unam eamdemque trium deitatem, naturam, substantiam, virtutem, regnum… condemnatus sit» (DS 501).

those of the Catharis or the Albigenses, after which came the Christological confession (cfr. DS 801).

The council also opposed the teachings of Joachim of Fiore who stated, against what had been set forth by Peter Lombard, that it was not possible to speak of Father, Son, and Holy Spirit as a *«summa res»* in such a way that in addition to the three persons of Father, Son, and Holy Spirit, there was also a common essence. This teaching posited some sort of a «quaternity». Joachim also envisioned the unity in God as that of a collectivity, just as many humans are one nation or many faithful are one Church (cfr. DS 803)[90]. With respect to this, the council stated as follows:

> We believe and confess... that there is a certain incomprehensible and ineffable *summa res* that is really the Father, the Son, and the Holy Spirit; at the same time three persons and each of them separately, and in this way, in God there is only one Trinity and not a quaternity, because each one of the three persons is that reality (*illa res*); in other words, the substance, the essence or divine nature that alone is the beginning of all things, beyond which no one can be found. And that *res* is not generating, nor begotten, nor proceeding, but it is the Father who begets... (DS 804).
>
> Therefore, although the Father is one, another one the Son, and another one the Holy Spirit, they are not another entity, but what the Father is, the Son and the Holy Spirit are also entirely, in such a way that we must believe according to the Catholic and orthodox faith that they are consubstantial. The Father who from eternity begets the Son gave him his substance... (DS 805).

The second Council of Lyon and the Council of Ferrara-Florence attempted to unite the churches of the East and the West by resolving the thorny issue of the *filioque*. We shall leave for later the study of this issue, and hence we will address again the basic affirmations of both councils. We believe that a few indications will suffice at this point. The profession of faith of Emperor Michael Paleologus was read during the second Council of Lyon (1274). It begins as follows:

---

90 On the Trinitarian doctrine of Joachim, cfr. DI NAPOLI G., «La teología trinitaria di Gioacchino di Fiori» in *Divinitas* 23 (1979) 281-312. About Joachim and Pietro Lombardo, COURTH F., *Trinität. In der Scholastik*, Freiburg-Basel-Wien 1985, 77-86; FÖSCHNER F., «Der Trinitätsbegriff Joachims von Fiore» in *WiWe* 58 (1995) 117-136.

We believe in the Holy Trinity, Father, Son, and Holy Spirit, one omnipotent God and in the complete divinity in the Trinity, co-essential and consubstantial, co-eternal and co-omnipotent, with one will, power, and majesty, creator of all creatures and from whom everything proceeds, through whom everything was made, in whom everything exists…[91]. We believe that each one of the persons in the Trinity is the unique true, full and perfect God (DS 851).

It further points out that «the Holy Trinity is not three gods, but one unique, omnipotent, eternal, invisible, and immutable God» (DS 853)[92].

We also recognize in these texts the understandings that have been paving the way since the end of the fourth century. The trend aimed at more strongly accentuating the divine unity and focusing less on the distinction between the persons is very clear, especially with respect to their external acts. Nevertheless, these texts also insist on the perfect divinity in each of the persons and their identification with the divine essence.

In regard to the Council of Florence, the second of the «councils of union» (years 1439-1442), mention must be made of the Trinitarian affirmations contained in the decree for the Greeks (cfr. DS 1300-1302) and the decree for the Jacobites (cfr. DS 1330-1333). For the moment we will address only a few phrases of this last decree:

The Catholic Church… believes in only one true, omnipotent God… Father, Son, and Holy Spirit, one in the essence, triune in the persons. The unbegotten Father, the Son begotten from the Father, the Holy Spirit who proceeds from the Father and the Son… These three persons are only one God and not three gods, because the substance of the three is only one, one in essence, one in nature, one in divinity, one in boundlessness, and one in eternity. In all, they are only one entity in which no opposition is raised in the relationship («omniaque sunt unum ubi non obviat relationis opposition») (DS 1330).

---

91 It is worth noting how the prepositions that Constantinople II applied respectively to the Father, to the Son, and to the Holy Spirit are applied here to the Trinity without any differentiation.

92 On the meaning of the second Council of Lyon, cfr. the letter of Paul VI to Cardinal Willebrands on the occasion of the celebration of the seventh centennial of the council in 1974; AAS 66 (1974) 620-625; there he recognizes that the unity, as achieved in this council, could not be accepted in the minds of Eastern Christians (623).

The pages that follow in this treatise will help us to better understand the affirmations of these medieval councils. With respect to the last phrase that we have quoted, we only point out the strong accent on the divine unity which we must affirm in everything that is not an obstacle to the plurality of the relationships. We will again address most of these texts in our systematic reflection. It will be useful for us to already be familiar with them.

Part two

From the «Economy» to the «Theology».
The systematic reflection on the One and
Triune God

«Trinitas in Unitate». The internal life of God: the processions, the relationships, and the divine persons

The historical summary that we have presented has shown us how the analysis of the Church has been driven to reflect on the divine life, on what God is in himself, precisely to guarantee the truth of salvation that God offers us in Christ. The «economy» has necessarily led to the «theology». We ended our historical review (apart from references to some medieval councils) in the final stage of the formulation of Trinitarian dogma. In our systematic analysis, we will also include the contributions made by Saint Augustine as they were indeed a major determining factor in Western theology, as well as the writings of medieval theology, especially those of Saint Thomas. We will always attempt to ensure that our reflection is based on the historical-saving manifestation of God, which is the only path we can pursue in our attempt to reach the mystery of God. In Chapter 3 of this treatise, we took as the point of departure the two missions of the Son and of the Holy Spirit which are referenced in Gal 4:2-6. In turn, in this chapter, we will attempt to determine how these missions lead us to the being of God, following the path of theological reflection that had already been addressed in the tradition of the Church.

The classical doctrine of God, so frequently inspired by the systematic thought of Saint Thomas, has addressed the one God before addressing the triune God[1]. In the case of Saint Thomas Aquinas, the order of the exposition corresponds to the order of our own knowledge. It is not a matter of giving priority to one dimension over the other[2]. We will be referring widely to Saint Thomas in our

---

1   In the *Summa Theologiae*, the study of God is placed at the beginning of part I, in q. 2-43. It continues immediately thereafter with creation, which for Thomas is still part of the treatise on God (which is part III), because it addresses the emergence of creatures from God. The first two parts address what pertains to the divine essence (q. 2-26) and what pertains to the Trinity of persons (q. 27-23). Although many of the issues addressed in part I seem to us philosophical in nature, we must not forget that our distinction does not correspond to the mentality of the thirteenth century. Based on the Scriptures, Saint Thomas also argues concerning these issues. On the other hand, the divine essence refers to the triune God. Regarding the Trinitarian thought of Saint Thomas, addressed in a subsequent bibliography, cfr. SALVATI, «"Cognitio divinarum Personarum…". La reflexión sistemática de Santo Tomás sobre el Dios cristiano» in *EstTrin* 29 (1995) 443-472; also ABRAMOWSKI L., «Zur Trinitätslehre des Thomas von Aquin» in *ZThK* 92 (1995) 466-480; VANIER P., *Théologie trinitaire chez s. Thomas d'Aquin*, Montréal-Paris 1953; ÉMERY G., *La Trinité créatice. Trinité et création dans les commentaires aux Sentences de Thomas d'Aquin et ses prédécesseurs Albert le Grand et Bonaventure*, Paris 1995; ibid., «Essentialisme et personnalisme dans le traité de Dieu chez saint Thomas d'Aquin» in *RevTh* 48 (1998) 5-38; SCHMIDTBAUR H.Ch., *Personarum Trinitas. Die trinitarische Gotteslehre des heiligen Thomas von Aquin*, St. Ottilien 1995. Regarding further information, in general terms, about the topics we are now addressing, cfr. KASPER W., *Der Gott Jesu Christi*, 337-347; ROVIRA BELLOSO J.M., *Tratado de Dios uno y trino*, 569-514; STAGLIANÒ A., *Il mistero del Dio vivente*, 534-543; SCHEFFCZYK L., *Der Gott der Offenbarung*, 350-370; GARCÍA MURGA J.R., *El Dios del amor y de la paz*, 242-250.

2   Cfr. *STh* I, 33,3 ad 1.

subsequent analysis, although the order that we will follow will be somewhat different. Our analysis of the unique divine essence will be included at the end because there is no other unity in God than that of Father, Son, and Holy Spirit. The divine essence is not something prior to the persons (evidently, Saint Thomas also agrees with this), because it subsists only in the three; but we can only speak about these three based on the historical saving manifestation of God, because the Father has sent his Son and the Holy Spirit. For this reason, we have already referred to the «missions» of the Son and the Holy Spirit, and we will address them briefly again[3]. Beginning with these *ad extra* divine missions, we will consider the eternal generation of the Son and the procession of the Holy Spirit, in other words, the divine «processions», according to Western theological terminology. Our brief review of the history of the theology of the first Christian centuries has given us the elements to understand these ideas.

1

From the divine missions to the «processions»

God sent his Son and the Holy Spirit. Based on the historical appearance of Jesus and the experience of the Spirit, the New Testament has already reached the conclusion that both exist prior to their mission in the world as it was entrusted by God the Father. In the first councils, the faith of the Church was defined based on the divinity of the Son and the Spirit, who are only one God with the Father. In subsequent reflection on the divine omnipresence, the question emerged as to how someone who is already everywhere can be sent to a place. Augustine himself posed this question[4]. The answer is that in this case, mission and manifestation, that is, being visible, have the same meaning. It is a new type of presence with different characteristics from those that are inherent in the omnipresence of God. In the case of the incarnation of the Son, the clear innovation that appears is that

---

3   In classical systematic thought, and in a very consistent manner, the missions take the last place. If we consider the immanent Trinity, the missions *ad extra* are the consequence of the internal life of the Trinity. Cfr. THOMAS AQUINAS, *STh* I 43. If, on the contrary, we prefer the order of our knowledge based on the revelation of the New Testament, from the missions *ad extra* of the Son and the Holy Spirit, we can then move to the consideration of what these are in relation to the Father, in the inner life of God. Cfr. in this respect *STh* I 43,7.

4   AUGUSTINE, *Trin.* II 5,7f (CCL 50,87-90); THOMAS AQUINAS, *STh* I 43,1.

the mission means a unique and unrepeatable perceived manifestation[5]. The mission of the Spirit is related at the same time to the visible manifestations that were present in the coming of the Holy Spirit in Pentecost[6].

This points to the different divine persons because the missions for which both persons were sent are different. The Father has sent, but he is not sent. He cannot be sent because he does not proceed from any other[7]. The Son is sent and he sends. The Holy Spirit is sent and he does not send. The manifestation or the fact of becoming visible, which is the new modality of presence of the divine persons, takes place in time[8]. We are speaking about the entrance of the divine persons into the history of humanity for the fulfillment of salvation. Therefore, this is a new type of qualitative presence, a free and personal presence[9]. The missions reveal to us the unity and the differentiation in God. According to Saint Thomas, they show us the procession of the one sent with respect to the one who is sending[10]. Therefore, the fact that God the Father has sent the Son and the Holy Spirit into the world shows us that they come from God. They come from God the Father into the world, but with this coming, it is revealed to us that they come from God also as it relates to his own being, in a different way from that in which all creatures come from him. Therefore, these divine missions lead us directly to the issue of the origin in God himself of the Son and the Holy Spirit, to the «generation» of the Son and the «procession» of the Spirit. In traditional theological vocabulary, mention is made of the divine «procession», but it has the Father as the ultimate beginning. As the Father has sent the Son and (together with the Son) has sent the Holy Spirit, in this same way the Son receives his being from the Father as the Holy Spirit also receives it from the Father, although with the participation of the Son. In due time, we will address the characteristics of this

---

5   Cfr. AUGUSTINE, *Trin.* II 5,9 (91-92); THOMAS AQUINAS, *STh* I 43,1. The mission shows the relationship (*habitudo*) of the one being sent with respect to the one who is sending, and on the other hand, it shows the *habitudo* with respect to the term of the one to which he is sent. Hence, with respect to this second aspect, it is said that the Son was sent into the world because he was visibly sent. It is clear that he was already in the world prior to that.

6   Cfr. AUGUSTINE, *Trin.* IV 20,29; 21,30 (201-202).

7   AUGUSTINE, *Trin.* IV 20,28 (198-199). Cfr. note 13, contained in chapter 2. Cfr. BONAVENTURE, *Breviloquium* I 5,5 (cfr. the entire context).

8   THOMAS AQUINAS, *STh* I 43,2; cfr. AUGUSTINE, *Trin* II 4,7ff (169ff).

9   Cfr. the distinctions of AUGUSTINE, *De presentia Dei liber* (Ep. 187, *ad Dardanum*) (CEL 57,81-119); cfr. also KASPER W., *Der Gott Jesu Christi*, 338.

10 THOMAS AQUINAS, *STh* I 43,1. The mission in God is involved in the procession of origin. Hence, the Father cannot be sent. Even in the *hypostasis* of the incarnation of the Father — the theoretical possibility of which is not ruled out by Thomas — he would not be «sent»; cfr. ibid. I 43,4.

intervention. This has been the rationale that has guided Christian theology in a more or less explicit manner from earlier days.

2

The divine «processions»: the generation of the Son and the exhalation of the Holy Spirit

According to Saint Thomas, in the general sense that one thing comes from another, all the «processions» entail an action. When applying this understanding to God, the Angelic Doctor states that not all the divine actions have their effect in the external range of action. The effect may remain in God himself. This is precisely the peculiarity of the divine processions and that which determines their differentiation with respect to the creation. There is not only a divine action outward, but there is also a divine action that remains within God[11]. This is a decisive aspect of the originality of Christian teachings about the one and triune God. He has in himself a fullness of life that has no need for creation. If we do not acknowledge this fullness of the intimate life within God, we inevitably return to the simplex nature of the one God. In their overly contrary and excessive views, Sabellius and Arius reached the same conclusion: the denial of the *ad intra* divine life. Based on these assumptions, every action of God needs to be external, because within the only one God there can be no room for any internal fruitfulness. However, this is not the God of our faith, as we have had occasion to evidence.

Our historical review has already confronted us with the question of the generation of the Son and the procession of the Holy Spirit. Reflection on the first one has been taking place since the very beginning of theology. We know about the speculations of the Apologists, which were continued by countless authors who have based their analyses on the analogy of the word uttered by humans. The fact that Son is the Word gives room for this comparison[12]; but even the ancient authors who did not want to engage in this type of speculation (founded

---

11 Cfr. THOMAS AQUINAS, *STh* I 27,1.

12 Hence, the frequent use of Ps 45(44),2: «eructavit cor meum verbum bonum». Cfr. among others, TERTULLIAN, *Prax* 7,1; 11,2 (Scarpat, 156;166); ORIGEN, *In Joh.* I 24,158; 38,280 (SCh 120,136;200); NOVATIAN, *Trin.* 15,83 (FP 8,152); DIONYSIUS OF ALEXANDRIA, in ATHANASIUS, *De sent. Dyon.* 23 (Opitz II/2, 63); cfr. THEOPHILUS OF ANTIOCH, *Ad. Aut.* II 22 (BAC 116,813).

on Isa 53:8, «generationem eius quis enarrabit»), have referred to the generation of the Son. The analogy of generation is determined by the same Father-Son biblical terminology. The theology of the «procession» of the Holy Spirit has been developed to a lesser degree and even the term itself is characterized by a higher degree of vagueness[13]. The procession of the Spirit has also been called *spiratio*, in view of the original meaning of the term «spirit» that is associated with wind and with a gust.

Latin theology has encompassed, under the common concept of «procession», both the generation of the Son and the procession or exhalation of the Holy Spirit. Eastern theology prefers to speak of generation and procession without including them within a generic concept. There are indeed good reasons to speak in this way because in God everything is unique and unrepeatable. We will attempt to use these two differentiated concepts in the following analysis. If we also continue using the concept of procession in its broad sense, it is not due to lack of sensibility to these issues and reasons. It is not always easy to change terminology when we have behind us the full weight of the Western tradition, which is our normal environment. On the other hand, without ruling out anything that we have just said, there is also a reason for this usage to be this way; it has its *raison d'être:* according to the Christian tradition the Son and the Spirit have in common the fact that they do not have in themselves the source of their being, unlike the Father. To a certain degree, the generic term «procession» accounts for this differentiation between the Father on the one hand, and the Son and the Spirit on the other. Something similar happens with «mission», although with the diverse characteristics of the mission of the Son and that of the Spirit, in these two instances, the same term «sending» is already used in the New Testament.

Consequently, the generation of the Son and the procession of the Holy Spirit, to which we have access from their missions, are the expressions of the life and internal truthfulness of the one and triune God. Theology has resorted to comparisons based on the created world to explain the unity and the Trinity in God. We have already read about the old metaphors of fountain and river and channel; of sun and ray; of root, trunk, and fruit. These were comparisons taken from subhuman nature. The theology of the Apologists concerning the procession of the Logos had already taken into account the human intellect. Beginning with

---

13 What is usually said about this procession is what it is not: it is not creation or generation; hence, the symbol *Quicumque* DS 75; «non factus, nec creatus, nec genitus, sed procedens».

Saint Augustine and with a clear awareness of the infinite distance that separates humanity from God, Western theology has preferred to use the comparison of the internal life of the human mind in order to address to a certain degree the mystery of the eternal truthfulness of the divine life. Eastern theology has been more reluctant to use images because of the tendency to emphasize the ineffable and mysterious nature of God and of his Trinitarian life. Independent of the value that each one can give to these analogies, knowing them is absolutely necessary for us. Otherwise, we cannot understand a decisive chapter of Christian theology which continues to have an influence in our times.

2.1. THE DIVINE PROCESSIONS AND THE ANALOGY OF THE HUMAN MIND. AUGUSTINE AND THOMAS AQUINAS

As we have already mentioned, Augustine used comparisons taken from the human psyche in order to shed light on the mystery of the Trinity. He did not attempt to reach God through the human being, but rather he tried to penetrate the divine image which the creator has imprinted in the human soul. Hence, indirectly, he could derive some insight which would draw us closer to the Trinitarian mystery. Without this reference to Gen 1:26-27, it impossible to understand the meaning of the attempt made by Augustine in this regard. According to Augustine, the human soul has been created in the image and likeness of God, of the Trinity as a whole, because God tells us according to Genesis: «let us make man in our own image, in the likeness of ourselves»[14]. As stated by the Bishop of Hippo, this image is quite unequal in comparison with God's image, although it is still an image[15]. The human soul contains the triad of mind, love, and knowledge[16], or also of memory, intelligence, and will[17]. The mind has been created in such a way that it always remembers, understands, and loves itself[18]. Nevertheless, human beings will be in the image of God when the soul does not recognize and love itself alone, but also God. Only in this way, will humans participate in the wisdom that pertains to God[19]. In this triad, the Son, as Logos, is related to

---

14   Cfr. AUGUSTINE, *Trin.* VII 6,12 (266f). HILARY OF POITIERS has preceded him in underlining this aspect, *Trin.* IV 17-19; V 8-9 (CCL 62,119-122;158-159).

15   Cfr. AUGUSTINE, *Trin.* IX 2,2 (294).

16   AUGUSTINE, *Trin.* IX 5,8 (300); IX 12,18 (309), mind, knowledge, and love, and these three are one.

17   AUGUSTINE, *Trin.* X 11,18 (330); cfr. also *Conf.* XIII 11,12 (CCL 27,247), the triad of being, knowledge, and will.

18   AUGUSTINE, *Trin.* XIV 14,18 (445).

19   AUGUSTINE, *Trin.* XIV 12,15 (442f); also XIV 16,22 (451), the image must be reformed by the one who formed it; XV 20,39 (516ff), the contemplation of and the delight in the eternal Trinity must be the light of him who is created after his likeness.

reason or knowledge. In the knowledge of things we have a word within us, and by saying it we engender it inwardly, and it does not take leave from us because we are born. As an analogy to this, God begets his Word, and his Word does not become separate from him[20]. This Word is equal to the Father[21].

Only in knowing itself can the human mind love itself[22]. As we will see in what follows, the Holy Spirit is in relationship with the will and love because these come after knowledge. When he used these images, Augustine was clearly aware that the Word of God and our word are not comparable. The presence of the image of God in the soul does not eliminate this key differentiation[23].

Based on those assumptions, medieval theology, primarily the thought of Saint Thomas, developed the theology of procession as deriving from the intellectual act that befits the generation of the Word. We have just stated that there is an action in the divine processions which does not have an external object but which remains in the agent himself. The most eloquent example in this respect for Saint Thomas is the intellect, the action of which —understanding— remains in the one who understands[24]. The procession of the Word is called generation because it is done as an intelligible action, and the conception of the intellect is the actual likeness of the thing that is understood. This conception exists in the divine nature itself because being and understanding are the same in God[25]. Saint Thomas further clarified that the procession via the intellectual action shares in its likeness and that it can be called generation because the one who generates engenders a fellow person. Because of the modality of his procession, the Son is like the Father. For this reason, the name of Son is in its full sense because it comes from the generation that makes him like the one who begets him. On the other hand, the procession by the will is not according to its likeness, because in this will there is no likeness with the object that is desired. Rather, in the will there is an impulse and a movement towards something[26].

20 AUGUSTINE, *Trin.* IX 7,12 (304).
21 AUGUSTINE, *Trin.* XV 14,23 (496).
22 AUGUSTINE, *Trin.* IX 3,3 (295f).
23 AUGUSTINE, *Trin.* XV 15-16 (497-501).
24 THOMAS AQUINAS, *STh* I 27,1.
25 THOMAS AQUINAS, *STh* I 27,2: «conceptio intellectus est similitudo rei intellectae; et in eadem natura existens, quia in Deo idem est intelligere et esse».
26 THOMAS AQUINAS, *STh* I 27,4. Already found in AUGUSTINE, *Trin.* IX 11,18 (309).

The procession out of will or love is traditionally reserved for the Holy Spirit. The first point that we find in tradition is that the Spirit is «from God» (cfr. 1Cor 2:12)[27]; however, the Spirit is not begotten because otherwise there would be two sons within God, contrary to the explicit affirmations in this respect found in the New Testament (cfr. John 1:14,18; 3:16,18; 1John 4:9).

Indeed, Saint Augustine related the person of the Spirit to will and love[28]. In the «Trinity», when considering the one who loves, the one who is loved, and love, the Holy Spirit is the last one[29]. As we have already evidenced, something similar applies to his triads about memory, intelligence, and will or mind, knowledge, and love. When the mind loves itself we have in the first instance the mind and love, but love assumes the knowledge that the mind has of itself[30]. In this way, it holds the third place. Hence, from the perspective of Augustine, when we see the typical characteristics of each of the divine persons, we must address the Holy Spirit as love.

Saint Thomas stated that in the intellectual nature, together with the acts of reason, are the acts of will:

> According to the act of the will we find in ourselves another procession, in other words, the procession of love, because the one who loves is in the one who is loved in the same way as things that are said or understood are in the one who understands by way of the conception of the word. Hence, together with the procession of the Word there is another procession in God, which is the procession of love[31].

Intellect and will are not different things in God. Nevertheless, as it pertains to the modality of love in that it only proceeds from the conception of the intellect, the procession of love in God is different from the procession of the Word[32].

27 IRENAEUS, *Adv. Haer.* V 12,2: «God took out the Spirit from himself»; Cfr. ORBE A., *Teología de san Ireneo* I, Madrid 1985, 547.
28 AUGUSTINE, *Trin.* IX 12,17 (308): «sicut dei verbum filium esse nullus christianus dubitat, ita caritas esse spiritus sanctus»; also VI 5,7 (235f), love and the unity of the Father and the Son.
29 Cfr. AUGUSTINE, *Trin.* IX 2,2 (294f), although Augustine clarified at this point that he has still not mentioned the divine Trinity at all.
30 AUGUSTINE, *Trin.* IX 3,3; 5,8 (296;300f). Cfr. TURRADO A., «Agustín (San)» in *Diccionario teológico. El Dios cristiano*, 15-25 (and its subsequent bibliography); ROVIRA BELLOSO J.M., «La fe se hace teología refleja (S. Agustín)» in *EstTrin* 29 (1995) 419-441.
31 THOMAS AQUINAS, *STh* I 27,3.
32 THOMAS AQUINAS, *STh* I 27,3, ad. 3: «…nihil enim potest voluntate amari, nisi sit in intellectu conceptum… ita licet in Deo sit idem voluntas et intellectus, tamen quia de ratione amoris est quod non procedat nisi a conceptione intellectus, habet ordinis distinctionem processio amoris a processione verbi in divinis».

Therefore, even though in God everything is identified with the divine nature, the processions stand out in terms of the order of one with respect to the other, because the second procession presupposes the first one. The distinction between the two is also founded on the diversity of the likeness that is present in one case over against the other one:

> Likeness belongs in one way to the Word and in another way to love. It belongs to the Word insofar as it is a certain likeness of the thing that is understood, as the begotten is the likeness of the one who begets. Nevertheless, it belongs to love, not because love itself is likeness but insofar as likeness is the principle of loving. However, we cannot say that love is begotten, but that what is begotten is the principle of love[33].

Consequently, according to Saint Thomas, the procession of the Holy Spirit must be seen in unison with that of Word, and at the same time it must be differentiated from it. These are the only two processions that take place in God because the only actions that remain in the agent are those of understanding and loving. The act of feeling, which might also seem to have this characteristic, is not inherent within the intellectual nature. For this reason, we cannot think of God in terms of more processions than those of the Word and of love, because God understands and loves his essence, his truth, and his goodness. God understands all things with a simple act, and with a simple act he loves them. As a result of this, there cannot be a procession, either from the Word —*ex Verbo*— or from love —*ex amore*[34].

As we have stated before, we can assess in different ways these speculations that appear in the writings of both Saint Augustine and Saint Thomas regarding the divine processions. Clearly, we are not speaking here about a binding doctrine, and we cannot say that it is followed very closely today in Catholic theology. Nevertheless, it is still necessary to be aware of this doctrine in order to understand many of the aspects of Western theological tradition, and even though these aspects do not depend on this speculation, they have been very frequently enlightened by its conjectures.

---

33 THOMAS AQUINAS, *STh* I 27,4, ad 2: «Similitudo aliter pertinet ad verbum, et aliter ad amorem. Nam ad verbum pertinet inaquantum ipsum est quaedam similitudo rei intellectae, sicut genitum est similitudo generantis: sed ad amorem pertinet, non quod ipse amor sit similitudo, sed in quantum similitudo est principium amandi. Unde non sequitur quod amor sit genitus: sed quod genitum sit principium amoris»; also I 30,2, ad 2. Cfr. already Augustine, *Trin.* IX 11,18 (310).

34 THOMAS AQUINAS, *STh* I 27,5.

The analogy with the human soul that knows and loves itself has not been the only alternative in the history of theology for explaining the fruitfulness of the *ad intra* divine life; to a lesser extent, the analogy of interpersonal love has also been used. Augustine spoke of the three of the Trinity as being analogous with the one who loves, the one who is loved, and love itself, although he primarily referred to the human mind that knows and loves itself[35]. We can find some indications, however, that interpersonal love also has been considered, at least indirectly, by the Doctor of Hippo[36]. This is the line of thought that has been followed more clearly by Richard of St. Victor († 1173), who preceded Saint Thomas by more than a century. It is worth briefly analyzing his *De Trinitate*, which presents another way of posing the difficulty of the plurality in God and of divine truthfulness *ad intra*. Even though Richard of St. Victor did not pose the issue of «processions» as directly as Saint Thomas, his explanation responds to this same difficulty, in other words, «justifying» the existence of one plurality in the one God.

Richard of St. Victor turned to reason in an attempt to enlighten the mystery in which we believe, looking for the *rationes necessariae* to explain the Trinity[37]. The point of departure is that in God everything is one; everything is simplex. All the attributes are only one and the same thing. There is nothing more than one Supreme Goodness[38]. Diversity in God is based on the perfection of *caritas*; there is nothing better or more perfect than *caritas*. Essentially, *caritas* is draw to the other. For this reason, love per se cannot be the perfect realization of itself[39]. Therefore, in order for there to be *caritas*, there must be plurality of persons. In order for God to have this supreme love, there is a necessity to ensure that there

---

35 AUGUSTINE, *Trin.* IX 2ff (294ff). Cfr. GALOT J., «La génération éternelle du Fils» in *Greg* 71 (1990) 657-678.

36 AUGUSTINE, *Trin.* VIII 10,14 (290-291): «Quid amat animus in amico nisi animum? Et illic igitur tria sunt». *In Joh.* XIV 9; XXXIX 5 (CCL 36,148;348). Let us not forget, on the other hand, that Augustine opposed the trend that considers the triad that is made up by man, woman and their children as the image of the Trinity: *Trin.* XII 5,5ff (359ff).

37 RICHARD OF ST. VICTOR, *De Trinitate* prol; 1,4 (SCh 63,52f); 70). On the Trinitarian theology of Richard of St. Victor, cfr. PIKASA X., «Notas sobre la Trinidad en Ricardo de San Víctor» in *EstTrin* 6 (1972) 63-101; SCHNIERTSHAUER M., *Consummatio Caritatis. Eine Untersuchung zu Richard von St. Victors De Trinitate*, Mainz 1996. On the necessary reasons, cfr. 88-91. These are necessary because they are found in God himself.

38 Cfr. RICHARD OF ST. VICTOR, *Trin.* II 18 (142).

39 RICHARD OF ST. VICTOR, *Trin.* III,2 (168): «Nihil caritate melius, nihil caritate perfectius... Ut ergo pluralitas personarum deest, caritas omnino esse non potest».

is someone who is worthy of it. This is the same conclusion that is reached when we begin with the idea of happiness, which is united with *caritas*: «as there is nothing better than *caritas*, there is nothing more joyous than *caritas* (sicut nihil caritate melius nihil caritate iucundius)». If the divinity is the supreme happiness, there is a need for the plurality of persons so that love is joyous, because he who loves also wants at the same time to be loved by the one he loves[40]. If God (the Father) would not wish to communicate to another one his love and his happiness, he would exist with *defectus benevolentiae*. If he were not able to, he would not be omnipotent. These two things must be excluded in him. The plurality of persons, a requirement for joyous love, demands that the two persons be equal and coeternal: «supreme *caritas* demands equality of persons (caritas summa exigit personarum aequalitatem)», and always in unity of substance. Otherwise, there would be more than one God[41].

After taking into account the plurality, we must proceed specifically to the Trinity[42]. In this respect, the following question emerges: why would not two suffice? The answer of Richard of St. Victor is that perfect *caritas* demands that the other one be loved as each one loves. There must be a *consortium amoris*. Not generating a *condilectus*, that is, the one loved together with oneself, would be a great sign of weakness. It would be a sign of a selfish love; however, when the *condilectus* not only «generates himself» but also desires himself, we have the sign of maximum perfection. Because of this, the consummation of *caritas* demands the Trinity of persons. Moreover, the fullness of happiness excludes any defect that *caritas* could have. For these reasons, the *dilectio* and the *condilectio* must go together. With only two there would be no one to communicate the delights of *caritas*[43]. The *condilectio*, that joint love, takes place «when a third one is loved in harmony with the two, when he is loved "socially". The affection of two is inflamed in *caritas* in the fire of love for a third one»[44]. Hence, with the exis-

---

40 RICHARD OF ST. VICTOR, *Trin.* III 3 (172).

41 RICHARD OF ST. VICTOR, *Trin.* III 4-7 (174-182).

42 RICHARD OF ST. VICTOR, *Trin.* III 11 (190-194); Cfr. SCHNIERTSHAUER M., *Consummatio Caritatis*, 129ff.

43 RICHARD OF ST. VICTOR, *Trin.* III 13-14 (196-200). BONAVENTURE, *Breviloquium* I 2,3: «Et ideo, ut altissime et piissime sentiat, dicit, Deum se summe communicare, aeternaliter habendo dilectum et condilectum, ac per hoc Deum unum et trinum».

44 RICHARD OF ST. VICTOR, *Trin.* III 19 (208f): «Ubi a duobus tertius concorditer diligitur, socialiter amatur, et duorum affectus tertii amoris incendio in unum conflatur». The terms used by Richard of St. Victor to point out this fact are quite varied: *concordialis, condelectari, confoederatio…*; cfr. SCHNIERTSHAUER M., *Consummatio Caritatis* 134.

tence of the third person it is possible to achieve the *caritas* of concord and harmony and the solidarity of love. They are never alone («concordialis caritas et consolidalis amor ubique nusquam singularis inveniatur»). In order that this solidarity of love can take place, the three must be equal, coeternal, and so forth. The being of the three is common to each of them and at the same time extremely simplex («summe simplex esse est singulis commune»)[45].

The above argument has shown that two persons do not suffice for perfect love and for perfect happiness. Nevertheless, we can ask ourselves: why only three? Why is it not possible to multiply indefinitely the divine persons? We have already seen the solution given by Saint Thomas: only the acts of intelligence and will remain in the agent. For this reason, there can be only two processions in God. Richard of St. Victor followed another course: the Father gives being and love and does not receive them; the Son receives them and gives them; the Holy Spirit only receives them. The Father is solely gratuitous love; the Holy Spirit is solely love that is «owed», in other words received; the Son, in the center of them, has received love, on the one hand, with respect to the Father, and gratuitous love, on the other hand, with respect to the Holy Spirit[46]. If there were more persons who would give and receive, there would be confusion among them, because each person is the same as his love, «qualibet persona… est idem quo amor suus»[47]. Because of this, the divine persons cannot multiply themselves, because if they were to do so they would lack their uniqueness, and each of them would not have one kind of love as his own exclusive characteristic. The difference in the kind of love does not lead to a diversity of grades nor to one being greater and the other one being lesser. If, according to this analysis of love, there cannot be more than three persons, because of the reasons we already have seen, neither can there be less. Having one *condignus* (one who is wholly worthy) is the perfection of one; having a *condilectus* is the perfection of one and the other[48]. For this reason, in the procession of the Son we see the communion of honor, because he is the *condignus*. In the procession of the Holy Spirit, we see the communion of love, because he is the *condilectus*. Following tradition, Richard refers to the Son as *genitus*, begotten. The names Father and Son lead us to this designation. The Holy Spirit is neither *genitus* nor *ingenitus* because on the one

45 RICHARD OF ST. VICTOR, *Trin.* III 21-22 (212-216).
46 Cfr. RICHARD OF ST. VICTOR, *Trin.* V 16 (344).
47 RICHARD OF ST. VICTOR, *Trin.* V 20 (352).
48 RICHARD OF ST. VICTOR, *Trin.* V 8; VI 6 (322; 388).

hand he is not the Son, but on the other hand, he has been created according to his nature, and for this reason, he cannot be called «unbegotten». In this respect Richard was not especially original[49]. In view of the fact that in the logical order the *condignus* comes before the *condilectus*, the procession of the Son is prior to that of the Holy Spirit[50].

These are two modalities or two attempts at addressing the mystery of the internal life of God which have had and continue to have an influence on theology to the present. There is no doubt that the Augustinian-Thomist direction has enjoyed a prestige in history that cannot be attributed to the line of thought of Richard regarding interpersonal love. Nevertheless, this line of thought has grown in value in recent times. We will return to this issue when we analyze the conception of person. Meanwhile, let us keep in mind the basic ideas of these two lines of thought, used in history as approximations of the ineffable mystery in the internal life of God. Despite the basic inadequacy of any possible explanation, we must affirm that the *ad intra* fruitfulness of divine love is an essential piece of information about the Christian conception of God. This is precisely what the classic conceptions of the generation of the Son and the procession or exhalation of the Holy Spirit attempt to depict. We arrive at them based on the *ad extra* missions through which God is revealed. Reflection in faith under the action of the Spirit has discovered that these temporal missions have their eternal foundation in the immanent life of God himself.

Eastern theology has not followed these analogies with human psychology and interpersonal love in order to shed light on the mystery of generation and breath or exhalation. It has maintained a rather more *apophatic* attitude (that is, God can only be described in terms of what he is not) as it relates primarily to the procession of the Holy Spirit. For example, it is worth quoting John of Damascus who addressed the issue in this way: «The modalities of generation and of procession are incomprehensible. We know that there is a difference between generation and procession, but we do not know what this difference is»[51]. It is worth noting with respect to this text that generation (in the case of the Son) and procession (as related to the Holy Spirit) are differentiated. As we have already shown, the generic concept of procession was not used.

49 RICHARD OF ST. VICTOR, *Trin.* VI 16 (420f).
50 RICHARD OF ST. VICTOR, *Trin.* VI 6-7 (386-390).
51 *De fide orthodoxa* I 8 (PG 94, 822); cfr. also I 2 (793); 17-8 (817-824).

In this presentation of the divine processions we have deliberately left aside the topic of the procession of the Holy Spirit from the Father and from the Son, although Western authors that we have quoted clearly assume it. Nevertheless, we will analyze this issue in greater depth when we address the person of the Holy Spirit. At that point, we will have all the information at hand that will enable us to understand the question that has been posed throughout history as it relates to the procession of the Holy Spirit and ecumenical problems that unfortunately have not yet been overcome and that are related to this procession[52].

3

The divine relationships

300 In classic systematic thought regarding Trinitarian theology, the topic of relationships in God is addressed following that of the processions. There is no doubt that this is another fundamental category of doctrine about the Trinity which must be addressed in close relationship with the one that we have been addressing up to this point. In fact, according to traditional theology, relationships in God are derived from the processions, in other words, from the fact that in Father, Son, and Holy Spirit we have an order in the «procession». As we have already had occasion to realize, the names Father and Son suggest the idea of relationship. Therefore, we can accept as the point of departure that the fact of the generation of the Son and the exhalation of the Spirit determine the existence of relationships with God. The Cappadocians, Basil and Gregory of Nazianzus, had posited the idea of relationships in Trinitarian theology. The Father and the Son have the same substance because they are the one who begets and the one who is begotten. Relational names, as is the case of «father» or «son» or «offspring», do not point to the substance of any being, but to a relationship. In the case of God, they point to the relationship of the Father with respect to the Son and vice versa. There are certain names which apply to persons or to things in themselves, while there are others which refer to their relationship with other

52 We have listed some important texts on the teachings of divine procession (some of which have already been quoted at the end of the previous chapter, while others will be referenced later on as they relate to the specific issue of the procession of the Holy Spirit): DS 850; 851, 853 (Second Council of Lyon); 1300-1302; 1330-1331 (Council of Florence). As we have already suggested, teachings, when addressing the processions, have no commitment to any speculative model for «explaining» the processions.

things. Man, horse, and ox belong to the first category; son, slave or friend belong to the second category, because they only point to the relationship with the term with which they are compared. Hence, when speaking about father and his «offspring», (as in the example of Eunomius), this does not necessarily imply two substances because both one name and the other only have meaning as they relate to the one they are compared with in the relationship[53].

3.1. THE RELATIONSHIPS IN GOD ACCORDING TO SAINT AUGUSTINE

With this background in mind, Saint Augustine turned this relationship into one of the masterpieces of his Trinitarian theology. It is worth noting that in his work *de Trinitate* he hardly used the term *relatio*[54], but rather he used *relativum*, «relative» and other equivalent expressions, for instance, *ad aliquid, ad aliud*, and the like. Let us briefly analyze the steps followed by the Doctor of Hippo[55]. We begin with the premise that Augustine found in the tradition: the simplex nature of God. This can lead to a false consequence: in view of the fact that in God there can be no accidents, everything that is affirmed must be according to his substance. However, different concepts are proclaimed concerning the Father and the Son. Therefore, in view of the fact that difference cannot be accidental due to the divine simplex nature, this diversity must of necessity refer to his substance. Consequently, the Son cannot be God in the same way as the Father.

In order to face this possible objection, Augustine posited a distinction which cannot simply be categorized as either substance or accident. In fact, there are no accidents in God, but not everything is proclaimed in him according to his substance. There are other things that are proclaimed *ad aliquid*, with respect to the other, as it is related to another. According to Aristotle, the category of relationship is accidental[56]; but accidents have their origin in mutability which is not present in God. Because of this, by being immutable, the aspect present in God in regard to relationships has no accidental nature. As it applies to God,

---

53 It is worth remembering some of the fundamental statements of the Cappadocians: BASIL, *C. Eun.* II 5 (SCh 305,22): «Father and Son do not designate substance but properties»; II 29 (118): divinity is shared in common, and among the properties we have both Fatherhood and Sonship. GREGORY OF NAZIANZUS, *Or.* 29,16 (SCh 250,210), Father is not a name of essence or of activity but a name of relationship that indicates how the Father is with respect to the Son and how the Son is with respect to the Father; cfr. ibid. 31,9 (290f).

54 Perhaps the only exception is found in *Trin.* V 11,12 (241): «ipsa relatio non apparet in hoc nomine (Spiritus sanctus)…».

55 Cfr. mostly *Trin.* V (CCL 50,206-227).

this introduces a new criterion for division of categories: that which is referred to as *ad se* and that which is referred to as *ad aliquid*. Precisely for this reason, the Father and the Son are always Father and Son; there is no change or mutation in them[57]. Therefore, in the utter simplex nature of the divine being we must maintain the distinction between what is said of God in himself and what is said of God in relationship with another: «Therefore, even though the Father and the Son are differentiated, this does not mean that they have a different substance, because differences do not refer to their substance but to their relationship (*relativum*), and this relational nature is not an accident, because God is not mutable»[58]. Reference is made to God as Father and Son in relative terms and not in absolute terms. Therefore, nothing keeps their substance from being the same, and nothing can prevent their substantial diversity, even though the two are not the same. As a result of this, the names Father and Son enable us see the relationship that is established between the two, that of Fatherhood and Sonship. There is only a Father because there is a Son and vice versa. In the previous tradition we have been confronted with this argument quite frequently.

A greater difficulty is found in Augustine when there is a need to address the Holy Spirit. This term is not relational, and on the other hand, it does not seem inherent to any of the persons because the Father and the Son also are «spirit» and they are «holy»[59]. Nevertheless, the relational nature of the Holy Spirit, which does not appear in his name, does appear when he is called «gift». The New Testament paves the way for using this term (cfr. Acts 2:38; 8:20; 10:45; 11:17; also John 15:16 and so on, on the Spirit who is «given»). Augustine could, in this respect, turn to the previous Latin tradition, most specifically that of Hilary of Poitiers whom he knew and quoted with praise[60], and for whom «gift» is used as another personal name for the Holy Spirit. However, the relational term forces us to determine for whom the Holy Spirit is a «gift». With different nuances, in

56 Different references to the Aristotelian categories in *Trin.* v 1,2; 7,8; 8,9 (207); 213f; 215f; *Conf.* iv 16, 28-29 (CCL 27,54).

57 Cfr. LADARIA L.F., «Persona y relación en el De Trinitate de san Agustín» in *Miscelánea Comillas* 30 (1972) 245-291, especially 257.

58 AUGUSTINE, *Trin.* v 5,6 (211): «… quamvis diversum sit Patrem et Filium esse, non est tamen diversa substantia: quia hoc non secundum substantiam dicuntur, sed secundum relativum; quod tamen relativum non est accidens, quia non est mutabile».

59 Cfr. *Trin.* v 11,12 (219f), also for the following text.

60 Cfr. HILARY OF POITIERS, *Trin.* II 1 (CCL 62,38), cited, even though there are modifications by AUGUSTINE, *Trin.* VI 10,11 (241). In this passage no mention is made of *donum* but of *munus*. The terms are equivalent.

the New Testament we have already seen that the Spirit is from God and he is from Christ; he is given by the two of them. As a result of this, and because this relationship must be established formally between the two, the Holy Spirit appears as given by the Father and the Son who together are the sole beginning of the third person[61].

Even though Augustine has not formulated this directly, from his texts we can see that the eternal generation of the Son and the procession of the Spirit are the generations that give origin to these relationships. On the other hand, the relational names of the Scriptures enable us to know the «processions» that will originate them. It is not especially difficult to understand the generation of the Son. The relationship that is established between the Father and the Son shows this type of «procession». Conversely, the Holy Spirit, who is a gift, does not proceed as born but as given «non quomodo natus, sed quomodo datus»[62]. As a «gift», the Holy Spirit proceeds from the one who gives him. Perhaps this doctrine of relationships has influenced the issue of the procession of the Spirit from the Father and from the Son which we have already analyzed and which will require our attention further ahead. Here we have an interesting example of the relationship between the economic Trinity and the immanent Trinity. If Augustine has stated that the Spirit is «economically» a gift, this has also led him to state that he proceeds as «given». According to this thinking, the «gift» of the Holy Spirit should already correspond to the generation of the Son in the immanent Trinity. Nevertheless, Augustine did not follow this train of thought. The confusions to which this terminology would have led are quite evident.

Considering that God is immutable, the eternity of the three persons is derived from the mutual relationships. As frequently happens in Trinitarian theology, this issue is clearer as it relates to the Father and the Son. If the being of the Father is that of being «father», this condition cannot be acquired at a certain point in time, and instead, must be eternal. Therefore, the Son is also eternal, unlike what the Arians thought. The eternity of the Holy Spirit poses greater difficulties. As has been already explained, this name does not point to a relationship, and the gift of the Spirit to humanity is certainly not *ab aeterno*. Does the Spirit begin to exist when he is given? With difficulty, Augustine found a way out by making the distinction between «gift» and «given» (*donatum*). The Holy Spirit

---

61   *Trin.* v 14,15 (223): «...relative ad Spiritum Sanctum, unum principium».
62   *Trin.* v 14,15: «Exit enim non quomodo natus sed quomodo datus...».

is eternally a «gift», and consequently he is also «givable», although we cannot say that he has been «given» forever[63]. Therefore, the third person existed just as the other two have, from the beginning. The intra-Trinitarian relationships that refer to the third person are also eternal, and as a result of this, they are immutable.

The point of departure for Augustine was certainly a strong emphasis on divine unity[64]. However, with his doctrine of relationships he was able to affirm the distinction between the persons without affecting the unity of the essence. We must differentiate between what is said of the divine essence and what is said in particular about each person. What is proclaimed about the divine essence —which is common to all the persons— is what is proclaimed *ad se*. What is proclaimed *ad aliquid*—with respect to the other— can refer to an *ad extra* relationship, with respect to creatures, and then it is proclaimed about the whole Trinity (for instance, that God is creator), because the Trinity is the only one beginning of everything that has been created. Nevertheless, it can also refer to the *ad intra* relationships, and in that case it is said of one of the persons in his relationship with the others. The absolute affirmations made about each of the persons also refer to the others because this is what the simplex nature of the divine essence demands. Otherwise, we would be speaking of tritheism. Hence, the Father is light, just as the Son and the Holy Spirit are light. However, the three are not three lights, but only one light. The same thing applies to wisdom, and finally to the divine being himself. The three are God, although only one God[65].

Consequently, the plural is excluded from everything that is said about God *ad se*. This does not imply disregarding the differentiation between Father, Son, and Holy Spirit. As we already saw before in Tertullian, Augustine resorted to John 10:30 to show the unity and the differentiation in God: «Ego et pater unum sumus... unum secundum essentiam, sumus secundum relativum»[66]. The sin-

---

63 Cfr. *Trin.* v 15,16 (224).

64 Cfr. especially the first three books of *Trin.*, where there is a clear tendency when speaking of God as one (Father, Son, and Holy Spirit), to apply a series of passages of the New Testament which clearly refer to the Father. Nevertheless, in spite of this, it is clear that the Father is the beginning of all divinity: *Trin.* IV 20,29 (200): «...totius divinitatis vel si melius dicitur deitatis principium pater rest».

65 *Trin.* VII 3,6 (254): «Lumen ergo pater, lumen filius, lumen spiritus sanctus; simul autem non tria lumina, sed unum lumen. Et ideo sapientia pater, sapientia filius, sapientia spiritus sanctus; et simul non tres sapientiae, sed una sapientia; et quia hoc est ibi esse quod sapere, una essentia pater et filius et spiritus sanctus. Nec aliud est ibi esse quam deum esse. *Unus* ergo *deus pater et filius et spiritus sanctus*». Cfr. also VI 7,9 (237f): God is triune, but not triple. Echoes of these ideas are found in the symbol *Quicumque* (DS 75), and also in the Sixteenth Council of Toledo (DS 528).

66 *Trin.* 6,12 (266); cfr. other quotations of the text in v 3,4 (208) 9,10 (217); VI 2,3 (231).

gular in God refers to his unique divine essence. The plural is excluded on this level, because in view of the divine simplex nature it would lead to tritheism. It can only refer to the relationships, which do not affect the unity of the essence.

Severinus Boethius, following the Augustinian line of thought, posited a very curious although convincing affirmation: «the substance contains the unity; the relationship multiplies the Trinity»[67]. Boethius also stated that not all relationships presuppose a differentiation in level of action as is the case between servant and lord. The relationship in the Trinity is that of one peer with another peer and one fellow with another fellow, of one who is the same as the other[68].

3.2. THOMAS AQUINAS. THE REAL RELATIONSHIPS IN GOD

The doctrine of Augustine regarding the relationships was addressed and improved by Saint Thomas. It is based on the fact that everything that is in God is either absolute or relational[69]. The relationships in God are real. There is an actual fatherhood and sonship, because otherwise there would not really be a Father and a Son, and this would be exactly the same heresy as that of Sabellius. The processions in God take place within the identicality of God's nature. Because of this fact, the beginning and the one who proceeds are in reference and «inclined» one to the other[70]. Hence, there is a differentiation with respect to creatures that have a real relationship with God, although not the other way around, since God has made them because God has willed it[71]. Relationship and essence in God are the same, since there can be nothing in God as an accident within a subject. Therefore, relationships are distinguished from essence only insofar as in relationship we are dealing with the respective nature in relationship with the other one. This is not the case with the essence[72].

BOETHIUS, *Trin.* VI (PL 64,1254f): «Sed quoniam nulla relatio ad se ipsum referri potest, idcirco quod ea secundum seipsum est praedicatio quae relationem caret, facta quidem est trinitatis numerositas in eo quod est praedicatio relationis; servata vero unitas in eo quod est indifferentia vel substantiae, vel operationis, vel omnino eius quae secundum se dicitur praedicationis. Ita igitur substantia continet unitatem, relatio multiplicat trinitatem: atque ideo sola sigillatim proferuntur atque separatim quae relationis sunt…».

BOETHIUS, *Trin.* VI (PL 64,1255): «Sane sciendum est, non semper talem esse relativam praedicationem, ut semper ad differens praedicetur: ut et servus ad dominum, differunt enim. Nam omne aequale aequali aequale est, et simile simili simile est, et idem ei quod est idem idem est; et similis est in Trinitate relatio, Patris ad Filium et utriusque ad Spiritum sanctum; ut eius quod est idem ad id quod est idem».

Cfr. THOMAS AQUINAS, *In I Sent.* d. 26, 1,1.

Cfr. THOMAS AQUINAS, *STh* I 28,1.

Cfr. *STh* I 28,2: «in Deo non est realis relatio ad creaturas».

STh I 28,2: «Quidquid in rebus creatis habet esse accidentale, secundum quod transfertur in Deum habet esse substantiale: nihil enim est in Deo sicut accidens in subiecto, sed quidquid est in Deo

In turn, the relationships are distinguished among themselves, and this differentiation is real, although it does not take place according to God's essence in which there is the utmost unity and simplicity, but according to relationship[73]. It is precisely the differentiation between the persons that leads us to these precisions. Otherwise, this differentiation would be compromised. These real and distinct relationships in God are founded on his action which leads to the internal processions. As we already know, they are the procession according to the action of the intellect, which is the procession of the Word, and the procession according to the will, which is the procession of love, that of the Holy Spirit. In each of these processions, we find two opposite relationships. One is that of the one who proceeds from the beginning, and the other one is the beginning himself. We already know that the procession of the Word is known by the name «generation». The relationship in the beginning of living beings is called «paternity» or fatherhood. The relationship of the one who proceeds from the beginning is referred to as «filiation» or sonship. As we can see, these are two opposite relationships. The procession of love does not have a name of its own. Nevertheless, the relationship with the one who is the beginning is called «exhalation», and on the contrary, that of the one who proceeds from the very beginning is generically called «procession» and also «passive exhalation»[74]. In this way, according to Saint Thomas, we have four real relationships in God. Let us keep this information in mind for the following analysis of the concept of the «person» in God.

The theology of relationship in God shows us that he exists in the fullness of life and communion, and he is the one and unique God who is contrary to a monad closed in on itself. It is quite evident that when thinking about relationship in God our multiple human relationships necessarily come to mind. Nevertheless, even though this analogy could be helpful, we must not fall into a naive tritheism. In our daily experience, first we *are*, and then we begin with a relationship, even though we may acknowledge the importance of the latter. Regardless, our being is not identified with any intra-human relationship. Our relationship with God determines what we are, but we are always dealing with a contingent rela-

---

est eius essentia… Relatio realiter existens in Deo, est idem essentiae secundum rem. Et non differt nisi secundum intelligentiae rationem, prout in relatione importatur respectus ad suum oppositum, qui non importatur in nomine essentiae».

[73] Cfr. STh I 28,3.
[74] Cfr. STh I 28,4; also 29,4; 30,2. Also BONAVENTURE, *Breviloquium* 1 3,4.

tionship. God has created us because he has willed it. We could very easily not exist. In view of the extreme simplex nature of the divine essence, the relationships in God are identified with essence itself. God has no relationships. God is a diversity of real relationships that have a beginning and an end in himself. God is love, and his life is essentially one of communication. God exists only in the internal relationships and never outside of or beside them. They are not something «subsequent» to the divine being. They are eternal, just as the being of God is eternal. It is not that God existed first, and then his relationships followed. By virtue of this fullness of his internal life, God has been able to go beyond himself in the incarnation, as he also has been able to carry out the creation that receives from God its full meaning. Reality created as contingent, differentiated from God, has its foundation on the differentiation that the relationships mean within God himself[75].

The relationships do not contradict the divine unity, but rather the latter is shown precisely in the relationships and not outside their scope. In turn, the differentiation of the relationships makes sense only within the scope of the divine unity. In its Decree for the Jacobites, the Council of Florence formulated the well-known principle: «everything [in God] is one, and the differentiation of the relationship does not stand in the way» («omniaque unum sunt, ubi non obviate relationis opposition» DS 1330)[76]. It is not simply a matter of saying that the divine relationships «oppose» the unity, as the latter does not «oppose» the Trinity of persons. God would not be more «triune» without the unity of his essence, as he would not be more «one» if there were no relationships. In fact, the divine unity is also expressed in them. This divine unity is not undermined or hindered by the mutual relationships that make up the persons, as we will see in the following paragraphs.

---

75 Cfr. on the relation of the creation with the Trinity, LADARIA L.F., *Antropología teológica*, Casale Monferrato-Rome, 1995, 64ff.

76 SAINT ANSELM is usually quoted as a precursor of this formula. Cfr. *De proc. Spiritus sancti* 1 (Opera, SCHMITT F.S. (ed.), v. 2, 180-181: «Sic ergo huius unitatis et huius relationis consequentiae se contemperant, ut nec pluralitas quae sequitur relationem transeat ad ea, in quibus predictae simplicitas sonat unitatis, nec unitas cohibeat pluralitatem, ubi eadem relatio significatur. Quatenus nec unitas amittat aliquando suam consequentiam, ubi non obviat aliqua relationis oppositio, nec relation perdat quod suum est, nisi ubi obsistat unitas inseparabilis». Neither the unity nor the distinction can be affirmed at the expense of one another. The formulation of Anselm seems more complete than that of the Council of Florence. On the relationships in God, cfr. also DS 528; 570; 573.

4
The divine persons

The concept of relationship in God leads us directly to the analysis of the question of persons. As stated by W. Kasper, the relationships that are contrasted in God are simply the abstract expression of the *hypostasis* of the three divine persons[77]. As we have seen, both in the theology of Saint Augustine and that of Saint Thomas, as well as in the Council of Florence (cfr. DS 1330), the relationship is what distinguishes God, and the person is what is distinguished. Both concepts are hence closely related.

4.1. THE CONCEPT OF «PERSON» AS SEEN BY AUGUSTINE

308 In our brief history of Trinitarian dogma[78], we have seen how Tertullian introduced the term *persona* in the Latin theological vocabulary as opposed to substance. With the concept of person still not fully clear, reference was made to distinction in God. The terminology of the «three *hypostasis*» was introduced in Greek theology, especially Alexandrian theology. This led to difficulties and misunderstandings because it could have been interpreted in the sense of an excessive separation and not as a simple distinction between the «three». The Council of Nicaea did not yet make a clear distinction between *hypostasis* and *ousía*. In the *Tomus ad Antiochenos* (year 360), Athanasius eliminated the prejudices against the use of the expression «three *hypostasis*». This is not necessarily an Arian formula, just as the expression «one *ousía*» is not necessarily Sabellian. The Cappadocians had already based their Trinitarian theology on the differentiation between *ousía* and *hypostasis*. Instead of this last term they also used as its equivalent, the term *prósopon*, which is perhaps more related in its origins to the «person» of Latin scholars.

Augustine, in his *de Trinitate*, reflected on and analyzed in depth the term «persons». After having used this term in the first chapters of his work in a more or less imprecise and general way, at a specific point of his presentation, especially in book VII, he began his direct analysis toward this issue. Greeks spoke of

77 Cfr. KASPER W., *Der Gott Jesu Christi*, 342.

78 On the history of this term MILANO A., «La Trinità dei teologi e dei filosofi. L'intelligenza della persona in Dio» in PAVAN A.-MILANO A. (eds.), *Persona e personalismi*, Napoli 1987; by the same author, *Persona in teologia*, Napoli 1984.

one essence (*ousía*) and three *substantiae* (*hypostasis*), while Latins referred to one essence or substance and three persons[79]. In Latin, we must prefer the term *persona* because *substantia*, which is equivalent etymologically to *hypostasis*, could be mistaken for essence because of the traditional use of these words in the Latin language. Nevertheless, this does not mean that *persona* is an adequate term, and it does not imply that it met the expectations of Augustine. The word has been used because it has not been possible to find a better one: «dictum est tamen tres personae, non ut illud diceretur, sed ne taceretur»[80]. In effect, when we are faced with the three, Father, Son, and Holy Spirit, and we call them persons, we use the same expression which we employ when referring to three people, in spite of the differentiation that exists between humans and God. We are forced out of necessity to use this term which is less inadequate than others.

Augustine has already told us that Father, Son, and Gift (as we know, this is the name of the Holy Spirit) are relational names. However, when we say that Father, Son, and Holy Spirit are three persons, are we only speaking of the relationships that unite them, just as when we talk about three friends or three neighbors, and we say something about them? In other words, the three persons are in a relationship, but is this so because they are «persons» or because they are Father, Son, and Gift? Is «person» a relational term? In our speech, we say that one is the neighbor or the friend *of* another one. In the same way, when referring to the divine persons, we speak about the Father *of the* Son, the Son *of the* Father, or the Gift *of* the two of them. In this way, we are showing that we use relational terms. Nevertheless, when we mention the person of the Father we are not speaking about the Son but about the Father himself. The consequence is that the concept of person is not spoken of as it relates to another one, but rather *ad se*[81]. Augustine faced a difficulty that cannot be overcome. It has been mentioned before that the plurality in God came from the relationship and that there was no room for the plural in everything that it said *ad se*. We are not dealing with three

79 Cfr. AUGUSTINE, *Trin.* VII 4,7 (CCL 50,255); also V 8,10 (217). Augustine already assumed that there is equivalence between the Greek terms which he did not quote in the original, but in the translation into Latin, (*essentia, substantia*) and the Latin terms, «una essentia vel substantia, tres personae».
80 AUGUSTINE, *Trin.* V 9,10 (217); cfr. also VII 4,7 (255); cfr. LADARIA L.F., «Persona y relación en el De Trinitate de san Agustín» in *Miscelánea Comillas* 30 (1972) 245-291, especially 268ff.
81 Cfr. AUGUSTINE, *Trin.* VII 6,11 (261-265), a key text for understanding the Augustinian concept of the person; cfr. LADARIA L.F., *Persona y relación…*, 271ff. It seems that Augustine still thinks about one «being» of the Father that is in a way previous to his being «Father», and the same thing applies to the other persons. He tends to base the relationship on an absolute, a being which is in a certain way «previous» to it.

gods, or three wise men, or three lights; instead, we are facing a plural that is mentioned *ad se:* three persons. The three are in a relationship as Father, Son, and Gift[82], but not as «persons». Augustine clearly realized that the plural in God came from the relationships, although the concept of person was for him an absolute one. He was not able to pursue this *aporía*, this difficulty[83]. Augustine did not try to define person directly; however, in this context, he pointed out the fact that person is something singular and individual, «aliquid singulare atque individuum»[84]. It is to be noted that he used the neuter in his approach to the concept.

4.2. FROM BOETHIUS TO THOMAS AQUINAS

Saint Thomas was capable of letting the *aporía* of Augustine remain along with the elements that the Doctor of Hippo himself gave it. Nevertheless, before studying his thinking process, we must dwell, although briefly, on some authors who have had an influence on subsequent thought.

We will begin by mentioning Boethius (+524), who was the one who posited a definition of person that has been and is still the necessary point of reference in Western theology: «persona est naturae rationalis individual substantia»[85], the person is the individual substance of the rational nature. The context in which Boethius addressed the issue of person is Christological, although he wanted his definition to be valid also from Trinitarian and anthropological points of view (including the angels as well). The first element of the definition is «substance», the substratum of being. However, this must be individualized, or in other words, it should not be exchanged for another one. Our rational nature defines this individuality even further: it is precisely in this nature that we humans experience the incommunicable. This element is necessary because by itself individuality is nothing more than a realization of nature and does not lead us yet to the domain of that which we normally understand as «personal»[86]. Consequently, only rational beings are «persons», and they have the individuality that renders them unrepeatable.

---

82 Cfr. AUGUSTINE, *Trin.* IX 1,1 (293). The three persons are related *ad invicem.*
83 Hence, he is forced to accept this «absolute» plural as well as the plurality of relationships; Cfr. *Trin.* VII 6,12 (262); VIII proem. 1 (268).
84 AUGUSTINE, *Trin.* VII 6,11 (263).
85 *Liber de persona et duabus naturis* 3 (PL 64,1343).
86 Cfr. KASPER W., *Der Gott Jesu Christi*, 342; MILANO A., *La Trinitá*, 51ff.

Richard of St. Victor modified the definition introduced by Boethius. According to him, person is the «naturae rationalis incomunicabilis existentia», the incommunicable existence of rational nature[87]. He ruled out «substance» and stressed the relational element. Richard arrived at this definition primarily by taking into account the divine persons. He pointed out the difficulty of applying to God the definition of person given by Boethius. If mention is made of *substantia* in the definition, we run the risk of thinking that the three persons in God are three substances or essences. Hence, we would fall into tritheism. Using the term *subsistentia*, which is too close to *substantia*, can entail a similar danger[88]. On the other hand, person means the *quis*, while substance is the *quid*[89]. There is clear differentiation between the two terms. Hence, what is proposed is the substitution of *substantia* with *existentia*, a word that points to the essence, *sistere*, that which is inherent in oneself and at the same time the precedence, the *ex* of the being of each one[90]. Only because of this are the divine persons distinguished, in view of the fact that they have the same quality and there is no unlikeness or inequality between them. In God there is unity according to the mode of being, *iuxta modum essendi*, although there is plurality in the mode of «existing», *iuxta modum existendi*[91]. The differentiation comes from the origin[92]. Precisely, the properties of persons are derived from the diverse modalities of «existing», as they relate to precedence or non-precedence. That which is inherent in oneself is the being of oneself; that which is common to the two is not their own being. The Father does not proceed from anyone, he «*ex*-sists» based on himself, while the other two persons proceed from him. The Son proceeds from the Father and has someone else who proceeds from him. The Holy Spirit proceeds from another one, and there is no one that proceeds from him[93]. The personal property is that characteristic which makes each one of us what one is, and for this reason there are as many persons in God as «incommunicable exis-

---

[87] RICHARD OF ST. VICTOR, *Trin.* IV 23 (SCh 63,282). A detailed presentation of the concept of person in the thinking of Richard can be seen in SCHNIERTSHAUER M., *Consummatio Caritatis*, 147-177.
[88] RICHARD OF ST. VICTOR, *Trin.* IV 3,4 (232-238); 21 (280). It is possible that BOETHIUS had already noticed these problems. In his *De Trinitate* (PL 64,1247-1256), he hardly used the term *persona*, and rather, talked extensively about relationship.
[89] RICHARD OF ST. VICTOR, *Trin.* IV 7 (242f). We saw how Augustine still spoke about the *aliquid* in relation to person (cfr. the text that is referenced in footnote 84).
[90] RICHARD OF ST. VICTOR, *Trin.* IV 12 (252f).
[91] RICHARD OF ST. VICTOR, *Trin.* IV 19 (272). Ibid. (270): «possunt essere plures existentiae, ubi non et nisi unitas substantiae».
[92] RICHARD OF ST. VICTOR, *Trin.* IV 15 (260).
[93] Cfr. RICHARD OF ST. VICTOR, *Trin.* V 13 (336).

tences»[94]; hence, the definition of divine person as «divinae naturae incomicabilis existential»[95]. Based on this definition of divine person, we arrive at the definition of person in general, which we have already discussed.

In the plurality of divine persons there is a «different harmony» and a «harmonious difference»[96]. In view of the fact that love is such a determining factor in the modality of explaining the processions, the divine persons, in addition to their modality of procession, are characterized by their modality of love, because in practice one and the other coincide. Each person is the same as his love, according to this text that we all know[97]. The difference lies in love and not in dignity or in power. In this way, the vision of Richard shows us how the person, in his identity and his incommunicability, is at the same time open in love. Even more so, love is what determines his unrepeatability. Undoubtedly, we are dealing with a very rich intuition: that which is unrepeatable in each one of the persons is the way in which the person reaches out because of love —in other words, the manner in which the person is related to the others. This is the «incommunicable» element, more than the substance. This is basically the most important thing for Richard as it relates to the divine persons, but we may think that with specific differences, we can also apply the principle to humans. The quality of love determines what we are. In another context, Augustine had already posed a similar argument[98]. In God there is only one love, although it is different in each one of the persons[99].

In receiving and giving love, the Son expresses the image of the Father who is the one who originally gives love. This is not the case with the Holy Spirit who, according to Richard, does not give love (*ad intra*). For this reason, the Son is Word, wisdom, because through him we have the revelation of the Father, source of wisdom, and because the Fatherly glory is manifested through him[100]. The glory of the Father appears in the Son, «as great as he is and in view if the fact that he willed it, he was able to have a Son like this one, equal in everything to him»[101].

---

94 RICHARD OF ST. VICTOR, *Trin.* IV 17-18 (264-268).

95 RICHARD OF ST. VICTOR, *Trin.* IV 22 (280f).

96 RICHARD OF ST. VICTOR, *Trin.* V 14 (338).

97 RICHARD OF ST. VICTOR, *Trin.* V 20 (352): «Erit ergo unicuique trium idem ipsum persona sua quam dilectio sua»; «qualibet persona… est idem quod amor suus».

98 Cfr. AUGUSTINE, *In I Ep. Joh.* 2,14 (PL 35,1997).

99 RICHARD OF ST. VICTOR, *Trin.* V 23 (360).

100 RICHARD OF ST. VICTOR, *Trin.* VI 12 (404-406); cfr. AUGUSTINE, *Trin.* VI 2,3 (230-231). The Son is word, image, all the names that are related in reference to the Father.

101 RICHARD OF ST. VICTOR, *Trin.* VI 13 (410).

The Holy Spirit is attributed this name, which inherently also pertains to the Father and to the Son, because he is the one who sanctifies; he is the love that is held in common with the two. The Holy Spirit is given to humanity when love of the deity is inspired in the human heart (cfr. Rom 5:5); «insofar as we give back to our creator the love we owe, we are shaped according to the property of the Holy Spirit»[102]. The persons are distinguished by the love that unites them. This clearly evidences that the unity and the differentiation in God do not oppose each other.

4.3. THOMAS AQUINAS: THE PERSON AS A CONTINUOUS RELATIONSHIP

We must take time to address Saint Thomas specifically, because his definition of divine person as a relationship is especially useful. He was able to solve the *aporía* of Augustine to which we have already referred. Thomas fundamentally accepted the Boethian definition of person that is applicable to all rational beings[103]. Nevertheless, he was well aware of the fact that the term does not apply to God in the way that it does to creatures, but it applies to God in a transcendent way. Even more so, in view of the fact that the name *persona* indicates the dignity which is denoted in «subsisting in the rational nature», it is especially the dignity of the one who belongs to God in view of the greater dignity of his nature[104]. Thomas analyzed the elements of the definition of Boethius in order to apply them to God. In the case of God, the rational nature simply means the intellectual nature, because in him reason does not imply a discourse. The principle of individuation in God cannot be comprised of matter. For this reason, «individual» in God is also incommunicable. The «*substantia*» refers to God insofar as it means existing by oneself[105].

---

102 RICHARD OF ST. VICTOR, *Trin.* VI 14 (412f; cfr. VI 10).

103 Cfr. THOMAS AQUINAS, *STh* I 29,1.

104 Cfr. THOMAS AQUINAS, *STh* I 29,3. From substance in Boethius, we move to *subsistere*. In *Pot.* 9,4, the person is defined in general as «substantia individua rationalis naturae… idest incommunicabilis et ab aliis distincta». Consequently, person in God is described as «subsistens distinctum in natura divina», and also «distinctum relatione subsistens in essentia divina». Cfr. FRANCO F., «La comunione delle persone nella riflessione trinitaria della "Summa Theologia"» in *Ricerche Teologiche* 8 (1997) 271-301, in addition to the bibliography mentioned in footnote 1.

105 Cfr. THOMAS AQUINAS, *STh* I 29,3 ad 4. Thomas, unlike Richard, will attach more significance to relationship than to origin in definition of the divine person.

However, the decisive step for the Trinitarian theology of Thomas has to do with whether the name person means relationship[106]. Thomas was well aware of the difficulty he faced: the term under analysis is spoken of in the plural of three, and one does not say *ad aliquid* (as Augustine already mentioned), which seems contradictory. Because of this, some have thought that the name person means the divine essence. Nevertheless, this cannot be so, because in this case, speaking of three persons would give rise to the slander of the heretics, and this term has been used precisely to avoid it.

In order to present his solution, Thomas focused on what is peculiar to the divine persons. Beginning with the definition of Boethius, he asked himself: what is the individual? It is what is distinct in itself, distinct from others. In any nature, the person is what is differentiated, distinct «in its nature». In this way, in the case of humans, flesh, bones, and soul pertain to the definition of the *human* person, although they do not belong to the definition of the person in general because they are qualities that individualize human beings. Nevertheless, in God the distinction is made because of the relationships. We must turn to them in order to discover the concept of the *divine* person:

> Differentiation in God is only made according to relationships of origin... Nevertheless, relationship in God is not like an accident inherent within a subject, but it is the divine essence itself. Hence, we can say that he is subsistent in that the divine essence subsists. Therefore, in that God is the deity, in the very same way the divine paternity is God the Father, who is a divine person. Thus, the divine person means the relationship insofar as it continues[107].

The concept of person is not equivocal, but it is not univocal either. The subsistent and continuous relationship defines the divine person, although not the human or angelic relationship, because the relationship does not determine the individuality in this nature, as we see in the case of God. In God, the individual substance —in other words, the one which is distinct and which cannot be communicated (uninterchangeable, irreplaceable)— is the relationship. Hence, when

---

106 Cfr. THOMAS AQUINAS, *STh* I 29,4, «Utrum hoc nomen persona significet relationem». We will refer to this article in the lines that follow.

107 THOMAS AQUINAS, *STh* I 29,4, corpus; cfr. also ibid. 34,2; 40,2; 42,4: «Eadem essential quae in Patre est paternitas, in Filio est filiatio». On the concept of person and the Trinitarian theology of Thomas, cfr. GRESHAKE G., *Der dreieine Gott. Eine trinitarische Theologie*, Freiburg-Basel-Wien 1997, 111-126.

dealing within the divine scope, far more so than within the human scope, the concept of person gives meaning to oneself and opens oneself to others. Thus, the divine persons are differentiated because they are in relationship. Therefore, the differentiation is not derived from separation but from relationship, and their unrepeatable being is not characterized by being closed toward others or isolated, but rather by each giving himself to others. The divine persons, Father, Son, and Holy Spirit, are persons insofar as they are in relationship. Divine unity is not the unity of a solitary existence, but rather it is the unity of perfect communion. In Father, Son, and Holy Spirit there is no «previous» substratum to this gift of being. The divine persons are not «before» beginning the relationship because they exist insofar as they are in relationship.

In our analysis of this topic, we have followed the traditional order, which is that of Saint Thomas, from processions to relationships and from relationships to persons. This would be the order of our knowledge based on the divine missions. Nevertheless, this does not mean that it is the order of «being». What comes first, person or relationship? The person comes first, naturally, not in chronological, but in logical order. It would seem that relationships are established because there are persons, and hence persons would be first. Precisely because Father, Son, and Holy Spirit are persons, they have a relationship, and not the other way around. What is concrete should proceed from what is abstract[108]. The use of the category of relationship has helped maintain the distinction of persons, affirming at the same time the unity of their essence. However, the starting point of Saint Thomas in his Trinitarian doctrine is the person of the Father and not the divine essence[109].

Affirming three persons in God does not mean multiplying the divine essence. The only thing that is clearly differentiated in God is what is contrasted *ad invicem*. In actuality, it is impossible to differentiate, for instance, wisdom and goodness[110]. Only as a result of the relationships can we speak of this differentiation in God. This leads to the issue of the «three» persons. In view of the fact that the relationships are four in number, Thomas asked himself why there are

---

108 Cfr. KASPER W., *Der Gott Jesu Christi*, 343; MALET A., *Personne et amour dans la théologie trinitaire de saint Thomas d'Aquin*, Paris 1956, 84 : « ... Saint Thomas concède que, si on considère la relation comme relation elle suit l'hypostase » ; cfr. ibid. 92, with a quotation from *In I Sent.* d. 23, a.3.

109 Cfr. MALET A., *Personne et amour dans la théologie trinitaire de saint Thomas d'Aquin*, 87; GRESHAKE G., *Der dreieine Gott*, 110f. Cfr. among other places *STh* I 33,1; 39,8, the Father is the «beginning that does not come from the beginning».

110 Cfr. THOMAS AQUINAS, *STh* I 30,1.

only three persons. As we said before, the relationships constitute the persons, insofar as they are actually differentiated. This actual differentiation, which appears between their relationships, is due to their relational opposition. Fatherhood and Sonship offer no difficulty whatsoever. They are opposing relationships, and hence they belong to two persons. The active exhalation pertains to both the Father and the Son, but it does not have any relational opposition to Fatherhood nor to Sonship. It is separated from the person of the Father and of the Son, and it is appropriate to both. The procession (passive exhalation) is appropriate to the other person, the Holy Spirit, who proceeds through the path of loving. The persons are only three because the active exhalation is not a property, since it does not apply to only one person. Hence, there are four relationships, although only three persons. Only three of these four relationships are «continuous»: the Fatherhood which is the person of the Father, the Sonship which is the person of the Son, and the procession which is the person of the Holy Spirit[111].

The plurality of persons is the reason why Thomas believed that God is not solitary. The Fathers had already insisted on this issue[112]. Even though the angels and the saints were with him, God would be alone if there were no plurality of persons, because solitude is not eliminated by association with someone with an alien or different nature[113]. It is also said that one person is alone in one garden even though there are animals and plants (cfr. Gen 2:18 and following). The doctrine of persons and relationships presented by Saint Thomas is by no means an abstract speculation concerned only with logical coherence. Rather, it shows the fullness of life in God, which is incompatible with solitude. Even though Thomas does not state this, the impression is given that solitude in God would mean an imperfection. In the fullness of the Trinitarian life the three persons «accompany» each other. The idea of interpersonal communion in God seems to be present here, although certainly in a veiled manner.

The persons are not differentiated from the divine essence *secundum rem*. It is always the concept of divine simplicity that is opposed to such a differentiation. The relationships in God are not accidents, and as a result, they must be identi-

---

111 Cfr. THOMAS AQUINAS, *STh* I 30,2.

112 Cfr. HILARY OF POITIERS, *Trin.* IX 36 (CCL 62A,410): «Deus… neque in solitudine neque in diversitate consistit».

113 THOMAS AQUINAS, *STh* I 31,3: «Licet angeli et animae sanctae simper sint cum Deo, tamen, si non esset pluralitas personarum in divinis, sequeretur quod Deus esset solus vel solitarius. Non enim tollitur solitudo per associationem alicuius quod est extraneae naturae… Consociatio angelorum et animarum non excludit solitudo absolutam a divinis».

fied with the essence, even though the persons are differentiated one from the other in a real way. Relationship, as compared with divine essence, does not differ as to entity or substance. Rather, there is only one distinction— that of reasoning. Nevertheless, insofar as the relationship is contrasted with its opposite relationship, there is an actual differentiation because of their mutual opposition. Therefore, we can (and must) affirm some things about each one of the persons which are not the case with the other persons[114]. Otherwise, the differentiation between the persons would not be true, and we would succumb to Sabellianism. Using this same reasoning, the traditional Trinitarian formula of an essence of three persons, or three persons of the same essence, makes sense because in God the essence is not multiplied, although the persons are multiplied[115].

On the other hand the persons are identified by their relationship[116], and by virtue of their relationship we distinguish each of them from the others. In this respect, we can state with greater clarity that the persons are differentiated because of their relationship more than because of their origin. Indeed, from the active point of view, origin means that someone proceeds from a subsistent person, in other words, in a sense it assumes that the person is already in existence. In the same way, from the passive point of view, it means that it is the path that leads to the subsistent person, although the person is not yet in existence. Following this principle, instead of alluding to *generans* and *genitus*—the one who begets and the one who is begotten— we choose the terms Father and Son because these names point to the relationship. Furthermore, only the relationship, not the origin, makes and differentiates the person[117]. On the other hand, we must bear in mind that their relationship not only distinguishes the persons but also unites them. The «opposition» that we see between them has to be understood as reciprocity[118].

---

114 Cfr. Thomas Aquinas, *STh* I 39,1.

115 Thomas Aquinas, *STh* I 39,2: «Quia in divinis, multiplicatis personis, non multiplicatur essentia, dicimus una essentia esse trium personarum, et tres personae unius essentiae». This formula must be preferred to «tres personae ex eadem essentia» because with the *ex*, which means origin, we might suppose that one thing is the *persona*, and another, the essence from which it proceeds.

116 Cfr. Thomas Aquinas, *STh* I 30,2; 40,1, in addition to the texts that have already been mentioned.

117 Thomas Aquinas, *STh* I 40,2 ad. 2: «Personae divinae non distinguuntur in esse in quo subsistunt, neque in aliquo absoluto; sed solum secundum id quo ad aliquid dicuntur. Unde ad earum distinctionem sufficit relatio». Cfr. the rest of the article; also I 33,2. Bonaventure has followed a somewhat different line, which further expresses the procession; cfr. for instance, *In Sent.* I d. 27, q.2; *Breviloquium* I 4,6.

118 Cfr. Bourassa F., *La Trinità*, in Neufeld K.H. (ed.), *Problemi e orientamenti di teologia dogmatica*, Brescia 1983, 337-372, 351.

The persons, made by the opposing relationships, are distinguished also by their
«properties» or «notions»[119]. The notion is the means for knowing the divine
person. We cannot grasp the meaning of divine simplicity. We must name God
by means of what we apprehend, in other words, by means of what we discover
in the things we sense from which we receive knowledge. In the case of simple
forms, in order to speak about them, we use abstract names, and we use concrete names to speak about continuous things. Because of the simplex nature of
God, we also refer to him using abstract names. We must use them in order to
differentiate between the persons. Therefore, these are abstract properties and
notions, as would be the case of Fatherhood and Sonship[120].

The concrete properties of the persons are deduced from the relationships
of origin by virtue of which they are multiplied. The Father cannot be revealed to
us as coming from another one, but instead as having others who come from him.
Because of this, the nature of innascibility (not coming into existence) and fatherhood belong to him. The Son comes from the Father; the property or notion
that characterizes him is sonship. The Father and the Son have in common the
active exhalation or breathing, and the procession belongs to the Holy Spirit. In
this way, we have five «notions» or «properties», and one of them is common to
two persons: the breathing or exhalation, which is common to the Father and
the Son. As their name implies, these notions or properties are inherent in their
persons. The notional acts that correspond to these notions or properties must
be attributed to the differentiated persons[121]. All these properties refer to the
intra-Trinitarian life.

Together with notions or properties, we must take into account the concept
of appropriations, that is, the manifestation of persons. We already touched on
this concept when we began our analysis and referred to the question of the economic Trinity and the immanent Trinity. We use the term appropriations when
the essential properties, which on their own pertain to the whole Trinity, are applied to a specific person because of the way in which this person is manifested.

---

119 Cfr. THOMAS AQUINAS, STh I 32,2-3
120 THOMAS AQUINAS, STh I 32,2: «…et huiusmodi sunt proprietates vel notiones in abstracto
significatae, ut paternitas et filiatio. Essentia significatur in divinis ut quid, persona vero ut quis,
proprietas autem ut quo».
121 Cfr. THOMAS AQUINAS, STh I 41,1; cfr. also I 41,3. BONAVENTURE, *Breviloquium* I 3,1: «For the healthy
understanding of this faith (of the Trinity) the holy doctrine shows that in God there are two
emanations (processions), three hypostases, four relationships, five conceptions and… only
three personal properties»; cfr. also ibid. 3,2ff.

In the same way, in the essential divine attributes, which correspond to the Trinity as a whole, we find a manifestation in the persons. According to Thomas Aquinas, these manifestations are «appropriations»[122]. Similarly, Bonaventure pointed out the fact that appropriations lead to the knowledge of the persons, although this does not mean that the attributes to which they are given possession are uniquely their own[123].

Perhaps one of the clearest examples of appropriations is found in the beginning of the Creed, when we call the Father «almighty» and «creator of heaven and earth». Undoubtedly, these names also pertain to the other persons. The three are almighty, and despite this fact, in God there is only one omnipotence. The three persons also participate in only one beginning of creation (cfr. DS 800; 851, and the like), but there is no doubt whatsoever that for the Father, as the beginning within the Trinity, it is especially appropriate to say that he is also the beginning of creation, although he is never the creator at any point in time without the other two persons. Among other examples, Saint Thomas pointed to appropriations of power and strength to Father; of wisdom to the Son; and of goodness to the Holy Spirit. It is not a question of saying that each of the persons has these properties exclusively. Nevertheless, there is also no doubt that they are especially appropriate for the person to which they are attributed: in the case of the Father, power for the reason that has been already mentioned; in the case of the Son, wisdom (cfr. 1Cor 1:24,30), insofar as he is the Logos or reason of the universe; and in the case of the Holy Spirit, goodness, insofar as goodness is related to love[124]. We have already seen that the Fathers referred to the Spirit as the perfecting cause of all things. We can assume that by perfecting all things the Spirit grants them his goodness.

Undoubtedly the use of appropriations is based on the Bible, and it is founded on tradition. It also is found frequently in both the liturgy and theology. Nevertheless, it is worth posing the question of whether the scope of appropriations is as broad as we have assumed at certain times in the history of theology, or rather,

122 Cfr. THOMAS AQUINAS, STh 39,7. Saint Thomas emphasizes that through creatures we can reach the knowledge of the essential properties of God, though not of the persons. Nevertheless, as we here turn to the traces that God has left in creatures for the manifestation of the persons, we also turn to the essential attributes for this purpose. Hence, the appropriations assume faith in the Trinity and knowledge of what is inherent in the divine persons.

123 Cfr. BONAVENTURE, Breviloquium 1 6,1.

124 Cfr. THOMAS AQUINAS, STh 1 39,8. Cfr. the other examples that are quoted in the same article. They coincide partly with those that are pointed out by BONAVENTURE, Breviloquium 1 6,1ff; cfr. these examples in LOMBARD P., Lib. Sent. 1 d. 32; 34,3-4.

whether we must leave more room for what is specific and inherent in each of the persons with respect to divine *ad extra* behavior in the creation and in salvation. The principle according to which all divine actions toward the world are held in common in the whole Trinity should not cause us to forget that this principle, which is indeed only one principle, is in turn, a principle which bears the distinction within itself. In view of the fact that the saving act must reflect in some way the being of God himself, the relationships that are inherent in each Christian in regard to each of the divine persons perfectly fit this concept. This can also apply to creation, which is indeed an act of the three persons. Nevertheless, in the New Testament we already find the differentiation between the action of the Father who is the ultimate origin of all things and that of the Son who is the mediator (cfr. primarily 1Cor 8:6; also John 1:3,10; Col 1:15-16; Heb 1:2). Quite early, as we have seen in our historical analysis, mention was also made of the Holy Spirit *in* whom everything exists. In this way, we already see reflected in the creating act an orientation toward salvation in Christ, the unity and the distinction of the Trinity which wills to include humanity in its divine life. As a result of this, we can assume that these diverse ways of acting by the persons are a reflection of the intra-divine distinction and that the inherent intervention of each of the persons in the history of salvation has already been pre-shaped in it in one form or another and that this salvation will reach its maximum expression in the mission from the Father by the Son and the Spirit[125]. Naturally, with these considerations we do not challenge the legitimacy or even the necessity of the concept of appropriation, but only some of its applications. The unity of the Trinity in the creating and sanctifying act does not necessitate keeping the distinction of the persons in the Trinity from also being reflected in their outward actions. Rather, we could imagine that if creation, and consequently the divine acting *ad extra*, is only possible because God is triune, this dimension must be reflected in all his acts, although this does not mean that in all of them we can see a revelation of the Trinity[126].

---

[125] In the work quoted in the previous note, Saint Thomas considered that the diverse use of the prepositions *ex*, *per* and *in* is only adequate for each of the persons. Let us note that in the Second Council of Lyon, the three prepositions referred to above are used indistinctly to refer to the whole Trinity (DS 851). However, we have also seen that this has not been the use given in previous stages of the tradition.

[126] In this context, we must take due note of the new approach to the concept of appropriations presented by GRESHAKE G., *Der dreieine Gott*, 214-216, where rather than the classical concept that is based on attribution to one person of what is common to the three, the opposite alternative is proposed: beginning with the perichoretic (successive) unity between the persons, each one of

A final highly important theological concept that has acquired far more value of late is that of the *perichoresis* or *circumincessio*. These expressions state that the divine persons are not only in relationship with the others, but they are in the others. They imply that between them there is not only an *esse ad* but also an *esse in*. The basis for this doctrine is found in the New Testament and specifically in some words of Jesus according to the gospel of John: «I am in the Father and the Father is in me» (John 14:10-11); «so that you will know for certain that the Father is in me and I am in the Father» (John 10:38; cfr. 17:21). These expressions gave rise to the idea of mutual «inhabitation» of the Father and of the Son that was enriched later on with the explicit mention of the Holy Spirit.

The mutual inhabitation of the Father and the Son is the expression of the unity of «power and spirit», according to the Apologetic Father Athenagoras[127]. Dionysius of Rome saw in the mutual inhabitation of the three divine persons the guarantee of the Trinity which is gathered within the monarchy of the Father (cfr. DS 112). The thought of Hilary of Poitiers (quoted in this context by Thomas[128] and very frequently indeed by modern theologians) was based on mutual inhabitation when he attempted to show the unity of the nature of the Father and the Son and the perfect generation of the Son begotten from the Father:

> What is in the Father is in the Son; what is in the unbegotten is in the only begotten…. This does not mean that the two are the same, but that one is in the other, and there is nothing in one without respect to the other. The Father is in the Son because the Son has been born from him, and the Son is in the Father because he receives his being as

them having properties in common with the rest, and because of this, what is inherent in each person becomes inherent in the divine communion or the divine essence: in this way God is almighty because the Father exists, and everything is based in the gift of the Father. God is truth and redeeming love because the Son exists, and so on. I believe that this alternative could be seen as a complement more than as a traditional alternative to the unity, and the distinction of God must be seen as equally primary and original. The Father actually gives the Son everything that he is (and both give it to the Holy Spirit), except Fatherhood (and Sonship), and in this respect, the discourse or reasoning of the properties that are common to the three persons, although possessed by each of them according to the personal specificity of each of them, makes sense in this respect. It is clear that if, as we will see further ahead, the concept of relationships of origin and of «processions» in God is challenged, the question of the divine unity is then posed differently. Cfr. the next chapter.

127 Cfr. ATHENAGORAS, *Leg. pro Chris.* 10 (BAC 116,660); the context is that of the generation of the Word.

128 Cfr. THOMAS AQUINAS, *STh* I 42,5.

Son from no one else.…. In this way, they are one in the other, because as everything is perfect in the unbegotten Father, it is also so in the only-begotten Son[129].

He who is in God is God, because God does not dwell in a nature which is different and alien from him[130].

John of Damascus was the first one to use in this Trinitarian sense the word *perichoresis*, which will become the technical term for expressing this reality about which theology had reflected from ancient times[131]. In Latin, mention will be made of *circumincessio*, which sometimes turns into *circumsessio*. Considerable use is made of these terms later in history, and they are derived from a twelfth century Latin translation of John of Damascus. These terms are not found in Saint Thomas, who undoubtedly addressed the issue of the unity of the essence, and the fact that each person is identified with the essence is what enables the Father to be in the Son and vice versa. Thomas added that the procession of the intelligible Word is not *ad extra*, but it remains in the one who expresses it. The same thing can be said of the Holy Spirit[132].

The Council of Florence viewed *perichoresis* as the consequence of the unity of the divine essence: «As a result of this unity, the Father is fully and wholly in the Son, fully and wholly in the Holy Spirit; the Son is fully and wholly in the Father, fully and wholly in the Holy Spirit; the Holy Spirit is fully and wholly in the Father, fully and wholly in the Son (DS 1331)»[133]. Both in the Christological use and in the Trinitarian use, circumincession is helpful for expressing unity in diversity. With the unity that comes from the common essence and from mutual love, each one of the persons is in a profound union and communion with the

---

129 HILLARY OF POITIERS, *Trin.* III 4 (CCL 62,75).

130 HILLARY OF POITIERS, *Trin.* IV 40 (145); cfr. also V 37-38 (192-193); VII 31.33 (298.300); Basil of Caesarea, *de Sp. sancto*, 18,45 (SCh 17bis, 406); AUGUSTINE, *Trin.* IX 5,8 (300), on the mutual inhabitation of the mind, the word, and love.

131 JOHN OF DAMASCUS, *De fide orthod* I 8.14 (PG 94, 829.860), etc. Cfr. DEL CURA S. «Perikhóresis» in *Diccionario teológico. El Dios Cristiano*, 1086.1094. The expression began to be used in Christology in order to refer to the unity of Christ in the two natures: cfr. GREGORY OF NAZIANZUS, *Ep.* 101 (PG 37,181), although it is used in its verbal form. The theologian from Damascus also uses the term in this sense; Cfr. III 4.7 (1000.1012).

132 Cfr. THOMAS AQUINAS, STh I 42,5; also ibid. 39,2, in which Thomas saw the formula explicitly set forth in the Scripture «tres personae unius essentiae», in the text of John 10:30, «the Father and I are one», and also John 10:38 (cfr. John 14:10), «the Father is in me and I am in the Father». It seems that the *perichoresis* is, hence, equivalent to the unity of essence and not simply a consequence of it, as would be the case in other passages.

133 This is a quotation of FULGENTIUS OF RUSPE, although it was believed at that time that it came from Augustine, *De fide… ad Petrum, liber unus*, I 4 (PL 65,674).

other two. Hence, this evidences a basic dimension of the divine unity, which is the unity of the Trinity. The inhabitation of each person in the others certainly respects the *taxis*, the order of the processions. Nevertheless, at the same time, it shows a radical similarity among them, the perfect communion in which the term distinction is more acceptable than the term differentiation[134]. Circumincession is not something that blends with unity and distinction, which have already been predetermined. It is not just a static «being in» the other that is the simple consequence of unity in the divine essence. This has been a frequent interpretation that can certainly find its foundation in the Council of Florence; however, without excluding this dimension, we can also consider that mutual inhabitation is at the same time an essential element of this unity, which is also found in the dynamic interaction of the three persons. This is the direction pointed to in the meaning of the Greek term *perichoresis*[135]. Unity and distinction in God are such that they imply being one *in* the other, and not only *with* or together with the other. Together with the relationship (*esse ad*) which is distinguished in the divine unity, *perichoresis* (*esse in*) unites by maintaining the distinction. Reciprocal inhabitation expresses and actualizes to a maximum degree the unity of the persons in their distinction. At the same time, this union reveals to us the communion with God to which all human beings are called. In fact, according to John 17:21-22, those who believe in Jesus must become only one entity *in* the Father and the Son[136]. Intra-Trinitarian *perichoresis* is also shown, as is the whole mystery of the one and triune God, in the economy. The actions of the Son and of the Spirit in fulfilling the plan of the Father are carried out in an in-depth unity, from the incarnation of Christ by the act of the Holy Spirit, to the resurrection by the act of the Father, where the intervention of the Holy Spirit is also present (cfr. Rom 1:4; 8:11). In this chapter about the unity of God, *unitas in trinitate*, we will analyze once again some aspects that are related to this issue.

---

134 Cfr. Von Balthasar H.U., *Theologik* II, *Wahrheit Gottes*, Einsiedeln 1985, 137.

135 Hence, for instance, in John of Damascus; cfr. Huculak B., «Costituzione delle persone divine secondo S. Giovanni Damasceno» in *Antonianum* 59 (1994) 179-212.

136 This has been emphasized by Kasper W., *Der Gott Jesus Christi*, 346f. We will analyze this issue in the chapter that addresses the divine unity.

5

The modern set of problems concerning the person in God: the «three persons» in the divine unity

In God, there are three persons in unity of essence. This dogmatic formulation has given rise to theological reflection on «person», a term which has moved from the Trinitarian and Christological field to the anthropological one. Two aspects have shown themselves to be especially fruitful in this reflection. First, it has been emphasized that person is the individual; unlike nature, it is the *quis,* not the *quid,* with its unrepeatable and non-interchangeable nature. A second aspect is that of relationship which was clearly understood by Augustine and developed by Thomas Aquinas. We have mentioned before that this dimension for Thomas specifically addresses the «divine» person and not the angelic or human person. Nevertheless, it should not surprise us that, always using the same term as an analogy, we have moved from *theo*logy to anthropology, and with the passage of time these elements have also found a place in theological and philosophical reflection concerning the human person[137]. In its typical fluctuations, theology has been in turn influenced by philosophical approximations on this issue. In the past few decades, theological discussion on the concept of the divine person has reflected this complex evolution, the details of which we cannot continue to address at this point, except when they have an effect on the basic objective of our study.

5.1. UNITY OF CHARACTER OR INDIVIDUAL IN GOD? ALTERNATIVE PROPOSALS FOR THE TERM «PERSON». KARL BARTH AND KARL RAHNER

Ever since the early days of the Modern Age, around the end of the Fifteenth Century, the philosophical concept of person has been evolving, and now it refers to a being who possesses himself in self-awareness and freedom[138]. K. Barth († 1968)

---

137 Cfr. Bueno de la Fuente E., *La «persona» en perspectiva teológica,* in González de Cardedal O. - Fernández Sangrador J.J. (eds.). *Coram Deo, memorial Juan Luis Ruiz de la Peña,* Salamanca 1997, 329-344.

138 Cfr. regarding this evolution, Rovira Belloso J.M., *Tratado de Dios uno y trino,* Salamanca 1993, 615-635; Greshake G., *Der dreieine Gott,* 127-168; Milano A., *Persona in teologia,* Napoli 1984; ibid., *La Trinità dei teologi e dei filosofi. L'intelligenza della persona in Dio,* in Pavan A.-Milano A. (eds.), *Persona e personalismi,* Napoli 1987, 1-286.

The Living and True God

324

was the first to realize the difficulties that can emerge in the field of theology if this concept of person is accepted with all its consequences and applied to the three divine persons. This would mean that in God there are three centers of consciousness, three wills, three freedoms, three individuals who are capable of self-determination. Hence, we could arrive at statements that are quite close to tritheism. Therefore, this led to the change in terminology that Barth proposed: the term *persona* should be substituted with «disposition» (*Seinsweise*), as this term would not run the risk of an inadequate interpretation, which is the case in the traditional term. This terminological proposal is framed within a very clear theological context from which it receives its meaning.

Barth began with the event of revelation, in which God is manifested in an indissoluble unity as the God who is at the same time revealed, the event of the revelation, and the effect of the revelation on humanity. This same God, who is an indestructible unity, is revealer, revelation, and revealed being, and he is attributed at the same time with a diversity in himself precisely in these three ways of being or dispositions[139]. Therefore, according to revelation, God is «an indestructible unity in himself, but at the same time, in his indestructible unity, he is three times the same in a diverse manner»[140]. In the unity of their essence, the Father, the Son, and the Spirit are the only God, and in the diversity of their persons, they are precisely the Father, the Son, and the Holy Spirit. Only in the incarnation of the Son do we find the starting point for understanding that in God himself there is a differentiation, that it is inherent in God being «once again» God in humanity, in the form of which nature he is not himself[141]. The God who is revealed in the Scriptures is one of the three specific ways of being that exist in his mutual relationships —Father, Son, and Holy Spirit. The Lord is the «You» who reaches out to the human «I» and hence is revealed as his God[142]. God is God in a triple repetition (*dreimalige Wiederholung*), and only in this repetition is he the only God[143]. In God there are not three «personalities»; there are not three «I», but only one «I» that is repeated three times[144].

139 Cfr. BARTH K., *Die kirchliche Dogmatik* I/1, München 1935, 315.
140 BARTH K., *Die kirchliche Dogmatik* I/1, 324.
141 BARTH K., *Die kirchliche Dogmatik* I/1, 334.
142 BARTH K., *Die kirchliche Dogmatik* I/1, 367.
143 BARTH K., *Die kirchliche Dogmatik* I/1, 369.
144 BARTH K., *Die kirchliche Dogmatik* I/1, 370.

Barth strongly insisted on the «personality» of God. We can never turn his «He» into a neuter, an «it»[145]. At the same time, Barth stressed God's unity. He quoted the well-known text of the Eleventh Council of Toledo, which stated that the Trinity «quae unus et verus est Deus nec recedit a numero nec capitur numero» (cfr. DS 530). The Trinity, which is the only and true God, cannot be separated from the number nor is it understood through the number. Therefore, the plurality does not point to an increase in quantity. On the other hand, all the limitations that we attribute to the unity are overcome in God himself. God is neither solitude nor isolation. The unicity of the revealed God includes the distinction and the order of the three persons, or even better, of the three «ways of being» or «dispositions» (*Seinsweise*)[146]. The revelation leads us to deduce that God is not an impersonal power, but…

…an «I» who exists in himself and for himself with his own thought and will….And in this way, he is at the same time God as Father, Son, and Spirit…. The only God —in other words, the only Lord— is the only personal God, in the modality of Father, Son, and Holy Spirit[147].

There is no property and no action of God that is not that of the Father, of the Son, and of the Holy Spirit. Nevertheless, there are differentiations between them which we can never minimize in any manner whatsoever into a common denominator. The differentiations come from the different relationships of origin; however, the three «ways of being» or «dispositions» are equal in their essence and in their dignity, without any decrease in their divinity. The Trinitarian doctrine is the denial of any modalism and any subordinationism. The unity and the Trinity in God belong together. One does not come into being at the expense of the other. In the opinion of Barth, the term *Dreieinigkeit,* which would be equivalent to «triunity», summarizes the unity and Trinity in God.

As we have shown, Barth wanted to avoid any danger of tritheist statements. Because of his terminology of the «ways of being» or «dispositions», others have accused him of being «modalist». Nevertheless, we must bear in mind that he clearly affirmed the differentiation in God himself and not only in his way or

---

145 On different occasions, Barth talked about the personality of God without subsequent clarifications; cfr. BARTH K., *Die kirchliche Dogmatik* I/1, 125; 143; 214; 370.

146 BARTH K., *Die kirchliche Dogmatik* I/1, 374.

147 BARTH K., *Die kirchliche Dogmatik* I/1, 379.

modality of manifesting himself. Barth's concrete teachings about Father, Son, and Holy Spirit are clear in this respect. It will suffice to quote a phrase: «God is Father in the creation, because before that, he is Father in his essence as Father of the Son»[148]. However, once we have pointed this out, we could wonder if the use made by Barth of the concept of person in God is the most adequate one. Barth affirmed the divine personhood. Of this there is no doubt, but in tradition, the concept has served to show the distinction in God and not the unity, as it appears that Barth attempted to demonstrate. On the other hand —and this criticism has been also aimed at Rahner who will be analyzed in what follows— the one who self-possesses himself is only one aspect of the modern concept of person, because relationship is also included[149]. On the other hand, when Barth alluded to the concept of person, the modern evolution of this concept was also evidenced. His definitions of the personal God found their origin in this concept, even though he only addressed it partially and applied it to God in his unity and not in his Trinity. We must relate to this fact the emphasis on divine unity in which only one repeated «I» is the «You» who is God for human beings. Is there no other purpose for pronouns that can describe the relationships of humans with God? In the saving economy, the Father and the Son, who are undoubtedly and certainly in divine essence one same thing (cfr. John 10:30), appear more as an interchangeable «I» and a «you» than as a repeated «I». It is also true that we must maintain the distinction, although not adequately, between the immanent Trinity and the economic Trinity; however, it appears that, beginning with Christian revelation, it is difficult to see the relationship between Father, Son, and Spirit as the repetition of an «I».

In the Catholic sphere, Rahner supported the concerns of Barth. We cannot simply say that Rahner set forth a simple substitution of the term person. He was well aware that this term was determined by a multisecular use[150]. Nevertheless,

---

148 BARTH K., *Die kirchliche Dogmatik* I/1, 404; the text is found in the formulation of the thesis with which he begins to speak about God the Father.

149 Cfr. MOLTMANN J., *Trinität und Reich Gottes*, München 1980, 161ff; KASPER W., *Der Gott Jesu Christi*, 350ff. Cfr. also MILANO A., *La Trinità dei teologi*....., 199: «Ora però non si può evitare di chiedersi come un teologo così rigoroso e sottile come Barth traga tanta sicurezza nel negare ai Tre della Trinita d'essere degli "Io"…». The same MILANO, ibid., wonders if we are dealing with the idealistic concern of seeing only one person in God; cfr the entire context, 183ff.

150 RAHNER K., «El Dios trino como fundamento…» in *MySal* 2/1, 387: «The term "person" is a fact. It has been approved by its use during more than one thousand five hundred years. There is still no term that is really better, which can be understood by all, and which can be subject to fewer false interpretations. Hence, it is worth keeping this term, even while knowing that … it does not fit in all aspects the expression of what we are attempting to affirm»; cfr. ibid. 341; also *Trinidad*, in

he was also aware of the difficulties that are derived from the fact that in the normal way of understanding the concept, and in view of the historical evolution of the words which the Church cannot control, the expression «three persons» may be equivalent to three different centers of consciousness and activity, which would lead to a heretical understanding of the dogma. We must attempt to avoid the understanding that the three persons in God are considered as three subjectivities, which would lead to tritheism.

Beginning with this concern of avoiding falling into tritheism, and at the same time respecting the peculiar characteristics of each of the «persons», Rahner developed his outline of the theology of the Trinity.

Consistent with his basic axiom, Rahner began with the idea that when God wills to communicate with humans, it is the Son who must appear historically in the flesh as a man, and it must be the Spirit who turns the acceptance of the whole communication into faith, hope, and love that is offered by the world. All of this assumes the freedom of God. Nevertheless, if God wants to freely communicate with himself, he is no longer «free» to do it in any other way, because then this self-communication would not be telling us anything about Father, Son, and Holy Spirit[151].

In view of the fact that the communication of God to humanity must take into account the structure of human beings, four double aspects can be emphasized (which are later reduced to two basic modalities) that must be present in this divine self-giving: a) origin-future, b) history-transcendence, c) offer-acceptance, d) knowledge-love (considered in their unity because knowledge is not consumed in itself but extends toward the love of what is known)[152]. We can easily see that origin, history, and offer are united in opposition to their contrary elements. This is the original divine initiative, the offer of self-communication which is the fundamental plan on which the world has been delineated. Nevertheless, we can ask ourselves why we should also include knowledge (or truth) in these four double aspects. It is because we are addressing the manifestation of the truth of God, of his essence; and this manifestation has an offer, an origin, and a history, which calls for acceptance in love.

Sacramentum Mundi VI, 758. Cfr. HILBERATH B.J., *Der Personbegriff in der Trinitätstheologie in Rückfrage von Karl Rahner zu Tertullians «Adversus Praxean»*, Innsbruck 1986. AA. VV., *La teología trinitaria de Karl Rahner*, Salamanca 1988.

151 RAHNER K., «El Dios trino como fundamento…» in *MySal* 2/1, 419ff.

152 RAHNER K., «El Dios trino como fundamento…» in *MySal* 2/1, 421ff, also for the following text.

The opposite aspects are also interrelated. Future and transcendence are united with relative ease. In any case, we must bear in mind that the future is not simply what has not yet arrived, but it is the modality of the communication of God who gives himself to humanity as the consummation of the human being himself. Hence, as it relates to the future, we must speak about the possibility of accepting an absolute future. The offer of God entails acceptance of this offer and includes its acceptance because this is the work of God himself. Self-communication that claims to be absolute and initiates the possibility of being accepted —and accepting it— is what we call love.

In this way, these two modalities, truth and love, are the two modalities of divine self-communication. This communication, insofar as it is truth, means that it has a place in history. In turn, this communication, insofar as it is love, means the opening of this history toward transcendence, toward the absolute future. The two dimensions are intrinsically united and are mutually conditioned, but they are not identical. «The divine self-communication does not take place in unity and in differentiation with history (of truth), and in the spirit (of love)»[153].

Hence, Rahner intended to proceed to the immanent Trinity, once it has been determined that «economically» this is the way in which God has communicated himself. This self-communication could not be considered true if it were not derived from the dual way in which God communicates himself in his internal life, in the immanent Trinity. The Father gives himself to the Son and to the Holy Spirit. This dual modality of outward self-communication must be appropriate to God in himself, because otherwise God would not have truly communicated. This communication of God has two different created effects —the humanity of Christ and the grace created in humanity— which are different in themselves. Nevertheless, the communication of God does not, in itself, account for these effects. They are the consequence of the two modalities of divine self-communication in the heart of the Trinity and not the difference between them[154].

If we wish to express what the imminent Trinity is, that it is derived from the economy, we are faced with the only God, because he is at the same time the being without origin, the one who is articulated for himself in truth, and who is received and accepted by himself with love. Only in this way can God self-communicate outwardly with freedom. This real differentiation in the only God is possible

329

153 RAHNER K., «El Dios trino como fundamento…» in *MySal* 2/1, 429.
154 RAHNER K., «El Dios trino como fundamento…» in *MySal* 2/1, 429f.

because of a dual self-communication of the Father with which, on the one hand, he communicates within himself, and at the same time, he determines the differentiation in that which is communicated and received. Insofar as we have this unity and differentiation, what is communicated receives the name of «divinity», «divine essence». The differentiation between the one who originally communicates himself and that which is uttered and received must be understood as «relative» (relational). It is the consequence of the nature of the divine essence. Nevertheless, this relationship that is distinguished in God should not be considered less significant. Because the Trinity has the most real existence, this does not mean that the relationship is less real[155].

After presenting these assumptions, Rahner discussed the *aporía* (the difficulty of delving into) of the concept of person in Trinitarian theology. When we refer to God, we cannot speak of three persons in the ordinary sense of the word. When we say that there are three persons in God, this does not mean a multiplication of the essence as it happens with human beings, nor the «sameness» of the personality of the three persons. (If we say three people, the three people, as human beings, are equal or the same, even though we know they are different). In God, there is a conscious distinction although it is not based on three subjectivities, but rather it is based on the fact that the conscious being is present in only one real consciousness. The triple subsistence is not qualified by three consciousnesses. Precisely because of this, Rahner stated that in the heart of the Trinity there is no reciprocal «you» between the Father and the Son[156]. Hence, it

---

155 RAHNER K., «El Dios trino como fundamento…» in *MySal* 2/1, 431-432. Cfr. also KASPER W., *Der Gott*, 354.

156 Cfr. RAHNER K., «El Dios trino como fundamento…» in *MySal* 2/1, 412, footnote 70: «Because of this, within the Trinity there is no reciprocal "you" either. The Son is the self-expression of the Father, but he cannot be conceived at the same time as the "announcer". The Spirit is the "gift" who does not give himself in turn». Also ibid. 434: «…in God, there are not three centers of activity or subjectivities or freedoms. Both because in God there is only *one* essence, and as a consequence of this, only *one* absolute being in himself and also because there is only *one* self-announcement of the Father, the Logos, who is not the one who announces but the one who is announced, and there is not properly a *reciprocal* love (which would imply two acts) between the Father and the Son, but a loving self-acceptance…». Cfr. LONERGAN B., *De Deo trino II. Pars systematica*, Romae 1964, 195f: «in divinis ad intra nemo decit nisi Pater». This issue is further expanded by SCHOONENBERG P., *Der Geist, das Wort und der Sohn. Eine Geist-Christologie*, Regensburg, 183-211. Cfr. on this position of Rahner, VON BALTHASAR H.U., *Teodramática* IV, Madrid 1995, 297, who questioned whether in this case the concept of self-communication can be consistent also outside the framework of the economy. Also cfr. GONZÁLEZ A., *Trinidad y Liberación*, San Salvador 1996, 35ff. The ones that are at stake are the relationships between the immanent Trinity and the economic Trinity; cfr. GRESHAKE G., *Der dreieine Gott*, Freiburg-Basel-Wien 1997, 197f; HOLZER V., *Le Dieu Trinité dans l'histoire. Le différend théologique Balthasar-Rahner*, Paris 1995, 121ff.

would seem that we must interpret that the «you» which is the Father of Jesus according to the gospels (cfr. Matt 11:25; Mark 14:36, and the like) is a consequence of the incarnation.

Consequently, according to Rahner, the subsistence per se would not be in itself «personal» in the present sense of the word. In other words, it would not be a center of activity. The German author was inspired by the definition of Saint Thomas, «subsistens distinctum in natura rationali» in order to posit the formula «the only God subsists in three different modes of subsistence (*Subsistenzweise*)». Based on his fundamental axiom which we have already discussed, Rahner pointed out that «the unique self-communication of the only God takes place in three different modes in which he gives himself as the only and identical God. God is the concrete God of each of these ways of giving himself, which naturally have mutual relationships without being merged modalistically»[157]. The meaning of subsisting is illuminated when we see that we ourselves are founded on that…

…point of our own existence in which we discover, with the first and the last of these experiences, what is concrete, irreducible, unmistakable, and irreplaceable… Here our main axiom is confirmed again. Without the historical-saving experience of Spirit-Son-Father, we could not conceive of anything as being the only God in his differentiated subsistence[158].

The concrete divinity exists of necessity in these three modalities of subsistence. It is not necessary to contemplate on a divinity who is the real foundation prior to these forms. The first form of subsistence constitutes God as Father, as a beginning without origin of the divine self-communication and self-mediation. In this way, there is no one «God» previous to this first form of subsistence[159]. Rahner granted that it is true that these formulas do not say a great deal about Father, Son, and Spirit as such. Nonetheless, the same thing occurs with respect to other terms of Trinitarian theology, as is the case with the term «relationship».

---

157 RAHNER K., «El Dios trino como fundamento…» in *MySal* 2/1, 437; in the same context (cfr. 447ff) Rahner justified the terms of his proposal and pointed out the fact that the expression which he proposed is the one that comes closest to the traditional use given by Barth; cfr. also 410, no. 76, in which he referred to the *tropos thes hyparcheos* of the Cappadocians which would be equivalent to «mode of existence or way of being». See, for instance, BASIL OF CAESAREA, *De Sp. sanct.* 18,46 (SCh 17bis, 408).

158 RAHNER K., «El Dios trino como fundamento…» in *MySal* 2/1, 437-438.

159 The person of the Father is a concrete face which God adopts when he is considered in turn in his aseity and in his paternity. Cfr. HOLZER V., *Le Dieu Trinité dans l'histoire…*, 121.

However, the mode of expression for subsistence offers the advantage with respect to the term «person», in that it does not suggest the multiplication of essence and of subjectivity[160].

We can see clearly that the obstacle Rahner wanted to avoid was tritheism. We can also see that his concerns coincided to a great extent with those of Barth. With Barth, he insisted on the need to exclude three autonomous centers of awareness and action in God. Nevertheless, based on Rahner's terminology of «*modes* (or ways) of subsistence» and Barth's «*modes* of being», we should not reach the conclusion that these authors are simply *modalists*, even though their attempts may have been, and indeed have been, subject to discussion. We saw this earlier in regard to Barth, and we can say the same thing regarding Rahner. For him, the Trinity is not merely economic, but it is also immanent. The modes of self-communication of God acting outwardly respond to what God is in himself. As with Barth, Rahner also insisted that the starting point is the Father; there is no divine essence prior to these three modes of subsistence, differentiated, while at the same time united in their real relationships. Once we have made this basic statement, however, what we can and should ask ourselves is whether with his proposal Rahner reached the conclusion he would have liked to reach and whether his considerations should not be completed by others and even corrected by them. This is the reason that his Trinitarian theology, and most specifically the issue of the «person» in God, has generated discussion in recent times. Naturally, in this criticism we have also run the risk of going to the opposite extreme of tritheism, which we intended to avoid.

We have already spoken of the enrichment experienced with the concept of person in the recent past. It is not only the individual who self-possesses himself and is aware of himself as the subject and center of activities. In the modern concept of person we also see the involvement of communication and love, in short, relationship. The terminology of the three persons can thus help us see that God is relationship and that he is communion. With due caution and while certainly trying not to present the three divine persons according to the model of three human persons, should we speak only of a repetition of the «I» in the Trinity, as Barth did, excluding any intra— Trinitarian reciprocal «you», as stated by Rahner? Many voices have been raised in Catholic spheres which have pointed out that the divine persons are characterized by awareness of themselves and by

---

160 Cfr. RAHNER K., «El Dios trino como fundamento…» in *MySal* 2/1, 439.

their freedom, because they exist in themselves not only in distinction from the others, but also in relationship with them[161]. The formulas of the three ways of being or the three modes of subsistence do not express the dimension of the mystery which is unity in intersubjectivity. Rather, they run the risk of denying it. We have already mentioned the problem that this poses in the relationship between the economic Trinity and the immanent Trinity, because it is clear that, in the first one, Jesus is facing the Father in a relationship of dialogue. Was Rahner really basing his thought on the economic Trinity for the concrete development of his Trinitarian theology? Indeed, in the discussion around the issue of person in God, yet another problem has surfaced. Even admitting that the concept of person in modern times insists on the idea of subject and individuality, among others, Barth and Rahner have not only not rejected that concept, but instead have accepted it, although they have not applied it to the three «persons» in traditional language, but to God himself as an absolute subject. If the persons were based on this «subject», it is clear that thereafter it would be difficult to speak about three. God is the subject of his self-revelation (Barth) or of his self-communication (Rahner)[162], but the Christian tradition has spoken of the unity of substance or of essence, although not the unity of the subject, whether it be the subject of his self-revelation, according to Barth or of his self-communication, according to Rahner[163]. Therefore, if we certainly cannot think that in God there are three diverse self-consciousnesses, this does not necessarily lead us to deny three centers of consciousness and action, three «agents»[164].

Chapter 9

333

---

161 Cfr. BOURASSA F., «Personne et conscience en théologie trinitaire» in *Greg* 55 (1974) 471-493; 677-720, esp. 483, 489. With this statement it is not so clear that the condition of the issue set forth by Barth and Rahner addresses all the aspects of the issue itself. Cfr. what is stated in footnotes 149 and 156.

162 KASPER W., *Der Gott Jesu Christi*, 366. Also MILANO A., 249. The transcendental method that is based on the human subject does not help Rahner to be open to the three «subjects» in God. The influences of the psychological doctrine of the Trinity are clear. Has this theology also helped eliminate the «we» of Trinitarian theology? Cfr. the observations of RATZINGER J. on Augustine and primarily on Thomas Aquinas: *Zum Personverständnis in der Theologie*, in *Dogma und Verkündigung*, München-Freiburg 1973, 205-223, 223.

163 Cfr. KASPER W., *Der Gott Jesu Christi*, 366; cfr. also GRESHAKE G., *Der dreieine Gott*, 141-150.

164 Cfr. KASPER W., *Der Gott Jesu Christi*, 352; ROVIRA BELLOSO J.M., *Tratado de Dios uno y trino*, Salamanca 1993, 626; 634ff. The terminological proposals of Barth and Rahner also have been criticized from the pastoral point of view; according to KASPER W., *Der Gott Jesu Christi*, 351: «One cannot invoke, adore and glorify a different mode of subsistence»; cfr. also O'DONNELL J., *The Mystery of the Triune God*, London 1988, 104.

J. Moltmann has basically been the one who has more consistently —I would even dare say, more radically— founded his Trinitarian theology on the communion of the persons. In this way, he positioned himself on the opposite extreme from Barth and Rahner. Moltmann believed that in the history of theology there has been no danger of tritheism and that the struggle against it has simply been a way of hiding the «modalist» tendencies[165]. He insisted that the above-mentioned authors accepted the contemporary concept of person in quite a fragmented manner[166]; the «I» can only be understood in relation with the «You». This is, as a result, a concept of relationship. Personality and sociality go together. The first cannot exist without the second. Hence, we cannot begin with the idea of absolute subjectivity in God, because based only on that, we would be operating with simple monotheism.

Nevertheless, on the other hand, Moltmann also believed that the use of the concept of substance in Trinitarian theology faced certain difficulties. It is not a biblical concept. Furthermore, if we see the unity of God on that plane, this is understood as a «neuter», as something that is not personal. In view of the fact that changes in the absolute subjectivity and the unity of substance are unfeasible, a third way opens before us in order to speak about the divine union[167]. This was for Moltmann the *perichoresis* (the coming to a subject in a circular way); only by beginning with this can we reach the *union* in God:

> Only the concept of union (*Einigkeit*) is a concept of a mediated and open unity. God is not a «united» God (*einiger*). This assumes a self-differentiation of the personal God and not only a modal differentiation because only persons can be «united» (*einig sein*), and not ways of being or modes of subsistence... The union of the «Tri-unity» (Die *Einigkeit* der *Drei-einigkeit*) is already determined by the communion (*Gemeinschaft*) of Father, Son, and Holy Spirit. There is no need whatsoever to further ensure it by specific teachings about the unity of the divine substance...[168].

---

165 Cfr. MOLTMANN J., *Trinität und Reich Gottes. Zur Gotteslehre*, München 1980, 161.

166 Cfr. MOLTMANN J., *Trinität und Reich Gottes*, 154-166. Kasper has been clearly influenced by Moltmann in his criticism of Rahner.

167 The term used by Moltmann is *Einigkeit* (also *Vereinigung*) and not *Einheit*. It seems that the purpose of this terminology is that of suggesting a dynamic element. This is the reason why it has been translated as *union* and not *unity*. We could also think in terms of *unification*.

168 MOLTMANN J., *Trinität und Reich Gottes*, 167.

An individualistic concept of person places relationship in second place, once the «I» is already constituted. When faced with this conception, we must stress the fact that the two dimensions —that of the «I» and that of the relationship— are closely and intimately united. Because of this, Moltmann pointed out the fact that Father, Son, and Holy Spirit are not only differentiated because of their personality, but at the same time, because of this differentiation, each of them is also with and in the other. The three persons are united by their mutual relationship and by their mutual inhabitation. The two concepts of person and relationship are also original to the Trinity. On the one hand, the relationship assumes the person. On the other, there is no person if not in relationship. The two concepts arise simultaneously and in connection. According to Moltmann they are united «genetically». The forming of the persons and their manifestation in their relationship are the two sides of the same coin, of the same reality[169].

Based on this Trinitarian theology, Moltmann attempted to derive consequences for political theology; monotheism understands God in terms of authority and control. The Paschal mystery of Jesus gives another version of supremacy; God is understood as communion, and hence freedom is at the same time union and communion. Understood in this way, the Trinity is a social program. Human beings created in the image of the Trinity are called to this type of union, to this *perichoresis*. «The experience of the community of Christ corresponds to the perichoretic unity of the triune and one God (*drei-einig*)»[170]. The mutual inhabitation of the persons shows us that there is no subordinationism in the Trinity[171].

Moltmann wished to eliminate to a certain degree the distinction between the economic and the immanent Trinity. The positive function of this distinction lies in safeguarding the freedom of the grace that God gives us. The cross appears only in the saving economy and not in the immanent Trinity[172]. Nevertheless, the distinction reveals itself as inapplicable and invalid when we begin with the idea that in God freedom and necessity do not oppose each other, but rather coincide in love. God loves the world with the same love that he is in him-

---

169 MOLTMANN J., *Trinität und Reich Gottes*, 189.
170 MOLTMANN J., *Trinität und Reich Gottes*, 174. Cfr. the development of this issue in the last part of the treatise, 207-239.
171 MOLTMANN J., *Trinität und Reich Gottes*, 191. Eliminating the danger of subordinationism is a constant in the authors who foster a social model in the Trinity and also in those who criticize the forming of persons as being derived from the relationships of origin. Cfr. the following analysis in this chapter and in the next one.
172 MOLTMANN J., *Trinität und Reich Gottes*, 168; 176-177.

self[173]. In this way, we can think of a temporal and historical God. Moltmann spoke of the «constitution» of the Trinity, and to this end he resorted to a great degree to traditional concepts. He also addressed the issue of a Trinitarian life, of the immanent Trinity, of the communion of love of the three persons in mutual inhabitation[174]. Nevertheless, at the same time, God is open to creation, to time, and to history. In this way, the question of unity in God of Father, Son, and Holy Spirit, is an issue of eschatology, of the consummation of Trinitarian history in God himself[175]. Trinitarian history is not as yet complete because we are still living in times of sin, death, and the like. Each one of us has to collaborate so that the forces of evil are defeated, so that division is overcome, and so that the forces of union are the ones that prevail. Trinitarian history will be fulfilled when in the eschatological consummation God will be all in all (1Cor 15:28). God will be glorified in creation, and creation will be glorified in God[176].

Here we are faced with a conception of the unity of the Trinity that is illustrated as «open» and that at the same time raises several questions. Is the divine freedom maintained in the economy or is God fulfilled in it? What is the link that closely unites the «three»? Is this union only the result of the procession? On the other hand, Moltmann believed that the persons are in relationship, although he did not admit that the relationship is the person or that it forms it. He believed that this leads to modalism. Yet, in his opinion, the Father is certainly in relationship with the Son, although this fact does not cause him to be, but simply presupposes his existence[177]. As we can see, the clear will to eliminate the danger of modalism raises the question of whether we might be going to the other extreme. We are not abandoning the concept of unity of the nature in God, although it is becoming quite difficult to avoid the impression that this nature is possessed by the three who began the relationship in a second «moment»:

173 MOLTMANN J., *Trinität und Reich Gottes*, 169.
174 MOLTMANN J., *Trinität und Reich Gottes*, 179ff.
175 MOLTMANN J., *Trinität und Reich Gottes*, 167.
176 MOLTMANN J., *Trinität und Reich Gottes*, 178.
177 MOLTMANN J., *Trinität und Reich Gottes*, 189. We must return to this issue in the next chapter.

The concept of substance reflects the relationships of the persons within the common divine nature. The concept of relationship reflects the relationship of the persons among themselves. The persons of the Trinity *subsist* in the common divine nature. They *exist* in their mutual relationships[178].

5.3. SELF-CONSCIOUSNESS AND ALTERITY OF THE
DIVINE PERSONS

«The doctrine of the Trinity cannot be confined to the [false] alternative between a "monosubjective" rigid conception and a "social" conception of the Trinity»[179]. In fact, in recent attempts made in the field of Catholic theology, the efforts have been focused on avoiding these two extremes. In the brief review of the criticisms addressed to Barth and Rahner, on the one hand, and to Moltmann, on the other, what we wish to present at this point has already been suggested. If the unity of the divine essence excludes three self-consciousnesses in God, this should not lead us to exclude three agents, three «subjects», nor with due caution need we surrender an enlightenment of the mystery of the divine unity that takes into account alterity(otherness) and intersubjectivity.

Still within the framework of traditional scholastic theology, B. Lonergan spoke of Father, Son, and Holy Spirit as three individuals who are referenced by their relationships, each one aware of himself and aware of the others with whom he is referenced. There are three divine and conscious individuals, which does not mean that there is a plurality of consciousnesses, because in God the essential act and the notional acts are not really differentiated. Nonetheless, when there is a plurality of individuals, there is also a plurality of conscious individu-

---

178 MOLTMANN J., *Trinität und Reich Gottes*, 189. As we can see, attempts are made at avoiding the concept of «subsistent relationship». Naturally, in this brief presentation, we are not attempting to reach an ultimate clarity in the thought of Moltmann. It will suffice to point out the basic line of thought and the problems this raises, as it relates to everything that we have said about the Trinity in relation to the Paschal mystery. Cfr. GRESHAKE G., *Der dreieine Gott*, 188-171, who sees in Moltmann the danger of a certain tritheism; PANNENBERG W., *Teología Sistemática*, Madrid 1992, 363, believes that Moltmann has not fallen into this tritheism and has opposed a non-trinitarian unity of God, though he has not been able to set forth in a more adequate way his ideas with respect to the constitution of the Trinity based on the Father, on the one hand, and its being based on mutual relations on the other. Indeed, greatly inspired by J. Moltmann, L. Boff made attempts to look for a third way between Greek theology and Latin theology in the communion of the *perichoresis*, in order to express unity and differentiation in God: cfr., primarily, BOFF L., *La Trinidad, la sociedad y la liberación*, Madrid 1987; also, *La Trinidad es la mejor comunidad*, Madrid 1990.

179 WERBICK J., *Dottrina Trinitaria*, in SCHNEIDER TH. (ed.), *Nuovo Corso di Dogmatica*, Brescia 1995, 573-685, esp. 636.

als. Hence, we can assume that there are «three reciprocally conscious individuals through only one consciousness that is possessed in a diverse manner by each of the three»[180]. Lonergan was followed almost literally by Kasper[181] who also referred to the «dialogue» that characterizes the divine persons: «The divine persons do not only exist in the dialogue, they are the dialogue»[182]. Similarly, F. Bourassa stressed that what individuates the different (opposite) persons is not an absolute individuation, but rather the mutual nature of the relationships, which is truly a reciprocal communication in the fullness of the divine substance: «All I have is yours…» (John 17:10). The divine «I» is not only infinite, but it is also the complete communication of its infinite nature. It promotes to infinity the one to whom it is being communicated. In this way, the communication of the Father to the Son begets the latter in his fullness, as the only God with the Father. The person is constituted in such a way as to exist in his fullness in the personal intercommunication. Each one is personally conscious and free in his personal property, exercising the same infinite consciousness. In this way, each person is a complete communication of himself, and the perfect communication implies total harmony, infinite unity in fullness of consciousness, love, and freedom. A reciprocal personal communication, total and infinite, opposes independence and limitation. As a result of this, there are not three distinct consciousnesses in God, but rather a perfect unity of substance and love. There is no yours and mine. Nevertheless, this consciousness is personal. The divine consciousness is one, although the divine «I» is not the «I» that is common to the three persons, but the differentiated «I» of each of them. Each divine person is aware of himself aware and aware of what God is, and that is why this is an awareness in communion, an awareness exercised by each one in communion with the rest. «Inner unity in God, vastly aware and full of love; not the inert and solitary union of a unique person, but community of life of the Father and the Son who is his only love»[183].

---

180 *De Deo trino…*, 193: «Tria subiecta sunt invicem conscia per unam conscientiam quae aliter et aliter a tribus habetur»; cfr. 186-196. However, even though Lonergan speaks of three individuals, he does not believe that the three persons are «I» or «you» intra-Trinity (cfr. footnote 156); cfr. about the issue, McDermott J.M., «Person and Nature in Lonergan's De Deo Trino» in *Ang* 71 (1994) 153-185, especially 182-185.

181 Kasper W., *Der Gott Jesu Christi*, 352: «In the Trinity we find three subjects that are reciprocally conscious in view of a unique and identical consciousness that is "possessed" by the three subjects in a different manner in each case».

182 Kasper W., *Der Gott Jesu Christi*, 353. In this respect, he kept his distance from Lonergan.

183 Bourassa F., «Personne et conscience en théologie trinitaire» in *Greg* 55 (1974) 719; cfr. also for the preceding part, 717; 720; by the same author, *La Trinità*, in Neufeld K.H.(ed.), *Problemi e orientamenti di teologia dogmatica*, Brescia 1983, 337-372, especially 352-353: «La coscienza di sé

Other Catholic authors have followed more resolutely the approach of dialogue and the analogy of inter-human relations which were clearly suggested in some of the theologians whom we have just quoted. In Augustine, we saw only some traces of this line of thought, although there is no doubt that the psychological analogy prevails in him. More decisively, Richard of Saint Victor based his ideas on the analysis of inter-human love. Indeed, it is quite easy to see that this orientation is highly regarded in most recent Catholic theology. Together with the category of the «I», which we saw prevailing in Barth, that of the «we» in God has also been used explicitly, although in very different ways, depending on the authors.

The model developed by H. Mühlen has had considerable influence and has also sparked some discussion: the Father is characterized as the «I», the Son as the «you», and the Holy Spirit as the «we» of the Father and the Son, the «us in person»[184], the hypostatized us, as we could say. Mühlen perceptively pointed out that «we» can never be the plural of the first person because strictly speaking the first person does not tolerate the plural. There is only one «I», but there can be several of «you» or «they». At the same time, «we» is the plural of the first and second persons, the plural of the Father and the Son. Marriage gives an image of this «us» or «we». Marriage is neither yours nor mine, but ours. No doubt Mühlen took the position of traditional Western theology, which has seen the Holy Spirit as the mutual love of the Father and the Son and the expression of their unity, as was the case with Augustine and a considerable part of the Western tradition. While acknowledging the validity of his intuition, some critics have wondered whether Mühlen had justified the exclusiveness of the application of pronouns to the Father and to the Son and what they tell us about the personal properties of the Father and the Son. Could they not be applied as well to the

esercitata personalmente da ciascuna delle persone in Dio è, per ciascuna, la coscienza di *essere* Dio, e ciò in commune con le altre Persone, e la coscienza di se come *distinta* dalle altre, ma in una *relazione* di tutta la propia esistenza *all'altro*... Questo significa una vita divina vissuta da ciascuna persona, divinamente, quinde unicamente, infinitamente e totalmente *per l'altro*». «Questa coscienza personale di una esistenza vissuta per l'altro, in una reciprocità così totale e infinita, è il culmine dell'unità».

[184] Cfr. MÜHLEN H., *Der Heilige Geist als Person in der Trinität in der Inkarnation und im Gnadenbund*, Münster 1963, especially 100-168; cfr. by the same author *Una mystica persona*, München-Paderborn-Wien 1968, 196-200. The Holy Spirit is a person in two persons in the heart of the Trinity, which corresponds to the ecclesiological formula that is set forth by the axiom: a person in many persons.

Holy Spirit? On the other hand, if this is the «we» of the Father and the Son, would the Spirit's personal property be misrepresented and distorted[185]?

J. Ratzinger used a similar metaphor, by also introducing the idea of the plurality of subjects and dialogue in God:

> From its origin, the concept of person expresses the idea of dialogue, and God is the essence of the dialogue. It points to God as the essence which lives in the word and subsists in the word as «I», «You», and «We». This knowledge of God reveals his own essence to humans in a new way[186].

Based on Augustine, Ratzinger defined person as the phenomenon of total relationship that can only fully take place in God, although he also pointed toward what, in one way or another, every personal being is, and thus also what humanity is[187]. Nevertheless, Christian theology contains no simple principle of the «I — you» dialogue of modern times. This simple principle of dialogue in God is not present, although in him we always have the «us» of Father, Son, and Holy Spirit. This principle is not present in human beings either, who exist only in the continuity of the people of God, and ultimately in Christ who unites the «we» of humanity and the «you» of God[188].

Von Balthasar also used the image of the «we», but not the «we» of the three, as in the case of Ratzinger, but of the Holy Spirit as the «we», the eternal dialogue between the Father and the Son, in a line of thought that has points of agreement with Mühlen[189]. However, he also used the image of matrimonial fecundity which emerges in the son[190]. According to this metaphor, the Spirit would

---

185 Cfr. for instance MILANO A., *Persona in teologia*, 256f; GRESHAKE G., *Der dreieine Gott*, 163; 194. GONZÁLEZ A., *Trinidad y liberación*, 198ff. We will raise this topic again when we address the person of the Holy Spirit.

186 RATZINGER J., *Zum Personverständnis in der Theologie*, 210.

187 RATZINGER J., *Zum Personverständnis in der Theologie*, 213. Cfr. also RATZINGER J., *Introducción al Cristianismo*, Salamanca 1971, 151-153, 159: «The "I" is at the same time what I have and what least belongs to me… a being that understands himself perfectly well understands that *in* his being he does not belong to himself, and that he arrives at himself when he leaves himself and is oriented again as a reference of his real originality».

188 RATZINGER J., *Zum Personverständnis in der Theologie*, 222.

189 Cfr. MÜHLEN H., *Spiritus Creator*, Einsiedeln 1967, 152.

190 Cfr. VON BALTHASAR H.U., *Theologik II. Wahrheit Gottes*, Einsiedeln 1985, 54ff, in which he quoted SCHEEBEN M.J., according to whom, the mother —who is the link of union between the father and the son— could be the image of the Holy Spirit. Nevertheless, Scheeben himself was aware that this idea was quite alien to the tradition. We have already seen how Augustine expressly rejected it. In far more generic terms, JOHN PAUL II on several occasions used this analogy

appear rather as the fruit of the unity of the Father and the Son. Von Balthasar believed that with this image the idea of the exclusive «I-you» dialogue is complemented, and despite all the differences, it would also correspond to the *imago Trinitatis* that is placed into human beings. It not only overcame the limitations of the «I» in the Augustinian concept, but it also enabled the *condilectus*, the co-beloved, who in the line of thought of Richard of Saint Victor was brought in from outside, to emerge instead from the internal understanding of love[191]. It is quite clear that this image cannot be seen in absolute terms without the risk of falling into tritheism[192]. Nonetheless, it can assist us in showing that the unity of the two is expressed and guaranteed in a third one and that the perfect love between the one who loves and the one who is loved cannot be evidenced without the *condilectus* who emerges from within this same love.

With some differences and nuances that we must acknowledge, Catholic theology has attempted to illumine the mystery of the divine persons in their unity and in their distinctiveness, combining the elements of self-possession self-consciousness, and inter-human relationship. In the case of both their unity and their distinctiveness, tradition offers valid elements, although the introduction of these elements in theological thought cannot be explained without the influence of anthropological and philosophical evolution.

Self-possession in consciousness and self-awareness, as well as in the condition of the «individual», are recognized as elements that comprise the concept of the divine person. In this respect, the proposal set forth by Rahner has not been significantly addressed, even though due attention has been paid to warning of the danger of tritheism. At this point, it is absolutely necessary to stress, as

of the family: «It has been mentioned in a beautiful and profound way that our God —in his most intimate mystery— is not solitary, but a family, because he carries in himself fatherhood, sonship, and the essence of the family that is love» (Homily in Puebla on January 28th, 1979, 2). Also in the «Letter to Families» dated February 2nd, 1994, 6, John Paul said that the divine «We» is the eternal model of the human «we», primarily of this human «we» that is made up of a man and a woman, created in the divine image and likeness. Cfr. on this issue, AA.VV., *Misterio cristiano y existencia humana*, Salamanca 1995.

191 VON BALTHASAR H.U., *Theologik II. Wahrheit Gottes*, 56f.

192 The author himself stresses that none of the models can be understood in absolute terms. Cfr. *Teodramática 3.*, Madrid 1993, 482f; by the same author, *Theologik II*, Einsiedeln 1985, 35, 39: the interpersonal model does not attain substantial unity in God, the «intrapersonal» model does not express the real and permanent «being face to face» of the *hypostasis* in God; cfr. also WERBICK J., *Dottrina Trinitaria*, in SCHNEIDER TH. (ed.), *Nuovo Corso di Dogmatica*, 617f, 639f. As it relates to the different attempts to base the divine unity in personal communion, there are different results; cfr. in that respect, O'DONNELL J., «The Trinity as Divine Community» in *Greg* 69 (1988) 5-34. Also on some aspects of the problem in current theology, see HILBERATH B.J., *Der dreieinige Gott und die Gemeinschaft der Menschen*, Mainz 1990.

is the case, in fact, in Catholic theology, that the three «subjects» have only one self-awareness, only one freedom, only one love and knowledge[193]. Each one of them is self-possessed and is aware of himself in the relationship with the other persons and in full communion with them. Each one is different in the radical relationality (the person is the relation) in such a way that the being of each of the persons — Father, Son and Holy Spirit— and the correspondence with the other two are identical[194]. In the divine persons, we see that the being of each of them coincides in relationship with the rest in perfect communion of one love. The self-possession of each one of the persons is identified with the full gift to the other two. Only as it relates to the others does each divine person have his own «identity».

In fact, and in keeping with the words of Jesus, we could reflect, «All I have is yours and all you have is mine» (John 17:10) and «May they all be one, just as, Father, you are in me and I am in you» (John 17:21), with the necessary inclusion of the Holy Spirit in a union of persons that fully eliminates «mine» and «yours», although still maintaining the distinction that corresponds to «I» and «you». The unity is not only a being «with» but a being «in» the other one, in a perfect communication which is a reciprocal inhabitation. Here we can see the clear differentiation from the human person, who although always in relationship and open to the others, exists in a certain tension between being oneself and being in relationship with the other (which is why we can close ourselves off from both God and our fellow humans). Even in the most perfect communion that we can

193 In this respect, mention can be made of a certain consensus; cfr. in addition to the authors quoted before, MILANO A., *Persona in teologia*, 242-246; NICOLAS J.M., *De la Trinité à la Trinité. Synthèse dogmatique*, Fribourg 1985, 147f: there are three conscious and free persons, although only one consciousness; GRESHAKE G., *Der dreieine Gott*, 122: «In God there is only one consciousness, one knowledge, one love, one free action, but all of these actions are not the realizations of nature, but of personal individuals. In other words, the subjects of these actions are three self-awarenesses, three centers of knowledge, three freedoms...» Personally, I would prefer to state «three self-aware, three free, etc.», in order to give more relevance to the person. We can legitimately question the appropriateness of the use of categories of «individual», of «you» and «I» in God in the immanent Trinity. It would suffice to speak of the reality in self-possession. This is what is stated by GONZÁLEZ A., *Trinidad y liberación*, 194, inspired by the categories of X. Zubiri, although he naturally adds that this self-possession is evidenced in full communion and in total delivery of one person to the other. Even though I am aware of the difficulty, I do not include in my analysis these precisions or explanations, because if in the *salutis* economy the persons appear as an «I» and as a «you», we must assume that there is something in the immanent Trinity that corresponds to this way in which Father, Son and Spirit make themselves known in the saving economy.

194 Cfr. WERBICK J., *Dottrina Trinitaria*, in SCHNEIDER TH. (ed.), *Nuovo Corso di Dogmatica,*, 652; GRESHAKE G., *Der dreieine Gott*, 184f; ROVIRA BELLOSO J.M., *Tratado de Dios Uno y Trino*, 636. The intimacy and the relationship are one and the same.

imagine, we cannot make others share or participate in everything that we are, nor participate fully in what the ones who surround us are and have. However, in God, the persons exist in total surrendering, giving up of oneself and in absolute giving.

All the images and models that shed light on access to the mystery, and that are based on human reality, must acknowledge the fundamental limitations of those images and models over against the infinite superiority of God and the impossibility of limiting God to our human schemes. If theology further explores the divine mystery, it should be even more aware of the *apophatic* moment which should always characterize the mystery, even though without being absolute. Any image would be relativized from the very beginning, if only because Jesus has not used it when he has assumed the task of explaining in human terms the divine nature of his person[195]. Naturally, this does not mean that we should disregard the secular efforts of theology or the constantly renewed attempts at explaining our hope.

Father, Son, and Holy Spirit subsist in the unity of their unique divinity, truly differentiated from one another by virtue of their reciprocal relationships. This, however, not only makes them distinct, but also unites them in an infinite love and in a mutual understanding. Unity and distinction are not in opposition in God. The biblical expression of the unity of the Father and the Son (cfr. John 10:30; 14:9-10, etc.; cfr. also Heb 1:3 —the Son being the radiance of the glory of God and the imprint of his substance) points to the unity in the distinction, but certainly goes beyond whatever we can imagine.

On the other hand, we must bear in mind that there is no repetition in God, and as a result of this, the Father, Son and Holy Spirit are not only differentiated, but each one of them is a person in a differentiated manner. We have already referred to this issue. We saw that at least beginning with St. Augustine, the use of the plural «three persons» generated various problems. Necessity is what forces this. Each of the persons is identified with the divine essence in such a way that God does not «grow» with the addition of Father, Son and Holy Spirit. Different teachings and interventions from earlier times, warned against «multiplication» in God. For example, Pope Hormisdas in the year 521 stated: «Unum est sancta Trinitas, non multiplicatur numero, non crecit augmento…» (DS 367). The Eleventh Council of Toledo (675) emphasized that God is Trinity, but that

---

195 Cfr. Von Balthasar H.U., *Theologik ii*, 61.

he is not «triple»[196]. Each person is not without the others; however, this does not mean that each person must be completed because he lacks something in himself. Each person is God entirely. This is another reason why in God there is no room for any addition or multiplication. The relationship of each person with the other two, without whom there is no divine person, on the one hand necessarily relates to the divine being, but on the other hand, is shown in the pure and overwhelming overflowing of love which is not directed toward compensating for any type of deficiency or fault.

---

[196] «Quae non triplex, sed Trinitas et dici et credi debet. Nec recte dici potest, ut in uno Deo sit Trinitas, sed unus Deus Trinitas » (DS 528); is inspired in AUGUSTINE, *Trin* VI 7,8 (CCL 50,238); cfr. VII 1,2 (249); the same council: «nec minoratur in singulis nec augetur in tribus» (DS 529); «nec redecit a numero nec capitur numero» (530). The explanation of Pius VI is also interesting in the papal bull *Auctorem fidei* — 1794: God is one «in three different persons», although not «differentiated in three persons» (DS 2697). Several interventions have repeated this idea: cfr. among others DS 470, 490, 501, 800, 803f, Lateran IV against Joachim of Fiore; 1880... There is evidence of the difficulty that the «number» in God has posed since ancient times in VON BALTHASAR H.U., *Theologik* III. *Dei Geist der Wahrheit*, Einsiedeln 1987, 110ff. Cfr. AMBROSIUS OF MILAN, *De Spiritu sancto* III 13 (CSEL 79,189): «Quomodo pluralitatem recipit divinitatis, cum pluralitas numeri sit, numerus autem non recipiat divina natura?»; BASIL OF CAESAREA, *de Sp. Sanc.* 18,44-46 (SCh 17bis, 402-410), each *hypostasis* is named on its own.

The Father, the Son and the Holy Spirit

As we have seen, the concept of divine person as a subsistent relationship means that in God there exist three different centers of self-possession and activity in perfect communion, in which even though they can be considered as three «I's», they exclude any «yours» or «mine» (Cfr. John 16:14-15). We have also emphasized that in God there is no increase or decrease that results from the differentiation of the divine persons. Rather, the divine essence is entirely possessed by the Father, the Son, and the Holy Spirit —each one in his own way, as each one of them is in his own way a «person» in God. For this reason, it cannot be sufficient for us just to make this reflection, which is necessarily somewhat generic, as was our reflection in the previous chapter. It is not enough merely to speak of the Trinity of persons; we must also analyze *who* are the Father, the Son, and the Spirit. Therefore, in this chapter we will proceed with a differentiated analysis of the inherent characteristics of each of the three. We must address this topic in a more systematic way than we have already done in our brief historical review.

1

The Father, the origin without beginning

According to the theological tradition that begins with the Fathers of the Church, the Father is the one who assures the unity of the Trinity because he is the only source of the divinity. We know that there is not a divine essence «prior» to the persons. Similarly, there is no divine nature that is «above» them (cfr. DS 803-804). Instead, this nature is entirely possessed by the three persons, each one of them in his own way. The Father possesses it in a more frontal or original way, giving it and never receiving it, although always in relationship with the Son and the Holy Spirit. In other words, his original possession of the divinity cannot be considered independently from the other two persons. We also know that when in the New Testament mention is made of God, this is in general terms, although not pertaining exclusively to the Father[1]. In this sense, we would have to identify the God of the Old Testament with the Father. In view of the fact that there is no previous divine essence, it is clear that we speak primarily of him when we refer to the infinite, eternal, omnipotent God (cfr. the Creed). W. Kasper strongly empha-

---

1 Cfr. RAHNER K., «Theos en el Nuevo Testamento» in *Escritos de Teología* I, Madrid 1963, 93-167; cfr. some nuances in GALOT J., «Le mystère de la personne du Pere» in *Greg* 77 (1996) 5-31.

sizes this[2]. Nevertheless, some objections have been raised against this conception. Undoubtedly, not with the purpose of denying the biblical information, but rather to demonstrate that in light of the Christian revelation God the Father does not ever exist without the Son and the Holy Spirit, the affirmations of the Old Testament about God cannot be understood as though they exclusively referred to the first person[3]. However, we must still address the personal identification of the Father of Jesus with the God of the Old Testament. Whatever is said about God as the ultimate source of everything that exists primarily refers to the Father. However, we cannot assume that these affirmations exclusively refer to him, because he is not the beginning of everything that exists independently from the mediation of the Son and the perfection that is granted to everything by the Holy Spirit.

God is manifested as Father, as we all know, in the life of Jesus and above all, in his resurrection from the dead. We believe in the God who has brought Jesus back from the dead, and with this fact he has definitively and irrevocably shown his Fatherhood (cfr. Rom 10:9; Phil 2:11; Acts 13:32-33, among other places). In our review of the basic affirmation of the New Testament, of Patristic theology, and of the catechism, we have already noted the main affirmations that refer to the Father. Now we must compile and complete this information in a more systematic way[4].

1.1. SOME ELEMENTS OF THE TRADITION

We know that if, in Christian terminology, mention is made of the Father analogously with human fatherhood, in the same New Testament, the text also makes us realize that the Father of Jesus is the *analogatum princeps* of all fatherhood. To be exact, he deserves the name of Father (cfr. Matt 23:9: «call no one on earth your father…»; Eph 3:15, «the Father from whom every fatherhood in heaven

---

2 Kasper W., *Der Gott Jesu Christi*, Mainz 1982, 187-197, in which in effect, the *De Deo Uno*, is considered to be teachings about the Father. Cfr. also Staglianò A., *Il mistero del Dio vivente*, Bologna 1996, 590ff.

3 Cfr. Schulte R., «La preparación de la revelación trinitaria» in *MySal* 2/1, 77-116, esp. 80-87; Von Balthasar H.U., *Teodramática 3. Las personas del drama: el hombre en Cristo*, Madrid 1993, 470. In the next chapter we will address this issue again.

4 Regarding the Father, in addition to the bibliography that has already been quoted and that we will continue to use, cfr., among others, aa.vv., *Dios es Padre*, Salamanca 1991; Bouyer L., *Le Père invisible*, Paris 1976; Torres Queiruga A., *Creo en Dios Padre. El Dios de Jesús como afirmación plena del hombre*, Santander 1978; Durrwell F.X., *Le Père. Dieu en son mystère*, Paris 1988; Galot J., *Découvrir le Père. Esquisse d'une théologie du Père*, Louvain 1985; Pikaza X., «Padre» in *Diccionario teológico El Dios cristiano*, 1003-1021.

or on earth takes its name…»). Mention has been made of the Father as origin and source, as well as of his «monarchy». Nevertheless, this does not in any way exclude the Son and the Holy Spirit. All these designations attempted to emphasize the exceptional role that the Father has in the Trinity and in the saving economy. Some expressions in ante-Nicene theology can have a certain «subordinationist» sense to our ears. However, we have also seen how the divinity of the Son and the Holy Spirit were vigorously affirmed. The Arian crisis forced the development of clearer formulations concerning the equality of the three persons. The Father is the beginning of the Son and of the Holy Spirit, who are God as he is. These considerations did not lead to a «decrease» in the person of the Father, but very much to the contrary, his greatness as «beginning» lies precisely in this role. Gregory of Nazianzus had emphasized that if the Father were only the principal cause of things that are created, he would be so in a poor and mean way. The Father is «ἀρχή» in fullness as he is the Father «of the divinity and of the goodness that is adored in the Son and in the Holy Spirit»[5]. The Father is the «beginning», and for that reason, the Son and the Holy Spirit cannot be considered to be less[6]. The Father cannot simply be identified with the divine essence, because he is God communicating that essence fully to the Son and to the Holy Spirit. The monarchy inherently involves the whole nature and not merely only one person[7]. The nature of the beginning which is inherent in the Father, in order to have its full meaning, requires the divinity of the Son and of the Holy Spirit. According to Gregory of Nyssa, when making a distinction between the cause and what emerges from it, we are only pointing out the difference of modalities of existing and not any difference in essence or nature[8].

---

5 GREGORY OF NAZIANZUS, *Or.* 2,38 (SCh 247,140). Cfr. AUGUSTINE, *Trin.* IV 20,29 (CCL 50,200): «totius divinitatis vel si melius dicitur deitatis principium pater est».

6 GREGORY OF NAZIANZUS, *Or.* 30,7 (SCh 250,240), the Father is «greater» (cfr. John 14:28) refers to the cause, but the fact that the Son is «equal» (cfr. John 10:30) refers to the nature. We have already referred on several occasions to the interpretation of John 14:28 made by the Nicene authors. The Father is greater as to beginning, but the Son is not lesser because he receives everything from him. The divine Fatherhood is evidenced precisely in the full gist of the divinity; cfr. also AUGUSTINE, *Trin.* IV 20,27; VI 3,5; (CCL 50,195.233). ATHANASIUS, *C. Arian* I 20; III 6 (PG 26,53.333), the Father is only Father in relation to the Son.

7 Cfr. GREGORY OF NAZIANZUS, *Or.* 30,2 (SCh 250,178). Cfr. also BASIL OF CAESAREA, *De Sp. Sanct* 18,45 (SCh 17 bis, 404-406).

8 GREGORY OF NYSSA, *Quod non sunt tres dei* (Jaeger III,156) *Contra Eunomium* I 497 (Jaeger I,170). Mention is made in these texts of the *pos einai* and the *tropos tes hyparcheos*. Cfr. also CYRIL OF ALEXANDRIA (PG 75,185B), the Son, upon existing as possessor himself of the essence of the Father, has in himself fully the Father.

The idea of the primacy of the Father as source and origin of the divinity has been maintained even when the equality of the three persons has been affirmed and clearly recognized, as we have seen before[9]. It has been precisely the reflection on the meaning of the Fatherhood of the first person that has excluded any subordinationism in the Nicene authors. Several magisterial statements coming from different levels have underlined this truth, for instance, different councils held in Toledo, most specifically numbers Six, Eleven, and Sixteen of the years 638, 675 and 693, respectively[10]. In these and other texts, clear mention is made of the fact that the Father has no beginning and that he is unborn[11]. The equality of the three persons is compatible with this differentiation.

As the beginning and source of the divinity, the Father does not in turn have a beginning. He is unbegotten. Many Church Fathers have made use of this designation and have taken it as the characteristic of the person of the Father[12]. The excesses in the use of this term by Eunomius have not been a reason to avoid this designation. Many authors have considered his unborn being as the most relevant property of the Father. For Bonaventure, the *innascibilitas* would be the reason for this primal fullness of the divinity of the Father[13]. On the contrary, for Thomas, this is certainly a property, a notion of the Father, although it is only negative. It only says that the Father is not the Son[14]. It is clear that there cannot be another unbegotten because if that were the case there would be more than one God. In effect, we are already aware of the relationship that has been established between the divine unity and the only beginning without beginning who is the Father.

According to Saint Thomas, the Father is the unbegotten and the beginning without beginning, but he is also the one who begets the Son, and he is, together with the Son, the beginning of the Holy Spirit. Primarily, we speak of the «Father»

9 THOMAS AQUINAS, *STh* I 33,1 ad. 2: «Quia licet attribuamus Patri aliquid auctoritatis ratione principii, nihil tamen ad subiectionem vel minorationem quocumque modo pertinens, attribuimus Filio vel Spiritui Sancto».

10 Cfr. DS 490; 525; 568. For more recent times cfr. LEO XIII, enc. *Divinum illud Munus*, of the year 1897 (DS 3326).

11 Cfr. DS 60; 75 (Quicumque); 441; 470; 490; 525; 569; 572; 683; 800 (Fourth Lateran Council); 1330ff (Florence); cfr. also 1862, *Professio fidei tridentina*.

12 Cfr. HILARY OF POITIERS, *Trin.* II 6 (CCL 62,43) : « Ipse ingenitus, aeternus, habens in se semper ut semper sit ». Cfr. LADARIA L.F., «Dios Padre en Hilario de Poitiers» in *EstTrin* 24 (1990) 443-479, esp. 446-447. We have already mentioned the Cappadocians in our chapter that addressed the history.

13 Cfr. BONAVENTURE, *In I Sent.* 29, dub. 1: *Breviloquium* I 3,7: «Innascibilitas in Patre ponit fontalem plenitudem». Cfr. CONGAR Y., *El Espíritu Santo*, 571f.

14 Cfr. *STh* I 33,4 ad. I.

in his relationship with the Son and only secondarily with respect to creatures[15]. God can create because he is Father, and not the other way around. There is a close relationship between the divine processions and the creation. The first are the cause for the second[16]. Saint Thomas considers the name Father as being more appropriate for the first person than that of *genitor* or *generans*, because these latter designations point to the generation *in fieri*, whereas in the case of the Father the generation has already taken place. The designation of things refers primarily to its perfection in the end. Because of this, as we have already pointed out, Thomas gives preference to the «relationships» over the «origin»; hence, the name «Father» is more suitable. Fatherhood and generation more properly refer to God than to creatures, because the generation will be even more perfect the closer the form of the begotten is to the one who begets. There is no greater proximity than the one which exists between the Father and the Son, because in the divine generation the form is numerically the same between the two. Nevertheless, this cannot occur in the case of creatures because in them we are dealing only with the same species (the Father and the Son are the same God, which is evidently not what is seen in human generations). However, the most decisive element in the section that Thomas devotes to the name of Father as inherent to a divine person[17], is the use that is made of the idea of the person as a subsistent relationship. The subsistent paternity is the Father:

> The proper name of a person means that which is appropriate to the person which is different from the rest… And that which distinguishes the person of the Father from all the rest is his paternity. Consequently, the common name of the person of the Father is this name Father, which describes his paternity[18].

The justification for these affirmations must be found in Thomas' definition of the divine person as a subsistent relationship. The paternity means that the Father *is* insofar as he is Father and that there is no being prior to his being Father. He is not like a human father who, before being father, at some point in time began to be so. «Being» and «being Father» coincide in the first person of

---

15 *STh* I 33,3: «Per prius paternitas dicitur in divinis secundum quod importatur respectus personae ad personam».
16 *STh* I 45,6: «Processiones divinarum personarum sunt causa creationis»; cfr. ibid. 45,7.
17 *STh* I 33,2; the previous explanation also refers to this article.
18 *STh* I 33,2 corpus. Also I 42,4 ad. 2; I 40, 4 ad 1: «quia Pater est, generat»; the relation is prior to the notional act, as the person precedes the action.

the Trinity. He is «being» in pure giving. «The meaning of his being is not in the substance that subsists in him but in the love that is communicated in him»[19]. Insofar as the Father is a beginning without beginning and from him comes everything in the final sense, based on his «Fatherhood» we can understand his being as a gift and an opening up. Hence, the Father is the pure capacity of giving and fully giving. Hilary said that the divine nature is communicated to the Son just as it is possessed by the Father[20]. If it were not present in God this total giving would be due to a lack of capacity or to lack of will. In both cases, the same property of God would be affected. During the Arian controversy, as we have seen, the idea of the total lack of «envy» of the Father played an important role to indicate that his giving to the Son is complete. In this way, his love is shown as the fundamental dimension of the being of the Father, and consequently it also determines the generation of the Son and the procession of the Spirit. As a result of this, his Fatherhood is fontal love, his love that is given. Maximus the Confessor stated: «God the Father, moved by an eternal love, proceeded to the distinction of the *hypostasis*»[21]. We need not think that his love is opposed to his «nature». In God, necessity and will cannot be opposed (cfr. DS 526). All is one in its utmost simplicity.

1.2. THE FATHER, BEGINNING OF THE SON AND THE HOLY SPIRIT

«The Father only-begot the Son from his substance» (DS 1330, Council of Florence, Decree for the Jacobites). We take this phrase, which is the result of a long tradition, as a starting point in our reflection on the generation of the Son. Let us note the double aspect of the affirmation: The *Father* begets *from his substance*. This idea is constantly repeated, beginning in the Council of Nicaea[22], as is reported by Thomas Aquinas: the Son is «of the substance of the Father»[23]. How-

---

19 KASPER W., *Der Gott Jesu Christi*, 198.
20 *Trin.* VIII 43 (CCL 62A,356): «Talis data est quails et habetur». Cfr. LADARIA L.F., «Dios Padre en Hilario de Poitiers», 455f.
21 *Esc. In de div. nom.* (PG 4,221), quoted by CONGAR Y., *El Espíritu Santo*, 577. Cfr. also the other texts quoted in this place.
22 «Begotten from the Father… in other words, of the substance of the Father» (DS 125). XI Council of Toledo (DS 526): «Nec enim de nihilo, neque de aliqua alia substantia, sed de Patris utero, id est, de substantia eius idem Filius genitus vel natus est». Let us note the metaphor of the «uterus» that seems to be identified with the substance of the Father. Here, a «maternal» feature of the Father also appears which also touches on a personal aspect.
23 STh I 41,3. The Father conveys to the Son all his nature and not a part of it as happens with human generation.

ever, at the same time we must bear in mind that the divine processions, in the traditional conception, are personal acts insofar as they are acts of human reason and will. They are notional acts, inherent to each one of the persons. As a result of this, even though the Father begets the Son from his substance (or, *mutatis mutandis,* he breathes the Holy Spirit), the generation and the expiration are acts *of the Father.* We must remember in this respect a basic text of the Fourth Lateran Council:

> In God there is only the Trinity, not a «quaternity», because any one of the three persons is that reality (*res*), that is, the substance, essence, or divine nature, which is the only beginning of all things, out of which none other can be found. That reality, however, does not beget, nor is it begotten, nor does it proceed, but the Father is the one who begets, the Son who is begotten and the Holy Spirit who proceeds, in such a way that there are distinctions in the persons and unity in the nature (DS 804).

Therefore, the Father, not the divine nature, is the beginning of the Trinity. It is clear that the Father, as God, begets the Son from his substance, but he begets him as Father and not as substance or nature. «Christ gives thanks only to the Father who is God, but never to the divinity that would be fruitful in the Father»[24].

The name Father refers to the relationship with the Son. It is this terminology that is emphasized in the New Testament. However, the Father is also related to the Holy Spirit although this relationship is not expressed in his personal name. Nonetheless, by being the beginning of the Holy Spirit (together with the Son or through him), he belongs to him as much as the generation of the Son, even though in the course of history, primarily in early times, the Father-Son relationship has been the one that comprised most of the reflection. We saw that in the first moments of Christian theology it was not always stated clearly that God was Father *ab aeterno.* The intellectual generation of the Son or Logos does not appear clearly separated from the creation of the world. Beginning with Origen, the eternity of the Fatherhood is clear along with the Logos who is begotten *ab aeterno.* Because of this, he is the Son from eternity, although the generation is still not contemplated with total independence from the creation of the world. With the Council of Nicaea, this second issue has also been clarified. In fact, when

---

24 VON BALTHASAR H.U., *Theologik II. Wahrheit Gottes*, Einsiedeln, 1985, 123; cfr. ROVIRA BELLOSO J.M., *Tratado de Dios uno y trino*, 593.

the Fathers wanted to find the bases for the eternity of the Son, they argued by saying that otherwise God could not always have been Father. He cannot be eternal as Father if the Son is not eternal as well. In view of the fact that we cannot think of the being of the Father prior to his paternity, this Fatherhood is itself the guarantee of the eternality and of the same nature of the Son and the Holy Spirit.

The issue of the eternal nature of the Son and the Holy Spirit is therefore related to that of the essential relationship of the Father with the Son (and respectively with the Holy Spirit), without which the Father is not simply not Father, but he would not *be*. His being is being Father. If the issue is only perceived from the «chronological» point of view, the argument would not have much weight. If «logically» there were a being previous to being «Father», the question of whether or not the relationship with the Son would be established in a subsequent moment would not change things considerably. Nevertheless, the eternality of the Son points to somewhat more than what is merely «chronological». It enables us to see that the Father *is* insofar as he is the beginning and source of the divinity; insofar as he begets the Son and he *is* the beginning of the Spirit, he *is* only insofar as he gives himself. We saw the difficulties that Augustine faced when he came to the understanding that the concept of divine «person» is absolute. It seems that this led him to conclude that in the Father, the Son and the Holy Spirit, there was something «previous» to the relationships that unite and differentiate the three. The Doctor of Hippo was well aware that he had not found a satisfactory solution to the problem that had been posited. The idea of the subsistent relationship will finally tell us, as we already know, that there is nothing «previous» to the relationship in the divine person.

1.3. **THE FATHER, AN ABSOLUTE PERSON?**

These issues are still very significant at the present time, because on the one hand, the definition of the divine person as a subsistent relationship has been given an answer[25]. However, at the same time, the difficulties appear to be especially serious as they relate to the Father: «The Father... cannot be made as result of a relationship. He has to exist by himself»[26]. The reason is that he does not pro-

---

[25] Let us remember what we have said in this respect about MOLTMANN J. for whom the identification of the person with the relationship in Saint Thomas would be, in short, modalist; cfr. *Trinität und Reich Gottes*, München 1980, 189.

[26] MOLTMANN J., *Trinität und Reich Gottes*, 182.

ceed from any other person. What is more, in view of the fact that the origin and the fullness of divinity are in the Father, at first sight it would seem coherent that this original possession of divinity is prior to his being the pole of a personal relationship. This is what is stated by Y. Congar, even though he does not particularly insist on this[27]. Other Catholic authors, in their legitimate attempt at emphasizing the position of the Father as the source of the divinity, have followed a similar line of thought[28], although with different nuances. Additionally, in some texts of Kasper the concept of «absolute person» appears, as applied to the Father who, as we have seen, is for him the one God[29]. According to the German theologian, the human person can only reach its fullness when it finds a person who, not only in its intentional pretension, but in his real being, is infinite. Another good concept of the person as the unrepeatable «being there» of the being, necessarily leads us to the idea of the absolute, divine person[30]. We cannot take these affirmations of Kasper out of their context, however. Here it is not a matter of speaking about the Father as an absolute person and the Son and the Spirit as well, but of the philosophical problem of the personality of God as the «absolute», whom we could reach through reason. In view of the theological assumption to which we have referred, this «absolute» will be the Father. But this is a different issue or aspect of the Trinitarian problem than the relation-

27 CONGAR Y., *La Parola e il Soffio*, Roma 1985, 138: «Il Padre è la fonte della divinità, prima (logicamente parlando) di essere polo di opposizione personale. È quanto confessa il simbolo: lo credo in Dio (divinità fontale) Padre onnipotente». Naturally, we can wonder if the Father is not the source of the divinity precisely as the pole of the relationships. Cfr. further ahead.

28 Cfr. also GIRONÉS G., *La divina arqueología*, Valencia 1991, 25: «The origin of everything is the Father, not the Trinity in itself as a closed circle of its own reciprocity. This means that the Father explains and justifies his existence by himself, without any reference to the Son or to the Holy Spirit»; 31: «The person of the Father is then made by his *free opening to every communication* (of love), *to every relationship with the other*. He has this original faculty (without any dependence whatsoever), but this would not have been acknowledged if it had not been expressed in a dialogue with the Son and the Spirit and with the same persons about the creation»; 43: «... the Eternal Father is the beginning of all in a double way: absolute and relative. He is the absolute principle insofar as his person is the original identity with the divine essence. It is the relative principle insofar as he freely has willed to communicate, making the "Others" as the basis of the relationship»; cfr. in addition to the context especially 21-31; 37-44. Some orthodox theologians speak of the Father in terms that at first sight seem similar; cfr. SPITERIS Y., «La dottrina trinitaria nella teologia ortodossa. Autori e prospettive» in AMATO A. (ed.), *Trinità in contesto*, Rome 1993, 45-69.

29 This option is problematic, as we have already suggested. Cfr. PANNENBERG W., *Teología Sistemática* I, Madrid 1992, 353, who asks himself concretely (ibid. note 204) whether Kasper has enough understanding of God as Father and whether this is conditioned from the very beginning by the relationship with the Son. In the lines that follow we will address the position of Pannenberg on this issue.

30 Cfr. KASPER W. *Der Gott Jesu Christi*, 195, also 192. God is freedom and absolute person.

ships of the three divine persons. For Kasper, when we perceive the vision of God as complete freedom, because the person is expressed in relationship rather than in substance, we need not operate with a conception that the person might remain only in what is substantial[31]. For him it is also clear that the person is relational and that in this we find the highest expression of its being. It does not in any way exclude the Father from this general appreciation.

With different levels of emphasis we therefore have an understanding that the Father is the beginning and origin of everything in the Trinity, in keeping with a conception that is derived from the oldest tradition of the Church. In some current interpretations of these classic affirmations we tend to see in the person of the Father something «previous» to the relationship or in reference to the Son and to the Holy Spirit. According to this thinking, the Father would not be pure relationship, although his person certainly has a relational dimension. Logically, but not temporally, his person would *be* before being the Father; therefore the relationship with the Son and the Spirit come afterward as an event. Is this thesis convincing? Before offering an answer to this question we must bear in mind other aspects of the contemporary theological panorama that will show an opposite viewpoint.

1.4.   THE DIVINE PROCESSIONS UNDER STUDY

In this current panorama we find a position that in fact seems radically opposed to the one that we have just presented. In this way, we can see how W. Pannenberg opposes the differentiation of the persons in God according to their relationships of origin. He believes that this modality of acting leads to subordinationist positions because it places, on the one hand, the Father as the beginning and source of the divinity, and on the other hand, it places the other two persons as being subordinated to the Father in their divinity and dependent on him. This would have been the road followed by the Greek Patristics as well as by Western theology beginning with Augustine who, with this psychological analogy, interprets the Son and the Spirit as expressions of self-consciousness and self-awareness of the Father[32]. On the other hand, the same authors state from the biblical point of view that the concept of «generation» does not show clearly the pertinence of Jesus to the world of God. Rather, it is related to the moment of the baptism

---

31 Cfr. KASPER W. *Der Gott Jesu Christi*, 195-196.
32 Cfr. PANNENBERG W., *Teología Sistemática* I; Madrid 1992, 328-329.

of Jesus where he begins his public life. Of more importance in this respect would be the passages that refer to the sending of the Son into the world by the Father[33]. Nevertheless, the terms of origin are not adequately accounted for in terms of the reciprocal nature of the relationships between the divine persons[34]. Pannenberg supports his view primarily with Athanasius who strongly insists, although evidently he is not the only one doing so, on the fact that without the Son, the Father is not the Father. The divinity of the Father would consequently be «conditioned» upon the Son[35]. We cannot speak of God the Father without God the Son or without God the Holy Spirit.

Indeed, this principle is solidly founded on the tradition. It has been established clearly after the Council of Nicaea when it reflected more explicitly on the eternality of the Son and his equality with the Father. The relationships in God are reciprocal, and consequently, if the Son cannot subsist without the Father, the latter cannot subsist without the Son and without the Holy Spirit. Nevertheless, is it necessary for this purpose to abandon completely the idea of the relationships of origin? Do not they point in any way to the same names of the Father and the Son that not only have undoubted roots in the New Testament but that go back to the use made of them by Jesus himself? Indeed, even these names have their origin in the historical-saving experience; they also have something to say about the immanent Trinity.

The three persons exist only in relationship, and this also applies to the Father. Pannenberg states that that this is not only so with respect to the personal identity of the «three», but also with respect to their divinity itself. The Father only possesses the Kingdom by means of the Son and the Spirit[36]. Pannenberg not

33 PANNENBERG W., *Teología Sistemática*, 332-333.
34 PANNENBERG W., *Teología Sistemática*, 346; the Father is only such in the relationship, ibid. 337.
35 PANNENBERG W., *Teología Sistemática*, 349; PANNENBERG W. quotes ATHANASIUS, *C. Arian.* I 20 (PG 26,55): «Because if the Son would not have existed before having been begotten, the truth is that he would have not always been in God. But this is an unfair statement. Because when the Father existed he was always with the Son, and the truth is that he is the Son and he is the one who says, "I am the truth" (John 14:6)». And he comments: «With this bold idea, Athanasius radically questioned the traditional understanding of the divinity of the Father, according to which this divinity is not subject to any condition, while that of the Son and of the Spirit are derived from it. No, the divinity of the Father is conditioned upon the Son; he is the one who shows the Father as the only true God (*c. Arian.* 3,9; cfr. 7). Athanasius also spoke about the Father as "source of wisdom", in other words the Son (1,9), but in such a way that without the Son who comes from that source he cannot be called the Father».
36 PANNENBERG W., *Teología Sistemática*, 351: «…without the Son, the Father does not possess his Kingdom: only by means of the Son and of the Spirit does he have his monarchy. And this applies not only with respect to the event of the revelation but, based on the relationship of Jesus with the Father, we must state that this is also the case as it relates to the internal life of the triune God».

only insists on the mutual «conditioning» of the persons in their identity and divinity themselves, but he also states that the full revelation (and realization?) of the divinity of the triune God will take place in the delivery of the kingdom to the Father by the Son in the consummation of the *historia salutis* (cfr. 1Cor 15:24-28). The problem of the unity of the Trinitarian God cannot be clarified, according to Pannenberg, if we are only taking into account the immanent Trinity before the creation, without bearing in mind the economy of salvation. Undoubtedly, the distinction between the economic Trinity and the immanent Trinity is necessary because God is the same in his eternal essence as in his revelation. In other words, we must think of him both as identical to the event of his revelation and as different from it. Nevertheless, neither can we think of the unity of the Trinitarian God by disregarding his revelation and the economic-saving action of God in the world that is summarized in this revelation:

> In view of the fact that the monarchy of the Father and his knowledge are conditioned by the Son, it is absolutely necessary to include the economy of the divine relationships with the world in the issue of the unity of the essence of God. In other words, the idea of the unity of God has not been clarified yet by just saying that the contents are the monarchy of the Father. If the monarchy of the Father is not realized directly as such, but through the Son and the Spirit, the essence of the unity of the Kingdom of God will also be in that mediation. Or even more so, is this mediation the one that precisely defines the contents of the essence of the monarchy of the Father?[37].

Undoubtedly, for Pannenberg, the triune God is perfect in himself even before creation. «Nevertheless, with the creation of a world the divinity of God and even his existence become dependent on the complete fulfillment of the destiny of that world in the presence of the Kingdom of God»[38]. As we can see, the difficult problem of the relationship between the economic Trinity and the immanent Trinity opens before us. However, apart from this complex set of prob-

---

[37] PANNENBERG W., *Teología Sistemática*, 354; cfr. also 358ff; Pannenberg rejects the idea of the action of God in history, but on page 359 he writes: «The eternal divinity of the Trinitarian God, as well as the truth of his revelation, still have ahead of them the need to give their validation in history»; on page 360, it is «the final consummation of history that decides regarding that truth». Regarding Pannenberg's conception of history, that determines to a great extent these ideas on the «validation» of the truth of God, cfr., among other writings, *La revelación como historia,* Salamanca 1977; «Der Gott der Geschichte. Der Trinitarische Gott und die Wahrheit der Geschichte» in *Grundfragen systematischer Theologie,* volume 2, Gottingen 1980, 112-128.

[38] PANNENBERG W., *Teología Sistemática* I, 424.

lems, we remain with a significant parallelism that Pannenberg emphasizes: the full realization of the sovereignty of the Father in the eschatological consummation goes through the delivery that the Son makes of his kingdom (the Son to whom elsewhere the Father has submitted all things). In the immanent Trinity, there is no room to speak about the divinity of the Father without that of the Son and that of the Holy Spirit that «conditions» it. These factors do not affect the «monarchy» of the Father. Rather, it is the only way in which this monarchy can be realized. Monarchy does not mean superiority of the Father and subordination of the Son and the Holy Spirit.

Within the field of Catholic theology, some of the statements made by Pannenberg have been echoed and supported. Without addressing the difficult problem of the relationships of the Trinity with history, G. Greshake considers that the classical doctrine of the processions is an obstacle to the consideration of the Trinity as communion and of the divine unity as unity in relationship and not as something «prior» to it; hence, the questioning of the traditional principle, taken from different magisterial statements, of the Father as beginning of the divinity[39]. The concept of the «processions» could have been necessary in a «unitary» horizon, but this would not be the case today. Because of this fact, Greshake is quite critical of the current that is strongly represented in Catholic theology, which bases the Trinitarian theology of the Father as the beginning and source of the divinity from which the Son and the Holy Spirit proceed[40]. There is no unilateral descending line in the Trinity because the Father receives from the Son the being of Father. None of the two exist without the Spirit who receives in himself a relationship with the Father and the Son and glorifies both[41]. In any case, Greshake is well aware of the uniqueness of the person of the Father, seeing him as the gift-source in his being (*Ur-Gabe*), which means that he is the foundation who offers the Trinitarian communion its harmony that maintains and sustains it as one. He insisted, however, that this does not mean that the Father is the beginning of a genetic process, but that this position of being the first person is only conceivable in relationship with the other two and never inde-

---

39 Cfr. GRESHAKE G., *Der dreieine Gott. Eine trinitarische Theologie*, Freiburg-Basel-Wein 1997, 190ff.
40 GRESHAKE G., *Der dreieine Gott*, 194, with preference to Kasper and Von Balthasar.
41 Cfr. GRESHAKE G., *Der dreieine Gott*, 186. Within this context, Greshake also talks about the «monarchy» of the Father that is no assumption, but the result of the perichoretic joint act of the persons; ibid. note 498.

pendently of them[42]. In fact, we could wonder whether the classical conception of the processions, insofar as it places itself in close relationship with the constituent relationships of the persons, has not also emphasized an interchangeable position of the persons in regard to the characteristics of the giving and receiving of each of them. The Father, as this relative name states, cannot be thought of without the Son (and without the Holy Spirit).

These positions of recent Western theologians, who tend to reduce the value of the intra-Trinitarian «processions» and thus to relativize the classical affirmation of the Father as the origin and source of the divinity have, to a certain degree, a precedent in the Russian orthodox theologian S. Bulgakov[43]. For him, it is a mistake to speak of processions in terms of «production». The issue of origin should not be addressed, because in the Trinity no one has origin; all the persons are equally eternal. On the other hand, speaking about a logical origin although not a chronological order is for Bulgakov a solution that is not convincing. Hence, the Father is not «cause». This concept does not exist in divine procession. Each person is self-determined and produces himself[44]. The names designate the concrete correlations between the *hypostases*. Fatherhood is not limited to generation. We must also bear in mind that the relationships are always Trinitarian. The relationship with the Son is not sufficient to define the Father, but we must also take into account the relationship with the Holy Spirit[45]. Hence, the Father is related to the Son as the one who begets him and related to the Holy Spirit as the one who breathes him. Bulgakov also reacts against the idea of «co-listing» the processions, the generation and the aspiration, because they do not have a common denominator of procession. Each procession is what it is. Only in this way can we see that everything is in relationship with the three, and with the two «processions» we see the division of a Trinitarian and unique act.

42 Cfr. Greshake G., *Der dreieine Gott*, 207-208. Facing this characterization of the Father as the original gift, what is inherent to the Son is «being like a recipient» («Dasein als Empfang»), in the recognition and the correspondence of the gift and in its subsequent transmission. The Holy Spirit is characterized on the one hand purely as the receiver and on the other as the union of the Father and the Son; ibid. 208, 210. Echoes of the theology of Richard of Saint Victor are discovered quite easily in this respect.

43 Cfr. Bulgakov S., *Il Paraclito*, Bologna 1987 (the original is from 1936), 272ff.

44 Cfr. Bulgakov S., *Il Paraclito*, 285-286.

45 Cfr. Bulgakov S., *Il Paraclito*, 291ff. For Bulgakov the problem of the processions and of the relationships means the supremacy of the nature over the *hypostasis*. Nevertheless, in the three-hypostatic being of God there is no neuter, the «it» is not present.

Nevertheless, even as he reacts against this issue of origin, the Russian theologian strongly insists on the supremacy of the Father and his special position, which is the ontological and logical center of the union formed by the three hypostatic centers of the Trinity, that is, the one who is revealed in the other's *hypostasis*. Because of this, the initial *hypostasis*[46], the fundamental one, is properly the subject, and the other two are the predicate and the copula, which identifies the predicate with the subject[47]. The Father hence has a fixed position; he is always the first one, while the positions of the second and the third *hypostases* could be reversible[48]. The *filioque*, about which Bulgakov is quite open, would somehow deprive the Father of this peculiar position of being the only one who is revealed, while the other two reveal him[49]. Those who are the second and third *hypostases* thus depend on what the Father is and on the other-co-revealing *hypostasis*[50]. Naturally, this is not the point in time to pass judgment or to give an opinion on all of Bulgakov's Trinitarian theology which is, by the way, quite complex. It will suffice for us to state the fact that we cannot understand the Father without the other two persons and, hence without the relativity that is inherent in him. The characteristic of the «initial *hypostasis*» of the Father is clearly evidenced, and despite the criticisms of certain ways of understanding the divine processions, the concepts of generation and expiration continue to be used.

1.5.   THE FATHER AS RELATIONAL BEGINNING

This brief review of the thinking of some important theologians of recent years shows us, simplified to a certain extent, these two countercurrents. One insists on the relevant position of the Father as the beginning of the Trinity, which leads in some cases to even consider him an «absolute» person, in other words, with a being that to a certain degree would be «prior» (logically, though not chronologically of course) to his relationships with the other persons. The other one, which out of fear of the danger of subordinationism that can be coupled to the idea of the processions and the relationships of origin, believes that we must abandon these categories in order to be able to reach a concept of the unity of God which is based on the perfect communion of the three persons. Nevertheless, even in this

---

46 Cfr. BULGAKOV S., *Il Paraclito*, 139; 136ff against the idea of the «causality».
47 Cfr. BULGAKOV S., *Il Paraclito*, 284; 356.
48 Cfr. BULGAKOV S., *Il Paraclito*, 162-163.
49 Cfr. BULGAKOV S., *Il Paraclito*, 285ff.
50 Cfr. BULGAKOV S., *Il Paraclito*, 303ff.

case, we do not rule out that the original love and gift are inherent in the Father, and the Son and the Holy Spirit correspond to the gift, each one in his own way.

Undoubtedly we must avoid making the Father an absolute person when considering him independently from the Son and the Holy Spirit. It is the same name of «Father» which prevents us from considering him without any intrinsic relationship to the Son and the Holy Spirit. Without them, the Father simply is not. The fruitful concept of the persons as a subsistent relationship comes once again to our aid. Let us remember that for Saint Thomas it is the relationship more than the procession that makes the person. At the same time, however, the principle according to which the Father is the origin and source of the Trinity is so strongly anchored in the tradition that it does not seem possible to do without it. The reciprocity of the relationships makes it possible to avoid any subordinationism without relinquishing the traditional doctrine of the processions, or if we prefer not to use this generic concept, of the generation and the expiration. The Father is simply the Father; he is not greater than the Son insofar as he begets the Son (and is the beginning of the Holy Spirit). Only the Father is the source even though it is true that without the Son and the Holy Spirit who proceed from this source the Father cannot receive this name. We must affirm at the same time two things: the Father is the only source and beginning of the divinity, and at the same he does not exist, nor can he exist, without the Son and the Holy Spirit. In this respect, he is given over to them just as the Son and the Holy Spirit are given over to him. The Eleventh Council of Toledo in 675, stated as follows: «What the Father is, he is not with respect to himself, but with respect to the Son. Likewise, what the Son is, is not with respect to himself but with respect to the Father. Similarly, also the Holy Spirit does not refer to himself but in relationship with the Father and the Son when he is called the Spirit of the Father and of the Son»[51].

The first person of the Trinity, being the only source and beginning of the divinity, is such insofar as he relates to the Son and the Holy Spirit, insofar as he is with them in relationship. In other words, the Father *is* only insofar as he is the original giving of himself. The primary source of the divinity is pure complete giving to the Son and the Spirit. I believe that even with all the difficulties that

---

51 «Quod enim Pater est, non ad se, sed ad Filium est; et quod Filius est, non ad se, sed ad Patrem est; similiter est Spiritus Sanctus non ad se, sed ad Patrem et Filium relative refertur, in eo quod Spiritus Patris et Filii praedicatur…» (DS 528). And also: «…quia nec Pater sine Filio, nec Filius aliquando existit sine Patre. Et tamen non sicut Filius de Patre ita Pater de Filio, quia non Pater a Filio, sed Filius a Patre generationem accepit…» (DS 526).

are undoubtedly faced by our intellect, we must maintain these two contrasts: everything comes from the Father, but at the same time he is not more insofar as he is the beginning of the Son and the Spirit. Based on the saving economy that enables us to know the Father precisely insofar as he gives us the Son, we can, and even must, always with fear and trembling, attempt to look at the Trinity within itself. The fontal love of the Father is that which delivers everything to the Son[52]. And if in the economy it is love that moves it all, so also in the intra-Trinitarian scope this love must find its correspondence and foundation. The Father is not a closed person; he is from eternity the one who, by delivering himself, gives being to the Son and to the Holy Spirit. Love, which has its source in the Father, is the internal beginning of the life of the Trinity; it is love that makes the Father send the Son, whom he had already loved previously (John 17:24). Everything occurs in the Trinitarian life through the radical free nature of love that the persons exchange (which does not include «necessity» in the intimate life of God). This love is reflected in the free nature of the creation and redemption, because neither the creature nor the sinner has any right whatsoever to creation or redemption[53]. The possibility of the incarnation of the Son, of making himself mutable «in the other one»[54], so that humans can finally be children of God (cfr. Gal 4:4-6), is founded in the intra-Trinitarian genesis, in the love of the Father who, when begetting the Son, does not retain for himself alone the being of God. The delivery of the Son to the world out of love is therefore founded in this intra-Trinitarian self-giving. If the Son reveals the love of the Father, it would not be wrong to assume that he also shows in his self-giving for us, the infinite capacity of the self-giving of the Father[55]. The self-giving of the Son is founded in the abyss of love of the Father which is an infinite capacity of giving of love, substantial love for which he needs the begotten loved one in self-giving, and for expressing the full gratitude he also needs the «third one», the fruit and testimony of the unity of love that begets and thanks[56].

Chapter 10

363

---

52 Cfr. PANNENBERG W., *Teología Sistemática*, 339; despite the reservations on the idea of the procession, the initiative of the Father is evident.

53 Cfr. VON BALTHASAR H.U., *Theologik II. Wahrheit Gottes*, 128; cfr. the continuation on 130; this love is not blind, but rather «wiser» than we might think.

54 Cfr. RAHNER K., *Grundkurs des Glaubens*, 217-219.

55 Commissio Theologica Internationalis, «Theologia-Christologia-Anthropologia» in *Greg* 64 (1983) 5-24, esp. 23, there is an intimate correspondence between the gift of the divinity of the Father to the Son and the gift of the Son to the abandonment of the cross. Cfr. VON BALTHASAR H.U., *Theologik II*, 259; *Theodramatik IV. Das Endspiel*, Einsiedeln 1982, 106-107.

56 VON BALTHASAR H.U., *Theologik III. Der Geist der Wahrheit*, 404: «The divine Father is more than "benevolence", "fidelity", "mercy". In other words he is substantial love for himself (and not only

The Father is the source of divinity insofar as he is fontal love, referred in every way to the Son and to the Holy Spirit. There is no «absolute» being of the Father previous to this fontal Fatherhood. In like manner, his person is the relationship that necessarily implies the reciprocity of the other two persons. Nevertheless, at the same time it seems that we can say that the Son and the Holy Spirit receive their being from him. The Father is precisely so insofar as he gives everything, insofar as he gives to the Son all his substance and not just part of it (cfr. Fourth Lateran Council, DS 805), and evidently also, insofar as he is the genesis of the Holy Spirit. In Christ, the Father is manifested as just, good, rich in mercy, in the words and acts of Jesus that are, together and inseparably, the total revelation of the Father (cfr. DV 2,4). The generation of the Son and the procession of the Holy Spirit do not imply by their own nature any subordination:

> A beginning cannot be perfect if it is not the beginning of a reality that is equal to it. The Greek Fathers gladly spoke about the «Father-cause», but this is simply a term that is an analogical term, the deficiency of which enables us to measure the purifying use of the apophatism: in our experiences, the cause is greater than the effect. On the contrary, in God, the cause, as a fulfillment of the personal love, cannot yield lesser effects. He loves them equally in dignity; the same cause is the cause of their likeness… The Father would not be in a true sense a person if he were not *pros*, towards, entirely turned to other persons, fully communicated to them, to those whom he makes persons and hence equals, by the integrity of his love[57].

I believe that this passage summarizes superbly what we evidenced in our brief analysis of the history of the theology of the first centuries, primarily that which developed after Nicaea.

The Christian faith and Christology have reached the conviction that the Father, in the heart of the Trinity, is the beginning without beginning and the original love emerging from the mission of Jesus to the world. God, known now

when faced with a creature), for which he needs the begotten loved one in the self-giving and for the demonstration of the perfect *desprendimiento* of the unity of the two; he will also need the "third one", the fruit and the testimony of the unity of the love that begets and thanks». Cfr. also ibid. 406; ibid. 145: «The eternal gift has to be understood as an act of incomprehensible love, that the Son receives as such, and that is not passively as the Beloved, but because he as the Beloved of the Father, receives his *substantia*, he is at the some time lover with the Father, loves in correspondence with response to the whole love of the Father, prepared for all the love». The Father can only be in the eternal correspondence of the Son and of the Holy Spirit.

57 LOSSKY V., quoted by BOBRINSKOY B., *Le mystère de la Trinité*, Paris 1986, 268-269.

as the Father of Jesus, is he, who by means of his Son, has created the world. By virtue of his Fatherhood he can be creator. The Father is ultimately the one to whom the Son will hand over the Kingdom at the end of the ages (cfr. 1Cor 15:24-28). «Everything there is comes from him and is caused by him. To him be the glory forever» (Rom 11:36)![58]

2

The Son: the perfect response to the love of the Father

The giving over of the Son to the Father is as total as that of the Father to the Son. Even more so, from our point of view, this giving over is even more evident because in our categories derived from human experience, the existence of him who is Father does not depend on that of his Son, although the opposite applies. We already know that this is not the way that things are in God, but it is clear that it is easier for us to see the Son as made by his relationship with the Father (and with the Spirit) rather than the other way around. In him there can be no being prior to his being made the Son. If the God of the Old Testament is known as the Father of Jesus in the life, death, and resurrection of the latter, Jesus himself, in his revelation of the Father, is shown to us as the Son, in a unique relationship with God which is not shared with any one. According to the New Testament, he is the «only Son». Among the different Christological titles, that of Son of God already holds an especially relevant place in the Old Testament, and following on the Old Testament understanding, it has had a privileged place in the tradition. This has been the case because from the very beginning it has been possible to have the intuition that the unrepeatable relationship with God the Father that the term «Son» expresses, reveals to us in the most profound way the being of Jesus. The other titles receive their definitive explanation in light of this first one. According to the subsequent reflection, if the Father is the subsistent source of

---

[58] In order to complete this statement, I add the references of some of the main teaching declarations about God the Father (the numbers refer to DS): he is the «beginning without beginning», everything he has he has it from himself: 1331; he comes from no other: 75; 441; 485; 490; 525; 527; 589; 800; 1330. The Father is the one who begets, the beginning and the source of all divinity: 284; 525; 568; 3326. The Father begets the Son from his substance: 470; 485; 525-526; 571; 617; 805; 1330; without any decrease in himself he gives everything to the Son, 805. The Father as creator: 27-30; 36; 40-51; 60; 125; 150. Everything comes from him; 60; 421; 680; 3326. Cfr. DS, page 861; RAHNER K., *El Dios trino como principio y fundamento trascendente…*, 399-401.

Fatherhood, the Son is the subsistent recipient of Sonship, the opposite relationship to the paternity that makes up the person of the Father. We must not forget either that his relationships with respect to the Holy Spirit are in the same way those which make up the persons of the Father and the Son, although these appear less at the forefront in view of the fact that, as was already pointed out by Saint Augustine, these relationships do not appear in the name «Holy Spirit».

2.1. THE SON, THE BELOVED OF THE FATHER WHO CORRESPONDS TO THIS LOVE

Jesus the Son is above all the first object of the love of the Father. The proclamations of Jesus as Son and as Beloved go together in the New Testament on various occasions. The voice coming from heaven at the baptism of Jesus is especially significant in this respect, «You are my Son the beloved; my favour rests on you» (Mark 1:11; cfr. Matt 3:17; Luke 3:24); and also the voice coming from the cloud during the transfiguration, «This is my Son, the beloved. Listen to him» (Mark 9:7; cfr. Matt 17:5; Luke 9:35, and other variants). In the synoptic readings we see again the idea in the parable of the killer tenants of the vineyard: «He still had someone left: his beloved son…» (Mark 12:6; cfr. Luke 20:13). According to Col 1:13, Jesus who delivered us from sin, is «the Son that he loves». In the fourth gospel, the idea of the love of God the Father for the Son appears very frequently: cfr. John 3:35;5:20;15:9;17:23-24.26, a love which is reciprocated by Jesus because he, in turn, loves the Father (John 14:31). There is no reason why we should assume that this love is limited to the saving economy. At least, in the high priestly prayer, mention is made of the love of the Father for the Son before the foundation of the world (John 17:24).

The love of the Father for the Son has been spoken of in the tradition. Origen connected this love with the eternal procession of the Son[59]. We have already referred to love as the beginning of the generation of the Son in the case of Hilary. For Augustine, the Son is the beloved, together with the Father who is the lover and the Holy Spirit who is love himself[60]. For Richard of St. Victor also, the Son is the first object of the love of the Father, the *summe dilectus*, this being a love to which the Son responds[61].

59 Cfr. for instance, *In Joh* XXXII 10,121 (SCh 385,240), the Son of the Fatherly goodness and of his love. Cfr. ORBE A., *Hacia la primera teología de la procesión del Verbo*, Rome 1958, 398ff.
60 *Trin.* VIII 10,14 (CCL 50,290f); the reciprocation of love by the Son is expressed in VI 5,7 (236): «unus diligens eum qui de illo est et unus dilligens unus de quo est et ipsa dilectio».
61 RICHARD OF SAINT VICTOR, *Trin.* III 7 (SCh 63,180ff).

The Father gives to the Son everything he is, everything he has out of love[62], his divine being. It is worth noting that if, in the Father, the divine being is manifested in giving and delivery, in the Son it is both acceptance and reciprocation. Fatherhood and Sonship appear in their mutual intimate involvement. There is not one without the other, although the primacy of the original love originates in the Father. The Son is the perfect reflection of the Father's being and his love with which he gives himself to the Son and is the source of reason and wisdom, the sense of every sense[63].

The reciprocation of the Son to the love of the Father is manifested in the economy of salvation in his full compliance with the Father's will (cfr. Heb 10:7-9), in the obedience of Jesus to death and even death on a cross, which means the ultimate degree of emptying himself (cfr. Phil 2:6-8). When responding in his life to the Fatherly love and manifesting this love that the Father has for us, Jesus also reveals the love of the Father in him. Based on the information of the New Testament, some current theologians attempt in several ways to search deeply into the intra-Trinitarian mystery of the love of the Father and the Son. It is worth pausing for a moment to analyze some of these attempts.

H. U. von Balthasar, beginning with the correspondence that in a way must be evidenced between the economy and the theology, even reaches the point of speaking about an original *kenosis* of the divine persons in their mutual self-giving. In this way, by the mere fact of the generation of the Son, we would see in the Father a kind of emptying of himself, of a fundamental *kenosis* which would correspond to the total eternal self-giving of the Son. In turn, the Father's self-emptying would find its expression and manifestation in the historical-saving *kenosis* of Jesus the incarnated Son.[64] «The governing principle between Jesus

---

[62] And he even reaches the point of giving everything in order to give everything with the Son (procession of the Holy Spirit from the Father and the Son in the Western vision); cfr. Von Balthasar H.U., *Theologik II, Wahrheit Gottes,* 150-151.

[63] Von Balthasar H.U., *Theologik II,* 130: «About this abyss of love that is the foundation for everything, we must say at the time that it is everything but blind; even more so, it is the widest and hence it is the ultimate sense of every knowledge and every reason…».

[64] Von Balthasar H.U., *Theodramatik IV. Das Endspiel* 106-107: «It must be said that this "*kenosis* of obedience"… is founded in the *kenosis* of the eternal persons, the ones with respect to the others, as an aspect among the infinite real aspects of the eternal life. Cfr. also *Teodramática IV. La acción,* Madrid 1995, 300-304; *Teodramática II. Las Personas del drama,* 272, etc. On this aspect of this thought of von Balthasar, Gilbert P., «Kénose et Ontologie» in Olivetti M.M. (ed.), *Philosophie de la religion entre éthique et ontologie,* Padova 1996, 189-200, especially 190-195; Werbick J., «Gottes Dreieinigkeit denken? H. U. von Balthasars Rede von den göttlichen Selbstentäusserung als Mitte des Glaubens und Zentrum der Theologie» in *ThQ* 147 (1996) 225-240; Holzer V., *Le Dieu Trinité dans l'histoire. Le différend théologique Balthasar-Rahner,* Paris 1995,

and the Father in the mediation of his mission is the economic form of the eternal covenant between the Father and the Son…»[65]. The initiation of this covenant clearly has its genesis with the Father, but this implies the acceptance by the other persons, the total mutual agreement of divine love. In Jesus, there is a perfect identification between his spontaneity in the fulfillment of his mission and his full obedience with which this is carried out. This identification clearly shows the perfect co-divinity of the Son with the Father[66]. The self-giving of the Son shows the self-giving of the Father, who has surrendered everything that he is. Therefore there is a perfect correspondence between the Father and the Son, and for this reason the Son is the perfect image of the Father[67], but the Son, who in his obedience performs the works of the Father (cfr. John 10:37;14:9-10), also performs his own works, which are the reflection of the fontal love expressed in the obedience performed in his own flesh.

368

Pannenberg, on the other hand, refers to the Son's distinguishing himself over against the Father. Unlike the first man, Adam, who, wanting to be equal with God, separated himself from him, Jesus, who glorifies the Father as God and does not eagerly grasp for equality with God, is united with him (cfr. Phil 2:6)[68]. This self-distinction also serves as a component of the eternal Son in his relationship with the Father[69], which will reach its final consequence in the death of the Lord on the cross, which, by accepting it, Jesus confirms himself as the Son. The Father, who loves the Son, is affected by this death by virtue of his «com-passion»[70]. Pannenberg draws the conclusion that the Son's submission to the divinity of

---

238ff; MARTINELLI P., *Il mistero della morte in H. U. von Balthasar*, Milano 1996, 342-351; MARCHESI G., *La cristologia trinitaria di H. U. von Balthasar*, Brescia 1997, 516-535. As he himself states, von Balthasar takes the idea from BULGAKOV S., *Le Verbe Incarné*, Paris 1943; cfr. *Teodramática* IV, 253; 289ff; 300. On Bulgakov, cfr. CODA P., *L'altro di Dio. Rivelazione e kenosi in Sergej Bulgakov*, Rome 1998. Evdokimov has also set forth similar ideas.

65   VON BALTHASAR H.U., *Teodramática* III, 468.

66   VON BALTHASAR H.U., *Teodramática* III, 474-475.

67   VON BALTHASAR H.U., *Teodramática* III, 476: «The meaning of this fatherhood from eternity can be seen in the mission of the Son, which has the main task of revealing the Son of the Father that goes to the end… This fatherhood can only be the surrendering of everything that the Father is… As God, the Son must be equal to the Father, despite coming from the Father, and because the Father has expressed all his love in the Son without any reservation, the Son is the perfect image of the Father».

68   Cfr. on this topic in LADARIA L.F., «Adán y Cristo en la «Teología Sistemática» de W. Pannenberg» in RET 57 (1997) 287-307.

69   Cfr. PANNENBERG W., *Teología Sistemática* I, 336-337; 348: «only in the case of the Son does this self-distinction have the sense that the other person, from whom he differentiates himself —in other words, the Father— is for him the only God, basing his own divinity precisely in his submission to the divinity of the Father».

70   PANNENBERG W., *Teología Sistemática* I, 340-341.

the Father is already a component of the intra-Trinitarian divine being of the Son expressed in the historical-saving attitude of Christ, who in his obedience shows the opposite attitude from Adam, who pretended to be like God (cfr. Gen 3:5; Phil 2:6ff).

J. Moltmann also sees the Son's eternal obedience to the Father manifested and realized in the cross. The sacrifice of limitless love is already included in the exchange of love which constitutes the divine life of the Trinity. The fact that Jesus dies and surrenders himself on the cross is in relationship with the eternal obedience in which he delivers himself entirely to the Father[71]. From eternity, the love of the Father, which gives light to the Son, is the love that gives and begets. The love of the Son is his response to the Father who gives it all[72].

These and similar considerations do not lack legitimacy in principle. Nevertheless, it seems necessary to analyze them. On the one hand, it is clear that we have seen in the life of the immanent Trinity and in the exchange of love between the persons, the condition of possibility of the projection of the love of God *ad extra* in the saving economy. However, it does not appear with such clarity that we must interpret everything that has happened in the life of Jesus as a temporal reflection of an eternal «drama». It might seem difficult to take the correspondence between the economic Trinity and the immanent Trinity to this extreme. As we have pointed out, the immanent Trinity is not exhausted in the saving economy nor is it completed or taken to perfection by it[73]. What is realized in

---

71 MOLTMANN J., *Trinität und Reich Gottes*, 184: «On the other hand, the *sacrifice of love without any frontiers* of the Son at Golgotha is from eternity included in the exchange of essential love, which is the divine life of the Trinity. The fact that the Son dies in the cross and in this way delivers himself is included in his eternal obedience by means of which he delivers to the Father in all his being, through his Spirit which the Father receives. The creation is safe and justified eternally in the sacrifice of the Son which is the foundation that supports it».

72 MOLTMANN J., *Trinität und Reich Gottes*, 184: «The Father loves the Son with fatherly love that produces. The Son loves the Father with the love that responds, that surrenders». Cfr. also GRESHAKE G., *Der dreieine Gott*, 208.

73 Cfr. among others, the observations made to the thesis of von Balthasar, VORGRIMLER H., *Doctrina teológica de Dios*, Barcelona 1987, 193-194; SCHEFFCZYK L., *Der Gott der Offenbarung. Gotteslehre*, Aachen 1996, 409-410; HOLZER V., *La Trinité divine…*, (cfr. note 64), 238; 257; GRESHAKE G., *Der dreieine Gott*, Freiburg-Basel-Wien 1997, 280-281, that enable us to see at the time how in other instances of his work the same von Balthazar relativizes his thesis. I believe that it is better, as is the case in the New Testament, to reserve this terminology of *kenosis* to the Son's emptying of himself in the incarnation, without intending to project it in an original Trinitarian event to which we have no direct access to guarantee the perfect correspondence with the economy. Here we would also have to apply what we said regarding the second part of the «fundamental axiom» of K. Rahner (cfr. c 2). Other analogical uses of the term *kenosis* referred, for instance, to a certain hiding of God in the creation or to the «anonymity» of the Spirit who acts in the Church without making himself visible, which offer more similarities with the historical-saving *kenosis* of the Son to which the New Testament expressly refers.

the economy of salvation is certainly based on the internal life of God, although it is the fruit of divine sovereign freedom. Both extremes must be maintained. Certainly «between the Son in the eternal life of God and the Son in the earthly history of Jesus there is an intimate correspondence. Even more so, there is a real identity that is nourished by the unity and the communion of Jesus as Son with God the Father»[74]. Even more so, «in the internal life of God we see present the condition of the possibility of those events which, because of the incomprehensible freedom of God, we will find in the history of the salvation of the Lord Jesus Christ»[75]. The love of Jesus evidenced in the surrendering of himself to death in obedience to the Father must be the reflection of the love of the Father himself who finds the response in the Son. Without it being necessary to speak of *kenosis* or dispossession, we can think of the love of the Father for the Son as a total self-giving, even though we cannot know the modalities of this giving. This consequence is legitimate in view of the fact that he who sees Jesus who surrenders himself to the end, sees the Father (cfr. John 14:9). The obedience of Jesus to death and even the death on the cross is also in this sense a clear evidence of his perfect acceptance of the love of the Father, of his being in total gratitude and correspondence.

2.2. THE SON AS LOGOS AND IMAGE OF GOD

The Son, the first object of the love of the Father, is as such, the one who reveals him. The tradition, clearly based on the New Testament, has spoken of the Son as Logos and image of the Father. The understanding of the revelation underlies the two titles. Undoubtedly there is a close relationship between them. If the first one primarily refers to the aspect of hearing (cfr. also Mark 9:7), it is the vision that appears more directly emphasized in the second.

As we know, the image of the Word comes from the prologue of the gospel of John (cfr. John 1:1.14; 1John1:1; Rev 19:13). The ideas contained in the Old Testament regarding the word and the wisdom of God, which are known to us, are undoubtedly the basis of the use of this concept in the gospel, even though the

74 Commissio Theologica Internationalis, «Theologia-Christologia-Anthropologia» in *Greg* 64 (1983) 19.
75 Commissio Theologica Internationalis, «Theologia-Christologia-Anthropologia» in *Greg* 64 (1983) 11; the text continues saying: «Therefore, the major events in the life of Jesus express for us openly the new colloquium of the eternal generation where the Father tells the Son: "You are my Son. Today I have Fathered" (Ps 2:7; cfr. Acts 13:33; Heb 1:5; 5:5; Luke 3:22)». Also ibid. page 23: «the gift of the divinity of the Father to the Son has a close correspondence with the gift of the Son to the abandonment of the cross».

religious philosophy inspired by Philo may also have had an impact in the same sources in the Old Testament[76]. The concept of the Logos is also known in Hellenistic philosophy. Nevertheless, there is naturally a radical innovation in the concept of John: the completely personal Logos, who is the incarnate Son of God. Kasper points out that even with this fundamental difference in the content of this Logos, there is certain formal affinity between the philosophical concept and the concept of the New Testament regarding the Logos. The Logos reveals to us the meaning of the world, the revelation of being in both thought and word[77].

We will not repeat everything that has been said in our brief analysis of the history of Trinitarian theology. The idea of the Logos helped even the Apologists to shed light on the generation of the Son by the Father by means of an analogy inspired in the human mind and not in human generation. Augustine has made the relationships between the inner and the outer word of the human being the main subject of his *De Trinitate,* primarily in his last book[78]. The outer word is the sign of the one who shines within, as though the word was born in us when we speak about what we know. There is a word that is before the sound. This scheme can be applied to God:

> And, in this way, the word of God the Father is the only begotten Son, in everything equal to the Father, God of God, light of light, wisdom of wisdom, essence of the essence… When uttering, the Father begot, while at the same time as he expressed himself, his word was in every way like him himself[79].

For Thomas, who follows Augustine[80], «Word» is also a relational term, as is the case of Son. It is relative to the one to whom the Word belongs. For this reason, it can be the personal name of Son, because it is not an essential name[81]. The «generation» in God, which takes place by means of his intellectual life (cfr. previous comments on the processions[82]), is inside of God because in him being and self-consciousness will coincide. This is his word, in every way equal to him

---

76 Cfr. SCHNACKENBURG R., *El evangelio según san Juan* I, Barcelona 1980, 306-308.
77 Cfr. KASPER W., *Der Gott Jesu Christi*, 230ff.
78 Cfr. AUGUSTINE, *Trin.* XV 10-14 (CCL 50, 483-497).
79 Ibid. AUGUSTINE, *Trin.* XV 14,23 (496).
80 Cfr. AUGUSTINE, *Trin.* VII 2,3 (250).
81 Cfr. THOMAS AQUINAS, *STh* I 34,1. According to ibid. 34:2, the birth of the Son is expressed with different names because none of them can exhaust his perfection.
82 Cfr. THOMAS AQUINAS, *STh* I 27,1.

and thus of his same substance, contrary to what the Arians stated. The intellectual procession is called generation, and hence the name of Word is inherent to the Son and only to him[83]. It is the same substance because everything that exists in the nature of God subsists, «quidquid est in natura Dei, subsistit»[84]. For Thomas, the Word does not only mean something in respect to God, but also in respect to creation. In his substantial Word, in which he knows himself, he knows God and at the same time all things. In him created beings are made and known[85].

Together with the theology of the Logos, Thomas developed the tradition of the image. The New Testament, as we know, speaks to us about Jesus revealing the Father. As such, this is the «image of the unseen God» (Col 1:15; cfr. 2Cor 4:4). He is «the reflection of God's glory and bears the impress of God's own being» (Heb 1:3; cfr. 2Cor 4:6). This idea was developed under different modalities in

the Patristic age. Irenaeus coined the famous formulation *visibile Patris Filius*[86]. For Clement of Alexandria, the Son is the face, πρόσωπον, of the Father[87]. Tertullian seemed to consider him his «*facies*»[88]. These different names do not differ among themselves[89]. Nevertheless, if in the earliest times the incarnate Son was considered to be the image of God, in evident relationship with the revealing function of the Father which Jesus carries out, the trend of considering that this image refers to the eternal Father will soon prevail because he is equal to the Father in his divine dignity. The anti-Arian struggle is responsible partly though not fully for this change[90]. Augustine saw the relationship between Father, Logos, and image in the fact that they are all in relation with respect to the Father[91]. It is the consideration of the immanent Trinity which is the one that prevails. Also in the case of Saint Thomas, the condition of the image refers to the pre-exist-

---

83 Cfr. THOMAS AQUINAS, *STh* I 27,2; I 34,2.
84 Cfr. THOMAS AQUINAS, *STh* I 34,2.
85 Cfr. THOMAS AQUINAS, *STh* I 34,3; *De Ver*, q.4 a 5.
86 IRENAEUS OF LYONS, *Adv. Haer.* IV 6,6 (SCh 100,450): «invisibile etenim Filii Pater, visibile autem Patris Filius»; ibid. 6,7 (452-453): «Agnitio enim Patris Filius, agnitio autem Filii in Patre et per Filium revelata».
87 CLEMENT OF ALEXANDRIA, *Ped.* I 57,2 (FP 5,192-193): «The face of God is the Logos, by means of which he is made visible and known»; Cfr. also *Strom.* V 34,1 (SCh 278,80); VII 58,3 (GCS 17,42); *Exc. Theod.* 10,5 ; 12,1; 23,5 (SCh 23,80;82;108).
88 Cfr. TERTULLIAN, *Adv. Prax.* XIV 10 (Scarpat, 182); cfr. the whole set ibid. XIV-XV 1ff (178-186).
89 HILARY OF POITIERS, *Tr. Ps.* 68,25 (CSEL 22,335); «forma et vultus et facies et imago non differunt».
90 Cfr. CANTALAMESSA R., «"Cristo imagine di Dio". Le tradizioni patristiche su Col 1,15» in *Rivista di Storia e Letteratura Religiosa* 16 (1980) 181-212; 345-380. SIMONETTI M., «Esegesi ilariana di Col 1,15» in *Vetera Christianorum* 2 (1961) 165-182.
91 Cfr. AUGUSTINE, *Trin.* V 13,14 (CCL 50,220f); VI 2,3 (230f); VII 1,1-2 (245); 2,3 (249f).

ing Son, and this image is exclusively that of the Son by virtue of being related to his intellectual generation as Word[92].

All these considerations are only possible because Jesus has manifested himself to the world as the revelation of the Father. Without ceasing to be God, the Son can leave his state and become a creature[93]. In fact, from the incarnation we can deduce that the Son is the beginning through whom God acts *ad extra*. From this is derived the only saving mediation of Jesus (1Tim 2:5). The possibility of creation is based on the possibility of the incarnation, the ultimate «externalization» of God[94], and creation is fulfilled with the mediation of the Son (cfr. John 1:3-4, 10; 1Cor 8:6; Col 1:15-16; Heb 1:2). From the beginning, the concrete order in which we exist points to Christ (cfr. Col 1:16-17). This is what leads to the preposition «through» (*dià, per*) which was applied to the Son by the Second Council of Constantinople, following a long tradition. Regarding the incarnate Son, «God is with us» (Matt 1:23), made like us and sharing our condition, Jesus is the only mediator between God and humanity. Only in light of the actual life of Jesus can we speak of him as word and image of the Father, and only in light of his actual existence do these two titles received their full meaning.

The life of Jesus is one of reciprocity, fully available, thankful for everything that the Father has given him. Jesus does not seek glory itself, but honors the Father and lets his Father glorify him (John 8:49-50;8:54;17:1-5). In short, Jesus has not proclaimed his own kingdom but that of the Father. Similarly, at the end of times, he will hand over the Kingdom to the Father and will be fully subjected to him (cfr. 1Cor 15:24-28), which does not mean, as we know, that he to ceases to reign (Niceno-Constantinopolitan Creed). If the Father is God insofar as he gives, the Son is God insofar as he both receives and gives. The Son is the beloved who as such is also lover. In this reference to the Father who has given over everything, we understand that this self-giving to humanity is given in the freedom and spontaneity of obedience. In his relationship with the Father, Jesus is the Father's perfect image and can reveal his love to us in his life and death. Nicaea has spoken to us about the Son, telling us that he is *homoousios* with the Father. In this way the truth of our salvation, our true relationship with God in his Son is

---

92 Thomas Aquinas, *STh* I 35,2: «… sicut Spiritus Sanctus, quamvis sua processione accipiat naturam Patris, sicut et Filius, non tamen dicitur natus… Quia Filius procedit ut Verbum, de cuius ratione est similitudo speciei ad id de quo procedit».

93 As we already saw in chapter 2, there is no reason why we should consider the possibility that another person was incarnated.

94 Cfr. Rahner K., *Grundkurs des Glaubens*, Freiburg-Basel-Wien 1976, 213-225.

guaranteed as God gives us his Son for us to know and unites us with him. However, the *homoousios* not only tells us who Jesus the Son is, but also ultimately who God the Father is, who can communicate fully to the Son and can send him to share the human condition. Hence, in this way he can be in a close and intimate relationship with his creatures.

Nevertheless, Jesus is not only consubstantial with the Father, but also, although in a different way[95], with us (symbol of the union, DS 272, Council of Chalcedon, DS 301). This double consubstantiality must be seen in its profound unity, because the Father has given himself fully to the Son, and consequently the Son is consubstantial with the Father, and the Son in full obedience and answerability to the Father, can make himself in every way like us, except in sin, to give himself over to his end for us his brothers and sisters. In the perfection of this self-giving, God is not only human like us, as has been stated in the ancient councils and we have repeated, but also as has been set forth in the Second Vatican Council, he is the «perfect man» (GS 22;41), the one in whom the plan of God is fulfilled until his end as a human being; in following him we all become more human. In the unity of his divine-human nature, Jesus, because he fully loves God (and because he is pure response with his love to the Father in the Spirit) in an insuperable way, can deliver himself for humanity in order to make us share in the foundational love with which the Father has loved him (cfr. John 15:9; Gal 2:20; Rom 8:35, among other places)[96].

---

[95] His consubstantiality with human beings evidently cannot be quantitative. Jesus is only one God with the Father, but he is also only one man with us, even though he is intimately united with each one of us (cfr. GS 22).

[96] In order to complete the information, we add the reference to some key declarations of the teachings on the Son (the numbers refer to DS). It is *principium de principio*, 1331, *genitos sive natus* of the Father: 75, 125, 150, 1330, etc. It is of the nature of the Father, 76, 125, 126, 900, everything he has is from the Father 1331, the Father has give him everything except being the Father, 900, 1331, 1986, 3675. He is not part of the Father, 526, 805, he is not an extension of the Father 160. He is the only-begotten, 4f, 12-30, 125, 150, 178, 258, 357, 538, 900, 3350, 3352. He has not been created *ex nihilo*, 75, 125, 126, 150. Begotten without beginning, eternally, 1331, 357, 470, *ab aeterno* 75, 126, 150, 50, 526, 538, 547, 554, etc.

3
The Holy Spirit, communion of love

The difficulties that we face in our reflections about the Holy Spirit are evident. We could begin with what is already told to us in Acts 19:2; «No, we were never even told there was such a thing as a Holy Spirit…». In all our previous statements we have repeatedly seen how Trinitarian theology has revolved very frequently around the Father-Son relationship. The «personal» nature of both is even clearer than the nature of the Spirit, and his reciprocal relationships appear under the same names. However, we have also been able to see that the way of being a person in God is different in this case, due to the fact that in the Holy Trinity nothing is simply «repeatable». The use itself of the expression «three persons» already had caused problems for Saint Augustine[97]. However, in Chapter 3 of this treatise we have seen how the Holy Spirit, in his peculiar characteristics, appears in the New Testament as a subject, as a center of activity. Of course this fact does not eradicate the greater difficulty that has always revolved around the discourse related to the Holy Spirit[98].

[97] Cfr. the qualified observations of THOMAS AQUINAS, STh I 30,4, in God we cannot speak about gender and species; also I 30,3, in God the numbers do not indicate anything positive; they are only there to eliminate false conceptions. We have already referred to the problem posed by the application of «numbers» to God. Applying concretely this issue to the Holy Spirit, MOLTMANN J., *Trinität und Reich Gottes*, München 1980, 205, points out that the Holy Spirit is not a person in a univocal sense with respect to the Son, and both are not persons as is the Father. In God, there are no general concepts; everything is unrepeatable. In a similar way, PANNENBERG W., *Teología Sistemática* I, Madrid 348, the «self-distinction» (we have already referred to this concept in the preceding pages) does not mean the same for each person.

[98] On the Holy Spirit, in addition to the bibliography that we have been quoting and the one that we have mentioned in Chapter 2, cfr. HILBERATH B.H., *Pneumatología*, Brescia 1996; DURRWELL F.X., *L'Esprit Saint de Dieu*, Paris 1983; DURRWELL F.X., *L'Esprit du Père et du Fils*, Paris. Montreal 1989; LAMBIASI F., *Lo Spirito Santo. Mistero e presenza*, Bologna 1987; LAVATORI C.E., *Lo Spirito Santo dono del Padre e del Figlio*, Bologna 1987; GRANADO C., *El Espíritu Santo en la teología patrística*, Salamanca 1987; MOLTMANN J., *Lo Spirito della vita. Per una pneumatologia integrale*, Brescia 1994; WELKER M., *Spirito di Dio. Teologia dello Spirito Santo*, Brescia 1995; COLZANI G. (ed.), *Verso una nuova età dello Spirito*, Padova 1997; MARALDI V., *Lo Spirito e la Sposa. Il ruolo ecclesiale dello Spirito Santo dal Vaticano I alla Lumen Gentium del Vaticano II*, Casale Monferrato 1997; Commissione Teologico-Storica del Grande Giubileo dell'Anno Duemila, *Del tuo Spirito, Signore, é piena la terra*, Cinisello Balsamo 1997; GALOT J., *L'Esprit Saint, personne de communion*, Saint Maur 1997; GONZÁLEZ DE CARDEDAL O., *La entraña del cristianismo*, Salamanca 1997, 693-739.

This difficulty did not arise in our times, and our awareness of it is nothing new either. We were already warned about this by the Fathers. Hilary of Poitiers did not want to commit himself beyond the statement of the Holy Spirit's existence and divinity, as well his gift to humanity[99]. Gregory of Nazianzus spoke about the revelation of the Holy Spirit, after speaking of the Father and the Son, in such a way that the Church would have reached its clear and distinct manifestation only in time[100]. For Basil, the *tropos tes hyparcheos*, the way of being, of the Holy Spirit is ineffable[101].

Undoubtedly, these difficulties have been due partially to the fact that the Holy Spirit and his irreplaceable function in our salvation were relatively forgotten in certain eras, both in theological reflection and in the piety of Christian people[102]. This situation, which even continued to relatively recent times, is no longer our case. The interest in pneumatology is a sign of our times. We have already verified that for current Catholic theology it is quite clear that without the acts of the Holy Spirit, neither the life of Jesus can be explained[103], nor that of the Church (cfr. LG 4) or of Christianity[104]. Our brief analysis of the theology of the New Testament has persuaded us of this. The most recent catechism of the Church has also stated that as it relates to the unicity and the universality of the saving work of Christ, the Holy Spirit, the Spirit of Jesus, exercises his saving function beyond the visible frontiers of the Church, associating the Paschal mystery to all humanity (cfr. GS 22; John Paul II, *Redemptoris Missio* 28-29;56; also *Dominum*

---

99 Cfr. *Trin.* II 29 (GCL 62,64).

100 *Or.* 31,26 (SCh 250,236), the Old Testament clearly spoke of the Father, while the Son was spoken of in a somewhat more obscure manner. In the New Testament, the divinity of the Son appeared clearly, while the divinity of the Holy Spirit was only discrete. In current times, the Spirit is manifested in a clearer manner.

101 *De Spiritu sancto* 18,46 (SCh 18bis,408). According to CYRIL OF JERUSALEM, *Cat.* 16,24 (PG 33,953), we do not need to investigate the nature of the Holy Spirit because we cannot investigate what is not written. Other data on these difficulties of the Fathers will be found in VON BALTHASAR H.U., *Theologik III. Der Geist der Wahrheit*, 106-107.

102 The list of examples mentioned by CONGAR Y., *El Espíritu Santo*, Barcelona 1983, 188ff are impressive. Cfr. also MÜHLEN H., *Una Mystica Persona*, Münster 1968, 473ff; HILBERATH B.J., *Pneumatología*, 8ff; 212, states how, with the causes for this forgetfulness by the Church, mention of the spiritual movements, the limited theological interest for life and spiritual experience, the unilateral emphasis on the unity of the action of the persons in the historical-saving acts, and the separation of the economic Trinity and the immanent Trinity would have led to the «Christomonism» in the Western theology. In like manner, the Holy Spirit would have been forgotten in the study of grace.

103 This is not the time to repeat all that has been said in the previous chapters. Nevertheless, as a point of curious information, mention should be made that according to the Eleventh Council of Toledo (DS 538), Jesus was not only sent by the Father but also by the Holy Spirit (cfr. Isa 48:16).

104 Evidently, here we can not address the issues of ecclesiology and the theology of grace.

et Vivificantem, 23;53). Without the Holy Spirit, the salvation that Christ has brought us does not take place among us nor does it have effects on us. The Christian conviction that the Holy Spirit is God and not a creature is founded on this basic reality. The Holy Spirit is united with the Father and the Son in the baptismal formula and in the ancient confessions of faith of the Church. Without the Holy Spirit we cannot speak of the «Trinity». Following closely the teachings of the New Testament, the tradition has presented to us the Spirit as a gift of God who is God himself, the gift *par excellence* to humanity. Consequently he is the «closest» divine person to us[105] and is also the most «external» to God. Nevertheless, at the same time, the Holy Spirit, this overflowing of God towards us, is the expression of the union and the love of the Father and Son and as such, the most intimate part of the divine being. The Holy Spirit as a gift and the Holy Spirit as love have been the two great topics of pneumatology in the Western World[106]. We must address both aspects, which are also part of a more intimate relationship than what might seem to be so at first sight. We must also devote some attention to the issue of the «procession» of the Spirit.

3.1. THE HOLY SPIRIT AS GIFT[107]

In the New Testament, mention is made on many occasions that the Holy Spirit has been given, sent, and so forth. We are already familiar with many of these texts[108]. Nonetheless, in some passages of the Acts of the Apostles we find more specifically the designation of «gift». Hence, in Acts 8:20, the Holy Spirit appears as the «gift of God»; in 2:38 and 10:45, mention is made of the gift of the Holy Spirit. According to Acts 11:17, Peter refers to the same gift that the gentiles have received, clearly alluding to the Holy Spirit of whom he has spoken in the previous verse: «we realized then that God was giving them the identical gift he gave to us…». There is also the idea of the gift and of the Holy Spirit being related in Heb 6:4. In the tradition, the «gift of God» mentioned by John 4:10 (cfr. 4:14) has been identified with the person of the Holy Spirit: «If you only knew what

105 Cfr. MÜHLEN H., *Der Heilige Geist als Person*, Münster 1967, 279ff.
106 Cfr. THOMAS AQUINAS, *STh* I 37-38. Our following analysis will give us the occasion to refer to many of the magisterial statements regarding the Spirit. A systematic summary of these statements will be found in DS page 862; cfr. also RAHNER K., *El Dios uno y trino…*, 405-406.
107 Considerable material on this issue throughout history will be found in LAVATORI E., *Lo Spirito santo dono del Padre e del Figlio*, Bologna 1987.
108 Cfr. for instance, John 14:16; Rom 5:5; Luke 11:13: «…how much more will the heavenly Father give the Holy Spirit to those who ask him ». The parallel text of Matt 7:11 says that he will give «good things».

God is offering…»[109], although perhaps the attempt at identifying precisely this «gift» that refers to Jesus and to his saving work in more generic terms is probably excessive. Nevertheless, if we take into account the whole of the New Testament, we must give evidence that both by the direct designation of «gift» referring to the Spirit, and by the numerous references to his gift, the importance that this idea has had in the theological tradition is fully justified. It is true that Jesus the Son also has been given, delivered; however, this gift of Jesus has taken place once and for all (cfr. Heb 7:27; 9:12; 10:10; Rom 6:10). His historical life and his self-giving for us are in determined coordinates of time and space, whereas the gift of the Spirit is a constant gift. It is the expression of the perennial nature of the saving action of God fulfilled once and for all in Christ, although it is the Holy Spirit who is the one who constantly universalizes, updates, and internalizes it[110]. The Holy Spirit as the love of God poured out into our hearts (cfr. Rom 5:5; Gal 4:6), is given to us every day in the invisible mission that was alluded to so frequently by Saint Thomas.

God loves us, and this love is realized in us by the gift of his Spirit within our hearts. Precisely from the gift of God realized once and for always comes the perennial gift of the Spirit to the hearts of humans. If Jesus is God with us (cfr. Matt 1:23), God made humans as we are, and the Holy Spirit is the gift in us, God in humanity. He is the God who is external; he is the «ecstasy» of God[111]. Because of this, in the first Trinitarian formulas the Holy Spirit most frequently appears primarily in his historical-saving dimension more than in that of the immanent Trinity: the Spirit is *in* us. In the Spirit, God goes outside himself in his self-communication to humanity, and most especially to those who believe in Jesus. By the action of the Spirit the divine word is accepted, and we believe in God (1Cor 12:3). It is the inner anointing referred to in 1John 2:20, 27 that is commented upon by Augustine: «If his anointing teaches all of you, we work without any reason for this purpose… Your ears are touched by the sound of my words, but the Lord is internal…»[112].

---

109 In this way, AUGUSTINE, *In Joh. ev.* 15,16-17 (CCL 36,156); *Trin.* XV 19,33 (CCL 50,509); CYRIL OF JERUSALEM, *Cat.* 16,1 (PG 33,931ff).

110 JOHN PAUL II, *Dominum et Vivificantem*, 24: «The redemption is fully fulfilled by the Son, the anointed, who has come and acted with the power of the Holy Spirit, finally offering himself in the supreme sacrifice on the cross. And, at the same time, this redemption is constantly carried out in human hearts and consciences —in the history of the world— by the Holy Spirit, who is the "other Paraclete"». Cfr. also footnote 153 in Chapter 3.

111 Cfr. KASPER W., *Der Gott Jesu Christi*, 278.

112 AUGUSTINE, *In Ep. Joh.* III (PL 35,2004); cfr. ibid. IV 1 (2005); cfr. CONGAR Y., *La Parola e il Soffio*, 35.

We have seen the significance that the concept of gift has had in the thought of Saint Augustine who turns it into the personal name of the Holy Spirit when he looks for a relational name as that of Father and Son. Nevertheless, if the term «gift» is relational, it is clear that we are dealing with the gift *of* someone. In the New Testament, it is clear that the Father and the Son are the ones who give the Holy Spirit, with different expressions in the different passages. The Father sends the Advocate because Jesus requests it or the request is made in the name of Jesus (John 14:16, 26). Jesus is the one who sends the Advocate on behalf of the Father (John 15:26; cfr. 16:7). Jesus risen from the dead breathes on his disciples on the same Easter day (John 20:22). In Acts, it is Jesus risen from the dead and ascended to the right hand of the Father (2:33). In the writings of Paul we have seen the formula of the Spirit of Jesus, of Jesus Christ, and so on, at the same time as the Spirit of God or Holy Spirit. Therefore, it seems clear that the same Spirit is at the same time from God the Father and from Jesus[113]. We do not need to emphasize once again that the gift is united with the Paschal mystery of Jesus.

The relationship of the Spirit as gift of the risen Christ is constant in the tradition. We owe to Irenaeus of Lyon one of the most beautiful «definitions» of the Holy Spirit in his historical saving: the in-breathing. The Spirit is *communicatio Christi*[114]. For Hilary, the gift is the personal name of the Spirit, although the term is not used to indicate the effects and the acts which are known before Jesus. Thus, for instance, no mention is made of the «gift» in relation to the inspiration of the Old Testament which is attributed to the Spirit himself. For Basil, the Paraclete, the Advocate, as Spirit of Christ, bears the seal and reveals the Paraclete who has sent him[115]. Augustine with his concern for the relational name

---

113 We are not yet addressing the intra-Trinitarian problem of the «procession» of the Spirit.

114 IRENAEUS OF LYONS, *Adv. Haer.* III 24,1 (SCh 211,472); the Spirit emerges from the body of Jesus, ibid.: «de corpore Christi procedentem nitidissimum fontem» (274). Cfr. III 17, 2-3 (330ff, especially 334): «… quod Dominus accipiens munus a Patre ipse quoque his donavit qui ex ipso participantur, in universam terram mittens Spiritum sanctum»; cfr. the entire context, as well as III 9,3 (110-111): «Spiritus ergo Dei descendit in eum, eius qui per prophetas promiserat uncturus se eum, ut de abundantia unctionis eius nos percipientes salvaremur»; III 11,9 (170); V 20,1 (cfr. ORBE A., *Teología de san Ireneo* II, Madrid 1987, 304ff). The intimate relation of the Spirit with Jesus has also been evidenced by GREGORY OF NYSSA, *Adversus Macedonianos de Spiritu Sancto* 16 (Jaeger III 1,102-103): «The idea of the anointing suggests… that there is no distance between the Son and the Spirit. In fact, just as between the surface of the body and the anointing of the oil, neither reason nor the sensation know intermediaries. In the same manner, the contact of the Son is immediate with the Spirit. Therefore, the one who is about to come in contact with the Son by means of faith must first necessarily come in contact with the oil. No part lacks the Holy Spirit».

115 *De Spir. Sanc.* 18,46 (SCh 17,410). On the Spirit gift cfr. also ibid. 23,57 (452.454), gift that comes from God, although in the same context and commenting on Gal 4:6, the voice of the Spirit

also emphasized that the Holy Spirit is the gift of the Father and of the Son. We cannot doubt the attribution of the gift of the Holy Spirit to Jesus and concretely to the dead and risen Jesus.

At least in one place in the New Testament, the acts of the Spirit in the times of the Old Covenant are already seen in relation to the gift of Jesus, to the gift that the Resurrected One will give (cfr. 1 Pet 1:11, the Spirit of Christ in the prophets). Christian pneumatology wants at all times to save the unity of the history of salvation and thus contemplates the Spirit as united with Christ and his work that is made present in the Church and in each Christian. For this reason, the division in the history proposed by Joachim of Fiore († 1202) was not accepted. According to the Abbott of Calabria, at least in the most frequent interpretation of his thought, the first age of the world was that of the Father, characterized by the rule of their kings over their subjects. The second is that of the Son that reaches it ultimate point with the coming of Christ, characterized by the institutional visible Church and concretely by the priests who preach the word of God. Nevertheless, this must give way to the era of the Holy Spirit, that of the monks and the spiritual men, an era when the Spirit will be the one who will directly rule believers, rather than the hierarchical structure. If this interpretation were so, however, we would run the risk of considering that the act of the Spirit would not be intrinsically united to that of Jesus, but that in a certain sense it would overcome it[116].

Consideration of the Spirit as the gift of the Father and of the Son manifests the unity of the Trinity because thereby the unity of the saving economy is guaranteed. Seeing the Spirit in relation to Jesus does not mean seeing the Spirit in «subordination». The unity of the economy of salvation implies the mutual relationship of the three persons which corresponds to its mutual interelationality in the heart of the immanent Trinity. In view of the fact that the history of

---

(Abbá, Father) becomes the voice of those who receive him. The good comes from the Father by means of the only— begotten Son with the action of the Spirit. On the other hand, for Basil the knowledge of God follows the same inverse ascending rhythm: *De Spir. Sanc.* 18,47 (412); cfr. Ambrosius of Milan, *De Spir. Sanc.* 2,13 (csel 79,137). Didymus the Blind, *De Spirit. Sanc.* 4,12 (sch 386,154), the Holy Spirit is the fullness of the gifts of God.

116 The classic interpretation of Joachim has been discussed recently by Moltmann J., «Speranza Cristiana: messianismo o trascendenza? In dialogo teologico con Gioacchino de Fiore e Tommaso d'Aquino» in *Nella storia del Dio trinitario. Contributi per una teologia trinitaria*, Brescia 1993, 147-173. This is not the time to give a global judgment on the Trinitarian theology of Joachim to whom we have already referred. We are only interested in emphasizing the intimate relationship with the Father and with Christ in all the action of the Spirit.

salvation reaches its height in Jesus and specifically in the Paschal mystery, the gift of the Spirit by the risen Jesus manifests the unity of the Father and the Son. The Spirit is only given when Christ is the risen Lord[117]. Because of this, our analysis of the Holy Spirit as a gift brings to mind and completes what we discussed in Chapter 3 of this treatise regarding the revelation of the Trinitarian mystery in the life of Jesus[118].

In any case, our previous considerations tell us that it should be clear that the gift of the Spirit is on the one hand, an internal reality in the believer[119], and on the other hand, that this gift, coming in the final analysis from the Father, can never be seen separately from Jesus. These two aspects are inseparably united. The Spirit, one and the same, is present in the head and in the members as stated by the Second Vatican Council (LG 7). This dimension of being centered on Christ can never be sufficiently emphasized. Precisely because the Spirit has been and is in Jesus, can he dwell in human beings. Jesus is the Anointed of God, the Messiah, he to whom the Spirit has been given originally, so to speak, so that we humans can receive the Spirit through Jesus. We know that the Patristic tradition is quite clear in this respect. For Saint Thomas, the Spirit is «unus numero in Christo et in omnibus»[120]. And before him, Hugh of St. Victor said:

---

117 Cfr. CONGAR Y., *La parola e il soffio*, Rome 1985, 161; VON BALTHASAR H.U., *Teodramática 3. El hombre en Cristo*, Madrid 1993, 478-479: «The Spirit of Jesus is now [during his mortal life] totally occupied in heeding the Spirit within him; his eternal conformity with the Father, his eternal spontaneity and his authority in the Spirit are linked together and centered in his obedience to the Spirit of the Father. Because of this, before the death of Jesus, the Spirit will not yet be free for the believers, "for there was no Spirit yet" (John 7:39). He will not be free before the earthly mission has been "consummated". In the death of Jesus the Spirit is now also humanly "expired" and returned to the Father… so that in Jesus' Passover he can be "inspired" into the Church… and on Pentecost he can descend from the Father and the Son over the Church»; cfr. also *Teodramática 4. La acción*, Madrid 1995, 342.

118 ORBE A., *La unción del Verbo*, Rome 1961, 633, summarizes in this way the thought of the early Fathers of the Church on the gift of the Spirit from Jesus risen from the death: «In his Baptism in the Jordan is precisely when the human nature of the Spirit starts… The humanity of Jesus must turn into an adequate instrument of the Spirit for the rest of humanity… Only with the day of Resurrection, already fully spiritualized in his humanity and sealed by the Spirit, Christ begins to breathe the spirit on the Apostles». Ibid. 637: «Rather than the assimilation of the Spirit by the humanity of Jesus, it was the assimilation of Jesus by the Spirit… By virtue of his purpose to humanity, his immediate principle [of the Spirit] will be the incarnated Word as such. The Father himself does not pour the Spirit directly and immediately upon the members of the Church».

119 Cfr. recently on this issue, WOLLENWEIDER S., «Der Geist Gottes als Selbst der Glaubenden. Überlegungen zu einem ontologischen Problem in der paulinischen Anthropologie» in *ZThK* 93 (1996) 163-192.

120 THOMAS AQUINAS, *In Sent.* III d.13, q.2, a.1 ad 2; cfr. other references in CONGAR Y., *La parola e il soffio*, 84.

In the same way as the spirit of the person comes down and enters through the head to vivify the members, likewise, the Holy Spirit, through Christ, comes to all Christians. Christ is the head… the Christian is the member. The head is one, the members are many and only one body is formed with the head and the members, and in this only body there is only one Spirit. The fullness of this Spirit resides in the head, the participation in the members, in the limbs[121].

The Spirit whom Jesus had in all fullness is the same one who has been given to us and dwells in us. This is the reason for the preposition «in», which in the tradition is related primarily to the Spirit. We have seen how Basil clearly showed that there is no exclusive association, nor can there be an exclusive association of the prepositions to each of the divine persons. Nevertheless, this does not prevent us from stating this certain «preference» that has been so clearly evidenced in the teachings themselves (Cfr. DS 421, Second Council of Constantinople). In turn, we can make a clear distinction between the two uses of the preposition. On the one hand, it refers to the Spirit in whom all things exist, as is the case of the text to which we have just referred. However, it is precisely because the Spirit of the Lord is all-embracing (cfr. Wis 1:7) that he can be the gift within us[122]. Hence, it pertains to the Spirit especially to be «gift», because he can be in all at the same time, in both the head and in the members. He is capable of raising in humanity the adequate response to the Word, who is the Son by means of whom the Father addresses us.

3.1.1. «GIFT», PERSONAL NAME OF THE HOLY SPIRIT

How can «gift» be a personal designation of the Holy Spirit if the term refers to the saving economy? We know that Augustine posed the problem as to why we call the Holy Spirit gift if he had not been given before a specific point in time, although he had always been *donabile*[123]. In other words, this property belongs to his divine being. Saint Thomas posed the same issue and responded in a similar way. The Spirit is called «gift» in that he has the capacity to be given, because he has this property within himself[124]. For this reason, the name applied to the

---

121 HUGH OF ST. VICTOR, *De sacr. Chris. Fid.* II 1,1 (PL 176,415).

122 Cfr. the relationship set forth by BASIL OF CAESAREA, *De Sp. sanc.* 26,62 (SCh 17 bis, 472), the Spirit is the «place» of the saints, as the latter are the «place» of the Spirit.

123 AUGUSTINE, *Trin.* V 15,16 (CCL 50,224), he proceeds from eternity so that he can be given.

124 THOMAS AQUINAS, STh I 38,1 ad 4: «… donum non dicitur ex eo quod actu datur; sed inquantum habet aptitudinem ut posit dari. Unde ab aeterno divina persona dicitur donum». Cfr. the same article as it continues.

third person of the Trinity is legitimate and it is eternal, even though the giving takes place in time. In fact, as Saint Thomas says, this is the case because the gift refers to the one who gives it and the one to whom it is given. Because of this, the divine person who is a gift, is *from* someone in a double sense, either because of the origin or because of the person to whom the gift is given. As a result, from eternity he could be the gift of God even though he had not yet been given to humanity[125]. On the other hand, the Holy Spirit can be within another rational creature only insofar as he is given. No one can possess the Holy Spirit by his own acts: therefore, the fact of being given, and thus of being gift, is the responsibility of the divine person. In terms of his origin, he is gift of the Father and of the Son, and in this way he is personally differentiated from them from eternity. Seen from another point of view, the gift is also different from the person who receives it[126].

Nevertheless, according to Saint Thomas, the Holy Spirit is not only the gift of the Father and the Son, but he also gives himself because he is the possessor of himself, and he has the power to use or enjoy himself[127]. It is worth noting that in this respect, Saint Thomas stood some distance apart from the biblical idea of the Holy Spirit as the gift of the Father and of the Son, and he was fueled in this regard by the legitimate concern of insisting on the understanding of the equality of the persons. However, we must bear in mind that in the New Testament also, the Spirit is active in the distribution of the gifts that are his manifestations (cfr. 1Cor 12:7-11)[128]. Saint Thomas added that *donum*, as a personal name, «does not point to submission, but only to origin when compared with the one who gives the gift, but when compared to the one to whom it is given, it means free use and delight»[129].

Saint Thomas was not satisfied with these observations regarding the personal nature of the name of the gift within God. He also questioned more explicitly why the name is specifically suitable to the Holy Spirit[130]. According to

---

125 Cfr. THOMAS AQUINAS, *STh* I 38,2 ad 3.
126 Cfr. THOMAS AQUINAS, *STh* I 38,1.
127 *STh* I 38,1: «Et tamen Spiritus sanctus dat seipsum, inquantum est sui ipsius, ut potens se uti, vel potius frui...».
128 The idea of the active Holy Spirit in the gift is present in BASIL OF CAESAREA, *De Sp. sanc.* 16,37 (SCh 17,376): «When we receive the gifts, we first think of the one who gives them away...»; cfr. AUGUSTINE, *Trin.* XV 19,36 (513). «Tu qui dator est et donum», hymn of the service of readings for Pentecost; *Liturgia horarum. Editio typica* vol 2., Typis Polyglottis Vaticanis 1977, 799.
129 THOMAS AQUINAS, *STh* I 38,1.
130 THOMAS AQUINAS, *STh* I 38,2.

Augustine, the being of the Holy Spirit as gift is in relationship with his procession from the Father and the Son[131]. Saint Thomas, who had already spoken of the Holy Spirit as the love of the Father and the Son (we will subsequently address these issues), stated that the name gift comes from the fact that it points to irreversible and gratuitous giving. Therefore, it is love that primarily involves the gratuitous gift. Love is always the first and original gift because only through love can all the other gratuitous gifts be given[132]. Therefore, love is the gift *par excellence.* According to Saint Thomas, as the Holy Spirit proceeds by way of love —even more so, being love himself according to the Augustinian expression— he proceeds as the primary gift. Even though the Son is also given (cfr. John 3:16), it is said that the Holy Spirit is a gift because he proceeds from the Father *ut amor.* Therefore, the gift is his specific name, just as it is said that the Son is the image because he proceeds as Word[133].

Saint Thomas developed an understanding that is quite significant between the gift of the Holy Spirit witnessed in the Scripture (and thus the personal name of «gift» that the tradition that preceeds Thomas has furnished him) and Trinitarian reflection on the Spirit as love. The relationship between the two aspects emerges with great clarity. The specific capacity of being given, which is inherent in the Holy Spirit, comes from his condition as love. The gift of the Holy Spirit and the love of God are shown as related in Rom 5:5. Therefore, we might assume that even though the order of Saint Thomas in his presentation comes from within the Trinity toward the *ad extra* gift, the *historia salutis* has also had relevance when basing his reflection on the immanent Trinity. Nevertheless, there is still a problem if the gift of the Spirit, and consequently his inhabitation in us, is only considered in terms of «appropriations» and is not seen as something inherent in the third person[134]. In this case, all that has been said about the Spirit as a gift in the believer would be considerably minimized. We can, however, enlighten the teachings of Saint Thomas with the information of the New

---

131 Cfr. AUGUSTINE, *Trin.* IV 20,29 (CCL 50,200).

132 THOMAS AQUINAS, *STh* I 38,2: «Amor habet rationem primi doni, per quod omnia dona gratuita donantur». Earlier, AUGUSTINE, *Trin.* XV 18,32 (507) noted that it is said that the Holy Spirit is «propter dilectionem»; 19,35 (512), the Spirit is gift insofar as he is given to those who, through him, love God; cfr. also 19,37 (513-514).

133 Cfr. THOMAS AQUINAS, *STh* I 38,2.

134 Cfr. for all these problems, PRADES J., «*Deus specialiter est in sanctis per gratiam*». *El misterio de la inhabitación de la Trinidad en los escritos de santo Tomás*, Roma 1993, 419-428, according to whom Saint Thomas on some occasions is addressing this idea under the scheme of the appropriations, and only some texts would suggest an action of his own.

Testament and of the oldest tradition, which offer far more space to the inherent relationships of each of the persons with human beings. In this respect, we can interpret the condition of the gift of the Holy Spirit poured in our hearts as something «inherent» to the Holy Spirit, even though his presence always involves, in some way, the Son and the Father who give him and send him to us (cfr. Rom 8:9-11; John 14:16-17.23). The Holy Spirit who according to the classical conception has the attribute of «fecundity» in the heart of the divinity, eventually turns into fecundity[135]. There are no important reasons that can force us to consider this «fecundity», which is so important in the tradition, as a merely «appropriated» fecundity. The action of each of the persons of the Trinity is inseparable from that of the others. However, this does not mean that this action cannot have and does not have its own characteristic features that are different in each case.

3.1.2.   *THE SPIRIT AS A GIFT IN THE BELIEVER
         AND IN THE CHURCH*

All of these considerations can lead us to the conclusion that the grace of God in human beings must be related in a very special way to the person of the Holy Spirit[136]. He himself is the gift of God, personal love himself, communicated to humanity. By virtue of the Spirit and through the mediation of Christ, we have access to the Father (cfr. Eph 2:18). Even though the New Testament does not say anything directly in this respect, we can consider that the Holy Spirit is already also present in the creation, insofar as the Spirit is the overflowing of the love of God outwards which grants to the creature participation in the being and in the life that only is in harmony with God. This participation acquires its ultimate degree of participation in the divine life through grace itself. Because of this, in the gift of the Spirit to the Church and the believers on the day of Pentecost, through a new gratuitous act of God, we see the beginning of the new creation that must lead to the entire creation, and especially to the human being, to his fullness (cfr. Rom 8:23). If Jesus the Son is «image» of God and in him God has the capability of going out of himself, taking as his own the created reality, the Holy Spirit above all has the capacity to be diffused: « send out your breath and life begins; you renew the face of the earth» (Ps 104:30); «For the Spirit of the Lord

---

135 Cfr. CONGAR Y., *El Espíritu Santo*, 272.
136 Cfr. LADARIA L.F., *Teología del pecado original y de la gracia*, Madrid 1993, 253ff; KASPER W., *Der Gott Jesu Christi*, 278ff.

fills the world» (Wis 1:7)[137]. The Spirit perfects the creation, which is made with the mediation of the Son[138]. In the New Testament, the Spirit of Jesus is infused in the believers as the spirit of Sonship by which we can cry aloud «Abbá, Father» (cfr. Rom 8:15; Gal 4:6). At this point, the Holy Spirit deploys all his virtues. He is poured out and spilled forth from God in order to introduce humans into the life of God himself. Through the Spirit, the salvation that Jesus brought to us is made a reality in each and everyone of us. It is the supremacy of the uncreated gift that is God himself, which is over all the different gifts and graces that God gives us[139].

We must not forget that in this context the Spirit is also the gift to the Church, the body of Christ over which the Holy Spirit has rested. Despite the universality of his effects and without decreasing or minimizing what we have said about this, to a certain degree the Church is the «natural» place of the Spirit, just as the human nature of Jesus was during the time of his mortal life. It is worth remembering the formulation of Irenaeus: «Where the Church is, there is the Spirit of God and where the Spirit of God is, there is the Church and all its grace, because the Spirit is the truth»[140]. The Spirit constantly sanctifies the Church, he dwells in it, he introduces it in the fullness of truth, unifies it and directs it, enriching it with the different priestly and charismatic gifts and leads it to perfection (cfr. Second Vatican Council, LG 4), and this is his vital principle, his «soul» (ibid. 7; cfr. also numbers 5-8). The Holy Spirit is a guarantee of the Church's loyalty to the tradition as well as the energy that inspires towards the newness of the future[141].

---

137 Even though it is not mentioned expressly, we can assume that the Holy Spirit also intervenes in the giving of perfections to creatures to which SAN JUAN DE LA CRUZ refers, *Cántico espiritual* 5,4 (Complete works, Salamanca 1992, 599): «And, by just looking at them,/ with his own figure,/ he left them dressed in beauty… We can thus know that with only this figure of his Son, God looked at all things and gave them their natural being, communicating to them many natural graces and gifts, making them finished and perfect… By looking upon them as good they were made good in the Word, his Son. And not only did he not communicate to him his being and natural graces by looking at them, but also by means of the only figure of his Son he left them dressed in beauty, communicating them supernatural being…».

138 Cfr. BASIL OF CAESAREA, *De Sp. Sanc.* 16,38 (376-384); GREGORY OF NYSSA, *Quod non sunt tres dei* (Jaeger III 1,47-48.50); *De Sp. Sancto Adv. Mac.* (100). Cfr. LADARIA L.F., *Antropologia teologica*, Roma-Casale Monferrato 1995, 64-69.

139 Cfr. LEO XIII, *Divinum illud munus* (DS 3330).

140 IRENAEUS OF LYONS, *Adv. Haer.* III 24,1 (SCh 211,474): «Ubi enim Ecclesia, ibi et Spiritus Dei, et ubi Spiritus Dei, ibi Ecclesia et omnis gratia. Spiritus autem veritas»; JOHN CHRYSOSTOM, *Hom. Pent.* I 4 (PG 49,459): «If the Holy Spirit were not present, there would be no Church. If there is Church, this is an evident sign of the presence of the Spirit».

141 Cfr. HYPPOLITUS, *Trad. Apost.* Prol (SCh 11,40), the Spirit teaches those who are in the head of the Church; CONGAR Y., *El Espítitu Santo*, 240; VON BALTHASAR H.U., *Spiritus Creator*, Einsiedeln 1967, 97-98.

In the doctrine of grace and in ecclesiology, these issues are developed in greater detail, although at this point we cannot further pursue them.

The gift of the Spirit is associated with joy and delight (cfr. Gal 5:29). In the case of Augustine also, the gift involves «use» as well as love, joy and happiness[142]. The Father and the Son, as they love each other, enjoy each other in the Holy Spirit who is love, and our joy of God is similar to that of the Holy Spirit who is the gentleness of the Father and the Son[143].

Therefore, the Holy Spirit is the gift of God in person because through him we enjoy God. In the Old Testament he already appears with these characteristics. He is the gift of the Father and the Son seen in their unity, primarily with Jesus, the incarnate Son, exalted at the right hand of the Father, who sends him to the apostles and to the whole Church. In the Spirit, gift of the two, we see evidence of the union of the Father and of the Son. At this point we can consider the issue of the Spirit as union and love of the Father and the Son in the Trinity.

3.2. THE HOLY SPIRIT AS LOVE OF THE FATHER AND OF THE SON

This issue is inherently more complicated that the one that we have just addressed, because the point of support in the New Testament is more distant, and it also goes back to the earliest tradition of the Church. The starting point can only be the fact that according to the New Testament, the Holy Spirit is the Spirit of the Father and of the Son. This was clearly seen by Augustine, whose influence has been decisive in the development of the doctrine to which we must now turn.

On several occasions we have been faced with this issue during our exposition. The explicit relationship of the Holy Spirit with the love of God is undoubtedly clearly expressed in the New Testament. According to Rom 5:5 «A hope which will not let us down because the love of God has been poured into our hearts by the Holy Spirit which has been given to us». Mention is also made of the love of the Spirit in Rom 15:30. The Holy Spirit appears before us also in different places as a special factor of unity and fellowship between Christians and of communion between them and with God (cfr. 1Cor 12:3ff; 2Cor 13:13; Eph 2:18; 4:3). On the other hand, as we know, in the life of Jesus the Son of God, in his historical journey toward the Father, the Spirit plays an essential role when he «manifests

---

142 HILARY OF POITIERS, *Trin.* II 1 (CCL 62,38), «usus in munere»; cfr. ibid. 35 (70-71). AUGUSTINE, *Trin.* VI 10,11 (CCL 50,242): «Illa dilectio, delectatio, felicitas et beatitudo… usus ab illo (Hilary) apellatus est»; cfr. the context.

143 THOMAS AQUINAS, *STh* I 39,8.

to him» the will of the Father. Through the Spirit, Jesus offers himself to the Father. The same Spirit is active in his resurrection. The presence and action of the Spirit in Jesus is therefore not indifferent in the concrete fulfillment of the union of Jesus with the Father. The gift of the Spirit offered by the Father and the risen Son also manifests and is a clear evidence of the unity of the two.

We must keep this information in mind in order to understand the meaning of this doctrine of the Holy Spirit as an expression of love and communion of the Father and the Son. Although it is true that it does not have an *explicit* basis in the New Testament, there are also significant signs which offer a foundation and make it possible to understand the development that we must study. The Holy Spirit appears with these characteristics as a link of union between God and humanity and among humans. For this reason, the question as to whether this corresponds to a certain degree also to his personal being *ad intra* as a sign and expression of the unity of the Father and of the Son is quite legitimate. From the experience of the gift that the Church has received, we can have access to this profound aspect of the divine intra-Trinitarian life. We must bear in mind that this doctrine has been developed primarily in the West, but we cannot consider that it is fully alien to Eastern theology[144]. It was known, for instance, by Gregory Palamas: «The Spirit of the Almighty Word is like an ineffable love of the Father for this ineffably engendered Word. This is the same love that this same Word and beloved Son of the Father uses with respect to the Father»[145].

3.2.1. *THE HOLY SPIRIT AS LOVE IN THE TRADITION*

We have seen that Saint Augustine was the first one to develop this doctrine. Nevertheless, we can find some minor precedents in previous Latin theology. Marius Victorinus had referred to the Holy Spirit as *Patris et Filii copula*[146]. In

---

[144] «The love of the Spirit», probably the love that the Spirit places in us or that the Holy Spirit has for us; cfr. Fitzmyer J.A., *Romans*, New York-London... 1992, 725.

[145] Gregory Palamas, *Capita physica*, 36 (pg 150,1144-1145). In this century, this same doctrine has been addressed by Bulgakov S., *Il Paraclito*, Bologna 1987, 143ff: the Father, the Son, and the Holy Spirit renounce themselves reciprocally in the total love. The Holy Spirit is hypostatic love and happiness. The author uses also the Augustine scheme of the lover / beloved / love itself (160). The Father is the image of paternal sacrificial love; the Son of filial sacrificial love; the Holy Spirit of boundless joyful love (285-286). The Holy Spirit is the union of the Father and the Son (303f), he is the *hypostasis* of love (346). The doctrine of the Holy Spirit as love undoubtedly has a relationship with the issue of the procession of the Spirit, although not only, from the Father and from the Son. Cfr. Pannenberg W., *Teología Sistemática* I, Madrid 1992, 343, which attempts to make a clear distinction between the two issues.

[146] Cfr. *Himnos* I; III (sCh 68,620.650); also *Adv. Ar.* III 9 (ibid. 466).

Hilary of Poitiers we have some formulations that literally seem to anticipate those of Augustine, although in the complete context of his theology they do not seem to mean more than the expression of the unity of the Father and the Son evidenced in the fact that the Spirit was the recipient of the two of them[147]. Ambrose of Milan referred to the Spirit as *individuae copula trinitatis*[148]. We quote below one of the basic texts of Augustine:

> For this reason, the Holy Spirit also subsists in the same unity and equality of substance. Therefore, if the unity belongs to both Father and Son, or else they share the sanctity of love as though it were unity, because it is love and it is love because it is sanctity, it is quite evident that this love is not something different from that by which one is united with the other, so that by means of which the engendered is loved by the one who engenders and who in turn loves the engenderer. In such a way they exist «to preserve the unity of the Spirit by the peace that binds you together» (Eph 4:3), and not by way of the participation, nor by the gift of someone who is superior to them, but on the Spirit's own account[149].

The union between the Father and the Son does not come to them through something alien or through an external principle, but rather through the gift of themselves. The Holy Spirit, who has the same divine essence as the Father and the Son, is the love in whom the two of them are united. It seems that the Holy Spirit, *ad extra* gift, turns here also into a mutual *ad intra* communal gift. Augustine moved on from the Holy Spirit as «gift» to the Holy Spirit as love. The greatest gift of God is that of love, and at the same time, the greatest gift of God is the Holy Spirit[150]. For this reason, Spirit and love must coincide. In this way, love (*caritas*)

---

147 Cfr. LADARIA L.F., *El Espíritu Santo en san Hilario de Poitiers*, Madrid 1977, 278ff.

148 *Exp. Ps.* CXVIII, 18,37 (CSEL 62,441). Regarding the background of Augustine in the East, cfr. ABRAMOWSKI L., «Der Geist als «Band» zwischen Vater und Sohn — ein Theologoumenon der Eusebianer» in ZNtWis 77 (1996) 126-132; according to Ambrose, Athanasius has struggled against the idea. The expression *copula Trinitatis* is also present in DIDYMUS THE BLIND, *De Sp. sanc.* 47,214 (SCh 386,336).

149 AUGUSTINE, *Trin.* VI 5,7 (CCL 50,235); also V 11,12 (219), the Holy Spirit is «ineffabilis quaedam patris et filii communio». The formula of the Eleventh Council of Toledo (DS 527) was considerably inspired by Saint Augustine: «quia caritas sive sanctitas amborum esse monstratur».

150 AUGUSTINE, *Trin.* XV 19,37 (513): «…si in donis dei nihil maius est caritate et nullum est maius donum dei quam spiritus sanctus, quid consequentius quam ut ipse sit caritas, quae dicitur et deus et ex deo»; ibid. 18,32 (508): «Dilectio igitur quae ex deo est et deus est proprie spiritus sanctus est, per quem infunditur in cordibus nostris dei caritas per quam nos tota inhabitat trinitas. Quocirca rectissime spiritus sanctus, cum sit deus, vocatur etiam donum dei (cfr. Acts 8:20). Quod donum proprie quid nisi caritas intelligenda est, quae perducit ad deum et sine qua quodlibet aliud donum dei non perducit ad deum?».

is the name of the Holy Spirit, together with that of gift[151]. As we have already seen, Augustine had arrived at the idea of the Holy Spirit as love based on the so-called «psychological» analogy of the Trinity. Nevertheless, although to a lesser extent, he had also taken into account the analogy of intrapersonal love[152]. The Holy Spirit is the love by means of which the Father and the Son love themselves because it belongs to the two of them[153]. By being and demonstrating the *communitas amborum*[154], he receives as his own the name of love because, in view of the fact that it is common to the two, he is personally called by the name which describes the Father and the Son in their mutual communion[155].

In Richard of St. Victor we have seen more clearly this line of thought regarding interpersonal love[156]. The Holy Spirit —by being the beloved of the Father and of the Son, the *condilectus*— is the love in which the two, the Father and the Son, participate. In this way, they fulfill the perfection of love. In all the assumptions of Richard of St. Victor, it is clear that the Holy Spirit comes from the Father and the Son, but that he is not considered directly as the love of the two. Rather, he is perceived as the one who receives the love that the Son receives from the Father and who together with the Son, gives love in turn. The viewpoint of Richard is consequently different from that of Saint Augustine, even though it is quite clear that the thought of the Bishop of Hippo has influenced the fundamental intuitions of Richard of St. Victor.

For Bonaventure, the Holy Spirit is made by the «liberality» or generosity of the concord of the Father and the Son. Bonaventure followed the reflections of Richard to a certain extent when he stated that the mutual love that is commu-

---

151 Cfr. AUGUSTINE, *Trin.* XV 17,29 (504); 17,31 (505s): «…ipse dilectio est». Cfr. also VI 5,7 (236), the three persons characterized as the one who loves, the one who loves him, and love himself. Also, in VIII 10,14 (291); XV 3,5; 6,10 (465;472). Beginning with Augustine, a long tradition developed which has reached to the present and which sees in love the name of the Holy Spirit. In this way, GREGORY THE GREAT, *Hom. In Ev.* II 30 (PL 76, 1220) «Ipse namque Spiritus sanctus amor est»; cfr. ANSELM, *Proslogion* XXIII (Schmitt, V 1,117).

152 Cfr. AUGUSTINE, *Trin.* VIII 10,14 (290-291).

153 AUGUSTINE, *Trin.* XV 17,27 (513): «Qui spiritus sanctus secundum scripturas sanctas nec patris solius est nec filii solius sed amborum, et ideo communem qua igitur invicem se diligunt pater et filius insinuat caritatem».

154 Cfr. *In Joh. ev.* 99,7; cfr. also ibid. 8-9 (CCL 36,586; 587).

155 *Trin.* XV 19,37 (513): «Et si caritas qua pater diligit filium et patrem diligit filius ineffabiliter communionem demonstrat amborum, quid convenientius quam ut ille dicatur caritas proprie, qui spiritus est communis ambobus?»; ibid. (514): «Quia enim est communis ambobus, id vocatur ipse proprie quod ambo communiter»; cfr. ibid. 17,29 (507).

156 Let us remember what we have said in Chapter 9.

nicated is the most perfect love[157]. Also for him, Spirit, love and gift, mean the same reality, although under different aspects. «Spirit» emphasizes the strength that love produces. «Love» indicates the modality of the emanation of the Spirit as «nexus» between the Father and the Son. The «gift» is the consequence of the above because the Spirit is made to unite us[158]. In this case, as in Augustine, the relationship between the theology and the economy is emphasized. The Holy Spirit, nexus or link of the love of the Father and the Son, fulfills the union between Christians in the history of the salvation.

As we have pointed out, Saint Thomas spoke of the two names of the Holy Spirit: love and gift. We have seen how he inter-related them. Proceeding in his exposition from the theology to the economy, he first addressed the Spirit as love rather than as a gift[159]. The name love can be taken «essentially» and «personally». When taken in the personal sense of the word, it is a name that pertains to the Holy Spirit just as the name of the Son is the Word. The verbs for loving and other equivalent verbs (*diligere* for example) are used to express the modality of behavior (*habitudo*) of him who proceeds by way of love with respect to his beginning and vice versa. Consequently, when we speak of «love», we are referring to the love that proceeds[160]. The Holy Spirit is called love insofar as he proceeds through this route. As to love, the Holy Spirit is the «nexus» of the Father and the Son, because the Father loves his Son and himself with the same love, and the same applies to the Son. Because of this, in the Holy Spirit insofar as he is love, we find the same kind of behavior as that of the Father toward the Son and that of the Son toward the Father. Concerning his origin, the Holy Spirit is the third in the Trinity because he comes from the Father and from the Son. Nevertheless, according to this form of behavior (*habitudo*) to which we have referred, he is the link that exists between the two, as he proceeds from both of them[161]. In Saint

---

[157] *Com. Sent.* I d.10, a.1, q.1. Cfr. CONGAR Y., *El Espíritu Santo*, 116.

[158] Cfr. *Com. Sent.* I d.18, a.1, q.3, ad 4; *Breviloquium* I 3,9: «cum proprium sit Spiritus sancti esse donum, esse nexum seu caritatem amborum…».

[159] Cfr. THOMAS AQUINAS, *STh* I 37, «De nomine Spiritus sancti quod est amor»; question 38 addresses the gift and earlier, in number 36, mention has been made of the person of the Holy Spirit. He is mostly concerned about his «procession», which we will address in the next footnote.

[160] Cfr. THOMAS AQUINAS, *STh* I 37,1: «In quantum vero his vocabulis (amor, diligere) utimur ad exprimendam habitudinem eius rei quae procedit per modum amoris, ad suum principium et e converso; ita quod per amorem intelligatur amor procedens; sic Amor est nomen personae, et diligere vel amare est verbum notionale, sicut dicere vel generare».

[161] THOMAS AQUINAS, *STh* I 37,1: «Importatur in Spiritu sancto, prout est amor, habitudo Patris ad Filium, et e converso, ut amantis ad amatum. Sed ex hoc ipso quod Pater et Filius se mutuo amant, oportet quod mutuus amor, qui est Spiritus sanctus, ab utroque procedat. Secundum igitur

Thomas we find the idea of mutual love as it pertains to the Augustinian tradition, but he did not make significant use of it[162]. What prevailed in him was the image of the psychological Trinity and the procession through love, unlike the procession of the Son by means of intelligence[163].

3.2.2. THE CONTEMPORARY CATECHISM AND THEOLOGICAL REFLECTION

When it accentuates the idea of the mutual love of the Father and the Son or that of the procession out of their free will, the idea of the Holy Spirit as love has been strongly present, and it continues to be so in Western theology. The first aspect is quite often the one that is primarily emphasized in recent times[164]. Here, we can see the correspondence that is present in the tradition between love and the *ad intra* mutual surrender and the gift to humans, the link of union between the Father and the Son and the principle of union of people within the Church, the body of Christ. Some of these ideas have been addressed in recent Papal teachings. John Paul II developed them especially in the encyclical «Dominum et Vivificantem» that was issued on May 18th, 1986. It is worth reproducing some of the most significant paragraphs as they relate to the topic that we are analyzing:

> God, in his intimate life, «is love» (1John 4:8.16), essential love common to the three divine persons. The Holy Spirit is personal love as Spirit of the Father and of the Son. Because of this, the Holy Spirit «explores the depths of everything, even the depths of God» (1Cor 2:10), as an *uncreated love-gift*. We can say that in the Holy Spirit, the intimate life of the one and triune God becomes entirely a gift, an exchange of the reciprocal love between the divine persons and because of this the Holy Spirit God «exists» as a gift. Therefore, the Holy Spirit is the *personal expression* of this gift, of this being-love. The Holy Spirit is a person-love. The Holy Spirit is a person-gift…

originem, Spiritus sanctus non est medius, sed tertia in Trinitate persona. Secundum vero praedictam habitudinem, est medius nexus duorum, ab utroque procedens».

162 In some references, in addition to the text that has been just quoted in *STh* I 37,2, the Father and the Son love themselves in the Holy Spirit, the «proceeding love»; 39,8.

163 Cfr. THOMAS AQUINAS, *STh* I 27,3-4, in which the idea does not appear and neither does it appear in *STh* I 36,2, where an explanation is given as to why the Holy Spirit also proceeds from the Son (otherwise, the second and the third person could not be distinctly separated), nor does it appear in *Comp. Theol.* 50. Cfr. more data on this issue in CONGAR Y., *El Espíritu Santo*, 116-120.

164 For example, MÜHLEN H., *Der Heilige Geist als Person*, Münster 1967; CONGAR Y., *El Espíritu Santo*, 218ff; VON BALTHASAR H.U., *Theologik III. Der Geist der Wahrheit*, Einsiedeln 1987, 144ff.

At the same time… it is love and gift (uncreated) and from this is derived as from a source (*fons vivus*) *every gift* offered to creatures (created gift)…[165].

In light of what Jesus says in the discourse in the Cenacle, the Holy Spirit is revealed in a new and fuller way. He is *not only the gift to the person* (to the person of the Messiah), but he *is a person-gift*…[166].

In the gift *made by the Son* we see completed the revelation and the gift of the eternal love: *the Holy Spirit*, who in the inscrutable death of the divinity is a person-gift, through the action of the Son; in other words, by means of the Paschal mystery, the Spirit is given in a new way to the apostles and to the Church, and through them, to mankind and to the whole world[167].

These passages very clearly emphasize that the condition of the person-love, person-gift in the heart of the divine life itself is the condition that determines and makes possible the giving of the Spirit to humanity. From the mutual love between the Father and the Son we move to the gift of the love that embraces all people. It is clear that in the order of knowledge and revelation, only through the gift given to the Church and to humankind on Pentecost can we reach the wealth of the love that unites the Father and the Son.

With the personal names of love and gift we emphasize two inseparable characteristics of the divine person of the Holy Spirit. On the one hand, we see expressed in him the divine life in its greater intimacy, the love that is the divine life. It is in this sense the deepest core of the Trinitarian life. On the other hand, it is the ultimate expression of divine communication toward the creature, the gift of the Father and the Son capable of introducing human beings into this divine intimacy that the Spirit himself expresses. The two aspects do not contradict each other. The inward communication is the condition that renders possible the «overflowing», the «ecstasy» of God that goes outside himself[168]. The Spirit

---

165 JOHN PAUL II, *Dominum et Vivificantem*, 10.
166 JOHN PAUL II, *Dominum et Vivificantem*, 22.
167 JOHN PAUL II, *Dominum et Vivificantem*, 23.
168 Cfr. KASPER W., *Der Gott Jesu Christi*, 278: «The Holy Spirit expresses the most intimate essence of God, the love that is given to himself, in such a way that what is most intimate is at the same time what is most external; in other words, the possibility and the reality of the being of God outside himself. The Spirit is likewise the ecstasy of God. It is God in the purest overflowing, God in the over-abundance of love and grace». HILBERATH B. J., *Pneumatologia*, Brescia 1996, 205: «The Holy Spirit is the encounter of love, the space where the Father and the Son overcome themselves and are united in love until they make up the unity. In this respect, spirit and love, the characteristics of the divine life, are at the same time the specific signs of the Holy Spirit».

is God-love, who in the heart of the Trinity leads to fullness and consummates at that time the saving work which is carried out by Christ once and for always by the initiative of the Father, and it is constantly fulfilled in human beings until the end of history through the Holy Spirit[169]. The Holy Spirit in this way closes and rounds out the circle of the being of God as love, a word that can summarize everything that is the divine life[170].

Because of all the above reasons, it is not surprising that in recent theology this is the special way in which the Holy Spirit manifests himself, insofar as he is the reciprocal love of the Father and of the Son, the being of God himself in different manifestations. For instance, it is stated that in the Holy Spirit we find «hypostatized» everything that we call the essence of the divine nature[171]. «The Spirit when understanding his «I», is eternally in himself as the «we» of the Father and of the Son and also when he is being «expropriated» in his *proprissimum*[172]. Does

this mean that the Spirit is only the union and the love of the Father and of the Son, in such a way that his personal property simply disappears in that of the other two? The Holy Spirit seals the union of the Father and the Son insofar as he is differentiated from them, insofar as the love of the two produces the «fruit» of the third person. In this way, the Spirit becomes the expression of love itself. In the economy of salvation, even as the Spirit was operative in the full communion of Jesus in his humanity with the Father, so also the full effusion or outpouring of the Holy Spirit on humanity is also the «fruit» of the return of Jesus to the Father. The love and the union of the two are realized or fulfilled only in a third one. However, from the love itself between the lover and the loved one (Augustine), the Holy Spirit seals the love of the two insofar as the two, in turn, love a third one, the *condilectus* (Richard of St. Victor)[173]. Augustine spoke of the Spirit

---

169 Cfr. JOHN PAUL II, *Dominum et Vivificantem*, 24.

170 Cfr. VON BALTHASAR H.U., *Theologik III*, 146-148; GRESHAKE G., *Der dreieine Gott*, 211, in the Holy Spirit the fullness of the divine life is personally palpable.

171 Cfr. DURRWELL F.X., *Le Père. Dieu en son mystère*, 1988, 146 : «everything that theological language refers to as divine essence, divine nature, is hypostatized in him»; cfr. also 148-149.

172 Cfr. VON BALTHASAR H.U., *Teodramática 2. El hombre en Dios*, 235. We have already referred on several occasions the known thesis set forth by MÜHLEN H. regarding the Holy Spirit as the «we» of the Father and of the Son. Cfr. page 291.

173 Regarding the Holy Spirit as fruit and expression of the love of the Father and the Son, cfr., among others, GRESHAKE G., *Der dreieine Gott*, Freiburg-Basel-Wien 1997, 210: «In this respect we see the double nature of the Holy Spirit. He is (1) a summary (*Inbegriff*) of the mutual love and the union of the Father and of the Son, and he is (2) the fruit that results from the love, and with this, in the sense of Richard of St. Victor, with the "third one", he is the guarantor of their love. Nevertheless, this double nature does not imply any duality»; cfr. also ibid. 156; KEHL M., «Kirche-Sakrament des Geistes» in KASPER W. (Hrsg.), *Gegenwart des Geistes. Aspekte der Pneumatologie*

who shows the communion of the Father of the Son[174]. Saint Thomas also stated that the Father and the Son loved themselves in the love which proceeded from them[175]. The relationship between the Father and the Son, which by no means can appear as «prior» to the infusion of the Spirit, does not reach its fullness without the latter. Only in the relationship with the Holy Spirit are the Father and the Son fully persons; they are united in paternal and filial love. The Father-Son relationship is not understood if it is not in this common love that they have in the Spirit who is at the same time their expression and their fruit. The three persons are equally important in God. Each one is constituted by the relationships of the other two, and as we have already mentioned, the «processions» or the intra-Trinitarian (*táxis*) order do not in any way imply superiority of certain persons over the others. None of them is, nor can be, without the other two. If we said that Father is the only beginning without beginning, he is not without the Son, and the same rationale must lead us to affirm that the Father and the Son, previous in the *taxis,* cannot be without the fruit of love of the two, the Holy Spirit.

The overflowing of the gift outward and the union of the Father and the Son in the intimacy of the divine life have been emphasized in different ways in the theological traditions of the East and the West[176]. In spite of this, we need not consider the two visions as though they are incompatible or alternative. The theological tradition offers the basis for both of them, and thus they can be considered supplementary. We need not assume that the analogies used in the West which are based on created realities, specifically human realities, have as their purpose the «explanation» of the divine mystery. God is presented to us as greater and more incomprehensible the more he comes closer to us and enables us to

---

heute, Freiburg-Basel-Wien 1979, 155-180, esp. 159: the Holy Spirit is at the same time the assumption and the fruit of the communion of the Father and of the Son; cfr. VON BALTHASAR H.U., *Theologik* II, 130; GONZÁLEZ A., *Trinidad y Liberación*, San Salvador 1994, 202; GALOT J., «L'origine éternelle de l'Espirit Saint» in *Greg* 78 (1997) 501-522, especially 517.

174 AUGUSTINE, *Trin.* XV 19,37 (513): «…communionem demonstrat amborum».

175 THOMAS AQUINAS, *STh* I 38,2, cfr. 38,1, LEO XIII, *Divinum illud* (DS 3330): «qui a mutuo Patris Filiique amore procedens…». The Holy Spirit is not only the love of the Father and of the Son but he also proceeds from the love of both of them.

176 VON BALTHASAR H.U., *Theologik* II. *Wahrheit Gottes*, 141: «The Eastern vision contemplates an ultimate self-overflowing of the Father through the Son in the amplitude and freedom of the Spirit that comprises everything. The Western vision contemplates the fact that the Holy Spirit turns into the response of the Son to the Father (that is only one common with the divine knowledge of the Son that comes completely from the Father and whom he has to thank for everything) the procession of the Sprit as a fruitful encounter of the love that gives and receives, that produces this love, absolutely as Spirit of love, in the common breath that goes beyond himself»; cfr. the rest of the text, pages 141-142.

know the mysteries of his love. Affirmation and denial must always be combined in our believing understanding of the mystery of the one and triune God. The revelation does not mean that the mystery ceases to be mystery. This is especially the case when we are dealing with the Holy Spirit because of the «anonymity» that characterizes the Spirit[177].

The position of the Holy Spirit in the center of the divine mystery is shown paradoxically in the lack of exclusiveness of the names that we apply to the Spirit. The name holy Spirit itself, as was pointed out by the Fathers, could also be suitable for the Father and the Son, because both are «spirit» and both are «holy»[178]. Love is the characteristic of God according to 1John 4:8.16. The Son has been given by the Father and has given himself. Since he holds as his own the names that are suitable exclusively for him, the Holy Spirit manifests the profound mystery of the divine being, precisely by enabling human beings to be in communion with God[179].

3.3.   THE PROCESSION OF THE HOLY SPIRIT

We have attempted to develop the basic lines of the theology of the Holy Spirit without focusing exclusively on the issue of the procession of the Spirit, even though we have needed to make frequent references to this element in view of the proximity of this issue with the ones that we have just addressed. We will now address this problem directly. This element is a doctrinal issue that has not yet been completely clarified in relations between the East and the West. In the past few years, some declarations have been made by the Catholic Church that can be expected to help us all reach a real understanding[180]. However, before speak-

---

177 In this way, GARRIGUES J. M., *El Espíritu que dice Padre*, Salamanca 1985, 63, the *tropos* of the third person is «anonymity»; BULGAKOV S., *Il Paraclito*, 336ff, spoke of the Holy Spirit as the unknown *hypostasis*.

178 Cfr. HILARY OF POITIERS, *Trin.* II 30 (CCL 62,65); DIDYMUS THE BLIND, *De Sp. Sanc.* 54, 237 (SCh 386,356f); BASIL OF CAESAREA, *De Sp. Sanc.* 19,48 (SCh 17 bis, 416); and mainly, AUGUSTINE, *Trin.* V 11,12 (CCL 50,219); THOMAS AQUINAS, *STh* I 36,1 ad 1, among many others.

179 Cfr. AUGUSTINE, *Trin.* VI 5,7 (235), that determines the relationship of God as love with the Spirit— love of the Father and of the Son; VON BALTHASAR H.U., *Theologik III. Der Geist der Wahrheit*, 148: «In this way "the most external point" of the divine essence —at the same time, identical with the "inner most center"— and when the Spirit is given as gift to the creature, in this gift we will find all the essence of the divinity and with this the "deification" of the creature». Also in ibid. 214, the gift of the Spirit to the creature does not annul our being as creatures and, hence, it does not eliminate the dialogue of humanity with God.

180 JOHN PAUL II, in his homily on the occasion of the feast of Saint Peter and Saint Paul, June 29th, 1995, before the ecumenical Patriarch of Constantinople, expressed the desire that someone could explain «la dottrina tradizionale del *Filioque* presente nella versione liturgica del Credo

ing directly about the controversial problem of the *filioque*, we must address the different approaches that have been taken in history regarding this problem before it became an explicitly controversial issue in the case of the different Christian confessions.

It is evident that we cannot believe that in the earliest times of the Church the issue had been posed in the same terms as they were proposed later on. For this reason, recalling some information contained in the New Testament and in the old tradition can help us address this issue with wider perspectives. Whatever we say here will help complete what we have been setting forth regarding the person of the Spirit.

3.3.1. THE PROCESSION OF THE SPIRIT IN THE EAST AND IN THE WEST

Before beginning our discussion, we must inevitably refer to John 15:26, the text to which the tradition as a whole has resorted. The Holy Spirit proceeds from the Father παρά του πατρός εκπορεύεται; although Jesus also participates in his mission (ibid.; cfr. 16:7), and the Spirit receives from him what is his (John 16:14-15). In 1Cor 2:13, mention is made of τό πνευμα τό έκ του θεου. We will not repeat at this point what we already know about the sending of the Spirit by the resurrected Jesus, nor that according to the New Testament, the Spirit is not only «of God» but also «of the Son» or «of Jesus».

We have already analyzed some elements of the old tradition. In general terms, it is believed that the Spirit comes from the Father, and that this is finally the guarantee of his divinity. Nevertheless, based on the indisputable fact of the gift of the Spirit by the Son, we also see a certain function of the second person in his procession.

According to Origen, even though the Spirit is clearly divine and therefore essentially different from creatures, he is the first of the beings who comes into existence by the action of the Father through the Son, according to the interpretation of John 1:3 made by the Alexandrian.

latino, così che sia mesa in luce la piena armonia con ciò che il Concilio ecumenico di Constantinopoli, nel 381, confessa nel suo simbolo: il Padre come sorgente di tutta la Trinità, sola origine del Fligio e dello Spirito Santo» (cfr. «L'Osservatore Romano», June 30th-July 1st, 1995). The clarification requested by the Pope took place in a Declaration of the Papal Council for the promotion of the unity of Christians, published in «L'Osservatore Romano», dated September 13th, 1995. The data that we will offer regarding the history of the problem can be completed with what is mentioned by PAATFORD A., «Le Filioque dans la conscience de l'Église avant Ephèse» in *RevTh* 97 (1997) 318-334.

Tertullian used the formula *a Patre per Filium*[181], but it could be that he was referring only to the gift *ad extra* of the Holy Spirit. The Spirit is the third one *a Deo et (ex) Filio*[182]. Tertullian affirmed this within the context of the Trinitarian comparisons with which we are already familiar and which point to a linear scheme: source, river, channel; root, trunk, branch... He also mentioned that the Spirit takes from Jesus (cfr. John 16:14), as Jesus takes from the Father[183].

Athanasius seemed to apply a similar linear scheme: the Father is light, the Son is brilliance, and the Holy Spirit illuminates us. The Father is source, the Son is river, and we drink from the Holy Spirit[184]. The concern of Athanasius in this context was simply that of making us realize how the participation that is immediate to the divine life takes place in the Holy Spirit. Other texts that refer to the internal life of God are somewhat more obscure. Everything that the Spirit has, he has from the Logos, παρά του λόγου[185]; however, he also quotes on another occasion John 15:26, where it is said that the Holy Spirit proceeds from the Father although he is sent and given by the Word, παρά του λόγου[186]. We know the parallelism of the Father-Son / Son-Spirit relationships that are presented by Athanasius[187]. Nonetheless, it is clear that we cannot look for a clear response to a problem that had not yet been posed at that time.

What was stated by Basil is not clear either. He agreed with the ideas of Athanasius about the proximity or the immediacy of the Spirit in us that makes us share the divine life[188]. The relationship between Jesus and the Spirit is primarily expressed in the following text: «He is all Spirit of Christ because he is intimately united to him by nature... as Paraclete he manifests the goodness of the Paraclete that has sent him, and in his own dignity he emphasizes the dignity of the one from whom he has emerged»[189]. If, in the first instance, the passage refers clearly to the saving mission, the meaning of the term «emerge» is not as evident.

181 TERTULLIAN, *Adv. Prax.* 4,1 (Scarpat, 150).
182 TERTULLIAN, *Adv. Prax.* 8,7 (160).
183 TERTULLIAN 25,1 (218):«*De meo sumet* (John 16:14), inquit, sicut ipse de Patre. Ita connexus Patris in Filio et Filii in Paracleto tres efficit cohaerentes, alterum ex altero ».
184 Cfr. *Serap.* I 19 (PG 26,573). SIMONETTI M., *La crisi ariana nel IV secolo*, Roma 1975, 494-500.
185 *C. Arian.* III 24 (PG 26,376).
186 *Serap.* I 20 (580); cfr. III 5 (632), the things received from the Spirit, *parà tou lògou* the strength to be.
187 *Serap.* I 25 (588s); certain indications of the Son-Spirit intra-Trinitarian relationship stated in Athanasius have been reported by CONGAR Y., *El Espíritu Santo*, 469. DIDYMUS THE BLIND, *De Sp. sanc.* 34,153 (286): the Spirit is «ex Patre et ex me (Jesus)», but we do not have the original text in Greek.
188 *De Sp. Sancto*, 26,63-64 (SCh 17 bis, 472-476).
189 *De Sp. Sancto*, 18,46 (410); 18,45 (408), the Holy Spirit unites the Father through the Son.

However, the intervention of the Son could be limited to the economy. We know that we owe to Gregory of Nazianzus the technical term of «procession» applied to the Spirit, although the person he proceeds from is the Father. The «procession» enables us to determine the property of the Spirit as it relates to the other divine persons. The Holy Spirit is not unbegotten; neither is he begotten[190]. The other two persons come from the Father, not to be confused, but united[191].

Mention can be made of the similar texts written by Gregory of Nyssa in which he suggested the intervention of the Son in the procession of the Holy Spirit that has its beginning in the Father. The person is one and the same, that of the Father, who begets the Son and from whom the Spirit also proceeds[192]. Therefore, it seems that the generation of the Son and the procession of the Spirit are related. Gregory also used the metaphor of the lamp that lights up a second one, and through this second one, a third one[193]. In other passages, the well-known text in the gospel of John is used: the Holy Spirit comes from the Father and receives from the Son (cfr. John 16:26; also Rom 8:9), although the problem of the internal relation is not excluded:

> In what has been caused, we see a new distinction between what is immediately from the first one and what comes through the mediation of the one who comes immediately from the first one…. The intermediary position of the Son reserves for himself the property of being the only-begotten, and the Spirit is not deprived of his natural relationship with the Father[194].

We could say that Gregory spoke in general terms of a procession of the Spirit *a Patre per Filium*, but without being exactly precise. The order (*táxis*) of the persons does not imply any chronological difference[195]. The Spirit proceeds from the Father. The intervention of the Son is not excluded, although to a certain

---

190 *Or.* 31,8 (SCh 150,290); ibid. 31,29 (292), the Holy Spirit does not lack anything, but there is a differentiation with respect to the Son in the relationship.
191 *Or.* 42,15 (SCh 384,82).
192 Cfr. *Ad Graecos ex comun. notionibus* (Jaeger III 1,25).
193 Cfr. *De Sp. Sancto adv. Mac.* (Jaeger III 1,93).
194 *Quod non sunt tres dii* (Jaeger III 1,56).
195 *Contra Eun.* 1 81 (Jaeger I 689): «As the Son is united with the Father and receives his origin from him, without being posterior to him… in this way also the Holy Spirit receives his origin, in turn, from the Son, because he is considered as previous to the *hypostasis* of the Holy Spirit only with respect to causality, without there being any place for temporal intervals in this eternal life»; GREGORY OF NYSSA, *Teologia trinitaria* (intr., translated by MORESCHINI C.), Milano 1994, 189-190.

degree, it is undetermined. What primarily matters is the divinity of the Spirit, which is ensured by the relationship with the Father, and not so much the strict problem of the «procession», which in these times is no longer an issue subject to discussion.

In the case of Cyril of Alexandria, we find some passages that point to the idea of the Spirit as inherent in the Son because he is from him and he receives from him. Some of these affirmations result from clear opposition to the statements of Nestorius. It was worth emphasizing that the Holy Spirit was inherent in Jesus also in the incarnation, in order to affirm the unity of the person of Jesus[196]. It seems that from the economy we move to the immanent Trinity. The Spirit is of the essence of the Son[197]; he is of the Father and of the Son, belonging to the Son[198]. He is even «of him»[199], but only with respect to the Father is the term ἐκπόρευσις used, which points out his relationship with the beginning without beginning. However, the verb προιέναι and other similar more obscure verbs also express the relationship with respect to the Son[200]. Theodoret of Ciro, who said that Jesus proceeds from the Father, accused Cyril of saying that the Spirit has his existence from the Son or through the Son. Nevertheless, Cyril did not change his opinion, and even after being antagonized, he continually stressed «of both of them». This is not the theology that we will see set forth later by Augustine, but we wish to point out that the Holy Spirit is united with the divine essence and that he is God like the Father and the Son. He is not a creature because he is of the Son. It seems that a relationship with the Son is affirmed in the procession of the Spirit, although still vaguely. The ultimate source from which the Spirit comes is the Father. Maximus the Confessor pointed out that the Holy Spirit, by his own nature, has his origin in the Father through the begotten Son[201].

We must also view some formulations made by John of Damascus († 749) before we address the thoughts of the Western theologians. John of Damascus primarily wanted to emphasize the divine unity from which we continue on to the «monarchy» of God the Father. He is the Father of the only-begotten Son and the *proboleus* of the Holy Spirit. The Spirit does not come as a result of the genera-

---

196 *Adv. Nest.* IV 1 (PG 76,173); cfr. CONGAR Y., *El Espíritu Santo*, 479ff.

197 Cfr. *Thesaurus* (PG 75,585;608): the Spirit is of the *ousía* of the Son, realized in the plenitude of the Holy Triad.

198 *In Ioel.* 35 (PG 71,377).

199 «Ex autou»; *De S. Trin. Dial.* 7 (PG 75,1093).

200 For instance, *In Joh ev.* 2 (PG 71,212); *Thesaurus* (PG 75,585;608;612); *Adv. Nest.* IV 1 (PG 76,173).

201 Cfr. *Quaestiones ad Thalassium*, 63 (PG 90,672).

tion, but he has another way of coming to be or of subsisting (τρόπος της ὑπάρξεως). The Spirit comes from the Father alone; only he can be called «cause», in such a way that the Son is not the cause of the Spirit, but he is the Spirit of the Son. This is not because he emerges *from* him, but because he comes *through* him (δι᾽ αὐτοῦ) from the Father. Through the Word, the Father produces the Spirit who manifests him. He is called Spirit of the Son, not as proceeding from him, but as proceeding from the Father through him[202]. Similarly, the Spirit rests on the Word and accompanies the Word, participating in his activity and making him evident. He is the image of the Word. Certainly we cannot say that John of Damascus taught the procession of the Spirit from the Father and from the Son. The procession of the Spirit is in a certain way related to the generation of the Son. We cannot exactly determine the difference that exists between one and the other: «By virtue of the faith we perceive that there is a differentiation between the generation and the *ekpóreusis* or origin of the Holy Spirit. The faith does not tell us of what this difference consists»[203]. John of Damascus saw the immanent procession and the gift of the Spirit in an intimate relationship.

In all, even though the formula *a Patre per Filium* does not intend to attach to the Holy Spirit an especially precise meaning, it can nonetheless be considered a line of thought which is found in the theology of the Greek Fathers. Above all, we must emphasize that the *ekpóreusis* itself is exclusively affirmed from the Father, because he is the only cause and the ultimate source of the Trinity. The intervention of the Son is not excluded. Even more so, it is affirmed by many, although in rather imprecise terms.

Western theology has followed other roads, mostly after Saint Augustine. Nevertheless, before we refer to this, we must point out the fact that the formula *a Patre per Filium*, which we saw in Tertullian, had been referred to by Hilary as something acquired. In spite of this fact, in view of the very limited development of his «immanent» pneumatology, we cannot exactly determine the meaning that he attached to it. Perhaps there were influences on him derived from Origen's line of thought, which is well known to us[204]. Ambrose was probably the

---

202 Cfr. *De fide orthod.* I 12 (PG 94,849); cfr. I 8 (832s), the Spirit does not come from (*ek*) the Son, but he is called Spirit of the Son. Cfr. GRÉGOIRE J., «La relation éternelle de l'Esprit au Fils d'après les écrits de Jean de Damas» in *Revue d'Histoire Ecclésiastique* 64 (1969) 713-755.
203 *De fide orthod.* I 8 (824); cfr. CONGAR Y., *El Espíritu Santo*, 484.
204 Cfr. LADARIA L.F., *El Espíritu Santo en san Hilario de Poitiers*, Madrid 1977, 302ff. Hilary also saw a parallel between the «proceeding» of the Father and the «receiving» of the Son, according to John 16:14-15. (*Trin.* 8, 20; CCL 62,331f). The Spirit is not begotten, but he is not created either.

first one to state that the Holy Spirit proceeds from the Father and the Son[205], even though in view of the context, it is difficult to determine to what extent he referred to the intra-Trinitarian procession or whether it is rather the gift of the Spirit to humanity.

The current of thought that began with Augustine, based on the background to which we have already referred, which sees the Holy Spirit as a gift of the Father and the Son and at the same time as mutual love and fruit of this reciprocal love, led Western theology, beginning with Augustine himself, to affirm the procession originating with the two first persons. The Father and the Son are the only beginning of the Holy Spirit who proceeds from the two of them[206]. Nevertheless, Augustine has been careful in stating that even though the Spirit proceeds from the two, he comes *principaliter* from the Father, because if he proceeds also from the Son, it is because the Father has given the Son this possibility. Everything that the Son is and that the Son has, and thus, also the fact that the Holy Spirit proceeds from him, has been given to him by the Father in his generation[207].

The fact that the Holy Spirit is considered love and gift of the Father and of the Son, leads us to reach the conclusion that he also comes from the second person, although the Father, from whom the Son receives everything, continues to be the sole source of the Trinity. It is worth pointing out the marked anti-Arian nature of the *filioque*. Upon associating the Son with the Father in the procession of the Spirit, the full communion of essence of the two, the consubstantiality of the Son with the Father, is most strongly evidenced. The medieval West would continue with these schemes, and as we will see later, the *filioque* has been affirmed by countless regional synods and councils. Anselm devoted a treatise to the procession of the Holy Spirit in which he strongly defended the *filioque* against the Greeks[208]. Similarly, Richard of St. Victor argued in favor of

---

205 *De Sp. sanc.* I 11,120 (CSEL 79,67).

206 Cfr. *Contra Maxim.* II 14,1 (PL 42,769), in addition to the text of *Trin.* with which we are already familiar.

207 AUGUSTINE, *Trin.* XV 17,29 (CCL 50,503f); «...nec de quo genitum est verbum et de quo procedit principaliter spiritus sanctus, nisi deus pater. Ideo autem addidi principaliter, quia et de filio spiritus sanctus procedere reperietur. Sed hoc quoque illi pater dedit non iam existenti et nondum habenti, sed quidquid unigenito verbo dedit, gignendo dedit. Sic ergo genuit ut etiam de illo donum commune procederet, et spiritus sanctus spiritus esset amborum»; XV 26,47 (529): «Filius autem de patre natus est, et spiritus sanctus de patre principaliter, et ipso sine ullo temporis intervallo dante, communiter de utroque procedit»; cfr. also *In Joh. Ev.*, 99,8 (CCL 36,587).

208 Cfr. *De procesione Spiritus sanctis* I 2.4.12.14.16 (Opera, SCHMITT F. S., ed., v. 2, 185.190.193.209-210.212-215.217), among other places; the Spirit can only be of the Son if he proceeds him. From the economy, we go to the immanent Trinity. The *principaliter* of Augustine is also mentioned

the procession of the two in view of the communion of power of all the persons[209]. The procession of the Holy Spirit is accomplished through the communion of love (the Spirit is the *condilectus*), just as the communion of honor is involved in the procession of the Son.

Saint Thomas pointed out the relationship that exists between the name of the Holy Spirit and the modality of his procession. Like Augustine and the authors that preceded him, he stressed the fact that the inherent name of the Holy Spirit is common in itself. This is due to the fact that he proceeds through the way of love. Therefore, the suitability of the name is in the first place determined by the fact that he is the Spirit of the two, of the Father and of the Son. The name is also appropriate because love —as the Spirit— is impulse, movement; in other words it is also inherent in the Holy Spirit. This name of «spirit» is likewise suitable for the person who proceeds through love. The adjective «holy» is also suitable. Holiness is attributable to those things that are ordered by God. If this person proceeds through the modality of love, by means of which God is love, «he is appropriately called Holy Spirit»[210].

Nevertheless, as we have already noted, in the case of Saint Thomas, the love of the Father and the Son plays an extremely limited role in the procession of the Holy Spirit from the Father and the Son. The fundamental reasons for which we must affirm the intervention of the Son in this procession are their opposite relationships:

> It is necessary to point out that the Holy Spirit proceeds from the Son. Otherwise, if he did not proceed from him, he would not be able to be distinguished personally from him in any way…. The persons are only distinguished among themselves by their relationships. In fact, the relationships cannot distinguish the persons if they are not opposite…. The Father has two relationships, one of which applies to the Son and the other to the Holy Spirit. In spite of this fact, precisely because they are not opposite, they are two persons…. Therefore, if in the Son and the Holy Spirit we cannot find more than two relationships by means of which each one of them is related to the Father, these rela-

by Anselm. Ibid. 14 (213). Cfr. GILBERT P., «La confession de foi dans le De processione Spiritus sancti de saint Anselme» in AA.VV. *L'attualitá filosofica di Anselmo d'Aosta*, Roma 1990, 229-262; BONANNI S., «Il *Filioque* tra dialettica e dialogo. Anselmo e Abelardo: posizioni a confronto» in *Lateranum* 64 (1998) 49-79.

209 Cfr. AUGUSTINE, *Trin.* V 8 (SCh 63,318ff).
210 Cfr. THOMAS AQUINAS, *STh* I 36,1.

tionships would not be opposite among themselves…. Hence, it would follow that the person of the Son and the person of the Holy Spirit would be only one[211].

The doctrine of the procession of the Holy Spirit through the road of love leads us to the same conclusion: love proceeds from the word, because we cannot love one thing if we do not conceive it and understand it through the conception of the mind[212].

According to Saint Thomas, the Greeks themselves understood that the procession of the Holy Spirit has a certain ordaining by the Son, because they stated that the Holy Spirit is likewise the Spirit of the Son or that he proceeds *a Patre per Filium*. He also added an interesting observation that enables to us to see the misunderstanding of terminology that could emerge around this issue. Previously in this treatise, we warned that many Greek Fathers, even though they recognize a certain intervention of the Son in the procession of the Spirit, do not refer to it using the term *ekpóreusis*. They reserve this term for his procession from the Father, because only the Father is the original beginning and the first source of the Spirit. However, Saint Thomas pointed out that in Latin the verb *procedere* is used to refer to any origin. For this reason, we can reach the conclusion that the Holy Spirit proceeds from the Son[213], although only in the Father can we find the original source of that divinity.

The formula of the procession of the Holy Spirit *a Patre per Filium* was also accepted by Thomas. In all truth, his explanation is Augustinian, based in the *principaliter* with which we are already familiar: the Son has received from the Father the reality that the Holy Spirit also has in proceeding from him. In this way, the Spirit proceeds, on the one hand, immediately and directly from the Father because the Father is the immediate principle, but on the other hand, he also proceeds «mediately», since he also proceeds from the Son who has received from the Father the possibility of being the beginning of the Spirit[214].

The Father and the Son are the only beginning of the Holy Spirit because in the common condition of the beginning of the Spirit they are not opposed in a relational manner. Thomas was already grounded in the principle according to which there is unity in God where there is no opposition in the relationship, a

211 THOMAS AQUINAS, *STh* I 36,2.
212 Cfr. THOMAS AQUINAS, *STh* I 36,2.
213 Cfr. THOMAS AQUINAS, *STh* I 36,2.
214 Cfr. THOMAS AQUINAS, *STh* I 36,3.

statement that will be formulated two centuries later in the Council of Florence[215]. It is a property that belongs to two subjects, as well as the two belong to (and are of) the same nature. However, if we consider the subjects of the inspiration, it is clear that we are dealing with two, because the Spirit proceeds from them because of the uniting love of the two[216].

This brief review of some representatives of the Eastern and Western traditions on this issue has enabled us to see the differences in approach to this topic, while also noting the points of similarity. These include acknowledgement of the Father as the ultimate source of the divinity, a presence of the Son in the procession of the Spirit —expressed in somewhat more obscure terms in the East— sometimes with the generic formulation «of the Father through the Son», and more strictly in the West, where beginning with Saint Augustine, mention is made concerning the procession of the Spirit «from the Father and from the Son» as only one beginning. In the West, the «economic» datum of the Spirit, gift of the Father and of the Son, has given way to the immanent datum of the procession of the two. Eastern theology has not taken this step, or at least it has not done so with the same clarity. On the other hand, it has placed more emphasis on the fact that the Spirit comes from Jesus, the incarnate Son. The Western theological conception has led to the introduction of the *filioque* into the creed and in the discussions that have emerged from it. This is precisely the problem that we will address at this point.

3.3.2. *THE «FILIOQUE» IN THE SYMBOLS AND IN THE CATECHISM*

The Augustinian doctrine of the procession of the Holy Spirit from the Father and the Son is echoed in the symbol *Quicumque* which probably emerged in southern France between the years 430 and 450 and which has enjoyed considerable authority both in the East and in the West. In it we find the formula «Spiritus sanctus a Patre et Filio, non factus nec creatus nec genitus, sed procedens» (DS 75). Leo the Great taught the same doctrine: the Holy Spirit proceeds from the two (year 447; DS 284). But still the *fides Pelagii papae* (Pelagius I, year 557) stated that the Holy Spirit «ex Patre intemporaliter procedens, Patris est Filiique Spiritus» (DS 441).

Cfr. THOMAS AQUINAS, *STh* I 36,4: «Pater et Filius in omnia unum sunt, in quibus non distinguitur inter eos relationis oppositio». Cfr. DS 1330.
216 THOMAS AQUINAS, *STh* I 36,4 ad. 1: «Peocedit ab eis ut amor unitivus duorum».

Chapter 10

405

The *filioque* was already present in the creed of Victricius of Rouen, a disciple of Ambrose, at the end of the fourth century[217], and in different Spanish creeds from the fifth century[218]. In the Third Council of Toledo (year 589), specifically in terms of the procession of the Catholic faith of Recaredo (previously Arian), it reads: «Likewise, the Holy Spirit must be confessed by us and it must be affirmed that he proceeds from the Father and the Son and that he is of only one substance with the Father and the Son» (DS 470). This clearly Anti-Arian affirmation is aimed primarily at affirming the consubstantiality of the Father and the Son, and of the Holy Spirit with the two of them. Furthermore, in the Fourth Council of Toledo in 633 it is affirmed once again that the Holy Spirit is neither created nor begotten, but that he proceeds from the Father and the Son (cfr. DS 490)[219].

In a synodical letter (Lateran Synod in 649), Pope Martin I affirmed that the Holy Spirit also proceeds from the Father. Some theologians were highly concerned about this in the East. Maximus the Confessor responded to some of these concerns by stating that the Latin Fathers spoke of the procession of the Holy Spirit by means of the Son. Maximus made a distinction between the ἐκπρεσθαι and the προιέναί. The Latin Fathers did not make the Son the «cause» of the Holy Spirit, but they affirmed the procession (*proeinai*) by means of the Son, and in this way they showed the identity of the essence. Hence, we can see a clear distinction between the *ekpóreusis,* which can only begin from the Father, the beginning from the first source or initial cause, and the *processing,* which does not imply this precision[220]. The problem does not seem to have had major consequences at that time. Also in England, a synod held in 680 in Hatfield, stated as follows: «Spiritum sanctum procedentem ex Patre et Filio inenarrabiliter». Hence, what had been stated by Pope Martin I was accepted.

---

217 Cfr. PL 20,246. Cfr. GARRIGUES J.M., *El Espíritu que dice ¡Padre!,* Salamanca 1985, 91ff.

218 Cfr. KELLY J.N.D., *Primitivos credos cristianos,* Salamanca 1980, 426-428, among others the First Council of Toledo in the year 400, although with additional information to the formula of the year 447, against the followers of Priscus to save the different *hypostases* of the Holy Spirit: it is neither the Father nor the Son, «sed a Patre [Filioque] procedens» (DS 188).

219 Cfr. the symbols of the Sixth, Ninth and Sixteenth Councils of Toledo (DS 490;527;569-570). The formulations of the last one are interesting: «ex Patris Filique unione procedit», «a Patre Filioque».

220 Cfr. additional data in GARRIGUES J.M., *El Espíritu que dice «¡Padre!,* 105ff. We saw that these distinctions in terminology are also present in Cyril of Alexandria.

So also in France, at the Synod of Gentilly in 767, it was stated that the Holy Spirit proceeds from the Son in the same way as he proceeds from the Father. Alcuin of York spoke strongly in favor of the *filioque* before Charles the Great. The latter protested before the Pope because the Council of Nicaea in 787 had accepted the confession of faith of the Patriarch Tarasios who incredibly professed that the Spirit does not proceed from the Father and the Son in accordance with the faith of the Nicene symbol, but from the Father through the Son[221]. Pope Adrian I defended the theologians from the East. The Council of Frankfurt held in 794 should have condemned the Eastern theologians, but Leo III, the successor of Adrian, once again defended the Second Council of Nicaea. The Pope accepted the doctrine of the *filioque*, but he did not wish to include it in the creed. He ordered the engraving of two plates, with the confession of Saint Peter, with the text in Latin and in Greek, but without the added text.

Fotius did not accuse Rome directly because of the *filioque*. There was no reason to do so because in the case of Rome it had not been included in the creed. Only when Henry II was crowned Emperor in 1014 was the creed introduced in Rome (until that time, it was not recited), and it was introduced with the added text that is common in the West. In the meantime Fotius, who had died in communion with Rome after having been excommunicated and deposed, had written since the year 867 against the Latin *filioque*, and he had formulated the thesis of the procession of the Holy Spirit only from the Father, a formulation that was more radical than those which had been set forth before. He insisted on the monarchy of the Father. Both the Son and the Holy Spirit come from the Father. In this way, every possibility of an intervention of the Son in the procession of the Holy Spirit was ruled out, something that had never been done before. The intervention of the Son in the mission of the Holy Spirit in the saving economy is fully deprived of any possible intra-Trinitarian correspondence. The theology of Gregory Palamas seemed to exclude the Son from the «hypostatic» procession of the Holy Spirit. Nevertheless, he gave it a place in the economic manifestation of «energy». Grace is offered by the Son, it is uncreated,

---

221 Cfr. Garijo Guembe M., «Filioque» in Pikaza X.-Silanes N., *Diccionario del Dios Cristiano*, Salamanca 1992, 545-554, 547; Congar Y., *El Espíritu Santo*, 496: «The *Filioque* had been introduced in the symbol in the last decade of the fourth century, and it was believed in good faith that it came from Nicaea-Constantinople, so that a long time before the fiery Humbert in 1054, the *Libri carolini*, circa 790, could accuse the Greeks of having suppressed it from the symbol!» Cfr. also ibid. 496ff.

but is not the Holy Spirit himself, but uncreated energy, the divinizing gift that is inseparable from the Holy Spirit[222].

We are familiar with the position of Thomas Aquinas who died when he was on his way to Lyon to participate in the activities related to the Second Council of that city in 1274. The Council had been summoned with the purpose of reestablishing union with the Greeks. The profession of faith of Michael Paleologus was read in the aula. It stated: «We also believe in the Holy Spirit, true, full, and perfect God, who proceeds from the Father and the Son, equal and consubstantial…» (DS 853). The Father and the Son are the one only beginning of the Holy Spirit (cfr. DS 850). The deeply longed-for union was not possible.

The issue was posed again before the Council of Florence (1439-1445). Some of the Greek representatives were very critical of the Latin position which they simply qualified as heretical. The memory of the mediating position of Maximus the Confessor, whom we have already mentioned, was able to unblock the discussion. It was impossible to even think that the holy Latin and Greek Fathers could have contradicted one another.

The accord of the union of Florence was subscribed to by the Emperor and thirty nine Eastern theologians, but it was not subscribed to by the main Eastern speaker, Marcus Eugenicus, and unfortunately, on that occasion it was not possible to complete the union. In turn, in the Council of Florence, the *a Patre per Filium* was understood in the sense of the *filioque*. What was not approved, however, was the opposite acknowledgement, in other words, that the *filioque* could also be equivalent to the *a Patre per Filium*. In this way, the diversity of points of view was simply reduced to the Western formula:

We define… that the Holy Spirit proceeds eternally from the Father and from the Son, and jointly from the Father and the Son he has his essence and his subsistent being, and from the one with the other he proceeds eternally as only one beginning and by only one expiration. At the same time we declare what the holy doctors and fathers told us, in other words, that the Holy Spirit proceeds from the Father through the Son, is inclined toward this understanding, and expresses, according to the Greeks, that the Son is cause and beginning of the subsistence of the Holy Spirit, as is also the Father, according to the Latin theologians. And because everything that *is*, is from the Father, the Father himself gave it to his only-begotten Son when he begot him, and

222 Cfr. CONGAR Y., *El Espíritu Santo*, 504: GARIJO GUEMBE M., «Filioque», 549-550.

besides being Father, the same fact that the Son precedes the Holy Spirit is what the Son also eternally has from the same Father, from whom he is also eternally begotten. We also assert that the addition of the word *filioque* was licit and right and reasonably included in the symbol, considering the truth and the need that was then urgent (DS 1300-1302).

The line of thought of the *principaliter* of Augustine is easily acknowledged in all the arguments that were set forth. It seems strange that it is stated that the Greeks also called the Son «cause» of the Holy Spirit. Rather, they reserved the expression for the Father, as is evidenced from some of the texts that we have analyzed.

3.3.3. THE ISSUE IN PRESENT TIMES

Even though the problem is not currently characterized by the virulence of those times, nevertheless we cannot consider that everything is completely solved. There are representatives of Orthodoxy who pose significant difficulties and do not wish to accept the Western conception. Despite this fact, there are others who do not believe that the *filioque* in itself is a reason to justify the separation[223]. Bulgakov thought that the *filioque* did not mean a dogmatic divergence between the Church of the East and the Church of the West. If there are no notable differences in the life of the corresponding Churches, this is a clear signal that there are no differences either as it relates to their faith[224]. Other Orthodox theologians insist on the simultaneity of the generation of the Son and of the procession of the Spirit and wish rather to see a mutual relationship between both without denying an intervention of the eternal God in the procession of the Holy Spirit who is the Spirit of the Father and of the Son[225].

---

[223] Cfr. the theses of Bolotov, at the end of the past century in CONGAR V., El Espíritu Santo, 627; thesis number 3 seems significant: «The opinion according to which the expression dia tou Hyiou had never contained anything else than a temporal mission of the Holy Spirit forces us to go against the interpretation of some texts of the Fathers».

[224] Cfr. BULGAKOV S., *Il Paraclito*, 208; 231; cfr. also page 145: «il Figlio nell'abbassamento di sé sacrificale, riceve anche simultaneamente lo Spirito, che procede su di lui dal Padre, che riposa su di lui e che passa attraverso (dià) lui, como reciprocità, risposta, anello dell'amore».

[225] Hence, BOBRINSKOY B., *Le Mystère de la Trinité*, Paris 1986 : « Le Fils sera don la *raison d'etre* de la procession de l'Esprit qui est à la fois l'Esprit du Père et l'Esprit du Fils. L'Esprit sera non moins lié—ineffablement—a la génération paternelle du Fils, reposant sur le Fils qui est pneumatophore de toute l'eternité. On peut donc concevoir que l'Esprit procède du Père seul, tout en se souvenant qu'il faut entendre 'Père du Fils' ... »; cfr. also 300 and 304: «Le Fils éternel n'est pas étranger à la procession du Saint Esprit. Mais, ajoutera la théologie orthodoxe; a) de manière ineffable; b) sans faire intervenir la notion de causalité et; c) sans mettre en question la caractère intrans-

Catholic theology tends rather to emphasize the compatibility and the complementary nature of the Eastern and Western formulas. This is the position reflected by the Catechism of the Catholic Church which points out that the complementary nature of both visions, if it is exacerbated, does not go against the identity of the faith that is confessed in the same mystery[226]. We must acknowledge that at this point there can be some misunderstandings which are derived from thinking that between the *ekpóreusis* of the Greek and the *procession* of the Latin there is an equivalence in meaning. We have seen how Maximus the Confessor and Thomas Aquinas were sensitive to these differences. In the case of the Latin position, any precedence is «procession». In the Greek position, the *ekpóreusis* is procession as the first beginning, and hence as a beginning of the Father. Therefore, only the Father is «cause». With differences that cannot be neglected, neither can we forget the points of coincidence with the *principaliter* of Saint Augustine. Moreover, the formula of Constantinople cannot be considered all-inclusive. In this respect, the «through the Son» is an explanation of the symbol that need not necessarily be contrary to it, as the *filioque* need not necessarily be contrary to the monarchy of the Father, source of all the Trinity, and only origin of the Son and of the Holy Spirit.

Formulas to reach a compromise have been constantly sought. For instance, «the Holy Spirit comes from the Father insofar as he is Father of the Son». It is worth noting that the symbol states that he proceeds from the Father. When the Father is mentioned, we are already thinking of a relationship with the Son, because otherwise the term lacks its meaning. The procession of the Holy Spirit is not a begetting[227]. The proposal of Moltmann has some points of contact with

missible de la proprieté hypostatique du Père, d'être seul Source et Principe de la divinité du Fils et de l'Esprit»; cfr. in the context the positive elements and the gaps that are found in the «filioquism». More information on the Eastern theology will be found in this same work, pages 294-305; see also Garijo Guembe M., «Filioque», 551-553. See also on this topic *Enchiridion Oecumenicarum* III, 2001ff; 2700ff. Cfr. Pirà B., *Lo Spirito Santo nella recente letteratura ortodossa*, in G. Colzani G. (ed.), *Verso una nuova età dello Spirito. Filosofia-Teologia-Movimenti*, Padova 1997, 155-237. Also Spiteris Y., «La dottrina trinitaria nella teologia ortodossa. Autori e prospettive» in Amato A. (ed), *Trinità in contesto*, Roma, 1993, 45-69. On the current ecumenical situation, cfr. Gamillscheg M.-H., *Die Kontroverse um das Filioque. Möglichkeiten einer Problemlösung auf Grund der Forschungen und Gespräche der letzten hundert Jahre*, Würzburg 1996.

226 CEC, 248. Cfr. the Declaration of the Papal Council for the Unity of Christians, dated September 13th, 1995.

227 Cfr. Garrigues J.M., *El Espíritu que dice ¡Padre!*, 129; hence the formula that proposes: «coming out (*ekporeuomenon*) from the Father, proceeding (*proion*) from the Father and the Son» (ibid. 98); ibid. 113: «Just as the Holy Spirit exists by nature according to the essence of the Father, in the same way he is by nature of the Son, insofar as he essentially emerges from the Father by

the above: he proceeds from the Father of the Son and receives his form from the Father and from the Son[228].

Without attempting to propose a concrete formula, but rather by explaining the sense of the *filioque* and its compatibility with the acknowledgement of the only source of the divinity in the Father, the declaration of the Papal Council for the Unity of Christians of 1995, to which we have already referred[229], points out that even though in the Trinitarian order, the Holy Spirit is consecutive to the relationship between the Father and the Son[230] because he has his origin in the Father insofar as the latter is Father of the only begotten Son, that relationship between the Father and the Son reaches its Trinitarian perfection only in the Spirit. In the same way as the Father is characterized as Father by the Son whom he begets, the Spirit, who has his origin in the Father, characterizes in the Trinitarian mode the Son in his relationship with the Father. The Father begets the Son only by inspiring the Holy Spirit, and the Son is begotten only insofar as the inspiration goes through him. It is worth noting that the Trinitarian order is maintained because the Father is characterized as such by the Son and not by the Holy Spirit[231], but this does not mean a chronological difference or a subordination. Only in the Holy Spirit is this relationship characterized from the Trinitarian point of view. The procession of the Spirit from the Father cannot do without the fact that this Father is Father insofar as he begets the Son.

As we can see in these different positions, which are not only personal, but also have an official nature, what they are attempting to precisely emphasize is the Trinitarian nature of all the intra-divine relationships. The Father-Son relationship cannot be considered independently from the Holy Spirit, the mutual gift of love in which they are united and love each other. Without the Spirit, the

---

virtue of the begotten Son». The Latin formula would be: «ex unico Patre unicum Filium generante se exportans (*ekporeuomenon*), ab utroque procedit (*prochoron*)». Cfr. by the same author, «La clarification sur la procession du Saint-Esprit et l'enseignement du Concile de Florence» in *Irénikon* (1995) 501-506 ; and «A la suite de la clarification romaine sur le Filioque» in NRTh 119 (1997) 321-334, primarily shows how the action of the Son and of the Holy Spirit are complementary in the work of salvation.

228 Cfr. MOLTMANN J., *Trinität und Reich Gottes*, München 1980, 203. Cfr. also, «Lo spirito della vita» in *Per una pneumatologia integrale*, Brescia 1994, 347.

229 Cfr. footnotes 180 and 226.

230 According to the same «Declaration», the Holy Spirit does not precede the Son, because the Son characterizes as Father the one from whom the Spirit has its origin, which is the Trinitarian order. Nevertheless, the breathing of the Spirit starting in the Father is done through and by means of (the two senses of *dià* in Greek) the generation of the Son.

231 Cfr. GALOT J., «L'origine éternelle de l'Esprit Saint» in *Greg* 78 (1997) 421-476, especially 516-517; of the same, *L'Esprit Saint, personne de communion*, Saint Maur 1997, especially 122ff.

Father-Son relationship cannot be fulfilled[232], and the procession of the Spirit from the Father cannot be considered independently from the Son. The Trinitarian *taxis* does not imply subordination although it implies mutual reference. The «order» does not imply eliminating the mutual interdependence of the persons. Perhaps this line of thought can contribute to understanding between the Church of the East and the Church of the West.

We must bear in mind that East and West still remained together after the Western introduction of the *filioque* into the symbol. The theology of Augustine was prepared before Chalcedon, where the value of Constantinople I was acknowledged. At that time, the Latin theologians could not understand the difference in meaning that the term «proceed» has in Greek and in Latin. When the West received the creed of Constantinople, the *filioque* had probably already been introduced even into different Western symbols (that of Victricius of Rouen, the *Quicumque*, as we have seen). This background must have been taken into account when assessing the introduction of the *filioque* in the symbol of Nicaea-Constantinople by the Pope, even though it is true that this was done without keeping in mind the Eastern Churches.

This is the reason why in past years certain voices have been heard that support the suppression in the Catholic Church of this addition to the Creed, which undoubtedly, should not mean the disapproval of the theological evolution that gave rise to the *filioque*. The different theologies and the formulas that have been condensed can represent valid approximations to the mystery and can even be supplementary among themselves if the diversities are not exacerbated. Among the important Catholic theologians, Congar was one of those who most clearly stood up for the suppression of the *filioque*, provided that…

---

232 The need to always see the three persons in relationship has led us to pose the problem of the presence of the Spirit in the generation of the Word. Cfr., for instance, DURRWELL F.X., *L'Esprit Saint de Dieu*, Paris 1983, especially 154ff, developed also in *Le Père. Dieu en son mystère*, 147ff, God begets «in the Spirit». Cfr. also CANTALAMESSA R., «*Utriusque Spiritus*. L'attuale dibattito teologico alla luce del'Veni Creator» in *Rassegna di Teologia* 38 (1997) 465-484, especially 477ff, in which he refers to the pre-cosmic anointing of the Son by the Father in view of the creation that the Fathers have known; cfr. ORBE A., *La unción del Verbo*, Romae 1961. We must bear in mind, however, that the personal nature of this «spirit» is not always clear. Some Fathers, for instance, Gregory of Nyssa, have even seen the anointing to be at the exact time of the generation: *Contra Apolinarem* 52 (PG 45,1249-1250). It does not seem from the context that we can derive many consequences from this *ab aeterno* anointing in relation to the presence of the Spirit in the generation of the Son. It is legitimate and even necessary to insist on the Trinitarian nature of all the intra-divine life and of the relationships between the persons; nevertheless we do not see with the same clarity how we can alter the traditional order of the divine processions.

…in the dialogue in qualified events with the Orthodox Churches, the non-heretical nature of the *filioque,* correctly understood, has been clearly evidenced and acknowledged, along with the equivalence and complementary nature of the two dogmatic expressions, «of the Father, absolute source, and of the Son», «of the Father through the Son»… On the other hand, Eastern theologians should not go beyond the «of the Father alone», and of the implications of the monarchy of the Father and of the demands of the texts of the New Testament[233].

It would also be necessary that the people in the East and the people in the West be duly prepared for this step that would be taken. It is also worth referring to Kasper who offers a different opinion, pointing out that if the Orthodox theologians acknowledge that the *filioque* is not heretical, the West need not give up its tradition which it naturally does not wish to impose on the others[234]. Personally I believe that returning to a common confession of the faith that unites, while taking into consideration the legitimate variety in the theologies, would undoubtedly be highly desirable. Let us expect that in a not-too-distant future, conditions could be present for that purpose.

The Catholic Church has already taken some steps in this direction. Ever since Benedict xiv (year 1742), the *filioque* is not compulsory for Catholic Churches with an Eastern rite. On May 31st, 1973, the Catholic hierarchy of Greece also suppressed it only in the recitation of the creed in Greek in the celebrations of the Latin rite. Pope John Paul ii recited the original creed of Constantinople in the solemn celebration of Santa Maria Maiore in the centennial year of the First Council of Constantinople (381-1981). He did exactly the same thing in the Basilica of Saint Peter on June 29th, 1995, when he was with the Patriarch of Constantinople, Bartolomeus i. Earlier, in 1925 Pius xi, in a celebration in Greek, had done the same[235].

---

233 CONGAR Y., *El Espíritu Santo,* 639; similarly, GARRIGUES J. M., *El espíritu que dice ¡Padre!,* 133, 149.
234 Cfr. KASPER W., *Der Gott Jesu Christi,* 272.
235 Cfr. VON BALTHASAR H.U., *Theologik* iii, 190. On the decisions of suppression of other churches and ecclesiastic communities, as well as of the commission «Faith and Constitution», cfr. CONGAR Y., *El Espíritu Santo,* 638-639.

The recent declaration of the Papal Council for the Unity of Christians to which we have referred on several occasions, states how the Holy Spirit rests on the Son[236], and during the life of Jesus the Spirit guides him in his love of the Fa-ther. In our third chapter, we have addressed this issue at length. This function of the Spirit in the economy is derived from an eternal Trinitarian relationship in which the Spirit, in the mystery of his gift of love, characterizes to a certain extent the relationship of the Father and the Son. Von Balthasar sees in the different modes of relationship of Jesus and the Spirit during the lifetime of Jesus the justification of the two different conceptions of the procession of the Spirit. The Spirit *in* him, in the incarnate Son who will later deliver him over to humanity, is the meaning of the economic formula of the *filioque*. Likewise, the Spirit who remains *on* him, hovers over him and encourages him, is the meaning of the *a Patre procedit*[237]. The formulas of «from the Father and the Son» or «from the Father through the Son» pose the advantage of considering the Trinity as a whole and the relationship of each person with the other two and not separate dyads, as could happen if we were only to consider the Father-Son and the Father-Spirit, or the Father-Son and Son-Spirit relation[238].

In fact, the issue has to do with the adequate relationship between Christology and pneumatology. On the one hand, the Spirit is not only the Spirit of God, but the Spirit of the Son, the Spirit of Jesus, gift of the resurrected Lord. On the other hand, the Spirit, worker of the incarnation of Jesus, comes and acts upon him and not only guides and follows the evangelization, but also prepares and precedes it. Jesus gives the Spirit, but at the same time the Spirit rests on him. Christology and pneumatology can never be separated. Hence, the reflection on the *filioque* opens a series of perspectives that are not exhausted in the strict Trinitarian doctrine. Likewise, in Christology, as we have

---

236 An idea very similar to orthodoxy, in BOBRINSKOY B., *Le Mystère de la Trinité*, 303: «La descente de l'Esprit sur Jésus au Jourdain apparaît donc dans la vision théologique orthodoxe comme une icône, une manifestation dans l'historie, du repos éternel de l'Esprit du Père sur le Fils».

237 Cfr. VON BALTHASAR H.U., *Teodramática* 3, 477.

238 VON BALTHASAR H.U. strongly encourages the *filioque* which he sees united with the idea of the God love and the Spirit as love of the two. On the other hand, he states that John 1:26 must be understood with reference to the economy and not to the Trinitarian life. Cfr. *Theologik III. Der Geist der Wahrheit*, 189-200. Also, in his time BARTH K., *Kirchliche Dogmatik* I/1, München 1935, 500ff, was a great defender of the *filioque*, if the Spirit given by the Son does not share in the eternality of the Son, the foundation of our union with God disappears.

seen, and also in ecclesiology, anthropology, and the theology of the sacraments, there will undoubtedly be a reflection of the consequences of this complex relationship[239].

[239] Cfr. CONGAR Y., *El Espíritu Santo*, 540-544, on the ecclesiological consequences of the *filioque* and the problem of whether the «Christomonism» and the relative oblivion of the Holy Spirit in the West must be considered as the consequence of this doctrine. There are reasons to think that it is a «doubtful» dispute. Cfr. also ibid. *La parola e il soffio*, Rome 1985, 142ff. BULGAKOV S., *Il Paraclito*, 277-278, believes that there is a relationship between the *filioque* and the idea of the Pope as the vicar of Christ. Cfr. also BOBRINSKOY B., op.cit, 302-303, who suggests far more delicately and gently the ecclesiological repercussions. Only out of curiosity is it worth stating that Saint Thomas considered that it is a similar mistake to deny the primacy of the Pope and that the Holy Spirit proceeds from the Father: *Contra errors graecorum* II 32 (quoted by CONGAR Y., *El Espíritu Santo*, 639-640). At any rate, we must avoid any hasty and exaggerated conclusions. Cfr. the considerations of CANTALAMESSA R., «*Utriusque Spiritus*», 470-471: if the deficiencies of the Western Church have been due to the *filioque*, his virtues and positive aspects would necessarily have also been due to the *filioque*.

«Unitas in Trinitate». The One God in the Trinity. Properties and modalities of action

1

The unity in the divine essence

1.1. THE UNITY OF THE FATHER, THE SON AND THE HOLY SPIRIT

After having analyzed the classical doctrine of the Trinity from the professions to the persons, based on the *historia salutis*, we have quite broadly addressed the characteristics of the Father, the Son, and the Holy Spirit. At this point, we must address the issue of the unity of the divine essence. I am aware that this is not the approach of a substantial line of thought in the theological tradition which, as we have had the occasion to evidence, has chosen instead to base its arguments on the unity of the divine essence[1]. However, the unity of God is not a unity prior to the trinity of the persons, even though it cannot be considered either as posterior or as subsequent to it. On the one hand, we are dealing with the unity of Father, Son, and Holy Spirit, although on the other, with a unity that is not always there and that is not a result of a process of the union of the three[2]. The New Testament presents to us the «only true God» (cfr. John 17:3) as the Father of our Lord Jesus Christ and as the one who gives us the Holy Spirit, the one with whom both the Son and the Spirit are intimately united. This is the God-Father who never exists without his Son and without his Spirit. Therefore, mention has been made in the tradition of the Church that the one God is Father, Son, and Holy Spirit in the unity of their essence in their *homoousía*. The divine essence is unique, although possessed by three persons, but this fact of being possessed by the three is also part of this essence. We are already aware of the evolution that has taken place in the division of the issues addressed in the old treatises *de Deo uno* and *de Deo trino*[3].

419

---

1 However, the most economic-salvific point of departure that has found its way into Catholic theology in recent times has enabled our proposal to be the mostly widely followed; cfr. PORRO C., *Dio nostra salvezza. Introduzione al mistero di Dio*, Leumann, Torino 1994, 189ff, 235ff; and mostly GRESHAKE G., *Der dreieine Gott. Eine trinitarische Theologie*, 184-185, 196ff, among other references.

2 Cfr. WERBICK J., *Teologia trinitaria*, in SCHNEIDER TH. (ed.), *Nuovo corso di Teologia Dogmatica*, volume 2, Brescia 1995, 573-685, 659.

3 Cfr. chapter 1 of this book.

We have already referred in this treatise to the option of some theologians who, precisely when faced with the difficulty of this classical division, choose to consider that the issues of the treatise *de Deo uno* are really issues of a «treatise» on God the Father. In fact, the Father has been considered in the tradition as the foundation of the unity of the Trinity in that he is the beginning of the divinity. On the other hand, the God of the Old Testament is identified in the New Testament with the Father of Jesus. Consequently, the one God is the Father. All of the affirmations about omnipotence and the eternality of God, among others, are addressed[4]. In the Creed also, the one God is identified with the Father of Jesus. Therefore, we cannot deny the foundations of this position. Nevertheless, we can wonder if they are absolutely convincing. The identification of the God of the Old Testament with the Father is evident. There is, however, a great difference between this and assuming that the Old Testament is only a revelation identifying the one God; there is really no justification for that understanding. It is not possible to accept without nuances a «succession» in the revelation of the divine persons, as a hasty reading of a known text of Gregory of Nazianzus might suggest[5]. The behavior of the God of the Old Testament is only possible because this God is the «Father». In other words, it is possible because he exists since the beginning of time only in relationship with the Son and with the Holy Spirit and in the exchange of love between them. This revelation of the one God, whom we later recognize as the Father of Jesus, is precisely preparing us for the revelation of the one and triune God. Therefore, if it is clear that the God of the Old Testament is identified with the Father simply because this God is the «Father», the progressive revelation of God is at the same time and in an incipient manner that of the Trinity of persons in the unity of the divine essence.

4   Cfr. the previous chapter. But even in these cases, reflection on the divine unity is not fully addressed in this study about the Father. We also take into account the unity of the Trinity; cfr. KASPER W., *Der Gott Jesu Christi*, 354-377.

5   GREGORY OF NAZIANZUS, *Or.* 31:26 (SCh 250,326): «The Old Testament clearly announced the Father, although it announced the Son in a rather obscure way. The New Testament openly announced the Son to us and only suggested to us the divinity of the Spirit. Now the Spirit is present amid us and grants us a more clear vision of himself...». GREGORY OF NAZIANZUS, *Los cinco discursos teológicos*, (Translation by J.R. Díaz Sánchez-Cid) Madrid 1995, 254. We have already referred to this passage in footnote 100 of the previous chapter. There is no doubt whatsoever that this is true to a considerable extent. However, it cannot be interpreted in a unilateral way. Cfr. the continuation of our text.

The full revelation of God is only possible in the mutual understanding of the unity in the divine Trinity. In the Old Testament we do not find the full revelation of the one God as Christians profess this God. A revelation of the Trinity that is juxtaposed in a way with the revelation of the divine unicity that the Old Testament proclaims so clearly is not the only aspect that is missing. Indeed, our one God is God the Father, Son, and Holy Spirit. The revelation of the common divine essence and the revelation of God as Father, Son, and Holy Spirit mutually imply each other:

> We could say that the revelation of the fullness of the divine «common» essence and the revelation of God as Father, as Son (Word), and as Holy Spirit run parallel. In other words, both revelations make up a unity and grow at the same time and in the same understanding, because they are the *sole* manifestation… of the one God, Father, Son, and Holy Spirit[6].

Consequently, we must take into account that there is a progressive manifestation of the one and only God in the history of salvation and of the old and the new covenant, and that every progression made regarding the knowledge of this divine unity is at the same time a growth in the knowledge of the tripersonal God. For reasons that are evident, this tripersonal God could still not be made explicit in the Old Testament[7]. On the contrary, through the explanation of the personal differentiation in God, we enlighten the knowledge of the unity of the divine being, and the features of Christian monotheism are gradually shaped[8].

---

6 SCHULTE R., «La preparación de la revelación trinitaria» in *MySal* II/1, 77-116, 87. Ibid. «…in view of the fact that God is the one and only God, and consequently, in view of the fact that the progressive manifestation of this one and only God is also one and only in the only history of salvation of the old and new covenant…, every "progress" regarding the knowledge about God "in himself" ("essence") is also a progression in regard to the knowledge of the faith in the "special" mystery of this God who is definitively manifested as tripersonal; and vice versa: in every explanation of a "personal differentiation" in God, the knowledge of the divine essence is also expanded at the same time».

7 Commissio Theologica Internationalis, «Theologia-Christologia-Anthropologia» in *Greg* 64 (1983) 5-24, esp. 9: «The monotheism of the Old Testament has its origin in supernatural revelation, and because of this fact, it holds an intrinsic relationship with the Trinitarian revelation».

8 Cfr. SCHULTE R., «La preparación de la revelación trinitaria» in *MySal* II/1, 87; also 80-81. Cfr. also, although from another point of view, VON BALTHASAR H.U., *Teodramática 3. Las personas del drama: el hombre en Cristo*, Madrid 1993, 470: «The idea of a successive revelation of the three divine persons is absurd because they are essentially immanent, one with respect to the others. In the pre-Christian revelation with God, only the living (Trinitarian) God may have been revealed, although not formally in his Trinity…». God could not have been able to establish any covenant with humanity without his Word and his Spirit.

Even though it is clear that currently we cannot follow them in many of their concrete affirmations, there is still a permanent core of truth in the teachings of the Holy Fathers who saw the Trinity revealed back in the Old Testament.

These reflections are an excellent justification for our systematic analysis because the affirmations about the one God do not refer to a divine essence that unfolds and expands into the three persons at a second or later stage. They do not refer exclusively to the God who is shown as the Father of Jesus at a subsequent point in time. Both the one God and the triune God are God the Father, Son, and Holy Spirit. Both the unity and the differentiation belong to the three of them. Undoubtedly, all of this points out the need to abandon the old terminology of the unity of the divine essence. This is the divine reality that is common to the three persons[9]. However, as we have already stated, this essence is possessed by the Father, the Son, and the Holy Spirit. It is possessed by each one of them entirely and in each one's own way. Indeed, when we speak of the unity of the essence, we cannot forget that it is a most profound unity that is evidenced, at the same time, in the greatest personal differentiation. In turn, it is worth affirming the two extremes, as we can see in the mystery of Jesus who dies in the cross abandoned by the Father and who is brought back to life by his divine power. It is the unity of the divine love, the supreme expression of this being «only one thing» of the three persons who exist solely in the unity of their mutual self-giving and therefore in their unyielding differentiation:

> Each divine *hypostasis* maintains its mystery, one that is impossible to solve: the Father, all self-giving (*relatio*) and who, in spite of this, can be the one who gives himself; the Son, as a Word uttered in response, who in his delivery to the Father can share the originating power of his Father and together with this power cannot only be love but can also make love emerge; the Spirit, the most sublime and sovereign divine freedom and at the same time total generosity and altruism, who exists only for the Father and for the Son[10].

---

9 Cfr. CEC, 252: this term points out the common divinity of the three persons. They are together with the terms —equivalent in use— of substance and nature that point to the divine being in his unity.

10 VON BALTHASAR H.U., *Theologik* III, 199-200.

In the selfless love —an internal reality that is communicated to creatures—
we see the highest expression of what is common to the three persons[11]. Mention is made in John 10:30 that the Father and the Son are one and the same, and
the neuter gender is used. The Fathers have attached great significance to this
fact because this neuter gender eliminates the danger of Sabellianism or Patri-
passianism (only one thing, but not only one person). However, this is a unity
of the persons. It is primarily manifested in their love and in their giving. It is not a
unity that that can be conceived without them[12]. Basil of Caesarea affirmed
that «in the divine nature and not combined unity we see the communion of the
divinity»[13]. For Augustine also, the one and only God is the Trinity[14].

Obviously we must avoid every danger of tritheism. We cannot think about
the «independent» existence of the three persons who only become a unity
which has the characteristics of a group at a second stage[15]. If in our systematic
thought we address the unity of God after having spoken about the three persons, it is not because we wish to consider this unity as subordinated with respect
to the personal distinction. The two aspects of the divine being are likewise
original. It is because, as we have already stated, the divine unity is not simply
the unity of a unipersonal God, that of an abstract divine essence; neither is it
just the unicity of the Father, but instead it is the unity of the Father, the Son, and
the Spirit. This is the way in which this unity has been manifested in the *historia
salutis*, and this is the only *raison d'être* for this order in our exposition.

---

11 ORIGEN, *In Rom.* IV 9 (PG 14,997): «…we can love God because we are loved by God. And in fact,
Paul himself speaks of the Spirit of love (Rom 15:30). God is called love, and Christ is called the
Son of love (Col 1:13). And if we know that the Spirit is love, the Son is love, and God is love, it is
obvious that we know the Son and the Holy Spirit from a source of fraternal divinity, whose abundance is disseminated into the abundance of love in the heart of the saints to make them share
in the divine nature, as taught by the Apostle Peter (2 Pet 1:4)».

12 TERTULLIAN, *Adv. Prax.* 22,11 (208) about the *unum* of John 10:30: «non pertinet ad singularitatem
sed ad unitatem, ad similitudinem, ad coniunctionem, ad dilectionem Patris qui Filium diligit
et ad obsequium Filii qui voluntati Patris obsequitur». HILARY OF POITIERS makes a distinction
between the *unitas* that is evidenced between the persons and the *unio* which does not distinguish
them, which would be Sabellian; cfr. *Trin.* IV 42; V 1; VI 8,11 (CCL 62,149,152,203,207), and mostly XI 1
(530): «id quod uterque in proprietate sua unus est, sacramentum unitatis ad utrumque».

13 BASIL OF CAESAREA, *De Sp. sanc.* 18,45 (SCh 17bis,406): ἐ τῇ κοινωνίᾳ τῆς θεότητός ἐστιν ἡ ἕνωσις;
ibid., the Father is in the Son and the Son is in the Father because each one is as the other one.
This is precisely what makes them both be only one thing.

14 AUGUSTINE, *Trin.* I 2,4 (CCL 50,31): «…quod Trinitas sit unus et solus et verus Deus»; XV 5,7 (468):
«… unum Deum, quod est ipsa Trinitas»; Symbol «Clemens Trinitas» (DS 73): «Clemens Trinitas
est una divinitas».

15 Cfr. FOURTH LATERAN COUNCIL, against Joachim of Fiore: «Verum unitatem huiusmodo non
veram et propriam, sed quasi collectivam et similitudinariam esse fatetur, quemadmodum
dicuntur multi homines unus populus, et multi fideles una Ecclesia…» (DS 803).

This is perhaps the ideal time to offer a brief balance in regard to the problems that we have already addressed in our analysis, although we are now viewing them from the concrete perspective of the relationship between the unity and the Trinity in God. Moltmann does not agree with the line of thought that is based on the only divine essence, because he believes that this can only lead to modalism. Yet we have also realized that his method is not free from the opposite danger either. God ends by being too dependent on the world and on history, and the final divine unity is simply an eschatological reality. Nevertheless, the starting point beginning with God as a subject, which primarily attempts to avoid the danger of tritheism (the line followed by Barth and Rahner), was not satisfactory in every sense either. In Barth the repetition of the «I» is more essential than the Father-Son relation that is presented to us in the New Testament. In turn, the correspondence between the historical-saving dialogue and the internal life of the persons in God faces considerable problems in the case of Rahner[16]. However, this cannot keep us from acknowledging their merit as they indeed begin from what is personal, from the idea of the subject and the person of the Father, and not from the impersonal idea of the substance. Nothing in God can be impersonal; nothing can be «neutral». There is no «neuter». However, as we saw before, the idea of person that is used is also insufficient because the relational dimension is not adequately taken into account. The «personal» unity of God cannot be that of the absolute person, but rather of the three persons in their reciprocal relationship. At the same time, this unity is a primary and not a derived fact.

We have also seen how the unity of the triune God, the unity of the essence of the «tri-one» God, has been based in the tradition on the origin and on the unique source of the divinity which is found in the Father. Nevertheless, it is worth stating at the same time that the Father is also relational, that he is fully in relation to the Son and to the Holy Spirit, and that he is not such a Father without this relationship. There is no being of the Father that is prior to or independent of his fatherhood. Hence, the Father is completely committed to communicating his being to the Son and (with the Son, through the Son) to the Holy Spirit. The Father is, on the one hand, the origin, the source; however, he is also the relationship. The Father gives being to those who only exist in their relationship to him. Nevertheless, at the same time, he *is* insofar as he is Father; he *is* insofar

16 Cfr. chapter 9.

as he begets the Son and is the origin of the Holy Spirit, insofar as he is related to the other persons. The relationship of origin, which is not a unilateral dependence by any means, leads to the unity and the communion of the three persons. In this way, the substantial unity and the distinction of the persons in their own personal union are two inseparable aspects of the divine being. There is no previous essence to the persons, as there is no absolute subject either. I believe that if we understand correctly the sense of the fatherhood of the first person in the intra-divine *taxis*, we rule out the danger of subordinationism when we emphasize the mutual relationships of the three. We also rule out modalism, because we do not begin with the absolute individual subject. Finally, we also rule out tritheism because the unique principle of the divinity is recognized in the Father. In this way, in the person of the Father we find, at the same time, the source of the unity and that of the Trinity. We affirm the essential unity that allows no room for the exclusion of the internal relationships in God, but that exists precisely in them. The persons are relative one to the other, and they are so, not independently of the relationships of origin, but precisely because of them, because the first origin is the «Father»[17]. The Father is not thinkable without the Son and without the Holy Spirit (although we have already mentioned on many occasions that the language is less clear in the case of the third person). In other words, he «depends» on them, as much as they depend on him. Nonetheless, we should not only emphasize the *origin*, but even more so the *relationship* between the persons[18] that unites them at the same time as it make them distinct, without disregarding any of the two aspects. The unity of God is evidenced in the exchange of mutual love, which is the communication of the being in this distinction. The supreme unity is not that of the isolated monad, but that of the God of love and perfect communion, the Father, Son, and Holy Spirit[19].

---

[17] From whom the other persons proceed, although he does not «precedes» them; AUGUSTINE, *Trin.* VI 2:3 (231): «non praecesit genitor illud quod genuit».

[18] We have already noted the position of Thomas Aquinas who preferred the term «Father» rather than *generans-genitor* (cfr. *STh* I 33,2). The first one attaches to the relationship primacy over origin. As a consequence of this, the Father begets because he is Father, and he is not Father because he begets. There are indeed very powerful reasons to prefer this position to the opposite one.

[19] See the considerations made by GRESHAKE G., *Der dreieine Gott*, 196f. In God we must exclude any «something» that could be thought of without relationship and beginning with which we could form the unity from the relationships.

We mentioned that in God there is nothing «neutral», everything is «personal»[20]. The fact that Father, Son, and Holy Spirit «are only one» (cfr. John 10:30) is not something different from the fullness of life that the three have in common. This divine essence has traditionally been considered as ineffable and inaccessible to humanity[21]. Nevertheless, in spite of all this, nothing prevents us from attempting to draw closer to this mystery, which will seem to grow even more the closer it is manifested to us.

The Scriptures already offer us a basis for this attempt. In the New Testament, and most specifically in the writings of John, we can see different «definitions» of God (it is worth noting that we use «definition» quite inadequately) which have been the starting point for subsequent reflections. We already know some of them. Undoubtedly the most decisive and conclusive is «God is Love» (1John 4:8,16); but also: «God is Spirit» (John 4:24); «God is light» (1John 1:5,7; cfr. 1Tim 6:16); God is the living God *par excellence* (cfr. Matt 16:16;26:63; Ps 18:47; John 6:51; 1John 1:1-2, etc.). Some of these expressions also apply to Jesus: light (John 1:49; 9:5); life (John 1:4;11:25;14:6). Undoubtedly, these words are not meant to be metaphysical definitions of God. They refer to the saving manifestation of God in Christ. When faced with the world's darkness, death, and hatred, they present to us the action of God who offers salvation in Christ. Nevertheless, and indirectly, they also tell us something about God himself. In Jesus, we see the manifestation of what has always truly been in the divine life, the life that comes from the Father and that is shared by the Son and the Spirit. These expressions and other similar ones point to a fullness of being[22] without any dependence, toward the totality of goodness and of life that does not include the limitations of any order to which we humans are subject. They suggest a fullness of the personal being, of total self-possession and knowledge, of full transparency and infinite freedom.

---

20 Cfr. FOURTH LATERAN COUNCIL (DS 803-804), texts that to which we have already referred. The *summa res* is the Father, Son, and Holy Spirit, and in them we fully find the divine essence of each one in communion with the other two. Cfr. the declaration of Eugene III after the Council of Reims against Gilberto Porretano (year 1148). No division can be set forth between the nature and the person (DS 745).

21 DIONYSIUS THE AREOPAGITE, *Cael. Hier.* II 3 (SCh 58bis,77ff), God exists beyond every essence (οὐσία) and every life. Cfr. further ahead footnote 48 in chapter 12 (on the analogy).

22 God is the one who is (cfr. Exod 3:14). Only he «IS». Cfr. CEC 213. THOMAS AQUINAS, *STh* I 13,11, «the one who is» is the name that is most adequate for referring to God. *STh* I 12,4: God is the *ipsum esse subsistens*.

In fact, the tradition of the Church from ancient times has linked the absolute divine simplicity with the being, the «spirit», of God (cfr. among other references, DS 566, 800, 3001)[23]. Thus we have been able to deduce the fullness of life in God, «every reason, every ear, every eye, every light»[24]. Therefore, we can derive the only ineffable divine essence from these metaphors which are undoubtedly quite distant, seeing them as the fullness of the being which implies the fullness of life and of self-possession, the full identity with himself in complete freedom. Therefore, he is fully personal[25].

The «definition» of God as love adds a decisive precision to this list of divine properties. In fact, the being in fullness and full self-possession acquires their supreme expression in the perfect giving of himself. Only the one who possesses himself can give himself fully, and the full possession of himself is manifested in this self-giving. The biblical teachings of the God who is love, which give its ultimate meaning to the other metaphors to which we have already referred, inform us that the divine perfection is not lived in the modality of narrow-mindedness or isolation, but in that of giving in love. This is not a question of saying that there is first self-possession and then love and self-giving. On the contrary, love tells us how this divine self-possession is, which being penetrated fully by him, gives God's being its definitive meaning. As a result of this, the capacity and the reality of infinite love must be considered as part of the most intimate being of God. Each one of the persons has God's being in his own way. Even more so, they not only have God, but, as mentioned by Richard of Saint Victor, each person is God's love. Nevertheless, this love is also common to the three persons, and this is what really gives evidence to their profound unity. Although different in its modality, the full loving gift of himself to the others, the expression of full self-possession, is common to the three persons. In this way, love is that which unites them and what distinguishes them, as we saw earlier in the case

---

23 Already in TATIAN, *Ad Graecos* 5 (BAC 115,578). AUGUSTINE, *De Civ. Dei* XI 10 (CCL 48,332): «Quae habet (Deus), haec et est»; cfr. the whole of chapter 10 (330-332) ; *De Trin.* I 12,26 (66); V 4:5 (209), among other references.

24 IRENAEUS OF LYONS, *Adv. Haer.*, II 13,3 (SCh 294,116); cfr. subsequent examples of the Fathers, as well as references about the origin of these clauses in ORBE A., *Antropología de san Ireneo*, Madrid 1969, 95. It is worth noting that Saint Thomas spoke in the first place of the simplicity when he began to talk about what God is, or even more clearly, about what God is not, *STh* I q.3, introd. Cfr. also BASIL, *C. Eunom.* II 29 (SCh 305,122).

25 ZUBIRI X., *El Hombre y Dios*, Madrid 1984, 168: «God, absolutely absolute reality is absolute dynamicity; he is an absolute "living himself"». Cfr. the context. ZUBIRI X., *Naturaleza. Historia. Dios*, Madrid 1987, 481: «God is… a pure personal love. As such he is ecstatic and enthusiastic».

of the relationship. In God, what unites is what distinguishes, being is giving, and giving implies the other. This is by no means solipsism. Thus, the tri-unity of the divine being reveals to us the meaning of the being, the sameness in the differentiation, the self-possession in the self-giving[26].

As a result of this, the «definition» of the love of God shows us what is most profound in the being of God: the divine essence which we cannot grasp and is always surrounded by mystery. Even though the texts of the New Testament that we have already mentioned refer more directly to the *ad extra* giving, they also permit us to see something of the divine life itself (from the economic Trinity to the immanent Trinity). Precisely because God must be seen as fully personal, the unity and the divine unicity cannot be understood in solitude and isolation[27]. The Father gives to the Son and the Spirit this fullness of being in love, and he can only exist in this communication. Therefore, the personal love is not uniper-sonal. He is tripersonal because love pertains to his essence:

> Love creates a close and profound communion of persons among humans, although not an identity of essence. On the contrary, God is love, and his essence is absolutely simple and unique. Because of this, the three persons have a unique essence. Their unity is unity in essence and not only communion of persons. This Trinity in the unity of the unique essence is the inexhaustible mystery of the Trinity that we can never un-derstand rationally, but rather, it can only be accessible to the understanding of the believer as a hint (*in Ansätzen*)[28].

26 GILBERT P., *La semplicità del principio. Introduzione alla metafisica*, Casale Monferrato 1992, 356: «La metafisica è a la ricerca del principio più universale e più necesario. L'universale è comunione; il necessario è stabilito fra ciò che è realmente differente. La tensione tra l'uno e il molteplice o tra l'identico e il differente è asunta da ciò che è al tempo stesso universale e necesario, uno e diverso, vale a dire dallo spirito capace di cogliersi in atto nell'azione espressa. La sostanza che subsiste in conformità a questa struttura dello spirito è la "persona". La persona si riconosce identica a sé es-sendo dinanzi all'altro vale a dire, differente, in seno ad uno scambio gratuito, di cui "persona" ne è la sola origine». Cfr. Also GILBERT P., *Kénose et Ontologie*, especially 195-200.

27 KASPER W., *Der Gott Jesu Christi*, 364: «In this way, the person does not exist in any other way than in self-communication with others and in recognition by other persons. Because of this, it is impossible that the unity and the unicity of God are understood as solitude, precisely because from the very beginning God is thought of as personal. Here lies the most profound foundation, on which the theist conception of an impersonal God cannot maintain itself». In the same sense, SCHEFFCZYK L., *Der Gott der Offenbarung*, 433: «the God who in his essence is personal love, can-not adequately be thought of in any other way than as Trinitarian». GRESHAKE G., *Der dreieine Gott*, 198-200: love is at the same time what distinguishes and what unites; cfr. in the context the quotation of Bonaventure: «Si unitas divina est perfectissima, necesse est quod habeat plurali-tatem intrinsecam» (*Q. dis. de Trin.* 2,2f).

28 KASPER W., *Der Gott Jesu Christi*, 365; ibid. 372: «The unity of God… as communion of the Fa-ther, Son, and Holy Spirit, is determined as unity in love».

We can ask ourselves if the incomprehensibility of the divine essence does not mean the incomprehensibility of divine love[29], the incomprehensibility of the total self-possession in communication and in full communion which at the same time is based on and expresses the original unity of the Father, Son, and Holy Spirit. In recent Catholic theology we find a consensus, which continues to grow, concerning the identification of love with the divine essence, although with differing colorations[30]. Saint Augustine had already identified love with the Trinity in his famous sentence: «vides Trinitatem si caritatem vides»[31]. The most profound unity that can exist in the triune God is consequently that of love[32].

Thus, as we can see, unity and differentiation are not contradictory. The unique divine essence should not be seen in opposition to the plurality of the persons, nor should it be seen as previous to them. Rather, it can be considered as the same unity and communion between them[33], which does not mean that

29 Based on the revelation of the New Testament we can correct a unilateral apophatism: MILANO A., «*Analogia Christi*. Sul parlare in torno a Dio in una teologia cristiana» in *Ricerche Teologiche* I (1990) 29-73: «... di Dio possono ben darsi dei nomi, e tra questi il più alto, è quello riconosciutogli da Giovanni: *agape*... L'*agape* è sul serio 'id quo magis cogitari nequit' ed è pertanto il nome più propio di Dio».

30 In addition to the authors we have just quoted, cfr. VON BALTHASAR H.U., *Theologik II. Wahrheit Gottes*, 130: «the identical love with the essence of God»; this love is the one that gives meaning to all; cfr. ibid. 140-141,163; SCHEFFCZYK L., *Der Gott der Offenbarung*, 413, God in his personal essence; MONDIN B., *La Trinità mistero d'amore. Trattato di teologia trinitaria*, Bologna 1993, 295-299; PORRO C., *Dio nostra salvezza. Introduzione al mistero di Dio*, 309ff; STAGLIANÒ A., *Il mistero del Dio vivente*, 597. Commissio Theologica Internationalis, «Theologia-Christologia-Anthropologia», 14: «The mystery of God and of man is manifested as a mystery of love». The paragraphs that are devoted to the love of God in the CEC (218-221,231) are quite significant: «Ipsum Dei esse est amor... Ipse aeterne est amoris commercium: Pater, Filius et Spiritus Sanctus, nosque destinavit ut huius simus participes» (221); «Ipsum Dei esse est veritas et amor» (231). In the field of orthodox theology, cfr. STANISLOAE D., *Dios es amor*, Salamanca 1984, 88; also, SPITERIS Y., «La dottrina trinitaria nella teologia ortodossa. Autori e prospettive» in AMATO A. (ed.), *Trinità in contesto*, Rome 1993, 45-69, especially page 58, about ZIZIOULAS J.: «L'amore non è una conseguenza o una "proprietà" della sostanza divina... ma ciò che *costituisce* la sua sostanza».

31 AUGUSTINE, *Trin.* VIII 8,12 (287); also, *Trin.* XV 17,29 (504): «substantia ipsa sit caritas et caritas ipsa sit substantia sive in patre sive in filio sive in spiritu sancto»; cfr. XV 6,10 (472). LOMBARD P., *Sent.* I 32:5: «Et sicut in Trinitate dilectio est, quae est Pater, Filius et Spiritus sanctus, quae est ipsa essentia deitatis; et tamen Spiritus sanctus dilectio est...».

32 BERNARD OF CLARAVAL, *De diligendo Deo* 12,35 (PL 182,996): «Quid vero in summa et beata illa Trinitate summam et ineffabilem conservat unitatem nisi caritas? Lex erit ergo, et lex Domini, caritas, quae Trinitatem in unitate quodammodo cohibet et colligat in vinculo pacis».

33 See also, FORTE B., *Trinidad como historia. Ensayo sobre el Dios cristiano*, Salamanca 1988, 18f; PANNENBERG W., *Teología sistemática* I, 361f: «The way in which this idea is addressed (that of the divine essence as such)... must be seen... if we can think about the concept of the divine essence as the synthetic compendium (*Inbegriff*) of the relationships between the Father, Son, and Spirit, unlike that other ontological idea of the essence that Augustine felt compelled to assume», 362f: «The Trinitarian faith of Christianity is only concerned with the concrete life that

this unity is a consequence of the union of the three. The unity and the Trinity are both absolutely primary and original; none of them is «previous» to the other. Both of them have their only foundation in the Father, who in turn exists only in relationship with the Son and the Spirit. Methodologically, it could be valid to take either one or the other as a starting point, but always bearing in mind that there is neither logically or ontologically a priority of one over the other. Christian monotheism is the monotheism of the triune God revealed in Jesus. God is in himself unity and plurality, and because of this, in the overabundance of his love, the love that he is in himself, he can give himself to the world —something which is not necessary— and by being love in himself, he can be love for us.

In short, the whole Trinitarian doctrine can turn into a commentary regarding what was said in 1John 4:8, 16[34]. In our human experience, God is, on the one hand, what unites[35], but on the other hand, he is precisely what lets the other one be what he is. The Trinity creates communion, although it does not absorb or eliminate the differences. The one who loves *is* and lets the other one *be*[36]. If we can apply to God this human experience by analogy, we can understand how love is based at the same time on the ultimate union and on the supreme distinction of the persons (clearly bearing in mind the basic difference that we have already noted between the unity of the divine essence possessed by the three and communion between people, even though we want to conceive it as very intimate). In this way, we can speak of God who comes to us and makes himself one

is differentiated in itself from the divine unity. In this way, the doctrine of the Trinity is in fact a "*concrete monotheism*" which is differentiated from certain ideas about the one God, who is to be found in an abstract other world and regarding an abstract unity that excludes from itself any plurality and in fact, turns the one God into a mere correlation of this world and the plurality of what is finite». Regarding the «concrete monotheism», cfr. KASPER W., *Der Gott Jesu Christi*, 358f. Cfr. also DEL CURA S., «El Dios único cristiano. Apología del monoteísmo trinitario» in *Burgense* 37 (1996) 65-92; especially page 88 on the origin of the expression «concrete monotheism». RAHNER K., «Über die Eigenart des christlichen Gottesbegriffs» in *Schriften zur Theologie* 15, Zürich-Einsiedeln-Köln 1983, 185-194, especially 190. God is not only the giver but the gift himself. This is only possible in a Trinitarian conception.

34 Cfr. PRENTER R., «Der Gott, der Liebe ist. Das Verhältnis der Gotteslehre zur Christologie» in *ThLZ* 96 (1971) 401-413, especially 403: «*God is love*. And why not simply say: God has loved us…? Why not say simply God *has* for us an infinite love, and thus he has loved us so much? Why not simply: God is full of love for us? Why: God is Love?»; quoted by PANNENBERG W., *Teología sistemática* I, 461; cfr. also SÖDING TH., «*Gott ist Liebe*». *1 Joh 4,8.16 als Spitzensatz biblischer Theologie*, in SÖDING TH. (Hsg), *Der lebendige Gott. Studien zur Theologie des Neuen Testaments* (Festschrift W. Thusing), Münster 1996, 306-357.

35 AUGUSTINE, *Trin.* VIII 10,14 (290): «Quid est ergo amor, nisi quaedam vita duo aliqua copulans vel copulare appetens, amantem scilicet et quod amatur?».

36 God creator, who creates out of love, gives the creatures his own consistence.

with us (God with us) and of the Spirit poured into our hearts (God in us), without negating in any manner whatsoever his transcendence and the incomprehensibility of his mystery (God the Father, God above us)[37]. God dwells in unapproachable light (1Tim 6:16); no one has ever seen God; the only Son has revealed him (John 1:18). As a result of this revelation through Jesus we are confronted with the light of his mystery. For this reason, only in love do we have access to the knowledge of God. He who loves has been born from God and knows him and, on the other hand, he who does not love, cannot know him (cfr. 1John 4:7-8)[38].

1.4. THE UNITY OF GOD AND THE UNITY OF MEN

The unity of the triune God is such that in this unity, and duly accentuating all the differences, we humans have a place. The so-called «high priestly prayer» of Jesus (John 17) is the foundation for such a consideration, so that we can use it as the beginning of our reflection[39].

The first verses of the chapter address the mutual glorification of the Father and the Son, and they culminate in verse 5 with the supplication that Jesus be glorified by the Father with the glory he had with him before the creation of the world. In this glorification we see the Father's glory. This is the eschatological revelation of the eternal being of God. God possess the glory of his divinity from eternity. This is the mutual glorification of the Father and of the Son. Now, because of the Son's humanity, it also embraces him insofar as he is a man, because his humanity, in the resurrection and the ascension, fully participates in the eternal life of God. Precisely because the humanity of Jesus is introduced in this eternal «doxology», can believers also be part of it. The Son is glorified «in them» (John 17:10). This glorification takes place by means of the «other Advocate», the Spirit of truth whom Jesus will send and who will guide the disciples to the whole and full truth, because it will communicate to them what he has heard from Jesus (John 16:14: «He will glorify me, since all he reveals to you will be taken from what

---

37 Cfr. GRESHAKE G., *Der dreieine Gott*, 532. Cfr. ATHANASIUS, *Serap.* I 28 (PG 26,596).

38 Cfr. JÜNGEL E., *Gott als Geheimnis der Welt*, 446ff; Jüngel states that we recognize the love of God when he sends his Son to the world, thus exposing him to the absence of love. In this way, God shows himself not only as the one who loves, but as the event himself of love. God does not will to love himself without loving the world. In the mission of the Son to the world God enters into the absence of love and in this way makes offensive man worthy of love. The identification of God with love does not enable the simple reductionism of Feuerbach. Love is only true when it comes from God. Cfr. also the very rich and suggestive analysis of love in ibid. 430-446.

39 Cfr. KASPER W., *Der Gott Jesu Christi*, 369ff. I am inspired by this author for the following explanation.

is mine»). The purpose of the Trinitarian doctrine is doxology insofar as it is part of the mutual glorification of the Father and the Son; however, we humans are introduced into this glorification. This glorification means our salvation: «the glory of man is God», as Irenaeus stated[40]. The ultimate purpose of humanity is found in the glorification of the one and triune God and in being totally accepted into the full life of the Trinity. This is possible because this divine unity does not eliminate and rule out the difference, but rather it takes it up into itself. Being, and being with the other, is the same thing within God[41]. Because of this, God can take the creature into his bosom, without the creature ceasing to be creature[42].

Our salvation, that is, our relationship with God and our participation in his life, is derived from these characteristics of the one and triune God. Eternal life lies in the knowledge of God: «to know you, the only true God, and Jesus Christ whom you have sent» (John 17:3). Jesus, the one sent by the Father, is in this way indissolubly associated with the «only God». The unity of the Father and the Son is, at the same time, the foundation of the union of believers with God and of union among themselves: «May they all be one, just as, Father, you are in me and I am in you, so that they also maybe be in us, so that the world may believe it was you who sent me. I have given them the glory you gave to me, that they may be one as we are one» (John 17:21-22). The unity is founded on the gift that God has offered to his followers: the «glory» that the Father has given him in the participation of the divine life that he has received[43]. All the actions of Jesus on earth

40 Irenaeus of Lyons, *Adv. Haer.* III 20,2 (sCh 211,388).

41 Cfr. Kasper W., *Der Gott Jesu Christi*, 373.

42 This is the basis for the intrinsic relationship between the creation and the Trinity. Only because there is otherness in God can the other one, the creature, emerge without being dependent on him. The unity of the divine action in creation must be affirmed because, as the three persons are inseparable, God is the sole beginning of creatures. Augustine has stated this in quite an elegant manner in *Trin.* I 4,7 (ccl 50,36): «…sicut inseparabiles sunt, ita inseparabiliter opererunt». Nevertheless, this does not mean that this beginning does not contain in itself the distinction, and that as a result of this, in the inseparable action of the persons, each one does not participate in the manner that is intrinsic to him. Cfr. Ladaria L.F., *Antropologia teologica*, Casale Monferrato-Roma 1995, 64-69.

43 Cfr. Schnackenburg R., *El evangelio según san Juan*, III, Barcelona 1980, 238ff. The glory and the unity are also seen together in Rom 15:5-6. On the relationship between the unity of the Father and of the Son and that of humans, expressed in the glory, Marzotto D., *L'unità degli uomini nel vangelo di Giovanni*, Brescia 1977, 192: «Gesú e il Padre sono una cosa sola e espressione ne è la Gloria che il Padre ha dato a Gesù, poiché da sempre lo ha amato, ma Gesù ha dato questa Gloria ai discepoli ed essi credono in lui. L'unità originaria si apre ad accogliere altri, che divengono una cosa sola anch'essi "in noi", "come noi", "dal momento che noi siamo una cosa sola"»; cfr. ibid. 198f. Simoens Y., *La gloire d'aimer. Structures stylistiques et interprétatives dans le Discours de la Cène (Jn 13-17)*, Roma 1981, 248 : «"Un", dans le rapport au Père et à Jesus, ils reçoivent

tend to create this union, to make all of us children of God. In addition, according to John 17:26, the love with which the Father has loved Jesus must also be in all Christians. The unity among Christians is founded on the unity of the Trinity[44].

What commands our attention is the fact that in the high priestly prayer no mention is made of the Holy Spirit, yet he is amply mentioned in the previous chapters. We therefore cannot assume that the union of humans with the Father and the Son and their presence among their children is fulfilled without the action of the Advocate, the Spirit of truth. Although we do not intend to force a precipitate harmony, it is worth noting that the concepts of glory and Spirit are associated on repeated occasions in the New Testament (cfr. 2Cor 3:6-9:18; Eph 3:16; 1Pet 4:14)[45]. A Patristic tradition, which cannot be ruled out by any means, is what maintains this intimate union and even reaches the pure and simple identification of the two concepts[46]. The unity between the Father and the Son is based at any rate on how Christ communicates his glory, in that he is of one being with the Father. For this reason, we can correctly speak of the true participation of humanity in the life of the one and triune God rather than only refer to it in a figurative sense. This unity enables God to come to us in the descending line of the *exitus:* Father-Son-Spirit, which is inverted in the ascending movement of the *reditus.* «For through him (Christ), then, we both in the Spirit have free access to the Father» (Eph 2:18), because Jesus with his death has broken down the dividing wall between people and specifically between Jews and Gentiles (cfr. Eph 2:11-17). In view of the fact that the divine unity is seen in the differentiation between the persons, so also the unity that is found within the Church in the

---

en don la gloire qui définit l'identité même de Dieu». Cfr. also GS 24, although the text does not refer directly to the introduction of human beings into the divine unity.

44 Cfr. SECOND VATICAN COUNCIL, LG 1.4, etc., with the famous quotation of SAINT CYPRIAN OF CARTHAGE, *De Or. Dom.* 23: «de unitate Patris et Filii et Sipritus Sancti plebs adunata». Cfr. also TERTULLIAN, *De Bapt.* 6,1 (CCL 1,282) : «Ubi tres, id est pater et filius et spiritus sanctus, ibi Ecclesia, quae trium corpus est».

45 Cfr. DURRWELL F.X., *L'Esprit Saint de Dieu,* Paris 1983, 22f; by the same author, *Le Père. Dieu en son mystère,* Paris 1988, 28: «The power, the glory, and the Spirit are inseparable».

46 Cfr. JUSTIN, *Dial. Tryph.* 49,2-3 (BAC 116,383); cfr. MARTÍN J.P., *El Espíritu Santo en los orígenes del cristianismo,* 196-200, about the relationship between these concepts and also with those of *kháris* and *dynamis;* IRENAEUS OF LYONS, *Adv. Haer.* IV 14,1-2 (SCh 100,538-546), both the glory and the Spirit work the communion with God; HILARY OF POITIERS, *In Mt* 2:6; 12,23 (SCh 254,110;172), *Tr. Ps.* 56,6 (CSEL 22,172); AMBROSIASTER, *Com. 2 Cor.* 3,18 (CSEL 81,219f). The most attractive passage is that of GREGORY OF NYSSA, *Hom. In Cant.* XV (PG 44,1117): «The link of this unity is the glory (cfr. John 17:22). On the other hand, if we examine very carefully the words of the Lord, we will discover that the Holy Spirit is referred to as glory. This is in effect what is stated: *And I have given them the glory you gave to me* (John 17:22). In fact, he had given them the same glory, when he told them, *Receive the Holy Spirit* (John 20:22)».

image of the Trinity, reflects differences and does not look for uniformity (cfr. 1Cor 12:4-30; Rom 12:4-9; Eph 4:9-13). The unity between human beings can only be seen in their respect for the distinctiveness of persons, groups, and peoples.

«Unum Deum in trinitate et Trinitatem in unitate veneremur» (*Quicumque* Symbol, DS 75). We cannot consider the divine unity without having the Trinity in mind, nor can we reflect on the Trinity while forgetting about the unity. Any statement that takes into account only one of these aspects must always be corrected, because it is simply complementary. The unity in the love that has its source in the person of the Father, who in turn, is only in relationship with the Son and the Holy Spirit, helps us to think simultaneously upon the two inseparable aspects of the divine being. Love is in the «beginning» of the Trinity, and through the Son it is also love that closes the circle of the Trinity, that is, the Holy Spirit —love in person— insofar as he is the fruit of the love of the Father and of the Son[47]. If everything that exists comes from the creating love of the one and triune God, in the overflowing of the eternal exchange of love which is the intimate life of God, we can conclude that the giving of himself in complete generosity is the ultimate meaning of everything that exists: «The meaning of the being is the full generosity and disinterestedness of love»[48]. This is the way in which Catholic theology in past times has referred to a «Trinitarian ontology»[49] in which love is seen as the most profound heart and core that gives meaning to all reality[50]. In view of the fact that the Trinity is also the origin of creation, these

47 Based on a similar consideration, PANNENBERG W., *Teología Sistemática* I, 466, states that the divine essence, the «divinity as a whole» is more evident in the Father as origin and in the Holy Spirit as love (common essence).

48 KASPER W., *Der Gott Jesu Christi*, 377. Cfr. also the whole context.

49 The expression was coined by HEMMERLE K., *Thesen zu einer trinitarischen Ontologie*, Einsiedeln 1976. The ontology that is derived from faith should have its starting point in love, in giving oneself to others. The concept of the Trinity has revealed love as the core of the mysteries of Christianity, but also in everything that it is (ibid. 36). From the same author, *Auf den göttlichen Gott zudenken. Unterwegs mit dem dreieinen Gott*, Freiburg 1996. Cfr. also GRESHAKE G., *Der dreieine Gott*, 454-464; STAGLIANÒ A., *Il mistero del Dio vivente*, 602-606. Commissio Theologica Internationalis, «Theologia-Christologia-Anthropologia», 14: «… The mystery of God and of men is manifested to the world as a mystery of love. Derived from this consideration and under the guidance of the Christian faith, we can deduce a new universal vision of all things… In the center of this "metaphysics of love" we no longer have, as has been the case in the old philosophy, substance in general, but rather, the person who has love is the most perfect and utterly perfective act».

50 HEMMERLE K., *Thesen zu einer trinitarischen Ontologie*, 55: «Since he did not spare his own Son but gave him up for the sake of all of us, then can we not expect that with him he will freely give us all his gifts?» (Rom 8:32). This fundamental experience of the faith is based on the death and resurrection of Jesus. This is the experience in which Jesus has delivered himself for us, but his delivery is the delivery of *God*. In it, his being is fully transformed, because with his ultimate

considerations are justified. Naturally, above all, they apply to humanity. The delivery of Jesus to death reveals to us the mystery of love and self-giving that is the divine life. In following Jesus, for whom everything was made, we become real human beings, as the Second Vatican Council (GS 41) clearly reminds us. This involves entering into the true meaning of life which starts within the life of God himself. This primacy of the person and of the relationship with God enables us to integrate those experiences that do not fall into any system: solitude and guilt, sadness and failure[51].

The revelation of this ultimate meaning of being is seen in the life of Jesus, image and revealer of the Father, who is at the same time the beginning, the root, and the source of the Trinity. Those who see Jesus, see the Father. Those who see Jesus can understand God as the full generosity of love. His life, death, and resurrection open before us the mystery of the Trinitarian communion in its magnanimous love. In the eternal Trinitarian love we find the condition of the possibility of the temporal *kenosis* of the Son. In order to arrive at a meaningful definition of being as giving and full altruism, we must begin with Jesus' revelation of the Father and with him the mystery of the Holy Trinity, the only God. We are introduced into the mystery by means of faith and baptism which we receive in the name (and not in the names)[52] of the Father and of the Son and of the Holy Spirit and by means of which we are joined in relationship with the death and resurrection of Jesus, and we begin to be part of the Church, which is his body. The Church has as its law the new commandment of loving one another as Christ has loved us (cfr. John 13:34), and that is the strongest seed of unity for humankind as a whole (cfr. LG 1:9).

self-giving, his being is assumed into the rhythm of God (by his self-giving). Ibid. 57, «He who believes in Christ… believes in a love that is in the beginning, in the center and at the end».

51 Cfr. KASPER W., *Der Gott Jesu Christi*, 377, ibid.: «It is finally an interpretation that leads to hope, an anticipation of the eschatological doxology behind the veil of history».

52 Cfr. CEC 233; *Catechismus Romanus* II 2,10; cfr. KASPER W., *Der Gott Jesu Christi*, 359.

2

The ways of acting and the properties (attributes) of God

The one and triune God whom the Christian faith confesses is shown to us in his revelation to humanity as «the one who is» in the fullness of self-possession, in the eternal exchange of love between the Father, Son, and Holy Spirit. The doctrine of the properties (attributes) of God, manifested in his actions, is better understood in light of the Trinitarian revelation, the only one that manifests to us the most profound being of God. Hence, this traditional teaching, which we will only be addressing briefly[53], can be considered as an extension of our reflections on the divine essence.

We have frequently been faced with the issue of the incomprehensibility of God. It is a consequence that is derived from his infinite and immeasurable nature[54]. As we have already pointed out, Thomas Aquinas referred to God as what «he is not» rather than as what he is[55]. His existence is known because of his effects. Nevertheless, as a result of the lack of proportion between effects and cause, we cannot know him perfectly according to his essence[56]. Perhaps for this reason we frequently find lists of properties of God, long lists that point out the fact that they cannot be encompassed with only one expression. In the Scriptures, these divine properties are deduced from God's ways of acting, and these properties and modalities of action comprise a whole. Obviously, it is equally impossible to fully cover the divine immensity with long lists of words. Nevertheless, there is no doubt that the enumeration and the diversity of approxima-

---

53 The recent manuals notably differ in the attention they give to this topic. A very important space is devoted to this subject by SCHEFFCZYK L., *Der Gott der Offenbarung*, pages 419-597, after having addressed the essential problems of Trinitarian theology. It is also addressed, although more briefly, by STAGLIANÒ A., *Il mistero del Dio vivente*, 597-601, and GRESHAKE G., *Der dreieine Gott*, 214-216. Both underline the Trinitarian nature of these properties.

54 Cfr. GREGORY OF NYSSA, *Contra Eunomio*, III 1,103 (Jaeger II,38). It is worth reproducing a text of PANNENBERG W., *Teologia sistemática* 1,368: «The worst ravings in the field of the knowledge of God are not evidenced when men are aware that their understanding is always below the greatness of that subject, but rather, when they mistake their limited ideas for this knowledge».

55 THOMAS AQUINAS, *STh* 2, beginning. Nevertheless, we can also make affirmative statements about God: *STh* I 13,12. Cfr. JOHN OF DAMASCUS, *De fide orthod.*, I 2,4 (PG 94,795.799).

56 THOMAS AQUINAS, *STh* I q.1 a.2. On the incomprehensibility of God in the Apologetic Fathers, we can refer to PANNENBERG W., «Die Aufnahme des philosophischen Gottesbegriff als dogmatisches Problem der frühchristlichen Theologie» in *Grundfragen systematischer Theologie*, Göttingen 1967, 296-346, especially 332ff; cfr. also BASIL OF CAESAREA, *De Fide*. (PG 31,681): «Neither words can describe, nor any mind can encompass the majesty and the glory of God. They cannot be expressed with a word or with a concept nor can they be comprehended as they are».

tions give us a more vivid impression that we are confronted with someone who clearly surpasses us. It is precisely the boundless and overflowing wealth of the love of God that is manifested in the abundance of the divine properties, which are in fact an articulation of that main and central idea. By no means should we think that these long lists are opposed to the principle of divine simplicity. Rather, the human impossibility of actually understanding it is what forces us to have this plurality of approximations.

In the pages that follow we will not attempt to submit an exhaustive study of this issue. We will simply offer some indications about the teachings of the Bible and the tradition in order to continue reflecting on the current problems related to divine immutability and impassibility.

2.1. DIVINE PROPERTIES IN THE BIBLE

The most profound affirmations about God in the Bible are not found in an abstract language about God but rather in the various prayers. When God is worshipped or when we implore God, when we speak to him with our hearts, when we experience his infinite goodness, is precisely when we human beings can go deeper into his mystery. Hence, we should not be surprised that in the Old Testament it is the Book of Psalms which most frequently speaks about the greatness of God and lists his great benefits offered to humanity that show the very nature of his being. Thus, for instance, we can refer to Ps 103:3-9:

> He who forgives all your offenses, cures all your diseases, redeems your life from the abyss, crowns you with love and tenderness, contents you with good things all your life, renews your youth like an eagle's. Yahweh acts with uprightness, with justice to all who are oppressed…; Yahweh is tenderness and pity, slow to anger and rich in faithful love; his indignation does not last forever…

Psalm 145 is also a hymn of praise and glory that humanity cannot encompass:

> Great is Yahweh and worthy of all praise… They will bring out the memory of your great generosity, and joyfully acclaim your saving justice. Yahweh is tenderness and pity, slow to anger, full of faithful love. Yahweh is generous to all, his tenderness embraces all creatures… Your kingship is a kingship forever, your reign lasts from age to age. Yahweh is trustworthy in all his words, and upright in all his deeds… (Ps 145:3.6.7-9.13-14. Cfr. also Ps 71, and Psalms 72,84 and 146).

The faithfulness of the divine God is also expressed in the prophets (cfr. for example, Jer 31:3; Hos 2:21-22). In fact, the works and actions of God, which are the historical experience of his love for his people, are the ones that established the criteria in these texts. Following this, then, the statements about his divine greatness and power appear. These passages and other similar ones seem to be comments or echoes of Exod 34:6-7, the invocation of Moses: «Yahweh, Yahweh, God of Tenderness, a merciful and compassionate God, slow to anger, rich in faithful love and constancy, maintaining faithful love to thousands and forgiving fault, crime, and sin…».

The inscrutable riches of the being of God is manifested in «he who is» *par excellence,* the «living one»; life belongs to him (cfr. Jer 10:10; Ps 36:10; Dan 6:27, etc.; in the New Testament life will appear in Jesus, cfr. John 1:16). But other expressions show the power of God and his transcendence over the earth. God is beyond our knowledge (Job 36:26); he is the Most High (Ps 7:18;73:11;78:56). His power is omnipotent: whatever God wills is done (Ps 115:3; Jer 32:17; Job 42:2). The omnipotence of God is manifested in his fidelity to the covenant established with his people (cfr. Ps 111). Based on the marvels of creation, the Lord appears clothed with majesty and glory (Ps 104:1ff; cfr. 113:4). The heavens declare the glory of God (Ps 19:2), but cannot contain it: «Why, the heavens, the highest of the heavens cannot contain you. How much less this temple built by me!» (1 Kings 8:27; cfr. Isa 66:1). The omnipresence of God is expressed in Ps 139:7-8: «Where shall I go to escape your spirit? Where shall I flee from your presence? If I scale the heavens you are there, if I lie flat in Sheol, there you are». His throne is in heaven. God's eyes keep careful watch. His eyes explore the sons of Adam (Ps 11:4; cfr. 14:2; Jer 23:24). The permanent omniscience of God is emphasized in Ecclesiasticus 42:18-20: «He has fathomed both the abyss and the human heart and seen into their devious ways; for the Most High knows all there is to know and sees the signs of the times. He declares what is past and what will be, and reveals the trend of hidden things…». God does not pass away; he exists from ever and for ever, unlike his actions and works. Ps 102:24-28: «Your years run from age to age. Long ago you laid earth's foundations, the heavens are the work of your hands. They pass away but you remain…; but you never alter, and your years never end». Because of this, God is frequently referred to as the «rock», a metaphor that expresses the soundness of the support that he offers to all people alike (cfr. Ps 18:32, among many other references). The everlasting nature of the love and the power of God are expressed in Psalm 136, which contemplates at a glance the whole creation of the world, the liberation of his people from Egypt, and the loving care of God for his creatures[57].

Many of these topics are assembled in a text of Ecclesiasticus:

> He who lives forever has created the sum of things.
> The Lord alone will be found just.
> He has given no one the power to proclaim his works to the end,
> And who can fathom his magnificent deeds?
> Who can assess his magnificent strength
> And who can go further and tell of all his mercies?
> Nothing can be added to them, nothing subtracted,
> It is impossible to fathom the marvels
> When someone finishes he is only beginning,
> And when he stops he is as puzzled as ever.
> Human compassion extends to neighbors,
> But the Lord's compassion extends to everyone.
> (Ecclesiasticus 18:1, 7, 13).

The holiness of God is another of his most characteristic properties. According to Ps 22:4, God is «the Holy one». «Holiness» only applies to God in the Old Testament. What is holy is originally that which is separated from this world. That is why it pertains to God. But this separation entails the non-existence of sin and impurity. In this way, holiness is the expression of the divine mystery. It is the good and the goodness of God himself that becomes the mystery of salvation insofar as this holiness is communicated. Mention is made on two occasions in the Book of Leviticus (Lev 11:44-45;19:2) that this holiness must be imitated by human beings. If in the first text it has to do with the precepts of ritual purity, in the second passage, the imitation of the holiness of God is identified with abiding by the divine commandments in reverence for parents and in keeping the Sabbath, as well as by abstaining from idolatry. Yahweh has sworn by his holiness. In this way, he seems to identify this holiness with himself (cfr. Amos 4:2). The holiness of God is shown primarily in love and in mercy: «I will not give rein to my fierce anger, I will not destroy Ephraim again; for I am God, not man,

---

57 Cfr. for more information ROVIRA BELLOSO J.M., *Tratado de Dios uno y trino*, 253-292; PASTOR F.A., *La lógica de lo inefable. Una teoría teológica sobre el lenguaje del teísmo cristiano*, Roma 1986, 131-147; GONZÁLEZ DE CARDEDAL O., *La entraña del cristianismo*, Salamanca 1977, 3-59.

the Holy One in your midst, and I shall not come to you in anger» (Hos 11:9). Hence, there is an intrinsic relationship between the holiness of God and his merciful love for humanity. Holiness is related to divine power and greatness (Isa 6:1-6); however, it is not a destructive power, but rather it is his love that saves by forgiving. For this reason, God, because he is the savior[58], becomes the Holy One of Israel (cfr. Isa 1:4;10:20;43:3,14)[59].

The New Testament does not offer us such a long list of divine properties. Nevertheless, some of these elements are repeated. The face of God must be seen in Jesus. With his words and his actions, he reveals to us the goodness and mercy of God (cfr., for instance, Luke 8:38-49; Luke 15, the three parables of the lost sheep, the lost coin, and the lost son). This is why he prefers the poor and forsaken, publicans and sinners. Specific mention is made of the mercy of God in Luke 1:45,78 (cfr. also 6:36[60], among other places). God is «rich in mercy» (Eph 2:4).

The omnipotence of God is also expressed with all clarity: «For nothing is impossible with God» (Luke 1:37; cfr. Matt 19:26). God asserts his omnipotence in order to save humanity. According to Revelation, God is the one «who is, who was, and who is to come» (Rev 1:4.8;4:8). The reminiscences of Exod 3:14 are clear[61]. On certain occasions, in this volume we repeat in connection with the expressions of Revelation that we have just mentioned, the term *pantocrátor* which is so frequently used in the tradition (Rev 1:8;4:8;11:17;15:3;16:7.14;19:6.15; 21:22; cfr. 2Cor 6:18). In some of these same contexts, God is called the «holy» (Rev 4:8;6:10;3:7;15:4;16:5)[62]. The expression is repeated in other places of the New Testament in reference to God (cfr. John 17:11; 1Pet 1:15; 1John 2:20) and also to Jesus (cfr. Luke 1:35; Mark 1:24; John 6:29; Acts 3:14;4:27). According to Revelation, God the Father and also Jesus are «the first and the last» (Rev 1:8;1:17;2:8; 21:6;22:13). This is an expression that undoubtedly can be related to divine eternality. For God «a day is like a thousand years and a thousand years are like a day» (2Pet 3:8; cfr. Ps 90:4). The divine eternality also appears in Rom 16:26.

---

[58] Cfr. Exod 15:2. God is the savior because he has freed the people from the Pharaoh.

[59] Cfr. ODASSO G., «Santidad» in ROSSANO P.-RAVASI G.-GIRLANDA A., *Nuevo diccionario de teología bíblica*, Madrid 1990, 1779-1788.

[60] Cfr. Matt 5:48, a parallel text in which the heavenly Father is called «perfect».

[61] In other passages, God appears as existing before the aeons or *eones*: cfr. Eph 3:9; Col 1:29; he is the king of ages, 1 Tim 1:1,17. Cfr. also Heb 1:8, which quotes Ps 45:7.

[62] In these last texts, the term *hágios* is not used, but rather *hósios*.

God is «invisible» although he is made known by Jesus (cfr. John 1:18; Col 1:15; 1Tim 1:17; 6:15-17). He is immortal (cfr. 1Tim 1:17; 6:16); incorruptible (Rom 1:23; cfr. Wis 2:23-24).He is also the «Most High». In this way, according to Luke 1:32, Jesus is the «Son of the Most High», and the Spirit is his power (cfr. Luke 1:35; Acts 7:48; Mark 5:7; Luke 8:28). Divine transcendence is strongly underlined in this way; however, at the same time, people can also be «children of the Most High», according to the words of Jesus in Luke 6:35 (cfr. Ps 82:6).

God is also «good». Even more so, God is the only one to whom this adjective is suitable (Mark 10:18). He is true; he is the only one that possesses justice (cfr. Rom 3:4-5).

We could continue with this list, although it could easily turn into a simple accumulation of data. It is worth pointing out that many of these characteristics and properties of God, which clearly express his transcendence over everything that has been created, can be communicated to those who believe in God, without questioning by any means the divine transcendence. In Jesus, we can share the justice of God (cfr. Rom 3:26). In him, we have access to the life that is only God's, to the eternal life that is a participation in the eternality of God himself (cfr. John 6:39-40, 54-58). In him we also share in the divine love (cfr. 1John 4:7-21). For those who believe, «everything is possible», as there is nothing impossible for God once all the distances have been bridged (cfr. Mark 9:23, 11:23; Matt 21:21). These two dimensions of the divine properties are interrelated in the New Testament. On the one hand, as was the case in the Old Testament, divine transcendence is still emphasized, but on the other hand, simultaneously, mention is made of participation in the life of God (cfr. John 10:34; Ps 82:6, «you are gods») through the saving action of Christ and the gift of the Spirit. The closeness of God can be saving precisely because it infinitely goes beyond all human powers and capabilities. In the transcendence and the proximity of God we can find the possibility of salvation for humanity, but if they are unrelated, neither one nor the other is enough. God himself (the Father, in this context), and not only Jesus, is on some occasions, especially in the pastoral letters, the «savior» who wants all humanity to be saved and attain the knowledge of truth (1Tim 2:3-4; cfr. also 1Tim 1:1; 4:10; Titus 1:3; 2:10; 3:4). In the texts of the traditions we will find both the divine greatness and majesty and his closeness to human beings. These are the two contexts that are emphasized, although in different ways.

In Saint Clement, also known as the Roman Clement, we similarly find a combination of the properties that speaks to us about the great and omnipotent God and of the properties that take into account the divine pardon and mercy:

> You, Lord, created the universe;
> You, faithful in all generations,
> Righteous in your judgments,
> Admirable because of your strength and greatness, wise when creating,
> Intelligent when soundly establishing what exists,
> Good with the visible things,
> Faithful with those who have trusted you,
> Merciful and compassionate[63].

Basil of Caesarea introduced a distinction between divine properties which will be important in later times. On the one hand, God is incorruptible, immortal, invisible; these are negative properties, we also say, however, that he is «good, just, creator, judge, and other similar things. In the same way, since the former terms mean a denial and a rejection of what is alien to God, these new ones now express an affirmation and the existence of what pertains to God»[64]. Gregory of Nyssa stated that incorruptibility, integrity, happiness, goodness, wisdom, power, justice and holiness are inherent to the three persons[65]. Within the context of praise and invocation, Augustine also accumulated an impressive list of divine properties:

> Oh supreme, optimum, most omnipotent, most merciful, most fair, most secret and most present, most beautiful and most strong, stable and inapprehensible, immutable and he who changes everything, never new and never old, renewal of all things, who brings down the arrogant to decrepitude. Always active, always at rest: you reap although

---

63 SAINT CLEMENT, *Ad. Cor.* 60,1 (FP 3,148f); also ibid. 59,3: «… in order to know you, the only Most High in the highest, the Saint who rests among the saints, who humbles the arrogance of the proud… the one who can enrich and impoverish, who can kill and make someone live, who creates life… who sees into the abyss, the witness of human work, the help of those who are in danger…». It is worth taking into account the nature of the invocation in this list of divine properties which have been inspired by biblical prayers; ROVIRA BELLOSO J.M., *Tratado de Dios uno y trino*, 336. We will see evidence of the same in other texts.

64 *Contra Eunom.* I 9 (SCh 299:200); also 10 (206).

65 *De Fide* (Jaeger III 1,66). Also, *Or. Cath. Magna.* 24 (PG 45,64).

you have no need; you guide, you fill and you preserve; you create, you nourish, and you make things ripe; you seek although you really lack nothing; you love, but you do not feel agitated; you are jealous and at the same time you are confident; you repent without suffering; wrath comes upon you, but you are at peace; you change the works but not your plan; you receive what you find when you had never lost it; you never need, you rejoice at what you win; you are never miserly but you demand your interests. We give you so that you owe us, and who has something that is not yours? You pay the debts without owing anything, you pardon them without losing anything. And have we said, my God, my life, my sweet one? Or what is said when one speaks about you? But woe betide those who do not speak about you because they are dumb even though they talk[66].

Here again, we find a combination of negative and positive properties. While some of them can be considered to be abstract based on the consideration of the «supreme being», on other occasions, such as those that relate to wrath or to repentance, the concrete biblical and historical inspiration is clear. Despite the fact that the philosophy of Plato, particularly Middle Platonism and Neo-Platonism, is undoubtedly an element that had an influence on the thought of the Fathers, it is certainly not the only factor and even less so, the determining factor[67]. The text of Augustine also points out the difficulty of speaking about God, while at the same time there is the need to do so.

John of Damascus († circa 749) offers especially long lists of divine properties. We have chosen one of them among the several that are found in his *De fide orthodoxa*, on this occasion within the context of a profession of faith:

We believe in only one God, one only beginning, without any beginning, unbegotten, unmade, who does not know destruction or death, eternal, immense, uncircumscribed, unlimited by any term, with infinite power, simple, uncompound, incorporeal, free from any flow, passion, and any mutation and alteration, invisible, source of every goodness and justice, intellectual light and light that has not been lit, power that is not understood in any measure and that is only embraced by his will... who is creator of all things, the cause of all visible and invisible things; who preserves all things; who is

66 AUGUSTINE, *Conf.* I 4 (CCL 27,2-3; cfr. also 3 (2).
67 In general terms and referring to this question, specifically dealing with the Apologetic Fathers, see PANNENBERG W., *Die Aufnahme des philosophischen Gottesbegriffs*, 296ff.

the providence in regard to all things; who contains and rules all things, superior in essence, life, word and thought; he is light itself, goodness itself, life itself…[68].

As we have already stated, Saint Thomas believed that we should speak about what God is not, rather than about how God is. Therefore, it is a negative path in which we must mentally eliminate what is not suitable for God. This is the way in which we can reach the simplicity, perfection, goodness, boundlessness, immutability, eternity, and unity of God[69]. After having taken into account what God is (or, rather, what he is not) in himself, we address the works and actions of God, those that remain in him and those that give rise to an external effect. In this way, we first speak about what corresponds to the intellect of God (his knowledge and his life), and after this, we speak about what corresponds to his will (his love, his justice, and his mercy). Finally, we speak about his power and his happiness[70].

This tradition has been noted by the First Vatican Council in the constitution *Dei Filius*:

> The holy, Catholic, and apostolic Roman Church believes and confesses that only one is the true and living God, creator and Lord of heaven and earth, omnipotent, eternal, immense, incomprehensible[71], infinite in intellect and will and all perfection; who, being a singular spiritual substance, completely simple and immutable, has to be considered different from the world in both reality and essence, completely happy in himself and by himself and ineffably sublime, prevailing over everything that exists or that can be conceived beyond himself (DS 3001).

In this list of divine properties we do not find even one that refers to the concrete acting of God toward humanity: his goodness[72], his mercy, his love…

---

68 JOHN OF DAMASCUS, *De fide orthodoxa*, I 8 (PG 94,808); cfr. also other elements in I 2; I 5; I 14 (792;801;860).

69 Cfr. THOMAS AQUINAS, STh I qq. 3-11. Cfr. what we have already pointed out in footnote 55. The principle of «negative theology» comes from Pseudo-Dionysius the Aeropagite: in God what is true are the negations because the affirmations are imperfect, cfr. *De cael Hier.* II 3 (SCh 58,79; cfr. 77-81).

70 Cfr. THOMAS AQUINAS, STh I qq. 14-26. With this classification, Thomas combined the «metaphysical» attributes with those that are shown in the divine revelation.

71 Cfr. the FOURTH LATERAN COUNCIL (DS 800). God is incomprehensible and ineffable.

72 Nevertheless, reference will be made to the goodness of God at a later point in DS 3002, and it is even placed before his omnipotence when addressing more directly the creation: «Hic solus verus Deus bonitate sua et "omnipotenti virtute" non ad augendam suam beatitudinem nec ad adquirendam…».

This omission finds an explanation if we consider the structure of the constitution *Dei Filius*. In the first place, in this constitution mention is made of God the creator of all things who can be known by the light of reason. However, immediately after, it is added that God, «on account of his infinite goodness» has devoted human beings to a supernatural end, in other words, to participation in the same divine gifts that the human being can never get to know through his intelligence[73]. Divine revelation is required in order to have this knowledge. Hence, we cannot say that consideration of the divine goodness and the love of God to humanity is outside the scope of the Council.

Several different attempts have been made at classifying these divine properties or attributes[74]. I do not believe it would be worthwhile to spend much time addressing these classifications. In short, they are all aimed at the fullness of life and the fullness of being in God, which is the fullness of love. This leads to the tendency to deny in God all our limitations, physical, spiritual, and moral. God is the immense and the eternal one, as compared with our limitation and our mortality. Nevertheless, he is the one who loves and who grants pardon, as compared with our hatred and our rancor. He is the one who forgives, as stated by Hosea (11:9), because he is God and not a man. He is the «holy» *par excellence*. He is the good God who stands in opposition to our wickedness, the faithful God who stands in opposition to our infidelity, the truthful God who stands in opposition to our lies. The positive and the negative go together. There can be no full giving if it is not in the full freedom of the possession of oneself to the exclusion of every type of limitation. By contrast, this fullness cannot be the fullness of selfishness and obstinacy, but one of full giving. Both self-communication and life take place first of all in God himself. This is the assumption of his communication to humanity.

73 DS 3006: «... sed quia Deus ex infinita bonitate sua ordinavit hominem ad finem supernaturalem, ad participanda scilicet bona divina, quae humanae mentis intelligentia omnino superant...», cfr. also DS 3007 and the following ones; DS 3025.

74 Cfr. AUER J., *Gott, der Eine und Dreieine*, Regensburg 1978, 356-580, classifies them according to the way in which they refer to the being of God and to his life and action. Among the first ones, he emphasizes three groups: those that refer to the aseity, those that are transcendental, and those that refer to the denial of what is creaturely. In the case of the second ones, he classifies them in turn into three groups, according to their relationship with knowledge, will and action and the being of the triune God. He is partly followed by ROVIRA BELLOSO J.M., *Tratado de Dios uno y trino*, Salamanca 1993, 338ff. According to PANNENBERG W., *Teología Sistemática* I, 426ff, some attributes are related to the idea of God «in general», while others are related to the concrete action that we know through the revelation. SCHEFFCZYK L., *Der Gott der Offenbarung*, Aachen 1996, 419-508, also makes a distinction between the properties that we know about through the saving action and those that pertain to the being of God. For a more detailed analysis of this issue, see these works.

In the previous pages, we were addressing the fact that our experience makes us feel our limitations both physically and morally. God is free from both of these. Nevertheless, we must dwell briefly on this issue. In fact, the legitimate and justified tendency for us to deny in God any limitation leads us to presume that he exists in pure perfection, a perfection from which we must exclude and rule out every change and every suffering. We have seen that according to the First Vatican Council, God is immutable[75] and perfectly happy, and he has not created the world to acquire happiness nor to increase it in himself. Therefore, we must be very clear that all these affirmations have an obvious meaning. They are binding for us, and hence they are not a subject of discussion. The question is only whether these affirmations have said everything there is to say. In fact, other considerations may be and should be included, and these have already been addressed occasionally throughout our previous analysis. In his love for humanity, the Son of God, obeying and complying with the will of the Father, was incarnated and suffered his passion and the painful and disgraceful death on the cross. We cannot doubt that the one who suffers and dies is the Son of God, although it is also true that he suffers and dies as a man[76]. This is an inevitable consequence that is derived from the unicity of being which is present in Jesus. It is the result of the fact that in his one person the eternal Word has hypostatically taken up the human nature.

Patristic reflection arrived at the idea of the *apatheia* in God in order to remove from him all human passions and sufferings, clearly opposing the vision of Greek mythology. This, however, has not been its only thesis. Quite frequently some of the texts written by Origen have been quoted in this respect. These texts are based on the *kenosis* of Jesus who has suffered for us the «passion of love». It has even been stated that the Father, the God of the universe, also suffers in a certain way and takes upon himself, as Jesus does, our way of being. In this way, by taking pity on us, he also experiences the *passio caritatis*. Out of love he places himself in a situation that is incompatible with the greatness of his nature when he takes upon himself the human sufferings on our behalf[77]. Undoubtedly, this

---

75 Cfr. the Council of Nicaea (DS 126); also the Sixteenth Council of Toledo in the year 693 (DS 569).

76 It is worth pointing out the formula of IGNATIUS OF ANTIOCH, *Ad Rom.* 6:3 (FP 1,156-157): «Allow me to be imitator of the passion of my God», which certainly refers to Jesus.

77 ORIGEN, *Hom. Ez.* 6,6 (SCh 352,229-231): «In the first place, he has suffered because he has descended and has been manifested. Hence, what is this passion that he has suffered for us? The passion of love. And the Father himself, God of the Universe, full of indulgence, of mercy and of

is by no means an attempt at attributing to God a human passion, nor is it abandoning the doctrine of the *apatheia,* while making clear differentiations in this respect. The *apatheia* is assumed, although it is completed in the light of revelation. Divine impassibility cannot be that of a God who is insensitive to the fate of the world. Therefore, the «passion of love» places the Son and the Father himself in a situation that does not correspond to their greatness. There is no confusion between the human and the divine nature. Rather, the suffering of God is inherent to his nature, which is none other than love[78]. It is the suffering of someone who feels sorrow, of someone who is not heartless, and not of someone who is rather limited[79]. During the Middle Ages, Saint Anselm also pointed out the difficulty involved in trying to reconcile his divine impassibility with his mercy[80].

In the past few years, the issue of the impassibility of God as it relates to his immutability has been posed again. Contrasted with the certainly unquestionable idea of a God who is only transcendent and who is beyond all the vicissitudes of the world, the implication of God in history and his participation in the destiny of human beings has been emphasized. According to the Old Testament, God feels wrath, punishes and relents (cfr. Gen 6:6; Exod 32:7-14; Ps 78:34ff; Isa 63:7ff; 61:1ff; Jer 18:7-10, etc.). Most of all, it is necessary to consider the fact that the Son of God was incarnated and has fully shared the fortune of human beings, «but has been put to the test in exactly the same way as ourselves, apart from sin» (Heb 4:15; cfr. Council of Chalcedon, DS 301). Rahner defended the idea of the mutability of God «in the other» in order to take seriously the affirmation of John 1:14, «and the Word *became* flesh». The Logos is the subject of this becoming, according to the biblical affirmation. He is the subject of the

peace, is it not true that he suffers in a certain way? Or is it that you ignore the fact that when he is involved in human affairs, he experiences a human passion? God takes his son upon himself with his way of being; the Lord your God as a man takes his Son on himself (cfr. Deut 1:31). Therefore, God takes upon himself our way of being, as the Son of God took our passions. The Father himself is not impassible. If we beg and pray to him he has pity, he feels sorrow, he experiences the passion of love and places himself in a situation that is incompatible with the greatness of his nature, and he takes up human passions upon himself for us». Cfr. also *Hom. Ez.* 13,2 (SCh 352,411); *Com Mt.* 10,23 (SCh 162,259); *Sel in Ez.* 16 (PG 13, 812). Cfr. the brief though substantial study of FÉDOU M., «La souffrance de Dieu selon Origène» in LIVINGSTONE E.A. (ed.), *Studia Patristica* XXVI, Leuven 1993, 246-250.

78 Cfr. FÉDOU, «La souffrance de Dieu selon Origène», 246ff.

79 Cfr. ORIGEN, *Sel. In Ezechielem* 16 (PG 13,812); also HILARY OF POITIERS, *Tr. Ps.* 149,3 (CSEL 22,867-968), who believes that the divine immutability can «become» moderated with human mutability, more concretely, with penitence and conversion.

80 Cfr. ANSELM, *Proslogion* VIII (ed. Schmitt 1,106).

change and of the transformation that he experiences in his human life, in our history. He is the one who is in himself immutable, but can change «in the other», in the creature. In other words, he can make himself a man; he can make himself another thing in time. This possibility should not be understood as a sign of internal need or limitation. On the contrary, it is the height of the divine perfection that would be less if the Son of God could not become something smaller and still continue being what he is[81]. As a result of this, it is not a matter of doubting the divine perfection and the immutability which is indeed inherent in this person, but rather of emphasizing the capacity of «getting out of» himself out of love for humanity. The need to reexamine the meaning of these two divine properties comes from Christological consideration. The mystery of the incarnation forces us to reflect on the meaning of divine immutability and to consider the mystery of the cross as it relates to that of impassibility. In this way, we can see the intimate relationship between the two. In fact, it would be more appropriate to reintroduce the biblical idea of the «faithfulness» of God into his plans of love that last forever, from age to age (Ps 33:11), amidst all the vicissitudes of human history.

In our exposition of the revelation of the mystery of divine love in the cross we have already found some authors who have directly addressed the topic of divine suffering. Can God remain insensitive to the pain and isolation of his Son Jesus on the cross? Can God remain insensitive to the suffering of so many of his children in his Son at all times and in all places[82]? If, on the one hand, certain ideas of divine immutability and impassibility seem to be hardly compatible with the image of God presented to us in the Old Testament and even more so, in the New Testament, on the other hand, we must avoid the evident excesses of con-

---

81 Cfr. RAHNER K., *Grundkurs des Glaubens*, 217-221. VON BALTHASAR H.U., «El misterio pascual» in *MySal* III/2, 144-335, 154: vis à vis what the heretics say «the immutability of God had to be affirmed in such a way that it would not imply that when the pre-existing Logos was incarnated, nothing real would occur in him and we have to keep this real event from leading to theopaschism»; also *Teodramática 3. Las personas del drama. El hombre en Cristo*, Madrid 1993, 480: «It is not God in himself who changes, but rather it is the immutable God, the one who begins this relationship with creaturality, and this relationship gives a new face to his internal relationships, a face that in all truth is not purely external, as though this external relationship did not really affect him...»; cfr. also id., *Theologik* II, Einsiedeln 1985, 258-259.

82 In addition to the authors that have already been quoted in Chapter 3, pages 72-89, cfr. KITAMORI K., *Teología del dolor de Dios*, Salamanca 1975; GALOT J., *Dieu souffre-t-il?*, Paris 1976; KASPER W., *Der Gott*, 235-245; GESCHÉ A., *Dieu pour penser I. Le mal*, Paris 1993. We can see the analysis of the positions held by some current theologians in DEL CURA ELENA S., «El "sufrimiento" de Dios en el trasfondo de la pregunta por el mal» in *RET* 51 (1991) 331-373; and earlier, VIVES J., «La inmutabilidad de Dios a examen» in *Actualidad Bibliográfica* 14 (1977) 111-136.

sidering that God is fulfilled or perfected in history, that his divine being is not fully made from all eternity, and that only in his participation in human fate does he reach his true fullness. It is clear that the mutability or the suffering of God cannot be the result of his not fully being or of an imperfection, but rather of the perfection of his being. We have already said that the fullness of the being of God is manifested in his love, in the intra-Trinitarian gift, and in the outward gift, in creation, and most of all in the salvation of humanity, as a free overflowing of the infinite love that he is in himself. In this way, the «passion of Christ» is the *passio caritatis* that was mentioned by Origen, the infinite capacity of sympathizing with those who suffer and of remaining by their side and even taking their place.

In the document that we have already mentioned on several occasions, *Theology-Christology-Anthropology*[83], the International Theological Commission addressed this problem and referred to some of the ideas that we have already suggested in these pages. We must clearly affirm the ideas of the immutability and the impassibility of God that find their roots in the Holy Scripture and in the tradition. Nevertheless, we do not have to conceive of them in such a way that God remains indifferent to human events. Thus, it is worth reproducing the most significant passages:

> God, who loves with the love of friendship, wants us to respond to him with love. When his love is offended, the Holy Scriptures speak about the suffering of God, and on the contrary, if the sinner repents and turns to him, he speaks of his happiness (cfr. Luke 15:7). «The health of pain is closer to immortality than the astonishment of those who do not feel» (Augustine, *Enarr. In Ps* 55:6). The two aspects mutually supplement each other. If one of them is neglected, the concept of the God that has been revealed is distorted and misrepresented…
>
> In our times, the aspirations of humanity look for a Divinity that is undoubtedly omnipotent, although not indifferent. Even more so, this Divinity should be moved mercifully by the misfortunes of humanity, and in this sense the Divinity should be a «co-sufferer» of their miseries. Christian piety always rejected the idea of a Divinity that was not touched in any way by the vicissitudes of his creation. Christian piety was even prone to accepting that, as compassion is a most noble perfection among people, the same compassion also exists in God in an eminent way and without any

---

83 Cfr. footnote 7. The texts that we have already quoted are on pages 20-24 of the text in Latin.

imperfection whatsoever. In other words, this is the «inclination… of the commiseration, and not the lack of power» (Leo I)[84] so that it can be compatible with eternal happiness. The Fathers referred to this perfect mercy with respect to the misfortunes and suffering of human beings as the «passion of love», of a love that fulfilled and conquered suffering in the passion of Jesus Christ (cfr. Gregory Thaumaturgus, *Ad. Theopompum*)[85].

Because of this fact, there is a lesson that we can derive from the expressions of the Holy Scriptures and of the Fathers, as well as from modern attempts at purifying this in a reasoned sense…

The same ideas or other similar ones have also been taken up in most recent times in the teachings of John Paul II:

450

The understanding and conception of God as a being who is necessarily most perfect certainly implies that in God there is no pain derived from limitations or wounds. However, in the depths of God lies the love of the Father who, when faced with the sins of men, according to the biblical language, reacts to the point of exclaiming: «I regret having made them» (Gen 6:7)… Frequently, the Holy Scriptures speak to us about a Father who feels compassion for man and shares his suffering. In short, this inscrutable and unutterable «*suffering*» *of the Father will engender* most of all the admirable *economy of the redeeming love* in Jesus Christ… In the words of Jesus the redeemer, in whose humanity we see the «suffering» of God, a word that talks about eternal love and that is full of mercy will be heard loudly: «I feel sorry for all these people» (cfr. Matt 15:32; Mark 8:2)[86].

---

84 DS 293 «inclinatio fuit miserationis, non defectio potestatis». (The text refers directly to the incarnation. Nevertheless, it seems adequate to take from this event precisely the criteria that are required to understand all the acts of God with respect to human beings.) The comment in parentheses is mine.

85 Cfr. JOHN PAUL II, *Dives in misericordia* 7; AAS 72 (1980), 1199ff.

86 JOHN PAUL II, *Dominum et vivificantem*, 39. Before the passage quoted in the text: «The "conviction in regard to sin" (John 16:8)….Should the inconceivable and unutterable *pain be revealed*, which as a consequence of sin, seems to be suggested in the *Holy Scriptures…* in the depth of God and, to a certain degree, in the very heart of the Trinity?»; also ibid. 41: «If sin has engendered suffering, up until now the pain of God in the crucified Christ receives its maximum human expression through the Holy Spirit. In this way, we see the paradox of the mystery of love: God suffers in Christ rejected by the creature himself». Cfr. also *Dives in misericordia* 4.5.8.

As a result of this, the «suffering» of God does not imply an imperfection or a need, but an infinite capacity of loving: the capacity of the Son to take upon himself all our suffering, the capacity of «compassion» of the Father. It is, on the contrary, an expression of his supreme perfection, of his fullness of life and being. It is clear that only in the light of the revelation of God in Jesus Christ can we focus in this way on the issue of the divine properties. Although it is true that we must affirm the possibility of the knowledge of God as it is derived from the creation (cfr. DS 3004), and that what can be discovered about God in this way is not irrelevant for theology, it is also quite true that our ideas about God must be open to a profound scrutiny in the light of the definitive manifestation of the being of God which is before us in the Christian revelation[87].

---

[87] On the one hand, the biblical revelation has to correct ideas that we could shape philosophically about God. Nevertheless, in view of the fact that faith must be rational, philosophical knowledge can sometimes also criticize the hasty images that we think can be legitimized by revelation; cfr. SATTLER S.-SCHNEIDER TH., «Dottrina su Dio» in SCHNEIDER TH. (ed.), *Nuovo corso di dogmatica*, Brescia 1995, I, 65-144, especially 130.

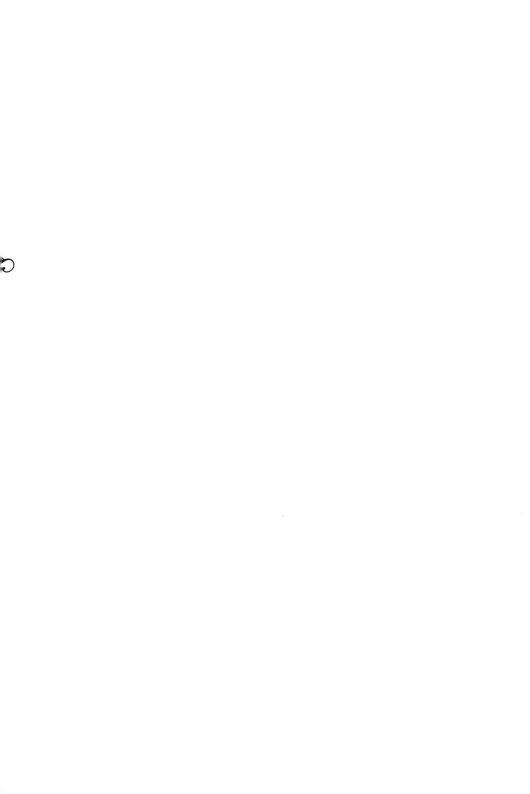

The «natural» knowledge of God and the language of analogy

The knowledge of God derived from creation

We have access to the knowledge of the Trinity only through the revelation that was evidenced in Christ and that we receive with our faith. Only in this way can we discern the depth of the divine mystery revealed in Christ, whom God in his infinite goodness has desired to share with us. Nevertheless, the teachings of the Church clearly affirm the possibility of acquiring the knowledge of God through creation. On certain occasions, and even though we must clearly determine the meaning of this term, mention is made of the «natural» knowledge of God, because it is acquired from the data offered by «nature». This knowledge is contrasted with that which we can attain from «supernatural» revelation. These concepts can be found in the constitution *Dei Filius* of the First Vatican Council, which, after having affirmed the possibility of the knowledge of God derived from creation, stated that God has revealed himself and his decrees through another, supernatural, way (cfr. DS 3004). This understanding corresponds to the supernatural purpose to which God has destined humanity: participating in his own divine goodness (cfr. ibid. 3005). For this reason, mention can be made of the *supernaturalis revelatio* (DS 3006)[1]. We will briefly analyze the statements seen in the Scriptures regarding the possibility of learning about God through creation, and subsequently we will address the definition of this possibility in the First Vatican Council.

1.1. THE KNOWLEDGE OF GOD DERIVED FROM CREATION IN THE SCRIPTURES

The possibility of knowing God through creation is also seen in the Scriptures. Through creation, God has enabled us to catch a glimpse of part of himself. According to Ps 19:2, «The heavens declare the glory of God; the vault of heaven proclaims his handiwork». The classical passage that addresses this issue in the Old Testament is Wis 13:1.3-5:

---

1   On the concept of «supernatural» in the First Vatican Council, we can see POTTMEYER H.J., *Der Glaube von dem Anspruch der Wissenschaft. Die Konstitution über den katholischen Glauben «Dei Filius» des Ersten Vatikanischen Konzils und die unveröffentlichen theologischen Voten der vorbereitenden Kommission*, Freiburg-Basel-Wien 1968, 100-107. Cfr. also SEQUERI P., *Il Dio affidabile. Saggio di teologia fondamentale*, Brescia 1996, 55ff.

Yes, naturally stupid are all who are unaware of God, and who, from good things seen, have not been able to discover Him-who-is, or by studying the works, have not been able to discover the Artificer. If charmed by their beauty they have taken these for gods, let them know how the Master of these excels them. And if they have been impressed by their power and energy, let them deduce from these how much mightier is he that has formed them, since through the grandeur and the beauty of the creatures we may by analogy, contemplate their author[2].

The author of the book of Wisdom begins with the possibility of the knowledge of God through things that have been created. Furthermore, he not only justifies this principle; he takes it for granted. He does not explain what steps can lead us to attain this knowledge. It is stated that in fact not all people reach this knowledge. Within this context, those who do not know God through his works are not «atheists»[3], but pagans who let themselves be carried away by the cult that is centered on the natural elements or on the heavenly bodies or luminaries, to such an extent that they mistake them for God, the Creator of all of them (Wis 13:2-3). We can reach God through creation, «by analogy», ἀναλόγως. Here, we find this term applied for the first time to the human process of the knowledge of God. With this term we point to a certain proportionality, which is evidently very distant, between the two terms of a comparison[4]. Nevertheless, these people are not capable of discovering it; they are unable to take the leap from the creature to the Creator. The beauty of things that have been created is what enthralls them[5]. They are attracted and drawn by what they see. For this reason, even though they cannot be excused, their guilt is less, and at a certain point we can find an explanation for the fact that the beauty of creation deceives them (cfr. Wis 13:6-9).

Far more serious is the sin of those who have been tempted by idols and who have called God objects made by human hands. (Wis 13:10ff; cfr. Ps 115:4-8). Their mistake is far more serious and inexcusable. The phenomena of nature, although

---

2 For a detailed analysis of the text, cfr. VÍLCHEZ LÍNDEZ J., *Sabiduría*, Estella 1990, 348-362; more briefly BUSTO J.R., *La justicia es inmortal. Una lectura del libro de la Sabiduría de Salomón*, Santander 1992, 115-116; MÜLLER Ph., «Weisheit 13,1-9 als "locus classicus" der natürlichen Theologie» in *MünThZ* 46 (1995) 395-407.

3 The Old Testament also reports the case of those for whom God has no significance, those who act as though he does not exist: cfr. Ps 10:3-4;14:1.

4 The following section will give us the occasion to analyze this topic in greater depth.

5 AUGUSTINE, *Conf.* x 27,38 (CCL 27,175): «What kept me far from you were those things that would not have existed if they did not exist in you».

not the works of human beings, can permit us to perceive something of the mystery of God.

In the New Testament we also have the basic text of Romans 1:19-23:

> For what can be known about God is perfectly plain to them, since God has made it plain to them. Ever since the creation of the world, the invisible existence of God and his everlasting power have been clearly seen by the mind's understanding of created things. And so these people have no excuse: they knew God and yet they did not honour him as God or give thanks to him, but their arguments became futile and their uncomprehending minds were darkened.

What first attracts our attention in this text, similar to that which we evidenced in the book of Wisdom, is the verification that the knowledge of God through creation has not always led to the honor and glorification of God, which should be its consequence. Thus we can understand that the knowledge of God cannot simply be limited to its intellectual aspect. God is no «neutral» object of knowledge, as are other objects. In the undistorted and righteous knowledge of God moral factors come into play, along with the attitude of thanking him and glorifying him. Without these attitudes of worship and acknowledgement, knowledge itself degenerates into idolatry, and the truth of God is exchanged for a lie. We revere and worship the creature rather than the Creator (cfr. Rom 1:23-25). The pure vision of the person who contemplates is essential in order not to corrupt the undistorted image of God. Another aspect is of the utmost importance for adequately understanding the text: a manifestation of God is already evidenced in the creation[6]. It is God himself who is revealed in this way, although knowledge of him is certainly still imperfect if we compare this with his revelation in Jesus. Therefore, we are not dealing here with a simple activity of people who have a mastery of knowledge. The verb that is used in verse 19, φανεροῦν[7], is the same that Paul uses for instance, in Rom 3:21, to refer to the revelation of the justice of God in Christ.

The possibility of knowing God through creation, even while bearing in mind the real difficulties that this entails, must be maintained as a principle that cannot be dismissed[8]. Throughout the Middle Ages, mention was made of

---

6 Cfr. SCHLIER H., *Der Römerbrief*, Freiburg-Basel-Wien 1977, 51ff.

7 FITZMYER J.A., *Romans*, New York 1993, 279ff; this verb means to make public or to reveal.

8 AUGUSTINE, *Sermo* 241:2 (PL 38,1134): «Ask the beauty of earth, of the sea… Ask the beauty of the sky… Their beauty is like a confession».

the two «books» —the Book of the Creation and the Scriptures— through which we can know God. The attempts to show the existence of God through human reason, dispensing with the actual value that we must attach to each particular argument, have this fundamental legitimacy that comes from the Scriptures themselves and from the tradition that is founded on them.

1.2. THE FIRST VATICAN COUNCIL AND THE SECOND VATICAN COUNCIL

In the nineteenth century we find some interesting occurrences of teachings about the natural knowledge of God. When faced with traditional fideism which believes that we must give up on a rational justification for faith, the Church had to maintain its rational nature. Because of this, not only the possibility of the knowledge of God is affirmed, but also that of the evidence or demonstration of the existence of God and the infinity of his perfections under the light of reason (DS 2751ff; 2765ff; 2811-2814)[9].

The constitution, *Dei Filius,* of the First Vatican Council, to which we have already referred, contains the main declaration of the ecclesiastical teachings on this issue:

> The holy Mother Church supports and teaches that God, the beginning and end of all things, can be known with certainty through the natural light of human reason based on the things that are created; "ever since the creation of the world, the invisible existence of God and his everlasting power have been clearly seen by the mind's understanding of created things" (Rom 1:20) (DS 3004; cfr. the corresponding canon of DS 3026).

In the same context, those who deny the existence of God are anathematized. This is the first time that the teachings of the Church are confronted with modern atheism (cfr. DS 3021ff; Second Vatican Council, GS 19-21)[10].

It is especially worth pointing out some aspects contained in this definition. In the first place, it is not isolated. It is not a matter of legitimatizing a natural theology together with or in place of the one that comes from divine revelation.

---

9   We also evidence the condemnation of the opposite mistakes that are derived from «rationalism» that wants to enclose faith and theological truth within the limits of human reason; Cfr. DS 2738-2740; 2775-2777; 2850-2861; 2904-2909.

10   Cfr. SESBOÜÉ B.-THEOBALD Ch., «La parole du salut» in SESBOÜÉ B. (ed.), *Histoire des Dogmes* IV, Paris 1996, 206ff; 274ff.

This is not the intention of the Council. «Natural» knowledge is itself a condition of faith, and it cannot be separated from reason. Faith is a free, personal, and responsible answer to the revelation of God. If this possibility of «natural» knowledge of God did not exist in responsible faith itself, faith would be impossible. It would be blind. Evidently it is not a matter of ensuring that this knowledge derived from the created reality is chronologically prior to contact with revelation or with faith. Rather, faith itself includes a certain «natural» knowledge of God that does not need to be expressly stated in an instinctive manner[11]. Additionally, we must bear in mind that this is an affirmation of a possibility, of a *quaestio iuris*, not of a fact. As we have already seen, the texts of the Bible that are within another context are not optimistic with respect to the positive results of this «revelation» of God in the creation. Even the First Vatican Council seemed to follow this line of thought when, after the text that has been quoted above, it pointed out that there are truths regarding God that are not inherently accessible to reason, but that in the current status of the human condition, they cannot be known by all of us easily or with certainty and without possibility of error (Cfr. DS 3005)[12].

To what did the Council refer when it spoke of the *natural* light of reason and therefore indirectly of the human «nature»? This is an abstract affirmation that does not intend to address the problem of the conditions in which humans have been, and have made use of their reason. Hence, we are not dealing specifically with fallen nature or with «pure nature». «Nature» in this context appears to be identified with the creation; this is the Creator God, beginning and end of all things, who can be known by natural reason through the things that have been created[13]. Hence, natural knowledge is differentiated in this context from the knowledge that people acquire through the revelation that takes place in Jesus and that has already been prepared for by the Old Testament. The Council clearly distinguished the two orders of knowledge (Cfr. DS 3025).

The Council affirmed that God can be known with certainty through natural reason, *certo cognosci posse*. The phrase *et demonstrari*[14] was expressly rejected.

---

11 Cfr. POTTMEYER H.J., *Der Glaube von dem Anspruch der Wissenschaft*, 179-180.

12 Cfr. DS 3875; CEC 36-38.

13 Cfr. POTTMEYER H.J., *Der Glaube von dem Anspruch der Wissenschaft*, 196-200. It seems that the Council was quite skeptical about the idea of «pure nature»; abundant information on the idea of nature in the First Vatican Council, in VON BALTHASAR H.U., *Karl Barth. Darstellung und Deutung seiner Theologie*, Köln 1951, 315-335.

14 Even though the expression, which we have seen used prior to the First Vatican Council, has been also used in the different documents after this council; Cfr. DS 3538, the anti-modernist oath; 3890, PIUS XII, encyclical *Humani Generis*, which adds further that this demonstration can be

A milder formulation would have been preferred, although with the *certo* a merely subjective knowledge was excluded because it was not founded on an objectively justified basis. It does not seem that the means by which we can reach this certain knowledge in each case is part of the definition[15].

The possibility of this knowledge was affirmed once again in the Second Vatican Council, which reproduced in DV 6 the text of the First Vatican Council to which we have just referred. Nevertheless, number 3 of this constitution is also important, in which mention is made «that all things came to be through the Word (cfr. John 1:3), and it offers men, in the things that have been created, a perennial testimony of himself» (cfr. Rom 1:19-20). Following the thought of the biblical texts to which we have referred, perhaps less evident although also present in the First Vatican Council[16], the Second Vatican Council confirmed that in the creation there is a manifestation of God, and consequently it is the divine initiative that is the basis of every possible knowledge of God through the things that have been created (cfr. GS 15.19).

Therefore, we are not faced with an initiative of human beings that goes against or that is apart from divine revelation. Rather, as conceived by *Dei Verbum*, it is the beginning of a process that will find its culmination and its definitive meaning in the fullness of the revelation that is Christ. In fact, even though it is not possible to know the Trinity based on the creation alone, but rather only monotheism can be known; this God, imperfectly known, is the one and triune God[17]. The ancient tradition of the Church has been able to see the diversified acts of the three divine persons in the creation, following the guidelines of the intervention of these persons in the *historia salutis*. In the Second Council of

evidenced without the help of grace (not only without the revelation). After having admitted this possibility, it would probably be adequate to add that this does not seem to be the most frequent case. Cfr. Second Vatican Council LG 16, on grace that can even act in atheists. See more in the following paragraphs of our text.

15 Cfr. POTTMEYER H.J., *Der Glaube von dem Anspruch der Wissenschaft*, 187.202; VON BALTHASAR H.U., «El camino de acceso a la realidad de Dios» in *MySal* II/1, Madrid 1969, 41-74, 57-58. The CEC 36-38 widely uses the text of the First Vatican Council.

16 Cfr. POTTMEYER H.J., *Der Glaube von dem Anspruch der Wissenschaft*, 199, in which it is stated that the expression *manifestatio naturalis* appears frequently in the records of the council. In the Second Vatican Council, the subject that appears in the New Testament about the creation through the Word is also reflected. Cfr. Col 1:15-18; 1Cor 6:8; Heb 1:2. On the other hand, the terminology of «natural-supernatural» is avoided.

17 Indeed, in view of the fact that creation as such is not an appeal to participate in the divine life, we cannot know the Trinity through creation. From creation, God appears as the only beginning of all things. By means of the creation, we can know what pertains to the unique divine essence, and not what pertains to the plurality of the persons; cfr. THOMAS AQUINAS, *STh* I 32,1.

Constantinople this line of thought would reach its fullest expression: only one God and Father from whom everything comes; only one Lord Jesus Christ through whom everything was made; only one Holy Spirit in whom everything exists (cfr. DS 421)[18]. If the Creator is the one and triune God, the knowledge that we acquire from the creation must refer one way or another to the God who creates in order to save us, and who creates through his Son who will save us in the fullness of times by taking up the human condition.

We cannot rule out (although we might possibly also think the opposite) that the way that leads to the «natural» knowledge of God is at least in many cases a way that is guided and oriented by grace. By means of this knowledge the human being is led, although in an imperfect way, to his ultimate and only purpose[19]. Natural knowledge of God does not imply a knowledge that is not related at all to the God of salvation. The revelation of God in creation and the revelation that culminates in Christ should not be confused although neither should they be separated[20]. In view of the unity of the divine plan that surrounds the creation and the salvation of humanity and that sees in the latter the most profound meaning of the former, it seems difficult to imagine that the first manifestation of God in creation in fact has nothing to do with his ultimate purpose for humanity. This knowledge is founded on a manifestation of God, on a divine initiative, and there is no reason why it should not be guided by God himself throughout the process. Therefore, the «natural» knowledge of God in the concrete order in which we exist is not the knowledge of God in hypothetical «pure nature»[21]. It is the knowledge that, with all the difficulties we have seen,

---

18 Cfr. CEC 258; 290-292. Cfr. on the history of this subject, LADARIA L.F., «Dios creador del cielo y de la tierra» in SESBOÜÉ B. (ed.), *Historia de los Dogmas* 2, Salamanca 1996, 29-73.

19 Cfr. VON BALTHASAR H.U., *Karl Barth…*, 335; ROVIRA BELLOSO J.M., *Tratado de Dios uno y trino*, 293-306.

20 Cfr. Commissio Theologica Internationalis, «Theologia-Christologia-Anthropologia» in *Greg* 64 (1983) 5ff.

21 Commissio Theologica Internationalis, «Theologia-Christologia-Anthropologia» in *Greg* 64 (1983) 9: «Christian theism does not exclude, but rather assumes to a certain degree natural theism, because Christian theism has its origin in God who has revealed himself through the completely free plan of his will. On the other hand, natural theism intrinsically corresponds to human reason, as taught by the First Vatican Council. Natural theism should not be mistaken for the theism / monotheism of the Old Testament nor for historical theisms, in other words, for the theism that is professed in different modalities by non-Christians in their religions. The monotheism of the Old Testament has its origin, and hence has an intrinsic relation with the Trinitarian revelation. Historical theisms have not been derived from "pure nature", but from nature that is subject to sin and which at the same time is subjectively redeemed by Jesus Christ and elevated to its supernatural end». It is worth noting that no knowledge of God that has been historically produced, and not only that of religion, is born from «pure nature». In this context, the mean-

refers to the Scriptures and to the teachings of the Church, although it is still possible to begin with creation. This is the first manifestation of God who, in the actual order in which we exist, already moves toward the full revelation in Christ. In fact, we cannot understand the message that he gives us if in humans there is no «pre-notion» and desire for God[22]. On the other hand, upon defending this principle, the Church strives against every fideism. The possibility of «natural» knowledge of God guarantees the freedom and responsibility of the act of faith[23], which must be justifiable before reason if it cannot be established based on pure rational assumptions.

The knowledge of God, although still imperfect, if it is authentic, is a step on the way to the acceptance of the revelation of God in Jesus Christ. It seems appropriate to assume that there will be in many cases a dimension of personal «surrender» to Christ, and this will not only be the result of a reasoning process. God cannot be an object of reason as other things are[24]. If God is present to us as a personal gift, the way in which humans can have access to God will be through this self-delivery[25]. Hence, God does not reveal himself to us simply as a «neutral»

ing of «natural theism» does not seem clear to me; cfr. ibid. 8-9, in truly natural theism there is nothing that really contradicts the tradition centered on Christ. It seems that attempts have been made at excluding that theism «that questions the possibility or the fact of revelation» as something that really is not in tune with reason (ibid.). Evidently this is no «natural» theism because the one that is founded on creation cannot challenge or exclude the possibility of revelation. From the text that is referred to in the previous footnote, we can deduce that it is a knowledge founded on creation.

22 Cfr. Commissio Theologica Internationalis, «Theologia-Christologia-Anthropologia» in *Greg* 64 (1983) 7; this «pre-notion» in Christ is surpassed and overcome, and it reaches a fulfillment that goes beyond the desires of humanity.

23 FIRST VATICAN COUNCIL, *Dei Filius* (DS 3008): «...plenum revelanti Deo intellectus et voluntatis obsequium fide praestare tenemur»; (DS 3009): «Ut nihilominus fidei nostrae "obsequium rationi consentaneum" (cfr. Rom 12:1) esset...»; cfr. also DS 3035; SECOND VATICAN COUNCIL, DV 5: «When God reveals himself we have to pay him the *obedience of the faith* (Rom 16:26; cfr. Rom 1:5; 2Cor 10:5-6) by means of which the human being trusts entirely and freely himself to God, paying "to the God that is revealed the homage of understanding and of will" (*Dei Filius*)». Cfr. SECOND VATICAN COUNCIL, AA 4: «Only with faith... can we know God always and in every place».

24 Cfr. GILBERT P., «Prouver Dieu et espérer en lui» in *NRTh* 118 (1996) 690-708.

25 ZUBIRI X., *El hombre y Dios,* Madrid 1984, 196: «But the fundamental nature of God is, according to what we saw, personal self-giving. In his virtue, man has access in a binding manner to God in a tension that has a very precise nature: a tension that is the human correlation of the giving tension, in other words, the tension of the delivery. The delivery corresponds to the gift. The complete form of the access of humans to God is "delivery"»; cfr. ibid. 197; 239; 258: «Every knowledge of God is the arrangement of a scope of a possible delivery because God is basically the reality of our I, and hence, knowledge of him opens in and of itself the area of my fundamental nature. Therefore, between knowledge and faith in God there is a unity that is not a mere convergence but rather, an intrinsic and radical unity». VON BALTHASAR H.U., *Karl Barth,* 323: «By its own nature the human spirit is so fully subject and submitted to his Creator and Lord, that his basic act —in the sphere of nature and before we must speak of the revelation through the

object of knowledge. In view of the fact that his knowledge is the foundation of our being, through him we are shown the magnitude of our deliverance. Within all knowledge of God, part of the attitude that we know as faith can be present in an initial manner[26]. It is the full giving over to God that is revealed in the homage of our understanding and will. The characteristics of this knowledge are derived not only from the person who knows and from knowledge itself, but also from the God who is revealed so that it can be known. The same experience occurs in the beginning of every search for his footprints that humans can undertake[27]. We can know God only because he is manifested to us. The God whom we know «naturally» is the God who has created us from eternity in order that we may share his intimate life. Because of this, his knowledge is not normally achieved by means of an intellectual exercise. Only by loving can we know the one who creates out of love, because everything that comes from God comes from love[28]. Only from the love of God revealed in Christ can we know the «theological law» of the knowledge of God from creation.

2

The issue of analogy

With our brief reflection on the text of Wisdom 13 we have addressed the concept of «analogy», which in the sense of proportion, relation, and similarity, was known to Greek philosophy[29]. We saw how the biblical text used the concept of analogy as a means for acquiring the knowledge of God. It would be possible to achieve this knowledge by comparison, similarity, and proportion from his cre-

---

word— cannot be any other than something similar to faith». Because of this, when people are asked to have faith before the divine revelation, we are not asking of them something irrational or against their very nature (ibid.).

26 Cfr. AMBROSIASTER, *Com. Ep. Rom.* 1:19 (PL 17:57): «opus fecit per quod possit agnosci per fidem».

27 AUGUSTINE, *Solil.* I 3 (PL 32,270): «Deus quem nemo quaerit nisi admonitus»; cfr. ANSELM, *Proslogion* I 1 (Schmitt, v.1, 97-100).

28 Cfr. SCHMAUS M., *Dogmatik* I, München 1948, 204; SCHEFFCZYK L., *Der Gott der Offenbarung*, Aachen 1996, 70. In this respect, there seems to be a remarkable consensus in Catholic theology. JOHN PAUL II, *Varcare le soglie della speranza*, Milano 1994, 31, also states that the answer to the question of the existence of God is not only an issue for the intellect, but also for the will of humans and even more so for their hearts.

29 Cfr. PLATO, *Timeo* 31-32 (Plat. Werke, 4:40-42); ARISTOTLE, *Metafisica* IV 2,1003a32-b7 (REALE G., ed., 130-132). Cfr. for the entire first part of this chapter, GILBERT P., *La patience d'être. Métaphysique*, Bruxelles 1996, 91-107.

ation. Evidently, in theological discourse, the «analogy» in which God is one of the subjects, must be related to creation. Therefore, the creature is in a relationship with God[30]. This relationship, the terms of which we must clarify, enables us to have knowledge of God, while at the same time it permits us to speak with a proper sense about God, despite his incomprehensibility. This knowledge and this language are possible because humans, as creatures, are related to God and fully dependent on God. The philosophical and theological tradition has thus referred to an analogy of being, *analogia entis*[31]. This issue has created difficulties and considerable discussion in the ecumenical dialogue of recent decades as well as in Catholic theological circles. Nevertheless, before beginning to address these theological problems, it is worth remembering some of the traditional ideas.

2.1. SOME CLASSICAL CONCEPTS

Analogy (etymologically, that which goes upward or beyond) means, among other things, comparison. We use it frequently in our daily language without even realizing that we are doing so. Our world makes us constantly experience things that are partly the same and partly different. An every day example will suffice to clarify this. The phenomenon of life constantly appears before our eyes in its multiple manifestations. In this way, we speak about the life of a plant and the life of people, which of course have many things in common (both plants and people are born, grow and die), although they also have very profound differences. We also refer to a school, which can be the place where the first concepts are taught, or it can be a highly specialized center of higher education. The same word may also describe a current of thought in the different sciences or branches of human knowledge. All these different meanings of the term have common elements, but at the same time, there are significant differences between them. To a greater or lesser degree, we make frequent use of analogy.

30 Thomas Aquinas, *Summa Contra Gentes* 2,18: «Creatio est ipsa dependentia esse creati a principi a quo instituitur, et sic est de genere relationis».
31 Cayetano and Suarez were the first ones to use this terminology. Saint Thomas did not use it directly. He rather mentioned that it is «ens est analogicum», «nomina dicuntur de Deo et creatura secundum analogiam, id est proportionem», «ens analogice dicitur»; cfr. *STh* I 13,5 corpus, and ad 1; ibid. 10 ad 4, among other places. This expression was popularized in the twentieth century in theology as a result of the work by Przywara E., *Analogia Entis*, München 1932; again in *Analogia entis. Metaphysik. Ur-Struktur und All-Rhytmus*, Einsiedeln 1962; the origin of this expression is erroneously attributed to him on certain occasions; Cfr. Terán Dutari J., «Die Geschichte des Terminus "Analogia entis" und das Werk Przywaras. Dem Denker der "Analogia entis" zum achtzigsten Geburtstag» in *Philosophisches Jahrbuch* 77 (1970) 163-179.

Based on the classical concepts, analogy falls within two extremes: univocity and equivocity[32]. Equivocity is evidenced when the same term means two completely different things. In all languages, we have these cases of equivocity. For instance, we speak of the «capital city» or «capital gains»; the word «capital» is used with two completely different meanings. Likewise, we speak of a bank on which to sit or a bank in which to deposit money. On the other hand, there is univocity when the terms point to a specific reality: man, horse. Undoubtedly, we can ask ourselves whether it is correct to believe that analogy is a third genre at which we arrive after we know the other two, or whether the analogy is more original per se. For instance, as mentioned by W. Kasper, univocal affirmations are only possible because they can be differentiated from others and related to them. Hence, univocity presupposes the possibility of comparing, and in this way, it assumes something that contains in itself uniformity and diversity[33]. Therefore, analogy is a primary form of language. Only by beginning with analogy can we understand what is univocal and equivocal.

In traditional terminology, a distinction is made between analogy of proportionality and that of attribution, also referred to as proportion. The latter is present when the term under analysis is actually related to several realities, although it belongs to each of them in a different manner. Inherently, it is made up of three terms, two of which refer to a third one, which is the attribute, that is, that which is attributed to the other two. Aristotle already spoke of this when he referred to being: «Being can be seen under several meanings, although always in relation to a unique term, to one specific nature… being is taken in multiple meanings, but in each meaning every designation is in relation to a unique principle». Within this context, the most famous example of health and of the term «healthy» is used. Everything that is healthy is related to «health»: the man or animal who has health or who can receive health, the food that preserves it, and the medicine that generates it[34]. It is quite clear that this term is properly used in

---

32 THOMAS AQUINAS, *STh* I 13,5: «Iste modus communitatis medius est inter puram aequivocationem et simplicem univocationem».

33 Cfr. KASPER W., *Der Gott Jesu Chriti*, 125; Cfr. also with a more direct reference to the relationship of humans with God, RAHNER K., *Grundkurs des Glaubens*, Freiburg-Basel-Wien 1976, 80.

34 ARISTOTLE, *Metafisica* (Cfr. note 29). SAINT THOMAS has also resorted to this example; *STh* I 13,5: «sicut multa habent proportionem ad unum, sicut sanus dicitur de medicina et urina in quantum utrumque habet ordinem et proportionem ad sanitatem animalis, cuius hoc quidem signum est, illud vero causa; vel ex eo quod unum habet proportionem ad alterum, sicut sanum dicitur de medicina et de animali, in quantum medicina est causa sanitatis quod est in animali… Significat proportionem ad aliquid unum; sicut sanum, de urina dictum, significat signum sanitatis animalis, de medicina vero dictum, significat causam eiusdem sanitatis».

all the cases, although in a different manner in the case of each of them. In the different successive attributions, the term has the same meaning. Hence, we are not dealing here with a univocal term. Nevertheless, it applies to a diversity of real subjects «that receive a unique predicate that is attributed in different manners»[35]. These attributions are in proportion to health, which in the «healthy animal» is fulfilled in a more complete way. However, in all cases, there is a reference to this «health» in which concrete subjects participate in a diverse and relative manner. «Health» is not a reality, but an ideal or maximum predicate that is related to many realities and that is applied more or less according to each of the cases. The analogue is not a term that has been fixed definitively and the sense of which is fulfilled forever in the same way. «The analogous attribute combines all the subjects under an ideal form, but it has its meaning in a proportional manner to its concrete applications. In this way, we can see that this is not a concept the sense of which is fulfilled once and for always»[36].

This example of the Aristotelian tradition is used by Saint Thomas, although without deriving for the time being any subsequent conclusions, in order to justify the «analogous», although not the univocal or equivocal, language about God:

> In this way, some things of God and of creatures are spoken of by analogy and not in a purely equivocal or univocal way. In fact, we cannot talk about God if we do not do it from creatures…. Everything that is said about God and creatures is said insofar as there is a certain direction of the creature toward God as his beginning and cause, in whom all the perfections of things preexist in an excellent way[37].

Nevertheless, we could ask ourselves whether this analogy of attribution or of proportion is enough to speak about God. In fact, as mentioned by Aristotle, there is no proportion between the infinite and the finite[38]. Within the context to which we have already referred, Saint Thomas pointed out that God is not a measure that is in proportion to things that are measured. From this, we can state that God and the creature cannot be contained under the same genre[39]. God and the creature cannot participate in «being» as an analogous attribute

---

35 GILBERT P., *La patience d'être. Métaphysique*, 93-94.
36 GILBERT P., *La patience d'être. Métaphysique*, 94.
37 *STh* I 13,5.
38 ARISTOTLE, De Caelo, 275a14; Cfr. GILBERT P., *La patience d'être. Métaphysique*, 98.
39 *STh* I 13,5 ad 3: «Deus non est mensura proportionata mensuratis. Unde non oportet quod Deus et creatura sub uno genere contineantur».

spoken about each of them. In the same way, there is no generic quality of «goodness» in which both God and humans participate. There is no third term that «mediates» between God and human beings. Therefore, in this sense it does not seem that the analogy of attribution is adequate for human language about God and for theology. The proportion or attribution runs the risk of reducing or condensing everything *ad unum*, although this is something that cannot be done between God and the creature. We cannot resort to a higher genre of «being» that encompasses each of them.

However, we have also referred to another type of analogy, that of proportionality. The analogy of distribution or proportion works with three terms (although the number could be expanded): in other words, the analogous attribute, health, in the case of the classic example, which is the predicate of two or more different realities. On the contrary, the analogy of proportionality works with four terms: A is to B as C is to D. The classic example would be: sunset is to day as old age is to life, or the steersman is to the ship as the ruler is to the city. This analogy of proportionality can be extrinsic or intrinsic. In the examples that we have set forth, it is evidently an extrinsic attribution. We are now in the field of metaphor. In short, most of the examples that can be alluded to are in fact metaphor. Nonetheless, we also resort to the same scheme when referring to the act of being. In that case, we are faced with a situation in which what is suitable is proportionality per se: «If we apply this structure to metaphysical discourse which ends in what is absolute, we would be faced with the following type of analogy: the creature is to being as the Absolute (God) is to being»[40].

The analogy of proportionality is also faced with objections when we wish to use it in the field of theology. These objections are based on the fact that by comparing the «being» of God with that of creatures, we return again to the common being, which would equally have as its predicate God and that which is created. The being of God is beyond every type of genre and species. Nevertheless, unlike proportion, proportionality does not refer to the one, but rather refers to a similarity of proportions. On occasion it has also been objected that proportionality is impossible because one of the terms is infinite. However, what proportionality cannot offer per se is offered by the category of «creating cause», which is capable of articulating the communication that encompasses all entities as the key to the gift of being. The gift of being extends outward. According

---

40 Muñiz Rodríguez V., «Analogía» in Pikaza X.-Silanes N., *Diccionario Teológico. El Dios cristiano*, Salamanca 1992, 44-49, 46.

to Saint Thomas[41], being must be understood as the «act of being», since the act is the dynamic movement that makes up being in its most pertinent reality. The verb «to be» in this way indicates an act, an action and not a state or condition. Therefore, the relationship between the infinite Creator and the finite creature can be expressed as a relationship of two modalities of an act:

> Even though the finite and infinite cannot be limited to a proportion, they can proportionalized, because the finite is equal to the finite as the infinite is equal to the infinite. In this way, there is a similarity between the creatures and God, because as God is in relation to what is suitable for him, in this same way, the creature is so in relation to his properties[42].

The analogy of proportionality concerns the reality of entities in their act of being. There is no evidence of a reciprocal relation between two things, except for the similarity of one relation with another one.[43]

Proportionality presupposes that the finite act and the infinite act exercise the same structure of the act, even though the finite cannot do so in a greater way because it receives its proportionality from the infinite. Thus, the analogy of proportionality cannot only be helpful for relating creatures among themselves, but also for creatures with the Creator, if the relationship of existing with the essence is adequately articulated[44]. In this way, we do not run the risk of making God an object of human concepts that encompass God and the creature at the same time. Analogy does not render the whole human language about God useless, although, as a last resort, it refers us to its mystery[45]. This is a process that finally does not offer a precise definition, but rather opens us to him who is

---

41 Cfr. *STh* I 3,4; I 5,1, Cfr. Gilbert P., *La pacience d'être. Métaphysique*, 100-101.

42 Thomas Aquinas, *De Veritate* 23,7 ad 9., quoted by Gilbert P., *La pacience d'être. Métaphysique*, 101. Cfr. Przywara E., *Analogia Entis*, Einsiedeln 1962, 135-141.

43 Cfr. *De Veritate* 2,3 ad 4, quoted by Gilbert P., *La pacience d'être. Métaphysique*, 106. Bonaventure, *In II Sent*. 16 1,1 ad 2: «in convenientia proportionis non est similitudo in uno, sed in duabus comparationibus».

44 Gilbert P., *La pacience d'être. Métaphysique*, 197: «If the finite being is exercised in a finite essence, the infinite existence is exercised in an infinite essence».

45 Cfr. Przywara E., *Analogia Entis*, 137: «Everything comes down to the ultimate and irreducible Prius of God». Cfr. ibid. 138ff; 210. The three classical steps of analogical human language about God are the *affirmation* in God of the perfection and goodness of this world; the *denial* of the limitations of these perfections in God; the *eminence*, the perfections that we can see in this world, free of their limitations that exist in God in an eminent degree, that exceeds the adequate comprehension on our part; cfr. Thomas Aquinas, *De Potentia*, q.2 a.5.

greater than our word and our thought. On the one hand, creatures exist in relation to God from whom they have received and constantly receive their being. Hence, there must be a certain similarity between the Creator and the creatures, because each of them is in relation to what is more suitable to them. Nevertheless, the dissimilarity between them is even greater. There is no possible comparison between the infinite Creator, who in his all-embracing freedom creates, and the creature which only exists in reference to God. We cannot encompass both of them in a common concept, as we cannot do so with our thought or with our words[46]. Thus, understood in this way, the analogy does not mean encompassing God and the creature within the same context and with the same language, but it precisely directs us to the mystery, to what is beyond ourselves. Insofar as it is founded on the fact of the creation, because in it every possible similarity of the creature with the Creator is based, God is not positioned in the human context, but humans are placed in the context of God. As we know, the creation is the beginning point of the manifestation of the divine revelation. This information is important for our subsequent reflections.

Within this context, it is worth remembering the definition of the Fourth Lateran Council, held in 1215: «there is no similarity that can be seen between the Creator and the creature without an even greater dissimilarity that can be seen between them»[47]. The likeness and unlikeness cannot be placed on the same plane, as could happen between creatures themselves. In every similarity that can be evidenced between the Creator and the creature, we must always point to a greater dissimilarity. This affirmation of the Fourth Lateran Council is for us a clear point of reference that we cannot avoid. The context of the definition is Trinitarian theology and not a philosophical discourse about God. In the Christian tradition, there has always been an awareness of the inadequacy of our concepts and words when we speak about God, although this has not simply entailed a silence regarding God[48].

46 This is a mysterious proportionality, «because among the magnitudes that are compared, the second one remains unknown in its existence: God and his being»: ROVIRA BELLOSO J.M., *Tratado de Dios uno y trino*, Salamanca 1993, 321.

47 DS 806: «Quia inter creatorem et creaturam non potest similitudo notari, qui inter eos maior sit dissimilitudo notanda». The context of this phrase and the evangelical examples that it contains are indeed interesting: the union of Christians with Christ and the union between the Father and the Son cannot be limited to a common denominator (cfr. John 17:22). This is also the case of the perfection of God and that of human beings who are called to imitate his perfection (cfr. Matt 5:48); cfr. DS 803;804, God is «incomprehensible and ineffable». Cfr. PRZYWARA E., *Analogia Entis*, 251-261.

48 We are familiar with the maxim of DYONISIUS THE AEROPAGITE, *De Coel. Hier.* II 3; BASIL OF CAESAERA, *Hom. de Fide*, (PG 31,464); AUGUSTINE, *De Trin.* V 1,2 (CCL 50,207): «pie tamen cavet,

The doctrine of analogy has had great significance for the philosophical tradition of «natural theology». Nevertheless, in past times, the problem has been addressed in great depth in its strict intra-theological scope. This topic has given rise to significant discussions among Catholic and Protestant authors. Specifically, the issue of the substitution of the traditional analogy of being for the analogy of faith has been set forth, primarily due to the efforts of K. Barth. This has led to a more widespread discussion about the function of analogy in theological discourse and the place that the analogy of being can have in our theological reasoning, which must begin with the revelation and the Christian faith[49].

2.2. THE CRITICAL EXAMINATION OF KARL BARTH AND THE
CATHOLIC REACTION: THE «ANALOGIA CHRISTI»

Barth has shown his profound astonishment when faced with the idea of the analogy of being, so that it is possible that he did not understand it in its literal sense. According to him, with the analogy that is used by Catholic theologians, the being of God is placed on the same level as the being of humans, without bearing in mind the abyss between the two. For Barth, the knowledge of God himself can only come from the word of God. When faced with attempts made by some Protestants to approach a natural knowledge of God in a similar way to that of Catholic theology as it was expressed in the First Vatican Council, Barth could only answer with a clear «no». For Barth, the *analogia entis* is the invention of the anti-Christ, and this is the reason why it cannot be Catholic. Any

---

quantum potest, aliquid de eo sentire quod non sit»; ibid. VII 4,7 (255); *Sermo* 52,6 (PL 38,360): «Si enim quod vis dicere, si cepisti, non est Deus: si comprehendere potuisti, cogitatione tua te decepisti. Hoc ergo non est, so comprehendisti; si autem hoc est, non comprehendisti»; THOMAS AQUINAS, *STh* I 1,7; I 2 prol.: «primo considerandum est an Deus sit; secundo quomodo sit, vel potius quomodo non sit»; I 13,1: «…non tamen ita quod nomen significans ipsum, exprimat divinam essentiam secundum quod est»; I 13,2, etc. But there cannot be negation or denial without a certain knowledge: *Pot.* q.7 a.5. First Vatican, *Dei Filius* (DS 3016): «At ratio quidem, fide illustrata, cum sedulo, pie et sobrie quaerit, aliquam Deo dante mysteriorum intelligentiam eamque fructuossissimam assequitur, tum ex eorum, quae naturaliter cognoscit, analogia, tum e mysteriorum nexu inter se et cum fine hominis ultimo; nunquam tamen idonea redditur ad ea perspicienda instar veritatum, quae proprium eius obiectum constituunt». GREGORY OF NAZIANZUS, *Or.* 28,9 (SCh 250,118): «Likewise, he who tries in an orderly way to investigate the nature of" He is who is" (Exod 3:14) could not only say what he is not, but after having said what he is not, he will also have to say what he is».

49 In fact, we have been able to reproach the doctrine of analogy and the theological use made of it because this doctrine has been based excessively on the creation but not on Christ. The relationship of faith and the intellect has been analyzed without really turning our attention to Jesus; cfr. MILANO A. «Analogia Christi: Sul parlare intorno a Dio in una teologia Cristiana» in *Ricerche Teologiche* 1 (1990) 29-73, esp. 29.32 and the following ones 35.63.

other reason would not be a serious one[50]. This has led him to the fundamental denial of every *vestigium Trinitatis*, of the imprints of the Trinity on creation, which have a long tradition in the Western world. For him, the *analogia entis* also means accepting a similarity between the Creator and the creature in the fallen world[51]. The image of the fallen world has no capacity to reveal God, as we do not have the capacity to recognize God in it. The only possible interpretation of the word of God is the one that the word itself gives. The word of God takes place in the creature who is opposite to him, but not in the world per se[52]. In the opinion of Barth, it does not make sense to talk about one «being» that the creature and the Creator jointly share, in spite of their «greatest dissimilarities»[53].

This does not mean, however, that Barth does not resort to the concept of analogy[54]. He holds to the *analogia fidei* in opposition to the analogy of being. As is well known, the expression comes from Rom 12:6. We must limit our analysis to some of his basic affirmations regarding this subject. Without abandoning the idea of the total dissimilarity between the Creator and the creature, Barth affirms that in this full dissimilarity there still prevails the human possibility of grasping (*ergreifen*) in faith the promises of God. This human capacity can still respond to the capability that God has of fulfilling his promises. The human himself does not have this capability, but it is based on the destiny that God has given us. By virtue of this capacity, we can recognize the word of God in a sure and clear way. It is true that it is not the same, although it is similar, to the surety and clarity with which God reveals himself in his word. Hence, in faith, there is a correspondence between him who is revealed in the knowing, and the object of the thought, the word of God in the human word. This *analogia fidei* falls within the line of thought expressed in Paul which speaks of knowing God as we

---

50 Cfr. BARTH K., *Die Kirchliche Dogmatik* I/1, München 1935, VIII-IX: «I believe that the *analogia entis* is the invention of the anti-Christ and I also think that as a result of it, one cannot be Catholic. At the same time, I have taken the liberty to consider that all the other reasons that we can have in order not to become Catholic have a very narrow vision and are not very serious».

51 Cfr. BARTH K., *Die Kirchliche Dogmatik* I/1, 40.

52 BARTH K., *Die Kirchliche Dogmatik* I/1, 172-173.

53 Cfr. BARTH K., *Die Kirchliche Dogmatik* I/1, 252. Barth seems to believe in the analogy of proportion. Here we cannot go into the details of his thought. Cfr. among other studies, POHLMANN G., *Analogia entis oder Analogia fidei. Die Frage nach der Analogie bei Karl Barth*, Göttingen 1965; CHAVANNES H., *L'analogie entre Dieu et le monde selon saint Thomas d'Aquin et selon Karl Barth*, Paris 1969; recently, PALAKEEL J., *The use of Analogy in Theological Discourse. An Investigation in Ecumenical Perspective*, Rome 1995, 13-66; TORRANCE A.J., *Persons in Communion. An Essay on Trinitarian Description and Human Participation with special reference to Volume One of Karl Barth's Church Dogmatics*, Edinburgh 1996, 120-212.

54 Cfr. among other places, BARTH K., *Kirchliche Dogmatik* I/1, 252.255.

are known by him (cfr. Gal 4:8-9; 1Cor 8:2-3; 13:2). Therefore, humanity can know the word of God insofar as this is known by God himself[55]. Faith is evidenced in the person, although its foundations are found in God, the object of faith, rather than in the person. The fact that the person believes is an action of God. The person is the subject of faith, not God. The person is the one who believes:

> Nonetheless, the fact that man is the subject of faith is like being in parenthesis as a predicate of the subject God, in parenthesis in the same way as the Creator embraces his creature, the merciful God toward sinful man, but in such a way that the being of the subject of man prevails, and precisely the «I» of man as such only exists from the «You» of the subject of God[56].

For Barth, there is no continuity between the being of God and that of the human being. There is no similarity between God and fallen creation, but there is a similarity between God and the person who believes. Stated more precisely, through faith a person can recognize God in a manner similar to the way in which God is recognized in his word. Therefore, we cannot speak of the analogy of being, because the fallen creation can tell us nothing about the being of God, but in faith there is a real knowledge of God. This is what leads to the «analogy» between likeness and the lack of likeness, between equality and the inequality. Thus, because the concept of analogy is necessary, there cannot be total similarity between God and human beings because this would mean either that God has ceased to be God or that the human has become God. Neither can we speak about a full dissimilarity, because in that case we would not be able to say anything coherent about God himself. This intermediate point between similarity and dissimilarity is what is called «analogy»[57]. The words we use to refer to God are always his and not ours. He chooses our words as an expression of his truth:

> His truth is not ours, but our truth is his. What we do is our knowledge of his creation that takes place with intuitions, concepts and words. He has his truth hidden from us in him as the Creator of those truths and our Creator. Everything that we decide was, is,

---

55 Cfr. BARTH K., *Die Kirchliche Dogmatik* I/1, 265-266.
56 BARTH K., *Die Kirchliche Dogmatik* I/1, 258.
57 Cfr. BARTH K., *Die Kirchliche Dogmatik* II/1, Zürich 1946, 254-255.264-265.

and will be true previously in him.... Our words are not ours but belong to him. And insofar as he makes use of them as his property, he also puts them at our disposal[58].

This analogy has its ultimate foundation in Jesus Christ because this correspondence of the human with God takes place in God, and only based on him can we speak theologically and consciously about the human being[59]. The analogy of faith is also solved in this way and turns into the analogy of relationship[60].

The analogy of faith, which is equivalent to the analogy of relationship with God with a Christological basis, is opposed to the analogy of being which Barth considers a simple philosophical effort, and as a result, an attempt to encompass God within human categories. Has Barth really understood the meaning in Catholic thought of the analogy of being? Catholic theology has followed different paths in confronting this radical criticism of Barth, of which he did not seem to be aware[61]. As the fundamental modality of the Catholic Church, which is more than a principle from which one can derive something, the analogy of being is primarily a *reductio in mysterium*, the ultimate concealment of God which begins in creation and appears most of all and paradoxically in the incarnation itself and in the cross[62]. It is the accentuation in Christ of the similarity between God and humanity, although this in truth implies insisting on the concealment of God. Hence, it seems that it would be the opposite of what Barth had feared[63].

---

58 BARTH K., *Die Kirchliche Dogmatik* II/1, 258-259. Cfr. VON BALTHASAR H.U., *Karl Barth. Darstellung und Deutung seiner Theologie*, Köln 1951, 118-119.

59 Cfr. the developments of *Die Kirchliche Dogmatik* III/2, Zürich 1948.

60 BARTH K., *Die Kirchliche Dogmatik* III/1, 1970, 207: «The analogy between God and man is simply existence understood as a relation between an "I" and a "you" that are facing each other. This analogical existence is primarily a constituent of God [reference to the Trinitarian doctrine], and consequently, it is also so in the case of the man created by God. If we were to eliminate it, it would be like suppressing both the divine in God and the human in men».

61 Cfr. PRZYWARA E., *Analogia entis*; by the same author, «*Analogia entis*» in LThK I 470-473; «*Analogia fidei*», 473-476.

62 Cfr. PRZYWARA E., «*Analogia entis*» in LThK I, 471; cfr. also *Analogia entis*, 247ff; by the same author, «Der Grundsatz "Gratia non destruit, sed supponit et perficit naturam". Eine ideengeschichtliche Interpretation» in *Scholastik* 17 (1942) 178-186; cfr. on the problem, CANISTRÀ S., «La posizione di E. Jüngel nel dibattito sull'analogia» in *ScCat* 122 (1994) 413-446, 428ff.

63 This issue has always been emphasized by JÜNGEL E. to whom we will refer later, *Dios como misterio del mundo*, Salamanca 1984, 367 (Orig. *Gott als Geheimnis der Welt*): «If it would only be a matter of honoring God as the "totally other" one, nothing would be more adequate for achieving this than the *analogia entis* that has been so strongly condemned and attacked. Precisely because of this, this can be suitable for a theology that responds to the Gospel».

In the dialogue with Barth, G. Söhngen[64] and H.U. von Balthasar[65] attempted to place the analogy of being within the scope of the analogy of faith, of the correspondence between God and the human that takes place in Jesus and is only discovered by faith in him. The Word of God that assumes human nature is our analogy of faith which assumes the analogy of being[66]. On the other hand, von Balthasar strove to show that for Barth himself, it is faith itself that assumes the existence of a free person, of a real interlocutor of God. «Only false gods envy man. The true God enables men to be what they are and what they have been created for»[67]. In the Barthian conception of creation, as that which assumes that God can set up the covenant with humanity[68], there would be a way to overcome the incompatibilities that at first sight might seem irreconcilable. The revelation of God presupposes a world different from him and to which he can manifest himself. The human being, always by the gift and the grace of God, is a true subject. The grace of God is efficient in the freedom of his creatures, and because of this, they can be facing God not only passively but also to a high degree in a more active way. This is the way in which von Balthasar summarized his considerations regarding the Barthian *analogia fidei*:

There is a correspondence between the Creator and the creature, certainly such that any other order in which it is considered rests on an absolute unilateralism, both on the part of the Creator and of the one who receives grace. Nevertheless, the creature comes in such a way from God that the creature receives from God not only the act of receiving, but that of responding. Or, stated in other words, the creature also receives the power to respond, and of responding in such a way that this «autonomous» response continues being a receiving to the highest degree. This is what is referred to as theological analogy[69].

---

64 Cfr. especially, Söhngen G., «*Analogia fidei*. Die Einheit in der Glaubenswissenschaft» in *Cath* 3 (1934) 113-136; 176-208; «*Analogia entis oder analogia fidei*» in wiwe 9 (1942) 91-100; most recently, *La sabiduría de la teología por el camino de la ciencia*, in *MySal* 1/2, 995-1070, especially 1017-1018, in which they attempt to relate the analogy of the Catholic being and the analogy of the Protestant creation in the reference of both to the analogy of faith.

65 Cfr. Von Balthasar H.U., *Karl Barth*, 118f.

66 Cfr. Söhngen G., *Analogia fidei*, 208; cfr. Canistrà S., «La posizione di E. Jüngel nel dibattito sul'analogia», 425.

67 Cfr. Von Balthasar H.U., *Karl Barth*, page 122, quoting *Kirchliche Dogmatik* 7, (III/3, Zürich 1951²) 98-99.

68 Cfr. Von Balthasar H.U., *Karl Barth*, 129.177.

69 Von Balthasar H.U., *Karl Barth*, 123.

The answer given by von Balthasar falls within a scope that is analogous to that of the relationship between nature and grace: there is no «pure» nature. The «natural» knowledge of God, as we have seen, is evidenced by means of the creation which takes place «in Christ», according to the testimony of the New Testament. Faith must discover this correspondence with God within the scope of the creature, not because it is creation but because it is «in Christ». Therefore, the analogy of being makes real sense in the light of Christ, in the light of the analogy of faith, and in a certain correspondence with the certainly «autonomous» creation that is consistent with itself, although it has come into existence in view of grace and of the self-communication of God[70]. It is clear that all knowledge of God is based on a previous revelation by God himself, and that the human being, when faced with this revelation, can only be in a situation of adoring surrender. This revelation must basically be seen in Christ, the center of this revelation; but precisely in him we discover that God can be revealed in creation and in history. Hence, the incarnation presupposes the order of creation, not identical with it, but directed and oriented toward it. Therefore, the creation can contain images and analogies that lead us to God. In his social nature, God is capable of the covenant, and this is the assumption in order that Jesus may become our brother. The human is the being that exists in correspondence with God. In this space that God himself opens we cannot deny the value of the symbols of creation, although only in light of the incarnation are they fully eloquent[71].

The creation turns into a real potential for revelation as soon as its Christological sense is understood. God has given it the aptitude for his plans. God himself uses it, and no other hands make it serve other purposes. In obedience to the Creator, the creature does what it would not be capable of doing on its own. The resurrection of Jesus is the culminating example. By having him overcome creation, God leads it toward the goal to which he has destined it[72]. Despite sin, creation is not fully corrupted. It has not lost its capacity to reflect God.

---

70 Cfr. Von Balthasar H.U., *Karl Barth*, 128-129; 131ff.
71 Cfr. Von Balthasar H.U., *Karl Barth*, 177-179. In this context, von Balthasar notes that Barth uses the term *Dasein* for referring to God and to the creature in his book on Saint Anselm, *Fides quarens intellectum. Ansems Beweis der Existenz Gottes*, Munchen 1931, 178-180.
72 Cfr. Von Balthasar H.U., *Karl Barth*, 181. Cfr. also Rahner K., *Grundkurs des Glaubens*, Freiburg-Basel-Wien 1976, 221, the creation is the «grammar» that God himself establishes in order to manifest himself.

In this way, the God who is Logos made flesh is the beginning of every analogy[73]. Through Jesus we reach God, not because he reveals him from below upwards, but rather because in Christ God is expressed from above downwards. Jesus not only expresses the Logos, the only subject in him, but by virtue of the Trinitarian relationships, he is also the expression of the entire triune God. In the analogy that is evidenced in the *Verbum-caro*, we discover the measure of all other philosophical or theological analogies. Only this analogy is the means by which the Logos himself unites all things and raises them to his level, because he is the foundation, the end of all things that have been created. All things have their definitive place in the analogy that encompasses every aspect of the Word made flesh. Nevertheless, even in the Christological analogy, the original and infinite distance between God and the creature prevails, and this is a distance that the human cannot measure or take in with his gaze[74]. In the recapitulation or summing up of all things in Christ, the creature does not disappear, but is transfigured in the infinite distance of the divine persons in their unique nature. We know something about this distance because of the relationship of Jesus with his Father in which we will share more intimately when the time for this transfiguration occurs[75]. In this way, we can see that the possibility of a coherent knowledge and language about God begins to open starting from faith in Christ, and also that it is founded on the Word of God made man. It is not that the human being wants to capture and imprison God in his categories, but

---

73 Cfr. Von Balthasar H.U., *Theologik II. Die Wahrheit Gottes*, 284-288, chapter entitled «*Verbum-Caro und Analogie*». By being the hypostatic union, the definitive union of God and the man, Jesus is the *analogia entis concreta*, but by no means can this go beyond and exceed this analogy in direction of his identity. The *inconfuse* of Chalcedon must be saved at every point in time; cfr. Marchesi G., *La cristologia trinitaria de H.U. Von Balthasar*, Brescia 1997, 219-251; Holzer V., *Le Dieu Trinité dans l'histoire*, Paris 1995, 66.74.86.202ff, among other places. Milano A., *Analogia Christi*, 65: «Se Gesù Cristo ha pensato, detto e fatto tutto "in maniera conforme a Dio", allora è da lui, e non da altri che bisogna apprendere come pensare e dire "le cose divine". La struttura formale dell'analogia… si può solo portare allo scoperto mediante l'analisi del discorso sul Dio venuto in Gesù di Nazaret che ormai è il solo discorso davvero corrispondente a Dio…».

74 Cfr. «El camino de acceso a la realidad de Dios» in *MySal* II/1, 41-74, esp. 61: «The analogy of being between God and the creature does not enable the comparison based on a third neutral member (the "notion of the being" because this is not possible), nor the comparison based on a formal proportion that is maintained equally between both extremes… nor the reduction of the one (the creature) to the other (God), in such a way that in this attribution the creature will be at a distance from the Creator so that the creature himself can verify and measure. Conversely, in this way the gaze of the creature could encompass the distance from God to creation. In any type of comparison, the way is paved for the *maior dissimilitudo* (DS 806)».

75 Cfr. *Theologik II*, 288. Von Balthasar states in this context the «proportionality» —the relation of relations— between the God-creature relation and the one that exists between the Father, the Son and the Holy Spirit. Cfr. Holzer V., *Le Dieu Trinité*, 181.184.

it always begins with the revelation of God in Christ in whom we find the ultimate foundation of the whole of creation[76]. For this reason, based on Christ's created reality, we can speak about God. In the creation in Christ, there is a «similarity» with the one whom our reality faces, although always within the greatest dissimilarity of the mystery that cannot be encompassed. The analogy is the distinction between the Creator and the creature, in the profound relationship of the definitive covenant in the blood of Christ. This mystery in Jesus has been manifested to us. Nevertheless, as we pointed out at the beginning of our treatise, this does not mean that the mystery disappears, but that we are more immediately confronted with it. God is always the greatest and the highest *Deus semper maior*, although in a new way, according to the Augustinian expression[77], which is so dear to E. Przywara. This new modality is not one of occult and inaccessible mystery, but one of infinite wealth that is given to us and that we are able to share, and of the fullness which we have already received. God has revealed himself in human words. The person who sees Jesus sees the Father.

2.3.   THE «GREATEST SIMILARITY» ACCORDING TO E. JÜNGEL

In past Protestant theology, the issue of analogy was raised again by E. Jüngel[78]. We have already referred to his opinion about Barth, which is based on his historical studies of the philosophical and theological tradition and on his confrontation with E. Przywara. For Jüngel, analogy is precisely the best instrument to maintain the total otherness of God, and for this reason, it cannot be used in a theology that is inspired by the gospel. John 1:18 tells us that no one has ever seen God but that the only Son has revealed him. If the first part of that phrase has been used by tradition to insist upon the unutterability of God, the second part has not been used to generate theological issues around the axiom that is only found in the former[79]. The process that has led to the affirmation of the

---

[76] Cfr. MILANO A., *Analogia Christi*, 67. The nature that is capable of grace is the one that enables us to speak of an *analogia entis*, always based on the new creation that is both manifested and acted in Christ.

[77] AUGUSTINE, *En. in Ps.* 62,16 (CCL 39,804): «Semper enim ille maior est, quantumque creverimus».

[78] Cfr. on the analogy in RODRÍGUEZ GARRAPUCHO J. F., *La cruz de Jesús y el ser de Dios. La teología del Crucificado en Eberhard Jüngel*, Salamanca 1992, 182-193; MARTÍNEZ CAMINO J. A., *Recibir la libertad. Dos propuestas de fundamentación de la teología en la Modernidad: W. Pannenberg y E. Jüngel*, Madrid 1992, 227-239; GAMBERINI P., *Nel legame del Vangelo. L'analogia nel pensiero di Eberhard Jüngel*, Brescia-Roma 1994; CANISTRÀ S., «La posizione di E. Jüngel», 413ff.

[79] Cfr. JÜNGEL E., *Gott als Geheimnis der Welt*, Tübingen 1977, 317-321.

unknowability of God, even the «agnosticism» about him[80], has not duly taken love into account. The love of God has only been expressed in language as «cause», and for this reason, the distance between God and humanity that is characterized by the infinite superiority of God can never be closed. «The God as love brought into language remains within the dimension of the originator which is located *supra nos*. This is precisely the *theological* weakness of the classical form of the doctrine of analogy»[81]. According to Jüngel, faith in the incarnation is that which forces us to reformulate the issue and even to deny the premises of the metaphysical tradition which permits the suspicion of lack of meaning in the incarnation itself. Consequently, it is a matter of seeing whether there is a theological use of analogy that corresponds to faith in the incarnation of God. Faced with these reservations as they relate to anthropomorphism, Jüngel wondered whether there is no anthropomorphism «that is rendered possible, that is offered, and that is demanded by God himself»[82]. Contrary to what had been the opinion of Protestants, and specifically that of the early Barth, analogy is not the instrument that can be used to think about God and the world in unison using the same system. Conversely, analogous language about God does not have any other purpose than that of maintaining its mystery.

On the other hand, Jüngel referred to the gospel as analogous speech about God. It is the analogy of «Advent» that leads to the language of the arrival of God to humanity. The God who comes into the world resorts to what is evident in this world in order to illuminate it from within and to place it at the service of something that is even more evident. It is obvious, for instance, that someone gives everything he has to ensure the increased value of a treasure found in the field. «But this evidence appears in a completely new light when it approaches language as the parable of the greatness of God which enables us to find him»[83]. The being of God is revealed by his Advent. God is no longer someone unknown; God reveals himself by resorting to intra-mundane evidence, and by becoming word he comes into language. Because of this, we cannot be operating with general principles in order to understand how to speak about God. We can only

---

80 Cfr. JÜNGEL E., *Gott als Geheimnis der Welt*, 381: «The traditional theological use of analogy that we have been able to see in Kant is predominantly agnostic, and it is precisely the result of the perfection of God».
81 Cfr. JÜNGEL E., *Gott als Geheimnis der Welt*, 381.
82 Cfr. JÜNGEL E., *Gott als Geheimnis der Welt*, 283.
83 Cfr. JÜNGEL E., *Gott als Geheimnis der Welt*, 390.

know this through the speech of God that has already been uttered. We must assume that this language «corresponds» to God[84].

The event whereby God becomes word is called «revelation». «In this event… the analogy of faith takes place, and in this scope, human words do not fall within the proximity of God, but God, as word, comes close to humanity in human words»[85]. According to Jüngel, the difference between God and humans, which is the essence of the Christian faith, is not that of greatest dissimilarity, but that of a similarity which is greater at every moment within a dissimilarity that is still extremely vast between God and humans. It is the distinction and the similarity between the humanity of God and the humanity of people. It is in the even greater similarity whereby the Christian faith confesses the incarnation of the word of God in Christ. In this way, the man Jesus is the parable, the comparison (*Gleichnis*) of God. This Christological affirmation is the axiom of a hermeneutic of the «utterability» of God. It is the starting point of a doctrine of analogy that makes the gospel have its appropriate value as a «co-respondence» which is typical of the gospel[86]. Nonetheless, immediately following this statement, Jüngel mentions that the correspondence of human language to God is not an inherent possibility of this language, but it comes from God himself[87].

We do not mask reality by resorting to parable and to metaphor. Indeed, on the contrary, language becomes more direct and insightful. What is spoken turns concretely into the expression of language. The parables have been used specifically by Jesus to speak about the kingdom of heaven. The parable is not a thesis. One does not say that the kingdom of God *is*, but *it is like*. We begin with a story that can engage the listener. The kingdom of God comes to him in the parable if the listener surrenders to the parable. These parables of the kingdom show a basic distinction between the kingdom of God and the world. Consequently, this is a dissimilarity and a way of being far apart from each other, although this dissimilarity is so great that it appears in a similarity and a closeness that is even greater. Because of this fact, even though the parable speaks in the language of the world, it speaks about God with truth and reverence. We are no longer speaking about the listener, the closest to himself, but about the fact that God himself

---

84 Cfr. JÜNGEL E., *Gott als Geheimnis der Welt*, 391.
85 Cfr. JÜNGEL E., *Gott als Geheimnis der Welt*, 371.
86 Cfr. JÜNGEL E., *Gott als Geheimnis der Welt*, 394.
87 Cfr. JÜNGEL E., *Gott als Geheimnis der Welt*, 395.

is near him. God comes to humankind, even closer than the human being can get close to himself: *intimior intimo meo*[88].

Here we are faced with the analogy of Advent. The similitude is greater because there is greater proximity. God, in the man Jesus, was present among human beings. This reality permits us and even forces us to speak about God as a man, of his even greater generosity and impartiality, and thus we can speak about God as love. Love is not only the originating cause, as we stated earlier, but love, insofar as it is through love that God comes to us, is also what enables us to speak about God, because love approaches language. Love is capable of the word, *capax verbi*[89]. God is distinguished from the human being by uniting with him in Jesus Christ. Nevertheless, the foundation of this union is not creation, but election in Christ, by virtue of which God elects the human for himself. Anthropology is based on this election. By saying «yes» to Jesus Christ, God says «yes» to the person and calls him into existence. This «yes» is based on the fact that God says «yes» to himself within the heart of his Trinitarian love[90]. God finds the person outside himself, *extra se*[91]. Only the analogy of faith can be the basis for theology. For Jüngel, the analogy of being can mean a historical phase that takes place, while at the same time it is perceived in greater depth. The analogy of faith is beyond the historical phase. It is not against it or at its side, because it takes us closer, in a more radical way, to the origin, into the divine election itself[92].

88 AUGUSTINE, *Conf.* III 6,11; Cfr. Cfr. JÜNGEL E., *Gott als Geheimnis der Welt*, 402-404.
89 Cfr. JÜNGEL E., *Gott als Geheimnis der Welt*, 408.
90 JÜNGEL E. sees a fundamental relationship between the «yes» of God to himself in the heart of the Trinitarian relationships and the «yes» of God to humans when he chooses them in Jesus Christ. «It is the "yes" of the free divine love that the triune God speaks to himself and hence also to his creature, which is thus created in his own correspondence». «Die Möglichkeit theologischer Anthropologie auf der Grunde der Analogie. Eine Untersuchung zur Analogieverständnis Karl Barth» in *Barth-Studien*, Gütersloh 1982, 210-232, especially 222-225; cfr. CANISTRÀ S., «La posizione di E. Jüngel», 442-443.
91 Here we can see a difference of emphasis with respect to Catholic theologians. While the latter emphasize the consistence —indeed relative— of created reality, Jüngel underlines the foundation of everything in Christ and hence, the lack of foundation «in himself». This leads to the trend among Catholic theologians to see the analogy of being as part of the analogy of faith (creaturely consistence of the creation in Christ), while Jüngel rather tends to show the incompatibility between both.
92 Cfr. CANISTRÀ S., «La posizione di E. Jüngel», 442-446. PANNENBERG W. also sets forth his criticism against the use of analogy. According to him, there can be an analogy of theological use with profane use, but not with respect to God himself. God makes our words his, and gives our praise its definitive meaning: «Analogie und Doxologie» in *Grundfragen systematischer Theologie*, Göttingen 1967, 181-202.

Reflection on the foundations of humans in the world within the divine election in Christ has certainly also been a positive factor in Catholic theology, which has also been concerned in recent years with focusing the doctrine of analogy upon the incarnation. It is only through the God who speaks and whose word became flesh that he comes to us, and it can make sense to speak about a human «co-respondence»[93]. The human being has come into existence because he has been chosen in Jesus Christ even before creation (Cfr. Eph 1:3ff). Thus, the human being is determined by this presence of God, by the *Deus intimior intimo meo,* according to the formula of Augustine of which Jüngel reminded us.

Does this mean, then, that one must invert the formula of the Fourth Lateran Council, as proposed by Jüngel? In the coming of God to the world, we have a greater closeness amid an even greater remoteness. Is the similarity greater than the dissimilarity between God and humanity? Undoubtedly, we cannot minimize the closeness of God to humans. The fact is that Jesus has been made our brother, tested in everything just as we are, except without sin (cfr. Heb 4:25). God truly comes to humanity. He is capable of renouncing himself out of love. In Jesus we have the God who is close, who comes to us in his love; but is it not precisely the manifestation of this love which makes us see with clarity the great distance between God and us?

> When we are speaking about the mystery within the scope of the revelation of grace, the emphasis falls on the positive incomprehensibility of God. The fact that the absolute God, superior to any contradiction, deigns to come down to the level of the creature will always exceed any possibility of understanding; and even more so, that he loves this creature and even honors this creature with such love that he takes on himself all the guilt, that he dies for that guilt amidst the pain, the darkness, and the awful divine abandonment and that he gives himself as a "victim", for the food and drink of the whole world. The distance, greater in every sense to anything else, between human nature and humankind and the divine nature is precisely manifested in

---

[93] It is worth noting the play on words that the authors in the German language use constantly when addressing these problems, between *sprechen* (to talk) and *entsprechen* (to correspond).

the "great similarity" (*in tanta similitudine*, DS 806) of the temporal giving of his divine being to humanity and in the assumption by God of human nature[94].

The same closeness of God who comes to us shows the great dissimilarity. Paradoxically, the love with which he comes close to us opens us to the *maior dissimilitudo*.

Without attempting to force words to an extreme, it will be useful to consider the record of this «similarity» in the New Testament. Jesus has come to us in flesh similar to that of sinful flesh (Rom 8:3); he has been made similar in every way to his brothers and sisters (Heb 2:17); he has been tested in every way like humans, except without sin (Heb 4:15). However, in the ascending line, the similarity is projected toward the future. Our similarity with God (or with Christ) is reserved for the final consummation: «We shall be like him, for we shall see him as he really is» (1John 3:2). The well-known axiom of the «exchange» of the Fathers tells us that he has become what we are, so that we could become what he is. If the first part, the coming down of Jesus, has been accomplished, this is not the case of the second part, which is still waiting for the consummation. Jesus closes the infinite distance between the Creator and the creature, although we do not accomplish this. The capacity to close the distance is precisely additional evidence of the *maior dissimilitudo*. The ὁμοούσιος ἡμίν of Chalcedon must remind us, and never let us forget, that only Jesus is the ὁμοούσιος τῶ Πατρί. The great similarity (and perhaps in this respect, it clarifies and gives full meaning to the reading of the Fourth Lateran Council) shows us a greater dissimilarity that is only overcome by the love of God in this great manifestation of «dissimilar» closeness. The analogy that is founded on love and on freedom is also found in the difference between God and humanity, even though the difference is emphasized, with due legitimacy at the time, over against the similarity because of the infinite divine condescension.

This topic is also connected with that of the relationship between the economic Trinity and the immanent Trinity that we have been addressing from the very beginning of our treatise[95]. The coming of God to humanity does not ex-

---

94 VON BALTHASAR H.U., «El camino de acceso a la realidad de Dios» in *MySal* II/1, 63; Cfr. also *Theologik II. Wahrheit Gottes*, 67: «… this shows with the utmost clarity that Jesus, also in his full human nature, is still the totally other, the unrepeatable, the interpreter of the Father».

95 Some Catholic critics have pointed out some ambiguities in Jüngel in this respect; cfr. LAFONT G., *Dieu, le temps et l'être*, Paris 1986, 293; BERTULETTI A., «Il concetto di persona e il sapere teologico» in *Teologia* 20 (1095) 117-145, esp. 124.

haust his mystery. Even more so, it opens the mystery to us in greater depth. The incomprehensibility of God is evidenced to us in its highest greatness in the event of Christ and not despite it. We saw in Chapter 2 the justified reservations when we were faced with some possible interpretations of the «vice versa» of the formulation of the fundamental axiom of K. Rahner. The being of God is not perfected or fulfilled in the saving economy, although neither is it «exhausted» in it. Through Christ, and primarily when faced with the abyss of love that Christ reveals to us, we can only resort to considering that in everything we might think or say about God and in everything that we as creatures are, we are at an infinite distance from the mystery of love that is revealed to us in Christ, who was crucified and who rose from the dead for us.

Epilogue

«How hard for me to grasp your thoughts, how many, God, there are! If I count them, they are more than the grains of sand; if I come to an end, I am still with you» (Ps 139:17-18). The author of this psalm addressed with just a glimpse the greatness of the divine designs and the majesty of God himself. The divine designs are already beyond the capacity of human beings. Nevertheless, if something impossible should happen so that we would consider these divine designs to have come to an end, we would still have God himself, who is always with us. The book of Deuteronomy expresses admiration for the proximity to the people of the sovereign God who carries out prodigious works that have never been heard or seen before: «And indeed, what great nation has its gods so near as Yahweh, our God, is to us whenever we call to him?» (Deut 4:7).

The nearness of God to his chosen people is simply the prefiguration of his nearness to all humanity, because his Son has been made one of us and «has been united in a certain way to every man» (GS 22). God, through the incarnation of his Son, is «God with us», in a way that neither the sages nor the prophets of the Old Testament could have even suspected (cfr. Isa 7:14; Matt 1:23). The doctrine of the one and triune God has shown us the nearness of God by his assumption of humanity: the intra-Trinitarian love is the origin of the love of God to human beings manifested when he sent his Son and the Spirit into the world. In this way, the «immanent» Trinity has been shown to us as the origin and the end of the history of salvation. The initiative of the mission of the Son and of the Holy Spirit comes from the Father who is the beginning without beginning, and Jesus will hand over the kingdom to the Father when all things have been subjected to him (1Cor 15:24-28). As we stated at the beginning of our treatise, the fullness of the human being and his ultimate purpose is God alone. Because of this, God is the sole object of theology. The God who sends to the world his Son and the Holy Spirit is the God whom we can call Father. He is the one who invites us to participate in and share his life as children in his Son when communicating to us the Spirit of sonship (cfr. Gal 4:4-6; Rom 8:14-15). This is the salvation to which God has destined us when choosing us in Christ before the creation of the world. The only-begotten Son, through the condescension of his love, also becomes the first-begotten among many brothers and sisters, and when uniting us to him, he also unites us with one another. He has been made what we are in order to perfect us in what he is[1].

---

1   IRENAEUS OF LYONS, *Adv. Haer.* v praef.; cfr. ORBE A., *Teología de san Ireneo* I, Madrid-Toledo 1985, 48-51, among other places.

Only because God is at the same time one and triune is the incarnation of the Son possible, and only because he can share our condition can we finally be what he is. In this way, the Trinity, the incarnation, and grace end by being, in their mutual interrelation, the key mysteries of Christianity[2], the axis that integrates in harmony all the other truths of our faith. In the Church, the body of Christ, we receive the super-abundance of his saving gifts, the Word and the Sacraments. While we are in pilgrimage in this life, we already have the first-fruits of the Spirit and of the future goodness that we expect to enjoy one day in all fullness. The salvation that Christ gives us is the prolongation of the over abundant life of God. Only with the starting point of the divine Trinity does each and every one of the mysteries of our faith have meaning, and based on the Trinity alone is the mystery of our existence finally coming to light. The gifts of God are no longer simply the object of our gratitude which moves us to praise, but rather, the gift that God makes to us is himself, a consequence of the mutual gift of love of the three divine persons. Within the scope of this love which, as we have seen, is always the first gift, we see our lives unfold. Only because God is triune can he create, and only because of that can he receive us into his heart. Saint Irenaeus has stated this in words that are very difficult to surpass:

> The Spirit prepares men for the Son of God. The Son leads men to the Father, and the Father grants men the incorruption of eternal life that each one of us can have only from God. In this way, as those who see the light are within the light and perceive its clarity, in the same way those who see God are in God and share his clarity. According to this, those who see God are the ones who share his life[3].

The life of God has been manifested in Christ, and we humans have been enabled to share it. This is the scope in which our existence is developed in this world. Living in God is our definitive destiny in the many dwelling places in the Father's house (cfr. John 14:1-3), as many (again quoting Irenaeus) as there will be members in the body of Christ[4].

2 Cfr. RAHNER K., «Sobre el concepto de misterio en la teología católica» in *Escritos de Teología* IV, 53-101, 91ff; also «Reflexiones fundamentales sobre antropología y protología en el marco de la teología» in *MySal* II 1, 454-468, 458; GONZÁLEZ DE CARDEDAL O., *La entraña del cristianismo*, Salamanca 1997, 8: «The Trinity prolonged its own life in men through the incarnation and grace. Trinity, incarnation, and grace are the core of Christianity, as expressions of the mystery that is God alone existing in the immensity and enclosed in the smallness of man».

3 IRENAEUS OF LYONS, *Adv. Haer.* IV 20:5; cfr. ORBE A., *Teología de san Ireneo* IV, Madrid 1996, 288-290.

4 Cfr. IRENAEUS OF LYONS, *Adv. Haer.* III 19,3 (SCh 211,382).

Therefore, Christian salvation is the work of the one and triune God, and it has this God as its beginning and goal. This is the unknown God, the one that humanity looks for without realizing it, the only one who can satisfy our desires because «it is in him that we live and move and exist» (Acts 17:28). Therefore, reflecting on the mystery of God does not mean standing at a distance from that which surrounds us. Rather, it is letting the air that we breathe penetrate us and discovering the one who is more within us than our own intimacy in order to open up to our brother and sister in whom God is also reaching out to greet us.

Our words about God, although always inadequate, should lead us to trusting prayer. It is not by chance that the best among the old treatises, *de Trinitate,* end with a prayer, and some of the modern ones do likewise. The study of the mystery of God should invite us to adoration, thanksgiving and praise[5]. It is impossible to speak adequate words, although we have so much more awareness of God expressing himself in the acts and words of Jesus. We can also end our journey by glorifying God with the words of Paul in the Eucharistic liturgy:

> Oh, the depth of the riches and wisdom and knowledge of God! How inscrutable are his judgments and how unsearchable his ways! For who has known the mind of the Lord? Or who has been his counselor? Or who has given him anything that he may be repaid? For from him and through him and for him are all things. To him the glory for ever! Amen (Rom 11:32-35).

Through him, with him, in him, in the unity of the Holy Spirit, all glory and honor is yours, Almighty Father, forever and ever. Amen.

---

5 AUGUSTINE, *En. In Ps.* 32,1.8 (CCL 38,254): «Ineffabilis enim est, quem fari non potes. Et si eum fari non potes, et tacere non debes, quid restat nisi ut iubiles? Ut gaudeat cor sine verbis, et inmensa latitudo gaudiorum metas non habeat syllabarum ». *Trin.* v 1,1 (CCL 50,206) : «[Deus] de quo semper cogitare debemus, de quo digne cogitare non possumus, cui laudando reddenda est omni tempore benedictio».

General Bibliography

I include in this bibliography the general works and not the monographs that only related to a concrete and specific point of our treatise. In order to avoid repetitions, those works that are quoted more frequently do not always appear in the notes with the complete reference. This complete reference can be found in this bibliography. Except in very few cases, I simply point at the recent works.

FEINER J.-LÖHRER M. (ed.), *Mysterium Salutis. Grundriss heilsgeschichtlicher Dogmatik II/1*, Einsiedeln-Zürich-Köln 1969.

ARIAS REYERO M., *El Dios de nuestra fe. Dios uno y trino*, Bogotá 1991.

AUER J., *Gott der Eine und Dreieine*, Regensburg 1978.

BOBRINSKOY B., *Le Mystère de la Trinité. Cours de théologie orthodoxe*, Paris 1986.

BONANNI S., *La Trinità*, Casale Monferrato 1991.

BREUNING W. (bearbeitet von W. BEINERT), *Gotteslehre*, in BEINERT W. (Hrsg.), *Glaubenszugänge. Lehrbuch der Katholischen Dogmatik* 1, Paderborn-München-Wien-Zürich 1995, 201-362.

CIOLA N., *Teologia trinitaria. Storia-Metodo-Prospettive*, Bologna 1996.

CODA P., *Dios Uno y Trino*. Revelación, experiencia y teología del Dios de los cristianos, Salamanca 1993.

CONGAR Y., *El espíritu Santo*, Barcelona 1983.

COURTH F., *Il mistero del Dio Trinità*, Milano 1993.

DURWELL F.X., *Nuestro Padre. Dios en su misterio*, Salamanca 1990.

FORTE B., *Trinidad como historia. Ensayo sobre el Dios cristiano*, Salamanca 1988.

GARCÍA-MURGA J. R., *El Dios del amor y de la paz*, Madrid 1991.

GRESHAKE G., *Der dreieine Gott. Eine trinitarische Theologie*, Freiburg-Basel-Wien 1997.

JÜNGEL E., *Gott als Geheimnis der Welt*, Tübingen 1977.

KASPER W., *Der Gott Jesu Christi*, Mainz 1982.

LAFONT G., *Peut-on connaître Dieu en Jésus-Christ?*, Paris 1970.

MELOTTI L., *Un solo Padre, un solo Signore, un solo Spirito. Saggio di teologia trinitaria*, Leumann, Torino 1991.

MOLTMANN J., *Trinität und Reich Gottes*, München 1980.

MONDIN B., *La Trinità mistero d'amore. Trattato di teologia trinitaria*, Bologna 1993.

MÜLLER G.L., *Katholische Dogmatik. Für Studium und Praxis der Theologie*, Freiburg-Basel-Wien 1985, 226-252; 390-413;415-476.

NICOLAS J.-H., *Synthèse dogmatique. De la Trinité à la Trinité*, Paris 1985, 25-265.

O'DONNELL J.J., *The Mystery of the Triune God*, London 1987.

PANNENBERG W., *Systematische Theologie* I, Göttingen 1988. Spanish: *Teología sistemática* I, Madrid 1992.

PEÑAMARÍA DE LLANO, A., *El Dios de los cristianos: estructura introductoria a la teología de la Trinidad. Tratado de Dios uno y trino*, Madrid 1990.

PIKAZA, X.-SILANES, N. (ed.), *Diccionario Teológico. El Dios cristiano*, Salamanca 1992.

PORRO C., *Dio nostra salvezza. Introduzione al mistero di Dio*, Leumann, Torino 1994.

RAHNER K., «El Dios trino como principio y fundamento trascendente de la historia de la salvación» in FEINER J.-LÖHRER M. (ed.), *Mysterium Salutis. Grundriss heilsgeschichtlicher Dogmatik* II/1, Einsiedeln-Zürich-Köln 1969. Spanish: *MySal* II/1, Madrid 1969, 359-449.

ROVIRA BELLOSO J.M., *Tratado de Dios uno y trino*, Salamanca 1993.

SCHEFFCZYK L., *Der Gott der Offenbarung. Gotteslehre*, Aachen 1966.

STAGLIANÒ A., *Il mistero del Dio vivente. Per una teologia dell'Assoluto trinitario*, Bologna 1996.

VIVES J., «*Si oyerais su voz*». *Exploración cristiana del misterio de Dios*, Santander 1988.

VON BALTHASAR H.U., *Theodramatik*, Bd. I: *Prolegomena*, Einsiedeln 1973; Bd II/1: *Die Personen des Spiels. Der Mensch in Gott*, Einsiedeln 1976; Bd II/2: *Die Personen des Spiels. Die Personen in Christus*, Einsiedeln 1978; Bd. III: *Die Handlung*, Einsiedeln 1980; Bd IV: *Das Endspiel*, Einsiedeln 1983.

VON BALTHASAR H.U., *Theologik*. Bd. I: *Wahrheit der Welt*, Einsiedeln 1985; Bd II: *Wahrheit Gottes*, Einsiedeln 1985; Bd. III: *Der Geist der Wahrheit*, Einsiedeln 1987.

VORGRIMLER H., *Doctrina teológica de Dios*, Barcelona 1987.

WERBICK J., «Dottrina trinitaria» in SCHNEIDER Th. (ed.), *Nuovo corso di dogmatica*, Brescia 1995, vol. 2, 573-683.

Index of Authors

Index of Authors

497

S

Sattler, S
PAGE 151

Salvati, G.M
PAGES 54, 103, 287

Scarpat, G
PAGE 187

Scheeben, M.J
PAGE 94

Scheffczyk, L
PAGES 29, 31, 43, 45, 50, 58, 152, 287, 369, 429, 428, 436, 445, 463

Schelle, U
PAGE 126

Schiersee, F.J
PAGE 120

Schlier, H
PAGES 85, 457

Schlosser, J
PAGES 76, 79

Schmaus, M
PAGE 463

Schmidt, W.H
PAGES 152, 153

Schmidtbaur, H.Ch
PAGE 287

Schnackenburg, R
PAGES 34, 82, 126, 138, 371, 432

Schneider, G
PAGE 79

Schneider, Th
PAGES 44, 62, 151, 337, 341, 342, 419, 451

Schniertshauer, M
PAGES 296, 311

Schoonenberg, P
PAGES 61, 330

Schulte, R
PAGES 152, 348, 421

Schürmann, H
PAGE 88

Schütz, Ch
PAGES 129, 155

Seibt, K
PAGE 227

Sequeri, P
PAGE 455

Sesboüé, B
PAGES 149, 163, 229, 234, 261, 262, 273, 277, 278, 458

The Living and True God.
The Mystery of the Trinity

This book was printed on *thin opaque smooth white Bible paper*, using the *Minion* and *Type Embellishments One* font families.

This edition was printed in D'VINNI, S.A., in Bogotá, Colombia, during the last weeks of the second month of year two thousand nine.

Ad publicam lucem datus mense februari in praesentatio Iesu in templo